AF520680

TRADITION AND MODERNITY IN EIGHTEENTH-CENTURY GOA (1750-1800)

INDO-PORTUGUESE STUDIES – 1

TRADITION AND MODERNITY IN EIGHTEENTH-CENTURY GOA (1750–1800)

MARIA DE JESUS DOS MÁRTIRES LOPES

CENTRO DE HISTÓRIA DE ALÉM-MAR
UNIVERSIDADE NOVA DE LISBOA

MANOHAR
2006

First published 2006

translation by Oscar Noronha

ISBN 81-7304-689-1

Published by
Ajay Kumar Jain *for*
Manohar Publishers & Distributors
4753/23 Ansari Road, Daryaganj
New Delhi 110 002

Printed at
Lordson Publishers Pvt Ltd
Delhi 110 007

Distributed in South Asia by
FOUNDATION BOOKS
4381/4, Ansari Road
Daryaganj, New Delhi 110 002
and its branches at Mumbai, Hyderabad, Bangalore, Chennai, Kolkata

Contents

Preface to the Second Portuguese Edition

We are glad to note that *Goa Setecentista: Tradição e Modernidade* is already out of stock and that the management of the Centro de Estudos dos Povos e Culturas de Expressão Portuguesa of the Universidade Católica Portuguesa was contemplating the publication of a second edition. This fact must not have been alien to the present circumstance of there being in Portugal an increasing interest for the Orient, which translates not only as research, but also by its actual knowledge. The number of researchers on Goa or visitors to it is ever increasing.

The commemoration of the voyage of Vasco da Gama to India at the present conjuncture as also the fact that the book was awarded the D. João de Castro National Prize, 1997 by the Comissão Nacional para as Comemorações dos Descobrimentos Portugueses must have undoubtedly contributed to its successful diffusion.

In this new edition, we have undertaken a careful revision of the text, deleting errors and making one or two minor additions, as is the case of the bibliography meanwhile edited and with interest for the subject. This is because, as is known, the Overseas historiography has been witness to a great progress in the last decade of this century, especially in the final years: national and international congresses, exhibitions, courses, did bring forth a considerable output which is important to take into account. We have not made any crucial alteration, as the text is still pertinent, as is its textual structure. Nonetheless, we shall continue to remain attentive to the Goan historical work, which, in fact, we are duty-bound to do.

We wish to thank the management of the Centro de Estudos dos Povos e Culturas de Expressão Portuguesa for the renewed confidence in this new edition and we hope that it might continue to merit the interest from researchers and the general public alike.

Lisbon
29 May 1999

Maria de Jesus dos Mártires Lopes

Preface to the First Edition

GIVEN ITS OBJECTIVITY, historical synthesis presupposes a meticulous and exhaustive analysis of the materials. Thus, the global vision of the Portuguese Overseas in a given age demands varied studies, historical monographs of the component parts. The Golden Goa of Albuquerque has given rise to reflection from researchers which, albeit far from exhausting the theme on sixteenth-century India, did cover, however, vast areas of historical research. There are only scattered studies on this or that aspect of eighteenth-century history of Goa. Here we must stress the great contribution made by a gallery of Goan or Portuguese-born historians, such as José Ferreira Barroco, Joaquim Heliodoro da Cunha Rivara, Filipe Nery Xavier, A.B. de Bragança Pereira, José António Ismael Gracias, João Baptista Amâncio Gracias and others, who have carted along a lot of material and left for posterity studies of great historical value. It is imperative, therefore, to have the data systematized in the light of new methodologies.

In the transition from the first to the second half of the eighteenth century, there were momentous political, social, economic and mental transformations – largely a result of Pombal's work – which forged in Goa a society whose features have remained up to our day. Indeed, the age began the great impulse of the New Conquests, whereby the Goan territory was quadrupled and imparted geo-political unity. Important Pombaline diplomas secured the civil equality of the Christian Goans with the Reinóis; and, consequently, they began to have access to the administrative and ecclesiastical cadres. In the field of education, Pombaline reform and the creation of diocesan seminaries contributed decidedly for the intellectual formation of the Goans, whose other face is reflected in the Pinto Conspiracy. Hence the choice of the period from 1750 to 1800 for our study.

From the spatial point of view, given the considerable

abundance of manuscript documentation and bibliography already available for certain themes, we were obliged to restrict our work only to the territory of Goa, excluding Daman, Diu and mission fields situated on the Indian subcontinent, Mozambique and the Far East. On the other hand, the natural scarcity of data on the latter-day dominions called the New Conquests compelled us to favour the study of the Old Conquests in the Goan territory.

Given the nature of the sources and in spite of their abundance as mentioned above, we do not have a complete response to some of the queries propounded by us. New studies will certainly permit us to plug the lacunae.

In order to understand our objectives, in the first part, we have sought to draw an institutional and economic picture of Goa in the mid-eighteenth century. It was not an easy task since there were no compact studies. We had to start by analysing the materials available to attain our goal.

Next, we dwelt on Goan society, with a view to characterising its constitutive strata and their level of participation in the different sectors of local life. In the treatment of these themes, the main difficulty encountered was that of the available documentation being of administrative nature, which did not always mirror social reality. We set our hands on all the data that directly or indirectly could help answer the issues outlined.

Religion, one of the essential aspects of this society and defining its own division (Christians, Hindus and Muslims) has been taken up in the longest chapter of this dissertation. It is perhaps the first time that the very rich material of the Pastoral Visits and the Church Rolls available in Goa has been utilized for such a purpose, besides a lot of other documentation.

The cultural aspects could not possibly be left out from our analysis, given its great importance in Goa down the centuries. The presence of many educational institutions has truly marked Goan culture profoundly and hence an entire chapter has been devoted to it.

The motivations and the political-cultural ideology that determined the Pinto Conspiracy have also attracted our attention. We have inquired to what extent this movement with a political mien can be viewed as a corollary to Pombal's social reforms, a consequence of the development of education and culture, and a partaking of European revolutionary ideals.

We believe that some facets of Goan society are more faithfully depicted in its daily life. Hence, we have attempted to analyse it in many of its aspects. Again, we faced several difficulties, given the scarcity of contemporaneous sources and the scanty information it provided. In many cases, we had to depend on ethnographic studies. In addition, had it not been for our Goan origin, the difficulties would have been still greater.

The present study was originally a dissertation on the History of the Discoveries and Portuguese Expansion, presented at the Faculty of Social and Human Sciences of the Universidade Nova de Lisboa, in July 1993.

From the very first moment, we counted with the support of some Professors, whose incentive and help allowed us to go ahead with this work. We cannot fail to highlight A.H. de Oliveira Marques who so readily accepted to guide the present study and to whom we owe a lot for his talent and historical rigor; Eugénio dos Santos for his intelligent guidance, ever ready to surpass distances and supply us materials; and Luís Filipe Ferreira Reis Thomaz who created in us a profound interest for eighteenth-century Goa and accompanied our work with perspicacious observations.

Many were the colleagues and friends who helped us with indications of great interest for our study. Although risking involuntary omissions, we cannot fail to mention the names of António Hespanha, António Montes Moreira, B.S. Shastry, Berta Mascarenhas Fernandes, Carmen M. Radulet, Denys Lombard, Eduardo Gonçalves Rodrigues, Ernestina Carreira, Fernando Castelo-Branco, Francisca Andrade, Geneviève Bouchon, João Pedro Ferro and Joseph Barros, who, unfortunately, are no more in our midst; Lívia Ferrão, Lotika Varadarajan, Manohar Sar Dessai, Maria Alcina Mártires Lopes, Maria Augusta Lima Cruz, Maria Ivone Clemente Gaspar, Maria dos Remédios Castelo-Branco, Percival Noronha, Raquel Soeiro de Brito, Sanjay Subrahmanyam, Susana Sardo, Vítor Rodrigues.

We would like to remember some institutions that supported

us during the long years of preparing this dissertation. To the Calouste Gulbenkian Foundation thanks are due for the scholarship granted and which was essential for the feasibility of research work in the Historical Archives of Goa for some months. We thank the Centro de Estudos dos Povos e Culturas de Expressão Portuguesa, of the Universidade Católica Portuguesa, in the person of its President, Eng. Roberto Carneiro, for granting us facilities to undertake this work when posted there. To Mário Lages, member of the Board of Directors of this Centre, we are indebted for the help and guidance given to us in handling the demographic data, in which subject, in fact, he is an acknowledged specialist. To Arch. Maria Cristina Pereira, Secretary of the said Centre, who patiently and perfectly typed the first version of this study, goes our appreciation and affection.

We are grateful for the support, stimulus and friendship given to us by Jill Dias, Director of the Centro de Estudos Africanos e Asiáticos of the Instituto Científica Tropical, to which we are presently associated.

Many were the archives, national and foreign, where we have had to work for years together and many were the facilities that their directors and employees extended to us: at the Arquivo Histórico Ultramarino, Isaú Santos, D. Luísa Abrantes, D. Benedita Galamba, Albino Resina and Carlos Leão; at the Arquivos Nacionais/Torre do Tombo, José Pereira da Costa and Inácio Guerreiro; at the Historical Archives of Goa, P.P. Shirodkar and Teresinha Almeida; at the Archive of the Patriarchal Curia of Goa, the Chancellor Rev. Benjamim Fernandes and Sister Elizabeth Souza; at the Xavier Centre of Historical Research (Goa), Teotónio R. de Souza.

Finally, to my husband who, with all his total dedication, removed all obstacles and created work conditions, making this task possible, and to my children who with their tenderness lightened the ordeal of research work, my gratitude.

Monte Estoril — MARIA DE JESUS DOS MÁRTIRES LOPES
April 1993

CHAPTER I

Institutional and Economic Aspects

AT THE BEGINNING of the second half of the eighteenth century, the territory called the Estado da Índia, or State of India, comprised Mozambique on the eastern coast of Africa, the districts of Goa on the Konkan coast, Daman on the Gulf of Cambay, and Diu on the coast of Gujarat, besides Macao and Timor in the Far East.[1] First, by the loss of the Província do Norte, or Northern Province (1739) and, then, by the disannexation of Mozambique (1752), the area administered by the Viceroys or Governors headquartered in Goa was considerably reduced.[2]

But the loss in territory (undoubtedly very scattered hitherto) meant a gain in unity. As a result, the separation of dominions as far-flung as Mozambique (1752) and later Macao (1844), on the one hand, and the acquisition of the *Novas Conquistas*, or New Conquests, adjoining the Portuguese territories of Goa, on the other, provided territorial continuity and viability to the Estado da Índia quite different from the earlier one.[3]

[1] 'The territory of Goa is a part of the Konkan, a narrow littoral strip situated on the foot of the very extensive Deccan plateau and which, over hundreds of kilometres, forms the Malabar Coast.' Cf. Mariano Feio, 'Problemas da geomorfologia de Goa', in *Garcia de Orta,* special issue, Lisbon, 1956, p. 39.

[2] The Northern Province included the following territories: Chaul, ceded by an agreement with Nizamaluco in 1521; Bassein and its lands, as a result of a treaty with the King of Gujarat in 1531 who also authorized the construction of a fortress in Diu; Daman, granted by the King of Gujarat in 1569, but which had to be obtained by force from the Abyssinian garrison post which was refusing to vacate the fortress (Padre M.J. Gabriel de Saldanha, *História de Goa (Política e Arqueólogica),* vol. I, Nova Goa, 1925, reed. New Delhi and Madras, Asian Educational Services, 1990, p. 66). About the disannexation of Mozambique in 1752, see fn 31 of this chapter.

[3] The area of the Old Conquests, including the island of Anjediva

In this context, the district of Goa became the cornerstone and vital part of the Estado da Índia, and the object of intense restructuring, as we shall see in due course.

GEOGRAPHY

The traveller crossing the Indian peninsula, from north to south, first notices the mountainous barrier of the Himalayas, the Hindu-Kush and the edges of the Iranian plateau, followed by the Indo-Gangetic plains, and finally, the Deccan or Indian tableland, whose edges comprise the ranges of the Western and Eastern Ghats. Between them and the sea, on the coast of the Bay of Bengal, there are important plains. On the other hand, by the Arabian Sea, there are only little coastal plains, sandwiched between the Western Ghats and the sea and cut up by the estuaries of the rivers coming down the ridge.

Goa is situated on one of these little mountainous amphitheatres, in which the Ghats come down in successive degrees toward the sea, from which they are separated by a little coastal plateau.[4] By stretching its territory up to the base of the ridge of mountains, the New Conquests of the second half of the eighteenth century gave the territory its natural limits and facilitated defence.

Set in the extreme south of the Konkan coast, between 14° 53'57" and 15° 47'59" north latitude, Goa adjoined the State of Saunto Varim or Sawantwadi to the north, separated by the river Tiracol; to the east and south was a conventional border, divided by waters, valleys, crests or slopes which divided it from the lands of Balghat (beyond the Ghats), like Belgaum and Supem, south of Kanara; and finally, on the western side it faced the Indian Ocean, or better, the Arabian Sea, with a coast having a total extension of 132.9 sq. km.[5]

(3 sq. km.), was about 755 sq. km., whereas that of the New Conquests touched 2,845 sq. km. Cf. Gerardo A. Pery, *Geographia Estatística Geral de Portugal e Colónias,* Lisbon, Imprensa Nacional, 1875, p. 381.

[4] Cf. Arístides de Amorim Girão, 'Razões geográficas da presença de Portugal na Índia', in *Garcia de Orta,* 5, no. 4, Lisbon, 1957, pp. 623-5.

[5] Cf. O. Boléo, *Apontamentos para uma Geografia Física de Goa,* Lisbon,

Three morphological strips can be distinguished in the territory of Goa, each with its own style of soil occupation and human activity: first, the littoral area, consisting of extensive laterite terraces and broad almost plain, underlying valleys, with extensive slopes. These platforms are a characteristic of the Goan scenery, occupying a great portion of its littoral, as in Bardez. Next comes an intermediate zone, marked by an abrupt narrowing of valleys and the 'sinuous introduction of prominent contours of the Ghat slopes'; and finally, a third zone, formed by the edge of the Deccan plateau.[6]

The first zone lends the Goan scenery a vivid contrast between the rugged, reddish and sterile laterite surfaces and the luminous green rice fields and orchards. It is also the most densely populated area of Goa.[7] Naturally, the intermediate zone, with the plateaux separating the deeply encased rivers and the spurs of the Ghats, only supports a lean cultivation of secondary cereals and cattle breeding, yielding poor revenue. Because of the lack of resources, it is much less densely populated than the fertile valleys of the littoral.

Finally, the Ghat zone, with a dense forest cover, is practically unpopulated, treaded only by a few cattle breeders.[8]

Agência Geral do Ultramar, 1955, pp. 9-10; and *Províncias Ultramarinas Portuguesas. Dados Informativos,* Lisbon, Agência Geral do Ultramar, 1961.

[6] See Raquel Soeiro de Brito, *Goa e as Praças do Norte,* 2nd edn., Lisbon, Comissão Nacional para as Comemorações dos Descobrimentos Portugueses, 1998, pp. 19-26, and ibid. 'Notas para o Estudo dos Modos de Vida em Goa', in *Garcia de Orta,* special edition, Lisbon, 1956, p. 183. On the orographic systems of Goa, see Bernardino C. da Costa, 'Geografia Física e Política', in *A Índia Portuguesa,* vol. I, Nova Goa, 1923, pp. 7-9 and *Províncias Ultramarinas ...,* pp. 46-7.

[7] On the laterite and geological formations of the territory of Goa, see B.C. da Costa, art. cit., pp. 15-25 and M. Feio, op. cit., pp. 46-8.

[8] *Ghat,* 'ridge of mountains, in general, and in particular the one that crosses the Indian peninsula from north to south ....' This is a single serra or ridge; its eastern part is called Eastern Ghats and the western, Western Ghats (cf. Sebastião Rodolfo Dalgado, *Glossário Luso-Asiático,* vol. I, Coimbra, 1919, pp. 426-7. The cattle breeders that traverse the Ghats are called Koulis. Referring to them, the Marquis of Alorna states that 'many of them used to live deep in the forests, an errant life, independent, and almost savage.

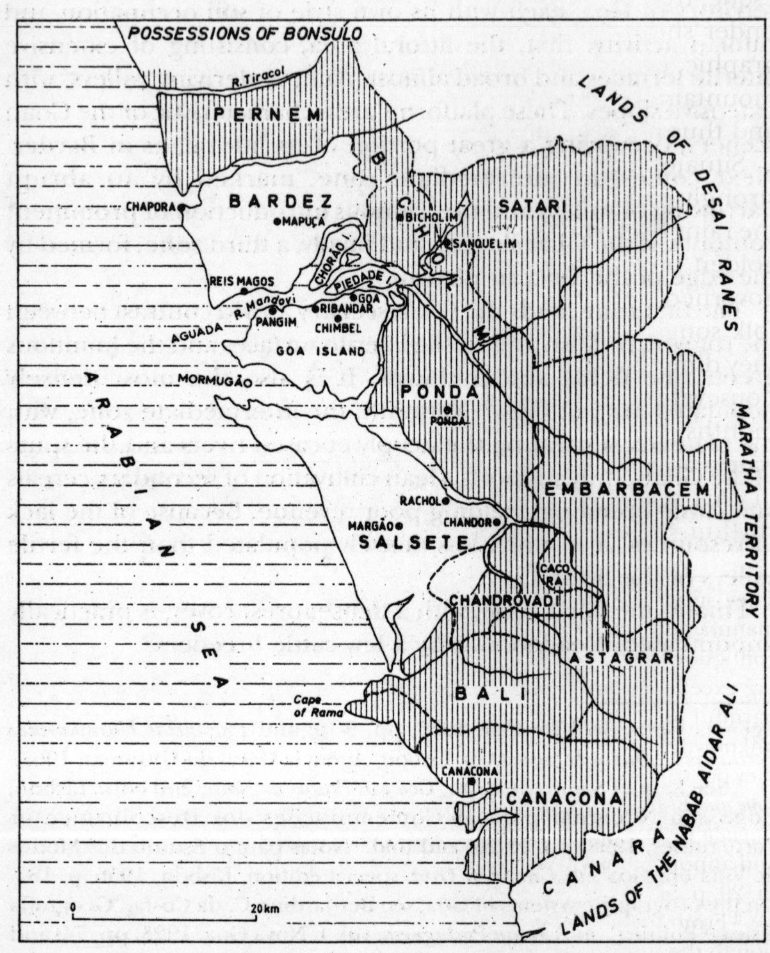

Map 1: The territory of Goa in the second half of the eighteenth century: Old and New Conquests, based on the *Carta Geographica dos Estados de Goa Levantada em os Annos d' 1776, 1777 e 1778 [...]. Foy novamente Copiada na dita Cidade em o Mes de Março de 1781*. Gabinete de Estudos Arqueológicos de Engenharia Militar, 1233/II – 2A – 24A – 111.

This great morphological diversity makes Goa very picturesque, freeing it from the monotony of the plains. In the period under study, the littoral was, as it had always been, the demographic, economic and political centre of the territory; but the mountainous region served as its barbican, facilitating defence, and thus not a totally useless counterweight.

Situated in the heart of the monsoon region, life in Goa is strongly conditioned by it. Not only Nature – truly seductive in the rainy season, with a wide gamut of green shades, soon turning golden brown in the dry season – but the ways of life too are governed by the monsoons that even provide themes for Goan folk songs.[9] They so influence the life of the locals that, when they diminish, prayers are said to God imploring rains. From the housewife who diligently stocks foodstuffs for the long rainy months, to the farmer who prepares the land to receive the waters and the fisherman who, on the other hand, cannot work in this season, human life in Goa proceeds in this cyclical rhythm.[10]

They survive on vegetables, and dairy products which they themselves manufacture roughly, not only for their sustenance but also to sell in the contiguous villages. ... They burn the woods to have land for sowing, allowing excellent construction timber to be devoured by the flames, which is harmful for their neighbourhood. ... Their customs are pure, and vice is unknown, however they do not recognise any authority whatsoever, nor do they pay tributes; for they are neither enlisted nor subjugated.' Cf. *Instrucções com que El-Rei D. José I mandou passou ao Estado da Índia, o Governador, o Capitão General e o Arcebispo Primaz do Oriente, no anno de 1774,* published and annotated by Cláudio Lagrange Monteiro de Barbuda, Pangim, 1841, fn. 29, p. 54.

[9] From the choral group *Gavana* the following songs stand out in allusion to the monsoons: *'Pausu boglek paulo mhuje maim doria gazota!* (repeat) *Doriach'deger boisun mhuje maim laram mejitam!'* Translation: My mother, the rains are about to come, the sea is roaring! (repeat) Seated on the riverbank, my mother, I count the waves! (repeat). And another one, as follows: *'Doddam vazoi re, magir pausu ietolo. Danu-danu ... tari meutoli. Tanddela, tauzam mari, tauzam, mari!'* Translation: Play quickly, the rain is about to come. Hurry up, it is time to cross over to the other side. Row, boatman, row,!

[10] See R.S. de Brito, op. cit., p. 26. Cf. the circular of Archbishop D. Francisco de Assunção e Brito, dated 20 August 1779, that 'to ask for rain, he ordains prayers for 3 days, and as the need goes, to recite the respective

The climatic conditions are quite regular, not only from the viewpoint of the average annual temperature levels and thermal amplitude but also as regards humidity and rainfall.

Thus, the months from June to September have a higher rainfall – they constitute the rainy season, the south-east monsoon, more commonly known only as the monsoon. In October, it rains much less and November is almost dry. From this season onwards the pressure rises, the temperature falls slightly and consequently the thermal amplitudes are greater, especially in the hinterland. It is a transition to the new, fresh and dry season stretching from December to March – that of the north-east monsoon, known as the *época do terral*. In March, temperatures begin to rise quickly, touching quite high levels, mainly in May when the south-west monsoon is pre-announced by thunder and a very hot and humid atmosphere. June witnesses the 'eruption' of the monsoon that in July spreads throughout India.[11]

It can thus be said about Goa's rainfall that the year is divided into three periods: with heavy rains from June to September; weaker rains in May, October and November, and December to April being dry months.[12]

Situated almost at sea level, Goa has a climate that is thus very different from that of the more mountainous neighbouring territory. This produces a marked originality both in the natural and human landscape.[13]

In comparison with the territorial limitations of Goa (approximately 3,600 sq. km), the navigable extent of its rivers is quite considerable, totalling about 250 sq. km. Thus a good part of its commerce is even today done by waterways, especially by the rivers with a greater discharge, the Mandovi and the

---

prayer at Mass' (Casimiro Cristóvão de Nazareth, *Mitras Lusitanas no Oriente* ..., 2nd edn., Lisbon, 1897, p. 316).

[11] R.S. de Brito, op. cit., pp. 27-9. The transition of the monsoon from the NE to that of SW is sudden; hence the word 'erupt'. On the other hand, the passage of the monsoon from SW to that of NE is very slow (cf. O. Boléo, op. cit., p. 85).

[12] Cf. R.S. de Brito, op. cit., pp. 20-1.

[13] Ibid., p. 23.

Zuari.[14] As regards the hydrographic network, as stated by Mariano Feio, 'it shows a clear structural influence, by the recurrent direction of the water courses to the Northwest or North-Northwest. There are only water courses or sections of them that, following the call of the sea, move directly towards the littoral.'[15]

Several rapids and falls are seen in the initial segment of some rivers of Goa, particularly the waterfall of Arvalem, in the taluka of Sanquelim, and Dudhsagar at Embarbacem, in the village of Sonaulim.[16]

During the south-west monsoon, the riverbeds naturally overflow and flood the bordering areas. Big deposits are drawn in its trajectory and this alluvium mainly constitutes the surface of the islands.[17]

[14] For data on the hydrographic network, see O. Boléo, op. cit., pp. 4-73 and B.C. da Costa, op. cit., pp. 11-14.

[15] Cf. M. Feio, op. cit., pp. 55-7.

[16] The Dudhsagar waterfall has a height of 165 metres, in the form of a dense water sheet 25 to 30 metres broad in the rainy season, but in the dry season it is reduced to a simple thread of water, the same happening with the Arvalem falls. Etymologically, the word *Dudhsagar* means sea of milk (*dudh* means milk and *sagar,* sea). But if etymology justifies fully the vocable given that the foamy waterfall produces the impression of milk, the Goan romanticist put together an interesting legend, which runs as follows: Close to the waterfall, there was a masterpiece of a royal palace in the Oriental style attesting to the magnificence of an opulent and powerful king. In it lived a princess of exceptional beauty of body and spirit, whose fame had spread all over the Konkan. Every morning the princess would come out of her palace, accompanied by a lady-in-waiting, and go to a tank of limpid and pure water, which the princess sipped from after ablution. One day, as she was stepping out of the tank, she crossed sight with a prince whose riveting gaze offended her modesty. Lo and behold, she poured the liquid from the jar, forming a curtain of milk, hiding the nakedness of her body from the indiscreet sight of the prince, whereas the lady hastened to cover her with a purple blanket. To perpetuate the memory of the fragrance of her virtue, the goddess Laxmi created a waterfall, suggestive of milk, surrounded by an Eden-like nature. A picture of this fall can be seen in A. Lopes Mendes, *A Índia Portuguesa,* vol. II, New Delhi and Madras, 1989, reedition of Asian Educational Services, on pp. 110-11.

[17] The alluvium dragged into the rivers obliging the abandoning or

Thus two zones can be distinguished in the district of Goa: the island section – corresponding to the taluka of *Ilhas* (Islands) – with a curious topography, a type of delta common to the rivers Mandovi and Zuari which, being easy to defend, was the initial zone of Portuguese occupation;[18] and the other zone is the continental part or terra firma, the larger part of which spreads out to the north, west and south of the Islands and where two topographical zones are still discernible: the *concelhos* (provinces, or *talukas*) of Bardez and Salsete, to the north and south of the Islands, respectively, and like them, fertile and densely populated lowlands which the Portuguese incorporated in their dominions in the second quarter of the sixteenth century. The continental part also comprised the hilly section of the Ghats and the transitional strip, all of which was conquered only in the third quarter of the eighteenth century and hence came to be known as the New Conquests.[19]

---

desilting of some ports. Hence, Goa Velha (aligned between the island of S. Jacinto and the Ponta da Senhora da Saúde), which before the arrival of the Portuguese had been a rich trading city, was abandoned, because of its siltation and, in the middle of the fifteenth century, was transferred to Velha Goa, on the left bank of the Mandovi. However, this city too – the capital of Goa until 1759 – had to be abandoned, not only for health reasons, but also because of the siltation of its port.

[18] The debris dragged by the Mandovi-Zuari system constituted an enormous internal delta, whose lowlands form the Ilhas archipelago. Truly only the main island – that of Tissuary or Goa – is bathed on the west by the Indian Ocean or Sea of Oman, all the others being in the interior of the estuaries. Among them are those of Chorão, the biggest after that of Goa, Piedade or Divar, Santo Estêvão or Jua, Vanxim or island of Capão, Acaró and the small island of Ratos.

[19] Cf. Map 1, referring to the territory of Goa, in this chapter. Since then the three coastal provinces (Bardez, Ilhas and Salcete) were called Old Conquests to which are joined two small islands of Anjediva and Tiracol. The New Conquests comprise four districts, divided into ten provinces – Pernem, Bicholim, Satari, Ponda, the five provinces called Zambaulim or Panchmahal and Canacona – situated essentially to the east, in the mountainous region of the Western Ghats. Cf. E.R. Hambye, 'Goa', in *Dictionnaire d'Histoire et de Géographie ecclésiastiques,* sous la direction de R. Aubert, Letouzey et Ané, Paris, n.d., p. 248. Also see the notes and appendix to the

EXTERNAL RELATIONS OF THE ESTADO DA ÍNDIA

The external situation of the Portuguese territories in India changed dramatically in the mid-eighteenth century. While the Mughals were supreme they most often enjoyed good neighbourly relations, perhaps because the Mughal Empire was a continental state without great pretensions to maritime hegemony.[20]

With the predominance of the Maratha Empire, the situation changed not only because of the physical proximity of their centre to the Portuguese possessions but because the Marathas sought to raise a naval force and control the surrounding waters, grudging the Portuguese the little that had remained of their erstwhile maritime hegemony.[21]

To add to this was the increasing tendency of the French and the English to evolve a policy of continental imperialism, being

---

Instrucções [...], referring to the provinces of Bardez, Salsete and New Conquests, pp. 15, 45-6 and I-IV, respectively.

[20] Regarding the rise and the decline of the Mughal Empire, see John F. Richards, 'The Mughal Empire', in *The New Cambridge History of India*, New Delhi, 1994. About the dissolution of the empire, see Percival Spear, *India, A Modern History*, new edn., University of Michigan Press, 1961, 1972, pp. 172-5; Vincent A. Smith, C.I.E. [...], *The Oxford History of India from the earliest times to the end of 1911*, 2nd edn., Oxford University Press, 1923, p. 465; Maurice Garden, 'A India: o comeco de um declino', in *Historia Economica e Social do Mundo*, ed. Pierre Leon, Port. transl., vol. 3, pt. I, Sa da Costa, Lisbon, 1983, pp. 219-20.

[21] [...] 'Shau Raja [the first branch of the Maratha reigning family; the second was Sambhaji Raja], taking advantage of the decadence of the Mughal Empire and the disloyalty of the Prince's Generals, runs about and plunders using his captains' armies in the large area from the kingdom of Cambay to Bengal, obliging all the provinces he crosses to pay him tribute, after devastating, looting and despoiling them of incredible riches. Sambhaji Raja's district extends from Talagy Angria's up to the extreme end of Kanara, and takes all of Konkan down to the lower Ghats for his tributaries, which includes the said Angria, the Bhonsales and similarly the entire district of Goa, which we never agreed to nor paid. The Sunda and the Kanara kings pay them considerable tribute'. *Instrucção do Exmo Vice-Rei Márquez de Alorna ao seu Sucessor o Exmo Vice-Rei Marquez de Tavora [...]*, by Filippe Nery Xavier, 2nd edn., Nova Goa, 1856, pp. 29-30.

no longer satisfied, as the Portuguese and Dutch had been, with their littoral locations. Hence they aimed to work out complex alliances and be politically intrusive in the sub continent.[22] Whereas the French with Lenoir and Dupleix expanded particularly in Carnatic (Tamil Nadu and adjacent regions), the English, who had settled in Surat and Bombay since the seventeenth century, became active in regional politics, supporting the Marathas in their efforts to take hold of the Estado da Índia's Northern Province, i.e. the entire littoral belt between Daman and Bombay, and the Chaul enclave a little further south.

The English and French policy of conquest acted as a stimulus for the Portuguese: it invited them to emulate it and suggested that they proceed with the occupation of territories adjacent to their own. Hence the annexation of the New Conquests between the first and the second half of the eighteenth century, to which we shall refer a little later.

A NEW STRATEGY FOR THE ESTADO DA ÍNDIA AND NEIGHBOURING POWERS

Several researchers and historians of Portuguese India describe the eighteenth century as a period of decadence and crumbling of the Portuguese Empire in the East which, having already a reduced jurisdiction with assaults by the Dutch and the English, suffered the fall of Bassein and consequent loss of the Northern Province. This phenomenon of decadence is referred to quite frequently in the documentation of the period and certainly is moral and institutional rather than politico-military in nature.

Therefore, although in the middle of the eighteenth century Brazil continued to be the cornerstone of the Portuguese Empire, there was at the same time a renewed interest in the development

[22] For instance, Dupleix even supported the Nizam of Carnatic and came to use the title of Governor of south India, in the Mughal style. See *The Cambridge History of India*, vol. V, chaps. VI, VII, VIII, IX, X and XIV. About the activities of the French Company of East Indies, see S.P. Sen, *The French in India, 1763-1816*, 2nd edn., Munshiram Manoharlal, New Delhi, 1971.

of the Estado da Índia. There could be several reasons to explain this attitude on the part of the Lisbon government. In fact, the remittances of Brazilian gold had reached their peak in 1720 but thereafter, they began to fade slowly but steadily.[23] This fall in gold production, with serious consequences for the economy, must have compelled the rulers to turn their attention to Goa. Having been the long-time glory of the overseas epic, in 1750, thanks to the annexation of some territories, it was recovering morally and economically from the drain caused by the loss of the Northern Province in 1739.[24]

It must be noted in fact that, despite foreign competition

[23] At the present state of research, it is not possible to establish strictly the values of Brazilian gold production in the eighteenth century. Virgílio Noya Pinto in *O Ouro Brasileiro e o Comércio Anglo-Português (Uma Contribuição aos Estudos da Economia Atlântica no Século XVIII),* Brasiliana, vol. 371, 2nd edn., S. Paulo, Companhia Editora Nacional, 1979, pp. 112-17, locates the great production in the years 1735-54 and points to an annual average between 14,134 and 15,760 kg. However, he states that 'the analysis of the gold cargoes in the fleet, the news about embezzlement and various forms of smuggling convince us that the Brazilian gold production is beyond the calculations allowed by the documents'. Hence he considers that the production must have been raised to a level between 18 and 20 tonnes annually. On this subject, also see A.H. de Oliveira Marques, *História de Portugal,* vol. II, Lisbon, Palas Editores, 1983, pp. 380-1, and Guy Martinière, 'A Implantação das Estruturas de Portugal na América (1620-1750)', in *Nova História da Expansão Portuguesa,* directed by Joel Serrão and A. H. de Oliveira Marques, vol. VII, *O Império Luso-Brasileiro 1620-1750,* coordinated by Frédéric Mauro, Lisbon, Estampa, 1991, pp. 241 ss.

[24] The loss of the Northern Province caused a significant reaction from the central government that sent one of the biggest expeditions till then prepared for the East, with more than 2000 soldiers. The Viceroy, Count of Ericeira, and Marquis of Louriçal, D. Luis Carlos Inácio Xavier de Meneses, freed the provinces of Bardez and Salcete from the possession of the Bhonsles (1741) and during the government of his successor, Viceroy D. Pedro Miguel Almeida e Portugal (1744-50) the fortresses of Alorna, Bicholim, Avaró, Tiracol, Rarim and Neutim passed on to the Portuguese dominions. Cf. A. da Silva Rego, *O Ultramar Português no século XVIII,* Lisbon, Agência Geral do Ultramar, 1970, pp. 83-7 and Jaime Cortesão, 'Domínio Ultramarino', in *História de Portugal,* ed. Damião Peres, vol. VI, Barcelos, 1934, pp. 671-2.

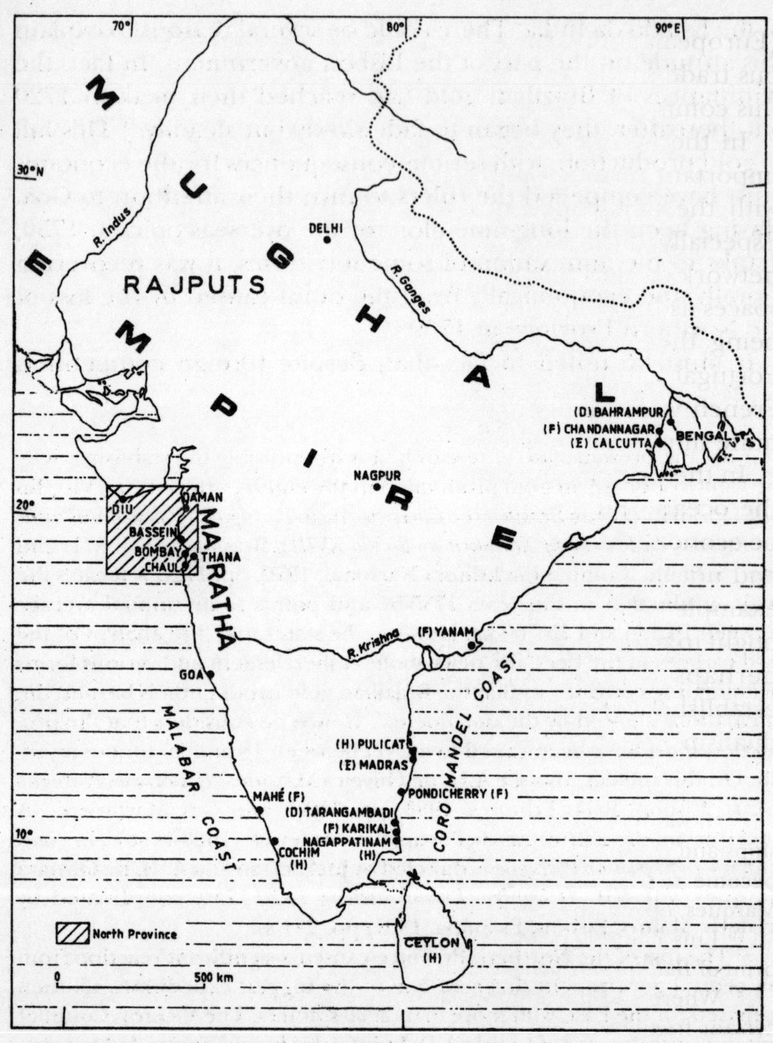

MUGHAL EMPIRE, RAJPUTS, MARATHAS
River Indus, River Ganga, River Krishna
Calcutta – Bassein – Daman – Bombay – Thana – Madras – Pondicherry – Cochin – Coromandel Coast – Ceylon – Northern Province
H – Dutch, F – French, I – English

Map 2: India in the beginning of the eighteenth century – Mughals and Marathas

(European and Asiatic), Portugal continued to enjoy a prosperous trade traffic with Asia, and Goa was an important centre in this commercial network.[25]

In the middle of the eighteenth century, Goa witnessed an important turning point in its history; it was related intimately with the new conception of the Portuguese Eastern Empire. Especially in the sixteenth century, this empire was essentially 'a network of maritime routes, with only some little discontinuous spaces as indispensable points of support on land, the network being their only reason of being'.[26] But times had changed. Portugal had lost its naval superiority: the Dutch, English and French were ploughing the eastern seas, and also conquering quite important positions.

In the new circumstances, instead of stopovers sprinkled over the ocean, there was need to have some territories that would be economically, strategically and politically viable in themselves and not by virtue of the said network. On the other hand, the example of the French and English conquests in Hindustan ought to have stimulated the Portuguese. The Marquis of Pombal, perhaps influenced by the theory of the colonial pact,[27] established a general orientation to do away with 'colonial dualism', and to make each province directly dependent on the

[25] 'It was worth trading with Goa even with a much smaller number of ships and *carreiras*, for it was undoubtedly much easier for an emigrant to become rich in India than in Portuguese Africa.' Cf. A.H. de Oliveira Marques, op. cit., p. 436.

[26] Luís Filipe Ferreira Reis Thomaz, *Goa: une société luso-indienne*, offprint of *Bulletin des Études Portugaises et Brésiliennes*, Paris, 42-3 (1983), p. 24.

[27] Whereas in the administrative and political aspect England granted certain freedom to its colonists in America, in the economic sector it adopted the 'colonial pact', whereby the colonies had to bring in revenue for the metropolis. Thus the English factories were supplied with raw materials from the colonies, and, once manufactured, the articles would return to the same to be sold. The English ships did the sailing and the colonies could not trade with anybody other than the mother country (cf. A. da Silva Rego, *O Ultramar Português no século XVIII*, Lisbon, Agência Geral do Ultramar, 1970, pp. 9-10). It may be noted, however, that in relation to Goa, the theory of the colonial pact was not applied in the same manner as, for example, with Africa.

central government. In fact till then the overseas territories used to be frequently grouped in pairs, one being dependent on the other. Thus, Angola was a subsidiary of Brazil, Mozambique of India and Guinea of Cape Verde. This situation was irreversibly abolished and, from then on, each colony had its own management in all spheres.[28]

Now the Goan territory had no unity; it was irregularly contoured and had enclaves dependent on local sovereigns who exposed the frontiers to incursions by enemies. The Northern Province was a source of wealth for a part of the Goan population, yet no effort was made to reconquer it.[29] Instead, right from 1740, there was a military and diplomatic ascent, which at the end of the eighteenth century, allowed the incorporation of the territories adjacent to the provinces of Bardez, Ilhas and Salcete (New Conquests), more or less quadrupling the earlier area and thus forging the territorial unity that has come down to our days.[30]

The idea of making the Estado da Índia an autonomous entity, with its own pace of development and without letting the decadence of another to reflect on it must have prompted the administrative separation of Mozambique in 1752, and that of Macao and Timor in 1844. Thus, all subaltern positions were abolished.[31]

Quite evidently, there were plans, mainly in the second half of the eighteenth century, for the restructuring and renewal of the Estado da Índia. Writing to the future Governor and Captain-

[28] Ibid., p. 19.

[29] In the first half of the eighteenth century, the Northern Province was so prosperous that it could well be said to represent, *mutatis mutandis*, a replica of the 'Golden Goa' of the sixteenth century. Its churches, convents, House of Mercy, squares, mansions, busy roads, and intense internal trade lent the city of Bassein in particular, features peculiar to developing regions. Ibid., pp. 72, 74 and 75.

[30] Cf. A.H. de Oliveira Marques, *Historia de Portugal*, vol. II, pp. 438-9.

[31] The royal decree of 19 April 1752 separated Mozambique from the Estado da Índia. On the reasons for this separation, see A. da Silva Rego, op. cit., pp. 197-9. Macao, Timor and Solor were disconnected from the Estado da Índia and became one province by the royal decree of 20 September 1844.

General of the Estado da Índia, D. José Pedro da Câmara, the monarch, D. José, stated that he was not ordering the 'succouring of the same State in the ordinary manner, but yes to have it restructured and founded afresh: by uprooting the vices which have hitherto contaminated it; and by planting in the lands that they have infected, Christian, political and military virtues, aimed at the rebirth of the reputation and glory of the Portuguese name in Asia.'[32]

From the political and military point of view, this perspective of reorganization did not necessarily mean conquering new dominions. Quite the reverse. The central government, containing the enthusiasm of the Goan people who, from the very first moment of the loss of the Northern Province, nurtured hopes of its speedy reconquest, ordained that only the existing territory should be maintained. It was therefore determined that, though the vitality of Goa was intrinsically connected to possessing the Northern Province, its military reconquest should not be desired so early; it was necessary to have a more favourable local conjuncture for its recovery – be it the death of the Maratha sovereign or some treaty sanctioning it. These directives emanating from the central power are quite clear, both in the Instructions given by the monarchs to the Governors and Viceroys of the Estado da Índia as well as in the very Instructions furnished by the outgoing Governors to their successors.[33]

[32] Royal letter accompanying the *Instrucções. ...*

[33] That is what is mentioned in the royal Instruction to the Count of Ega of 31 March 1758: The King states his 'firm intention of preserving what exists, without the honour of restoration and much less of conquest ever crossing your mind.' Cf. A.H.U., *Índia,* maço 28-A (290) and códice 513, ff. 1-10. The same spirit prevails even in 1774, for in D. José's *Instrucções* to the Governor D. José Pedro da Câmara, he ordains that 'all the possessions in Portuguese Asia be reduced ..., by seeing to it, on the one hand, that this moderation and abstinence from restoring and making new Conquests be and remain unconditional until His Majesty orders the contrary; and on the other hand that all care be employed by the Government of Goa to promote and spread trade. ...' The Government of Goa should, therefore, 'preserve their own things without the least intention of conquering another's property'. Cf. *Instrucções* ... Quinta Instrucção, Chap. I, pp. 43-4.

The Northern Province was never reconquered. However, the evolution of the political and diplomatic situation of the Estado da Índia, surrounded as it was by Asian kinglets, did allow certain fortresses and dominions contiguous to the Goan mainland to be conquered in the second half of the eighteenth century in order to ensure its stability in the face of constant enemy threats.

Which were these powers? What were the means of defence for the Portuguese power vis-à-vis other local sovereigns? Were diplomatic relations in accordance with a plan for reanimating Goan trade and life in general? Let us attempt some answers.

About the year 1750, there were local rulers and potentates of which some could be more or less regarded as friends, others as tacit or avowed enemies. Thus the King of Kanara whose power extended theoretically from Chaul up to Cape Comorin, lived 'in good peace and correspondence' with the Portuguese government. Since the Portuguese factory of Mangalore was situated in his district, it suited the Portuguese to follow a policy of peace and good neighbourliness, this being crucial to sustain Goa, which could hardly produce rice that was sufficient for four months of the year.[34]

In the past, the Zamorin was the most powerful sovereign on the Malabar Coast and the worst enemy of the Portuguese. But in the period under consideration the Muslims residing in the territory had undermined his power, and this made him re-approach Portugal. The Portuguese held a factory in his dominions, at the Calicut port itself.

Given their hinterland position above the Ghats and being mere *sardessaiados* dependent on the Mughal king, the Nawabs of Kittur and Xaunur meant little to Portugal, 'but nonetheless we live in good friendship and correspondence with them, and we can easily call them our friends', wrote the Marquis of Alorna.[35]

The kingdom of Sunda or Sundém comprised an extensive part of the Vijayanagar of yore, occupying two-thirds of its territory. The king lived, by and large, in peace and harmony

[34] *Instrucção* [...], pp. 8-10.
[35] Ibid., p. 15.

with the neighbouring territories of Goa, which were allies out of common interest, as evidenced also by the treaties signed with him. Several reasons, however, such as their immediate neighbourhood, the need for supplies, the fact that numerous Dessai vassals of the Estado da Índia owned lands (*dessaiados*) in the province of Ponda, the nearest neighbour of Goa, made the Viceroys keep good relations with him.[36]

The Angrias, Hindu corsairs who had acquired some political power, were the 'scourge' of the Malabar coast, from the end-point of Diu to Calicut. They were truly feared and held in awe by all. They frequently solicited the friendship of the Viceroys of India who discreetly deferred negotiations, engaging them with an ostensible peace inasmuch as not to be obliged in any manner whatever. The main goal of these negotiations was to prevent naval depradations by these pirates and the consequent trade instability.[37]

[36] About the Sunda kingdom, its extension and the reasons that led the Viceroys to maintain good correspondence with it, see *Instrucção*, pp. 15-24. A brief summary of the treaties with the Sunda is found in the *Instrucção*, pp. 16-17. Also see Julio F. J. Biker, *Collecção de tratados e concertos de pazes que o Estado da Índia Portugueza fez com os reis e senhores com quem teve relações nas partes da Asia, África Oriental desde o princípio da conquista até ao fim do século XVIII*, Lisbon, 1885, pts. VII, pp. 10-15, 30-2, 46-7, 132-7; VIII, pp. 1-4; IX, pp. 11-13, 46, 103-25. With regard to trade relations as a whole, the kingdom of Sunda used to supply pepper to Goa and receive munitions and arms that it required. The King of Sunda even obtained permission to open a pepper shop in Goa. Besides this, other items sold by this king in Goa included oranges, milk products and a certain type of textiles used by the more humble people and known as *cambolins* (coir mantle). See B.S. Shastry, 'Commercial Relations between the Portuguese and the Sonda chiefs: 1593-1764', paper presented at the Vth International Seminar on Indo-Portuguese History, Cochin, 1989. Regarding the contents of the designations *'sardessaiados'* (*sar-deshmukhi)* and *'dessaiados'* (*deshmukhi)*, see the Glossary.

[37] The Angria dominions were divided between two brothers: Talagy Angria, with headquarters in Vijaydurg, commonly called Guirim, the more powerful and closer neighbour of Goa; and Managy Angria, who had settled in the region presently called Kulabo, close to Bombay. Guirim is at 16° 37' N latitude and 73° 22' E longitude and is a distance of 193 English miles from Goa. Cf. *Instrucções* ..., pp. 24-9.

The reigning Maratha family was divided into two branches: that of Shahu Raja, its supreme prince, with his court in Satara; and that of Sambhaji Raja, with his court in Kolhapur. They were notorious in India for their atrocities and the terror spread by their hordes through all the provinces they passed. Their troops seemed so disorganized that the Viceroy the Marquis of Alorna used to say that he did not fear to attack an army of 50,000 Marathas with a body of 5,000 regular troopers.[38]

The council of Shahu Raja comprised four or five ministers, of which Nana, the son of Baji Rao, had wrested the Northern Province from the Portuguese. He was, undoubtedly, the most powerful of them all and reputed to be 'the greatest and most terrible enemy of this State'. The peace signed with him in 1740 was indeed only an illusory one, for he possessed a fleet and never missed a chance to attack the frigates from the north.[39]

The Sawant Bhonsales, Dessais of Kudal, had an open war with the Portuguese. The period of the three Bhonsale wars is well known in the history of Goa: they stretched right through the first half of the eighteenth century and contributed towards the good reputation of the Portuguese army among the Asian chieftains. Several times this enemy proposed peace to the Marquis of Alorna who did not proceed with the negotiations as they were not of advantage to the State.[40]

When we took up the issue of the Asian potentates, we had inquired about the dominant aspects of our diplomatic and military policy. For this end we think it necessary firstly to consider the positions normally taken by the Indian potentates in their contacts with the Viceroys and Governors of India. The picture that the Marquis of Alorna drew of them in the said Instrucção sums up the political aspects of the eighteenth century: 'Before having any relation with Your Excellency, they will make, as they

[38] Ibid., pp. 29-39. Gives further information on the Maratha form of government and the struggle for power succession.

[39] Ibid., pp. 45-6.

[40] Ibid., p. 37. Also see Maria de Jesus Célia dos Mártires Lopes, 'Panorama Político do Estado da Índia no século XVIII. Subsídios para a sua história' (photostat copy of the M.A. dissertation), Coimbra, 1969, pp. 31-8. Kudal is situated at 16° 1' N lat. and 73° 4' E long. to the north of Goa.

always do, all the diligence possible to identify, and examine the genius of Your Excellency, to find the manner and methods to be employed to make you agree to the peace ...'. And further he states, 'Experience shall show Your Excellency that all the business they proposed, whether friends or enemies, is either unjust to all the respects, or solely founded on their own interest. ...'[41]

Given the manner in which the neighbouring kings functioned, the Marquis of Alorna sought to forewarn his successor of possible shortcomings, advising him to always maintain an attitude of reserve and scepticism.[42]

In the midst of the extremely complex diplomatic issues with the neighbouring kings, calling for cautious reserve and pondered discretion, the Viceroys had at their service a gallery of Goans – Hindus, Muslims, Jews and Parsis – who were quite efficient in their role as *'línguas'* (State interpreters) and envoys to the Indian kings. Sometimes they constituted real interpreter families rendering important services as agents of Portuguese diplomacy in India.[43]

[41] Instrucção [...], pp. 44-5.

[42] The Marquis of Alorna recommends that, 'Y. Ex. should distrust all those who in order to propose some business, begin with adulation, flattery, deep submissions, avowals of sincerity, and of cordial affection, and believe, that then he is firmer in his decision not to comply with anything that he has promised.' Cf. Instrucção ..., p. 45.

[43] The families of the *'linguas'* that became well-known were: Vaga – Bogona Camotim who exercised the function from 1719 to 1751, Ananta Camotim Vaga (1752-93), Boguna Camotim (1793-1807) and Sacarama Naraina Vaga (1807-44). The Dumós were another family that also made their mark – Vitogi Sinai Dumó, Poqueá Sinai Dumó, Naraina Sinai Dumó. Among the non-Hindu interpreters, there figures a Muslim, Ismael Khan, who negotiated with Tulagi Angria Sarquel the preliminaries of the treaty of 6 November 1755; a Jew, who in the second quarter of the eighteenth century, mainly exercised the function of director of the Portuguese factory of Surat and rendered important service to the nation, mainly at the time of Baji Rao's invasion of Bassein; the Parsi Ruston Manock, who played an important role as representative of the Portuguese government in more than one conflict with the Nawab of Surat. Cf. Panduronga Pissurlencar, *Agentes da Diplomacia Portuguesa na Índia. Hindus, Muçulmanos, Judeus e Parses*, Bastorá, 1952.

The circumstances were particularly difficult. The enemies had the great and inevitable advantage of easily getting information of any move. 'There live in our Country,' writes the Marquis of Alorna, 'a great number of Muslims, Gentiles of the same colour, of the same dress, the same language, and of the same Law, as those of the enemy Country; ... they enter and leave this Country without any need to disguise themselves in order to find out what they wish; which is not the case with the Portuguese, for neither the headgear, nor the cabaan can camouflage them, and the language, and the colour betrays them very easily.'[44] Added to disclosing State secrets was the dissimulation and lack of truthfulness in the information, for what 'came to me through Gentiles and Locals, half of it was false and the other half doubtful ...'.[45]

In this context, the Viceroys and Governors of the State sought to act cautiously through a network of spies and of sepoys, whose zeal and loyalty often freed the rulers from seemingly insurmountable dangers. The Marquis of Alorna quite realistically gave a summary of the political situation as follows: 'The scarce State forces, the distance, the uncertainty of the aid, and the scant firmness of the alliances, oblige the one who governs the same State to be armed with a fund of prudence and maturity capable of giving up even the most secure of projects, fearing poor success, which could be irreparable, and to await a favourable occasion; and when it is not so, it will be more useful to keep the power of the Arms resting rather than embarking on an enterprise that could fail, and which, even if successful, would be difficult to keep.'[46]

This was the position of the relations that the Estado da Índia had with the local neighbouring powers about the year 1750. A decade later, while the political chessboard remained by and large the same, it did change in many other ways. Accordingly, the provinces of Canacona, Zambaulim, Embarbacem, Ponda and the jurisdiction of Cabo da Rama, which earlier belonged to the King of Sunda, came under Portuguese sovereignty in 1763,

[44] Instrucção [...], p. 48.

[45] Ibid., p. 107.

[46] Ibid., pp. 110-13.

upon being granted to them in exchange for protection and political asylum.[47]

The Marathas now stood adjacent to Goa on the north, through the Konkan territory, which they ruled. On the eastern side of Goa between them and the provinces of Ponda, Embarbacem and Zambaulim was the Ghat section.

The Bhonsales continued to be a threat to the Estado da Índia not only by their infidelity but also because of the position of their lands bound on the north by the provinces of Bardez and Pernem.

The local Muslim ruler Hyder Ali Khan, after fighting the English and the Marathas allies in the court of Bengal, conquered, in the court of Malabar, the kingdom of Mysore, the States of the King of Kanara and those of the King of Sunda; the latter, dislodged from his dominions in 1764, requested asylum in Goa, which he was in effect granted. Hyder Ali Khan's policy of conquest (1763) and then that of his son Tipu Sultan (1783) made them consider capturing Goa as being a natural strategic point in their empire. Thus there emerged in the political scene a new ruler, closer-at-hand and more powerful than the Marathas, representing a danger to Goa.[48]

In spite of the great difficulties facing the Estado da Índia with regard to the Asian chieftains, its most intimidating enemies

[47] Cf. Instrucções [...], Quinta Instrucção, p. 55.

[48] See the *Notícia dos princípios de hum mouro levantado chamado Aidar, e da sua elevação até adquirir o honorífico de Nababo Aidar Ali Can, e dos seus progressos, e conquistas,* cf. A.H.U., *Índia,* maço 24 (22). On his power and advances in the government of the Count of Ega, see this chieftain's letter to the Viceroy of 29 August 1761, in *Boletim do Instituto Vasco da Gama,* no. 2, Nova Goa, 1928, pp. 105-6; the letter from the Count of Ega to the King, dated 2 February 1763 (A.N./T.T., *Reino,* maço 602); the letter from the Count of Ega to Sebastião José de Carvalho e Mello, publ. by António de Sousa Vasconcelos Simão de Saldanha, *As Cartas de Manuel de Saldanha, 1° Conde de Ega ...,* Lisbon, 1984, pp. 253-4. Also see Ernestina Carreira, 'Portuguese India in the reign of Tipoo Sultan', in *Moyen Orient et Océan Indien,* vol. 6, 1989, paper presented at the Vth Seminar on Indo-Portuguese History, Cochin, January 1989. On the appropriation of the dominions of the King Sunda by Hyder Ali Khan and the asylum granted to the former by the Portuguese, see Instrucções ..., Quinta Instrucção, pp. 55-6.

were undoubtedly the Europeans established in these stations. Thus, save the Danes, headquartered in Tranquebar on the Coromandel Coast, with whom Portugal did not have any relations, and the Spanish in the Philippines with whom good trade relations had been set up, the rest tried all means within their reach to annul the Portuguese influence in Asia.

The Dutch in the seventeenth century had taken over the best of the Portuguese dominions in the spice zones. They kept up the same hostility in the second half of the eighteenth, and wished, for example, to establish an alliance with the Marathas in order to become the lords of Daman and by all means hinder Portuguese trade in the north.[49]

Keen as they were on building an overseas empire in India, the English adopted a policy that was damaging to the Portuguese sovereignty. From their direct attacks, through constant acts of piracy, to the hostilities disguised in the help rendered by way of arms and ammunition to the Asian peoples with whom Portugal did not have friendly relations, they sought by all means to feed the hatred against the Portuguese.[50]

After the wars between the French and English on the Coromandel Coast, Portuguese trade was practically extinct in these posts and in Bengal.

Thus, in 1739, by their policy of nurturing dissension, and because in these misunderstandings lay their strength, the English helped the Marathas in the war that ended up with the Portuguese losing their Northern Province.

As regards the French, whereas close to 1750, they maintained good relations with the Portuguese, helping them whenever possible, twenty-five years later, in 1774, they are referred to in the Instructions as 'having the same covetousness as the Dutch

[49] Instrucção ..., pp. 73-4.

[50] The commander Thomas Griffin often extorted from the Portuguese ships, sometimes seizing all the profits, at other times detaining and selling in public auction the ships and their cargo (cf. Instrução [...], pp. 75-6). See Sebastião José Ferreira Barroco, *Reflexões sobre a Cauza da Decadência do Estado da Índia* ..., Library of the Science Academy of Lisbon, Red Series, no. 34, ff. 16-20v.

and the English with greater boldness and much less strength'.[51]

In this context, what were the guidelines for the Viceroys in their political-diplomatic relations with the European empires in Asia? By and large, they did their best to keep their weather eye open on any hidden machinations, mainly from the English, since the Dutch and the French posed fewer dangers in the second half of the eighteenth century. This attitude made the Portuguese authorities to attribute to English influence any moves made against the Estado da Índia by the Marathas or other Asian rulers.

On the other hand, it was recommended 'to make the most of the rancour that Hyder Ali Khan bore against the English, and to employ all dexterity, and all artifice, to alienate from them the other Rulers of the Malabar Coast, Surat, and Diu, in the same manner in which he has done against us'.[52]

Furthermore, the correspondence maintained with the Governor of Bombay and the court of London always sought to unmask English intentions, protest the damage caused and even, in extreme cases, to threaten an alliance with France. However, an attitude of neutrality in the event of war among the European nations established in Asia had been proclaimed. However, these measures did not have the right effect, inasmuch as the Portuguese possessions were often the victims of extortion on the part of the English.[53] And although the latter seldom entered into direct conflict with Portugal, they were nevertheless the worst of the potential enemies of the Estado da Índia, constantly threatening it with economic stifling, besides orchestrating conspiracies and alliances likely to undermine it slowly and steadily.

[51] Instrucção [...], p. 77 and Instrucções ..., Sexta Instrucção, p. 60. On the European conjuncture, see Jorge Borges de Macedo, *História Diplomática Portuguesa. Constantes e Linhas de Força. Estudo de Geopolítica,* Lisbon, Instituto de Defesa Nacional, n.d., pp. 235-74.

[52] Instrucções [...], Sexta Instrucção, p. 58.

[53] Such was the case of the city of St. Thomas of Meliapore which Admiral Boscoven seized through a breach of faith, hauling down the Portuguese flag and hoisting in its place the English flag. Then he compelled all the Portuguese settled there to leave the place (cf. Instrucções [...], p. 76).

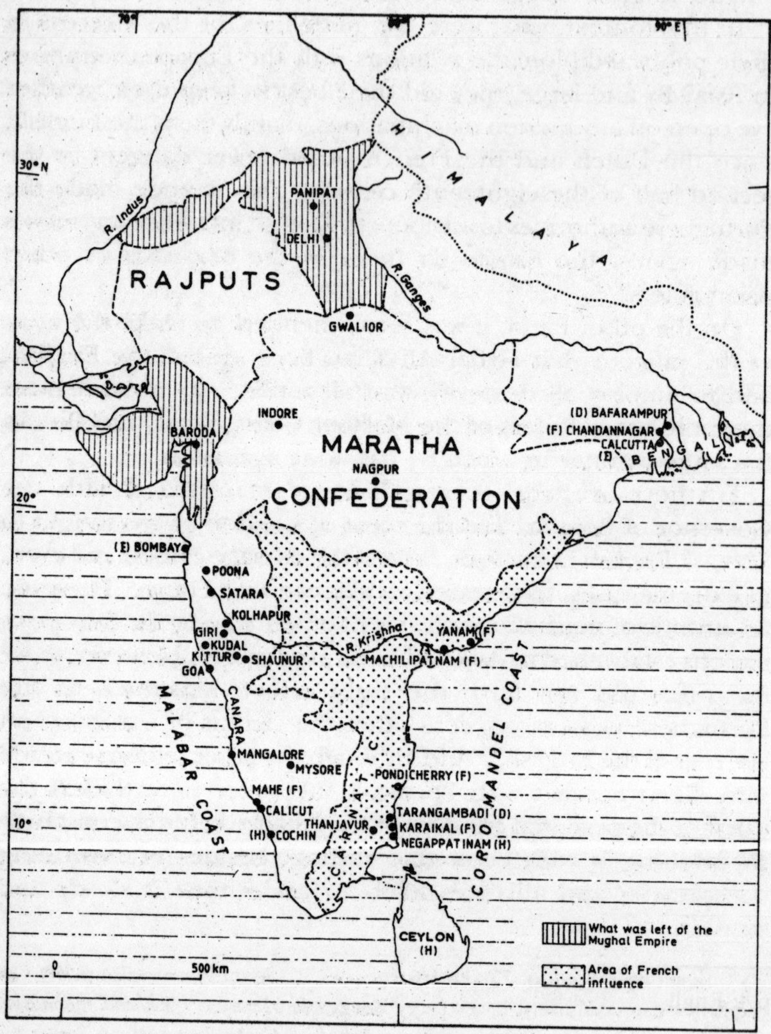

Legend: *D – Danes; H – Dutch; F – French; E – English*

Map 3: India between 1740–1761: the Maratha Expansion and the Europeans. The capitals of the kingdoms neighbouring Goa.

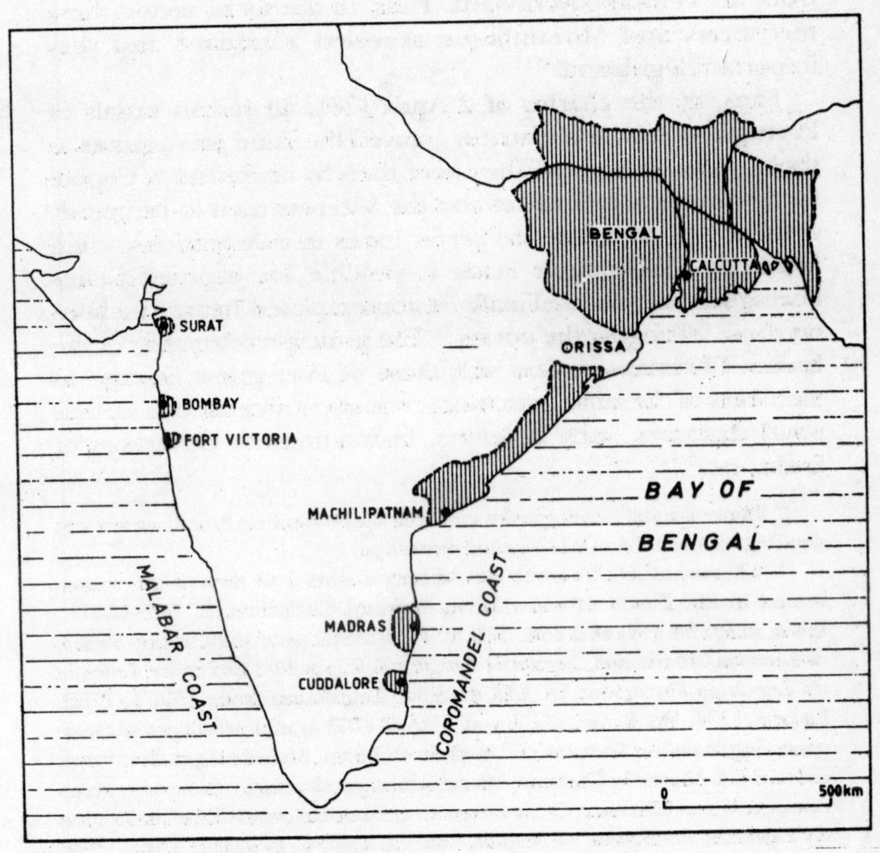

Map 4: English possessions in India during the late eighteenth century.

POMBALINE REFORMS

In the Portuguese colonial empire of the second half of the eighteenth century, Brazil and India, though very different in importance, were its cornerstones deserving of special attention from the central government. Thus, in the social sector, these territories and Mozambique received abundant and very important legislation.[54]

Thus, by the charter of 2 April 1761, all Indian vassals of Portuguese Asia, if Christians, enjoyed the same prerogatives as those of the Kingdom. They were thereby immediately eligible for all honours and offices and the Viceroys used to be greatly ordained to attend to and prefer locals in competitions, when found fit. The charter made it possible for baptised Goans Portuguese surnames. Finally, it contemplated heavy sanctions on those infringing the norms.[55] The principle of equality of the Indian Christians in Goa with those of Portuguese lineage, as members of the same community, was often reiterated in various royal diplomas, such as letters, instructions to Governors of India, etc.[56]

[54] There is a vast bibliography available on Pombaline Brazil; we are not dealing with it here as it is beyond our scope.

[55] 'Charter of law whereby His Majesty deems it fit that all the vassals settled in the *Estado da Índia,* being baptised Christians ...' (cf. A.H.U., *Índia,* maço 98 (95) and cód. 513, ff. 135v-138v), published in the *Boletim do Conselho Ultramarino, Legislação Antiga,* vol. II, pp. 30-2 and in the *Collecção da Legislação Portuguesa,* by A.D. da Silva, Legislation from 1750 to 1762, Lisbon, 1830. For Brazil, the law of 4 April 1755 grants privileges to those marrying Brazilian Indians and to their children, forbidding calling them *caboclos* (cf. Marcello Caetano, 'As reformas pombalinas e pós-pombalinas respeitantes ao Ultramar. O novo espírito em que são concedidas', in *História da Expansão Portuguesa no Mundo,* Vol. III, Lisbon, Editorial Ática, 1940, p. 260). Also as regards the local inhabitants of Macao, the charter of 2 April 1761 and the royal letter from 15 January 1764 order 'the curbing of the intolerable injustice of considering My Vassals Natives of this Country to be worse, and inferior circumstances than those born in My States of Europe, so as to be excluded from Governing Posts, and Public Administration' and ordains that they enjoy the same effects of inalterable justice which attends to all (cf. *Arquivos de Macau,* 3rd series, vol. XI, no. 5, May 1969, p. 266).

[56] Cf. letter from D. José to the Count of Ega, dated 10 April 1763

The territorial scope of the law of 2 April 1761 would be extended to East Africa in 1763, establishing the legal equality of the Portuguese born here in relation to the European Portuguese.[57]

Considering that the Goan Catholic had the same rights as a Portuguese, it was ordained to prefer the Indians in the administration of the parishes and, among the Reinóis, those who knew the local language, or else 'they cannot feed the sheep, whose bleating they do not understand'.[58]

Also in the ambit of the missions, preference for local Goans was safeguarded. It was thought that evangelization would yield good fruit if local priests were engaged in it. The expulsion of the Jesuits from the Portuguese dominions in 1759 and the need to replace them in the pastoral function had earlier made necessary an increasingly greater recourse to Goan ecclesiastics. It was even sought, as we shall later see, to establish a seminary 'in which boys of all the Oriental nations should be brought up in letters and good customs, who upon receiving education would return to their lands to preach the Gospel to their own folk, since from Portugal never could a sufficient number of preachers come'.[59]

(A.H.U., *Índia,* cód. 428, f. 15 and Instrucções [...], Instrucção Quarta, pp. 39-41); also see the replies given by the Count of Ega dated 8 and 12 January 1762 stating that he had executed whatever His Majesty had ordained in this regard (A.H.U., *Índia,* cód. 441, ff. 304v, 339-39v). In a proclamation and edict dated 31 October 1761 the same Governor copies the royal letter in favour of the locals of the State (A.H.U., *Índia,* cód. 442, ff. 225v-6, 227v-8).

[57] Diploma of 10 April 1763. Cf. A.H.U., *Índia,* cód. 1327, no. 76, cited by Fritz Hoppe, *A África Oriental Portuguesa no tempo do Marquês de Pombal, 1750-1777,* Lisbon, Agência Geral do Ultramar, 1970, pp. 165-6, 172-3.

[58] Cf. the reference to these royal determinations in the representation by the Chamber General of Bardez, dated 23 April 1766 (H.A.G., *M. Reino,* Book 139). Already on 28 January 1762, the Chamber General, in the person of its attorney, thanked the King for the selection of local clerics for the parishes of Salcete and requested the same for their province.

[59] 'Cópia da Ordem de S. Mag. sobre as Missões e administração dos colégios' of 2 April 1761 (A.C.P.G., *Cópia de Vários Documentos,* ff. [illegible]

It may be noted that in East Africa too a seminary and a missionary school were to be set up, modelled on the Goa seminary. They would be not only for the whites, mestizos and domiciled Indians, but also for the blacks. However, this did not materialize for lack of funds. In Angola and the islands of S. Tomé e Príncipe too, pastoral action was often exercised by local clerics.[60]

The juridical equality between locals and Reinícolas (born in the Kingdom), and the preference for the former over the latter, made it possible for locals to have access to ecclesiastical cadres. Also the ranks of the army were opened to them. In 1760, the sepoys were reformed and the local auxiliary corps of the Estado da Índia that had been created at the time of the Count of Sandomil were revived. The need and advantages of maintaining local troops had long since been proved, as they were more experienced in the military tactics of the Asian potentates. Besides, their numbers would swell the ranks of the army causing a psychological shock effect on the enemy.[61] A few more privileges were further conceded to the local militia, 'wishing to favour the above mentioned locals of this State, and to let them know that the big distance that separates them from my Royal presence, does not diminish the attention that I concede to all my faithful vassals...'.[62] In Brazil too auxiliary troops and local orderlies were recruited in order to compensate the dearth of Portuguese-born soldiers.[63]

---

in F.U.P., 18-1-8, 15, 3/5. Also cf. A.H.U., *Índia,* cód. 512, ff. 175-86 and cód. 153, ff. 121-29v).

[60] In May 1761 the Captain General was ordained to examine the possibility of instituting a seminary and missionary school in the old Jesuit school on the island of Mozambique. See Fritz Hoppe, *A África Oriental Portuguesa ...*, pp. 172-3.

[61] The sepoy reform of 5 December 1760 reduced its number (eliminated some and reformed others), raised the salaries of the Sub-Lieutenants and Sargeants and equalled the basic pay (cf. H.A.G., *M. Reino,* Book 133-A, ff. 41-41v).

[62] Cf. A.H.U., *Índia,* cód. 441, ff. 303v-304 and códice 513, ff. 138-9v.; H.A.G., *M. Reino,* Book 118-A, ff. [illegible], in F.U.P., 7-1-1, 13, 4/5.

[63] Cf. Caio C. Boschi, *As Directrizes Metropolitanas, a Realidade Colonial e as Irmandades Mineiras,* Belo Horizonte, 1987, p. 137.

The abolition of slavery of the 'chins' (Chinamen) was also declared. In 1760 it was abolished on the Continent and Islands, although maintained in Brazil and Africa.[64]

The themes of the charter of 2 April 1761 were restated more concretely in the charter of 15 January 1774 which sought to reform the government of the Estado da Índia. For this purpose it set up a veritable 'constitution' for political, civil and economic life. The royal instructions for the Governor and the Archbishop (1774) also contained fundamental directives on a number of public sectors.[65]

From the religious point of view, the same orientation was followed, that is, of 'preferring the local Indian secular clergy to the adventitious and regular local clergy of these Kingdoms...'.[66] Certain norms were thus established for filling up the titular offices in the Primatial See by preferring Goans and entrusting the administration of the parish churches to secular clerics who were almost totally Indians.[67]

These directives remained in force in their fundamental aspects during the second half of the eighteenth century. Indeed, D. Maria determined that 'if there should be competent and virtuous Goan clergymen, they should be preferred to the Reinícolas, for it is not fair to refuse them the bread of their land to the benefit of the others'.[68]

[64] Cf. the royal letter from the Count of Ega dated 20 March 1758 (A.H.U., *Índia,* cód. 513, ff. 12-14). Also, see another letter from the same date stating the reasons why slavery of the Chinese had to be abolished (A.H.U., *Índia,* maço 90 (99)). Also see the letter from Tomé Joaquim Corte Real to the Count of Ega dated 29 March 1760 to have the slavery of the Chinese stopped as being against the natural and divine law (H.A.G., *M. Reino,* Book 138-B, f. 288). We have dealt with this subject in greater detail in the study on 'Mendicidade e "maus costumes" em Macau e Goa na segunda metade do século XVIII', in *As Relações entre a Índia Portuguesa, a Ásia do Sueste e o Extremo Oriente. Actas do VI Seminário Internacional de História Indo-Portuguesa,* Macao, Lisbon, 1993, pp. 65-82.

[65] Cf. charter of 15 January 1774, in *Boletim do Conselho Ultramarino, Legislação Antiga,* vol. II, Lisbon, 1867, pp. 147-61.

[66] Cf. A.C.P.G., *Cópia de Vários Documentos ...*, ff. 64-66v, in F.U.P., 18-1-8, 23/5 and 24.

[67] Cf. Instrucções ..., p. 18.

[68] Cf. the letter from D. Maria to the Archbishop, dated 5 March 1779

This policy apparently had two aims: first, to charm and ensure the fidelity of the local population to the Portuguese Crown; second, to undermine the large, predominantly European, religious Orders. Despite their moral decadence, these Orders used to strongly overshadow the State that, governed by the theories of enlightened despotism, resented any competition with its authority.

It was perhaps to thwart the power of the European Orders that a policy of protecting the Orders and local congregations was designed at once. These guidelines were continued in the reign of D. Maria. Going back to the orders issued to the Archbishop in 1774 she determined that the earlier ban on the entry of locals into religious Orders of European origin be removed.[69] It was also provided that no Portuguese from the Kingdom would be admitted into the religious clerics established in Goa without express royal permission.[70]

It was in the same spirit of doing away with racial discrimination that the central government ordered the dress code at the Santa Monica nunnery to be made uniform. It so happened that there were nuns of European lineage (paternal or maternal) living together with Goan nuns, wearing black veils and white veils, respectively. Although nothing else but the colour was different, the sovereign determined that all of them should wear black veils, irrespective of their ancestry.[71]

(A.C.P.G., *Cópia de Vários Documentos* ..., ff. [illegible] in F.U.P., 18-1-8, 30, 1/5 and 31, 1/2).

[69] A.C.P.G., *Cópia de Vários Documentos* ..., ff. 91-91v, in F.U.P., 18-1-8, 33, 4/5 and 34, 1/5.

[70] Apropos the licence granted to Bernardo José Rodrigues, born in Portugal, to shift to the Estado da Índia, and profess in the convent of the clerics of Saint Augustine of Goa, on 21 March 1779, the Queen stated, however, that the said orders stand unaltered (A.H.U., *Índia,* maço 26 (296) and 55 (300); cód. 516, f. 182v; A.C.P.G., *Cópia de Vários Documentos* ..., f. 107, in F.U.P., 18-1-8, 38/4; H.A.G., *M. Reino,* Book 159-B, ff. 391-3).

[71] Letter from M.M. Castro to the Bishop of Cochin, dated 6 March 1779 (A.C.P.G., *Cópia de Vários Documentos* ..., f. 99, in F.U.P., 18-1-8, 36/4. Also cf. H.A.G., *M. Reino,* Book 159-B, f. 558, and A.H.U., *Índia,* cód. 516, f. 182 and maço 55 (300).

As regards the military reforms, at the time of the Marquis of Pombal it was sought to stabilize and activate one-third of the auxiliary troops and the body of orderlies in Goa and adjacent islands. This was in order to prepare local militia to stand up to the frequent and sudden incursions of the Indian armies.[72]

With the regimentation of the troops the barracks of the Brigadier General, who was the Commander-General of all the infantry, were set up at the house of St Roch, in the city of Goa, where the three regiments of that branch used to be stationed.

In addition, one-third of the auxiliary troops then comprising twelve companies with 50 men each, was raised by four companies, thus with 800 military men. For commander of this contingent – the *mestre de campo* – was chosen a *fidalgo* 'or distinguished person, respectable and of established reputation', the other command posts being staffed with nobleman 'of honour'.[73] Thus there was a very clear intention to discipline as well as dignify the auxiliary troops. They would have the same honours as the infantry and its officials were made to wear uniforms. The soldiers and the stationed troops would have similar arms and be similarly trained to use them.

However, the Ordinance Corps of Goa were also reorganized. Using the traditional structure of *ganvkari* and *thanadars*, one company was formed in each jurisdiction. Its Captains and Sub-Lieutenants would be elected from among the 'most distinguished' *ganvkars*. This act would be presided over by the *thanadar-mor* that would take up the post of *mestre de campo* of all the Orderlies. This was also designed to ban the 'barbarous title' of *thanadar-mor*, says the instruction of the Marquis of Pombal.[74] Furthermore, this corps also made it possible for the local authorities to recruit already trained youths to work as the so-called paid troops.

In the second half of the eighteenth century the locals were encouraged to be engaged in defending their own land. They were assured promotion to all the ranks, and it was even the nobility and the children of the most distinguished Brahmins

[72] Instrucções ..., Instrução Primeira, p. 4.

[73] Ibid., p. 4.

[74] Ibid., p. 4.

and Chardós were advised to come forward, as was the practice with the highest ranking *fidalgos* in the Kingdom.[75]

This same arrangement made the central government revoke the prevailing ban on locals becoming officers and soldiers in the three companies of the Goan artillery regiment.[76] This measure was meant to attract the locals to the army and to not exempt Goans from military service. However, alleging the traditional pacifism of the Indians and their lack of interest in the military profession, the councils of Bardez and Salcete quite often sought to bend the official policy such as to have the locals excluded from the militia. But we believe that the central leadership precisely only wished to compensate the falling numbers of Europeans in the ranks.

Whereas considerably significant measures were taken in the social sector, in the administrative field too some reforms were necessary. The historical vicissitudes faced by the Estado da Índia in the seventeenth century and the first half of the next occasioned the loss of important positions.[77] Nevertheless, the Governors or Viceroys continued to lead an ostentatious life and maintained an expensive court.

[75] Cf. the copy of the letter addressed to the Salcete chamber by the Marquis Inspector-General of the Royal Treasury, dated 28 February 1776 (A.H.U., *Índia,* maço 123 (113)). For research data on the Brahmins and Chardós, see Chapter II, pp. 114-27.

[76] The royal charter of 28 April 1773 had created the artillery regiment of the Estado da Índia. According to this statute, 'none of the ranks of officials, and soldiers of the Three Companies of Bombers, Miners and Artisans can be staffed with Persons, not born in these Kingdoms of Portugal, and of the Algarve'. The royal letter for the Governor Francisco da Cunha e Menezes, dated 5 October 1792, the ban was lifted which prevented the service of the locals in the commissioned companies of the artillery regiment (cf. A.H.U., *Índia,* cód. 520, ff. 38v-9).

[77] The dominions lost were the following: Moluccas (*c.* 1605), the kingdom of Pegu, Hormuz (1622), Malacca (1641), Ceylon, Cranganore (1662), Cochin and other fortresses, in favour of the English and the Dutch. In 1661, the port and island of Bombay was handed to the English, as dowry on the marriage of Infanta D. Catarina to the English sovereign Charles II. Between 1661 and 1663, the fortress of Barcelore, Mangalore, Honavar, Coulão and Cannanore and others on the Malabar coast, which successively fell into the hands of the Dutch; the establishments of 'Nagappatinam'

Adding to the troubles were the Portuguese descendants settled in India. Besides enjoying a privileged social status, they monopolized public offices, which they transferred from generation to generation or sold like their own property, even in cities or factories that no longer belonged to the Portuguese Crown. The Royal Treasury thus continued to pay the salaries of the assignments that, really speaking, did not exist.[78]

There were thus a number of redundant offices burdening the Public Treasury whose balance sheet was often in the red. On the other hand, other institutions better suited to the times had to be created.

This situation made the central government bring about a series of reforms, which were particularly numerous in the consulate of the Marquis of Pombal, even though it was difficult to accurately surmise their consequences. A man of the age of Enlightenment who had lived for a long time in Austria and England, he was conversant with the doctrines that had inspired the considerable reform activity that he undertook forming an organic and harmonious whole. The reforms decreed for the Estado da Índia were largely intimately related with others ordained for the Kingdom and other overseas possessions.

In India, the reforms touched several areas of public life and generally endeavoured to establish norms for bookkeeping, criteria for revenue collection, cutback of offices and expenses, rules for uniformity of the public law, etc. Thus, in the field of Revenue, in line with what happened in the Kingdom, the Board of Royal Revenue of the Estado da Índia (1769) replaced the then extinct Casa dos Contos (Treasury). After four years, the Revenue Council and the post of Superintendent was abolished, certainly after irregularities were noticed. It may be pointed that both on the Continent as well as Overseas, Revenue Boards had

---

and St. Thomas of Meliapore on the Coromandel coast; in 1699, Mombassa was occupied by the Muslims; in 1739, the Northern Province was conquered by the Marathas, with the help of the English (see Father M.J. Gabriel de Saldanha, *História de Goa* ..., vol. 1, pp. 146-7).

[78] See Marcello Caetano, 'As reformas pombalinas ...', op. cit., pp. 251-60 and L.F.F.R. Thomaz, *Goa: une société luso-indienne*, op. cit., p. 27.

been created to obviate the abuses of the Governors and of the earlier Revenue superintendents. In 1774 the new Goa customs regiment was established.[79]

Detailed reforms were thus enforced to cleanse this important sector of public life. The degradation of the public revenue collection agencies, incompetence, negligence and corruption of its agents called for an intense restructuring.[80] It may be noted, however, that notwithstanding these reforms, there continued to be several useless posts which only burdened the royal treasury.[81]

In the naval sector too there was a need for reforms, given that 'the referred forces are nominal, and not real, with great outcry, and insignificant service'. Hence, the arsenal directed by the Revenue superintendent of the Estado da Índia was put under the Intendant General of the Navy and its warehouses by the charter of 13 April 1773. Several measures were decreed for the administration of the arsenal and the service at sea. Also note the abolition of the *cartazes,* 'which in the happy times of Portuguese Asia, were of such glory and use ..., being impractical,

[79] By royal letter dated 10 April 1769 was created the Board of Royal Revenue of the Estado da Índia (cf. Instrucções ..., Instrucção Terceira, p. 33). In fact, this Instruction enumerates several laws promulgated for this sector of public life. In the 1760s and 1770s there came the Revenue Boards in all the captaincy-generals of Brazil which, directly subordinated to Lisbon, used to superintend all the public revenue (cf. A. H. de Oliveira Marques, *História de Portugal,* vol. II, p. 390). The charter of 13 April 1773 abolished the Council and the Revenue Superintendent of Goa (cf. Instrucções ..., Instrucção Terceira, pp. 35-6). On the structure of the Board of the Royal Revenue of the Estado da Índia at the end of the century, see the letter from [F.A.V. Cabral] to the Marquis Major-domo, dated 5 May 1800 (H.A.G., *M. Reino,* Book 179-B, ff. 611-12). See the Regiment of the Customs of the City of Goa in *Boletim do Conselho Ultramarino. Legislação Antiga,* vol. II, pp. 161-95.

[80] See Instrucções [...], Instrucção Terceira, pp. 33-8, enumerating the legislation promulgated for this sector of public life.

[81] See the letter from the councillor João de Saldanha Lobo to M.M. Castro, dated 13 February 1772, in which he refers to the measures taken by the Senate of Goa to limit the expenses and in which he enumerates, stating reasons, the diverse posts that 'have no utility'. Cf. A.H.U., *Índia,* maço 121 (111).

and of no effect, they degenerated into fraudulent and covetous pretexts for robbing the merchant Navies ...'.[82]

In the judicial field, the abolition of the High Court by the law of 15 January 1774 is impressive. This grand areopagus brought harmful consequences to the inhabitants of Portuguese India.[83] Hence the said statute abolished the post of Chancellor, creating a little later the post of State senior crown judge, on 24 May 1774, similar to what had existed in the early days of the conquest. It may be recalled that the jurisdictional, and even personal, conflicts between the Chancellors and Governors, were instrumental in increasing the habitual slowness of the ordinary service. The legislator believed that if the post of a single higher functionary – in this case the crown judge, was directly dependent on the House of Supplication in Lisbon – justice would be dispensed promptly.[84]

But this must have hurt a considerable number of interests;

[82] See Instrucções ..., Instrucção Segunda, pp. 21-32. Cf. the reference to the charter of 13 April 1773, cited earlier, that 'abolished the Council and the Revenue Superintendent of Goa, with all their functions: creating anew the post of Intendent General of the Navy and of its Warehouses', Ibid., pp. 35-6. The *Cartaz* was a 'passport or safe-conduct for sailing'. Its Arab etymology suggests that it had existed before the arrival of the Portuguese, who resumed it. Since 1502 the navigation of non-Christians in the Indian Ocean depended on the passage of safe-conduct by the Portuguese authorities; at the time under study, the *cartazes* were abolished (S.R. Dalgado, op. cit., vol. I, pp. 220-1 and L.F.F.R. Thomaz, 'Estrutura Política e Administrativa do Estado da Índia no século XVI', in 2nd *Seminário Internacional de História Indo-Portuguesa. Actas.* Lisbon, I.I.C.T., 1985, p. 525).

[83] Paragraph 1 of the charter of 15.1.1774 abolished the High Court of Goa and decrees and created the post of senior crown judge of the Estado da Índia (A.H.U., *Índia,* maço 26 (296) and H.A.G., *M. Reino,* Book 167-A, ff. 205-10 and Book 168-C, ff. 733-733v. Also cf. *Colecção da Legislação Portuguesa,* Lisbon, ed. A.D. da Silva, 1829, pp. 746-9). The Count of Ega in his letter to Sebastião José de Carvalho e Mello, referred quite minutely to the High Court of Goa. He said that it was not very united. Thereafter he profiled each of the members of the High Court: Chancellor, Attorney of the Crown, *juiz dos feitos, juiz do crime* (criminal magistrate), *juiz do cível* (civil magistrate). [A.H.U., *Índia,* cx. 94 (docs. under classification) published by A. Saldanha, *As cartas* (...), carta no. 1, pp. 103-14].

[84] Cf. fn. 82 of Chapter II.

hence under Queen D. Maria I, the law of 2 April 1778 brought back the tribunal with four high court judges and a Chancellor restoring the *status quo ante* as regards their authority and jurisdiction.[85] Curiously, there was a similar reaction in the Kingdom.

As regards the Church, two important measures were taken that fit into a whole set of wider reforms: the expulsion of the Jesuits and the extinction of the tribunal of the Inquisition.

Illuminism, with its pedagogic philosophy that was quite different from that of the Jesuits, was responsible for the Society losing its influence and attracting a general attack on itself. But it was the problem with the Jesuits of Brazil that precipitated the events. Of course, other factors included the State-Society troubles at the time of executing the Treaty of Limits in 1750; the reactions to the establishment of the Society in Grão-Pará and Maranhão in 1755; the problems caused by the law aimed at freeing indigenous peoples and suppressing the Jesuit missions, ordering the transfer of the administration of the Indians to State officials.[86]

Besides the difficulties in Brazil, the Jesuit opposition to enlightened despotism in the Kingdom also contributed

[85] Cf. H.A.G., *M. Reino,* Book 159-A, ff. 5-6, 65-6 and A.H.U., *Índia,* maço 52 (305).

[86] The treaty of Madrid in 1750 surrendered to Spain the colony of Sacramento and the territory of the septentrional bank of the Prata River, in exchange for all the lands and populations of the eastern bank of the river Uruguay, where the Jesuits had seven *reductions* with 30,000 indigenous people. This treaty is based on the principle of the natural frontiers and contains the doctrine of American autonomy. Thence the beginning of the fight with the Indians in the Jesuits *reductions,* one of the fundamental points of the conflict of the Marquis of Pombal with the Society of Jesus (cf. Fernando Castelo-Branco, 'Madrid, Tratado de', in *Dicionário de História de Portugal,* vol. II, pp. 883-4). The institution of the Companhia do Grão-Pará e Maranhão on 6 June 1755 to which were granted monopolies, provoked great reactions. The Jesuit Father Ballester, in a sermon at the Patriarchal Palace, referred to the said Company and proposed the formation of a spiritual company, whose profits would be paid in heaven a hundred fold. This won him his imprisonment and exile to Bragança (see Fortunato de Almeida, *História da Igreja em Portugal,* vol. III, p. 113).

substantially to their expulsion. The political theory that the monarch receives his authority directly from God gave the King total and supreme power. The execution of this programme implied the annihilation of ecclesiastical influence, particularly that of the Jesuits who enjoyed great influence and power in society. There being ministers hostile to the Society of Jesus in almost all the governments of Europe in the second half of the eighteenth century – Pombal, Aranda, Choiseul, Tanucci, Kaunitz – favoured the development of an anti-Jesuit sentiment.[87]

[87] By virtue of some incidents registered already at the end of October 1755, there was a rumour that the Jesuits were going to be expelled from the court, which in fact happened on 21 September 1757, when they were dismissed from the palace. Then, Pombal initiated a campaign with the Pope, accusing the Jesuits of engaging in illegal commerce in America and of instigating the people in the Kingdom. Pope Benedict XIV appointed Cardinal D. Francisco de Saldanha as a Visitor and reformer of the Society on the Continent and Overseas, by the brief *In Specula Supremae dignitatis,* of 1 April 1758. A little later, the patriarch of Lisbon banned the Jesuits from confession and preaching. The news of the attempt on the life of the King in September 1758 gave rise to a fresh outbreak of the campaign against the Society of Jesus. The general confiscation of the properties of the Order and the detention of many of its members followed this. The law of 3 September 1759 declared them denaturalized, proscribed and exterminated for having 'carried out the encroachment of the whole of Brazil and for being accomplices in the conspiracy against the king'. The pontifical brief of Pope Clement XIV, *Dominus ac Redemptor* of 21 July 1773 suppressed the very order, under pressure of the European courts. It survived, nevertheless, in Russia, with Catherine II who did not allow the promulgation of the pontifical brief. In 1814, Pope Pius VII re-established it universally (see F. Almeida, *História da Igreja em Portugal,* vol. III, pp. 110-28; Father João Pereira Gomes, 'Jesuítas', in *Dicionário de História de Portugal,* vol. II, pp. 589-93; J. Bacelar e Oliveira, *Bloqueio, sequestro e desterro dos jesuítas em Goa, segundo a 'História do Exílio' do P. José Caeiro,* essay, Lisbon, 1985; J. Veríssimo Serrão, *História de Portugal,* vol. VI, pp. 8-54 and bibliography cited by this author. On the Society of Jesus in general, see also Alain Guillermou, *Les Jesuites,* 2nd edn., col. 'Que sais-je?', Paris, P.U.F., 1992, and the bibliography indicated herein) and Jean Lacouture, *Os Jesuítas,* vol. I, *A Conquista,* trad. portuguesa de Maria F. Gonçalves de Azevedo, Lisbon, Estampa, 1993.

Although their suppression was decreed in Lisbon on 3 September 1759, it had been planned and also extended to Goa much earlier.[88] Accordingly, the extinction of the Society of Jesus in Goa took place in this year, in the administration of D. Antonio Taveira da Neiva Brum da Silveira (1750-5) and in the government of the Count of Ega (1758-65). They executed the sovereign's sharp orders quickly and cautiously, and this won them a royal commendation.[89]

In his letters to the Count of Ega, the King seriously accused the Jesuits of high treason, abuses and encroachments; of making war against the Portuguese armies and plotting to usurp the overseas dominions; and of being tainted by theological, moral and political errors.[90]

The expulsion of the Jesuits brought about some difficulties in their replacement, which we shall deal with in Chapter III. But it was perhaps a strong challenge for the formation of a

[88] Already in May 1751 the King had ordered the publication of edicts offering prizes to persons who brought to light the hidden assets of the Jesuits (A.H.U., *Índia,* cod. 1308, no. 206, f. 8). There are various orders to the Count of Ega against the Jesuits, dated the year 1758, such as the ban on their entry in the palace of Goa, their exclusion 'from ministries and secular incumbencies', as also commercial traffic. In March 1759 was ordered the extinction and transportation of the Jesuits to the Kingdom as also the general confiscation of all their properties. A hundred and twenty-seven Jesuits were imprisoned in Goa on the morning of 26 September 1759. They set sail for Lisbon only on 19 December 1760. Twenty-three died on board. Most of them were incarcerated in the fortress of S. Julião da Barra. The pontifical suppression of the Society in 1774 was observed in Goa in the archbishopric of Francisco de Assunção e Brito, with festivities in each parish (see E.R. Hambye, 'Goa', in *Dictionnaire d'Histoire et de Géographie Ecclésiastiques,* p. 295. Also cf. A.H.U., *Índia,* cód. 1308, no. 1119, f. 2v; no. 121, f. 3; cód. 513, ff. 60v-62v, 70-74v; cód. 441, ff. 196-202; cód. 444, ff. 4; A.N./T.T., *Reino,* maço 594).

[89] Cf. A.H.U., *Índia,* cód. 513, ff. 104-104v; maço 89 (100) publ. Por A. S.V.S. de Saldanha, *As cartas de Manuel de Saldanha, 1° conde de Ega ...,* pp. 137 and 160.

[90] Cf. letters of the King to the Archbishop of Goa, dated 28 March 1759 (A.H.U., *Índia,* cód. 439, ff. 57-58 and cód. 513, ff. 76v-78; letter from the King to the Count of Ega of the same date. Also see the notice on the main points of the abuses and encroachments by the Jesuits (A.H.U., *Índia,* cód. 1308, no. 125, f. 3).

local, Goan clergy who would soon have an important role in filling up the religious posts.

The extinction of the Holy Office in Goa in 1774 was also part of the Pombaline programme that had been introduced in the Kingdom. It was connected with the political-cultural environment of the Lights and the strengthening of royal power.

To add to this, the annexation of the territories from neighbouring chieftains in the second half of the eighteenth century made a policy necessary of social and religious tolerance toward the Goans. Accepting the usage and customs of the people and showing good will toward their religious practices could possibly win them over and have them settle and populate the New Conquests.[91]

After the death of D. José I and the fall of Pombal there was a reaction in favour of restoring the Inquisition. On 4 April 1778, the new Regiment of the Goa Inquisition was approved and the deputy of the Council-General, António Manuel Fragoso de Barros, travelled to Goa in order to have the same reorganized.[92]

Revived in 1778, the Inquisition of Goa would resume its activity only in 1782. It functioned precariously till 1812, when it was definitively abolished. The progress of the lights spreading through the sciences and philosophy had created an ambience that was clearly hostile to its activity. The Church should have utilized gentler means to uproot the 'vices of gentilism' than those proposed by the Inquisition. It was more important to instruct rather than punish![93]

[91] 'Carta de Marquês de Pombal ao governador e capitão-general da Índia D. José Pedro da Câmara, ordenando-lhe a extinção da Inquisição de Goa, datada de 10 de Fevereiro de 1774', publ. by F. de Almeida, op. cit., vol. IV, p. 319. Also cf. the provision of 8 February 1774 whereby Cardinal D. João da Cunha made it known that with the extinction of the Inquisition of Goa, all the jurisdiction earlier attributed to its ministers was now assumed by him (A.N./T.T., *Conselho Geral do St° Ofício, Papéis Avulsos,* maço 6-2434).

[92] See our study, 'A Inquisição de Goa na segunda metade do século XVIII', Lisbon, 1989, p. 241, offprint of *Stvdia,* 48 (1989).

[93] The Governor of Goa, in his letter dated 23 February 1792, referred to the unlimited power wielded by the Inquisition and to its consequences

In the area of local administration, the municipal councils merited particular attention. It may be noted that whereas in the Kingdom a number of councils were being abolished, new municipalities were being established overseas, which played an important role in the administration and public life of these dominions.

Although the fundamental law of 7 January 1774 abolished the statutes regulating the government of India, the royal charter of 15 January of the same year maintained the privileges of the Chamber of Goa and reorganized it. It would now have one president elected for a triennium, with status of *moço fidalgo,* with 'virtues Christian, political and of the common good'. It would also have four councillors, two being *fidalgos* and the other two 'belonging to the civil nobility of the citizenry'. Besides this, there was one city attorney and four guild attorneys, one syndic who was an expert professor of law 'well bred and zealous of the public welfare' (all annual), one scribe with service for life, and two monthly inspectors of weights and measures (Reinóis or Goans).[94]

The importance attached to this 'congress that represents the

---

fatal not only for the State but also for religion. As regards the question of reversal of the Catholics to Hindu beliefs, he stated that the Hindus did not take back those who had embraced a different religion (cf. H.A.G., *M. Reino,* Book 173, ff. 416-417v).

[94] The royal charter clarifies the form of election of the president. The electors of the city had to propose three *fidalgos* to the Mesa do Desembargo do Paço (Palace Replevin Court) presided over by the Governor. The market inspectors were appointed by the plurality of the votes of the Council among the honourable residents or civil Reinícolas or locals, without the social distinctions practised to date. Hence, less than six local market inspectors cannot be elected per year. They were elected every two months (January/February; March/April; May/June, etc.) (cf. Instituto Histórico e Geográfico do Rio de Janeiro, lata 205, doc. 1; H.A.G., *Acórdãos e Assentos da Câmara de Goa,* 7742, f. 13; *Collecção da Legislação Portuguesa,* pp. 745-6). In addition, Marcello Caetano, op. cit., p. 257, refers to the most important people who constituted the senate of the Council of Goa and to the role of the municipal council in local life. Its composition was not always the same: until 1773, it comprised three councillors, two ordinary judges and one attorney; from this date onwards, there was normally one *fidalgo* councillor and two nobles. Thus, it happened in 1773, 1776, 1777; how-

State of the People of the capital of India' was evident. For this very reason, the election of the president became triennial and the number of councillors was increased. Municipal administration was thus strengthened and governmental action stabilized.[95]

We have not come across any law that gave preference to Europeans in municipal posts, even though this was the reality. Around 1755 Indians became the representatives of professions when there were no whites and mestizos. Pombal's Instrucções in 1774 ordained that Goans should be given priority over Reinóis in the access to civil and military posts. The text of the statute does not specify in which of the two categories to include the *descendentes*, who constituted the largely mixed-blooded creole nobility who had been traditionally predominant in the local administration.

The same royal charter of 15 January 1774 created the municipal senates of Salsete and Bardez. These two provinces had to wait so long to have municipalities as they were rural areas. It may be noted, however, that Goa had a very old and rich experience of cooperative life – the *ganvkari* or village communities – and the institution of the Municipal Councils was perhaps fixed on the same foundations.[96] It is not always easy to discern the relations between the Chambers-General of the village communities and the Municipal Councils. Probably

---

ever, in 1790, this distinction ceases to exist but returns in 1792; in 1793, again there is no distinction. Finally, from 1795 to 1800 once again these distinctions are made (cf. H.A.G., *Assentos e Juramentos da Câmara de Goa,* 7762, ff. 3, 40, 76v, 264-264v and *Acórdãos e Assentos da Câmara de Goa,* 7742, ff. 17v-18; A.H.U., *Índia,* maço 42 (316).

[95] In the sixteenth century, the Council of Goa comprised ten persons, the *fidalgo* councillor, 2 noblemen councillors, 2 ordinary judges, the city attorney and 4 attorneys of the professions. In the second half of the seventeenth century (1654) it had 6 *fidalgo* councillors and 3 noblemen elected for three years; later it had only three councillors, one *fidalgo* and 2 noblemen. See C. R. Boxer, *Portuguese Society in the Tropics: The Municipal Councils of Goa, Macao, Bahia, and Luanda* (1510-1800), University of Wisconsin Press, Madison and Milwaukee, 1965, pp. 12-41. This work supplies important data on the evolution of the Chamber of Goa, mainly in the sixteenth and seventeenth centuries.

[96] Margão was raised to a township on 3 April 1778. The senate of the

the Portuguese had equated the village communities with the Portuguese municipal councils, for the charter of usage and customs had been granted way back in 1526.[97] The General Assemblies continued to exist concurrently with the Municipal Councils, although devoid of power, in favour of the latter. They were now called 'agrarian' and were mainly concerned with land cultivation and payment of certain taxes. This evolution attracted criticism and reaction from the attorneys of the General Assemblies, but the process was irreversible.[98]

The General Assemblies federating the ancient *ganvkari* played a major role in local administration and life in general. They would regulate the price of products, especially paddy, the basic commodity of subsistence, collect certain tributes, pay for welfare works and participate in the economic development of the land.

At crucial moments of Goan history the voice of its people was heard through their attorneys who submitted their position to the Governor or even to the monarch. To quote an example, when the Franciscans were being substituted with secular clerics in Bardez, its General Assembly rose to the occasion and vehemently, and successfully, argued the case.[99] Gradually, the General Assemblies inherited this capacity of making representations, being combative and dynamic in the local life. In

---

Council of Salsete, created on 15 January 1774, was extinct in 1779 and re-established on 23 March 1783. Cf. J.A. Ismael Gracias, 'Feriados Concelhios na Índia Portuguesa', in *O Oriente Portuguez,* vol. XII, nos. 1 and 2, Nova Goa, Imprensa Nacional, 1915, pp. 21-30. Also see Álvaro de Loyola Furtado, 'Os primórdios da imprensa e do jornalismo em Goa e no resto da Índia', in *Boletim do Instituto Menezes Bragança,* no. 116, Goa, Bastorá, 1977, pp. 5-38.

97 See A.B. de Bragança Pereira, *Etnografia da Índia Portuguesa,* vol. II, pp. 306-7.

98 See the 'Representação' of the General Chamber of Bardez, dated 2 May 1779 (A.H.U., *Índia,* maço 2 (246)).

99 See the 'Representação da Câmara Geral de Bardez' of 30 January 1770 (referred to in fn. 110 of Chapter III) (H.A.G., *M. Reino,* Book 148-B, ff. 577-8v, 579-81v). On this subject refer to the important códice at the Biblioteca da Academia das Ciências de Lisboa, *Série Vermelha,* no. 88, *Costumes, e estilos das Camaras, e Regimento. ...*

fact, Bardez Chamber General was keen on creating jobs for the locals, and hence encouraged the setting up of factories and reviving the Mapusa fair. Products and people flocked here from Goa and different parts of India, bringing considerable earnings to the Royal Treasury.[100]

Another statute that wished to favour the local Indians and promote the progress of Goa was the royal charter of 9 April 1778 that established a Legislative Board, as in the British colonies, comprising the Governor, three high court judges and the Government Secretary. It had the powers to establish any provisional alterations and reforms and to propose whatever it deemed fit for India, since only *in loco* could the case be known better.[101] Even though we cannot specify any concrete action taken by this Board, we find that the creation of such an institution in the Estado da Índia in that age certainly implies a good amount of autonomy for the area, which was unfortunately not kept up.

Reference must be made here to some noteworthy economic reforms introduced in the period under study as part of the same policy of revitalising the Estado da Índia.

The economic programme of the central government, and very especially that of the Marquis of Pombal, was no doubt influenced by mercantilist thought. The Marquis was indeed the great theoretician of the doctrine of the colonial pact which in fact presupposed that the colonies existed only to ensure a favourable trade balance for the metropolis.[102] But, given the economic crisis of the Portuguese Empire and the influence of 'learning', the colonial policy suffered some alterations in the second half of the eighteenth century. Pombaline reforms parti-

[100] See the proceedings of council of the Chamber of Bardez from 12 February 1785 to 21 November 1787 (Central Library, Panjim, Mss 46-B, ff. 8 and ss.). The Mapusa fair earned the Senate 1,500 xerafins, one-third of which reverted to the Royal Treasury. This fair is still held every Friday.

[101] Cf. *Annaes Maritimos e Coloneaes*, no. 2, December 1840, Lisbon, Imprensa Nacional, 1840, p. 79.

[102] The doctrine of the *colonial pact* is found formulated by Pombal, in its essential points, in the note of 31 January 1776 to the French Ambassador, Marquis of Blosset (cf. Marcello Caetano, op. cit., p. 259).

cularly echo these transformations, reducing the mercantilist exclusivism of the metropolis and encouraging production in the colonies, with a view to a better articulation between the metropolitan and colonial worlds.[103] From the social point of view, this openness in the mercantile system created an interest in racial equality and the assimilatory tendency referred to earlier.

Simultaneously, physiocratic ideas began to gan popularity in Europe and Portugal. The principle that agriculture was fundamental for the people's happiness and national prosperity did trigger State interest in this branch of economics.

Ever since the conquest up to the middle of the eighteenth century, agriculture in Goa was at subsistence level, disconnected from the great networks of Portuguese commerce in the East, and apparently, often in deficit. This obliged the importation of rice from Kanara. The people cultivated their lands only for their personal needs and not to sell the surplus. As a result, many fields used to remain uncultivated and some would be harvested only once instead of twice. Thus the territory, including the royal treasury, would have to spend a considerable amount of money on the purchase of food from outside.[104]

Throughout the second half of the eighteenth century great efforts were made to promote agriculture and industry as being the only means of reviving the Portuguese dominions in India. Royal provisions, books and pamphlets on methods of cultivation were sent to Governors in India, who sought to make the projects viable. The Count of Ega made considerable efforts to guide the people on how to cultivate their lands. Accordingly, he and his successors often subsidized the municipal councils, made improvements, and encouraged the people to plough uncultivated lands, undertake traditional agriculture and other more suitable ones.[105]

[103] See José Jobson de Andrade Arruda, 'A produção económica', in *O Império Luso-Brasileiro, 1750-1822,* coordinated by Maria Beatriz Nizza da Silva, *Nova História da Expansão Portuguesa,* vol. VIII, Lisbon, Estampa, 1986, pp. 90-1.

[104] See the letter from the Governor to M.M. Castro, dated 30 April 1777 (cf. H.A.G., *M. Reino,* Book 157-B, ff. 412-15).

[105] It was the case, for example, of the writings on cultivation, harvest

Keeping in mind the progress of agriculture, the Marquis of Pombal set up the post of Intendent General of Agriculture. The intendent-designate, Gustavo Adolfo Hércules de Chermont, knew little about the subject but was a resourceful, energetic and experienced man. He encouraged the cultivation of the lands traditionally tilled and to take up those till then uncultivated, all of which led to a considerable development of agriculture.[106]

The second intendent was Simeão Rodrigues Moreira who, in the footsteps of his predecessor, continued the campaign for promoting the agricultural land. Thus, between 1770 and 1790 approximately, a considerable increase was noticed in the annual production of rice and other food. The average annual production between 1777 and 1786 was 181 *khumb*, rising to 493 *khumb* in the years 1788-91. In the year 1790 alone the production was more than half of what had been produced in about 10 years.[107]

The production of rice, which is the staple food of the people, increased by 136 per cent between 1787 and 1791, as compared to the decade from 1777-86.[108]

---

and preparation of hemp, in French (cf. H.A.G., *M. Reino,* Book 163-B, ff. 559-69). Also see the letter from D. Rodrigo de Sousa Coutinho to F.A.V. Cabral dated 6 May 1799 informing the sending of pamphlets on the cultivation of the lands specified. These works were supposed to be distributed among the people of the India, for the King wisheed to 'give the inhabitants of his overseas dominions the lights and precise ideas for the advance of agriculture on which the happiness of the people so much depends' (A.H.U., *Índia,* cód. 520 ff. 165-6). The owners of coconut groves were obliged to plant one cotton tree for every ten coconut trees (cf. A.H.U., *Índia,* cód. 1308, ff. 7, nos. 186 and 442, ff. 181-181v).

[106] The Marquis of Pombal sent a provision on 21 April 1771, but only in 1776 his objectives were achieved with the creation of the Intendency General of Agriculture (cf. Instrucção ..., p. 10, fn. 14).

[107] One *kumb* has 20 *khandis.* One *khandi* is equal to 20 *kuddav* or *alqueires.* As weight, it corresponds to 20 hands or some 500 pounds. As one pound is 454 g, one *khumb* corresponds to 227 kg (cf. S.R. Dalgado, op. cit., vol. I, p. 333). See the Glossary.

[108] Whereas the average of the revenue of the emphyteutic fees of the new lands, in the years from 1777 to 1786, was 6,071 xerafins, in the half-

At the same time, there was some success in the cultivation of mandioca, cotton, pepper, coffee, flax, vegetables.[109] For the last decade of the eighteenth century there are indicators of good results in the production, though the data-source may not always be a reliable one.[110]

It may be noted, however, that agriculture did not prosper to the extent expected. This was perhaps due to various factors, such as the people's scrupulous use of traditional processes for rice cultivation; the introduction of shrub plantation and the

---

decade that followed it was 18,500 xerafins. It may be noted that the amounts in Salsete are always higher, their share in ten years (1777-86) being 63 per cent of this revenue soon followed by 30 per cent attained by Ilhas, 6 per cent by Bardez and 1 per cent by the New Conquests. As regards *bat* (rice without husk), the production was 246 *khumbs*: Salsete with 51 per cent, Ilhas with 29 per cent, Bardez with 14 per cent and the New Conquests with 6 per cent (cf. *Rezumo geral do que tem rezultado de utilidade a Goa com o Estabelecimento da Agricultura desde o anno de 1777 até ao fim de Dezembro de 1791, assim do rendimento do dinheiro das novas terras, como igualmente da produção do mantimento delle'*; H.A.G., *M. Reino,* Book 173, f. 305).

[109] In the year 1791, the production of mandioca was 21,996 ft, that is, 1,065 *khuddos* and 7 measures; that of cotton was 31,829 ft, 180 *arrobas* and 24 pounds; that of coffee, 14,449 ft, 184 *arrobas* and 102 pounds; flax, 18 *khandis,* 9 hands and 31 pounds; vegetables, 549 *khandis,* 5 *khuddos* and 7 measures. Planted were 2,01,618 ft of construction timber trees (44 per cent in Bardez, 44 per cent in Salsete and 12 per cent on Ilhas). Abundant documentation refers to the introduction and increase of these cultivation (cf. A.H.U., *Índia,* cód. 516, ff. 113, 201-2; cód. 517, ff. 61v-62v; cód. 518, ff. 78v-79; maços 126 (142); 131 (137); 135 (133); 150 (158). Also, see H.A.G., *M. Reino,* Book 158-A, ff. 146-150v, 151-152v; Book 160, ff. 58-59v; Book 159-C, ff. 766-8).

[110] Simeão Rodrigues Moreira was deported to India *'por escrever sinais alheios e não sendo destituido de préstimo'* (for forgery and was not devoid of merit) he became the intendent of the navy and agriculture. 'This Simeão used to talk a lot, write unceasingly, decorating the maps which he sent to that Court, not only with painting, but with exaggeration of advantages that never exist, both in Agriculture as in the referred industry [Combarjua], such that he made many god-fathers who gave him credit that his disguised service did not deserve' (H.A.G., *M. Reino,* Book 177-B, ff. 551-551v). See S.J.F. Barroco, *Reflexões sobre a cauza da decadencia do Estado da India ...*, Biblioteca da Academia das Ciências de Lisboa, *Série Vermelha*, no. 34, ff. 54v-56; 66-66v.

unsuitability of the plants to the soils; slackness, negligence and idleness; the distrust of the *ganvkars,* the owners of the village, who feared that the establishment of agriculture might bring innovation into their usages and customs, mainly their religion. These factors explain, then, to a certain extent, the opposition raised against the agricultural reform in Goa and also its poor results.[111]

The industrial field was active too because the setting up of factories was thought to be decisive for economic revival.

Hence proper conditions were to be created for industries to prosper in Goa. The textile industry was in need of technicians from other places in the Indian subcontinent; the manufacture of shroud laid ropes and possibly the gunpowder industry had to import expertise from Portugal. There were also times when Goan apprentices were sent to different places in India, namely Diu.[112] The workers were to be taught new treatment processes

[111] The Chamber-General of Bardez submits to the King, in the person of his attorney, that the Governor and the Inspector-General of agriculture have introduced shrub cultivation and other types of plants, 'wishing to give it the natural state of Europe, America and other lands of India, which have a great variety ...'. It states that the lands of Goa can produce rice, coconut and fruit trees. It may be noted that pepper requires very humid soil; hence, it is produced only in the south. The inspector of agriculture ordered it to be sown all over the land, so some of the seed never yielded; wheat grows but does not yield; cotton takes five to six years to do so. The construction timber trees (teak) are wild plants that grow in the forests of the north and the south. Cf. A.H.U., *Índia,* maço 2 (246).

[112] The efforts made towards sending sons of the soil to Bengal, Surat or even to Diu, to learning weaving was not successful, given their reluctance to leave their land. Cf. copy of the bond ..., of 14 October 1752, the letter of the Viceroy to the Castellan of Diu dated 5 January 1753 and the letter from the Marquis of Távora to the secretary of State, Diogo de Mendonça Corte Real, of 11 January 1753 (H.A.G., *M. Reino,* Book 125-B, ff. 570-81, 586-90). The Count of Ega, in his letter from 26 October 1758 to the Castellan of Diu, refers to the coming of weavers from Diu to Goa, even before their arrival in the territory. He orders that due contribution may be made for the sustenance of the families of the four dyers (cf. A.H.U., *Índia,* cód. 430, f. 277v). One *mestre* (master), one *contramestre* (assistant master), four *espadadores* (swingler) and *asseadores* (cleaners) from the Continent, reached the city of Goa around 18 February 1783 (cf. H.A.G., *M. Reino,* Book 163-A, f. 628).

and the manufacture of products, undoubtedly with a view to improving their quality.[113]

In the second half of the eighteenth century factories in Goa had varying degrees of activity: they included the Royal Factory of Silks and Textiles, the Factory of Ropes in the Royal Arsenal, factories producing flax linen,, coir, cotton, gun-powder and iron.[114] In fact, Simeão Rodrigues Moreira, whom we know already as the inspector of agriculture, later occupied the newly created post of intendent and inspector of factories and manufacturers of the Estado da Índia.[115]

[113] See the doc. cit. on the various stages for the preparation of hemp (A.H.G, *M. Reino,* Book 163-B, ff. 559-69 and A.H.U., *Índia,* cód. 494, ff. 20-27).

[114] The charter of the Count of Ega of 9 September 1762 approved and confirmed, in fulfilled of the royal orders, the 20 conditions for the establishment of the factory of silks and textiles, presented by the merchant Rama Chandra Camotim (A.N./T.T., *Junta da Real Fazenda do Estado da Índia,* Book 50, fls. 10v-13). On the manufacture of shrouds and of ropes, see the Instrucções ..., of M.M. Castro, dated 28 February 1782 (A.H.U., *Índia,* cód., 494, ff. 30-36v and H.A.G., *M. Reino,* Book 163-A, ff. 576-82); the letters of M. M. Castro to the Governor Frederico Guilherme de Sousa, of 15 and 22 March 1782 and the Governor's reply to M.M. Castro, of 4 March 1785 (A.H.U., *Índia,* cód. 517, ff. 105-106v; H.A.G., *M. Reino,* Book 161-F, ff. 1492-1504 and Book 164-E, ff. 1228-9). On the production of cloth in the Combarjua factory and the despatch of samples to the Kingdom in 1789, see H.A.G., *M. Reino,* Book 169-B, ff. 686, 687, Book 172-B, ff. 579-81; Book 174-B, ff. 591-603v; A.H.U., *Índia,* maço 158 (150) and cód. 496, ff. 59-60. Regarding the cotton cloth factory established in Mapusa, see the letter [from the Governor] to the Senate of the Bardez Council, of 22 January 1788 (H.A.G., *Cartas e Ordens,* 82v, 912; *M. Reino,* Book 172-B, ff. 516-17); in what concerns the cloth factory of Taleigão, see the letter from the Governor to M.M. Castro, of 12 April 1791 (H.A.G., *M. Reino,* Book 172-B, ff. 579-81 and Book 174-B, f. 617). On the gun-powder factory, see the letter from M.M. Castro to the Governor F.G. Sousa, of March 1783, in which reference is made to the 'weakness' of the gun-powder manufactured in Goa and to the manner in which the quality may be improved (A.H.U., *Índia,* cód. 517, ff. 146-146v). There is a reference also to an iron factory in Ponda and Zambaulim (New Conquests). On 31 December 1785, the Royal Treasury had a profit of Rs 32,819, 1 tanga and 54 réis (H.A.G., *M. Reino,* Book 167-A, ff. 205, 210).

[115] Cf. the letter from 24 March 1787 which refers to the said appointment (H.A.G., *M. Reino,* Book 169-B, f. 408).

Simultaneously, private manufacturers, independent from the royal factories, were encouraged in the hope of promoting the textile industry in the State.[116]

To increase production and save them from Indian competition, several protectionist measures were decreed for the factories of Goa, Daman and Diu, such as exemption from custom duties both in Goa and in the Kingdom on cloth manufactured in Portuguese India.[117]

Finally the impetus given to production in Goa managed to keep up the mercantilist programme of the Count of Ericeira, resumed by the Marquis of Pombal in the Kingdom and now extended to India, Brazil and Africa.[118]

Despite all these efforts by the central and local governments, the results of this industrial surge were short-lived. Indeed, here and there, production increased and improved in quality but its fruits did not last long. Sometimes, the expenses were higher than the revenue and some factories had to be shut down.[119]

[116] The coir industry, for example, engaged several private parties. In fact, this very interest made the Governor accept the conditions presented by D. António J. Cárcome Lobo to set up a coir factory (cf. H.A.G., *M. Reino,* Book 164-E, ff. 1228-9).

[117] Cf. diplomas of 8 January 1783, 8 March 1786, and 24 March 1787, regarding the exemption of duties on the factories in Goa (A.H.U., *Índia,* maço 12 (269), cód. 519, ff. 25-6; H.A.G., *M. Reino,* Book 169-B, f. 408, respectively). For this exemption to be effective, the cloth had to carry a certificate on its manufacturing process in Goa.

[118] In Brazil the industries of sugar, iron, naval construction and textiles were developed. 'The Portuguese government even developed a project – which never materialised – to set up a factory of printed cotton, hiring able Hindu weavers and inducing them to migrate, with their families, to Brazil, where they would get all the necessary support, including the fare to go from Goa to Bahia by the ships of the *Carreira das Índias.* Cf. Charles R. Boxer, *A Idade de Ouro do Brasil,* S. Paulo, Ed. Nacional, 1969, p. 310, cited by José Jobson de Andrade Arruda, op. cit., p. 131.

[119] Such was the case with the cloth and silk factories set up at the time of the Count of Ega. On 30 January 1766 the interim Governors informed the King that the expenses had been unfruitful (Cf. H.A.G., *M. Reino,* Book 138-B, ff. 483-483v). In 1780, there are reports of their closing down at an unspecified date many years earlier. The royal treasury spent on them an amount of 63,408 xerafins, 3 tangas and 52 reis. Some of the weavers were imprisoned and executed and others were sent away (cf. H.A.G., *M. Reino,*

What were the reasons for the failure? Possibly the same that did not allow agriculture to develop. Thus, the 'slackness' and 'idleness' of the inhabitants who were sometimes reduced to penury and ill health, added to other factors, namely the lack of proper investment and the consequent inability to make the Goan industries competitive.[120]

Commerce, which had brought prosperity to the city of Goa and contributed a lot to its development in the sixteenth century, was now in a critical state. The Viceroy, the Count of Ega in fact referred to its economic activity as being 'almost at the final paroxysm' and expressed fears about the financial situation of Goan businessmen.

Was there masterplan to revive the commercial activity of Portuguese India? Or, on the contrary, were its problems sought to be resolved empirically?

The need for a commercial revival made the central government and the local authorities develop an action plan to remove obstacles that had hindered its proper functioning. In this sense, a charter of D. João V banned foreign traffic and ships at the Goa port to prevent competition for the local

---

Book 159-A, f. 31). Cf. also the letters of D. Maria to the Governor Frederico Guilherme de Sousa of 20 February 1779 and of 8 January 1783 (A.H.U., *Índia,* cód. 206, ff. 74v, 105). As regards the cotton cloth (factories at Combarjua and Taleigão), already in 1787 it was known that its progress was not as rapid as that of the shrouds manufactured in the rope factory. Cf. letter from M.M. Castro to Francisco da Cunha e Menezes of 9 April 1788 (A.H.U., *Índia,* cód. 519, ff. 111-12). Besides this, in 1792, the cloth samples of the Taleigão factory sent to Portugal were sold with difficulty 'given their quality, width and effects' (Cf. H.A.G., *M. Reino,* Book 174-B, f. 617). Finally, the letter from F. V. Cabral to D. Rodrigo de Sousa Coutinho, of 2 March 1798, informed him about the closing down of the Combarjua factory (H.A.G., *M. Reino,* Book 177-B, ff. 551-551v).

[120] We have not come across studies on the Goan factories in this period. Nevertheless it is very commonly known from the documentation that certain habits of idleness and inertia were mainly responsible for the weak development of the same. By way of example cf. the letters of the Governor to M.M. Castro, of 8 March 1786 and of 1 March 1792, and the judgement by the senate of the Bardez Council of 12 March 1789 (cf. H.A.G., *M. Reino,* Book 69-B, ff. 410-12; Book 173, ff. 246-247v and Book 172-B, ff. 528-30).

commerce. However, the Viceroy the Marquis of Alorna considered the disadvantages that could result from this measure, since a great part of the merchandise, mainly cloth from Bengal and the Coromandel Coast, had been introduced in Goa by the foreigners. Considering this, the monarch did allow some tolerance, but inasmuch as to let the foreigners understand that they had to depend on the Viceroy's permission.[121]

On the other hand, it sought to put an end to the irregularities at the customs; and, during the consulate of the Marquis of Pombal, in 1774, a new customs regimen was established.[122]

Measures were also taken to defend sea trade from constant pirate attacks. Accordingly, every year a war frigate would guard the coasts, from Bombay to Daman and Surat.[123]

These protectionist measures were part of a policy of progress that also included concession of privileges to residents of Goa, Daman and Diu. Thus, from 1760 onwards, they were allowed to trade 'without reservation whatever on the Ports, nor commodities'. The traditional policy of direct State exploitation of trade did not pay off; it was now altered and replaced by very attractive conditions to stimulate participation by local merchants.[124]

[121] The reply of the King to the letter from the Viceroy of 15 January 1749 did not permit the free circulation of the foreign ships, but admitted some tolerance, not with the ships going directly to Europe, but with those going to the European establishments in Asia (B.N., *Pomb.* 742, f. 23). The charter of D. João V (referred to in a document of 16 March 1750) banned foreign commerce, but precisely the commerce of the French in Mozambique. In reply to the royal order the Marquis of Alorna, on 20 March 1750, stated his obedience, but nevertheless presented the disadvantages of this policy. Cf. A.H.U., *Índia,* maço 77 (1750).

[122] 'Regimento para a alfândega de Goa', 20 January 1774, already cit. in fn. 79 of the present chapter.

[123] See the letter from Luís Pinto de Sousa of 4 October 1795 to F.A. Veiga Cabral, on the royal order for the guarding of this coast, in order to protect and regulate the convoys from Daman and Diu. Simultaneously the pirates, especially the Marathas, would get intimated (cf. A.H.U., *Índia,* cód. 520, ff. 84v-85).

[124] A letter from the Secretary of State, of 29 March 1760, granted this privilege. Otherwise, neither those residing in Goa nor in the capital, Daman

Also, with the opening of the ports of Mozambique to foreign trade, the Crown certainly had the objective of promoting free circulation of products between India and eastern coast of Africa.[125]

Reference has been made earlier to the fact that goods manufactured in Goa were free from duty on the way out from this territory and upon entry in Lisbon. Besides this, the businessmen of Goa could load their Europe-bound merchandise on a priority basis.[126]

Other facilities, such as granting transhipment facility for goods and 1 per cent tax exemption to the Goan merchants for the reconstruction of the city of Goa, were among the provisions made for trade promotion. Further, by a charter of 1774, the system of *cartazes* was abolished and all seizures effected became the property of the ship commander.[127]

---

and Diu would survive or, much less, promote economic development of the people of Mozambique and the Rios de Senna. To date, the Crown had to bear losses resulting from monopoly on ports and commodities, whereas the Governors and *almoxarifes* (treasurers of the royal household or tax-collectors) enjoyed profits. Finally, this letter considered that the former system would not be acceptable even if it promised to bring profits to the Royal Treasury, as it would deprive privateers from the means of subsistence and progress.

[125] Law of 10 June 1755 on the general freedom of trade. The Portuguese subjects in Asia could trade in Mozambique and in the dependent ports in all the merchandise, except missanga, considered the trade monopoly of the Royal Treasury (see Fritz Hoppe, *A África Oriental* ..., pp. 139-43).

[126] By virtue of the preference given to the Goa businessmen in the loading of their cloth, they had to declare, in advance, the goods they wished to load on the voyage ship, so that the commander could regulate the quantity of goods he could freight on the northern ports. See the letter from D. Rodrigo de Sousa Coutinho to F.A.V. Cabral, of 28 March 1797 (A.H.U., *Índia,* cód. 520, ff. 101v-102 and H.A.G., *M. Reino,* Book 177-B, f. 423). On the exemption of duties on goods manufactured in Goa, refer to the letter from 29 January 1792 (A.H.U., *Índia,* maço 23 (294)).

[127] On the *cartazes* see the Glossary at the end. Cf. the charter of 27 January 1774 (A.H.U., *Índia,* maço 19 (267) and the Instrucções ..., Instrucção Segunda, pp. 27-8). Exceptions to this provision were the vessels of the Hindus who, in wartime, took arms, ammunition and other

At the beginning of the second half of the eighteenth century, mercantilist ideas were current in Portugal. As far as trade was concerned, this economic doctrine generally recommended the formation of majestic and monopolistic companies that would stand up to foreign competition. Their statutes granted them great privileges and freedom of action. Thus it happened with the Company of Agriculture of the Alto Douro; the Algarve Fishing Company; the General Company of the Grão-Pará and Maranhão and that of Pernambuco and Paraíba.

In relation to Goa, as early as 1750, The Overseas Council reflected upon the need to set up an Oriental Company, due to a decline in trade in India.[128] The Viceroy, the Count of Ega was of the same opinion, sometimes expressed in his correspondence with the Marquis of Pombal.[129] However, given the decadent state of the Goan navy and also the policy of granting several privileges to the Goan merchants, as referred to above, the Crown considered that it was presently inopportune to establish

---

banned goods to the State enemies. In this case, *baldeação* or *transbordo* (transshipment) meant the passage of one load of merchandise from one national ship to a foreign one or vice-versa, within the territorial waters. The royal charter of 2 March 1779 granted this benefit, both in the port of Goa, or in Lisbon (H.A.G., *M. Reino,* Book 159-A, ff. 78-79v). At first it was conceded only for the ports of Asia but, on 12 March of that same year, it was extended to the port of Lisbon and from here to the foreign countries (A.H.U., *Índia,* cód. 516, ff. 198-9). As regards the 1 per cent tax for the rebuilding of the city, it was imposed on the goods. In this way the merchants used to be burdened with this tribute, beside the 5 per cent they paid at the customs. The King acceded to their argument that they were afflicted with one tax that the other social classes did not pay and ordered the suspension of the said tax. On the said date and on 1 January 1780, he ordered that the revenue be recovered through some other source, whether *urrak,* coconuts, wines, or any other commodity of mass consumption in the city so that the merchants would feel less pressurized and the onus was shared by all the classes. [A.H.U., *Índia,* cód. 516, ff. 199 and maço 131 (137), respectively.]

[128] Opinion of the Overseas Council of 16 March 1750. Cf. A.H.U., *Índia,* maço 77 (62).

[129] See the letter from the Count of Ega to Sebastião José de Carvalho e Melo, of 20 December 1758, published by A.S.V.S. Saldanha, op. cit., p. 107.

companies in Goa. Thus, it would be 'unthinkable to deprive the trade of Goa, Daman and Diu of their only means of subsistence because of an untimely monopoly'.[130]

It may be understood, however, that the King did not ban the creation of private companies in the Estado da Índia though he opposed the establishment of companies under the State name and protection, because of the lack of means and ability to sustain them.[131] In fact, the Bengal company founded by the Count of Ega, modelled on the French and English companies, must have been running into losses already in 1760, and were therefore closed. It may be noted that, in the Viceroy's opinion, this decision, accompanied by the opening of the Mozambican ports in 1755, could be fatal to the trade in India.[132]

At the end of the century there was once again a great interest in setting up a large company, considering that otherwise Portuguese trade in Asia would never be truly national. In this sense, careful studies were made and a plan was drawn subject to examination by competent people (1779).[133] In fact it may be noted that the British East India Company was presently very prosperous and was certainly worthy of emulation by the Portuguese.[134]

[130] Cf. the two letters of Tomé Joaquim da C. Corte Real to the Count of Ega of 29 March 1760 (A.H.U., *Índia,* cód. 425, ff. 170-170v and cód. 441, ff. 242-3).

[131] Cf. the letter from Tomé Joaquim da C. Corte Real to the Count of Ega of 29 March 1760 (A.H.U., *Índia,* cód. 441, ff. 249-249v) and the letter from the same to D. João José de Melo of 2 April 1760 (A.N./T.T., *Junta da Real Fazenda do Estado da Índia,* Book 32, ff. 45v-46).

[132] Cf. A.S.V.S. Saldanha, op. cit., pp. 39-40, 163.

[133] See the letter from D. Rodrigo de Sousa Coutinho to F.A. Veiga Cabral in which he communicates the despatch of a trade plan elaborated by a great statesman with the help of two able businessmen, to be studies by competent people. However, the letter did not carry the plan along (A.H.U., *Índia,* cód. 520, f. 96v). See the document of the same date entitled: *Breve e útil ideia do Commercio Navegação e Conquistas d'Azia e d'Africa escrita por meu Pai D. Francisco Innocencio de Souza Coutinho-1779.* Could this be the said plan on the establishment of a company? (H.A.G., *M. Reino,* Book 177-B, ff. 431-2, 452v).

[134] The Portuguese minister in London, D. João de Almeida Melo e Castro, in his letter to Luiz Pinto de Souza, of 8 April 1794, refers to the

In these circumstances, though a large State-owned company was never formed, the Crown did sign agreements with private parties to trade with the East. Thus on 15 December 1752, Nicolau Grenier was authorized to send five ships to Goa, the first one in 1753, and in every consecutive year up to 1757.[135]

With the objective of restoring and promoting trade, the royal decree of 16 March 1753 established yet another agreement with Feliciano Velho Oldemberg. Accordingly he could send a ship every year to all the ports of India and China, for the following ten years. On 11 August 1753 the licence was extended to another four ships every two years, so he could send a *nau* in the monsoons of February 1756, 1758, 1760 and 1762. Oldemberg was thus able to send eleven ships to Goa and thence to the Coromandel Coast, Bengal and other ports of Asia for ten years.

Oldemberg's petition to ensure the continuation of this treaty by his children, in case of his death, allows us speculate on the profits made by this undertaking. Hence, the reasonably profitable conditions stipulated in the agreement speak not only for the monarch's interest in this arrangement, but also the desire to promote private enterprise in India. The diploma itself expresses His Majesty's desire 'that all His vassals take interest' in this economic activity.[136]

---

prosperous situation of the English East India Company. He mentions the extension of its territorial possessions, at the cost of the dominion of Tipu Sultan and the French and shows the importance of its trade (A.H.U., *Índia,* cód. 520, ff. 69-72v). It was set up on 31 December 1600 and on 20 March 1602 the *Vereenidge Oast Indische Compag'nie* (V.O.C.) was founded. On the origin of the European companies, refer to Maria Manuel Sobral Blanco, *'O Estado Português da Índia da Rendição de Ormuz à Perda de Cochim (1622-1663)',* vol. I, Lisbon, 1992, pp. 393-400, Photostat, Ph.D. dissertation, Holden Furber, *Rival Empires of Trade in the Orient 1600-1800,* Delhi, 1990, pp. 185 and ss. And José Sáinz Ramirez, *Imperios Coloniales,* Madrid, 1942, pp. 219, 398.

[135] On the conditions to which this agreement was subject, see J. Veríssimo Serrão, *História de Portugal,* vol. VI, pp. 162-3.

[136] On this subject, see the appendix to this chapter. We have underlined the conditions of the agreement which corroborate the royal orientation on the trade done by private parties. Also see J.V. Serrão, op. cit.,

Once the central government had concluded that conditions did not favour the formation of a national trade company for India, the better option he noticed was that of attracting private initiative to the Asian trade. This explains why the Crown encouraged private initiative in this trade, by conceding ample privileges and allowing a broad field of action, even in the choice of their trading methods. Hence, contrary to the general impression, it was still profitable to trade with the East – and one or two voyages were sometimes enough to make a businessman wealthy.[137]

What did trade in India consist of? Which regions were the trade contacts maintained with? Which were the regular trade routes? And what products were traded?

In order to avail of the suitable direction of the winds and the monsoons, the ships had to leave Lisbon for Goa in March or April and reach Mozambique in August, and make the onward journey to Goa, driven by the south-west monsoon in September. A few days after arriving in Goa there used to be the Northern expedition (Daman, Diu, Surat) and between 31 December and 2 January, the ships would begin their return journey to Portugal.

But practically speaking, these dates were sometimes not heeded. This would jeopardize the connections between the Kingdom-Goa and Goa-Northern Province voyages, and vice-versa, causing serious trade losses.[138]

---

vol. VI, pp. 163-4. Oldemberg counted on the protection of Diogo de Mendonça Corte-Real, but his son Martinho Velho belonged to the *Junta da Providência* (Welfare Board) that at a certain moment wished to overthrow Pombal. For this reason Oldemberg's trade company fell into disgrace. His son was imprisoned and the properties confiscated. Felix V. Oldemberg liquidated his enterprise on 6 May 1760 (cf. Fritz Hoppe, op. cit., pp. 301-2; and Herman Kellenbenz, 'Oldemberg (Oldenberg), Feliciano Velho', in *Dicionário de História de Portugal*, vol. I, directed by Joel Serrão, Lisbon, 1968, pp. 198-9.

[137] Cf. A.H. de Oliveira Marques, op. cit., vol. II, p. 436.

[138] There used to be a great delay in the preparation for the voyage to the north, by indolence or in order to wait for coconut plucking, preparation of areca and other local produce. In order to avoid these delays the goods and effects meant for the northern trade were not to be off-loaded

Besides this annual voyage to the north, there was a vigorous land and sea trade movement with various parts of the Indian continent.

The articles shipped from Goa to the Kingdom included mainly pepper, a variety of textiles, saltpetre and precious stones, including diamonds. Goa would receive in return 'drugs' for its hospital, books and magazines, timber, foodstuffs, etc.

The ships leaving Goa for Daman, Diu and Surat used to carry coconut, areca, and other local produce and return mainly with textiles. The Goa-bound ships used to carry leaf tobacco at Bahia de Todos os Santos, Brazil, to be sold there, besides food provisions. It may be noted that between Brazil and India there were both legal and illegal commercial exchanges, which increased considerably in the period under consideration. Besides the said articles, Goa used to receive smuggled gold and silver from Brazil through Peru, and this favoured Goa's financial balance. On the other hand, a 'growing flow of Oriental riches heading for the South American market' was noticed in Bahia.[139]

Tobacco trade, which had been one of the main revenue earners for the Estado da Índia, was now decadent. The central government sought to obviate this decline by ordering the annual

---

in Goa; only the entry of the same would be registered in the book of lading and without many formalities causing delay. Cf. the letter from M.M. Castro to F.G. de Sousa, of 14 March 1780 (H.A.G., *M. Reino,* Book 168-C, ff. 829-30 and A.H.U., *Índia,* cód. 517, ff. 2v-3v); and the letter from this Governor to M.M. Castro, of 8 March 1786 (H.A.G., *M. Reino,* Book 169-B, ff. 410-12).

[139] Cf. José Roberto do Amaral Lapa in his study, 'O Brasil e a navegação portuguesa para a Ásia (Séculos XVI, XVII, XVIII)', *Estudos Históricos,* no. 7, Marília, 1968, pp. 98-100, which refers to a considerable maritime movement in Bahia, in the eighteenth century, with ships from the Indian Ocean and the concourse of Oriental products. See Celsa Pinto, 'At the dusk of the second empire: Goa-Brazil commercial links, 1770-1820', in *Purabilekh-Puratatva,* vol. VII, no. 1, January-June 1990, Goa; and Philomena Anthony, 'Colonial Brazil and Goa – Visible and Invisible Links'. The foodstuffs going from Brazil to Goa were mainly sugar, cheese, orange sweets. India exported to Brazil, textiles, clayware, tea, precious stones.

despatch of tobacco from Bahia de Todos os Santos to Goa, for consumption by its inhabitants.[140]

The said trade was in the hands of Hindu businessmen; that is to say, it was monopolized by three or four Hindu houses. The conditions set up in the agreement included that of being able to freely send out the necessary amounts in gold or silver for purchasing the product. Hence they never missed an opportunity to introduce in Goa, on their own account, tobacco bought at ports in the lands of neighbouring chieftains. For this purpose, they used to commit frauds in relation to Brazilian tobacco, discarding it as spoilt and ordering it to be burned. At the slightest delay in the arrival of the Brazilian tobacco, they would soon import the product from places on the Malabar Coast, causing huge losses for the Royal Treasury.[141]

[140] On 21 March 1779, M.M. Castro informed the Governor F.G. de Sousa of the embarking in Bahia of 4,000 *arrobas* of leaf tobacco. Of the 2,11,412 inhabitants of Ilhas de Goa, Salcete and Bardez, at least 67,087 were tobacco smokers (A.H.U., *Índia,* cód. 517, ff. 53-54v). For the year 1780 there is mention of an equal amount being sent and for the 1788 the amount of 5,268 *arrobas* (A.H.U., *Índia,* cód. 517, ff. 13-13v and cód. 519, ff. 155-155v). On 12 February 1790 there is an indication that the voyage ship had loaded 6,000 *arrobas* of leaf tobacco in Bahia and 2 rolls of cord tobacco (A.H.U., *Índia,* cód. 519, ff. 186-186v). On the amounts of these trade see also the works of Celsa Pinto and of Philomena Anthony referred to in note 152; José Roberto do Amaral Lapa, op. cit., enumerates some ships that in Bahia loaded tobacco for Goa and this in spite of the reduced number of ships that used to stop over in Brazil on the onward voyage to the Orient, in the eighteenth century.

[141] M.M. Castro, in a letter to F.G. de Sousa, of 8 March 1784, stated: 'As long as the Hindus hold the agreement for the same Commodity, and this is not managed by the Royal Treasury, so as to make the said Hindus lose all hope of introducing the said commodity on their account, bought at the ports of the neighbouring chieftains, the Bahia tobacco shall always be defective in Goa, however many precautions, and provisions may be taken in that Captaincy ...' (A.H.U., *Índia,* cód. 518, ff. 78-78v). Also in his letter of 12 February 1785 he referred to evasions by the Hindus; thus, the tests conducted on 150 bales of tobacco, revealed that only 14 or 15 were found 'spoilt', out of which some could be used, only one being totally rejected. Now earlier half had been set aside and there were times when about two parts of the despatch had been burned (A.H.U., *Índia,* cód. 518, ff. 146-146v).

The oscillation of prices, varying depending on the place of sale and the buyer, was yet another irregularity.[142] These frauds were sought to be curbed by first taking measures to superintend the quality of the Brazilian tobacco. So the bales would be opened and examined at Bahia, in the presence of the Governor and Captain-General and only the best of tobacco would be shipped; and in Goa tests would be conducted afresh in the presence of the Governor.

Simultaneously, it was sought to calculate the annual tobacco consumption in the Estado da Índia, in order to make proportional remittances with an addition to make up for the damages caused in transit. In an extreme situation just the right amount of tobacco could be bought in the neighbouring regions to guarantee the consumption until the arrival of the voyage ship. It is indeed noted that as a result of the measures adopted, the Brazilian leaf tobacco became popular with the inhabitants of India, thanks to its superior quality.[143]

Besides this so-called legal and official trade referred to above, there was another source outside the law and against State interests. Undertaken by the Portuguese settlers in India, with the support of some Hindu ethnic groups, it was full of promise and generated colossal fortunes. This process, which began in the seventeenth century, and continued up to the nineteenth century, reached its apogee in the period from 1750-1850, and owing a lot to Pombal's trade policies.[144]

[142] The locals bought tobacco for 2 xerafins per pound in Bardez and Ilhas, and the military personnel and white men for 6½ xerafins; in Salsete, its price was 8½ xerafins. Cf. the letter from M.M. Castro to F.G. de Sousa, of 9 April 1783 (A.H.U., *Índia,* cód. 517, ff. 151-62).

[143] Cf. the letter from M.M. Castro to Francisco da Cunha e Menezes, dated 12 February 1790 (A.H.U., *Índia,* cód. 519, ff. 186-186v).

[144] Having in mind the commercial development of the Kingdom and of the colonies, the Marquis of Pombal favoured the merchants. Thus, he contributed to the rise of the so-called 'indigenous capitalism' in the Estado da Índia. Very especially the Saraswat Brahmins and the Vanias were engaged in illegal private trade, occupying an important place in the Goan economy. See the following works by Teotónio R. de Souza in which he documents this Hindu dominance of the Goan economy: 'Glimpses of Hindu Dominance of Goan Economy in the seventeenth century', in *Indica,* XII, March 1975, pp. 27-35; 'Goa-based Portuguese Seaborne Trade in the

Equally important was the trade between Portuguese India and the East African coast, which always constituted one economic unit. Even after the administrative separation of East Africa from the government of Goa, in 1752, the central government continued to deal with Portuguese India as essentially one with Mozambique in the economic sphere.

The trade between the two territories thus continued to be under the administration of the Revenue Council of India which, by agreement signed with the merchants of Goa, Daman and Diu, ensured the annual despatch of merchandise to Mozambique.[145] It was incumbent on the government of India to guarantee the necessary loading for the annual trade voyage between the two territories, which the Crown used to regularly send money for.[146] In 1755 the Revenue Council of Portuguese India abolished trade administration though it permitted free trade to all the Portuguese subjects of Asia by paying the duties in Mozambique.[147]

It may be noted that trade freedom was declared in Portuguese West Africa on 11 January 1758, and by the decree of

---

Early Seventeenth Century', in *The Indian Economic and Social History Review,* XII, 1976, pp. 433-42; 'French Slave-Trading in Portuguese Goa (1773-1791)', in *Essays in Goan History,* ed. Teotónio R. de Souza, New Delhi, pp. 119-29. Also see Celsa Pinto, 'Goa Based Overseas and Coastal Trade (18th and 19th centuries)', in *Goa Through the Ages: An Economic History,* vol. II, ed. T.R. de Souza, New Delhi, pp. 176-8.

[145] On the trade relations between Goa and Portuguese East Africa, see the study by Fritz Hoppe, op. cit. mainly at pp. 122-8, presenting the trade organizational structure between India and Mozambique, giving greater importance, as is obvious, to the economic activity on the East African coast.

[146] Cf. the letter from the Marquis of Távora to the king, dated 18 January 1754, confirming the despatch of clothes to Mozambique in the previous monsoon; he further stated that he was going to add more to total 14,000 cruzados sent by the Crown for that purpose (H.A.G., *M. Reino,* Book 126-B, ff. 644-5). Also see 'Lista de roupas que tem ido para os portos desta costa da conta da carregação que veio de Goa em Março de 1753. Para as ilhas do C. Delgado para comprar escravatura e para, Quilimane para pagamento das obras da nova fortificação no Tangalane' (A.H.U., *Índia,* loose doc., unnumbered maço).

[147] Cf. Fritz Hoppe, op. cit., p. 171.

17 November 1761, ships on the Indian itinerary had to halt at Luanda on their return journey.[148]

Balghat pearls, tin, gunpowder, and, above all, cotton cloth were exported to Mozambique. The African products sent to Portuguese India included amber, slaves and especially ivory.

The sending of Indian articles, mainly cloth, had a vital importance for the external trade of the East African coast. Simultaneously, African ivory fed the Goan handicraft industry. The regularity with which Indian merchandise was sent every year to Mozambique confirms that these two territories were economically interdependent.

Thus, Daman and Diu had good traffic conditions and quick connections with Surat and Cambay, the traditional weaving and embroidery centres. They also had some cloth manufactures. Goa was slowly beginning to produce some textiles, as a result of the policy of industrial progress tried out in the second half of the eighteenth century. But Goa was above all a trading entrepôt for cloth from the Gujarat and Coromandel coasts, Balghat, and in lesser quantities, from Bengal and China.

Besides cloth, Daman used to export some rice and Goa used to send cashew liquor, arms, gunpowder and uniforms.[149]

With regard to the agents of the Afro-Asian trade, it was, undoubtedly, the Muslims and Hindus who predominated. Among the latter, the Banias (name in which the Jains were also included) stood out. Living exclusively from trade and mastering effective techniques, they managed to supplant any form of foreign competition. With the opening of the East African trade to Indians the Banias enlarged their business throughout the coast.[150]

Thanks to their great business acumen, Hindu merchants cornered the trade activities in that region, to the detriment of the Portuguese merchants. The excesses and offences committed by the Hindus and Muslims residing in Mozambique sometimes created a climate of hate on the part of the population.[151] It can

[148] Ibid., p. 170.
[149] Ibid., pp. 217-18
[150] Ibid., pp. 178-9. On the Jains, see the Glossary.
[151] Taking into consideration the opinions of his predecessors Baltazar

thus be stated that Christian merchants of Goa, Daman and Diu availed little of the trade facilities that the central government made available on the East African coast.

In order to preclude the difficulties it was sought, in the 1780s, to draw up a plan to regularize this trade. This was meant to bring Goa greater profits from the Indo-African traffic and finally revitalize that trade.[152] Particularly in the last two decades of the eighteenth century, an economic policy was developed to draw the very rich Oriental trade towards Goa and let Portuguese India benefit from it. Accordingly, it was sought to attract trade from Surat to Daman and prevent the smuggling of cloth.[153] Governor Francisco da Cunha e Menezes (1786-94) wished to establish a trade alliance between the merchants of Goa and Macao.[154] To make this plan feasible he proposed the formation of a society to supply cotton to Macao ships seeking this product on the Indian coast. This was done in order to divert to Goa the trade held by the Macao ships at ports on the Malabar Coast, particularly in Bombay.[155]

Manuel Pereira do Lago and Fr. José de Vasconcelos, the Governor of Mozambique, Pedro de Saldanha e Albuquerque, listed the excesses and offences committed by the Hindus and Moors residing in that territory (A.H.U., *Índia,* cód. 215, ff. 107-111v). Also, see Fritz Hoppe, op. cit., pp. 181-3, referring to the offences by the Banyas and to the governmental measures to curb their irregularities.

[152] See the royal letter from 15 March 1787, whereby a new plan and rules were formed for the Goa trade with Mozambique and other ports of the East African coast (H.A.G., *M. Reino,* Book 167-A, ff. 160-5 and A.H.U., *Índia,* maço 149 (155)). In his letter to the Governor F.G. de Sousa, dated 21 April 1784, M.M. Castro refers to decadent state of the Portuguese trade on the East African coast and to the measures to revive it (cf. A.H.U., *Índia,* cód. 518, ff. 72v-77).

[153] Cf. the letter from Rodrigo de Sousa Coutinho to F.A. Veiga Cabral, dated 28 March 1797 (A.H.U., *Índia,* cod. 520, ff.101-101v) and the letter from the Governor of Daman to Rodrigo de Sousa Coutinho.

[154] Cf. the letter from Francisco da Cunha e Menezes to M.M. Castro, dated 4 February 1788 (H.A.G., *M. Reino,* Book 169-B, ff. 428-33). See the copies of the proceedings of 15 November 1787 and 22 September 1790, in *Arquivos de Macau,* 3rd series, vol. IV, no. 5, Nov. 1965, pp. 270-1, 276-7).

[155] Cf. the document in annexe to the letter from the Governor F.C.

All these measures coincided with a wider royal project to combine trade of the possessions on this side of the Cape, and especially that of the East African coast, with the Indian and Chinese trade, with its headquarters in Goa.[156]

Not much is known about the outcome of this plan. The Macanese businessmen did not jump at it soon; they invoked their prior commitments, although the main reason was perhaps that the regular Goa-Macao-Goa voyage was not lucrative. It was nonetheless true that the Macao ships returned fully loaded from Goa and not in ballast as was earlier the case and this must have partly favoured Goan trade.[157]

Contemporaneous sources nonetheless speak of a decadent trade, sometimes citing reasons and even remedies to avert such a situation. Let us summarize the opinions.

In 1786, the governor stated that the limited funds in Asia (and without which there could be no traffic) did not let the Portuguese trade in these stations. In fact, they found more secure fortunes in Brazil and the few who came to India would finally end up going to Bombay, where they were the 'disguised treasurers of the English'. The latter, in collusion with the said businessmen, competed very badly with the Portuguese, both on the East African coast and in Macao. The landowners too were afraid to invest in trade whose profits were unstable and unpredictable.[158]

Menezes to M.M. Castro, dated 4 February 1788 and which relates to the conditions presented by the businessmen of Goa to attract to this city the cotton trade with China (H.A.G., *M. Reino,* Book 169-B, ff. 434-5). Also, see the letter from M.M. Castro to F.A. Veiga Cabral that documents the descent of the cotton from the Ghats and the facility in obtaining it this way (A.H.U., *Índia,* cód. 520, ff. 57v-58). Further cf. the copy of the proceedings of 8 October 1787, in *Arquivos de Macau,* 3rd series, vol. IV, no. 5, November 1965, pp. 272-3.

[156] Cf. the letter from F.C. Menezes to M.M. Castro, dated 4 February 1788 (H.A.G., *M. Reino,* Book 169-B, ff. 428-433v).

[157] See the copy of the proceedings of the Senate of Macao cited earlier, dated 22 September 1790, in *Arquivos de Macau,* 3rd series, vol. IV, no. 5, November 1965, pp. 276-7.

[158] See David Higgs, 'A Inquisição de Goa no fim do século XVIII', in *Ler História,* 24, Lisbon, 1993.

Besides these reasons, the Governor also mentioned the sloth and idleness of the inhabitants which made them prefer hunger to work, always resisting everything that would curb their habits, even the most ruinous ones. This must have also been the cause of the poor results obtained in agriculture and industry, as noted earlier.[159]

Another reason forwarded to explain the decline of trade was the non-compliance with the foreseen dates for the departure and arrival of ships. Thus, when the ships anchored in Goa only in December and January, it was no longer possible to undertake the expedition to the north. In that case, commercial exchanges between Goa and Daman, Diu, Surat would not take place. The merchants would also be unable to buy cloth in India to send to Portugal. At other times, late voyages to the north made it impossible to finalize the preparations in time as the ships left Goa by the first days of January. This made it impossible for the ships to sail inside the channel, and Mozambique and Senna would remain delinked from the Court. Their late arrival in Lisbon made it difficult to prepare for the subsequent voyage and delayed it too.

Several royal orders sought to put an end to this situation, determining that the ships should leave Lisbon at the latest by the end of February, and, on the return trip, leave Goa invariably between 31 December and 2 January, with or without cargo. With regard to the voyage to the north, it was ordained that, soon after its arrival in Goa and after having unloaded only the commodities necessary for consumption in this territory, they should leave for the septentrional locations.[160]

[159] Cf. letter from the Governor to M.M. Castro, dated 8 March 1786 (H.A.G., *M. Reino,* Book 169-B, ff. 410-12).

[160] Cf. the orders despatched on 10 March 1779 (A.H.U., *Índia,* maço 26 (196) and cód. 516, ff. 197v-198v). Also see the letter from M.M. Castro to the Governor, F.G. Sousa, dated 14 March 1780, about the dates on which the voyage ships should leave, whether from Lisbon port or the Goa port. It refers to the fact that the Governor was obliged to stay 12 days in Mozambique, 'the same being the number of days between 25 August, when he ought to have reached the said port and 7 September when he actually did, during this short time the monsoon would set in, so all his

Yet another reason indicated was the need for voyage ships, given the volume of goods transported from Goa to Portugal. It was said that two voyage ships were required instead of one, to allow the Goa businessmen to load all their goods and thus avoid losses.[161]

The sovereign was compelled to abolish 'liberties' and other privileges as they hampered navigation and trade.[162]

The obstacles created for the sale of goods on the Brazilian ports on the return journey caused the merchants many losses. Similarly, the fact that the ships to Goa passed through Bahia to receive tobacco, leaving Lisbon already late in April and May, seriously imperilled the date of arrival at its destination.[163]

The constant attacks by the Asian armies and the conflicts between the European powers sometimes created a climate hostile to the proper realization of commercial exchanges. D. José Pedro da Câmara feared that this would consequently ruin the factories, cause losses to merchants and contractors, and see the introduction and the competition of foreign and national goods, and reduction of the customs revenue.[164]

There were others who considered that the only sure remedy to curb the decadence of trade would be to establish a general

---

efforts to avoid it were in vain' (H.A.G., *M. Reino,* Book 168-C, ff. 829-30 and A.H.U., *Índia,* cód. 517, ff. 2v-3v). M.M. Castro in his letter to the Governor, dated 10 March 1779, stated that the abuse had reached such an extreme that in the last years the ships had left Goa in April and May. In this way the voyage ships had to sail outside the channel causing great inconvenience to the dominions of Mozambique and Sena (H.A.G., *M. Reino,* Book 159-D, ff. 1058-1058v). It may be noted that in earlier centuries this stopover was absent. This is perhaps why Fritz Hoppe states that it was not done at this time (cf. op. cit., p. 207).

[161] Cf. the letter from M.M. Castro to the Governor, dated 12 February 1785 (A.H.U., *India,* cód. 518, ff. 146v-147).

[162] Cf. the letter from M.M. Castro to the Count *Regedor* (A.H.U., *India,* maço 97 [96]).

[163] Cf. the letter from D. José Pedro da Câmara to M.M. Castro, dated 30 December 1778 (A.H.U., *India,* maço 126 [142]).

[164] Cf. the letter from D. José Pedro da Câmara to M.M. Castro, dated 24 December 1778 in which he refers to the declaration of war between France and England (H.A.G., *M. Reino,* Book 160, f. 7).

company for all of Asia and part of Africa. Earlier this position had first been defended by the Marquis of Alorna and then by the Count of Ega. And, as seen above, from the 1780s up to the end of the century, this idea was partially taken up again, though without results.[165]

Certainly, the decline of commerce in Goa cannot be attributed only to a single reason but to the convergence of various factors. First, it was the absence of a concerted policy. But other reasons, such as the lack of capital, scarcity of ships, absence of native initiative, that the extant documentation constantly points to, aggravated the situation. Apparently, the ultimate reason, which probably escaped the attention of contemporary authorities, was structural in nature; and the steady ascendancy of the English economic power in the Indian Ocean helped to defeat the Portuguese attempts to reverse the situation.

* * *

This was a period of great mutations, both externally, with the strength of the European powers in India, as well as internally, with the New Conquests, the redefinition of the Goan territory and the administrative separation of Mozambique.

There was a great desire on the part of the central authorities to follow these transformations and reform the economy, administration and society of the Estado da Índia. All this is obvious from the abundant legislation concerning India, which even appears disproportionate to the weak dimensions and low weight of the territory in the Portuguese Empire as a whole. It may be noted that India came soon after Brazil in the volume of expenses and even revenue, largely surpassing the Portuguese African territories.

Even if only some of the measures and projects produced the desired effects, it appears that at least the instant shipwreck of

[165] In the opinion of M.M. Castro, the only remedy would be to unite the funds of the company of Pará and Maranhão with those of Pernambuco and forming one company for Asia (December 1781) *Arquivo das Colónias*, vol. III, no. 15, Lisbon, Ministry of Colonies, 1917.

the Portuguese India was prevented, at the time of the English high tide in the Indian Ocean.

If, in the Portuguese Empire as a whole, it was not possible to have India reconquering the first position, the great reforms accomplished during this period had a profound and decisive impact on Goan society, conferring on it the characteristics it had in the contemporary times and which, in various ways, are strongly contrasted with those that had distinguished it in the earlier period.

APPENDIX

Conditions of the Trade Agreement with F.V. Oldemberg

By the royal decree of 16 March 1753 F.V. Oldemberg was granted permission to send his *nau N. Sr[a] do Bom Despacho* from Lisbon to Macao, which had to leave by 15 February 1754. All the commodities and goods deemed convenient could be loaded on the onward journey from the city of Lisbon and the return journey from Macao, paying the entry and exit duties in all the dominions of the Crown declaring that, out of the goods they had brought they would only pay duties in whole for those sold and consumed for this Kingdom, for those sold outside the Kingdom only 4 per cent would be paid by way of transhipment; for this end they would be sold in public auction at the Casa da India, as used to be done with the ships of Coromandel and Macao. Since the concession of the benefit of transhipment used to deprive the Royal Treasury of an important income and since that agreement meant a ban on sending another ship to China, F.V. Oldemberg was obliged to transport in his ship the Bishop of Macao and his family, bearing their expenses with the due decency. The said ship could stop over at all the Chinese ports but at the ports in India and those on the Coromandel Coast it could do so only by means of passports. The King permitted all the goods ordered by Oldemberg from outside the Kingdom and his conquests, on his own account and risk, to be loaded on the said ship, to pay only 4 per cent of the custom duties and these would be transhipped to the same ship. Oldemberg would be further obliged to bring on the said ship the necessary orders for the Royal Silk Factory of Lisbon, without charging freight up to the volume of 4 barrels; on the excess he would pay the ordinary freight. Among the conditions set by the decree of 11 August 1753 the main ones are the following:

1. Transportation of 100 soldiers on every small ship and 300 on every big ship.
2. Transportation of war ammunition for the Estado da Índia.

3. Importation of foreign goods into the Kingdom was not permitted to him whose entry was banned in the Kingdom.
4. He would pay eight contos of reis to the Royal Treasury for every ship that was granted permission by the Crown. This money would be deducted from the price of the soldiers' rations.
5. If the trade flourished and it was necessary to send another ship, besides the eleven, the King would grant him permission, in preference to any other person.
6. As soon as the first ship unloaded in Goa, it could leave for the ports of India, China and Coromandel and load goods for the city of Goa; the Viceroy would extend him all the necessary support.
7. If for any reason the said ship was unable to transport to Goa all the goods needed for loading the large vessels, the same ship could on its return trip halt at any of the ports of India, China and Coromandel, complete its load and sail on straight to Lisbon.
8. Of all the goods that Oldemberg redirected from the Asian ports to Goa with the aim of loading them for the Kingdom, he would be granted custom franchise; however, towards all that he sold or negotiated in the said city or any other port of Portuguese Asia, he would pay the respective duties towards the regiments of the respective customs.
9. Oldemberg was entitled to associate himself in this business indistinctly with any persons he wished, both from Lisbon and Goa, or from other parts of the Kingdom or Overseas, in great or moderate shares, forming a company or free association, as agreed with the parties, that is, during the entire monsoon period, or for a particular period of time.
10. He would be obliged to bring on the ten *naus* coming to Goa 1,500 quintals of saltpetre.

The decree of 24 December 1753 widened the conditions earlier granted as also conceded some others. Among them, the following stand out:

1. Oldemberg could buy or freight in any port of Asia all the vessels necessary with all the privileges, freedoms and exemptions.

2. Since Oldemberg's ship went ahead of the *naus* of the Crown which were to go in March 1754, it was supposed to take the soldiers to Mozambique, with the needful for their sustenance on land and their transportation up to Goa.
3. Exemption of duties for precious items and goods at the Goa customs and the ports of Asia.
4. The King allowed the Viceroy, Governor, cabos, ministers, soldiers and law officials and of the Revenue of the Estado da Índia, could be interested in this business.
5. Oldemberg could sign all types of agreements with foreigners.
6. And, in case of war, they would not suffer losses in their capitals.
7. Nobody could ship anything on these ships of this business, without express permission from Oldemberg.
8. He was allowed to load silver, gold, currency.
9. For the service of the same trade Oldemberg could depute in the Court up to twenty persons and in the city of Goa up to twelve and on the minor ports up to six for the jobs he deemed convenient; these people plus the crew of the ship of this business would indistinctly be free of all the public burdens.
10. If this trade increased so as to make one or more ships in one or more years loaded from Goa to the city of Lisbon, Oldemberg could send for all that he deemed fit, by paying for each of them four contos of reis as donation.
11. No event, even if for the urgent State requirement, could withdraw money from this business.

(Cf. A.N./T.T., *Junta da Real Fazenda do Estado da Índia*, Book 37, ff. 54-61v, 68-68v.)

CHAPTER II

Society

DRAWING A SKETCH of Goan society is not an easy task. There are no systematic studies done on its formation and evolution down the centuries; only some scattered and diffuse data is available, whose historical and sociological context is sometimes unclear.

However, there are well documented, almost exhaustive, works by Bragança Pereira on castes, religions and races of age-old India and, more particularly, on Goan society. But they are of ethnographic rather than historical nature. Hence an historical treatment of the social institutions of the territory becomes necessary.

Other difficulties stem from the very intricate nature of the theme. That is to say, there coexist different, or even paradoxical, social realities, together with a social structure inherited from its remote past now lost in time, constrained by the new social data that has emerged. In this context, the Portuguese expansion resulting from the spread of Christianity became the prime harbinger of European sociological models, as we shall see in due course.

Though this society naturally has its roots immersed in the India of old, the models, in fact more theoretical than real, furnished by the Hindu Dharmashastras, cannot be generalized.[1] Considering the groups that comprise it, their nature and interaction, the Goan social system does present certain peculiarities. Thus, for example, a Hindu Brahmin from Goa is not on a par with his counterpart from Hindustan, much less with the Christian Brahmin of Goa.

Serialization and systematization becomes quite difficult because of the great complexity and diversity of the social

[1] See the Glossary.

categories that exist in Goa, amenable to diverse religious, professional, or even ethnic criteria, depending on the analytical perspective adopted.

Goan society is above all a caste-stratified society, defined by Bragança Pereira as 'an endogamous social aggregate, animated by the spirit of hierarchy and insulation, regulated by customary norms consecrated by the Hindu religion'.[2] That was obviously a reference to the Hindu castes. Among the Christians, the caste system continued to exist, albeit devoid of the religious significance that was its principal justification, inasmuch as the determinant conditions had changed. It may be added that a high caste does not necessarily have a better economic status. However, the Brahmins having arrived in Goa after the Marathas (from whom the Chardós probably descend) they managed to get themselves admitted in great numbers into the Maratha communities, as Kulkarnis (scribes) and secured great economic advantages.

It would, therefore, be wrong to analyse Goan society based either on the classical scheme of the Hindus Dharmashastras, or on the Eurocentric structural model of society in the *old regime.* In fact, that society cannot be characterized exclusively based on the classes that were more intimately related with the European peoples.

In our study on Goan society we have come across difficulties inherent to the nature and content of the sources. The demographic data we possess is from official sources, which are not always dependable. Neither did we go into private family archives, although this would have greatly enhanced our work, nor were we successful in locating the parish registers of the time. Hence, in many cases, we only surmise certain tendencies and directions taken by Goan society without finding any concrete evidence to support them.

[2] A.B. de Bragança Pereira, *O sistema das castas. Ensaio Histórico-Sociológico,* offprint of *O Oriente Português,* vol. XVII, nos. 1-4, Nova Goa, 1920, p. 4.

POPULATION

A Note on the Sources

Population research on Goa in the second half of the eighteenth century has a corpus of charts that had been made by royal order. We did not find any for the period prior to 1753, which are followed by those of 1776. From then on the series up to the end of the period under consideration is regular indeed, with just a few omissions for the province of Salsete.[3]

Another aspect to consider in these charts is that they supply statistical data only on the Old Conquests. Being silent on the New Conquests, such sources become somewhat inadequate. These territories had been recently conquered and populated at the time and their Christian population was considerably smaller than that of the Old Conquests in the period under study; yet it would be important to know the number of inhabitants of these new dominions that more than trebled the area of Goa in the last years of the eighteenth century.[4]

Though age groups divide the actual population, examining them in detail is of little consequence to our work, as the age limits chosen for men and women do not match, making significant comparisons impossible.

Another great difficulty in using this numerical data lies in the absence of a single criterion for enumeration of the ethnic-religious groups. Indeed the charts of 1753, 1797 and 1799 distinguish between white Christians and locals, Hindus and Muslims, Negroes, Timorese, Chinese and Bengalis. However, the charts for the remaining years consider only the Christian and Hindu groups (and, in some cases, Muslim groups for Bardez). How does one compare numbers corresponding to different classes of population groups?

[3] Cf. Appendix II.1 to this chapter. We have not given the number of inhabitants of Goa in 1777, as it was wrong (19,405). There is no mention of the total number of inhabitants of Salsete for the years 1783 and 1790.

[4] The area of the Old Conquests, including the island of Angediva (3 sq. km.), was about 755 sq. km., whereas that of the New Conquests touched 2,845 sq. km. Cf. Gerardo A. Pery, *Geographia Estatistica Geral de Portugal e Colonias*, Lisbon, Imprensa Nacional, 1875, p. 381.

However, as the population charts always present two constant elements – the number of Christians and the number of Hindus – they allow us to see the population figures of these two main Goan social groups in the Goa islands, Bardez and Salsete.

Though the terms 'Hindu' and 'Muslim' have different meanings, since some population charts have clubbed these two social-religious groups under a single category, we were obliged (for the sake of uniformity) to do the same by adding the number of Hindus and Muslims. And we presume that in the population charts mentioning the word Hindu generically, the Muslims have been included. It may be noted that the number of Muslims is always small.

Evolution of the Total Population

From the statistical data as a whole what stands out is the marked population decrease between 1753 and 1799 (see Figs. II.1 and II.2) representing a total loss of 14.2 per cent, that is, 29,358 inhabitants. The 1780s were truly the great period of population loss. Between the years 1781 and 1789, there was a loss of 21,128 inhabitants (10.9 per cent); in relation to 1753, there was a decrease of 34,396 inhabitants (16.7 per cent), in 1789.

Wigh regard to the interpretation of the various percentages of the total population in the Old Conquests, it must be remembered that the number of years between the various periods is not identical. Between the first and the second there is a gap of 25 years; between the second and the third, 7.5 years; between the third and the fourth, 9.5 years. Thus the average annual decrease of total population between 1753 and 1776-80 is –0.13 per cent; between 1776-80 and 1781-90 this number rises to –1.3 per cent; and, in between the two last periods, the decrease stands at –0.52 per cent.

With regard to the province of Ilhas, it is seen that, taking the data grouped in Table 1, a steady decrease of population was registered in the entire period under study. In the province of Bardez, on the contrary, there was a slight increase of population between the beginning of the period under study and the quinquennium of 1776-80, which is the opposite of the tendency noticed in Ilhas. The same phenomenon is noticed in the

Christian Lady (Arquivo Histórico Ultramarino, LR, 387, Manuel da Cunha Maldonado and Joaquim António Roncon, *Usos e Costumes da Índia*, 1846-1847)

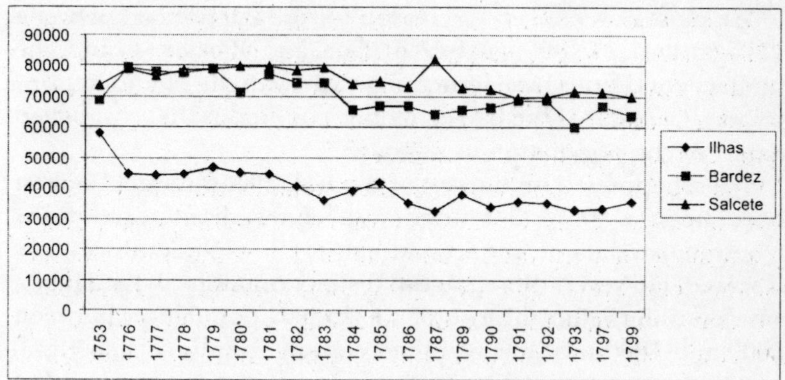

Fig. II.1: Province-wise evolution of the population.

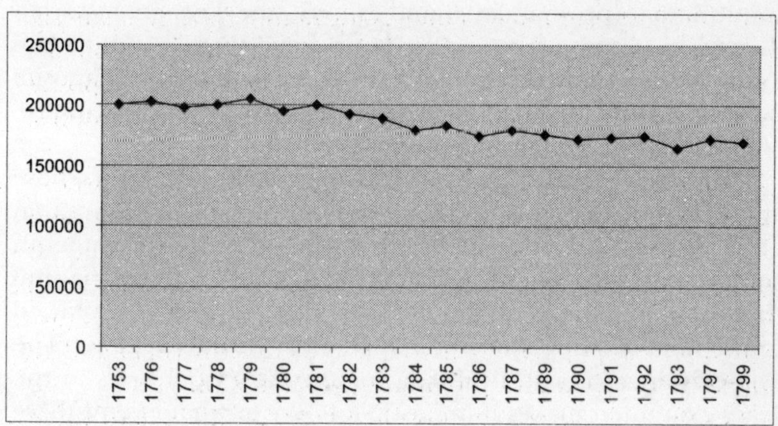

Fig. II.2: Total population evolution.

province of Salsete, and the question that comes to mind is whether or not this diminution in the province of Ilhas contributed towards this increase.

There would thus be a tendency for rural migration of the population, as suggested by the abandonment and depopulation of the old capital (old Goa). Logically, this must have led to the dispersion of its inhabitants, since the new capital, Pangim, was nothing more than a little urban aggregate. In other periods under study, both in Bardez and Salsete, the population tends to decrease as in Ilhas.

We must now explain the reason for the fall noticed between 1776-80 and 1781-90, mainly in Goa and Bardez. Could the sanitary conditions have something to do with the phenomenon? Or was it a result of the bad economic conditions that compelled a part of the population to migrate?

What happened on the rest of the Indian continent? Could it have been a general tendency of the Indian population? Quantitative data on the second half of the eighteenth century is scarce. However, there are two distinct opinions: Irfan Habib, who considers that the rise of the Indian population between 1600 and 1800 was slow (0.14 per cent per annum). The eighteenth century, marked by incessant wars, is seen as a period of economic blockade and total absence of growth.[5] In an essay on south India (present-day Tamil Nadu), the French historian Roland Lardinois arrives at the same conclusion.[6] Authors like Frank Perlin, André Wink and Chris Bayly, take the opposite position, based on qualitative data (expansion of agriculture, commerce, etc.) and not quantitative data.[7]

However, we would like to suggest some conjectures, for whose answers we do not have any numerical indicators. The acquisition of extensive territories in the second half of the eighteenth century did cause significant surges of migrations. It was natural that the populations of the Old Conquests should have shifted to the new, less populated and apparently healthy regions. The non-existence of statistical data for the New Conquests in the years examined makes it impossible to say to what extent these migrations influenced the decline of population in the Old Conquests.[8]

[5] Irfan Habib, 'Population', in *The Cambridge Economic History of India*, vol. 1, ed. T. Raychaudhuri and I. Habib, Cambridge, Cambridge University Press, 1982.

[6] See this author's 'Deserted Villages and Depopulation in Rural Tamil Nadu, *c.* 1780-*c.* 1830', in *India's Historical Demography: Studies in Famine, Disease and Society*, ed. Tin Dyson, London, Curzon Press, 1989, pp. 16-48.

[7] C.A. Bayly, *Indian Society and the Making of the British Empire*, Cambridge, Cambridge University Press, 1988. We are grateful to Prof. Sanjay Subramanyam for the information supplied to us on this subject.

[8] The royal letter of 15 January 1774 guarantees non-Catholic inhabitants their religious and civil usage and customs. Cf. A.L. Mendes, *A Índia*

TABLE II.1: ANNUAL AVERAGES OF THE TOTAL POPULATION BETWEEN 1753 AND 1799 BY PERIODS AND VARIATION PERCENTAGES BETWEEN PERIODS

Years	Ilhas		Bardez		Salsete		Total	
	Average	%	Average	%	Average	%	Average	%
1753	57,732	–	75,666	–	73,198	–	2,06,596	–
1776–80	45,128	–21.8	76,530	+1.1	78,292	+7	1,99,950	–3.2
1781–90	37,064	–17.9	67,677	–11.6	75,636	–3.4	1,80,377	–9.8
1791–9	34,279	–7.5	66,193	–2.2	71,032	–6.1	1,71,504	–4.9

Note: The amount for 1753 is the one furnished by the maps of that year; that of the subsequent periods is the average of the years that comprise it, according to the available data.

May we also recall that the measures for the economic restructuring, namely in the manufacturing industry and the agricultural sector, were not in keeping with the State's expectations and did not have great effect. The people could hardly satisfy their primary needs, caused partly by the high population density in the Old Conquests, would not be able to develop themselves either and would certainly be forced to migrate.

Though data about the volume of emigration is not available, we have quite a few references to Goan emigration to places

---

Portuguesa, vol. I, p. 147. After the conquest of Mordongoro, Zambaulim and Dumengoro, the Count of Ega ordered the publication of several indults and proclamations (for example, 5 June 1763; 12 September 1763), promising to preserve the usage and customs of these populations. He granted them the indult of enjoying all the privileges, exemptions and immunities they had under the King of Sunda. The Dessais of the said province could freely possess their *dessaiados,* pensions and belongings. Their leaseholds and pensions would be preserved; justice would be administered as done before and a high court judge intendent general was appointed. Further, criminals and debtors who had taken refuge in these lands were promised immunity. The same would be applied to those who had shifted from this province to lands in Ilhas, Bardez and Salsete. Cf. A.C.P.G., *Cópias de cartas régias* [...], in F.U.P., 18-1-8 (22/4 and 5); and H.A.G., *M. Reino,* Book 140-A, ff. 124-6 and A.H.U., *India,* maços 93 (91) and 96 (93).

outside their native land, especially Mozambique and to areas bordering the Goan territory on the north, east, and above all the south, particularly Mangalore. The *Róis da Cristandade* (Church Rolls) also refer to the number of Goan residents away in Mozambique and Balghat (beyond the Ghats).[9] Finally, deficient public health conditions, epidemics and endemic fevers may also have been responsible for the population decrease.[10]

Province-wise Population Evolution

During the second half of the eighteenth century, considerable efforts were made to restore the city of Goa. Reconstruction projects and basic sanitation were undertaken but the results were short-lived. Contemporaneous documents often refer to the unhealthiness of the old city of Goa and its suburbs.

Added to these circumstances were perhaps the consequences of the commercial decline, stressing the tendency for the depopulation. Obviously we cannot cut short and explain in a direct and simplistic manner the demographic fall in Ilhas by the crisis of the old city. However, we must remember that in the earlier centuries there was a vast body of State officials populating the city, its suburbs and some neighbouring islands, thanks to the commercial activity and a plethora of institutions. We can conjecture that the progressive disappearance of this body also caused a reverse phenomenon which was, with due reservations, partly responsible for depopulation in some parts of this province.

In the province of Bardez, there is a population increase from 1779 to 1781, and then a descending curve till 1787. Thus, between 1779 and 1780, there is an exceptional increase of population in Goa and Salsete, which seems to exclude the hypothesis of an internal migration. Did people come from the New Conquests? If yes, why only to Bardez?

[9] E.R. Hambye, op. cit., p. 317. *Róis da Cristandade* will be taken up in Chapter III.

[10] Recall the unhealthy state of the city of Goa and its consequent depopulation. There are isolated references to certain epidemics that razed the population, like that of 1766 in Chorão, when many inhabitants were killed and others migrated. Cf. Viriato de Albuquerque, 'Ilha dos Fidalgos', in *O Oriente Português,* I, 10 and 11 (1904), pp. 549-58.

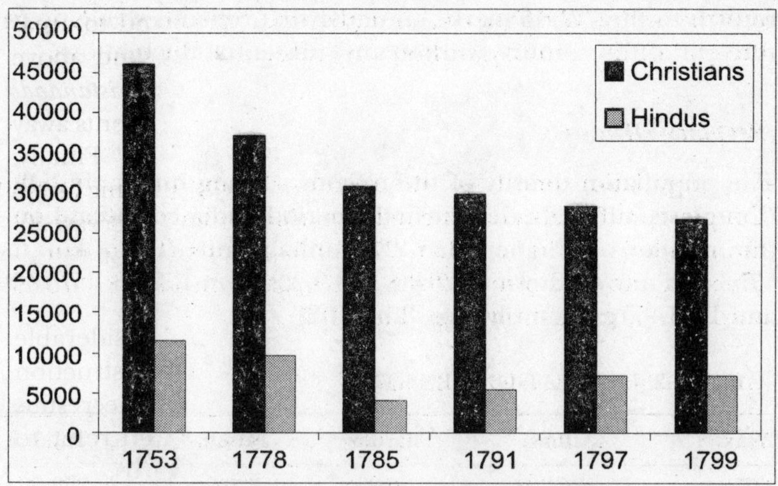

Fig. II.3: Evolution of the Christian and Hindu population in Ilhas.

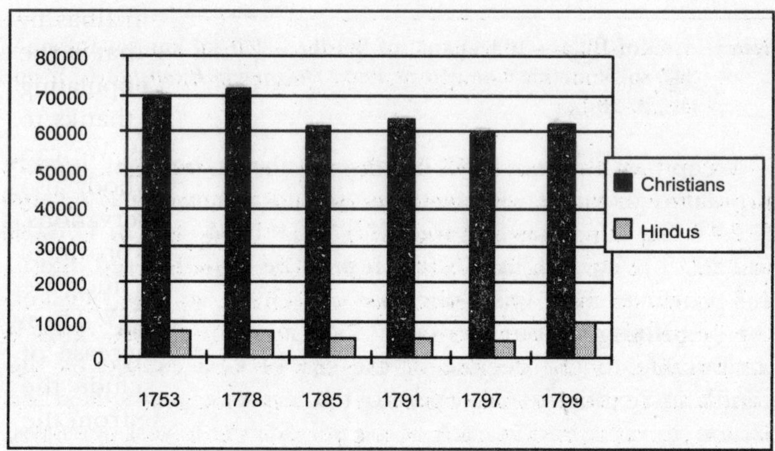

Fig. II.4: Evolution of the Christian and Hindu population in Bardez.

The population of Salsete grew between 1753 and 1777: there was an increase of 5,011, that is, 6.7 per cent. There was a marked decrease from 1782 up to 1786. In this year there was an enormous growth of population figures perhaps originally from Goa and Bardez. However, in the following year the population returns to the 72,845 mark, a number that remains stable up to the end of the century, without any substantial fluctuations.

Population Density

The population density of the regions coming under the Old Conquests suffered a decline in the period under consideration: the number was higher than 273.6 inhabitants (h)/sq. km. in 1753 and moved down to 264.8, 238.9, 227.1 in 1776-8, 1781-90 and 1791-9, respectively (see Table II.2).

TABLE II.2: POPULATION DENSITIES

Years	Ilhas	Bardez	Salsete	Total
1753	354.2	308.8	210.9	273.6
1776–80	276.9	312.4	225.6	264.8
1781–90	227.4	276.2	218.0	238.9
1791–9	210.3	270.2	204.7	227.1

Note: Area of Ilhas – 163 sq.km.; of Bardez – 245 sq. km.; of Salsete – 347 sq. km. (cf. Gerardo A. Pery, *Geographia Estatistica* (...), op. cit., p. 381).

Except for the year 1753, Bardez was always the most densely populated province, with averages oscillating between 270.2 and 312.4 h/sq. km. Ilhas followed with 276.9 h/sq. km. in 1776-80 and 227.4 h/sq. km. in 1781-90. It must be remembered that in this province there was a decrease of 143.9 h/sq. km. between the beginning of our period (1753) and the 1790s. This is attributable to the decline of the city of Goa caused by the population exodus to other parts of the territory, as stated earlier. Salsete, in turn, had in each of the periods the lowest densities, as seen from the respective table.[11]

[11] In the New Conquests, with a population of 79,675 inhabitants and area of 2,854 sq. km., the population density in 1810 was only 27.9 h/sq. km. See data in fn. 12.

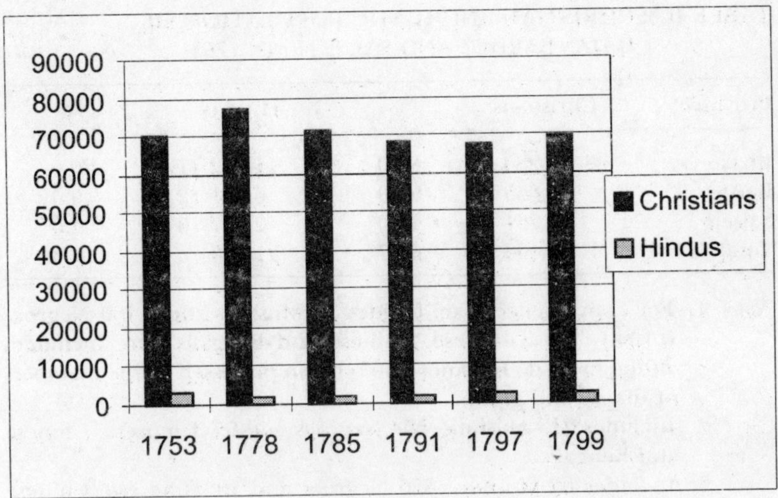

Fig. II.5: Evolution of the Christian and Hindu population in Salsete.

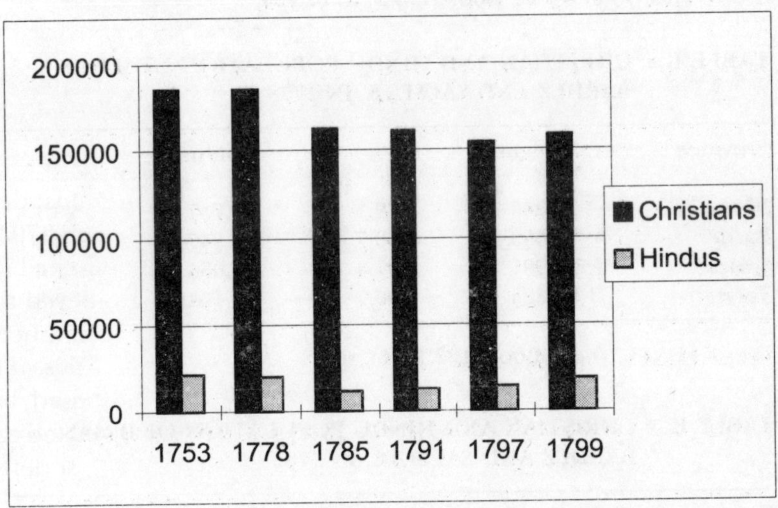

Fig. II.6: Evolution of the Christian and Hindu population in the three provinces.

Population in Ethnic-Religious Terms

Let us detail the number of Christians and Hindus, in order to see what each of the religious groups meant to the population as a whole (see Figs. II.3–II.6 and Tables II.3–II.8). The first

TABLE II.3: CHRISTIAN AND HINDU POPULATION OF ILHAS BARDEZ AND SALSETE, IN 1753

Province	Christians	%	Hindus	%
Ilhas	46,280	80.0	11,452 (1)	20.0
Bardez	68,865	91.0	6,801 (2)	9.0
Salsete	70,261	96.0	2,937 (3)	4.0
Total	1,85,406	89.7	21,190	10.3

Notes: 1. For convenience sake, besides 23 Muslims and 2,760 Negroes (black), 334 Timorese, Chinese and Bengalis were included, although we do not know the religion professed by the members of the second group.

2. Includes 213 Muslims, 554 Negroes and 95 Timorese, Chinese and Bengalis

3. Includes 62 Muslims, 886 Negroes and 10 Timorese, Chinese and Bengalis

Source: H.A.G., *M. Reino,* Book, 125-B, ff. 628-30.

TABLE II.4: CHRISTIAN AND HINDU POPULATION OF ILHAS, BARDEZ AND SALSETE, IN 1778

Province	Christians	%	Hindus	%
Ilhas	37,240	79.3	9,737	20.7
Bardez	71,593	90.7	7,347	9.3
Salsete	76,991	97.4	2,080	2.6
Total	1,85,824	90.7	19,164	9.3

Source: H.A.G., *Índia,* Book, 127 (141).

TABLE II.5: CHRISTIAN AND HINDU POPULATION OF ILHAS, BARDEZ AND SALSETE, IN 1785

Province	Christians	%	Hindus	%
Ilhas	30,900	88.0	4,081	12.0
Bardez	61,549	92.2	5,185	7.8
Salsete	71,204	97.0	1,987	3.0
Total	1,63,653	93.5	11,253	6.5

Source: H.A.G., *M. Reino,* Book, 167-A, ff. 93-6.

TABLE II.6: CHRISTIAN AND HINDU POPULATION OF ILHAS, BARDEZ AND SALSETE, IN 1797

Province	Christians	%	Hindus	%
Ilhas	29,873	84.6	5,434	15.4
Bardez	63,547	92.5	5,184	7.5
Salsete	68,359	97.5	1,792	2.5
Total	1,61,779	93.0	12,410	7.0

Source: A.H.U., *India,* maço 163 (146).

TABLE II.7: CHRISTIAN AND HINDU POPULATION OF ILHAS, BARDEZ AND SALSETE, IN 1797

Province	Christians	%	Hindus	%
Ilhas	28,410	79.7	7,250 (1)	20.3
Bardez	59,191	92.8	4,614 (2)	7.2
Salsete	67,577	96.5	2,478 (3)	3.5
Total	1,55,178	91.5	14,342	8.5

Notes: 1. Includes 1274 Negroes and 315 *pardos* (lit. 'brown people', probably half castes.
2. Includes 581 Negroes and 138 *pardos.*
3. Includes 505 Negroes and 96 *pardos.*

Source: H.A.G., *M. Reino,* Book, 179-A, ff. 239-42.

TABLE II.8: CHRISTIAN AND HINDU POPULATION OF ILHAS, BARDEZ AND SALSETE, IN 1799

Province	Christians	%	Hindus	%
Ilhas	26,771	78.7	7,238 (1)	21.3
Bardez	62,151	86.9	9,393 (2)	18.1
Salsete	69,279	96.6	2,406 (3)	3.4
Total	1,58,201	89.3	19,037	10.7

Notes: 1. Includes 1964 Negroes and 162 *pardos.*
2. Includes 499 Negroes and 156 *pardos.*
3. Includes 440 Negroes and 97 *pardos.*

Source: H.A.G., *M. Reino,* Book 179-A, ff. 237-41.

noteworthy fact is that in the second half of the eighteenth century Christians in the Old Conquests always outnumbered the Hindus. It was only in the second half of the nineteenth century that, due to migration, the Hindus began to outnumber the Christians in Ilhas and Bardez.[12]

From the comparative analysis of the Christian population in Ilhas, Bardez and Salsete, in the years 1753, 1778, 1785, 1791, 1797 and 1799, it is seen that the province of Salsete always showed a higher number of Christians, which remains true to our day, followed by Bardez and Ilhas in decreasing order.

From a comparison of these charts it is seen that the percentage of Christians in the territory grew from 89.7 to 93.5 per cent between 1753 and 1785. This growth is reversed between 1785 and 1799 when we find a slightly lower percentage of Christians than in the beginning of the period under consideration (1753).

Salsete records the highest percentage of Christians, fluctuating a little between 96 and 97.5 per cent, with no tendency for uniformity during the period.

With regard to Bardez, whose percentages vary between 86.9 and 92.8 per cent, there is an almost constant growth up to 1791

[12] The Christian population of Ilhas, Bardez and Salsete was larger than the Hindu population in the nineteenth century and the first half of the twentieth century. It was only in 1950 that Christians were indeed slightly outnumbered by Hindus due to Christian emigration. Thus, at this time, whereas there was a slightly higher number of Hindus in Bardez (52,353 Hindus as against 50,878 Christians), in Ilhas and Salsete there continued to be more Christians than non-Christians (36,254 Christians as against 35,572 Hindus in Ilhas and 93,815 Christians as against 22,517 Hindus in Salsete). Cf. the data supplied by the Statistical Services of Goa. We are indebted to Dr. Alberto Noronha, ex-Director of the said department, who furnished this data. In the second half of the nineteenth century the situation changes increasingly due to the emigration of the Christian Goans. Referring to this phenomenon, Orlando Ribeiro states that 'while the Hindu population increases and endures, representing the majority of the Goan inhabitants (42 per cent in 1881, 58 per cent in 1950), it is said that there are a hundred thousand Christian Goans spread through the world' (cf. 'Originalidade de Goa', in *Aspectos e Problemas da Expansão Portuguesa,* Lisbon, Junta de Investigação do Ultramar, 1962, p. 183).

whereas during this last decade the province touched its lowest (86.9 per cent).

The percentage of Christians in Ilhas is the most irregular of all the provinces in the territory. From 80 per cent in 1753, it touches 88 per cent some 32 years later and goes down by almost 10 per cent between 1785 and 1799. Hence, the phenomenon noticed in the territory as a whole must be attributed substantially to the Ilhas province. This is not surprising with the capital situated there, and fluctuations being normally more frequent in an urban society.

Curiously, the Salsete province not only has the highest percentage of Christians but also the highest percentage of priests, at least in 1753 and 1797 (see Tables II.9 and II.10). Ilhas too had a large number of priests. However, the percentage of priests for every Christian inhabitant is higher in Ilhas in the year 1753, as the number of Hindus in the province is considerable.

Though the sources do not specify their origin, there is reason to believe that these priests were Goans, given their importance

TABLE II.9: NUMBER OF INHABITANTS PER CLERGYMAN IN 1753

Province	Population	Prosbysters	Deacons	Sub-deacons	Total	Inhabitants/cleric
Ilhas	57,732	344	21	36	401	143.9
Bardez	75,666	192	13	44	249	303.9
Salsete	73,198	385	23	34	442	165.6

Source: H.A.G., M. Reino Book 125-8, ff. 628-30, see Table 3.

TABLE II.10: NUMBER OF INHABITANTS PER CLERGYMAN IN 1797

Province	Population	Prosbysters	Deacons	Sub-deacons	Total	Inhabitants/cleric
Ilhas	35,660	161	12	68	241	148.0
Bardez	63,805	246	35	163	444	143.7
Salsete	70,055	388	77	386	858	81.6

Source: A.H.U., *Índia,* maço 170 (163), see Table 8.

in the exercise of pastoral and missionary activity in the period under study, which we know from other sources, as we shall see in Chapter III. How do we explain such a density of ecclesiastical staff in Salsete? Why was it the most Christianized province? It may be recalled that the Jesuit missionary methods contributed, since the sixteenth century, towards a greater evangelization of the province of Salsete, which had been entrusted to them. The fact of the seminary of Rachol being in this province may also have been a determinant, since this made an ecclesiastical career more accessible.

A comparison of the total Hindu population in the Old Conquests with that of the New Conquests is not possible for lack of data. For a later period (1848), the number of Hindus is much lower in the Old Conquests than in the New Conquests.[13]

[13] There are bits and pieces of data on the Christian, Hindu and Muslim population of the New Conquests for the year 1810. In a chart of this date, there is an ethnic-religious detailing of the inhabitants of Ponda (covering Ponda, Astragar, Embarbacem, Chandrawadi, Bali and Cacora), Canacona and Cabo de Rama. But the population of Bicholim, Pernem and Tiracol is indicated as a whole, without detailing the social-religious groups, making it impossible to compare the number of non-Christians and Christians of the Old and New Conquests (Ponda: Christians: men 2,662 and women 1,761; non-Christians: men 15,403 and women 10,202; Muslims: men 566 and women 397, with a total of 32,620). Canacona and Cabo de Rama: Christians: men 1,706 and women 1,470; non-Christians: men 13,030 and women 11,040; Muslims: men 30 and women 40; Bicholim (including Mulgão and Usgão) with a total of 8,723); Pernem with 23,293 inhabitants and Tiracol with 456) (H.A.G., *M. Reino,* Book 190-C, ff. 850-9). I am grateful to Teotónio de Souza for the above data. The earliest information we have, with data about Christian and non-Christian population in the New Conquests, dates to 1848. It proves that the number of non-Christians of the territories of New Conquests is, in this year, much higher than that of the Old Conquests (in these statistics are included the Hindus of Angediva and the Tiracol fort). Thus, whereas the latter had 29,728 non-Christians, in the New Conquests their number rose to 1,01,806. The area of the New Conquests is certainly larger than that of the Old Conquests (2,845 sq. km. as against 755 sq. km.), but it also includes large forest areas and hence uninhabited countryside. The number of Christians in the Old Conquests was 2,13,361, whereas in the New Conquests it was only 18,595, which further stresses the presence of non-Christians in these lands. Hence in 1848 whereas in the Old Conquests there was a percentage of 87.8 per cent

Ilhas presented (save in the year 1799, when Bardez was leading) the highest percentages, followed by Bardez and Salsete with their considerably reduced Hindu population. Indeed Ilhas is the lowest populated province in 1753, but with the highest percentage of Hindus. Their number represents 5.5 per cent of the total population in the Old Conquests and about half of their Hindu population.

We have dealt with two majority social-religious groups of Goan society – Christians and Hindus residing in this territory, particularly in the Old Conquests, and for certain, largely their own locals. Another group, though a minority, used to be a part of this social world (as it does even today): the Muslims. Unfortunately, we only have at our disposal complete information for the year 1753 (see Table II.11). Beyond this, there are only partial indicators (for some years and only in the province of Bardez) and this circumstance does not allow any conclusion to be drawn. In relation to the existing population figures, the percentages are very low, oscillating between 0.08 per cent and 0.3 per cent. In Bardez, from 1781 to 1793 the percentage dwindled from 0.2 per cent to 0.1 per cent (see Table II.12).[14]

Christians for 12.2 per cent non-Christians (the number of Muslims was very small indeed – only 212 – representing 1 per cent), in the New Conquests the situation was the opposite, with 84.6 per cent Hindus, 14.4 per cent Christians and 1 per cent Muslims). The same is seen from the 1900 chart furnished by the Statistical Department of Goa, cited earlier. Indeed at this time, the number of non-Christians in the Old Conquests was 48,667 whereas that of the New Conquests was 1,61,111.

[14] According to Alberto C. Germano da Silva Correia, *Les Musulmans de l'Inde Portugaise. Histoire, Demographie, Anthropometrie, Morphologie médicale, Anthropo-sérologie, Ethnographie,* Bastorá, 1937, pp. 86-9, in 1749, the number of Muslims spread over Portuguese India would be about 2,953, of which only 203 lived in the territory of Goa (excluding the New Conquests, incorporated in the second half of the eighteenth century). A century later, in 1846, that number rose to 5,805 inhabitants. As this number includes 1,386 Muslims residing in the New Conquests, we note that the Muslim population in the Old Conquests was 4,419 inhabitants, there being, therefore, double the number in 1749. In 1878 the number came down to 2,738 inhabitants, but in the beginning of the century it rose to 4,478 inhabitants. The author also supplies population figures for various years of the

TABLE II.11: NUMBER OF MUSLIMS IN 1753

Province	Muslims	% of total population
Ilhas	23	0.04
Bardez	62	0.08
Salsete	213	0.30
Total	298	0.20

Source: H.A.G., *M. Reino*, Book, 125-B, ff. 628-30.

TABLE II.12: NUMBER OF MUSLIMS IN BARDEZ FROM 1781 TO 1793

Year	Muslims	%
1781	159	0.2
1782	171	0.2
1785	57	0.1
1786	49	0.1
1787	56	0.1
1788	53	0.1
1789	56	0.1
1790	58	0.1
1791	51	0.1
1792	57	0.1
1793	56	0.1

Sources: 1781 – AHG, *M. Reino*, Book 162A, ff. 366 a, b and c; 1782 – AHG, *M. Reino*, ff. 163B, ff. 409-11; 1783 – AHU, *Índia*, cx. 366; 1784 – AHG, *M. Reino*, Book 164E, ff. 1327; 1785 – AHG, *M. Reino*, Book 167A, ff. 95; 1786 – AHU, *Índia*, cx. 374; 1787 – AHU, *Índia*, cx. 379; 1789 – AHU, *Índia*, cx. 384; 1790 – AHU, *Índia*, cx. 388; 1791 – AHU, *Índia*, cx. 390; 1792 – AHU, *Índia*, cx. 393; 1793 – AHU, *Índia*, cx. 394.

Floating Population

The population charts of 1753, 1797 and 1799 provide indications on certain minorities, such as the Christian whites who, though few in number, did play a leading role and occupied an important

twentieth century also. In any case, the Muslims always were a minority in the Goan population.

place in contemporary society. An analysis of the data tabulated below leads us to the inevitable conclusion that their numbers dwindled almost to half, from the beginning of the second half to the final years of the eighteenth century (0.9 per cent of the total population in 1753, 0.6 per cent in 1797 and 0.5 per cent in 1799).

In the population charts the figure pertaining to the Luso-descendants was not made explicit. They were possibly included in the population group of the Reinóis, given their ethnic and social affinities.

It would be important to follow their evolution down these almost fifty years, but no detailed information is available. In any case, this decrease was perhaps the corollary of the policy of recruiting locals for the government in India.

It would be most interesting to examine the social component of this European minority, their origin and professional position. The lists pertaining to troops sent annually to India may throw some light on their social circle. In any case the data provided by these lists are rather incomplete and can serve only as indicators.[15]

On this topic we have data for 36 years, with a maximum of 835 Reinóis in 1758 and a minimum of 111 in the year 1763. In this period of time 13,913 persons arrived in Goa, that is, an annual average of 386.5 arrivals. We do not have the numbers for the return journeys.

Besides people originally from different parts of Continental Portugal some Azoreans were also in the expeditions to India. In 14 years, about 251 of those islanders arrived in Goa, probably for social, economic and professional advancement, nine of them from Madeira and two from Cape Verde.

The mortality index on the Lisbon-Goa voyages was quite high in the second half of the eighteenth century. At least 1,730 men died, over a period of 40 years, which means an average of 43.3 per annum.

[15] These lists do not always indicate the exact number of soldiers landing in Goa. In these cases, we arrive at this figure by subtracting the number of dead in transit and the number of those stopping over in Bahia and Mozambique from those who had embarked in Lisbon. Hence the approximate value of this data.

There were also a significant number of deaths registered in the Military Hospital of Goa, in spite of the constant appeals made by the monarch and the measures taken by the local authorities to check the situation. Over a period of 35 years, 5,641 men died, with a maximum of 259 in 1792 and a minimum of 3 in 1754, which was a great purge for the white population.[16]

It may be noted that a considerable number of military personnel used to leave Goa for other stations in India. In 32 years there were 2,628 desertions, which translated into an average of 114.3 per annum, with a maximum of 183 in 1752 and a minimum of 26 in 1800.

Probably, a large percentage of white men residing in Goa were from the forces, which can in fact be partially confirmed by comparing their respective sources of information. Children, women, some regulars and ecclesiastics (though considerably less than in the earlier centuries), a few civilians, used to probably make up this group of white Christians.

Besides this European, essentially ruling, minority, the three population charts of 1753, 1797 and 1799 mention other minorities that, on the other hand, occupied the lower echelons of society: Negroes, on the one hand, and the *'pardos'* Timorese, Chinese and Bengalis, on the other, as seen from the following tables.

TABLE II.13: WHITE POPULATION IN 1753

Provinces	Boys	Men	Girls	Women	Total	% of total pop.
Ilhas	145	408	140	456	1,149	2.0
Bardez	25	40	29	45	139	0.2
Salsete	71	226	61	220	578	0.8
Total	241	674	230	721	1,866	0.9

Source: A.H.G., *M. Reino,* Book 125-B. One has used the term boys/girls as in the document. We assume it refers to children under the age of 7.

[16] Note that the number of Goans in the list of dead in the Military Hospital is quite low.

TABLE II.14: WHITE POPULATION IN 1797

Provinces	Boys	Men	Girls	Women	Total	% of total pop.
Ilhas	63	179	45	645	932	0.80
Bardez	111	108	75	104	398	0.20
Salsete	24	20	8	6	58	0.03
Total	198	307	128	755	1,388	0.80

Source: A.H.U., *Índia,* Maço 170(163).

TABLE II.15: WHITE POPULATION IN 1799

Provinces	Boys	Men	Girls	Women	Total	% of total pop.
Ilhas	64	199	53	172	488	0.30
Bardez	86	69	73	106	334	0.90
Salsete	33	3	12	3	51	0.03
Total	183	271	138	281	873	0.50

Source: A.H.G., *M. Reino,* Book 179-A, ff. 239-41.

TABLE II.16: NUMBER OF NEGROES IN 1753

Provinces	Negroes	% of population
Ilhas	2,760	4.80
Bardez	554	0.70
Salsete	886	1.20
Total	4,200	0.02

Source: A.H.G., *M. Reino,* Book 125-B, ff. 628-30.

TABLE II.17: NUMBER OF NEGROES IN 1797

Provinces	Negroes	% of population
Ilhas	1,274	3.60
Bardez	581	0.90
Salsete	505	0.72
Total	2,360	1.40

Source: A.H.U., *Índia,* Maço 170(163).

TABLE II.18: NUMBER OF NEGROES IN 1799

Provinces	Negroes	% of population
Ilhas	964	0.020
Bardez	499	0.006
Salsete	440	0.006
Total	1,903	0.010

Source: A.H.G., *M. Reino*, Book 179-A, ff. 239-41.

They show that the number of negro slaves went down to less than half, at the end of the eighteenth century, whereas other communities remained more or less constant.

TABLE II.19: NUMBER OF TIMORESE, CHINESE AND BENGALIS IN 1753

Provinces	Timorese, Chinese, Bengalis	% of population
Ilhas	334	0.600
Bardez	95	0.100
Salsete	10	0.100
Total	439	0.002

Source: A.H.G., *M. Reino*, Book 125-B, ff. 628-30.

TABLE II.20: NUMBER OF TIMORESE, CHINESE AND BENGALIS IN 1797

Provinces	Timorese, Chinese, Bengalis	% of population
Ilhas	315	0.90
Bardez	138	0.20
Salsete	96	0.14
Total	549	0.30

Source: A.H.U., *Índia*, Maço 170(163).

TABLE II.21: NUMBER OF TIMORESE, CHINESE AND BENGALIS IN 1799

Provinces	Timorese, Chinese, Bengalis	% of population
Ilhas	163	0.004
Bardez	156	0.002
Salsete	97	0.001
Total	416	0.002

Source: A.H.G., *M. Reino,* Book 179-A, ff. 239-41.

The data is scarce indeed. It would be pertinent to examine to what extent the humanitarian measures inspired by Illuminism, and more specifically the Pombaline efforts to reduce slavery at some places, were successful.

Furthermore, we came across social components, albeit minor and unstable, like Brazilians, foreigners, Indians from neighbouring kingdoms, etc. These were, of course, concrete and specific references, with no data to quantify them.

Evolution of Birth and Mortality Rates

Table II.22 presents a summary of the population, numbers and percentages of births and deaths, whenever possible, in five-year groups.

This grouping by period seeks to leave out the insignificant variations of the original data and respective rates occurring whenever the basic population is quite limited. It is in fact common knowledge that demographic phenomena turn regular only with large numbers. This can be partially achieved by taking into account five-year population figures as a reference point for the phenomena that occurred during that period.

The birth figures for all of the Old Conquests are much higher in the initial period under study (1776-80). Between 1781 and 1799 the percentages are almost stable, with about 5 points lower than in the beginning.

As a whole, these figures remain at a level that can be regarded as perfectly compatible with the stage of demographic develop-

TABLE II.22: POPULATION IN ILHAS

Years	Population	Births per year	Rate %	Deaths per year	Rate %
1776-80	45,128	1,624	36.0	1,627	36.0
1781-5	38,507	1,217	31.6	1,814	47.1
1786-90	35,620	1,049	29.4	1,218	34.2
1791-3	33,908	915	27.0	1,235	36.4
1797-9	34,835	965	27.7	1,226	35.2

TABLE II.23: POPULATION IN BARDEZ

Years	Population	Births per year	Rate %	Deaths per year	Rate %
1776-80	76,531	2,492	32.6	2,167	28.3
1781-5	69,556	1,949	28.0	2,394	34.4
1786-90	65,798	2,151	33.0	1,917	29.1
1791-3	65,206	2,298	35.2	1,713	26.2
1797-9	57,675	2,237	33.0	1,862	27.5

TABLE II.24: POPULATION IN SALSETE

Years	Population	Births per year	Rate %o	Deaths per year	Rate %
1776-80	78,292	2,785	35.5	1,735	22.1
1781-5	76,400	1,956	25.6	2,152	28.1
1786-90	74,872	2,097	28.0	2,022	27.0
1791-3	71,141	1,843	25.8	2,029	28.5
1797-9	70,870	1,580	22.2	1,580	22.2

TABLE II.25: POPULATION IN THE 'OLD CONQUESTS' REGION

Years	Population	Births per year	Rate %	Deaths per year	Rate %
1776-80	1,99,676	6,899	34.6	5,528*	27.7
1781-5	1,85,276	5,229	28.2	6,531	35.3
1786-90	1,75,655	5,228	29.7	4,901	27.9
1791-3	1,70,255	5,056	29.7	4,975	29.2
1797-9	1,73,379	5,131	29.6	4,667	26.7

Note: *The average of this period has been made only with the figures of 1779 and 1780, as the figure for 1778 was obviously incorrect.

ment of the area. This indicates a reasonable statistical quality, although these estimations, beginning from the factors extrinsic to the data itself, cannot be demonstrated. But there is one pointer: the great regularity of mortality index in relation to the birth index. Thus, the birth rate depends on several conscious options (ethical, religious, etc.) whereas the laws of nature and the advance of medical sciences determine mortality. Now there is precisely a greater alteration of global valuation in all of the Old Conquests. And although it can argued that these variations too are attributable to a relatively small population under survey, it is perhaps significant that mortality should rise from 27.7 to 35.3 in the first two periods and later stay between 26.7 and 29.2.[17]

Considering the two together, the fact of the inverse proportions of birth and death in the first two periods, makes us wonder if it is the second phenomenon that determines the first one. That is to say, the birth rate goes down precisely because of a rise in the mortality rate. Demographically speaking, this is the inevitable conclusion. The explanation is the high mortality which, in our view, must be related to the following particulars recorded by history: dietary deficiencies, poor sanitary conditions, epidemics, etc.[18]

[17] For curiosity sake, it is stated that the Portuguese mortality rate in the beginning of the nineteenth century (1802) was 27.25. Cf. the data of INE, *Subsídios para a História da Estatística em Portugal*, II, Táboas Topográficas e Estatísticas, Lisbon, 1945, final chart.

[18] Although scarce, there are sporadic references. Thus, in Guirim (Bardez), alimentary deficiencies and trade reasons caused 442 persons to be out in Balghat (cf. *Rol da Cristandade*, Guirim, 1793, Book 3, f. 197v.) The Sirula roll (Parish of Our Lady of Help), 1781, registers 14 sick mendicants (cf. ibid., Book 2, f. 146). In the year 1764, there was a famine in Macasana (Curtorim - Salsete) that occasioned speculations in the price of rice (cf. *Visitas Pastorais*, Books 5-6, ff. 99, 102v, 100, 103; Books 11-12, ff. 166v, 172). Also once in a while people were affected by epidemics. There are reports of a contagious disease in Piedade, in 1753 (ibid., Books 3-4, f. 39), an epidemic in 1766 that razed the population of Chorão, compelling the inhabitants to migrate to other parts of Goa (cf. Viriato A.C.B. de Albuquerque, 'Ilha dos Fidalgos', in *O Oriente Portuguez*, vol. I, no. 10 and no. 11, Oct. and Nov. 1906, pp. 549-58). In 1780 an epidemic spread in S. Mateus, Azossim (Ilhas) and in 1785 in Mormugão (cf. F.N. Xavier, *Bosquejo*

From a generic data evaluation one can further note that the differences in the totals of births and deaths are relatively small. This is perfectly in accordance with the demographic theory and with the stage of sanitary development of the population. However, the total decline of population cannot be explained by the evolution of birth and death rates; the answer to which must be sought in emigration.

We may ask what could be the basic circumstances that occasioned the phenomenon. Historically speaking, we may consider the following: fascination by the New Conquests, where living conditions seemed more favourable than in the Old Conquests; expansion of trade with other regions, mainly in India and Mozambique; religious reasons, especially among the Hindus, who could freely celebrate their rites, which had official sanction only in the New Conquests.

The relative evolution of the birth and death rates of each of the provinces obviously follows the model of the whole, namely, the fall in births from the first to the second period, pronounced mainly in Salsete (with about 10 points of difference, more than double that noticed in Goa and Bardez, with 4.4 and 4.6 points, respectively).

This fall in Salsete is not connected with a rise in the mortality figures. The most significant jump in this demographic variable is noticed in Ilhas where from 1776-80 to 1781-5, there is a leap from 37 to 47.1 deaths per thousand inhabitants. Curiously, in this province of Ilhas, the birth rate also shows a much higher diminishing trend than the death rate during the period.

The opposite phenomenon showing a big positive difference between fertility and mortality is seen in Bardez. In Salsete the two rates are almost balanced. It is difficult to understand the historical reasons for these divergent phenomena. The province-wise differences in the sanitary conditions and medical assistance

---

Histórico das Communidades [...], (part referring to the description of the villages and communities), pp. 42 and 379). In 1788 there raged a big epidemic that strongly affected Mormugão, Chicalim, Verna. There were 11 to 12 burials daily in every parish (B.P.A.D.E., cód. CXVI/2-11, no. 28). In 1798 some people died of smallpox and in a second pestilence in Parrá (Bardez) (*Visitas Pastorais*, Books 27-29, f. 48).

during the period are apparently not a sufficient explanation for the same.

SOCIAL GROUPS: THEIR CHARACTERISTICS

If a study of the Goan population is quite difficult, mainly because of lack of information, analysing and characterising this society is no less difficult.

Heterogeneity is indeed one of its most peculiar aspects. It so happens that there was, and is, a peaceful coexistence of a Christian and a non Christian population, the latter comprising essentially Hindus and Muslims. Within each of these three large social-religious groups there are diverse castes and sub-castes. By their overwhelming numerical superiority and by their specificity, we shall begin analysing the social groups, beginning with the local Christians.

A prior issue is imperative. How does one explain the existence of castes among the local Christians? The Hindu abandoning his religion and converting to Christianity, shouldn't he have left automatically the place he occupied in the social hierarchy, which in India is intrinsically related to religion?

On their arrival in India, the Portuguese missionaries found a very hermetic and caste-stratified society. Whereas evangelization was limited to small groups, mainly consisting of outcasts, around the Portuguese positions, the problem was tackled with perspicacity. Their conversion to Christianity, like the adoption of Islam – both egalitarian religions – meant a social promotion from the edges into the mainstream. The problem arose as soon as evangelization began to spread and became systematic; this happened especially when it was extended to the higher castes too, for whom being equated with the outcasts who had converted earlier, was humiliating. Alienating or merely abolishing the age-old caste structure might have had serious consequences for conversion. This was perhaps one of the main reasons for castes persisting in Goan Christian society, constituting an odd example in history. In fact it is only in Goa and in Goan communities the world over that there are Christian social groups divided into castes. In Goa, they have lost their religious basis but are still present even today at the social level, through marriage, and quite influence their way of thinking. It may be recalled that the Portuguese society of the age also had its hierarchy: the nobles were proud of their ancestry and it was quite acceptable that men, equal in dignity before God, should have a hierarchy in this world based on their role in society.

Bragança Pereira believes that it was conversions made collectively that prevented the caste mechanism from disintegrating. 'If there had been isolated conversions, the *new Christians* would have assimilated the habits of the *old Christians*, and the castes would have disappeared, whether due to the difficulty for the converts to contract matrimony with members of the Hindu caste that they had left, or because of the pressure of the new Indo-Christian society, into which they had entered'.[19] In fact, in Daman there are no castes, for the locals were not converted en masse. Though this might be a plausible reason for the persistence of castes in Goan society, it may be noted that caste prejudices were firmly rooted in the Hindu mentality and strongly influenced their behaviour.[20]

From the sixteenth century the new converts did enjoy wide royal protection. It was sought to introduce them into the Christian society, by giving them surnames of the important families of the Kingdom and guaranteeing their livelihood by granting them certain posts, land concessions, etc. It may be noted, however, that the new Christians – in fact like the Portuguese who were not nobles – were able to exercise only a few functions, most of them subaltern.[21]

Equality before the law, sanctioned to the local Christians by the royal charter of 2 April 1761 and subsequent diplomas gave them unrestricted access to public posts, ecclesiastical boards, army ranks, as mentioned earlier. It may be noted, however, that

[19] Bragança Pereira, op. cit., p. 41.

[20] This position is also adopted by Leopoldo da Rocha who considered that even isolated conversion would not have succeeded in destroying caste prejudices. He justifies his statement by stating that this method of evangelization was unsuccessful in other parts of India. See *As Confrarias de Goa*, Lisbon, 1973, pp. 318-19.

[21] See Chapter III, pp. 290-2.

in practice there were indeed certain restrictions, which prompted the locals to complain to the monarch. In fact, the very Instrucções of D. José to the Governor and the Archbishop of India expose this situation and seek to curb the injustice.[22]

On the other hand, their preference for Reinóis rather than locals for posts requiring leadership and greater responsibility can sometimes be explained by the unwillingness of the locals to exercise certain functions and, particularly, their natural dislike for the military career.

We believe that, apart from certain exceptions confirming the rule, there was in fact during the second half of the eighteenth century a royal policy of promoting the Indians. However, it seems that many a time its practical application *in loco* was not perfect due to various factors that we shall analyse in due course, particularly the natural resistance from the European aristocracy that had been enjoying a top position and occupying important posts.

Local Christians were mainly employed in the teaching sectors, public administration and health, for which they in fact had shown a natural inclination, and on a smaller scale, in the army. A good number of Indians joined, first, the secular clergy and, then, the religious Orders. Their number in fact grew excessively and the authorities were compelled to take restrictive measures. We believe that the appearance of new a population agglomerate, the great deficiencies in health and primary education boards witnessed the recruitment of local personnel. In this regard, the local contribution was undoubtedly valuable, occupying as they did a great number of posts, albeit subaltern, but indispensable to ensure institutional functioning and social life.[23]

[22] Cf. Chapter III, pp. 208-9.

[23] Quite considerable is the number of appointments of Goans as teachers of Philosophy, Latin grammar, Rhetoric, masters of the 3 R's and catechism; as pharmacists, physicians, surgeons, etc. The appointments (generally interim) were made after an examination before the respective authority and masters of the subjects. Besides their ability and knowledge, good reports on their life and habits were also mentioned. We shall return to this topic in the chapter dealing with education. By way of example, we mention the permission granted to Joaquim Filipe Gonçalves, on

Christian Castes

Though great in number, the Christian castes of Goa can nevertheless be grouped under four broad divisions: Brahmins (Bamonn), Chardós (Chardde), Sudras (Sudir) and the lowest castes.[24] According to tradition, the Brahmins of Goa descend from the Senoys (Shenay) who came from Bengal in the twelfth and thirteenth centuries. Settled in Cortalim and Quelossim, they worked as Kulkornni or village scribes in almost all the *comunidades* of Goa, excepting perhaps the villages of the Salsete Kshatriyas.[25]

The opening of certain religious Orders to Indian vocations almost exclusively favoured the Christian Brahmins, for only the members of this caste used to get admission. Already the Fifth Provincial Council (1606) had banned conferring holy orders on members of the lower classes.[26] In fact, here and there, mainly

---

19 February 1778, to teach Latin Grammar in any province of Goa. He was born in Piedade (Divar), son of the *'advogado de número'* António Caetano Gonçalves and of Angelina de Albuquerque; was successful in the exam and good reports were given of his life and habits. Cf. A.N./T.T, *Junta da Real Fazenda do Estado da Índia,* Book 66, f. 141. The same happened to José Filipe de Sousa who was authorized on 31 October 1778 to exercise the post of physician. A resident of Calangute, he assisted in the Royal Hospital for a long time. The chief physician interviewed him. He knew rudiments of Latin and also had 'the best of conduct'. Cf. A.N./T.T., ibid., Book 66, ff. 204v-205.

[24] According to B. Pereira, the Christian castes of Goa are the following: 'Brahmins, Chardós or Chardi, Gaudde or Agris (salt men), Sudir (toddy tappers or distillers of local spirits), carpenters, masons, washermen, oil-men, barbers, fishermen, goldsmiths, ironsmiths, potters, Gauddis or Kunnbis (agricultural farmers), Mahars (*farazes*), Chamars (tanners).' They are by and large considered Sudras who are not Brahmins, Kshatriyas, Kauddis, Kunnbis, Mahars nor Chamars. *Etnografia da Índia Portuguesa,* vol. II, Bastorá, 1940, p. 47.

[25] See F.N. Xavier, op. cit., pp. 81-2. See the Glossary.

[26] In fact, the fortieth decree (third action) determined that only 'children of Brahmins or Prabhus or other castes reputedly noble' could enter the Church ministry, for through them the non-Christians and Christians would be better respected and known. Cf. J.H. da Cunha Rivara, *Archivo Portuguez Oriental,* fascicule 4, Nova Goa, Imprensa Nacional, 1862, p. 240.

the Luso-descendants and some Brahmins too were among those who best enjoyed the policy of promoting local Christians.[27] This is what happened, for example, in the medical boards, in the Tribunal of the Inquisition and the Revenue Board, in which towards the end of the eighteenth century almost all their functionaries were Brahmins, taking advantage of the prevailing policy.[28]

[27] See Appendix II.2 to the present chapter.

[28] Cf. letter from F.A.V. Cabral to M.M. Castro, dated 13 December 1794, in which he states that 'the measures of the exchequer have banished from this Revenue Board all the Portuguese, on the ground that only those should be added who began as clerks, and scribes of the different departments, circumstances that only fit the Brahmins, who entered in that manner into the service of the Board: so much so that in the absence of the present Treasurer General, who is a Portuguese from Goa, all shall be occupied and handed to the Brahmins within a few years.' Cf. A.H.U., *Índia,* maço 167 (165). We have come across some references to members of the Brahmin caste occupying ecclesiastical posts, like for example Nicolau Francisco de Abreu, born in Anjuna, congregant of St. Philip Nery who was the rector of the Chorão seminary. Cf. Father Caetano Francisco de Souza, *Instituições Portuguezas de Educação e Instrução no Oriente,* Bombay, 1890, p. 99 and Miguel Vicente de Abreu, *Noção de alguns filhos distinctos da Índia Portugueza,* Nova Goa, 1874, p. 5. The diocesan seminaries of Chorão and Rachol too, founded in 1761, were entrusted to the missionaries of the Congregation of St. Philip Nery, who were of the Brahmin caste. Cf. H.A.G., *M. Reino,* Book 177-B, ff. 547-8. In some other fields too this was the case. In the tribunal of the Inquisition, the third Inquisitor Pedro de Figueiredo of the Congregation of St. Philip Nery and the promoter, cleric Lourenço de Ataíde, were Brahmins. The Governor remarked, however, that the inquisitor was 'naturally more ignorant than the two referred Portuguese [inquisitors] for he never has never been outside Goa' and, he adds, 'very timid after his relatives were hanged in the [Pinto] revolution'. As regards the promoter he also finds him 'covered under the circumstances considered'; admiring nevertheless his good will when called to vote in the High Court. Cf. letter from the Governor to D. Rodrigo de Sousa Coutinho, dated 7 April 1800, H.A.G., *M. Reino,* Book 179-B, ff. 419-491v. In the field of health we know of Inácio Afonso, very experienced in medicine, though he was given to drinking. Brahmin participation was very limited. However, there are some references. The Marquis of Távora in his letter to the King dated 20 January 1754, refers to the establishment of a cavalry in Salsete, taking Brahmins as his officials (A.H.U., *Índia,* cód. 205, f. 10).

How does one account for the Brahmin participation in the Goan life? We do not have sufficient data to answer the question. However, it may be noted that they were in a better position than other castes, especially the lower ones, to avail of the privileges extended to the locals, by virtue of their social-economic status and cultural level. Complaints abound in official documentation against their lack of technical qualifications to exercise certain functions; but they quite possibly took advantage of the urgency in recruiting local personnel. At any rate, being in the dark about the background of such complaints, it is difficult to say whether they were genuine, or in what measure they resulted from mere jealousies felt by other social groups. In a small milieu like Goa, they could easily manage to whisper this or that in the ears of the Governors and others responsible for the administration.

It thus becomes difficult to judge the influence and rôle of this caste in Goan society. Keeping in mind that the intervention of the ecclesiastics was quite strong and significant here and that, in view of the recruitment policy, most of them certainly belonged to the Brahmin caste, we can surmise their influence with the local inhabitants. We come across Brahmin priests asserting themselves, for example, on issues like the *ganvkari,* even if infringing the norms laid down by the Constitutions; carrying out business and even blocking the conscription of Indian troops. Their action was clearly felt in other sectors of Goan society, such as the High Court, the court of the Inquisition, the Revenue Board, since they occupied managerial posts in these fairly powerful institutions.

It may be recalled that the anti-establishment revolt of 1787 – the Pinto Conspiracy – was planned and prepared by Brahmin priests, which proves how the members of this caste were conscious of their power.

Another caste present in the Goan society of the Old Conquests is the Chardó caste, sometimes called Ketri. There are many doubts about their origin and designation. Their Hindu counterpart is not known for certain. Orientalists like S.R. Dalgado, Bragança Pereira, P. Pissurlencar, F.N. Xavier, believe in the Maratha, Rajput or Vani ancestry among the Chardós.

There was perhaps a crossing of these last two castes in the earlier centuries, though presently this is not very common. Possibly, the Chardó caste also includes some Ranes (Ranne), who consider themselves to be of the Kshatriya caste.[29]

From these statements, Pissurlencar infers that the Christian Chardó caste is different and wider than the Hindu Kshatriya caste, since it includes blood from Kshatriya, Vaishya, and even Sudra castes if the Marathas of lower social strata are considered as such.[30] It may be noted that the Brahmins, Chardós and Vanis were regarded as the higher social classes, as can be deduced from a judgement of the Goa High Court, of 26 July 1674.

In the period under study (and the same happens in our day) there are Chardós only, and no Marathas, among Christians in the Old Conquests. There are only references to them – but as Hindu castes – in the New Conquests. This situation led to the wrong conclusion that there was no Chardó caste among the Hindus, or that all Chardós had converted to Christianity.

Besides references to Hindu Chardós, it is a fact that in certain village communities, Christian Chardós and Maratha Hindus belong to the same *vangodd* (common trunk).

In the opinion of Bragança Pereira, this confusion was caused by the change of name by the martial tribes in the New as well as the Old Conquests. The term 'Maratha' is a modern designation of the military tribes of the New Conquests, perhaps subsequent to the Maratha confederation. The change of designation from Chardó to Maratha could be due to the elevation of Shivaji, the Maratha who was promoted to the Kshatriya nobility in circumstances that need not be specified here.

According to F.N. Xavier, the Chardós reached a high position in the Old Conquests as compared to the Dessais and Hindu *ganvkars* of the New Conquests; this was by virtue of their conversion to the Christian faith and smooth assimilation of

[29] 'Members of a noble caste in the *New Conquests* of Goa, with bellicose tendencies'. Cf. S.R. Dalgado, op. cit., vol. II, p. 249.

[30] See P. Pissurlencar, 'Contribuição ao estudo etnológico da casta indo-portuguesa denominada 'chardó', à luz de documentos inéditos encontrados no Arquivo Histórico da Índia', offprint of *Actas do I Congresso Nacional de Antropologia Cultural,* Porto, 1934, pp. 1-7.

European habits.[31] It would indeed be interesting to see this acculturation come to pass, but the documentation is very scarce.

Meanwhile, we know that, in 1750, the Congregation of the Third Order of the Discalced Carmelites founded in Chimbel admitted members of the Chardó caste. A purely Goan congregation created by three diocesan priests, it advanced quite a lot. In the following year (1751) these priests applied for the establishment of a Carmelite seminary in the locality. Thus an exclusively Chardó religious community was formed.[32] Unavailability of data prevented us, however, from deciding up to what extent the Chardó caste was an instrument of Christian culture in Goa, given that the process of Westernization must have taken place precociously but subtly – perhaps with the aim of surpassing and neutralising the Brahmins – and did not leave behind any documentary evidence.

The great majority of the Goan population belongs to the Sudra caste that arrived soon after the Kunnbis in very remote times. It comprises many sub-castes such as the Gaudde (villagers), farmers (cultivating the lands), the Balagateers (Christians trading beyond the Ghats), fishermen, artisans (who take to their profession hereditarily).

Mention must be made of the Kunnbis, engaged in agriculture, who by their cultural backwardness, remain one of the most characteristic social groups of Goa.[33] They are supposed to be

[31] Cf. F.N. Xavier, op. cit., pp. 81-2.

[32] The priests João Baptista Falcão and Francisco Xavier dos Anjos applied for the founding of a seminary of the Carmelite Order in the village of Morombim-o-Grande, Chimbel. There is an application for permission dated 11 April 1755 for setting up the said seminary by the said priests. On 24 April 1778 the Carmelite religious are granted an annuity of 3,000 xerafins from the revenues of the properties confiscated from the Jesuits. The royal letter of 26 February 1781 to the Bishop of Cochin, the Governor and Administrator of the Archbishopric of Goa, confirmed this congregation and placed it under royal protection. In the next chapter on Religion, we shall return to this subject in greater detail.

[33] See F.N. Xavier, op. cit., pp. 78-9. Some data on their origin and way of life can be found in the article by António de Menezes, 'The Kunnbis of Goa', in the magazine *Goa Today,* Panaji, August 1969. Also see R.E. Enthoven, *The Tribes and Castes of Bombay,* vol. II, reed. Asian Educational Services, New Delhi and Madras, 1990, pp. 134 and ss and 284 and ss.

the earliest inhabitants of Goa, perhaps originally belonging to the same race that gave birth to the Kadamba dynasty. They were probably converted to the Christian faith in very a remote past which cannot be specified.

According to some authors, in their habits and concepts of life and the Beyond, they have some points in common with the Hindu Gaudde, to which we shall refer later. But presently the anthropologists argue that the Kunnbis are Dravidians and the Gaudde, Aryans.

They are still an ethnic group set apart by their culture and typical habits, with some of their dances and songs having become a part of Goan folklore. According to F.N. Xavier, the oldest stratum of the Goan population possibly comprised the Kunnbis, fishermen, artisans and the Gaudde of Bardez and Ilhas. Be it as it may, they constitute the bulk of the Goan agricultural population.

Finally, among the so-called lower social groups we have the *farazes* (animal flayers) and the cobblers or skin tanners, having a very low social status; they are generally despised by society, somewhat like the untouchables among the Hindus, even though the taboo of untouchability is not present among Christians. Europeans indiscriminately club them together as pariahs, but this Dravidian term is the name of a caste on the Coromandel, not current in Goa.[34]

Guarding against a simplistic relation between castes and the professional activities of their members – which would be fallacious at least with regard to the higher castes in Goa – we do see, however, by the report drawn up by the Viceroy, the Count of Sarzedas, in 1808 that, like the Hindus, Christian Brahmins too were businessmen, agents and legal attorneys of causes; the Chardós were warriors; the Sudras, sailors, the *farazes,* engaged in domestic work and menial jobs; and the Kunnbis, in land

[34] S.R. Dalgado notes that it is a wrong meaning attributed by the lexicographers to the word *pariah.* Indeed 'they [*pariahs*] are not known as miserable and abject nor are they refuse of society'. They have the same caste attitude as the Brahmins and Kshatriyas in relation to the castes they considered inferior and are very conscious of their habits and privileges. Cf. op. cit., vol. II, pp. 177-8.

cultivation.[35] As per the witness given by the Bishop of Halicarnasso, the greater part of the sepoys were *farazes* or pariahs of Goa.[36]

Hindu Castes

It is important to describe Goan Hindu society, with which Christian society is related and communicates so closely. Between the two there exist, if not genetic connections, considerable similarities which must be noticed for a better understanding of Goan society. In fact, this aspect comes out quite evidently among the new Christians, as we shall see ahead. However, we do not wish to emphasize this point overly, as it relates to an age-old social structure that probably did not suffer any perceptible alterations in the period under study.

Hindu society is divided into castes. They were initially established for ethnic reasons, with the aim of preserving the racial 'purity' of the conquerors. But this social fact was later transformed into a religious phenomenon sanctioned by their religion and holy books.

It is in India that the caste system presents its most finished example. If the Hindus are very tolerant with respect to dogmas and theological questions, they are nevertheless very strict about fulfilling the caste rules (in-caste marriage, living in common, remaining 'purity', meaning ritual purity).[37]

With the Hindu castes of Goa, there are the Brahmins, Marathas (military people), Vanis (merchants), Sonars (jewellers), Kansars (braziers), and two castes of untouchables: the Mahars *(farazes)* and Chamars (tanners) who could not have contact with the remaining castes.[38]

[35] Cf. A. B. Pereira, *Etnografia da Índia Portuguesa,* vol. II, p. 56.

[36] Instituto Histórico e Geográfico Brasileiro, lata 125, no. 8, 'Relatório enviado de Goa a M. de Mello sobre os assuntos da Índia, por seu primo B. de Halicarnasso.'

[37] There are many studies on castes in India, the most important ones being the following: Romila Thapar, 'Image of the Barbarian in Ancient India', in *Comparative Studies in Society and History,* 13, 1971; B.E.F. Beck, 'Indian Minstrels as Sociologists: Political Ethnologies depicted in a Local Epic', in *Contribution to Indian Sociology,* N.S., 16, 1, 1982, pp. 35-57.

[38] See Bragança Pereira, *Etnografia da Índia Portuguesa,* vol. II, pp. 25-47

Hindu Goldsmith (Arquivo Histórico Ultramarino, LR, 387, Manuel da Cunha Maldonado and Joaquim António Roncon, *Usos e Costumes da Índia*, 1846-1847)

The Brahmins play a dominant role in Hindu society and enjoy a privileged position; this status comes mainly from their educational function as guardians of society. From a tender age they are brought up according to the principle of superiority over other Hindus, an aspect that has in fact stayed with the Brahmin converts to Christianity.[39]

Although the Maratha ancestry of the Kshatriyas has been contested, they continue to defend this extraction. In fact, they believe themselves to be descendants of the Kshatriyas of old and the Rajputs, considered their modern representatives, and till date continue many of the practices of those two castes.[40] Like them, they are mainly given to the military career. To this caste belong the rajas of Baroda, Gwalior, Kolhapur, the Ranne and some Dessais of Portuguese India.[41] Earlier we dealt with

---

and Mariano Feio, *As castas hindus de Goa,* Lisbon, 1979, in which he makes a detailed description of the said castes.

[39] The Brahmin group include the Chitpavans, the Padhés, the Caradés, the Joshis and the Saraswats. The latter caste is the most numerous in Goa. In the Vedic age, the title of Brahmin was not yet hereditary. This term meant the word and the authors of hymns. Later it began to refer to the priests who recited them. Thus the term began to include the patronymic names too.

[40] Ever since the coronation of Shivaji Bhosale (1668) by a Kshatriya, the Marathas sought documents that would establish the relationship of the Bhosales with the Rajputs. One of the proofs they present is that the family names are the same as those of the Kshatriyas or the Rajputs. They further argue that there exist family ties between them established by marriages and some common habits too. But these proofs have been challenged, given that whenever a caste wishes to rise in the social scale they adopt family names, habits and principles of the branches from which the Marathas claim to descend. The Rajputs are hereditarily soldiers and landowners. They are a dominant race from Gujarat. Their social peculiarity is their clan division. They take it as their right to wear the sacred thread with the same formalities as the Brahmins. Cf. R.E. Enthoven, *The Tribes and Castes of Bombay,* articles 'Maratha' and 'Rajput', vol. III, Delhi, 1975, 1st edn., 1922, pp. 3-41 and 269-96, respectively.

[41] After dealing with these hypotheses on the origin of the word 'Maratha' and referring to the psychological features of the Maratha men and women, B. Pereira states that the similarity of surnames, marriage of pubescent girls, and the reclusion of the women, reveals the blood relationship between the Rajputs and the Marathas. Cf. *Etnografia da Índia Portuguesa,* vol. II,

the equally controversial relationship between this social group and the Chardós.

The Vanis, who are mainly businessmen, believe that they belong to the Vaishya *varna.* The Vaishyas were thus obliged by their sacred books to devote themselves to economic activity.

Any way, it appears that the *jati* division (subgroups within a caste) into *varna* or classes in the old and the normative religious texts is quite arbitrary and sometimes even unsure. Apparently, genealogies showing different castes were in good part arranged at a later date, so as to grant them legitimacy and status, all of which makes it quite difficult to view it critically and discern the truth.

Let us now see the level of Hindu participation in Goan society, through their professional activity, social position and the aspects that clothed their relationship with the Christians.

In the documentation of the times we found them sometimes as merchants, shopkeepers, tax collectors (tithes, customs, tobacco), brokers, usurers, jewellers, sepoys or sepoy captains, scribes, *ganvkars,* interpreters, etc.

Though it is difficult to establish the blood relationships of the various Hindu groups, it is evident that members of one family used to trade together – something very common among Hindu merchants. This is the case of the Camotins to whom there are many references. Many other cases could be cited but, only to illustrate, let us see Upea Camotim who asks for permission to open business establishments and requests the extension of this benefit to his brothers Chandrú Camotim, Suba Camotim and Pandu Camotim.[42]

---

pp. 30-2. The Ranne were members of a noble caste from the New Conquests, with warring tendencies (cf. fn. 29). The term Rajputs or Resbuts is applied to people of the military caste from Gujarat claiming to be descending from the Kshatriyas. The rajahs of Jodhpur, Bikaner, Kishengarh, Jaipur also belong to this caste. They are military men and landlords. Historically, they appear in the sixth century (see S.R. Dalgado, op. cit., vol. II, pp. 244-6).

[42] Upea Camotim asks the King to deign to grant him official permission to set up a cloth shop, another for foodstuffs and a third for retail contract (31 January 1750, date of the order). Cf. A.H.U., *Índia,* maço 77 (62).

The Camotins indeed played a very active role in Goan trade. Rama Camotim was a merchant, the 'biggest, dealing in all commodities and his shop has the largest clientele'.[43] In 1751 he seeks authorization to establish two *boticas* (shops), one for cloth and silks and the other for spices and food in retail and wholesale, each shop having three agents.

In 1762, Rama Chandra Camotim signed an agreement with the State which had 20 conditions, ratified by the Count of Ega, for the management of the Royal Silk and Cloth Factory, set up in the city of Goa.[44]

Gopala Camotim was another leading businessman that we come across in 1750 requesting the preservation of the Hindu custom of male children becoming the inheritors and in their absence the *crioulos* (adopted children), but never the girl-child. This was to prevent properties from passing on to the Crown Treasury in the absence of a male child.[45]

Further, the Camotins, or Kamat brothers, were Hindu Brahmins of Goa and rich businessmen who began gaining prominence in 1770. Even though their fortune was based on trade with the Portuguese world (Mozambique and Lisbon),

---

'Gopala Camotim paternal grandfather of the supplicant, and Nilca Camotim his cousin both businessmen, and wishing for the benefit of the former, ... his son Pondu Camotim Father of the supplicant, wished to introduce himself in the same cause Massana Sinay being head of his wife...'; this transcription documents again the business association of relatives. Cf. A.H.U., *Índia,* maço 77 (22). The same is noted with the application made by the merchants Narana Camotim, Roguna Camotim, Suba Camotim, Babulea Camotim and other heirs of Roulu Camotim and Crisná Camotim in which they ask for *namoxins* of the ex-Jesuits [A.H.U., *Índia,* maço 2 (246)].

[43] Cf. letter from D. João de Mello to the [Count of Ega], H.A.G., *M. Reino,* Book 181-A, ff. 215-215v.

[44] Charter whereby H. Exc. [Count of Ega] deems it fit to approve and confirm by virtue of the orders of H. Majesty the 20 conditions of the Royal Silks and Cloth Factory, established in the city of Goa (A.N./T.T., *Junta da Real Fazenda do Estado da Índia,* Book 50, ff. 10v-13).

[45] See the application of Gopala Camotim dated 28 February 1750. Cf. A.H.U., *Índia,* maço 77 (62).

they were linked with European trade circles, as correspondents, bankers, and intermediaries of the French.[46]

These and other cases are a proof of the active intervention of the Camotins in the economic activity of eighteenth century Goa, in their capacity as merchants, agents, brokers, tax collectors, that is, professional businessmen.[47]

About the Hindu Corondos we only know that they formed a society and were grappling with family disputes and large debts, after the death of their administrator.[48]

Equally important was the action by the Hindus as adjudicators at customs, a practice dating back to the seventeenth century.[49]

[46] Custam Camoty Mamay sent a cargo of 7 casks and 21 barrels, by order of the Count of Ega, to be delivered in Lisbon to Inácio Pedro Quintela, as the Countess of Ega was absent. 4 February 1765 [A.H.U., *Índia,* maço 89 (100)]. Bagraty Camotim and Essu Camotim, widows of Roulu Camotim and Crisna Camotim and their children Biquea and Narana Camotim, were tax collectors of the Cuncolim and Veroda county. See their application dated 3 March 1770, asking that they be kept in this occupation, since they had been removed before the stipulated time [A.H.U., *Índia,* maço 1 (247)]. Narana Camotim, Roguna Camotim, Suba Camotim, Babullea Camotim and Crisna Camotim, aspiring to the acquisition of the confiscated properties of the Jesuits, request that they be given the *namoxins* and other properties formerly belonging to the debtor Jesuits, in remuneration for the great 'discharge' that the supplicants have done. On the other hand, from the application of 22 March 1787 in which they ask for the handing of the papers, it is seen that the same was not granted [A.H.U., *Índia,* maço 2 (246)].

[47] See Teotónio R. de Souza, 'French Slave Trade in Portuguese Goa (1773-1791)', in *Essays in Goan History,* New Delhi, 1989, pp. 119-31, and Ernestina Carreira, 'Les Kamat et le commerce français en Inde: 1778-1819', in *Moyen Orient & Océan Indien, Middle East & Indian Ocean XVe-XIXe s.,* no. 7, Paris, Société d'Histoire de l'Orient, 1990.

[48] Biqueá Naique Corondó complains about the serious losses that he has suffered with the agreements made with the Royal Treasury. The Queen orders an investigation of the truth before she can proceed. See the petition made by this Hindu on 1 March 1779, with references to the Corondó society [A.H.U., *Índia,* maço 26 (296) and cód. 519, ff. 35v-36v].

[49] Norsu Naique was a custom duty collector as seen from the action that he proposed against the Attorney of the Crown and Revenue that he should be paid in this capacity 34,000 xerafins for the rights of cloths, loaded on the account of the *fundo do giro* (turnover fund). Cf. the letter to

Some of them were also private tax collectors for tithes and tobacco.[50]

We could refer to many other Hindus who actively participated in trade and other sectors of economic life. It seems, however, that those whom we have referred to demonstrate clearly the degree of Hindu dominance in this economy. As said in Chapter I, one of the serious problems of trade in Goa was the lack of funds available for business. It was just a few rich Hindus and rich merchants who, availing of a favourable financial situation, could invest large sums of money, drawing big profits.

Besides the association of members of a single Hindu family in the business, another prominent aspect is the continual exercise of a function by certain families, by virtue of its transfer from father to son. This was the case of the State *linguas* (interpreters). Vitogy Sinay Dumó, his son Poqueá Sinay Dumó and Gopala Dumó, who, besides being merchants and brokers, were also interpreters. The same happened with the Vaga family that for a century provided the State with interpreters. They are Boguna Camotim (who was the incumbent from 1719 to 1751),

---

D. João de Melo, administrator of this fund, dated 4 April 1763 (A.H.U., *Índia,* cod. 515, ff. 47, 48v-49v). Note that Filipe de Valadares Soto Maior observes that the non-Christians were involved in the embezzlement of custom duties in Diu. Cf. the letter from the same to the high court judge José Joaquim Sequeira Magalhães Lançóes, dated 29 January 1774 (H.A.G., *M. Reino,* Book 151, ff. 39-40). For the seventeenth century there is a study by Michael N. Pearson that gives detailed information and statistical data on the State revenue collectors in India between 1600 and 1670. The author shows the Hindu role, especially that played by the dominant groups of Saraswats and Vanias in the Goan economy (cf. 'Indigenous dominance in a colonial economy. The Goa rendas 1600-1670', in *Mare Luso-Indicum,* Tome II, Geneva, 1973, pp. 61-73).

[50] From the letter from Henrique Carlos Henriques dated 27 January 1763 to the Revenue Superintendent, it is seen that five Hindu tax collectors had been appointed for the payment of ecclesiastical revenue to the ecclesiastical ministers [A.H.U., *Índia,* maço 7 (229)]. Biquea Camotim and Narana Camotim were tax collectors of the Count of Cuncolim. Cf. letter of 3 March 1770 [A.H.U., *Índia,* maço 1 (247)]. Sadassiva Naique refers to the services rendered by his family members and ancestors as tax collectors. Cf. letter of 5 November 1779 [A.H.U., *Índia,* maço 16 (279)].

Ananta Camotim Vaga (1752-93), Boguna Camotim (1793-1807) and Sacarama Naraina Vaga (1807-44).[51]

These public agents rendered important services to the State, gathering accurate information about neighbouring chieftains, precluding surprises from them, advancing money in times of need, etc. For this very reason, the State generously compensated them with diverse favours, among which brokerships were common. It may be noted that the activities of the merchants, brokers, State interpreters complemented each other, for very often they fell upon the same person.[52]

Besides the important participation of Hindus in trade, we must mention their contribution in other sectors of the economy. For instance, as artisans, no doubt their traditional jewellery stood out in the Indian continent. We found, essentially, two Hindu jeweller families in the period under study: the Xette and the Chatim, with great importance in the territory of Goa. Indeed

[51] In fulfilment of the royal order, the Governor granted Ananta Camotim Vaga the basic pay of 70 xerafins and 40 réis per month; due to their age they did not exercise very frequently the charge of 'interpreter', but his nephew, Boguna Camotim Vaga, served with 'redoubled zeal' as assistant to the 'interpreter', with a salary of 10 xerafins per month. Cf. letter from M.M. Castro to Francisco da Cunha e Menezes, dated 30 April 1790 [A.H.U., *Índia,* cód. 519, f. 990 and maço 35 (282)] and letter from the Governor to M.M. Castro dated 7 April 1791 (H.A.G., *M. Reino,* Book 172-B, f. 576). Vast information on the interpreters can be found in Panduronga S.S. Pissurlencar, *Agentes da Diplomacia Portuguesa na Índia,* Nova Goa, 1952.

[52] On Vitogi Sinay Dumó and Poqueá Sinay Dumó, see the letter from the King to the Viceroy, dated 20 March 1764 (H.A.G., *M. Reino,* Book 137-A, ff. 37), the letter from the Governors to the King dated 31 January 1766 (H.A.G., *M. Reino,* Book 138-A, f. 102v) and a petition by Poqueá Sinay Dumó dated 19 February 1773 (A.H.U., *Índia,* maço 10 (272)). By this last document it is clear that Vitogi Sinay Dumó served as Balghat broker of the province of Bardez. He also solicited the post of broker of the *Ribeira das Naus* (shipyard), as remuneration of the services rendered. Cf. the opinion of the Revenue Superintendent, on that petition of 16 January 1760) (A.H.U., *Índia,* cód. 441, ff. 121-2). Gopala Dumó was a broker much esteemed by D. João José de Melo. He is referred to by the Bishop of Halicarnasso, cousin of M.M. Castro, in a report that is sent to him on the India affairs in 1774 (Instituto Histórico e Geográfico Brasileiro, lata 125, no. 8).

even after the eighteenth century, these two *vangodds* of the jeweller caste continued to exist.[53]

Curiously, we collected some information on that social group in a corpus of the *Junta da Real Fazenda do Estado da Índia* comprising letters of pardon, charters of guarantee, permission for the extension of security letters. There are jewellers accused of keeping or buying stolen ornaments. Later we shall deal with these aspects of behavioural deviations. This documentation allows also the appreciation of a great variety of ornaments available in Goa not only with private owners but also with the churches.[54]

Hindus are also found as sepoys or sepoy captains engaged in the defence of certain lands. Help sought from Indian troops, because of recruitment difficulties in the Kingdom and the defence needs, greater now with the acquisition of the New Conquests, made it imperative to have local military cadres. Some non-Christians who at wartime had helped the Portuguese were promoted to different posts, by virtue of their military conduct and as a reward for the services rendered. The relative frequency of requests for these posts convinces us that these

[53] According to F.N. Xavier, in Chorão there exist three *vangôdds* of jewellers, first the Fernandes, second the Vas, Chatim and Xette and third the Salkar. Cf. *Bosquejo Histórico* [...], p. 93.

[54] In the documentation collected there is clear reference to the jewellers Rama Chatim and Soirea Chatim and implicit reference to Pursea Chatim, Roulu Xette and Dessu Xette, accused of having stone jewellery and having bought stone ornaments. Thus, Rama Chatim was accused of having bought a stolen item of the crown of Our Lady of the Rosary, belonging to the church of Santa Cruz of Pilerne. See the charter of 10 March 1770 that was granted to him in order allow him to be cleared of the fault within one year (A.N./T.T., *Junta da Real Fazenda do Estado da Índia*, Book 68, ff. 72v-75. Later on we shall cite this corpus as *J.R.F.E.I.*). Also Soirea Chatim was accused of having contributed towards a theft that there was at the house of Luis Caetano. Cf. letter of pardon dated 4 May 1779 (A.N./T.T., *J.R.F.E.I.*, Book 69, ff. 124-5). Fondu Xette was alleged to have bought some *pingos de afogador* (necklace beads) from some thieves. Cf. letter of pardon dated 8 April 1780 (A.N./T.T., *J.R.F.E.I.*, Book 68, ff. 84v-85). There was a 'judicial inquest' of Siva Xette for receiving a stolen article. See the prorogation of the letter of [security] dated 15 September 1791 (A.N./T.T., *J.R.F.E.I.*, Book 78, deteriorated f.).

were offices quite sought after by the Hindus, perhaps because of the remuneration that went with it and by the social status they got. On the other hand, the fact that some of the sepoy captains had not formed a company and were at the same time in the service of the neighbouring kings shows the mercenary nature of these military men, all of which often caused their dismissal.[55]

We also noted the activities by Hindus in some sectors of Goan life. It is important to know about their status and position in society.

For religious reasons, since the first days of the Portuguese conquest, Hindus were banned from holding public functions. The main objective of this policy discriminating between Hindus and Christians was to induce them to convert, as is well documented by innumerable prerogatives and privileges granted to the neo-converts.[56] Still we do come across Hindus exercising

[55] Among the Hindus working as sepoy captains, we have Ramagy Porobo, Sambagy Rao, Chandaba, Rane Dessai, mercenary of the villages beyond Bardez, Gorqui Sinay, Sirpaty Ravo, Custangy Rao and Vasdeo Lassavanta Rao, Gorqui Sinai, Dulba Naique, Sar Dessai of the lands of Ponda and his children Nilba Naique and Panduranga Naique, Vencu Naique, Calé Porobo, chief *ganvkar* of Usgão, Rama Sinay, Narba Naique, Pataba Rau, Laca Naique (Cf. A.N./T.T., *J.R.F.E.I.,* Book 40, unnumbered f.; Book 41, ff. 88v-89, ff. 154-154v, ff. 194-194v; Book 46, ff. 180-180v; Book 54, ff. 31-2; Book 50, f. 107; Book 61, ff. 112v-113, ff. 131-131v; A.H.U., *Índia,* maço 48 (306); cód. 516, f. 136; maço 15 (271)). Working as sepoy corporals were Essobá Naique, Dessai of Ponda, Churgi Naique and Vitoba Porobu, Dessai of Calangute, who had come from the lands of the Sunda to serve the State; Rogu Saunto Vaddicar (A.H.U., *Índia,* cód. 447, f. 71; maço 1 (247)). In their requests the applicants invoke the good services rendered. Thus Gorqui Sinai states that he served in various negotiations with the neighbouring kings, even the Maratha. He went thrice to the Nana's court in Pune; also to the lands of the chieftain Sidi, executing services honourably (A.N./T.T., *J.R.F.E.I.,* Book 54, ff. 31-2). Rogu Saunto Vaddicar says that His Majesty had admitted him as a vassal on 15.1.1764 for having left the ex-Maratha that he was serving at that time (A.H.U., *Índia,* maço, 1 (247)). The Hindu captains discharged were Laca Naique, Dulba Naique, Ramagi Naique, Vasdeo Lassavanta Rao (H.A.G., *M. Reino,* Book 140-A, ff. 267-267v).

[56] Cf. Chapter III, pp. 291-2.

somewhat important functions in the second half of the eighteenth century, and even receiving royal privileges and honours. Some such privileges included being entitled to a palanquin, using the umbrella, not being imprisoned in the public jail, being exempted from the *xendi* tax, etc. For example, the Dumó interpreters were granted such benefits.[57] Also Sadassiva Caliana, master of the *Ribeira* (quay) of the Diu fortress, was appointed royal builder in return for his services. And at the request of Rama Chatim, the Queen granted him the office of the tester of the Royal Mint as long as he was competent for the post. These cases apparently wish to translate a certain openness of spirit, in which the criterion of competence overrules the ethnic-religious one.[58]

In spite of these and other occasional examples, it is natural that the Christians should have been called for a majority of the posts, especially those involving great responsibility, also because they constitute, as seen above, the overwhelming majority in the Goan society.

[57] Cf. the King's letter to the Viceroy, dated 20 March 1764, informing of the request of Poquea Sinai Dumó and solicits his opinion (H.A.G., *M. Reino,* Book 137-A, f. 37); the Governors' letter to the King, dated 31 January 1766, giving a favourable opinion (H.A.G., *M. Reino,* Book 138-A, f. 102). In his letter to the high court judge José Joaquim Sequeira Magalhães Lançőes, Filipe de Valadares Soto Maior invokes, with regard to the petition of Mulgi Rogunata, for 3 trienniums of major brokership at the customs in Diu, the banning by Church law that the non-Christians be allowed to have or serve public offices, confirmed by royal charter of 3 April 1582. F. Valadares further presents the grounds that the non-Christians were involved in a big way in the embezzlement of custom duties in Diu.

[58] By virtue of his merits, Sadassiva was appointed royal builder with a salary of 100 xerafins, by royal order, signed by the Marquis of Pombal on 3 February 1774 (A.N./T.T., *J.R.F.E.I.,* Book 60, ff. 134-134v). By petition of the jeweller Rama Chatim it is seen that the office of the tester of the Royal Mint belongs to D. Josefa Francisca de Cárcome Lobo, earlier deceased. The Queen declares that never should the property of such offices be deferred which demand personal effort, by succession. She further says that Rama Chatim should be employed therein, 'in case he is capable of serving in it and in no other way'. Cf. letter from M.M. Castro to Francisco da Cunha e Menezes dated 30 January 1786 (A.H.U., *Índia,* cód. 519, ff. 33-33v).

A careful reading of the requests for favours solicited by non-Christians makes us believe that often they applied for extravagant privileges, disproportionate to the services rendered. Expectedly, in such cases their requests would be turned down.[59]

Muslims

Documentation is very scarce with regard to the Muslim community. Some of them became prominent in the wars against the Bhonsles and the Marathas and, like the Hindus, they were granted military posts, by virtue of their feats and the defence needs (mainly corporal and sepoy captain). Special reference must be made here to Ismal Khan, the commander of the light navy of the Estado da Índia, for his good services since 1746, in consideration of which he was conceded a good number of benefits.[60]

[59] By way of example, we cite the petition of the Dessais of Bicholim, Vitogy Sinay, Suriá Rau and Suriagi Rau, dated 9 October 1753, in which they request the keeping of the annuities, appurtenances e revenues of their *dessaiado*, the leasehold in three life terms of two fields. The Crown attorney and the Viceroy note the baseless statements made in the applications when they say that they are possessors of certain rights on the lands. Hence, the application was not granted on 24 March 1756. Cf. A.H.U., *Índia*, maço 1 (247). We can also refer to the petition of Crisná Sinai Cabadi dated 6 December 1757, whereby he requested the village Agravaró or Chaporém and in their absence one of the fields Macazana and Casana Dunudém in the New Conquests in satisfaction of 22,000 xerafins which his father gave by the peace with the Marathas in 1739. D. João José de Melo, the Revenue Superintendent, gave an unfavourable opinion, arguing that on that occasion not only the applicant's father but also other persons had made donations. Hence, if it were conceded to the applicant, the same would have to be done to all others; this would mean an excessive diminution of the State revenue. The Revenue Superintendent further stated that donations imposed on similar occasions were considered as tributes and would never have remuneration. It may be noted, in fact, that the lands of the New Conquests used to bring considerable revenue to the State, due to which so many restrictions were put on granting them to private parties.

[60] Counted among the Muslims who held military posts, are, for example, Xeque Faquir Mahamede and Xeque Ali Naique as captains of the infantry

Like the Hindus, the Muslims were obliged to pay certain tributes, among them the *xendi* (capitation tax). Several times they applied for exemption from this onus which was finally abolished in 1840.[61]

There are only a few references to the economic activity engaged in by this community. Apparently, they were, as they are today, an urban mass, engaged in trade and small industry. At least some of them show signs of relative prosperity.[62]

---

working in the sepoy company; Faquir Sabo, Faquir Mamed Salbana, Daud Can, Abu Can, Amadagy Ismalgi, Issup Can, Moidin Can as sepoy captains; Xeque Abdulu Reyman as sepoy corporal (cf. A.N./T.T., *J.R.F.E.I,* Book 40, ff. 42v-43v; A.H.U., *Índia,* cód. 447, f. 10; A.N./T.T., *J.R.F.E.I.*, Book 41, ff. 94-95v, 100-1, 129-30, 145v-146, 177-177v; Book 46, ff. 117-117v; Book 54, ff. 18v-19; A.H.U., *Índia,* cód. 447, ff. 71v-72). Ismalcan applied for certain benefits, such as one field in Bicholim. From a document dated 16 March 1760 it is noted that it was granted to him. It may be noted that, by and large, many restrictions used to be imposed on the granting of land in the New Conquests, for their revenue not even covered the ordinary expenses [A.H.U., *Índia,* maço 173 (189) and maço 40 (315)].

61 *Sendi, xenddi* or *xendim* was a little tress of hair that the Hindus of many classes had. Cf. S.R. Dalgado, op. cit., vol. II, pp. 302-3. A.H.U., *Índia,* cód. 442, f. 197v. On 9 March 1797, the officials of the Council of Ponda complained about some violence practised by António de Assa, commandant of the same province, in order to take measures on many issues, among them that of exempted Muzavar Catib, Mulam and others tax from the annuity of the Muslims (A.H.U., *Índia,* cód. 215, ff. 122v-124). The tax was created on 10 July 1705 together with the *sisas,* imposed annually on the use of the said wood, from the age of 15 years. Its imposition was regulated according to the offices and trades that each exercised. It was abolished on 22 December 1840. Cf. Manoel Felicíssimo Louzada d'Araujo d'Azevedo, 'Segunda Memória Descriptiva [...], in *Annaes Maritimos e Coloniaes,* 3rd series, no. 4, Lisbon, 1844, pp. 131-2. Also see Teotónio R. de Souza, 'Xendi Tax: A Phase in the History of Luso-Hindu Relations in Goa (1704-1841 A.D.)', in *Studies in the Foreign Relations of India (From the earliest times to 1947),* Hyderabad, 1975, pp. 463-71.

62 Maomé Amazan Saibu was the owner of the ship *Infante D. João,* which had to be sold in Lisbon, as it was in a deplorable state (A.H.U., *Índia,* cód. 518, ff. 82v-83). The Muslims (as also the Banyas and other non-Christians) of the city of Goa requested against the making of the inventories of the properties of the dying, by the judicial authorities. This is because they used to make friendly partitions and pay the debts *pro rata,* with 'singular

Luso-descendants

The Portuguese expansion in the Indian Ocean made it possible for many Portuguese from the Kingdom to settle in Goa. The marriage policy undertaken by Albuquerque contributed towards the formation of a social nucleus – the Casados – who were of great political and social-economic importance in the sixteenth century. This body of Casados was the embryo of the Luso-descendant social group, though later more Reinóis, Portuguese couples and even families descended on India, leading to an increase in their number.[63]

There are different opinions on their social origin. Luso-descendant historians tend to highlight the noble and European component, whereas Brahmin researchers (who, from the eighteenth century, were bent on establishing the superiority of their caste over the European aristocracy) take pleasure in denigrating their social provenance. They considered it was mainly the plebeians who had settled in India to better their social-economic condition. Perhaps they were married to Goan women of the lower strata, the social outcasts (mainly the dancing girls), given the great difficulty of penetration into the caste-stratified Hindu society. On the other hand, the Luso-descendant historians argue that the settlers are of noble stock; in fact they recall the great bearing that this social group had on the Portuguese expansion, particularly in India, where they hoped to gain prestige and to resolve their economic problems. They maintain that the nobles in the East married Goan women from the higher castes. Now, we tend to believe that both noble and plebeian elements were at the root of this social group. The issues relating to the sixteenth century have been badly handled and not much documentation is available either. In the seventeenth and the eighteenth centuries, it is certain that members of the nobility preferred

harmony' and the crown judge António Correia Monteiro de Matos intervened by making the inventory (Cf. A.H.U., *Índia,* cód. 425, ff. 6-20). We would like to think that these two documents prove the participation of this social group in trade.

[63] On the Casados see C. R. Boxer, 'Casados and Cabotagem in the Estado da Índia, 16th/17th Centuries', in *II Seminário Internacional de História Indo-Portuguesa. Actas,* Lisbon, Instituto de Investigação Científica Tropical, 1985, pp. 119-35.

India to other stations because of the gifts they used to receive. Nonetheless the absence of serious and updated research on this subject makes generalizations impossible.

This social group comprised both individuals and families from the Kingdom who settled in India, crossing with others of the same origin (also called Castiços), as well as men and women from the Kingdom, who married locals in the East, and their descendants. Initially an open group with no caste spirit, they ended up transformed somewhat into an endogamic group open only to Europeans, on the ground of both their own aristocratic prejudices and segregation by other castes.

Luso-descendant communities settled mainly in the city of Goa and its suburbs (Ribandar) and also, from the beginning of the seventeenth century, in the Northern Province. Here, thanks to the climate and more advantageous land regime (the *prazos*), there rose a very prosperous colony of Luso-descendants that supplied men who became famous in the history of Goa.[64] In fact, some of these children of Bassein distinguished themselves in the military operations that resulted in the occupation of the New Conquests. The fall of Bassein, in 1739, made that group flow back, mainly to Goa.[65]

The military career was, no doubt, their main occupation. However, they also devoted themselves to other activities. Several

[64] In Ribandar there reside Luso-descendant families, in an aristocratic ward. Cf. A. Lopes Mendes, *A Índia Portugueza. Breve Descripção das Possessões Portuguezas na Asia,* vol. I, Lisbon, 1886. Reprinted by Asian Educational Services, New Delhi, Madras, 1989, p. 59. In Bassein, Chaul, Thana, Island of Salsete, Caranja, Asserim, there lived hundreds of Portuguese families since the seventeenth century and the city of Bassein began to be called Dom Baçaim inhabited as it was by numerous families with titles. See A.C. Germano da S. Correia, *Os Luso-Descendentes da Índia,* Bastora, 1946, pp. 2-3.

[65] Among the Luso-descendants born in of Bassein who became notable in the military campaigns of the New Conquests are Hermenegildo da Costa Campos and D. António de Noronha, better known as the Bishop of Halicarnasso. Germano Correia presents a small biography of the latter (ibid., p. 27). Besides them, many other Luso-descendants from Bassein distinguished themselves. See L.A. Rodrigues, 'Noteworthy 'luso-descendants' of Portuguese India', in *Boletim do Instituto Menezes Bragança,* no. 111, 1976, pp. 65-6.

Luso-descendants became well known in the field of sciences, letters, and religion, both in the East and in the Kingdom. Thus, they left behind quite detailed descriptions of the struggles with the Hindu and Muslim potentates, providing data of autobiographical, religious and memorialist nature.[66]

From the concluding years of the seventeenth century to the middle of the eighteenth century there was a great exodus of Luso-descendants to various parts of Hindustan, for economic reasons, where they reinforced the nucleus of Frenchmen residing on the Coromandel Coast, the English in Bengal and Bombay and the Dutch in Ceylon.[67]

Thanks to the military posts they occupied and because of their fidelity to the mother country, given their ethnic origin, the Luso-descendants had too accentuated a political relevance for even the Pombaline reforms to substantially alter. They also enjoyed a high social status and many Luso-descendants were, in the period under study, honoured with the titles of *cavaleiro fidalgo*, *moço fidalgo*, etc.[68] This privileged position of the descendant nobility may have been one of the reasons behind the Pinto Conspiracy plotted by the local nobility.[69]

Reinóis

We have dealt with Asian social-ethnic groups and the Luso-descendants or Eurasian groups that in spite of the mobility inherent to any population were of a relatively permanent nature.

[66] Ibid., pp. 33-5. Literature by the Luso-descendants, relating to their participation in the campaigns of the New Conquests, was highlighted by Carmen Radulet, 'A situação geopolítica do Estado da Índia no século XVIII: codificação histórica e literária das problemáticas', paper presented at the *II Congresso Luso-Espanhol sobre Descobrimentos e Expansão Colonial,* Fac. de Letras da Universidade de Lisboa, 13-15 October 1993.

[67] Germano da S. Correia, *História da Colonização Portuguesa na Índia,* vol. I, Lisbon, 1948, pp. 439-40.

[68] Filipe Nery Xavier presents a group of Luso-descendants honoured with titles of nobility. They are referred to in Appendix II.2 to the present chapter (cf. *Nobiliarchia Goana ou Catalogo das Pessoas* ..., Nova Goa, 1862, pp. 98-119).

[69] Cf. L.F.F.R. Thomaz, *Goa: Une Société Luso-Indienne,* op. cit., p. 27.

Next comes the social class constituted by Europeans from the Kingdom – Reinóis – whose stay in India was temporary, for in principle, it lasted only the term of their service mission.

The defence and the administration of the territory were, in the ultimate analysis, entrusted to this social group that, for this very reason, enjoyed quite an advantageous socio-political situation. A large part of the white population was naturally kept busy by military activity.

The going to India could mean social promotion, as was so often the case. Many were introduced into the nobility or higher degrees of nobility. The documentation available on this subject made possible the analysis of the types of titles, the conditions under which they were granted, the relation between titles requested and those granted, etc.[70] However, there were some difficulties. It is that, as regards its form, the requests for titles used to vary quite substantially. Some carry mention of the applicant's name, his curriculum, the title applied for, followed by the proposal of the Overseas Council or of the Governor, and finally, the royal decision. However, this is the most complete, but unfortunately, less frequent model. What is most common in reality are documents without one or more of these details. That makes systematization quite difficult. Hence the conclusions have to be necessarily cautious and restrictive.

The fact that the same individual sometimes solicited quite different titles led us to include in such a case a single request in more than one type, depending on the titles requested, and sometimes granted – which is always the case given that many requests did not receive royal orders.

[70] It is quite a large and rich documentation, spread through several archives. The most characteristic source, following its own norms, is found in the *caixas* of India (documents being classified) and in the *maços* also of eighteenth century India, at the A.H.U.; there is also some documentation in the corpus of the *Reino* of A.N./T.T.; here, in this archive, we collected more information in the documentary body called *Junta da Real Fazenda do Estado da Índia* which we have referred to earlier. In the codices of the *Monções do Reino* at the H.A.G., some copies of requests for titles are in the two archives mentioned above, but enriched with dispatches of later dates, allowing a more detailed follow-up of the evolution of certain processes.

We tend to think that hard statistics could lead to a simplistic and even distorted view of the reality, given the nature of the subject and the types of sources, not always complete and exhaustive. Hence, data quantification was not our first and last objective, but only a work aid to issue judgements with certainty.

For the period between 1750 and 1773 there are many requests for the habit of Christ, annuities, cost subsidies, sometimes accompanied by applications for title of *fidalgo,* the right of renouncing in favour of another person and even of concession of a post or a charge.[71]

This abundance of requests and of concessions can be explained by the urgent need for war corporals for the military occupation of new dominions (New Conquests), mainly between 1750 and 1770. Later on, the conquest went on giving place to the population, and hence, the lack of military chiefs became smaller. Thus, after 1773, an almost total absence of such requests is noted. It may be noted that from 1773 the number of requests for titles by Reinóis began to decrease.[72]

On the other hand, the number of applications by local Christians increased simultaneously who solicited the exercise of certain posts of doctors, pharmacists, bleeder surgeons, teachers of Latin grammar, school masters, etc. Curiously, it was precisely in the last quarter of the eighteenth century that such titles abounded.

A particular case to remember is that of the privileges conceded to volunteers going to India. It is noted that, contrary to what used to happen in earlier periods, now it is the custom for

[71] From the 82 applications that in the year 1750 asked for titles, 42 solicited such titles. In 1756 we have 26 individuals out of a total of 76 supplicants. Two years later, in 1758 – the year with the greatest number of applications during the second half of the eighteenth century, with 115 persons – a great number of requests of these titles are registered, that is 66. In the following years ard up to 1773 we also find some very significant figures, such as: 28 requests for 58 applicants in 1764; 24 for 42 persons in 1765.

[72] Indeed, in 1778 there was only one request and in 1779 two; after 8 years, in 1786, only one. After 10 years another one; finally one in 1797 and another in 1798.

the King to promote to the next post the vassals who served him in those stations.[73]

A commission in India could thus very often mean reinforcing the social-economic establishment or even aiming at a prestigious career, with a Continental projection. In fact, one decree of D. José I dated 30 March 1755 revoked the ban on rewarding with titles in the Kingdom the services rendered in the Estado da Índia. In this manner, the persons who rendered good services in India would be later recompensed in the Kingdom.[74]

The qualifications that the candidates ought to have seemed to be essentially the condition of nobility and that of volunteer to India. These would be, in principle, the two fundamental conditions for an individual to be able to receive these titles, though sometimes some applicants did not simultaneously have the two requisites. 'The greatness with which Your Majesty honours the *noble* soldiers, who settle *voluntarily* enlist in the service of the Estado da Índia, and the supplicant being one of them, may you deign to give him the honour of the habit of Christ with annuity [...]', thus read the form often found in the

[73] From the documents appended to the letter from João Lucas B. de Mesquita to M. Corte Real, dated 23 April 1752, it is seen that it was the 'style' to give each soldier who voluntarily agreed to settle in India, 5 months of 'single basic pay' (4,590 xerafins) and 4 months of 'single four-month basic pay' as cost subsidy (3,660 xerafins), which amounted to 8,250 xerafins (cf. A.H.U., *Índia,* maço 33 (53)). Also see the copy of the notice of the Duke of Lafões dated 12 June 1788 on the quite favourable royal conditions regulating the going of volunteers to India. They are the following: 1. They are not obliged to serve for more than six years and at the end of the period they shall not need permission to leave; 2. The return transportation from India to the Kingdom shall be borne by the Royal Treasury; 3. On expiry of the term they shall freely return to the Kingdom or remain in India, Brazil or any other dominion of His Majesty; 4. It shall be at his discretion to incorporate himself or not into the army again; 5. In the competitions they shall be preferred to others of the same grade who did not serve in India; 6. Before embarkation each shall receive five months of basic pay doubled for cost subsidy and 4 months of single basic pay (cf. H.A.G., *M. Reino,* Book 177-B, f. 583 and Book 180-A, ff. 54-54v). In the course of the second half of the eighteenth century, there were several edicts on topics more or less similar to this one.

[74] Cf. A.H.U., *Índia,* maço 63 (321).

documentation of the times, proving the conjugation of the condition of nobility aligned to the circumstance of being a volunteer.[75]

With eight years of service in India, the Portuguese returning to the Kingdom would qualify to apply for titles in reward of his services such as commendations, administration of chapels, *namoxi* of the temples, former Jesuits properties, fields, villages, different posts, etc., such as the habit of Christ, annuity, cost subsidy, right to transfer onto another.[76]

The fulfilment of the services rendered could be enjoyed by himself or by his family members or even by other persons named by him. Thus an individual could inherit part or all of the service done by another in India, under diverse forms such as marriage dowry, dowry to enter into a convent, *praças* (posts) of pious works and their maintenance, besides the above mentioned titles.[77]

There is a great disparity between the titles requested and the concessions granted in reality, not only as regards the number but also as regards its value. Thus, the number of applicants and requests is much higher than that of the titles granted in fact and also the amount of cost subsidy or annuity is also always lower than that asked for. The requests for titles were sometimes exorbitant and even abusive. The authorities sought, therefore,

[75] Cf. the petition of José Lúcio Correia de Sousa who goes to India as a volunteer soldier and belongs to the nobility. He asks for the habit of Christ, annuity of Rs. 1,00,000, cost subsidy of Rs. 2,00,000 (*'para se poder aviar'*, to let himself go) and status of *fidalgo.* With slight changes, this form appears frequently in the petitions of this nature.

[76] By way of example see the request for remuneration of the services rendered by Francisco Lopes. The applicant asks for habit of Christ and annuity for his wife and children. The Council opines that he should be granted the habit of the order of Santiago with 2,000 réis of annuity, given that any Portuguese may ask for remuneration of services after serving for 8 years in the Estado da Índia (A.N./T.T., *M. Reino,* maço 313).

[77] Cf. the royal charter of 2 November 1755 granting the benefit of the post of scribe of the extras of the Revenue of the *Contos* of the Estado da Índia for marriage dowry to D. Rosa Henriques de Castro. She was to enjoy this benefit during her lifetime, in partial remuneration for her father's services (A.N./T.T., *J.R.F.E.I.,* Book 40, ff. 24-24v).

to stop these solicitations. Thus, if the requests are many, the royal grants are relatively scarce.

In spite of it all, it seems to us that in the second half of the eighteenth century, the social promotion of the European Reinol from the condition of nobility had become relatively easy. There is no doubt that the number and value of the titles granted was much less than the ones applied for, but the excessive number of requests must be kept in mind vis-à-vis the many burdens which the State had to face.

Only a case-wise genealogical research, which was not possible for us to undertake, would confirm whether, as claimed, second children of nobles are predominant, who went to India to improve their economic status. Maybe such cases were not rare but there are not many documents stating this very clearly. The laws in force also protected the children of the *fidalgos*, who by offering their services in India, used to obtain the charter of the title of *fidalgo*.[78] It is important, therefore, to stress that the Portuguese *fidalguia*, by and large, chose to go to India in search of professional self-fulfilment, social promotion, or a solution to their financial difficulties.

SOCIAL TENSIONS

Since tensions are an historical invariable, let us see the level of its presence in this society.[79]

The very social system of castes presupposes division, rivalry, discord, and hence, latent social tensions. Let us remember that marriages could not, in principle, be held outside the respective caste and that the brotherhoods and confraternities used to normally join together people of a particular caste. The same was sometimes noticed in the village *comunidades*, and thus there existed Brahmin, Chardó and Sudra village communities. Even the relationship of the locals with the descendants and that of

[78] See Appendix II.3 to the present chapter.

[79] To prepare this material, as that of this chapter in general, we took prior help from the work by Manuel Tuno de Lara, *Metodologia de la historia social de España,* 4th edn., Madrid, 1979, which helped to clarify certain concepts of social history.

the Europeans with the locals was conditioned by these social norms.

Even in institutions like the Cathedral chapter or in the Inquisition, these divisions were present. The appointments to the chapter sometimes gave rise to such problems that they compelled the Marquis of Pombal to regulate the recruitment policy, as stated in Chapter I. The same happened with the appointment of church curates and with the recruitment for public offices.[80]

Without exaggerating like the Bishop of Cochin and Governor of the archbishopric of Goa, D. Frei Manuel de Santa Catarina (1780-2), for whom the caste system was a bane of Goan society, we do see that this *status quo* had implications upon social and private life, in the mentality, in the habits and customs of its members. However, there is an attitude of reverence to the established social order, inherited from times immemorial, which in some measure explains the reason for the almost non-existence of open conflicts.

Certain economic factors such as high prices and low salaries may have contributed to further aggravate those social tensions. We know that foodstuffs were very expensive and salaries very low, throwing many persons and families into poverty, but there are no reports of any mutiny or social agitation.[81]

[80] See the letter from the Bishop of Cochin, Governor of the archbishopric of Goa, to M.M. Castro, dated 20 March 1782, which describes perhaps exaggeratedly this belligerent ambience in Goa. Among other facts, it reports that he appointed the churches of Kanara with clerics whom he found better suited and named the individuals he found in a better position to head the deaneries. He did not pay attention to the recommendation letters as is customary. This resulted in a great confusion as some of the deans were Chardós, and being above the Brahmin parish priests; this disorder reached such proportions that a Visitor had to be sent to remove the guilty who, in his opinion, belonged to both the sides, even though the Brahmins were always the cause of the discord [cf. A.H.U., *Índia,* maço 134 (134)].

[81] The employees of the *Tribunal dos Contos* asked for a higher salary because, for the reasons mentioned, they experimented 'total poverty and misery'. They even mentioned that the King granted a rise to ministers of justice and to the ecclesiastics. Cf. letter from D. José to the Count of Ega,

The analysis of the documentation allows us, on the contrary, to find situations of conflict between people of different institutions. By way of example, we shall mention the frictions between the Governors and Chancellors of the High Court (the most frequent ones), between the Archbishops and that tribunal, between the Governors and Archbishops, between the regulars and the secular clergy, between the Municipal Councils and the Archbishop, etc.[82] These institutional conflicts sometimes assumed the nature of truly personal conflicts, as happened with the Viceroy, the Marquis of Távora and the Chancellor João de Mesquita Matos Teixeira, with the Viceroy, the Count of Ega, and the Chancellor João Baptista Vaz Pereira, making their relationships quite difficult.[83]

---

dated 30 March 1759, in which he asks for the opinion of the Viceroy, upon hearing the Revenue Superintendent (A.H.U., *Índia,* cód. 439, f. 31 and cód. 205, f. 252).

[82] There is proof of jurisdictional conflicts, for example, between the Chancellor of the High Court of Goa, José Joaquim de Seqúeira Magalhães Lançoes and the Governor, on 25 February 1783 [A.H.U., *Índia,* maço 119 (117)]; between the Archbishop primate and the High Court of Goa, caused by the behaviour of the brothers of the confraternity. Cf. the letter from M.M. Castro to the Bishop of Cochin, Archbishop primate elect of Goa, dated 17 April 1784 (A.H.U., *Índia,* cód. 518, ff. 87v-88), f. 107v; maço 1 (731); A.C.P.G., Cópia de cartas régias ..., f. 163, in F.U.P., 18-1-9 52/5 and 53/1; between the Crown attorney of the High Court of Goa, Sebastião José Ferreira Barroso and the Archbishop on 2 April 1790 [A.H.U., *Índia,* maço 158 (150)]; between the civil and ecclesiastical authority, that is, between the Crown Court and the Bishop of Cochin on 18 February 1782 [A.H.U., *Índia,* maço 139 (135)]; between the Governor Frederico Guilherme de Sousa and the chancellery on 21 February 1782 [A.H.U., *Índia,* maço 139 (135)].

[83] In his letter to the King, the Marquis of Távora gives a detailed account of various difficulties that he has had with the Chancellor. He reports what happened when he ordered the patent to be issued to António José de Melo, in the government of Bicholim. The Chancellor 'glossed' on the said patent in which he was addressed as *'senhoria'* (Lordship). As it had something to do with an express transgression of the last law of address, the Marquis of Távora wrote him a letter whose reply was late to come, containing insults to his person. He states that the Chancellor does everything possible to reduce the Viceroy's jurisdiction and that has 'glossed'

ILLICIT BEHAVIOUR

A study of Goan society brings us to the analysis of some behaviour referred to therein, which we can term as illicit. In the *Arquivo Nacional/Torre do Tombo*, in the corpus of the *Junta da Real Fazenda do Estado da Índia*, there is some documentation relating to the letters of pardon, bail bond letters, letters of security, which precisely allow this reflection.

As it deals with a subject that is quite difficult to study by its very nature and complexity, we decided to make a case-by-case analysis in order avoid hasty generalizations. We have always sought to keep in mind the material author, the attenuating and the aggravating factors.

In the overall account of the illicit behaviours noticed, theft was the most frequent and covered a great variety of objects,

---

many privileges, to the great surprise of the politicians and military men of the land. He further observes that almost all the doubts raised by the Chancellors apply to persons he suspects of being pleasant to him, the Marquis. He also states that he has been much importuned by the Chancellor in virtue of the pensions he has given the 'servants' who accompany him to India and points reasons why he could not do it in another way. See the letter from the Marquis of Távora to the King, dated 30 December 1753 (H.A.G., *M. Reino,* Book 129-A, ff. 29-43). The Chancellor on his part reports to the King his reasons. In a letter dated 25 January 1755 he states that he 'glossed' one letter from the post of the city captain to which Rodrigo Aranha da Fonseca had been appointed and lists his reasons. The opinion of the Overseas Council accompanying this letter was that the Chancellor had 'glossed' because there was no mention of the residence, which is not a matter for interpretation and which though the Chancellor could put doubts every time he wished, he should not form these doubts founded on extrinsic facts. The Chancellor is advised to avoid as far as possible to postpone the despatch of the papers to the chancery, raising doubts all at once in order not to multiply the interpretations and losses to the parties [A.H.U., *Índia,* maço 89 (100)]. Also see the letter from D. José dated 29 March 1758 on the complaints that the Marquis of Távora made about this Chancellor and the reply of the Count of Ega dated 10 December 1758. Thereby it is seen that the charges made against the Chancellor were as follows: removing of folios of the High Court book; extraordinary delay in the distribution orders of the lawsuits; of 'glossing' repeatedly the ranks and creating disorder in the coffer of the expenses of justice (cf. A.H.U., *Índia,* cód. 441, ff. 1-13v).

from rags (old bedsheets), guns, *bat* (husked rice), coconuts, poultry, cattle heads, up to furniture items, ornaments, etc. It seems to be the case of a relatively poor society in which the individuals venture out for very little, stealing articles of very low monetary value. Perhaps in this society theft was considered a very minor offence than what it was in contemporaneous European society. A similar case is noticed in the present Brazilian society, if compared to the European. ...

The type of objects stolen also allows us to catch a glimpse of a rural and pastoral society, where husked rice, coconuts, poultry, were essentials for the needs of subsistence.[84]

Also noticed were some thefts of ornaments or purchase of stolen jewellery, which we referred to earlier. Sometimes, the theft is perpetrated by the kaffir who steals for his master, thus becoming its material but not moral author.[85]

[84] From a total of 417 persons imputed and implicated in illicit behaviour, there were 77 theft cases, implicating 107 persons (25.6 per cent). Sebastião de Sousa was accused of robbing an old bed-sheet and another piece of cloth of the same type. Cf. letter of pardon dated 28 April 1777 (A.N./T.T., *J.R.F.E.I.,* Book 66, ff. 9-9v). António Manuel Fernandes was imputed of theft in the hospital larder. Cf. letter of pardon dated 30 May 1778 (A.N./ T.T., *J.R.F.E.I.,* Book 67, ff. 37-37v). José Fernandes and ten persons were imputed as accomplices in a theft of rice and some *'fatto'* (cloth). Cf. letter of pardon dated 6 June 1778 (A.N./T.T., *J.R.F.E.I.,* Book 67, ff. 43v-44). A document of 30 June 1780 explains the meaning of the term *'fatto'* [cf. A.H.U., *Índia,* maço 12 (269)]. Luís Caetano da Costa was accused of robbing buffaloes. Cf. letter of pardon dated 23 June 1778 (A.N./T.T., *J.R.F.E.I.,* Book 67, ff. 46v-47). Vicente António Gonçalves, *naik* of the court of the State senior crown judge was accused of theft of some mortgage, money and other things. Cf. letter of pardon dated 18 August 1778 (A.N./ T.T., *J.R.F.E.I.,* Book 66, ff. 176-7). Pandu Porobu was accused of being caught robbing the shop of Madu Naique. Cf. letter of pardon dated 12 December 1778 (A.N./T.T., *J.R.F.E.I.,* Book 67, f. 151v).

[85] This can be gathered, for example, from the charter of security issued on 4 September 1777, to Maria de Bragança to be free for one year from the amassing done. That is because her kaffir Sebastião had robbed money and given her 24 xerafins (A.N./T.T., *J.R.F.E.I.,* Book 66, ff. 63v-64). Also by letter of pardon granted on 17 April 1779 to António Pereira, his wife Maria Machada and their daughter Rosa Pereira, it is noted that a kaffir of theirs had robbed a few rupees (A.N./T.T., *J.R.F.E.I.,* Book 69, ff. 66v-67).

After theft, the largest numbers correspond to the delicts against physical integrity. Here, too, a kaffir or the servants were often made use of to commit the crime.[86] It may be noted, however, that by and large, these behavioural deviations are nothing more than incidents of small gravity; the documents refer to altercations, fights, quarrels, slaps, 'riots', beatings, etc. The description of these disturbances and the context in which they took place, as also the relatively low percentage of cases, lead us to conclude that this is not an aggressive society that promptly resorts to force to resolve their differences.[87]

Whereas it is certain that cases of homicide were registered, some were, nonetheless, perpetrated by military men Reinóis who were naturally part of the floating and adventitious population of Goa. Reference must be made to the assassinations committed by the *fidalgos* D. Henrique de Noronha, D. Gil and D. Francisco and that of Manuel Dassa Castelbranco who killed his father-in-law. Even though the documentation is often silent on the type of crime, there are references to death in the well, the death of kaffirs, etc.[88]

On the robbery of jewellery or purchase of stolen jewellery, see fn. 54 of this chapter).

[86] We counted 42 cases against physical integrity in which 88 persons were implicated (21 per cent), out of a total of 417 persons, as referred to above.

[87] For example, Sabina Rodrigues, widow and her children Isabel de Sousa and Cosme de Sousa, were accused of a theft, of beatings and wounding. Cf. letter of pardon dated 14 April 1757 (A.N./T.T., *J.R.F.E.I.*, Book 38, ff. 115v-116). Caetano Ferrão and Custódio Carvalho were 'judicially quested' about the slaps that they gave. See the proroguing for six months of the letter of security dated 29 February 1776 (A.N./T.T., *J.R.F.E.I.,* Book 63, ff. 137-8). Pedro Dias accused his uncle António Dias of slapping him with an open hand. Cf. bond dated 30 April 1774 (A.N./T.T., *J.R.F.E.I.,* Book 61, ff. 46-7). Tomás de Almeida and Domingos de Almeida were pulled up for spanking a sepoy. Cf. charter of 23 September 1777 freeing them from imprisonment to get acquittance within a year (A.N./T.T., *J.R.F.E.I.,* Book 66, ff. 65v-67). Inácio Henriques was questioned in the 'riot' case. See the letter of pardon dated 12 August 1779 (A.N./T.T., *J.R.F.E.I.,* Book 69, f. 160).

[88] See Appendix II.4 to this chapter.

Hindu shopkeeper (Arquivo Histórico Uttramarino, LR, 387, Manuel da Cunha Maldonado and Joaquim António Roncon, *Usos e Costumes da Índia*, 1846-1847)

There are also cases of falsification, normally of documents, weights and measures. Standing out in the first category is false registrations, the 'exclusion of the coconut trees in the list'; as regards the other categories, there is reference to illegalities in the weighing of husked rice and tobacco.[89]

Percentage-wise, there follow the deviations of corruption and those of connivance in the escape of prisoners. If, in relation to the latter type of illicit conduct, the material compensation is veiled, as regards corruption, this is undisputedly the main motivation. Although the percentage of corruption in the overall assessment of delicts is relatively low, it reveals that this fault was widespread in Goa, polluting its foundations and defrauding public and private finances. Indeed, the sampling in question mainly covers a group of persons who occupied small public offices like *naik,* scribes of the deanery, bailiffs, prison officials. As is well known, corruption existed not only at this level, but also in the high levels of administration and was undoubtedly responsible for some of the great evils of Goan society. We shall deal with this subject below.[90]

[89] Some *ganvkars* were accused of having falsified registrations in the village communities. By way of example, see the provision of 29 January 1776, proroguing for another six months the letter of security to José Crisóstomo de Ramos, José Pinto, Salvador de Menezes, Paulo de Menezes and Caetano Fernandes, *ganvkars* of Saligão (Bardez) (A.N./T.T., *J.R.F.E.I.*, Book 63, ff. 119-119v); and the charter of security of 1 February 1776 granted to José Dantas, Aleixo Pinto, Domingos Caetano Coutinho and Manuel da Cruz, *ganvkars* of Saligão (A.N./T.T., *J.R.F.E.I.*, Book 63, ff. 123-124v). As regards the falsifications in the weighing of tobacco, we cite, for example, Domingos Francisco Parrado and Remédios Gracias, tobacco contract workers, and Vitoba Porobo. Cf. proroguing of the letter of security of 23 October 1790 and letter of commutation of deportation of 2 April 1791 (A.N./T.T., *J.R.F.E.I.,* Book 77, ff. 178v and 179 and Book 78, ff. 27-27v, respectively). As regards false coinage, the accused were D. Gaspar Silvestre Bettencourt e Sá Machado (he was granted pardon on 22 June 1757), the goldsmith Rama Chatim, Rama Custam Chatim and Tucu Chatim (obtained proroguing of the letter of security on 8 February 1776) (cf. A.N./T.T., *J.R.F.E.I.,* Book 38, ff. 129-130v).

[90] We counted 12 cases of corruption implicating 15 persons in different administrative posts. Thus, António Xavier de Noronha and António de Noronha, the former when a physician of the Gunpowder Factory and the

Some trespasses are regularly ascribed to some definite professions: connivance in the escape of prisoners is, logically, always attributed to jailers, thefts of ornaments and purchase of stolen jewellery were blamed on jewellers,[91] extorsion of money to scribes, *naiks*, village corporals and other officials, as well as deviation of construction materials. Our opinion is based upon more conjecture because, as has already been mentioned, only rarely are the professions of the delinquents indicated.[92]

From the analysis of the penalties doled out, it is seen that many prisoners were pardoned and others obtained letters of

---

latter presently exercising the post, were punished for having received one measure of rice from each captive per month. They did not deny the fault, but stated that they had done so ingenuously, alleging that it was always the usual practice of their predecessors. See letter of pardon of 16 May 1758 (A.N./T.T., *J.R.F.E.I.,* Book 67, ff. 30-30v). The surgeon of the said institution was also accused of the same fault and he invoked the same arguments, as seen from the letter of pardon dated 19 May 1778 (A.N./T.T., *J.R.F.E.I.,* Book 67, ff. 36-36v). Filipe Neri do Rosário was accused of taking 3 tangas for every certificate from the book of registrations of entry and exit of the prisoners at the Rachol jail, when an official there. Cf. letter of pardon dated 5 April 1765 (H.A.G., *Alvarás e provisões,* ff. 23-24v). There was a judicial inquest of António de Vargas, bailiff of the office of the senior crown judge, for illegally receiving money for execution services. See the letter of pardon dated 27 April 1778 (A.N./T.T., *J.R.F.E.I.,* Book 67, ff. illegible). Henrique Pais, Diogo de Sousa and Caetano Pais, *naiks* of the Bardez Customs, were interrogated on the deviations and *coluyos* (collusion) of the rights and revenue of the Royal Revenue. See the prorogation for one year of the letter of security dated 7 September 1779 (A.N./T.T., *J.R.F.E.I.,* Book 69, ff. 171v-172). José Álvares de Sousa, scribe of the Bardez Chamber, contributed to the deviation of 7,670 xerafins which he extracted from the Tuesday coffer. He committed falsities, thefts, robberies, deviation of money. Cf. provision of 13 November 1779, proroguing for a year the letters of security (A.N./T.T., *J.R.F.E.I.,* Book 68, ff. 37v-39). António José da Silveira, *naik* of the *Tribunal dos Feitos* of the Crown and Revenue, was imprisoned for having received money higher than the stipulated. See the charter of bond dated 22 November 1788 (A.N./T.T., *J.R.F.E.I.,* Book 74, ff. 90-1). These examples clarify the manner in which subaltern functionaries sometimes extorted money from the largely poor population, who thus used to grow rich.

[91] See note 54 of this chapter.

[92] See note 90 of this chapter.

security and temporary charters of bail to be able to work to liberate them.[93] This leads us to think that, at least in the case of lesser offences, justice was not very strict and the idea was to correct rather than punish. In fact, the very form of the letters of pardon point to a reconciliatory attitude with God and society when, for example, it states that the pardon was granted 'in reverence to the wounds of O.L. Jesus Christ, for which stimulus H. Majesty usually grants pardon ...'. Many individuals obtained pardon on Good Friday, by which it was perhaps sought to take the message of Christian love to people among whom there were many neo-converts and pagans and also some of them implicated in illicit conduct.[94]

There are reports of some abuses committed by higher functionaries and by certain administrators of the Estado da Índia. Thus, some high court judges were accused of jurisdictional abuses, illegalities and corruption.[95] But in other sectors of public

[93] The following numbers are mere indicators. For 337 convictions/imprisonments there were 208 (61.7 per cent) letters of pardon, 56 charters of bond and 87 letters of security. In four cases, the deportation was commuted to pecuniary penalty and for change of place, for example, from Goa to Brazil. It must be noted that the sum of the letters of pardon, charters of bond, letters of security and commutation of penalty (351) is higher than the number of imprisonments (337). Since it is not always easy to follow the unfolding of the cases, the surplus (only 14) should be included in the group of charters of bond and letters of security that do not seem to be substantially different from each other.

[94] Indeed many convicts were granted amnesty in the Holy Week, 'for the love of God, given the holy time in which they asked for pardon'. This form with which by and large the letters begin is quite common. Cf., for example, the letter of pardon to António Xavier de Noronha and António de Noronha, dated 16 May 1758 (A.N./T.T., *J.R.F.E.I.,* Book 67, ff. 30-30v). We counted 40 cases of illicit conduct committed by Hindus, from whom 21 obtained letter of pardon; 8, letter of security, and 3, charters of bond.

[95] There are testimonies on irregularities committed by the following high court judges: Francisco Raimundo de Morais Pereira, sent on service by the Marquis of Távora, to Rios de Sena (H.A.G., *M. Reino,* Book 130-B, f. 370); José Luis França, referred to in the next footnote; João de Sousa de Meneses Lobo, against whom there was a process for having collected the amount of 3,20,000 réis by way of funeral expenses of D. João V and acclamation of D. José to the throne (A.H.U., *Índia,* maço 7 (279)); José

life, in the Revenue, in the army there were also serious quibbling, there being sometimes an veritable network of solidarity in the practice of infractions.[96] Some Viceroys and Governors also could not escape these accusations, as happened with the Count of Ega and D. João José de Melo.[97] The central government ordained in these cases, in the interest of public justice and morals, the judicial processing of the infringers and the confiscation of the properties.

Lobo da Veiga, for his conduct in Mozambique and Rios de Sena where he was send as prosecutor (H.A.G., *M. Reino,* Book 135-B, ff. 623-697v); José Joaquim de Sequeira Magalhães e Lanções, Feliciano de Ramos Nobre Mourão and António da Costa Correia e Sá (A.H.U., *Índia,* maço 40 (315), maço 124 (109) and maço 172 (186)).

[96] Included among the military men implicated in corruption cases were the infantry lieutenant Manuel Jansen. Cf. the letter from the Count of Ega dated 2 September 1761 (A.H.U., *Índia,* loose doc., unnumbered file); the commander of the ship *N. Senhora da Caridade e S. Francisco de Paula* for the smuggling of gold powder in Bahia. Cf. the letter of Francisco Xavier de Mendonça Furtado to the Count of Ega, dated 12 April 1764 (H.A.G., *M. Reino,* Book 137-A, f. 249); the Lieutenant Colonel and then Colonel Henrique Carlos Henriques (H.A.G., *Índia,* Book 168-B, ff. 403-417v); etc. José Luís França, influencing the Count of Ega led him to an ambitious trade. A society was formed comprising the Viceroy, the Count of Ega, Manuel Teixeira da Fonseca e Paiva, his *capitão de guarda,* and the Lieutenant and later Colonel Filipe de Landreset, the said high court judge J.L. França, Subá Camotim and upon his death, Vitogi Camotim. In his letter dated 28 January 1765 to [...], the high court Chancellor, José Baptista Vaz Pereira, makes quite a detailed report of the dishonesty of the said high court judge, consisting of sale of certain commodities at a high price, recourse to the State coffers. Cf. A.H.U., *Índia,* maço 33 (53).

[97] Influenced by José L. França, the Count of Ega undertook some business, such as that of the confiscated goods at the arrival of the ships and before going to the customs; which were later sold at high prices, 'his Palace being the main Business House, where the best pieces can be bought' (ibid). During their administration as interim governors, Filipe de Valadares Soto Maior and João de Mesquita Matos Teixeira were 'interested in the monopoly enjoyed in this capital of the foodstuffs necessary for the sustenance of its residents' [A.H.U., *Índia,* cód. 513, ff. 78-9 and maço 101 (88). H.A.G., *M. Reino,* Book 133-B, ff. 324-324v]. The General Chamber of Bardez accused the Governor, D. Pedro da Câmara, of some irregularities [A.H.U., *Índia,* maço 130 (138)].

VILLAGE COMMUNITIES

We cannot ignore the role played by the village communities in Goan society. An institution peculiar to India – every village having an agricultural community with its own government (council) – preserved its essential characteristics in Goa, better than in any other part of the Indian subcontinent.[98]

We are not going to deal with the origin and evolution of the village communities, on which there are specialized published works; what is important to analyse is its action in Goan society.

In the period under study there were no great changes made to the norms in force. As stated earlier, an edict from the Viceroy the Count of Ega, in 1763 guaranteed certain immunities and religious tolerance of the inhabitants of the New Conquests, and in the following year, by an addition to the regulation, debtors of the communities subjected to imprisonment and the auctioning and removal of the *sacadorias* (treasuries) was regulated.[99]

The Chambers-General – a federal council of various village communities – were obliged to pay the old and new tributes and cope with almost all the needs of the royal service. This explains how, in the peace with the Maratha and the Bhonsales, they contributed their own money. Public works like the construction of squares, road repairs, etc., were also entrusted to them.[100]

[98] See F.N. Xavier, op. cit., pp. 63-75.

[99] On this issue the following works may be consulted: F.N. Xavier, op. cit., in vol. III, pp. 1-39, the author presents an exhaustive bibliography on the subject. A.E. de Almeida Azevedo, *As Comunidades de Goa. História das Instituições Antigas,* Lisbon, 1890. Cf. José Maria de Sá, in 'Notas preliminares' to the *Bosquejo Histórico das Comunidades* ..., op. cit., vol. I, Bastorá, 1903, pp. 129-30 and Artur Teodoro de Matos, 'Sistema Tributário e Rendimento Fundiário de Goa no século XVI', in *Las Relaciones entre Portugal y Castilla en la Época de los Descubrimientos y la Expansión Colonial,* Salamanca, 1994, pp. 271-92.

[100] In their representation to the Queen, dated 18 March 1778, the General Council of the Bardez province, in an attempt to denigrate the role of the senates, highlights the beneficial action of the General Councils. Thus it states that they pay old and new tributes, spend money for the State, as they did in the peace with the Marathas and Bhonsles, build new fortresses with which the province is sown, repair the dilapidated ones, planing the public roads, etc. (A.H.U., *Índia,* maço 2 (246)). In 1771, the

Besides this, they took an active part in parish life where they had an important social and spiritual function, supporting teachers and contributing towards the expenses of the cult and welfare measures.[101]

It was on the village communities that the rural parish communities were modelled and to them is due (together with the confraternities), the permanence of pre-Christian traditions and caste. Thus, they contribute quite a lot towards the conservation, through the times, of remote family ties and allowed that, even among Christians, there should be Brahmins, Chardós and Sudras.[102]

* * *

General Council of Bardez had to contribute 54,000 xerafins for the continuation of the Tivim moat and repairs of the *tercenas* of Chapora. In 1776 the communities gave 3,90,000 xerafins for the reconstruction of the city of Goa and 30,000 xerafins as advance for the construction of the rice granary. Besides these expenses, the Bardez council had to pay for the sustenance of 200 sepoys. In 1777 the communities were entrusted with tax collection of ½ per cent for the works of the said city. Two years later, they began to pay 3:015:3:20 xerafins. In the following year, the salary of the judge of the Bardez communities was raised. In 1785, the Salsete council spent 21,275 xerafins on the moat and fortress of Rachol, 7,856 xerafins for the basic pay of the General of the province, two assistants, garrison post and interpreter of the fortress and 650 xerafins for the repairs of the *tercenas* and General's house. In 1795, it was determined that the communities should contribute to the Public Revenue a loan corresponding to one-third part of their revenues up to the amount of 3,00,000 xerafins and between 1795 and 1797 another loan of 3,30,595 xerafins was demanded from them. In 1799 the salary of the judge of the Salsete communities was also raised. Cf. José Maria de Sá, 'Notas Preliminares', in *Bosquejo Histórico das Communidades* ..., op. cit., pp. 129-31.

[101] Thus the village communities assumed various burdens such as the salary of the *mestre-capela*, the main instruments of education in those times, who used to teach the children reading and writing, besides singing and catechism. They used to also ensure the payment for the *boyas* of the Holy Viaticum, the expenses for the feast of Christmas, for the mass by the blessing of the new sheaves, etc. In this way, the village communities would allow the religious manifestations in the Goan villages to take place. To illustrate, see the action of the village community of Malar, in F.N. Xavier, op. cit., p. 165.

[102] See Hambye, 'Goa', in *Dictionnaire d'Histoire et de Géographie ecclésiastique* ..., earlier cited. The Bishop of Cochin, governor of the archbishopric of

The dominant note of this society is the great diversity of social groups, with different statuses and their unique life patterns. Naturally, each group had its role in the social dynamics; there stand out, however, some which, for various reasons, would impress certain originality, as in the case of the groups indicated below:

- the Europeans who were torch bearers of Christian and Western culture and played leadership roles. Hence, they used to consider themselves superior to the members of other strata of society;
- the Brahmins as a group, somewhat corresponding to the European, but autochthonous; were conscious of their social and cultural superiority and considered the Europeans violent and hardly discreet; their caste prejudices are, in fact, very clear in the *Nobiliarchia Bracmana*;
- the Luso-descendants, who were the bridge between the Europeans and the local Christians, with their habits, ways of life, food, etc., but also forming some sort of caste;
- the Chardós who stood apart from the other social groups, by their assimilation of the Western culture;
- the Kunnbis who, in spite of their very early conversion to Christianity, remained faithful to their customs of yore.

In this context, the meeting of cultures and mentalities was, naturally, very rich. The Pinto Conspiracy itself, whose mentors were Brahmins, shows, however, a contact with the liberal ideas in vogue in the Europe of the second half of the eighteenth century and, therefore, a notable cultural Westernization.[103]

If the crossing of races was much reduced, in virtue of the rigidity of the social caste system, the assimilation of cultures, that is, the 'spiritual crossing', was very intense. Hence Goa's main role was and shall always be that of the crossing of civilizations, in the past and the present.

Goa, in his letter dated 20 March 1782, to Martinho de Melo e Castro, notes the existence in Goa of Brahmin village communities in which no Chardó enters, of Chardó village communities in which Brahmins do not enter [A.H.U., *Índia,* maço 134 (134)]. We shall refer to the confraternities in next chapter.

[103] On this subject see Chapter V.

APPENDIX II.1

Population of Ilhas, Bardez and Salsete (1753-99)

Year	Provinces			
	Ilhas	Bardez	Salsete	Total
1753	57,732	75,666	73,198	2,06,596
...	...	...	...	...
1776	44,081	77,865	76,687	1,98,633
1777	–	77,716	78,209	–
1778	46,977	78,940	79,071	2,04,988
1779	44,978	71,119	77,926	1,94,023
1780	44,477	77,014	79,569	2,01,060
1781	40,543	74,406	78,397	1,93,346
1782	36,071	74,392	79,266	1,89,729
1783	39,183	65,614	–	–
1784	41,758	66,634	74,747	1,83,139
1785	34,981	66,734	73,191	1,74,906
1786	32,677	64,267	82,140	1,79,084
1787	38,326	64,609	72,463	1,75,398
1788	37,696	65,395	72,845	1,75,936
1789	33,871	66,288	72,041	1,72,200
1790	35,528	68,431	–	–
1791	35,311	68,731	70,151	1,74,193
1792	33,042	60,166	71,778	1,64,986
1793	33,372	66,720	71,495	1,71,587
1797	35,660	63,805	70,055	1,69,520
1799	34,009	71,544	71,685	1,77,238

Sources: A.H.G., *M. Reino,* 125-B, ff. 628-30; A.H.U., *Índia,* maço 126 (142); A.H.U., *Índia,* maço 125 (110); A.H.U., *Índia,* maço 127 (141); A.H.G., *M. Reino,* 159-A, ff. 252, 291, 292; A.H.U., *Índia,* maço 136 (129); A.H.G., *M. Reino,* 161-C, ff. 649-50 b; A.H.G., *M. Reino,* 162-A, ff. 366 a, b and c; A.H.G., *M. Reino,* 163-B, ff. 409, 410, 411; A.H.U., *Índia,* maço 145 (159); A.H.G., *M. Reino,* 164E, ff. 1326, 1327 and 1330; A.H.G., *M. Reino,* 167-A, ff. 94, 95 and 96; A.H.U., *Índia,* maço 150 (158); A.H.G., *M. Reino,* 169-A, ff. 305, 306 and 307; A.H.G., *M. Reino,* 170-B, ff. 485, 486 and 488, A.H.U., *Índia,* maço 158 (150); A.H.U., *Índia,* maço 162 (171), A.H.U., *Índia,* maço 163 (146); A.H.U., *Índia,* maço 166 (167); A.H.U., *Índia,* maço 167 (165); A.H.G., *M. Reino,* 173, ff. 237-9; A.H.G., *M. Reino,* 179-A, ff. 239-41.

APPENDIX II.2

Examples of Local Goans who Received Titles

The following can be seen from the work of F.N. Xavier, *Nobiliarchia Goana ou Catalogo das Pessoas ...*, Nova Goa, 1862, pp. 98-119. Thus, among the local Brahmins with titles of nobility are found António João Pinto, Inácio Pinto, José António Pinto (1770), from Candolim, Pedro António Álvares, from Margão (1798), José Maria Monteiro, from Candolim (1802). The number of Luso-descendants *agraciados* at the period under survey was bigger. Reference is made to the following names: António Caetano Prestes d'Abreu (1750), Alexandre de Sousa Pereira (1750), Caetano de Lemos de Meneses (1750), D. Francisco Henriques (1767), Manuel da Costa de Ataíde (1768), António de Melo Pereira (1751), Jacinto Monis Barreto (1751), Álvaro Caetano Moniz Barreto (1751), Tristão Pereira Coutinho (1755), Jorge Pereira Coutinho (1756), Fernando Seabra Neto (1757), José Francisco de Seabra Neto (1757), D. Luís Inácio de Noronha (1758), D. Diogo Pereira (1758), Manuel de Melo da Silva (1760), D. Cristóvão Pereira de Castro (1761), D. António José de Cárcome Lobo (1764), D. Francisco de Cárcome Lobo (1764), Luís de Melo (1764), André Lopes de Lavre (1764), Agostinho de Melo Lobo (1766), Francisco Xavier Lobo de Magalhães (1766), Sebastião José Lopes de Lavre (1766), Diogo Henrique Carlos Henriques (1766), João Pereira Coutinho (1766), D. Pedro de Meneses (1766), Francisco Xavier Henriques da Mota e Lacerda (1766), D. Francisco Xavier de Castro (1767), Diogo de Melo de Sampaio (1768), Vicente da Costa de Ataíde (1768), Diogo da Costa de Ataíde (1768), José da Costa de Ataíde (1768), Cristóvão da Costa de Ataíde (1768), Luís de Melo de Sampaio (1768), António de Mendonça Corte Real (1778), D. Lourenço Vicente Cristóvão (1781), D. José Francisco de Noronha (1781), Caetano de Sousa Pereira (1781), Vasco Luís de Carneiro de Sousa e Faro (1781), Xavier de Mendonça Corte Real (1781), João Manuel de Azevedo e Brito (1781), José Dionísio Carneiro de Sousa e Faro (1781), Joaquim Frederico de Lemos e Saldanha (1781), Joaquim Xavier Henriques de Lacerda (1782), Vicente José Dinis d'Ayalla (1783), José Joaquim Henriques (1785), Bernardo António de Lemos Telo de Meneses (1785), José Maria Telo de Meneses (1785), António Monis Barreto (1785), Francisco António de Lemos e Saldanha (1785), João Manuel António de Melo (1785), Cristóvão António de Melo (1785), António José de Melo (1785), Francisco Xavier de Mendonça Corte Real (1788), Diogo de Mendonça Corte Real (1788), João Joaquim de Mendonça Corte Real (1788), António José Correia da Silva (1790), Francisco António da Costa d'Ataide Teive (1791), D. José Maria de Castro e Almeida (1799).

APPENDIX II.3

Examples of Second and Illegitimate Sons who Went to India as Military Volunteers

By way of example, we cite Manuel Ventura de Araújo e Azevedo and Francisco José Araújo e Azevedo, noblemen, second children, both of whom were from Monção (Minho) who volunteered to go to India. Also João António de Madureira Prado Lobo, *fidalgo* of the House of Royal House, enlists voluntarily for India because 'he has a great desire to go to serve His Majesty in the Estado da Índia with the post, annuity and habit of Christ which Your Majesty be served in attention to the services of his said father and the *abandonment in which he was left, being the second child* and having no assets, on which to depend' (A.N./T.T., *Reino,* maço 317).

Among the illegitimate children there were, for example, Luís Ferreira Carneiro de Vasconcelos, António Ferreira Carneiro de Vasconcelos and José Ferreira Carneiro de Vasconcelos, illegitimate children of Luís António Ferreira Carneiro de Vasconcelos, military volunteers and belonging to a distinct noble families. They were given the habit of Christ, an effective annuity of 30,000 réis and cost subsidy of 60,000 réis each (17 March 1759, A.N./T.T., *Reino,* maço 314).

António Xavier de Barros e Alvim, illegitimate son of Colonel Gonçalo Xavier de Barros e Alvim, aged 20 years, volunteers to go to India. He asks for the first vacant post of Lieutenant. He is granted the habit of Christ, 30,000 réis annuity and 60,000 towards cost subsidy (26 March 1760, A.N./T.T., *Reino,* maço 314).

José Manuel Ferreira de Abreu, illegitimate son of Domingos Ferreira de Abreu, secretary of the Board of the Three Estates. Nobleman, 17 years of age, offers himself as a military volunteer. Asks for habit of Christ, annuity of 40,000 réis and cost subsidy of 3,00,000 réis. He is granted the habit of Christ, annuity of 30,000 réis and cost subsidy of 60,000 réis (6 April 1763, A.N./T.T., *Reino,* maço 316).

Alexandre José de S. Maria, illegitimate son of Hermano José Braamcamp, professed in the Order of Christ. The latter always accepts him as his son. Asks for habit of Christ, annuity of 1,00,000 réis and cost subsidy of 2,00,000 réis and is granted habit of Christ, effective annuity of 20,000 réis and cost subsidy of 40,000 réis (2 April 1765, A.N./T.T., *Reino,* maço 317).

Nuno Álvares Pereira, voluntary soldier and belonging to well-known nobility (of the principal families of the town of Alcochete) asks for habit of Christ, annuity of 1,00,000 réis, cost subsidy of 2,00,000 réis and right to renounce the habit of Christ to anyone of his choice. The Overseas Council was of the opinion of granting him the habit of Christ, effective annuity of 40,000 réis and cost subsidy of 80,000 réis. The process does not come with royal order. We know, however, that generally lower benefits were granted than those proposed by the Overseas Council. The father of Nuno Álvares Pereira was an illegitimate son 'recognized with noble status'. (11 April 1765, A.N./T.T., *Reino,* maço 317).

Manuel Inácio da Silva, illegitimate son of Tadeu Leopoldo Pereira da Silva, Sergeant-Major from Vizeu, nobleman, volunteer, asks for habit of Christ, annuity of 1,50,000 réis, right to renounce and cost subsidy of 2,00,000 réis. The king granted him the habit of Christ, effective annuity of 30,000 réis and cost subsidy of 60,000 réis (6 April 1767, A.N./T.T., *Reino,* maço 313).

João Zeverino de Sousa Mexia, son of João de Souza Mexia, *fidalgo* of the Royal House enlisted voluntarily as soldier to serve in India and asked for benefit of *fidalgo* status which his father had, habit of Christ, annuity of 1,50,000 réis and a cost subsidy considering the applicant's noble status. On 2 March 1754, the Overseas Council opined that a charter of the status that his father had to be passed, as this was the manner followed with the illegitimate children of *fidalgos* embarking voluntarily for the Estado da Índia (cf. A.H.U., *Índia,* loose document, no number on maço).

In this documentation we came across 15 requests from illegitimate children of noblemen offering to enlist for India, possibly expecting social promotion.

It may be noted that the monetary value of the benefits granted is always substantially lower than that applied for. We can cite more examples, but it seems that those mentioned above are explanatory on how the fringes of nobility sought India as a solution to their problems, especially social and economic problems.

APPENDIX II.4

Examples of Instances of Homicides by Portuguese and Luso-descendent Military Men

Though homicides are crimes against physical integrity, we have considered them separately, given that they are extreme cases. They total up to 33. Some military men were, in fact, accused of homicide. José Leal da Conceição, Captain of one of the companies of the auxilliary *terço* on the Island of Goa, is investigated on the deaths of José Ribeiro and Manuel José Gomes, father-in-law and son-in-law, stating that he had helped the soldiers of his company to assault them, who later died. See the letter of pardon of 22 April 1779 (A.N./T.T., *J.R.F.E.I.,* Book 69, ff. 69-70). Also José Porfírio, soldier of the 2nd regiment was imprisoned for the death of a squadron corporal of the same regiment. Cf. Letter of pardon of 15 May 1779 (A.N./T.T.,

J.R.F.E.I., Book 69, ff. 130-1). João Salgado de Faria e Araújo, infantry captain and keeper of the money and food of the royal arsenal and navy was denounced for killing the Hindu Custam Poy. Cf. Letter of pardon of 6 November 1779 (A.N./T.T., *J.R.F.E.I.,* Book 69, ff. 195-196v). The adjutant Tomás António de Sá e Morais was deported for 10 years to East Africa for the death of a sub-lieutenant of the Royal Legion of Volunteers. See copy of the sentence by the War Council of 16 June 1784 (A.H.G., *M. Reino,* Book 167-C).

On 13 May 1751 there appeared in the river Mandovi, close to Verem (Bardez), a corpse 'with a stone and two knife cuts' and it was found to be that of a servant of Francisco António Pereira Coutinho, *capitão-de-mar-e-guerra,* who was away in Mozambique. The latter was the son-in-law of D. Henrique de Noronha, in whose house the daughter stayed during the absence of her said husband. After some days a corpse and two bodies without a head were noticed which were found to be of a Franciscan friar called Frei António de S. Diogo, nephew of D. Henrique de Noronha and that of a kaffri belonging to the same priest. It was said that they had gone from the city of Goa to the house of D. Henrique and had not returned from there. The criminal high court judge found indications that the culprits were D. Henrique de Noronha and his three children D. Gil, D. Francisco and D. Luís. They were put behind bars, with the exception of D. Luís (the perpetrator of the crime) who was sent to China in a Macao ship. See Viceroy's letter to the King, dated 30 January 1752 (H.A.G., *M. Reino,* Book 124-A, ff. 172-5). On 22 March 1754 in his letter to the Viceroy, D. José ordered that, because they were such distinguished people, they were more blameworthy of a delict accompanied by circumstances of perfidy and lack of humanity. He further states that in similar cases an example of justice must be set which always deserves greater attention and must prevail over all other considerations (A.H.U., *Índia,* cód. 512, f. 197). On 12 February 1768, the interim Governors informed the King that D. Henrique de Noronha had died in prison and that (for the last seventeen years) his sons, D. Gil Anes de Noronha, were condemned to perpetual deportation to Timor, and D. Francisco Henriques with five years for Diu (the said document mentions 'Carlos Caetano Henriques', either by mistake or as being a part of the name). The Governors further mention the King's consideration that, given the distinguished status of these convicts and the rigorous and horrible imprisonment, they be pardoned [A.H.U., *Índia,* maço 78-A (55)].

Manuel D'Assa Castelbranco and João António D'Aassa Castelbranco were deported for the death of José Ro[...] [illegible], son-in-law of the former. Cf. Letter of pardon of 4 April 1760 (A.N./T.T., *J.R.F.E.I.,* Book 41, ff. 146v-147). See the charters of bail of 2 August 1766 and 10 January 1776 which refer to the two dead fallen into the well (A.N./T.T., *J.R.F.E.I.,* Book 50, ff. 13 and 14 and Book 63, ff. 111-112v). Some cases of kaffri deaths were also detected. Cf. Provision granted letter of security, dated 18 September 1790 (A.N./T.T., *J.R.F.E.I.,* Book 77, ff. 127); proroguing of letter of security dated 22 June 1776 (A.N./T.T., *J.R.F.E.I.,* Book 63, ff. 169-169v), letter of security of 24 November 1764 (A.N./T.T., *J.R.F.E.I.,* Book 54, f. 52), etc.

CHAPTER III

Religion

THE EXPANSION OF Christianity in Asia was a glorious feat indeed, arrayed with positive aspects in the context of the human and spiritual life of the peoples. And, in the words of Oliveira Marques, 'the commercial and military empire was thus redoubled and enlarged into a religious empire, more lasting and perhaps more interesting as revealing civilizational contacts.'[1] In no other part of the Portuguese Oriental empire did Christianity create such deep imprints on the landscape and life in general as it did in Goa, eloquently testified by its old city with its religious monuments and majestic See where, until a few years ago, the chapter intoned the psalms.[2]

Scattered as they are through the parishes and dotting the rural scenery, the church buildings of Goa stand out by their characteristic outline and also by their whiteness contrasting with the green shades of the fields and coconut groves. They are one of the unique landmarks that set Goa apart from the rest of India. They not only confirm the acceptance and adoption of Christianity in these locations but also blend with the history of a people who, essentially the spiritual children of Hinduism and Indian culture, did suffer influences from another source, forming a rich and original symbiosis.

Ever since India was conquered by the Portuguese, the right of the *Padroado* – many centuries old in Christian Europe and thus in Portugal too – was enlarged in these stations, comprising the *Padroado Português do Oriente.* Through it, the Papacy, pressed between the difficulties of Roman politics and the new tasks of

[1] A.H. de Oliveira Marques, *História de Portugal,* vol. II, Lisbon, Palas Editora, 1983, p. 217.

[2] In 1983, when for the first time we visited Goa, after it became a part of the Republic of India, we attended the part of the office sung by the old canons in the Cathedral.

evangelization resulting from the Western expansion, willingly and with some expectation, conferred on the Portuguese sovereigns ample privileges and also spiritual responsibilities and duties, as for example, that of the religious organization of Asia. Thus a kind of accord was established between the two parties which was given sanction by several pontifical bulls.[3]

How did Portugal correspond to this charge of evangelising India, assumed voluntarily by the country and confirmed by the Papacy? How was the Church in the East organized? What place did Goa occupy in this religious structure?

* * *

After having been under the spiritual jurisdiction, first of the Order of Christ, and then, of the diocese of Funchal (1514), Goa was raised to the category of diocese in 1534 and, in 1557, to that of Archdiocese and Metropolitan Church and Primate of the East.[4]

As a bishopric, its episcopal authority extended from the Cape of Good Hope to China, and on being promoted to arch-

[3] On the concept and the meaning of the expression *right of Padroado,* on the reasons that led to its institution, and finally, regarding its evolution down the ages, see the works of Father António da Silva Rego: *O Padroado Português do Oriente. Esboço Histórico,* Lisbon, Agência Geral das Colónias, 1940, pp. 3-15 and 23-30; *História das Missões do Padroado Português do Oriente. Índia* (*1500-1542*), vol. 1, Lisbon, Agência Geral das Colónias, 1949, pp. 99-102; *O Padroado Português no Oriente e a sua Historiografia* (*1838-1950*), Lisbon, Academia Portuguesa da História, 1978. See also the 'Rezumo e citação das Bullas dos Sumos Pontífices, que concederão a Jurisdicção Espiritual aos Senhores REIS e Infantes de Portugal em Todas as Terras e Ilhas Conquistadas e por Conquistar, que a poderão exercitar por Bispos para isso por eles eleitos tudo pela razão de Mestres da Ordem de Christo', in A.C.P.G., *Cópias de Vários Documentos,* ff. 3-75 (cf. F.U.P.), and study by Charles-Marital de Witte O.S.B., 'Les Lettres Papales Concernant L'expansion Portugaise au XVI siècle', in *Nouvelle Revue de Science Missionaire,* 1986.

[4] Like the other Portuguese territories in Africa and Asia, Goa too was subject, in its first times, to the spiritual jurisdiction of the vicar of the Order of Christ and, in 1514, it joined the diocese of Funchal. In 1534, by the bull *Aequum Reputamus* of Paul III, it was made into suffragan bishopric of the archbishopric of Funchal, whose diocese was elevated in 1533 to

bishopric, it headed two suffragan bishoprics of Cochin and Malacca. Added later were Macao, Funai (Japan), Cranganore, Meliapore, and others. Down the ages, some of them were separated from the ecclesiastical province of Goa.[5]

In this context, this Portuguese territory became the centre of Christianity in the East, and thus, also of the missionary expansion. The Asia-bound priests could board the ship in Lisbon only. It was normally in Goa that they would disembark, dispersing thence to the various missions. Goa and Lisbon were thus either the point of arrival or of departure for all the missionaries. It was finally a form of control on the movement of the religious agents for the East. It was also from Goa that the clerics and the economic resources, paraments and different articles (whether coming from the territory or from the Kingdom), were dispatched to the different missions of the Portuguese Patronage in the East, spread through East Africa, India, China, Japan and Oceania.[6]

As we shall shortly see, this picture changed with the coming of the missionaries directly dependent on the Roman Congregation of Propaganda Fide.

The situation of the Church of Goa, at the end of the first half

---

metropolitan status. In 1557 the bull *Etsi Sancta et Imaculata,* of Paul IV, raised the bishopric of Goa to archbishopric and dismembered it from Funchal. See the following works: *Memória Histórico-Eclesiástica da Arquidiocese de Goa 1533-1933,* Nova Goa, 1933, pp. 35-7 and 65; A.B. de Bragança Pereira, *História Religiosa de Goa,* offprint of *O Oriente Português,* vol. I, Bastorá, n.d. [1932-34], pp. 56-7; E.R. Hambye, op. cit., p. 318; Father Antônio Lourenço Farinha, *A Expansão da Fé no Oriente (Subsídios para a História Colonial),* vol. II, Lisbon, Agência Geral das Colónias, 1943, pp. 14-15; F.M. Bordalo, *Ensaio ...,* op. cit., pp. 146-7.

[5] The bishoprics of Cochin in 1558 and Malacca no longer belonged to the archdiocese of Goa. In India its spiritual jurisdiction extended to the south up to Calicut and to the north up to Diu and comprised almost all of the Mughal empire. In 1575 it received the bishopric of Macao and in 1588 Funai in Japan (*Memória Histórico-Eclesiástica ...,* p. 37).

[6] There is an account of this in *Relações das Missões* (read Reports) which their respective prelates presented every year. See, for example, those of 1760, 1762 and 1768. Cf. A.H.U., *Índia,* cód. 441, ff. 161, 161v, 173, 320, 320v, 324 and maço 108 (124).

of the eighteenth century and at the dawn of the second, is a result of the convergence of a series of factors and of problems that were long since beginning to be felt in the archdiocese. It is therefore important to trace the dominant line of the religious action in India during the earlier centuries for a better understanding of this epoch.

In the beginning of the sixteenth century, though religion was an essential element of the expansionist ideology, the commercial interests were indeed important. For this and other reasons, evangelization proceeded at a slow pace and was hardly systematic until the 1540s. The policy of religious tolerance and the practice of mixed marriages, tried by Albuquerque, helped a lot to create an open and mixed society in Goa where several creeds were respected as was in fact the case with other parts of the State of India (Daman, Diu, Malacca, Macao).[7]

But such a society did not last long in Goa. Meanwhile, with the Counter-Reformation, the policy of religious imperialism, which had sought to make 'of the Portuguese State of India a solid Catholic state and Goa a great ecclesiastical centre, the focus of Christian culture', began to gain ground in the Kingdom.[8] In this context, Albuquerque's policy gave way to a particularly violent intolerance, in the second half of the sixteenth century and in the seventeenth century.[9]

[7] On the ideological reasons that conditioned evangelization in the first years, see Luís Filipe F. Reis Thomaz, *Goa: une société Luso-Indienne,* offprint of *Bulletin des études portugaises et brésiliennes,* 42-3, Paris, n.d., p. 18. Also refer E.R. Hambye, op. cit., p. 285. Thus the mass conversions would have reduced the revenue of the State coming from taxes paid by the Hindus and Muslims. Also the moral laxity and the administrative and commercial corruption did not attract the population to Christianity. Luís Filipe Thomaz further refers to the fact that Christianity only had adepts among the marginalized elements of the lower castes (populations from the sea ports) and among the people directly connected with the Portuguese (women and soldiers' lovers, factory employees, slaves, etc.) Since there are already specialized and well-documented works like those we referred to and other older ones, which we shall cite opportunely, we shall not dwell on religion in Goa in the sixteenth and seventeenth centuries.

[8] L.F.F.R. Thomaz, op. cit., p. 19 (translated from the French).

[9] Cf. E.R. Hambye, op. cit., p. 286.

In fact, this new attitude towards the non-Christians saw the creation in Goa of institutions like the Inquisition; it engendered measures meant to favour the converts and to make life difficult for the Hindus. Such were, in fact, the directives from the Provincial Councils of Goa (1567-1606). It was thus a policy protecting the Christians and discriminating against the Hindus.[10] Bragança Pereira rightly states that in Goa the religious policy 'oscillated between the highest tolerance and fanaticism taken to the extreme extent'.[11]

Nevertheless, St. Francis Xavier's missionary activity and the introduction of new methods of evangelization by the Jesuits to attract the local inhabitants to the Christian faith decisively marked the second half of the sixteenth century. It was precisely between 1555 and the beginning of the seventeenth century that the greater part of the three provinces of Ilhas, Bardez and Salsete were Christianized due to the joint action of the religious orders (Franciscans, Dominicans, Jesuits) and the secular clerics.[12]

[10] It may be recalled, among other measures, that in 1537 there appears in Goa the 'Father of the Christians' who was supposed to deal with all the issues of the new Christians (see *O Livro do 'Pai dos Cristãos'*, ed. José Wicki, S.J., Lisbon, C.E.H.U., 1969, pp. X and XI). The royal letter of 23 March 1559 ordered the nomination of Christians, and never the non-Christians, to subaltern posts of Justice and of Revenue, who had to wear badges (A.L. Farinha, *A Expansão da Fé,* vol. II, pp. 32-5). Non-Christian ceremonies were prohibited in the lands of Goa and Daman (they were only allowed in Diu), by the royal provision of 1559. Under Governor D. Constantino de Bragança (1558-61) many temples were destroyed. In 1560 the Goa Inquisition was established (F.N. Xavier, *Bosquejo Histórico* ..., pp. 263-4, and E.R. Hambye, op. cit., p. 288).

[11] A.B. de Bragança Pereira, *O Sistema das Castas,* op. cit., p. 39.

[12] See E.R. Hambye, op. cit., pp. 286-7 and L.F.F.R. Thomaz, op. cit., p. 20. In 1564, nine-tenths of the population in Ilhas became Christian thanks to the action of the Jesuits and the Dominicans. The island of Chorão became totally Christian between 1560 and 1563. The evangelization of Bardez was entrusted to the Franciscans about the year 1556. On the presence and the activities of these regulars in Goa, see F. Félix Lopes, 'Os Franciscanos no Oriente Português de 1584 a 1590', in *Stvdia,* 9, C.E.H.U., January 1962, pp. 29-142. In 1625 three-fourths of its population was Christian. The province of Salsete, more traditional and the least touched by

In the following century, the policy of repressing the Hindus was strengthened. In the religious field, the general policy was to ban public cults of non-Christians, as a result of which Hindu temples were not allowed.[13] Inquisitorial activity was also intense, as well demonstrated by the numerous processes, the lists of the convicts and the autos-da-fé held in Goa at this time. Normally it targeted Christians, but could also affect non-Christians when found to be influencing or harming the religious life of the Christians. The edicts of the Holy Office enumerate a series of traditional practices, of more or less cultic nature, forbidden to Christians, in order to avoid, in the perspective of the tribunal, infiltration of Hindu beliefs in religious life.[14]

It was in the seventeenth century that the first symptoms of crisis within the Church began to be noticed. Indeed, the *Padroado-Propaganda* conflict began at this time with the setting up of the Congregation of the Propaganda Fide (1622) in Rome, followed by the creation of apostolic vicariates directly dependent on Rome and not on Goa. The appointment of Goan vicars in various regions in India, who had earlier belonged to the Patronage and, in some cases (for example, Mangalore) were subject to Portuguese sovereignty, led to a lot of trouble.[15] Besides

---

Christianity, was entrusted to the Jesuits who began their action in 1560. At the end of the sixteenth century there were 35,000 Christians in Salsete, distributed over 11 parishes. On the Christianization of Chorão, see A.B. de Bragança Pereira, *Historia Religiosa* ..., pp. 181-2 and Viriato A.C.B. de Albuquerque, 'Ilha dos Fidalgos', *O Oriente Português*, 10-11 (1904), pp. 549-58.

[13] The royal charter of 1629 prohibited temples and Hindu rites in Goa. Cf. A. Baião, *A Inquisição de Goa*, vol. I, p. 118. The use of Konkani (local language) was banned for preaching and catechism by Viceroy Francisco de Távora in 1684 and customary Hindu law, respected hitherto, eliminated (L.F.F.R. Thomaz, op. cit., p. 23).

[14] In the seventeenth century there were in Goa 2 autos-de-fé; in 15 years' time (1685-1700) 944 persons were sentenced. Cf. the table of 'autos held by the Inquisition' in Fortunato de Almeida, *História da Igreja em Portugal*, vol. IV, Porto, Livraria Civilização, 1971, pp. 315-16. Also see A. Baião, op. cit., pp. 263-95.

[15] Cf. E.R. Hambye, op. cit., p. 292 and A. da Silva Rego, *O Padroado Português*, p. 19.

this, there was also some softening of missionary fervour and pastoral zeal amidst the religious Orders, together with signs of poor discipline and corrupt habits.[16]

Many clergymen, regular and secular, predominantly of European origin, were engaged in pastoral activity in Goa. The parishes were generally entrusted to the Franciscans, Jesuits and Dominicans, who exercised the function of parish priests; and as, very often, they did not know the local language and were not very upright, they did not always exercise their pastoral tasks with due dignity.[17]

In the archdiocese of Goa too the political difficulties emerging from the Restoration in Portugal (1640) and the snapping of diplomatic ties with the Holy See left the archbishopric without a spiritual head for many years. The Cathedral Chapter, that had assumed the direction of the archbishopric, came into conflict with the Governor, because of his favouritism in ecclesiastical appointments. This problem was aggravated by the protest between the clergymen of Brahmin and non-Brahmin origin.[18]

Nevertheless, the evangelization of these lands went on, as proved by the founding of several colleges, novitiates, churches. New religious Orders were established in Goa in the course of the seventeenth century, such as the Carmelites and the Theatines (foreign), the friars of St. John of God (Reinóis) and the Oratorians (Goans). The convent of St. Monica too was founded for the nuns of the Augustinian Order. In the field of welfare, besides several hospitals and retreats, the Recolhimento de Nossa Senhora da Serra (for orphans of honest families) and Santa

[16] See A.L. Farinha, op. cit., vol. II, pp. 82, 106-14; Jaime Cortesão, 'Domínio Ultramarino', in *História de Portugal,* ed. D. Peres, vol. VI, pp. 665-6.

[17] See the royal letter to the Viceroy, the Count of Vila Verde, dated 24 March 1696, ordering that when the religious parish priests did not behave as true clergymen the churches be taken from them and handed over to whoever gave a better account of himself. Cf. A.H.U., *Índia,* maço 100 (85).

[18] Cf. E.R. Hambye, op. cit., p. 291.

Maria Madalena (for women needing rehabilitation) are to be highlighted.[19]

Generally speaking, the religious problems, in some measure latent, to which we have referred, became more evident in the first half of the eighteenth century. In fact, there were several difficulties in the wake of the very political situation, with the loss of Bassein and the forts of the north except Daman (1739), in favour of the Marathas.

The Goa church did not manage to respond to the innumerable needs of the missions spread throughout Asia and East Africa, for its clergy had lost their erstwhile qualities. Numerous but lax and disorganized, ambitious, without great religious fervour, it would be the cause of preoccupation for the authorities who sought to reform them but without much success.[20]

In the parishes as well, there were frequent abuses committed by the regulars, on the one hand, and the consequent jurisdictional conflicts among the prelates of the religious Orders and the diocesan bishop, on the other, were frequent.[21]

The Congregation of the Propaganda Fide was aware of this situation, reported to it sometimes exaggeratedly. Hence they adopted the policy of sending foreign missionaries and appointing vicars-apostolic for the lands of the Portuguese Patronage in the East on the grounds that Portugal was unable to fulfil the religious duties it had assumed as a patron. Truly,

[19] Ibid., pp. 326-8 and A.L. Farinha, op. cit., vol. II, pp. 85-9, 98-100 and 123-6 (in these last pages a summary is given of the main Orders founded in the seventeenth century).

[20] In 1703 Viceroy Caetano de Melo e Castro informed King D. Pedro II that there were many clergymen in Goa. Even among the Jesuits there was a certain apostolic inertia (E.R. Hambye, op. cit., p. 297).

[21] As an example, see the High Court judgement, dated 23 June 1749, regarding the controversy between the Archbishop and Father Procurator General of the Province of S. Tomé of the Regular Observants. One of the points of discord was the prior examination hitherto conducted by the Bishop of the Franciscans to whom the parishes had been entrusted. As is obvious, the Franciscan prelate considered this measure an encroachment on his rights and an abuse of authority by the Archbishop (A.C.P.G., *Ofícios e Portarias,* Book 1, ff. 113v-118v).

the Portuguese missions continued to decay, though also the missions under the responsibility of the Propaganda were not as successful as Rome had anticipated.[22]

The Inquisition, in the wake of what it had been doing in the earlier century, now further tightens its network of superintendence, with regard to the cultic practices of the Christians and the non-Christians too, which shows that the measures that had been adopted were not producing the expected results. Thus, many converted Hindus and converted Christians, whose reversion to Hinduism was feared, were targeted by the Inquisition, which led the businessmen to flee from State lands, to the great detriment of commerce. The 'Hindu dominance' in economic activity, to which we referred in the earlier chapter, may be kept in mind here.[23]

The Archbishops too, through their pastoral letters and administrative rules and by means of pastoral visits, seek to avoid non-Christian infiltration into Christian orthodoxy.[24]

By and large, the official religious policy followed at this time, in harmony with the orders proceeding from the King (which did not always coincide with the wishes of the Viceroy), was to permit certain non-Christian festivities, as long as they were held in private. Earlier, the French traveller Innigo de Biervillas, on his visit to India in 1736, had observed that the non-Christians had religious freedom, but could not have temples in the city of Goa. Besides, the non-Christians could not be

[22] Cf. A. da Silva Rego, *O Padroado Português no Oriente ...*, op. cit., p. 21.

[23] The edicts of the Inquisition dated 12 August 1733 and 14 April 1736 introduce a number of prescriptions that the natives of India had to follow in their religious practice, dress code, and habits (A.C.P.G., *Ofícios e Portarias*, Book 1, ff. 31-33v and 22-30, respectively). See the letter from D. João IV to Viceroy João de Saldanha da Gama, dated 1 April 1730, showing that the non-Christian businessmen fled to Bombay and other lands, in fear of the Inquisition (A.C.P.G., *Ofícios e Portarias*, f. 30 in F.U.P. 18-1-8/9).

[24] See, for example, the pastoral letter from D. Frei Lourenço de Santa Catarina, dated 1745, advising the Christians to abstain from certain practices like the *lavatórios* (ritual washings), the use of *murdanga* (tambour used by the dancing girls), the work 'behind closed doors' in the non-Christian households (A.C.P.G., *Ofícios e Portarias*, Book 1, ff. 70-1).

obliged to listen to the preaching of the Gospel, as it had sometimes happened.[25]

Generally speaking, the situation of the Church in the transition from the first to the second half of the eighteenth century, was not, in any way, flourishing. Much to the contrary, it betrayed signs of decadence: the State used to spend large amounts with the Church; the religious Orders were holders of great fortunes and sums of money which in critical moments they advanced to the State (it may be recalled that the Jesuits promptly gave monetary help to finance the Mombassa expedition, in exchange for mortgage of the islands of Panelem and Corjuem in their favour).[26] In the religious congregations and in the mission stations entrusted to them, there was a certain slackness and softening of the former religious proselytism. They stressed the animosity between the Jesuits and the other religious Orders, possibly because of the prestige and the prominent position that, among other reasons, came from its role in the education of the youth.[27]

As regards the secular clergy, there is no doubt that their numbers grew; nevertheless, their moral, religious and cultural formation was not always the best.[28] The symptoms of decline in

[25] See the letter from D. João V to Viceroy João Saldanha de Gama, dated 12 April 1731, prohibiting the celebration of *shigmo* (Hindu festival similar to our carnival) as it coincided with Lent (A.C.P.G., *Cópia de Vários Documentos,* ff. 32-32v in F.U.P., 18-1-8/9). Cf. the order of D. Pedro II in 1700 for the Hindus not to be obliged to listen to the preaching, because 'religion must be voluntary and introduced with all sweetness' (A.C.P.G., *Cópia de Vários Documentos,* ff. 15-16 in F.U.P., 18-1-8/9). Cf. Souvenir de Beaumont [pseudonym], *Voyage d'Innigo de Biervillas, Portugais, a la côté de Malabar, Goa, Batavia, & autres lieux des Indes Orientales,* Paris, 1736, p. 185.

[26] See A.L. Farinha, op. cit., vol. II, pp. 132 ss. According to Francisco de Sousa, in *Oriente Conquistado a Jesus Christo,* in 1703, the State spent 1,24,929 xerafins with the Church. Also see C.R. Boxer, *A Índia Portuguesa em meados do século XVII,* pp. 73-5, wherein he mentions some cases of Jesuits involvement in business.

[27] Cf. *Voyage d'Innigo de Biervillas ...,* pp. 185-6.

[28] Already in 1750 the number of clerics was considered excessive and measures were being taken to avoid so many ordinations. As this aspect remained after 1750, we shall take it up later.

the clergy were, mainly, of moral nature: bad fulfilling of the priestly duties, materialist spirit, lust, etc. It may be noted that the situation was particularly serious with the Franciscans, divided as they were into two parties. At the level of the faithful there was laxity in the religious practice, dissolution in matrimony, licentiousness, corruption...[29]

This is why there was a great desire for social reformation as a means to contain the abuses, whose causes were attributed to the political and economic decadence of the times. Truly, the pastoral decrees and the episcopal visits had multiplied, in order to check the main anomalies. And in 1720 D. Inácio de Santa Teresa was appointed Archbishop, not only as a prelate but also as a reformer of the abuses in the State of India.[30]

This moral crisis had in fact been long-drawn. It saw several settings and protagonists, and for several reasons, it was not contained. Let us see the turn it took at a later stage.

* * *

As we would like to submit, the second half of the eighteenth century is a turning point in the history of Goa. As a result, the annexation of new territories – New Conquests – populated by a large Hindu majority, caused a change in the religious policy commonly followed. An attitude of religious tolerance was adopted with regard to idols and Hindu practices and the preservation of the local habits and customs was guaranteed.[31]

The new cultural winds – the so-called Enlightenment – raging in Europe and in Portugal undoubtedly contributed to such a change. The religious foundations of the State were deeply shaken. The Inquisition was secularized and changed into a State tribunal. The Society of Jesus was expelled from the

[29] See the letter from the Marquis of Alorna to the King, dated 8 January 1750, reporting the clashes among the Franciscans (H.A.G., *M. Reino,* Book 122-B, ff. 211-14 and F.U.P., 122-B 1/1-1-5 and 2/1-3).

[30] For instance, see the pastoral letter of 1745, by D. Frei Lourenço de Santa Maria (A.C.P.G., *Ofícios e Portarias,* Book 1, ff. 55-72). Cf. E.R. Hambye, op. cit., p. 296.

[31] See fn. 8 to Chapter II.

Kingdom and the Empire. In the relations with the Holy See, a Gallican-type policy was opted for, tending to accentuate the independence of the State in relation to the Papacy.[32]

In Goa too, the Jesuits, one of the greatest pillars of the absolute monarchy in the throne-altar alliance, were expelled in 1759.

Notwithstanding the great power of the inquisitors, the Tribunal of the Holy Office was abolished in Goa, in 1774. In this ideological atmosphere, Albuquerque's policy of tolerance was resumed for some time, and religious activity in Goa, from 1750 to 1800, incontestably assumed new directions.[33]

REGULAR CLERGY

The religious Orders saw their power strongly shaken by the new political theory of enlightened despotism according to which the King received his sovereignty directly from God and exercised it over his vassals, without having to give them an account of it nor to convoke his representatives. Besides, the expulsion of the Jesuits represented a deep blow to the prestige and strength of the regular clergy.

In Goa, where the Jesuits played a prominent role in evangelization and education, the regular Orders of European origin also suffered a certain decline in the course of the second half of the eighteenth century.

Let us cast a glance on the religious congregations present in Goa and on their social action, in the 1750s, more precisely between 1757-8, that is, on the eve of the suppression of the Jesuits (1759).

The Franciscans, Dominicans and Jesuits – the three great religious orders headquartered in Goa from the first days of the conquest – continued to exist, and albeit morally decadent, they still held considerable influence in society. With more than two centuries of presence in Goa and having done considerable

[32] See Luís A. de Oliveira Ramos, *Projecções do reformismo pombalino,* Coimbra, 1984, offprint of the *Boletim do Arquivo da Universidade de Coimbra,* VI, 1984, pp. 597-8.

[33] See L.F.F.R, Thomaz, op. cit., pp. 24-5.

work in the sixteenth century in the field of Christianization, education and welfare in the Old Conquests, the regular clergymen having secured a strong acceptance in society. Their magnificent convents with novitiates, several colleges, hospices, etc., are a testimony to the social-religious action that they had with the populace.

Each of these three Orders took charge of vast areas in the Goan territory. Thus in 1757, twenty-four parishes in Bardez, with more than 70,000 souls, had been entrusted to the Franciscans; the Jesuits administered temporarily the twenty-five parishes of Salsete; the Dominicans presided over the religious administration of five parishes on the Island of Goa; the Augustinian monks, established there about 1570, had enlisted, on this date, two parishes in Ilhas, and even if they showed some symptoms of moral relaxation, they continued to work, possessing as they did some missions outside the Portuguese territory.[34]

The Augustinian nuns (since 1606), the Discalced Carmelites (1607), the Theatines (1640) and the Hospitaller Brothers of St. John of God (1685) completed the table of religious Orders of European origin headquartered in the territory. In 1757 all these congregations were based there, assisting the people, with the exception of the Disclosed Carmelites who, in the beginning of the eighteenth century, left the territory as they were no longer willing to pay obeisance to the Portuguese Crown.[35]

In the city of Goa, now quite depopulated, there existed thirteen regular houses with some activity. In the island of Chorão functioned the Jesuit noviciate. In Salsete, at the College of St. Ignatius, two professors of grammar and logic taught the

[34] See our study 'Um importante documento para a história da arquidiocese de Goa no ano de 1757: a Visita *Ad Limina* de D. António Taveira de Neiva Brum da Silveira', in *Arquipélago. Revista da Universidade dos Açores,* Série Ciências Humanas, no. V, January 1983, pp. 229 ff.

[35] See E.R. Hambye, op. cit., p. 327; for further information about the nuns of St. Monica in the eighteenth century see our study 'The Sisters of Santa Monica in the 18th Century. Details of their Daily Life', in *Goa and Portugal. History and Development,* ed. Charles J. Borges, Oscar G. Pereira, Hannes Stubbe, New Delhi, Concept Publishing Company, 2000, pp. 238-47.

people. In Bardez, there was the college of Reis Magos, now inactive.[36]

Besides these religious Orders, another two – of purely Goan origin – completed the list of congregations: the Oratorians of Goa, also founded in the seventeenth century (1682) and the Third Claustral Carmelites, created in 1750, to which we shall refer later. In fact, after this Order, no other was established in Goa, although certain congregations headquartered in the Kingdom, like that of the congregation of the Mission, did render an important collaboration in the religious activity.

In the period under study, the congregants of St. Philip Nery – the Oratorians – had acquired some prestige, by their knowledge of the local language as also being quite learned and leading an austere and virtuous life, imbued with religious fervour. They indeed successfully undertook missions on the islands of Goa and in the provinces of Bardez and Salsete.[37]

It may also be noted that owing to the new ideas of pedagogy and teaching that had spread in Europe and in Portugal with the philosophy of the Enlightenment, the Jesuit methods had become discredited. The Oratorians benefited from this, and they were called to take up teaching posts and official missions.

[36] The religious houses existing in the city of Goa, according to the report of Archbishop Neiva Brum in his *ad limina* visit of 1757, were: the convent of St. Dominic and the college of St. Thomas belonging to the same Order; the convent of St. Francis and the college of St. Bonaventure of the Franciscans; the convent of the Augustinian monks and the college of Our Lady of Populo; the monastery of the St. Monica nuns, belonging to the Order of Augustinian monks; the house of the Most Holy Name of Jesus, where the incorrupt body of St. Francis Xavier is preserved; the college of St. Paul-the-New for the education of the catechumens; the house of the Holy Cross of Miracles and the convent of Our Lady of Mount Carmel of the Oratorians (this one was given to them upon the exit of the Discalced Carmelites from Goa); the house of the regular clerics of Divine Providence with only four professors and the house of the Hospitallers of St. John of God, with only four clergymen, with no practice of hospitality. See our study 'Um importante Documento ...', pp. 244-6.

[37] Cf. the *Mapa das Feitorias, que os Religiosos denominados da Companhia de Jezu conservam na Ásia Portugueza ...* following by *Missoens, e Estabelecimentos que tem as outras Religions na Índia.* Cf. A.H.U., *Índia,* maço 28 (293).

Being *'canarins'* and knowing Konkani enabled them to provide religious assistance to the people of Ilhas, Bardez and Salsete, as also in the vast areas populated by non-Christians, that had been newly conquered (in 1757, Ponda, Piro, Ximpim, Tiracol had already been annexed).[38]

By and large the religious Orders possessed considerable assets that the pious faithful further augmented, with huge donations. They also enjoyed important privileges and were exempted, such as payment of tithes, stamp paper, etc.[39]

Especially the religious Orders that were established earlier in Goa, the Franciscans, Dominicans, Jesuits, and to a certain extent, the Augustinians, enjoyed a relatively comfortable situation, though the loss of lands in the Northern Province had diminished their revenue. This was apparently not the case with the nuns in the 1750's who, for the said reason and also because their expenditure was higher than their revenue, were grappling with great financial difficulties (at the time of joining, every nun brought along a retinue of servants, cortège of servants).

This deficient situation compelled the prioress to apply for new real estate, some of which was situated in the New Conquests. This gave rise to some controversy for the State Revenue of Goa was seeking its own financial solvency by means of the revenue from the new territories. Hence, some of the requests made by the nuns were not granted.[40]

[38] Ibid. At the Tiracol fortress there was a Franciscan in 1758; and one each at Piro and Ximpim.

[39] See the letter from the Marquis of Távora to the King, dated 14 January 1751 in which he states that 'in the small district of these Ilhas of Goa, Bardez and Salsete, the Religious Communities possess so many assets that it is worth reflecting on whether their intention of possessing others is worthwhile' (A.H.U., *M. Reino,* Book 123-A, ff. 141-2).

[40] See the letter from the Marquis of Alorna to the King, dated 21 February 1750, in which he opines unfavourably on the request for concession of the village of Mayem in Bicholim (New Conquests) for having lost 4 villages in Bassein. His position was based on the fact that the said village had still not been incorporated into the State as the peace had not been finalized and also because he considered that the present revenue of the convent was more than enough if the financial management was better

The latter-day Orders, for obvious reasons and the conditions in which they were established, had a less favourable position. In fact, in 1757, the Oratorians, complained that they were living only on their mass stipends and some 'voluntary oblations from generous Christians'.[41] Every religious congregation had been entrusted with mission stations outside the territory of Goa, to which they had to provide religious assistance. The Franciscans, the first religious order to settle in India, occupied vast regions in Hindustan – Cochin, kingdom of Quilon, Coromandel Coast. The Dominicans had established themselves in the islands of Cabo Delgado and the rivers of Macuame, Sena (Mozambique), Siam, Solor and Timor. The provinces of the Jesuits had jurisdiction over all of North India, Goa, Malabar, with jurisdiction over South India, China and Japan. In each of them, there were residences, missions or 'factories'. The Augustinians took care of Bengal. The Theatines were spread out in South India as well as in Ceylon and Indonesia. Finally, the Oratorians had a geographical division to a certain extent like that of the Theatines. Besides certain communities in Mozambique, they had spread through South India, and in South-East Asia – Malabar Coast, Fishery Coast and Ceylon. In this island, their action was particularly productive.[42]

For a long time, the religious Orders were not receptive to the entry of the Indians. In principle, they did not admit the

---

(A.H.U., *Índia,* maço 32 (289). By letter of 27 February 1750, D. João V solicited the opinion of the Marquis of Távora on other requests which he issued in the following terms: the King was to order that no nun should enter the convent with a servant (at this time, the number was above 226); the sovereign was to grant possession of the coconut garden and permit the acquisition of the land requested, but depending on royal confirmation (B.N., *Pomb.* 742, ff. 40-1 and H.A.G., *M. Reino,* Book 123-A, ff. 140-2). On 5 April 1752, D. José informed the Marquis of Távora that the request for perpetual possession of the coconut garden and the acquisition of lands with revenue of 6,000 xerafins had not been granted (A.H.U., *Índia,* cód. 205, ff. 189v-190).

[41] Cf. the *Mapa das Feitorias,* op. cit., in which they hand over all of it to the Superior and they 'live in common'.

[42] Ibid., and *Relação das Missões* of 1760, 1762, and 1768. Cf. A.H.U., *Índia,* cód. 441 and maço 108 (124).

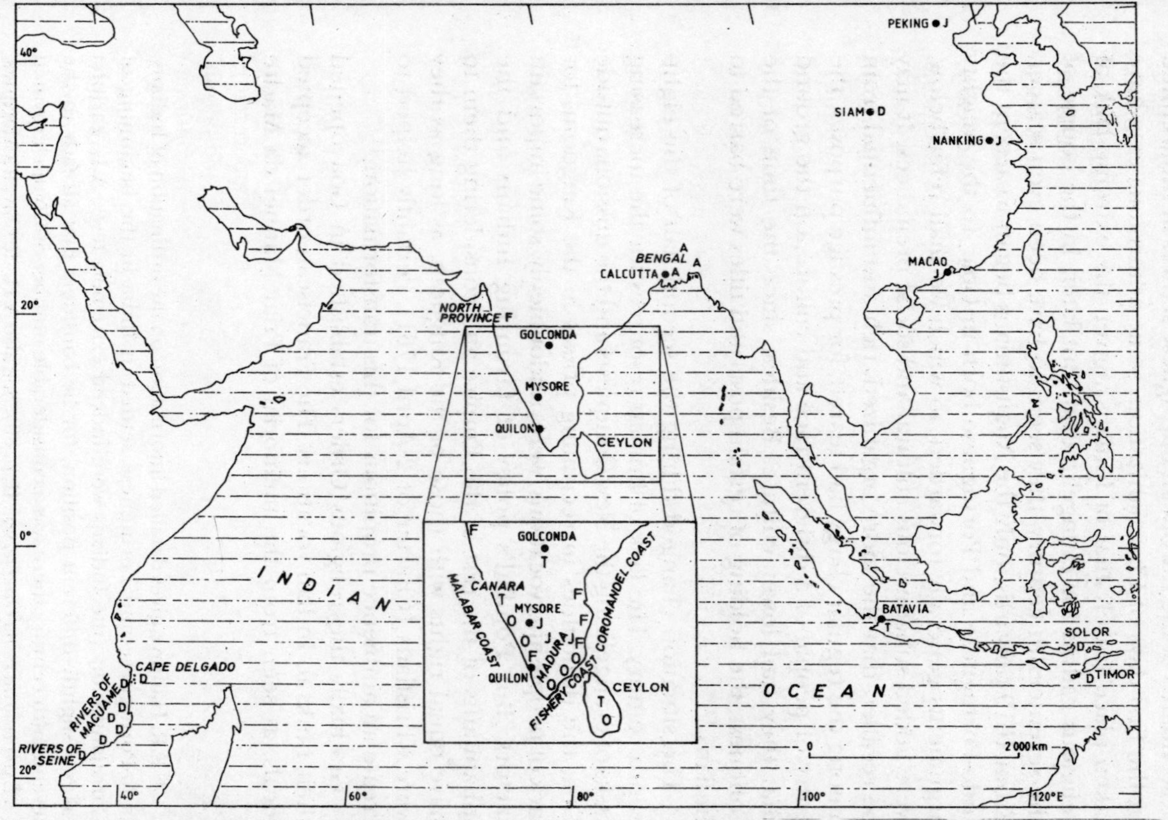

Legend: A – *Augustinians*; D – *Dominicans*; F – *Franciscans*; J – *Jesuits*; O – *Oratorians*; T – *Teatines*

Map III.5: Main missions of the religious congregations during the second half of the eighteenth century.

descendants of the European Portuguese settlers in India either. In the first days of Christianization, some admissions may have taken place (rarely that of Indians), given the extreme lack of religious cadres for evangelization. But later, in the course of the seventeenth century, they seem to have been even scarcer. From 1619 onwards, only the Augustinians began to accept the Indo-Portuguese and Portuguese born in Goa. To the weighty arguments generally forwarded, to which we shall refer below, were added subconscious cultural and social prejudices. It may be recalled that the more organized, rich and influential from among the regular clergy had feared, for prestige purposes, the entry of people of a different race and culture, on the ground that they had lower culture. Besides, since the time of the conquest, the holding of certain posts and titles were barred to Indians.[43]

The situation changed during the second half of the eighteenth century. The lack of human resources for the increasing tasks of evangelizing the New Conquests and the missions outside Goa, the difficulties in recruiting priests in the Kingdom, for lack of people and vocations, were, undoubtedly, some important factors. But Pombal's policy of favouring Indians and the inhabitants of the rest of the Empire and considering them to have equal rights with those of the Kingdom, as long as they were Christians (Charter of 2 April 1761), certainly helped to create an ambience propitious for this transformation.[44]

Gradually the religious Orders established in Goa opened their ranks to Indian vocations. The Franciscan order accepted locals, as seen from the memorial of Friar Manuel da Madre

[43] E.R. Hambye gives detailed information on the ordination of Indians, Indo-Portuguese and Portuguese settled in India in the beginning of Christianization (the Indians were indeed extremely few). A.L. Farinha takes a slightly different position, for he considers that already in the seventeenth century there was a considerable number of Goan clergymen (*A Expansão da Fé no Oriente*, vol. II, p. 80). See also A.H. de Oliveira Marques, accompanied by an elucidative excerpt from C.R. Boxer (*História de Portugal*, vol. II, Lisbon, 1983, pp. 203-4).

[44] On the Charter of 2 April 1761, see fn. 68 and 69 of Chapter I.

de Deus, Provincial of the St. Thomas province.[45] The foreign Theatines, compelled by their extreme dearth of regular clergy, included local people, and soon held the first ordination in 1751.[46] Ten years later, they proscribed the admission of Reinóis into the noviciate in India, there being no bar, however, for the locals.[47]

It can well be said that, theoretically speaking, there was a gradual turn-about: Whereas in the first half of the eighteenth century only Reinóis, and not Indians, were, in principle, admitted; in the second half of the century, on the other hand, the Reinóis could only enter with royal permission.[48] In practice, however, the entry of novices coming from Portugal into the various 'Religions' was not rare, and among them, of some deportees as soldiers, as it had long since been happening.[49]

The Congregation of St. Monica which, since its foundation

[45] Fr Achilles Meersman, O.F.M., 'The Question of Admitting Indians to the Franciscan Order', *Neue Zeitschrift fur Missionswissenschaft Nouvelle Revue de Science Missionaire,* XIII, Switzerland, 1957, pp. 29-33.

[46] By letter of 20 January 1750, the Superior of the Theatines in Goa, Father Carlos Joseph Fideli, reported to Father Alberto Caetano de Figueiredo the great affliction in which his House was on account of the lack of priests, and sought his intercession in Rome to solve the problem. (B.N. cód. 177, ff. 241-3). Two years later, the Marquis of Távora noted that Father Fideli had taken local novices and had not put them under the Congregation of the Propaganda Fide. His attitude was approved by the Viceroy and the King [A.H.U., *Índia,* maço, 19 (267)]. In December 1759, the missionary Francisco António, of the House of Divine Providence, writing to the Rev. Luís da Silva, giving news of the death of D. Carlos José Fideli, referred to the 'great blunder' of admitting Indians in the House. (B.N., Mss. 245, no. 129).

[47] Cf. H.A.G., *M. Reino,* Book 118-A, ff. 95-95v, in F.U.P., 7.1.1., 19/4 and 5.

[48] On 21 March 1779 permission was granted to Bernardo José Rodrigues, from the kingdom to go to India, to take the habit in the convent of the Augustinian missionary in Goa. Cf. letter from M.M. Castro to Governor Frederico G. de Sousa of the same date. Cf. H.A.G., *M. Reino,* Book 159-B, ff. 391-3 or A.C.P.G., *Cópia das Cartas Régias* ..., f. 107, in F.U.P., 18-1-8, 38/4, or A.H.U., *Índia,* maço 55 (300).

[49] See the Archbishop Primate's letter of 1777 in which he refers to the frequent entry into the 'Religions' of novices coming from the kingdom.

(1606), had been receiving only Portuguese and Indo-Portuguese women, now began to admit Indians with full right, probably in the transition from the first to the second half of the eighteenth century.[50] Within this order there were, as referred to in Chapter I, some discriminations, such as, the use of the black veil by the European nuns (daughters of European father or mother) and of the white veil by the Indians (daughters of an Indian father or mother). Also for the latter, if the opinion of the General Assembly of Bardez is to be believed, the dowry amount for entering into the convent was higher.[51]

In 1773, this selection criteria was eliminated and it was determined that the nuns of the white veils should begin to wear a black one and that this practice be sought to be avoided at the time of entry of the new nuns.[52] In the following year, D. Frei Manuel de Santa Catarina, administrator of the archbishopric of Goa, informed on the manner in which the issue had been settled, by accepting Goans to the black veil, as long as they had the qualities 'which the nuns of the choir ought to have'. The

Cf. A.H.U., *Índia,* maço 110 (126). On 14 March 1781, permission was granted to Teotónio Jorge da Silva to take the habit and to profess in any of the religious Orders of the Estado da Índia. Cf. letter from M.M. Castro to the Bishop of Cochin, administrator of the archbishopric of Goa, of the same date (A.H.U., *Índia,* cód. 517, ff. 29v-30 and 48v or maço 12 (269) or A.C.P.G., *Cópia de cartas régias* ..., f. 118, in F.U.P., 18-1-5, 41/4). It may be noted that the entry of the deportees into the religious orders was a practice coming down from earlier times and which the civil authorities turned against.

[50] Cf. E.R. Hambye, op. cit., pp. 294-5. On the founding of this congregation, refer Fr. Agostinho de Santa Maria, *História da Fundação do Real Convento de Santa Mónica da Cidade de Goa,* Lisbon, 1699.

[51] See the representation made by the Chamber General of Bardez, dated 18 March 1778, which refers to the discrimination in the European girls paying only 3,000 xerafins and the Indians 5,000 xerafins. Cf. A.H.U., *Índia,* maço 2 (246). But M.M. Castro in his letter to the Bishop of Cochin, dated 6 March 1773, states that the dowry was equal (H.A.G., *M. Reino,* Book 168-A, f. 125).

[52] Cf. this very letter in which he ordains the Bishop of Cochin that, on reaching Goa, he should study the means of doing away with that discrimination. Also see the draft of the letter of 21 March 1779, stipulating the same. Cf. A.H.U., *Índia,* maço 55 (300).

problem was more sensitive, in relation to the passage of the nuns of the white veil to the black one, both by their state and lay professions, as also because they were women dedicated to the service of the convent without any preparation. It was thus a question distinct from the first one and had rather to do with the internal regulation of the religious Orders. The cultural formation of the nuns came into question for a certain type of work and not of racial discrimination.[53]

But even at the end of the eighteenth century and beginning of the nineteenth, this distinction was still present with great advantage for the European nuns. Whence it is inferred that, in spite of the firm wish of the central government to equate the local Goan with that of the Kingdom, by suppressing colour and racial distinctions, there was still a great resistance to its application.[54]

It is known that in the late eighteenth century there were impediments for the entry of Indians in the Franciscan Order. In 1779 its Provincial refused to accept locals, calling them niggers and, in this condition, unable to enter the Order under statutory prohibition. In the following decade (1786), it was the same story, with the Superior stating that, for several reasons, it was not possible to accept Indians and sent for clergy who were Reinóis.[55]

[53] See the letter from D. Frei Manuel de Santa Catarina to M.M. Castro of 14 January 1780. Cf. A.H.U., *Índia,* maço 134 (134).

[54] In 1788 there were still 48 nuns of the black veil and 31 of the white veil (A.H.U., *Índia,* cód. 519, ff. 115-115v or H.A.G., *M. Reino,* Book 170-C, f. 993). In the beginning of the following century (1804), there were 42 nuns of the black veil and 19 of the white veil (A. Lopes Mendes, *A Índia Portuguesa,* vol. I, pp. 83-4). This means that at the first date the percentage was 60.7 for the black veil nuns and 39.3 nuns for the white veiled whereas in the beginning of the nineteenth century, the percentage stood at 68.8 against 31.2.

[55] M.M. Castro counters the reasons given by the Provincial not to admit the locals. Thus the argument that the Goans used to apply for the clerical state at a very early age and seldom had the vocation, the Secretary of State countered by showing that the situation was the same with the Reinóis. Cf. the letter from M.M. Castro to the Archbishop of Goa dated 15 February 1786 (A.H.U., *Índia,* cód. 519, ff. 66v-67v). See José António

It would be worth investigating whether or not a similar situation existed in other religious Orders. It would also be important to see if they were merely sporadic cases of resistance to a new mentality that was taking shape in the age of Enlightenment. We had no access to the list of ordinations held in the 'Religions' of Goa during the second half of the eighteenth century. This would have certainly clarified the matter. Nevertheless, we can easily imagine how the observance of the earlier laws, for more than two-and-a-half centuries, had created a particular way of life and a certain inertia that would take its own time to change. The royal charters of 1762 and 1774 were too recent and radical to be promptly accepted and executed. This is only a conjecture and needs corroboration!

We had the opportunity to refer to the scattered signs of intra-cloistral unruliness and degraded habits as noticed in the regular clergy. This situation, whose origin is difficult to pinpoint, however, kept on growing worse so much so that, in the final years of the seventeenth century or beginning of the following century, it became worrisome. In the second half of the eighteenth century, the convent of St. Francis, for example, was reduced, on certain occasions, to a 'lugubrious theatre of cruelties' and some clerics behaved so scandalously that the ecclesiastical authorities had to resort to the military forces.[56]

---

de Menezes, *Almanach Recreativo para 1883 ... Segundo Anno,* Nova Goa, Imprensa Nacional, 1882, pp. 136-41.

[56] There exists enough documentation with respect to the abuses by the Franciscans. Meanwhile, see the following documents about the tense situation in the convent of St. Francis which called for the intervention of a company of grenadiers: Copy of the letter from the interim Governors to the High Court judge Francisco da Silva Corte Real, dated 14 July 1767; copy of the letter from Henrique José de Mendanha Benevides Cirne to the Provincial of the Franciscans, Fr Matias de Santa Rita, dated 14 July 1767; copy of two letters of Francisco da Silva Corte Real to H.J. de M.B. Cirne, dated 16 July 1767; letter from H.B. Cirne to the Provincial, dated 1 August 1767 and the letter of pardon by Father Caetano de S. Matias [before 19 January 1768]. Cf. A.H.U., *Índia,* maço 104 (89). Also see the letter from the interim Governors to the King, dated 21 January 1768. Cf. A.H.U., *Índia,* maço 78-A (55). Among the priests who opposed the Provincial, were the guardian of the convent, Fr Nicolau de Santa Rita, main head of

Among the three main religious Orders established in Goa since the sixteenth century – the Franciscans, Dominicans and Jesuits – it was undoubtedly the first one that showed the greater signs of laxity. In fact the internal crisis, both in the Province of the Reformed Capuchins of the Mother of God, and mainly in the Province of the Observants of St. Thomas, was quite deep and assumed diverse aspects.[57] So the lack of knowledge of Latin on the part of some Reinol novices was notorious, for they used to come to Goa without being tested by good masters of Latin or by any examiner of the military orders. The same lack of preparation was noticed in local novices and even among certain clerics and prelates. Hence there was occasionally a want of good teachers for the novices.[58]

This ignorance was even greater among those friars who, being appointed in chapels and administering their coconut gardens, used to spend the greater part of their time out of the convent, a fact that contributed greatly for their contracting vices like gambling, incontinence, a materialistic spirit. ...[59]

The spirit of poverty too was unknown to some of them who engaged in trading activity and kept money, kaffris, personal attendants, unnecessary household goods. Fr Nicolau de S. Francisco was a flagrant case: known as a 'public contractor', he

---

the rebellion and Father Caetano de Santa Maria who self-inflicted blows and blamed it on the Provincial. Later, when quite sick, he confessed the truth.

[57] The Archbishop of Goa, D. Gaspar Leão Pereira (1560-7) founded in Daugim (suburbs of the city of Goa) a house for the members of the Franciscan order who wished to follow a more austere ideal. This house, under the patronage of the Mother of God, later turned into the headquarters of a new Franciscan province, known as the *Capuchins*, recollected, discalced, reformed (1622) (E.R. Hambye, op. cit., p. 325). See the letters of the Archbishop Neiva Brum to [...] dated 15 January 1757 [A.H.U., *Índia*, maço 91 (102)] and of the Governor F.A. Veiga Cabral to L. Pinto de Sousa Coutinho, dated 22 February 1797 on the laxity of certain reformed Franciscans.

[58] See fn. 65 of this chapter.

[59] See the letter from the Archbishop to [...] dated 15 January 1757, in which there is a reference to Franciscan chaplains living in some scandal [A.H.U., *Índia*, maço 91 (102)].

used to despatch cloths to different ports and sell rice by sacrificing 'the silence, gravity and modesty of the convent' to the 'tumult of the local population'.[60]

Here are some of the many deviations that these clergymen were accused of, as echoed in innumerable documents: the almost systematic breaking of the vow of obedience or simply a reminder of it, whereby some Franciscans were discourteous, insubordinate and even rebellious; the excessive number of clergymen and its harmful consequences; the establishment of colleges without the required authorization and certainly, last but not least, the neglect of the practice of Christian virtues, as enjoined upon them by the Founder.

Signs of laxity were visible among Dominicans and Jesuits too.[61] The latter carried out business and financial operations and sometimes charged exorbitant rates of interest. This was an old tradition and continued in the time of D. João V, who granted these missionaries the commercial licences they had requested, as they had managed to keep royal consideration and were always the first to extend financial aid at wartime. This is what happened in 1727, when the State had to approach the Jesuits for a loan, albeit at a high rate of interest, mortgaging to them the islands of Panelem and Corjuem, in order to make the Mombassa expedition possible. Their monetary help is also a proof of the great economic power of this religious Order.[62] When expelled in 1759, their adversaries accused them of having undertaken 'scandalous trade', which must be taken with a pinch of salt since the climate disfavoured them. Given the Franciscan agitation against the reforms undertaken by their Provincial, Archbishop D. António Neiva Brum da Silveira (1750-75) was

[60] Cf. the letter dated 19 December 1770 attached to the inquest of this friar, ordained by the higher authorities (H.A.G., *M. Reino,* Book 147-A, ff. 297-8).

[61] Fr Domingos da Conceição of the Order of Preachers went on deportation to Mozambique, for smuggling tobacco powder. Cf. letter from Governor Frederico Guilherme de Sousa to Martinho de Melo e Castro, dated 12 January 1782 [A.H.U., *Índia,* maço 136 (129) or H.A.G., *M. Reino,* Book 161-D, ff. 2177-9].

[62] See the Appendix III.1. *Hipoteca das Ilhas de Corjuem e Ponolem pela Coroa aos jesuitas: medidas para o seu desempenho.*

granted powers to 'subject, reform and punish them'.[63] On the lines of the Council of Trent, the prelate established strict qualifying norms for entry of the missionaries into the archbishopric of Goa, demanding credential letters on their moral conduct.[64]

Since most of the problems facing the clergymen resulted from their poor intellectual background, they had to answer a difficult test conducted by the Archbishop himself, and the Provincial of the Order was ordained to forbid novices from going to India without prior approval from good Latin masters or any examiner from the Military Orders.[65]

In order to put an end to the abuses rampant in appointments to churches of Bardez, D. António suggested to the King that the ecclesiastical revenue should be given to the parish priests who were actually assisting in the parishes; and if, in spite of this, the anomalies continued, the churches should be entrusted to another Order.[66]

[63] See the royal letter from D. José I to the Governor of India, dated 22 March 1769, in which he orders 'inquest' and to proceed on the regular observants of the Province of S. Tomé and in which he determines that they remain subject to the Archbishop (A.H.U., *Índia,* cód. 206, ff. 36v-37)

[64] The clergymen could only be admitted upon presentation of credentials 'on how they are of good life and saintly habits' and with legal age.

[65] This is what can be gathered from the reply of the State Council to the Archbishop's letter of 14 March 1758, published in our work, *Epistolário* ..., pp. 58-9. Also see, ibid., *O Arcebispado de Goa* ..., p. 209.

[66] *O Arcebispado de Goa* ..., pp. 209-10. D. António Taveira da Neiva Brum da Silveira arrived in Goa on 22 September 1750 to replace Archbishop D. Frei Lourenço de Santa Maria who had renounced the diocese. Together with the Chancellor, Matos Teixeira e Filipe de Valadares, he participated in the Twelfth Government Council (1756-8) and later in the Thirteenth Government Council (1765-8). He was quite instrumental in promoting the local clergy, admitting them to the holy orders and introducing measures for their welfare. 'The modesty, attractive manners and polish' of the Archbishop 'won the sympathy of the Goan people'. The Chamber General of Bardez was all praise for him, stating that he was 'a saintly prelate, eminent man of letters, zealous pastor' and 'Father of the Poor'. Although intransigent in matters of the faith, yet his generosity, spirit of Christian charity, as also his magnanimity in the offering of liturgical paraments to the churches was also referred to by his contemporaries. He set sail for the

In the pastoral letter of 8 January 1770, Neiva Brum suggests concrete measures to curb illegalities in the appointment to offices, the novices' lack of training, laxity in the observance of poverty, continence, chastity, humility, religious practice, discipline and obedience to the Superiors. He also considers the urgent need for appointing a reformer and reducing the number of clergymen.[67]

Archbishop D. Francisco de Assunção e Brito banned the Franciscans and the Augustinians from preaching and confession, thus provoking a climate of agitation in Goa (1776). The tempest died down thanks to the intervention of the wife of the Governor D. Ana Joaquina de Saldanha who succeeded in lifting the interdiction.[68]

The abuses committed by the regular clergy compelled the Archbishop, D. Frei Manuel de Santa Catarina (1780-1812), to consider the suitability of removing certain regulars from their congregations, who proved to be harmful, and then to proceed

---

kingdom on 4 March 1775, but died during the voyage, upon rounding the Cape of Good Hope, on 2 June of the same year.

[67] Cf. C.C. Nazareth, *Mitras Lusitanas no Oriente* ..., Lisbon, Imprensa Nacional, 1897, pp. 289-90. In our study, *O Arcebispado de Goa* ..., pp. 209-10, we refer to the main points of this pastoral letter.

[68] Cf. the letter from the Archbishop to the King about the Franciscan missionaries of the province of S. Tomé, dated 22 March 1782. Cf. A.H.U., *Índia,* maço 134 (134). See the letters of the Governor to the Marquis of Pombal, dated 21 April 1777 [A.H.U., *Índia,* maço 111 (125) and H.A.G., *M. Reino,* Book 157-b, ff. 348-348v] and of Feliciano Ramos Nobre Mourão to M.M. Castro, dated 30 April 1777. Cf. A.H.U., *Índia,* maço 125 (110). From the Augustinian Order, D. Francisco de Assunção e Brito took charge on 1 October 1774 and began his functions in March 1775, upon the return of his predecessor to the kingdom. Of 'a hardy and austere nature', he quarrelled with the people and the clergy (C.C. Nazareth, *Mitras* ..., p. 301). Indeed the Chamber General of Bardez accused him of acts of corruption and of impiety, for he had allowed the building of temples. The Governor too gave unfavourable information about him. The royal order of 7 April 1778 recalled him to the kingdom, in order to dwell on the state of the Church in India. He left Goa on 4 February 1783, and died on 10 December 1808 (cf. C.C. Nazareth, *Mitras* ..., p. 301; *Memória Histórico-Eclesiástica* ..., pp. 90, 125-6; E.R. Hambye, op. cit., pp. 297, 334).

with their reformation.[69] As earlier stated by the Archbishop Neiva Brum, he noted the urgent need for a reformer for the religious Orders, very especially for the Province of the Reformed of the Mother of God, which was directed by unworthy clerics. This right was conferred on the same Archbishop by the apostolic nuncio in Portugal, Vicente Ranuzi (1785), with full powers over the religious congregations.[70]

He initiated his action with the Franciscans, whose reform aimed especially at two aspects: the regular observance, mainly the practice of poverty, and the strict choice of missionaries.

His first reform decree of 23 May 1784 had a preamble in which he considered the missionaries to be the 'best deposit' to keep the Christian religion perfectly, and the division among the Franciscans being the principal cause of their decadence. He then referred to those sectors in which the anomalies were more frequent, such as receiving and preparing the novices for

[69] See the letter from D. Frei Manuel de Santa Catarina to the King, dated 13 March 1784, referring to the first steps taken towards the reformation of the religious Orders. Cf. A.H.U., *Índia,* maço 115 (122). The Discalced Carmelite Bishop of Cochin, D. Frei Manuel de Santa Catarina, having been appointed Governor and administrator of the archbishopric of Goa, arrived here on 3 October 1779; he took charge on 5 February 1780 and, later, on 19 July 1783, he was confirmed as Archbishop of Goa by the Pope, the investiture taking place on 21 November 1784. Considered virtuous, of a conciliatory nature and as a Visitor and reformer of the religious Orders of India by the apostolic nuncio in Lisbon (*Postquam per alias,* of 3 March 1785), he endeavoured the moralization and education of the clergy, the final establishment and endowment of the diocesan seminaries. He often expressed his opinion on the local clergy, perhaps somewhat exaggeratedly, as being ignorant, lacking moral and intellectual preparation. Hence the people did not hold him in great esteem. He died in Goa on 10 February 1812 (*Memória Histórico-Eclesiástica,* pp. 90, 125-6; E.R. Hambye, op. cit., pp. 297, 334).

[70] See the nuncio's brief referred to in a letter from 19 February 1785, granting the Archbishop of Goa all the rights and ample jurisdiction to be a reformer of the religious Orders set up in Goa. Cf. A.H.U., *Índia,* maço 101 (88). The letter from M.M. Castro to the Governor, Frederico Guilherme de Sousa, of 9 March 1785, informed him of the same [A.H.U., *Índia,* maço 86 (107), cód. 518, ff. 150-150v and H.A.G., *M. Reino,* Book 166, f. 22]. Also cf. the following fn.

the clerical state, the regular observance in its diverse aspects, like dress, food, practice of poverty.[71]

It may be noted that, in reality, the crisis was essentially the same that Archbishop Neiva Brum had discovered, wherefore it is understood that the problems still continued with the seraphic order in the 1780s, if not worsened further.

The decree also dealt with the more urgent issues relating to the Order: the lack of fit and competent missionaries for teaching; a moral conduct that was hardly demanding; entrusting chapels to ill-prepared clergymen; the celebration of Mass without proper care and the 'trading of the Mass'; the lack of diligence of the clergymen which made them have 'lads' in their service; the materialistic spirit; laxity in the vow of poverty.

All these questions were duly treated in the organization of the decree and some concrete measures were presented. Hence, in order to check the lack of educated missionaries, its author ordained a strict curriculum, with classes in Philosophy, Theology and Morals in the convent of Goa, and if the number of missionaries so demanded, in the college of St. Bonaventure too. Here Morals was given a lot of importance as a component, with periodic meetings held for the entire community.

Keeping in mind the good conduct of the regular clergy and seeking to avoid occasions that could lead to licentiousness in customs, the Archbishop imposed certain restrictions on their movement, forbidding them to go out alone or stay overnight outside the convent.[72]

[71] See J.A. Ismael Gracias, 'Reforma da Religião Franciscana em Goa no século XVIII', in *O Oriente Português*, year VII (1910), nos. 1 and 2 (Jan.-Feb.) and year VIII (1911), nos. 11 and 12 (Nov.-Dec.), pp. 1-14 and 251-69 respectively, in which are published decrees of the reform undertaken by D. Frei Manuel de Santa Catarina, which documents are fundamental for a study of this subject. As stated by the author, these sources are found in a book of registration of the St. Thomas Province. The author also publishes the brief announcement by Vicente Ranuzzi, dated 8 May 1784, sanctioned on 9 March 1785 and which reached Goa in the monsoon of that year (pp. 251-5).

[72] The missionaries would never go out seeking alms. They could do so for some literary activity and others in which the entire community were to participate. They could never take the help of companions, except that of

The issue of observance of choir obligations, in which the regulars were apparently not very zealous, was taken up in another decree by the Archbishop: the exemption from attending the 'prayed choir' that had earlier been granted to the definers was now withdrawn. It was also stipulated that no clergymen would ever fail in this obligation, and the community could either anticipate or delay to hold it, if so required.[73]

In the spirit of the statutes of the Order, humble work was to be greatly appreciated. Hence, the reformer could not fail to notice the liberty taken by the regular clergy of keeping private servants. It was, therefore, established that the matter would not be left to the discretion of the missionaries themselves, but yes to the Provincial or Curator of the convent, who would decide whether or not to authorize the clerics to have a helper.[74]

In order to curb the secular and materialistic spirit that affected some regular clergymen, he appointed a trustee to administer the alms. He also ordained severe vigilance on the cells, forbidding them to keep any unnecessary objects.[75]

This reform decree recommends the selection of persons proper both in the observance of rules and in the field of letters, making it compulsory that he be told his transgressions.

In the reform of the Franciscan Order undertaken by the Carmelite Archbishop, the education of the youth occupied an important place. Accordingly, he ordained the appointment of a *regent* who would be the senior-most emeritus professor to oversee literary exercises.[76]

Another important object of reform was, undoubtedly, good order in the mission stations. They were in a parlous condition

---

prelates or the masters. The most exemplary from among the laymen or lay brothers and priests, if necessary, were chosen to beg for alms. It was thus sought to make the clergymen lead a discreet life (ibid., pp. 8-9).

[73] Cf. the decree of 8 April 1788 (ibid., pp. 259-62).

[74] Lay brothers may be conceded to the weary missionaries and, when absolutely necessary to have 'lads', they had to be well bred and at least 20 years old (ibid., pp. 10-11).

[75] When some item was found in the cells it would soon be returned to the community or ordered to be sold in order to assist the needs (ibid., p. 12).

[76] Cf. the decree of 8 June 1786 (ibid., pp. 255-7).

indeed, for there were some unbearable members in their cloisters who had no knowledge of religion and their discipline. Hence, instead of edifying the unfaithful, they used to rather be an object of trouble and scandal for the Christians. As the abuses were rampant despite the prescriptions, the missionary had to present himself to the Archbishop at least eight days before his departure, in order to follow the orders. This was a precondition for sailing. Besides, the missionaries was not allowed to stay more than ten years in the mission stations, since that life was not totally compatible with the discipline of the cloister.[77]

Next to be taken up was the reform of the Augustinians, Dominicans and, in the 1790's, the Oratorians too, who, inasmuch as they were learned in the doctrine and highly educated, were, in his opinion, also in need of reform, so as to preclude any degeneration.[78]

Similarly, he believed that the reform of the regular clergy should have been done in such a way as to have European ecclesiastics directing the local regular clergy, by virtue of their genius. It may be noted that the central government advocated a diametrically opposite policy, favouring the recruitment of local personnel.

In his view, the reform measures enforced by him were bland and prudent. But they did attract strong opposition in the province of the Mother of God, whose clerics not only publicly

[77] The documents concerning the missions are the Archbishop's letter to the Franciscan provincial, dated 8 March 1788 which was, in fact, a circular for all the prelates of the religious Orders, and the decree of 4 December 1788 (ibid., pp. 258-9 and 262-6).

[78] Cf. the letter from D. Frei Manuel de Santa Catarina to M.M. Castro, dated 12 March 1787. He states that 'while it is true that even though externally they do not cause scandal, as regards their domestic governance and internal law, are the ones who are in most need of reform'. Much though he acknowledges the value of these clergymen, he is of the opinion that 'a body of locals cannot preserve itself without the Portuguese governing them, or an external reformer to visit, reform and keep them in subjection'. Cf. A.H.U., *Índia,* maço 1 (731). By letter from 30 March 1790 he considers that the reform of the congregants was timely, or else in a few years' time they would be spiritually and temporally ruined. Cf. A.H.U., *Índia,* maço 157 (147).

opposed them, but also undertook a propaganda campaign against them, engaging in satire and anonymous libels.[79]

The Archbishop received unconditional support from the central government and Rome, in the person of its apostolic nuncio in Rome, with his reform also meriting total acquiescence.[80]

We do not know to what extent these reform measures attained their objectives, which, at any rate, are difficult to pinpoint. There is a dearth of information given the fact that the archives of the religious houses did suffer great havoc, as stated earlier. Be that as it may, if they had failed to bring in a spiritual renewal, at least like a dyke they held back the torrent of degrading customs in the religious houses in Goa.

Besides the already existing religious Orders and congregations, yet another – and the last of them all, the Third Cloistered Carmelites – comes in the year 1750, blending perfectly with the new directives for religious activity in Goa and in line with the needs of evangelization in this age.[81]

[79] Letter from the Archbishop to M.M. Castro, dated 30 April 1792. Cf. A.H.U., *Índia,* maço 2 (713). Fr. Jerónimo de Jesus Maria refers to the reform of the Province of the Mother of God and to these difficulties raised by certain clergymen. Cf. A.H.U., *Índia,* maço 156 (148).

[80] See the excerpt of the letter from M.M. Castro to the Archbishop, dated 12 April 1788, and the copy of the letter from the apostolic nuncio in Portugal, dated 11 April of the same year, transcribed by J.A. Ismael Gracias, 'Reforma da Religião Franciscana em Goa', in *O Oriente Português,* nos. 1 and 2, 1910, pp. 266-9.

[81] Cf. the administrative rule of 10 December 1750 authorising the institution of the Third Cloistered Carmelite order in this diocese (C.C. Nazareth, *Mitras* ..., p. 279). Fathers João Baptista Falcão and Francisco Xavier dos Anjos and his predecessors, Father Francisco da Costa and the tonsured Paulo Mariano Falcão used to live for twelve years in some retreat houses, situated in the village Morombim-o-Grande, parish of Santa Bárbara (Ilhas). As there were other people who wished to keep them company in this secluded life, they began to construct another house and were duly authorized by the Bishop to have a public chapel with Our Lady of Mount Carmel as the patroness in village Chimbel (parish of Ribandar – Ilhas), on the plot of land gifted by Salvador Xavier de Moura. Since the founder of the houses along with his companions desired to serve Our Lady of Carmel, he secured his rule through a Carmelite missionary, he applied for royal

In fact, the members of this purely Goan institution were not regulars in the exact sense of the word, for they did profess perpetual and strict regular observance. They led an austere and contemplative life but also exercised some apostolate, thus compensating for the lack of priests in the new tasks of evangelization. Besides this, they also knew Indian or local languages, so important for successfully Christianising the overwhelming Hindu populations of the New Conquests.[82]

Archbishop Neiva Brum regarded as useful and necessary the desire that these priests had of setting up a seminary, given the fact that three Goan seminaries (directed by regulars) had become extinct. Time had indeed vindicated the Archbishop's belief about the utility of such a seminary, as in the 1570s, when the seminaries belonging to the Franciscans, Augustinians and Jesuits were no more, the seminary of the Soledade in Chimbel rendered yeoman service in training ecclesiastics.[83]

---

permission to set up this Order in the said houses. See the document accompanying the Archbishop D. António's letter to the King, of 1 April 1751. Cf. A.H.U., *Índia,* maço 24 (22).

[82] Ibid. This letter from the Archbishop, as also the other unsigned one, is elucidative. Both comment favourably on the founding of this congregation and important pieces of information on the nature that this institute should have. The Archbishop used to think that it was unnecessary for them to be rigorously religious but only cloistered clerics subject to the Bishop and independent from the superior of the Order of Carmel, except in the enjoyment of their privileges. After pondering on some aspects of the Archbishop's opinion as regards the type of foundation, the author of the other opinion concluded that the King should grant permission under two conditions: exemption from the choir and that the superiors of the Order should not send foreign missionaries and novices to Goa other than a visitor.

[83] The administrative rule of Archbishop D. Francisco de Assunção e Brito, dated 20 April 1778, stated that being of great use the seminary of the third Carmelite order, where there were 20 ecclesiastics of good conduct and in which he ordered some ecclesiastics be kept for correction through spiritual exercises, instituted in them two chairs of dogmatic and moral theology and rites (C.C. Nazareth, *Mitras* ..., p. 315). See also the letter cited in the earlier footnote and the letter [of the Archbishop to the King], dated 24April 1778 (H.A.G., *Monções,* Book 102-A, ff. 49-60). In 1786 these ecclesiastics maintained three classes of Latin, philosophy and theology. Cf. A.H.U., *Índia,* maço 28-A (290).

The action programme of its founders, who led an exemplary life, was to 'direct the youth and all those who applied themselves to minor and major studies, hear confessions, preach, evangelize, correct bad habits, instruct *ordenados* [*sic*], perfect the clergy, give Ignatian exercises and assist the dying'.

In 1758 the Archbishop approved the regulations of the hospice that these regulars had in Chimbel.[84] It was clearly a congregation with polyvalent functions, at once active and contemplative. Besides, though enjoying certain rights inherent to religious Orders, it remained diocesan *de iure* and, as such, was subject to the Bishop. This would help to preclude in future the jurisdictional conflicts that were so frequent in that age.[85]

Another aspect to consider was its economic sustenance. With its residence built on a plot of land gifted to them, and living as they did from its estate and Mass stipends, with no immovable properties in common, this congregation was no burden to the State Revenue which, as stated earlier, was spending a lot on the clergy whose expenses sometimes exceeded their revenue. However, later, in 1778, this congregation was granted an annual pension from the properties sequestered from the Jesuits.[86]

Archbishop D. António published the statutes of the congregation, which was highly favoured by D. Frei Manuel de Santa Catarina who, as a Carmelite keen on restoring his order that had been withdrawn from Goa around 1702, gave them the definitive rules in 1785.[87]

Queen D. Maria I confirmed the congregation of the Third Carmelite Claustral Discalced Order and placed it under her protection (1781). Later, in the last decade of the eighteenth

[84] Cf. C.C. Nazareth, *Mitras Lusitanas no Oriente,* Lisbon, 1897, p. 283.

[85] See E.R. Hambye, op. cit., pp. 328-9.

[86] By letter from 24 April 1778, referred to in fn. 83 of this chapter, an annuity of 3,000 xerafins was granted to it, from the income of the properties confiscated from the Jesuits. Also see the document referring to the properties to be applied to this congregation, dated 6 May 1784 [A.H.U., *Índia,* maço 145 (159) or H.A.G., *M. Reino,* Book 164-C, ff. 1095-1096v].

[87] Unable to re-establish the Carmelite Order, D. Frei Manuel de Santa Catarina instituted a corporation consisting of secular priests with the vow to observe the Carmelite rule, and built them a little convent and a church in 1782 (ibid., p. 321). Also see E.R. Hambye, op. cit., p. 329.

century, these priests asked permission for reestablishment, and at the same time presented their ordinations and statutes.[88]

The Third Carmelite Order had only two members in 1750, but in the 1770s the number went up to a score, and a little later to thirty clerics. After the suppression of the Jesuits they took over their mission stations, numbering five in 1800.[89]

From the social viewpoint, the founding of this religious institute appears to have been unprecedented and did create an impact on society of those days, for unlike the Theatines and the Oratorians, it was to receive not Brahmin members but candidates from the Chardó caste. As stated earlier, though the charter of 2 April 1762, revoking the provision of the Fifth Provincial Council of Goa, did qualify all local Christians for the religious Orders, in reality, it was mainly members of the Brahmin caste who benefited from these measures.

Again, as stated before, the Oratorian Congregation had been founded at the end of the seventeenth century, by priests of the Brahmin caste. The creation of the Carmelite institute at this juncture, with the said characteristics, made the regular state accessible to another stratum of the local population, thus making it possible for a larger number of Goans to benefit from the social privileges conceded by the Pombaline law.

This fact proved at the same time that, albeit very slowly, the law was beginning to have an effect, giving place to many changes in the Goan society. Ideally, other castes deserved to have an opportunity to join the religious Orders and get promoted socially

[88] See the letter from the Queen to the Bishop of Cochin, Governor and Administrator of the Archbishopric of Goa, dated 26 February 1781, confirming the Congregation of the Discalced Carmelites and taking them under her protection. For the greater health of their establishment she orders to find out what is the patrimony that can be consigned to them. [A.H.U., *Índia,* maço 13 (268), cód. 517, ff. 27v-28 and 33-33v; or A.C.P.G., *Cópia de Vários Documentos* ..., f. 111, in F.U.P., 18-1-8, 40/1]. See the ordinations and statutes of the Third Discalced Order of the Blessed Virgin Mary of Mount Carmel, present in the archbishopric of Goa. Cf. A.H.U., *Índia,* maço 164 (169).

[89] Cf. E.R. Hambye, op. cit., pp. 328-9. See the letter from Fr. Francisco da Paixão with the list of the Missions administered by the Carmel Convent in Chimbel (H.A.G., *M. Reino,* Book 179-A, f. 204v).

and culturally, in the second half of the eighteenth century, but apparently everything showed that this theoretical desideratum was not a practical reality.

Several reasons (dealt with in the first chapter and the present one), wherein political and economic factors carried a lot of weight must have prompted the central government to expel the Society of Jesus from the Kingdom and the remaining dominions (1759). As is known, the political theory of Enlightened Despotism had helped to reduce the immense power wielded by the religious Orders. The Society of Jesus was by far the economically most powerful religious Order and the one least touched and undermined by laxity in observing rules, as happened with the other Orders. Its penchant for regimenting the people, making them unsusceptible to State influence, if need be – as they had done in Paraguay – provoked distrust and jealousy on the part of the State. Its fidelity to the theory of the contractual origin of power competed with that of the divine right of kings underlying Enlightened Despotism. All this explains the elimination of the Society.

Now it is important to assess carefully the after-effects of the Jesuit expulsion on the religious set-up in Goa and the transformations that took place.

It must be recalled that the Jesuits had a religious, social and cultural action of great significance in this territory, especially in Salsete, where, at the time of their banishment, they were administering 25 parishes. Besides this, they were important agents of education (College of St. Ignatius in Rachol, the noviciate in Chorão), and had quite a few missions outside Goa, organized into four provinces: Goa, Malabar, Japan and the vice-province of China.[90]

Obviously, substituting them was not an easy task, above all in the missionary field, for some Bishops who resided therein were Jesuits and besides this there was a great dearth of missionaries.[91]

[90] Cf. our study 'Um Importante Documento ...', p. 245. See the *Mapa das Feitorias* ..., op. cit. or cód. 512, ff. 113-117v which lists the various missions, also indicating the number of missionaries.

[91] See the letter from the Count of Ega to the Secretary of State Tomé Joaquim da Costa Corte Real, of 7 December 1760, in which he takes stock

The Ignatians were replaced in the exercise of their functions by regulars of all other religious families (except the Theatines who were few) and by secular clerics. In order to proceed correctly, certain behavioural norms were prescribed for the selection of new missionaries.[92]

As the Jesuits were the strength of the Portuguese Patronage, their expulsion had an impact. As a result, from the third quarter of the eighteenth century onwards, the Patronage-Propaganda conflict began to aggravate further. By and large, it can be concluded that in the second half of the eighteenth century, the central government did not favour the religious Orders of European origin (Augustinians, Franciscans, Dominicans, and

---

of the results obtained and the difficulties that had cropped up in the missions. He considers the Bishop of Cochin and the Archbishop of Serra responsible for the delay in the substitution of the Jesuits. Cf. A.H.U., *Índia,* cód. 425, ff. 247-9 or cód. 513, ff. 149-153v or maço 99 (86). On 7 April 1761, King D. José I ordained the Count of Ega to proscribe and denaturalize the Archbishop of Serra and the Bishop of Cochin if they did not obey the royal determination to send them to Lisbon (A.H.U., *Índia,* cód. 513, ff. 155-157 and H.A.G., *M. Reino,* Book 118-A, ff. 74-5, in F.U.P., 7-1-1, 14/illegible and 7-1 illegible/2 and 3). This order is repeated in the following year by royal letter from 7 April 1762. Cf. A.H.U., *Índia,* maço 86 (107). But the issue remained unresolved and on 18 April 1764 the King ordained their imprisonment and also that of the rebel Jesuits, in order to place there parish priests by royal appointment. Cf. A.H.U., *Índia,* maço 86 (107). In 1770, the problem was still present, though the number of Jesuit missionaries residing therein had reduced, 'in the shadow' of the Bishop of Cochin and Archbishop of Serra (H.A.G., *M. Reino,* Book 143-A, ff. 245-245v).

[92] In order to substitute the Jesuits in the missions first the prelates of the religious Orders had to be convoked and declare which ecclesiastics could compete for the missions. For the selection of secular clerics too applications had to be made to the Archbishop since there was no sufficient number of regulars. To preclude the reluctance of the Jesuits in leaving the missions, the leaders of the Goa and Malabar provinces had to issue letters of obedience to their missionaries for the missions to be handed over to them undisputedly. The Jesuits would be kept for some time in the mission stations, for the purpose of teaching the new missionaries the dialect and the customs of the country. Cf. the opinion of Marçal José Machado, dated 31 October 1759 (H.A.G., *M. Reino,* Book 132-B, ff. 528-530v).

Jesuits) but supported the new congregations of local regulars (Oratorians and Third Claustral Carmelites). This attitude can perhaps be explained as being a means of counterbalancing the influence of the first group of religious Orders, which had to be abated. However, the State's great bet is now the formation of a local but secular clergy. In fact, the substitution of the regulars by the secular clerics in the parishes (generally sons of the soil) was at one time the cause and effect of the decline of the European religious Orders and the rise of the Goans. We shall deal with it in the pages that follow.

SECULAR CLERGY

Abundant legislation of those years highlights the preference to be given to local clergymen as against the regulars, invoking historical reasons, natural and canon law. Indeed in the first days of the conquest of Goa the European missionaries had assumed responsibility for its evangelization, because of the lack of Goan priests. Meanwhile, down the ages and, particularly, in the second half of the eighteenth century, many local ecclesiastics were ordained. Hence having recourse to the regular European clergy was unjustified, it being unfair 'to snatch the bread from the rightful owner'. Besides knowing the language, the locals fulfilled many other requisites that evidently made them more suited for the pastoral function. Employing the local clergy was a religious policy tried out in the first days of Christianization in the Orient. This orientation was now being taken up again with a renewed vigour.

It may also be noted that the State had contracted heavy burdens of endowment and maintenance of the religious Orders. Hence the interest in forming a secular clergy. In fact, having them did not cause conflict with the prelates of the religious Orders, very conscious of their privileges.

The progress of the policy was stimulated by the following factors: the results obtained in Bassein, whose population remained Christian even after the Maratha conquest in 1739, thanks to the action of the religious clergy; by the latter's contribution to filling up the void caused by the suppression of the Jesuits; and by the effects obtained in the parishes entrusted permanently to secular clerics and some mission stations.

Both by the devotion and the social-cultural promotion that it produced, the opening of the religious calling to the locals was so well taken by them that, in 1750, their number was regarded as excessive. Truly, the central government determined several times that measures be taken such as to prevent the dearth of ministers for churches as well as their unnecessary multiplication. Nonetheless, many clerics continued to be ordained in Goa.[93]

DIOCESAN SEMINARIES

The boost given to the diocesan seminaries, keeping in view the formation of the secular clergy and education of the youth was, so to say, the great challenge for the government throughout the second half of the eighteenth century. Both the civil and ecclesiastical authorities were convinced that this was the best means for educating the clergy and to spread virtues and learning in the population. Hence, their support for the founding of such institutions. The same was not the case with the creation of religious houses that was opposed by the government that at least did not wish to 'multiply the regulars'.[94]

[93] The Marquis of Alorna considers that the edict of the Archbishop D. Frei Lourenço de Santa Maria conferring major orders on the Estado da Índia gave occasion to an excessive number of clerics being ordained. Cf. the opinion of the Overseas Council of 12 March 1750 [A.H.U., *Índia,* maço 77(62) or cód. 214, ff. 65-65v]. On 6 March 1758, the King communicated to the Archbishop the revocation of the royal resolution of 15 March 1750 ordering the observance of the provision of 26 March 1726. By this royal provision the Archbishop had the powers to admit to the Orders, without depending on the opinion of the Viceroy, 'only those individuals who were necessary for the service of the Church, and employment in the Missions ...' (A.H.U., *Índia,* cód. 444, f. 67). At the end of the century, the central government continued recommending the same. See the letter from D. Rodrigo de Sousa Coutinho to the Archbishop, dated 6 March 1799, and that of M.M. Castro to the Archbishop, dated 7 March 1799. Cf. A.C.P.G., *Cópias de cartas régias ...,* ff. 251-251v, in F.U.P., 18-1-8 (21/5 and 21/1) and A.H.U., *Índia,* maço 157 (147), respectively.

[94] The Oratorians wished to set up a third house in the college of Rachol

Upon the expulsion of the Jesuits who, until 1759, had sustained a large number of teaching institutions in Goa, efforts were made to revive clerical training for locals, based on tradition followed in the Seminary of the Holy Faith set up in 1541. In fact this teaching establishment trained Asian ecclesiastics who, after being 'instructed and well formed', proclaimed the Christian doctrine in their lands, in different missions, with very useful results. The same was sought to be done in 1761, with the creation of the college for the boys and indigenous clerics of the East, aimed at ministering a solid Christian education, good philosophical and ecclesiastical preparation and the latest scientific knowledge, as seen from its statutes. Nonetheless, this plan did not come to be. We shall return to this topic in the next chapter.[95]

For several reasons, teaching was entrusted to the Oratorian fathers. The policy of accepting only local Indian clerics (a policy that was very pleasing to the central government) and the fact of their good moral conduct greatly influenced this choice.[96]

Meanwhile, 'for the convenience of the building and the purity of air', the new seminary was shifted from the college of St. Paul (city of Goa) to the old noviciate of the Jesuits on the island of Chorão where it functioned almost throughout the second half of the eighteenth century.[97]

---

which had belonged to the Jesuits (the first was that of the Miracles and the second to the Carmels). On this subject, the letter from Francisco Xavier de Mendonça Furtado to the Count of Ega, dated 4 April 1761 ordered to check out the viability of a foundation of secular clerics (A.H.U., *Índia,* cód. 512, ff. 208-208v or cód. 512, ff. 145v-146). On 23 April 1766, the Count of Oeiras informed the Count of Lousã that the King had till then not resolved, but had rather reflected on the difficulty of arranging local clerics. He continued: 'The King does not wish to multiply the regulars but rather the clerics' (A.H.U., *Índia,* cód. 515, ff. 148-149v).

[95] See fn. 42 in Chapter IV, and the text of the same page and following.

[96] See the letters of the King to the Archbishop and to the Prepositus of the Congregation of St. Philip Nery of the city of Goa, both dated 4 April 1761 (A.H.U., *Índia,* cód. 513, ff. 141-142v and H.A.G., *M. Reino,* Book 118-A, ff. 118-118v in F.U.P., 25/2 and 3 for the first missive; A.H.U., *Índia,* cód. 513, ff. 146-146v and A.C.P.G., *Cópia de Vários Documentos,* ff. 57-57v, in F.U.P., 18-1-8/9).

[97] Cf. the *Cópia do assento no. 1 que acusa na carta atrás* [letter from the

At the time of the founding of the seminary of Chorão (1761) the construction of another one was authorized, at Rachol. This was made possible by Archbishop Neiva Brum, by instituting the seminary with secular clerics of the 'habit of St. Peter' and giving them their statutes (1762).[98]

About ten years later, in 1774, this seminary closed down, apparently for economic reasons. Efforts made by the Archbishop, D. Francisco de Assunção e Brito (1774-83), to revive it were unsuccessful. It resumed activity only in 1781, in response to requests made by the people of Salsete.

In the same year (1781) a third seminary was built – that of the Good Jesus – in the city of Goa.[99] At one point of time, these three seminaries used to prepare a sufficient number of clerics to wholly secure the parishes of Goa and largely assist in the missions.[100]

The interest in seminaries ushered the recruitment of a teaching faculty with a scientific, pedagogic and moral formation.

Count of Ega to the Secretary of State, Francisco Xavier Mendonça Furtado], dated 20 January 1762 and the letter from the Count of Ega to the same, dated 15 January 1762 (A.H.U., *Índia,* cód. 441, ff. 362v and 361-2, respectively). These documents furnish further information on the revenue and expenditure that it involved, on the number of collegiates, the direction and the teaching faculty of the same. Always Oratorians were chosen to be the masters and Dominicans the directors. About the origins of the Jesuit noviciate in Chorão, which functioned till 1759, see Fr Bráulio Guimarães, 'Memória da Congregação da Missão em Portugal' (unpublished), A.P.C.M., Lisbon, n.d.

[98] Refers to diocesan clergy. The seminary of Rachol functioned in the old Jesuit College built in 1609 (first called College of All Saints and then, in 1622, renamed College of St. Ignatius). Set up by the provision of 4 January 1762, it was titled *Good Shepherd* and under the protection of Child God. On its statutes cf. C.C. Nazareth, op. cit., p. 288. About this seminary see *Memória Histórico-Eclesiástica da Arquidiocese de Goa* ..., p. 282, and Father Bráulio Guimarães, *Memórias* ..., op. cit., pp. 171-2.

[99] Letter from M.M. Castro to Frederico Guilherme de Sousa of 1781 re-establishing the seminary of Rachol and creating that of the Good Jesus (A.H.U., *Índia,* cód. 517, ff. 31 and 55-8).

[100] Letter from the Governor dated 6 February 1785. Cf. A.H.U., *Índia,* maço 147 (161). Also the Archbishop informed M.M. Castro on the conclusion of the works and on its activity. Cf. A.H.U., *Índia,* maço 1 A (128).

That explains the coming to Goa of priests of the Mission Congregation, who, besides having those requisites, were also versed in the methods of religious pedagogy. The three seminaries of Goa, hitherto with the Oratorians, then changed hands with the Lazarists who arrived in Goa on 3 October 1779.[101]

For several reasons, and particularly because of the jurisdictional conflicts emanating from the royalist principles adopted by the government, the Vincentians did not stay in the diocese as long as it was foreseen and desired.[102] But in spite of the short span, these priests were able to leave behind a notable work, not only at the seminaries but also in the assistance provided to the people, as we shall see in due course.[103]

---

[101] About the arrival of the Lazarists in Goa in several batches and on the fruitful work done in the seminaries, see Father Bráulio Guimarães, *Memórias ...*, op. cit., pp. 155, 163, 166, 170. On a single occasion there left for Lisbon ten ecclesiastics, in 1782. Further see the interesting letter from 31 December 1799, from António Luís dos Santos, priest of the Congregation of the Mission, who was the rector of the Seminary of Chorão, in which he referred to the need for creating a big seminary. He gave several examples of confirming the advantages that could come from it. Cf. A.H.U., *Índia*, maço 127 (141).

[102] The administrative acts of the Superior General of the Congregation were submitted to the royal sanction. The Italian padres of this Order, accustomed to the severity of the canon law, reacted adversely to this orientation of the Portuguese ecclesiastical authority. Besides, they faced difficulties in adapting themselves to the climate and the nature of the locals. Also the preference of the latter and that of the authorities in general for the Portuguese priests created certain susceptibilities. For all these reasons and with the due authorization they gradually left Goa heading to Lisbon and Italy. See Father Bráulio Guimarães, op. cit., p. 195, *passim* and the letter from 20 February 1785 of M.M. Castro to the Archbishop of Goa [A.H.U., *Índia*, cód. 518, ff. 161-3 or maço 155 (153) or A.C.P.G., *Cópia de Vários Documentos*, ff. 169-169v, in F.U.P., 18-1-9]. The letters of D. Frei Manuel de Santa Catarina to M.M. Castro, of 12 February 1787 and of 6 February 1788, as also that of M.M. Castro to the said prelate, dated 9 April 1788, show the evolution of this problem. Whereas in 1787 the situation appeared calm, in the following year everything indicated that the priests would go away, as they truly did [A.H.U., *Índia*, maço 1 (731); the last from A.C.P.G., *Cópia das Cartas Régias ...*, f. 209, in F.U.P., 18-1-9].

[103] The Governor informed, by letter from 6 February 1785, that many

In the 1790s, because of the exit of the 'Rilhafoles fathers' (as the Lazarists were known), the upkeep of the three seminaries became difficult. Hence the seminary of the Good Jesus had to close down in 1795, though the others remaining functional.[104]

The curriculum followed at the end of the century, in the seminaries of Chorão and Rachol, denotes a sound theological, philosophical, moral and literary training. The teaching and apprenticeship of the practical liturgy, ecclesiastical ethics, plain chant and especially Holy Scriptures were not neglected either. We shall return to this issue in the next chapter.[105]

It may be noted that the internal timetable, though not excessively strict, divided the day between classes, individual study, divine cult, rest and leisure.[106]

It is certain that even at the end of the century there were references to the state of ignorance and the disproportionate number of the secular clerics, the work of these institutions being apparently more quantitative than qualitative in nature. However, the opinions differ widely. It must be remembered that other regulars filled the void left behind by the Jesuits and the clerics ordained in the diocesan seminaries. And in the evening of the century, when along with the decadence of the religious Orders of European origin (Augustinians, Dominicans,

---

ordinands flocked to the three seminaries and that the Lazarists deserved praise for the zeal in their ministry [A.H.U., *Índia,* maço 147 (161) or H.A.G., *M. Reino,* Book 165-A, ff. 179-179v, 181]. Writing to M.M. Castro on 13 April 1791, D. Frei Manuel de Santa Catarina referred to the importance of the seminaries and the fruits they had already produced in Goa. Cf. A.H.U., *Índia,* maço 2 (713). Father Romualdo Ansaloni, Rector of the Seminary of Rachol, in his letter to the Queen, of 4 March 1789, referred to the work done in Goa, mainly in the field of educating the youth. Cf. A.H.U., *Índia,* maço 106 (83).

[104] Letter from Luis Pinto de Sousa to F.A.V. Cabral, dated 12 April 1795 [A.H.U., *Índia,* cód. 520, ff. 66v-67 and maço 86 (107); H.A.G., *M. Reino,* Book 177-B, f. 615]. Tobacco trade was the financial support of the seminaries. Cf. the copy of the letter from M.M. Castro to the Governor, dated 19 March 1781 (A.C.P.G., *Cópia de Cartas Régias,* ff. 122-6, in F.U.P., 18/1-8, 43/2-5 and 44/1-3).

[105] See in Chapter IV, fns. 65 and 66 and the text that refers to it.

[106] See Appendix III.2: *Daily Schedule at the Chorão Seminary.*

and Franciscans) there was also a lack of regulars for the mission stations, it was also the secular clerics who filled in this lacuna.

But the work of the diocesan seminaries grew as they opened their doors to the people by way of the so-called 'public classes'. And thus, to be fair, it must be said that, having no economic distinctions or caste prejudices, they constituted an important factor for cultural and social promotion,[107] to which we shall return in the next chapter.

SECULAR CLERGY IN THE PARISHES

The abundance of local secular clerics and the administration of parishes by regulars would frequently give rise to jurisdictional conflicts and to the question of permanence or not of the clergymen in the diocesan churches. This was an old issue and under D. Inácio de Santa Teresa (1721-40) and D. Fr. Lourenço de Santa Maria e Melo (1744-50), it caused tensions between the ecclesiastical authority and the regular clergy.[108]

With the suppression of the Jesuits, followed by the progressive

[107] The government order of 4 January 1798 established public schools of minor studies in the seminaries of Chorão and Rachol and the extinction of the royal teachers. It determined the admission in these schools of all students wishing to study (H.A.G., *M. Reino,* Book 179-A, f. 95).

[108] See E.R. Hambye, op. cit., pp. 293-4, in which he refers to friction between certain Archbishops of Goa and the regulars, on jurisdictional matters. Also see the judgement of 23 June 1749 on the controversy between Archbishop D. Frei Lourenço de Santa Maria and the prelate of the Observant Franciscans of S. Tomé, for apparently secondary reasons, but sufficient to generate conflict. Thus these regulars who were accustomed to pealing bells to their provincials in the churches of Bardez, were forbidden to do so, this being permitted only for the Archbishop, the Viceroys and Governors. They argued that this prohibition could not be, for the Archbishop did not have jurisdiction for it, once these said churches were *pleno jure* of the Order of Christ; hence, these bells depended on the Grand Master of the Order, and the Bishops had no jurisdiction for such a prohibition. The judgement referred to other provisions of the Archbishop, such as that of the parishioners recognising as parish priests only those Franciscans who carried a provision from the Archbishop. This determination was considered an encroachment on the jurisdiction of the patronage of the Orders ... (A.C.P.G., *Ofícios e Portarias,* Book 1, ff. 114-118v).

occupation of parishes of Salsete and some Islands by secular clerics, this problem of the participation or not of the regulars in parish work was mainly related to Bardez, where the Franciscans had been administering 24 parishes since the sixteenth century.

Above all it is important to see how the Franciscan parish activity went on. Whereas the Franciscans showed great zeal in the initial years of the conquest, by converting and spiritually assisting the populations, the same cannot be said of them in the eighteenth century, particularly in its third quarter.

Thus, many parish tasks, like confession, preaching, administration of the sacraments were undertaken by curates and local clerics whom the Franciscans 'hired' since they did not know the local idiom.[109] It must be stressed, then, that this issue assumed the nature of a linguistic problem. Documentation on the subject always invokes ignorance of the local idiom by the regulars.[110] It may be noted, on the other hand, that in the seventeenth century, the argument forwarded by the Franciscans to prevent the parishes from being administered by secular clerics was that the latter did not know the Portuguese language.[111] Now, around 1760, the secular clerics, under the protection of the Pombaline law that favoured the access of locals to offices, pushed for the

[109] Letter from [...] to the Archbishop, of 1766 (A.H.U., *Índia*, cód. 514, ff. 91-2)

[110] In all their 'representations' to the central government, the Chamber General of Bardez alluded to the ignorance of Konkani by the Franciscans. In that of 30 January 1770 they stated that these regulars 'did not do anything on their own for they did not know the language of this land, hence they got everything done through the sons-of-the-soil clerics and curates ...' (H.A.G., *M. Reino*, Book 148-B, ff. 577-578v and 579-581v).

[111] Thus, in 1648 the Viceroy Francisco de Távora, by suggestion of the Franciscans of Bardez, and in 1732, the central government imposed the use of Portuguese in Goa, instead of Konkani, the local idiom used for preaching and catechism. These provisions became dead letter, but were made use of by the Franciscans in order to oppose the effort of the Archbishop to having them replaced with diocesan priests. Cf. A. Meersman, 'The Suppression of Konkani in Goa', in *Z.M.R.*, LV, 1911, pp. 1-18, cited by E.R. Hambye, op. cit., p. 294 and L.F.F.R. Thomaz, op. cit., p. 23.

removal of Franciscans from Bardez, precisely on linguistic grounds – their ignorance of Konkani.

This fact was a cause for concern for the contemporary authorities, Archbishop D. António and the Governor D. João José de Melo (1768-74). The latter insisted that the Franciscans had 'spoilt' the Konkani chair that formerly their zeal 'had created, so that their flock, versed in it, would take the doctrine to the missions'.[112] Neiva Brum stated that way back in 1628 there were Franciscans already deficient in the local language. He portrayed the situation very realistically, stating that these regulars used to take help from secular clerics to fulfil the main parish duties – 'for even if some of them do understand the language of the land, they do not use it regularly in their ministry, either because they do not know it well enough, or in order to avoid the trouble ...'.[113]

Furthermore, the Franciscans used to not assist the parishioners completely, for they were engaged in other activities – for example, teaching. Professors of Philosophy and Theology teaching at colleges would spend time out of the parish. On the other hand, they were erratic in the church appointments, selecting clerics who were content with rectorships to reside in the churches, and would allot their fees for the definitors to assist in the convents. As a result, the ecclesiastical alms that were meant for the real parish priest for their *de facto* assistance in those parishes, were in fact used in the convents.[114]

Another abuse was the allotment of young clergymen to churches, entrusted to the parish priests, on the pretext of

[112] See the letter from D. João José de Melo to the Secretary of State F.X. Mendonça Furtado, dated 8 February 1770 (H.A.G., *M. Reino,* Book 143-B, ff. 595-7).

[113] Letter from the Archbishop to the same Secretary, of 1770. Cf. A.H.U., *Índia,* maço 134 (134).

[114] In 1758 the church of Candolim given to the definidor Fr. Manuel de Santo Eusébio, was served by Fr. Manuel de Assunção; the church of Pilerne, given to the definidor Fr. João de Santa Quitéria and that of Socorro (Sirulá), given to the definidor Fr. Vicente da Mãe de Deus, were served by other ecclesiastics. Cf. The reply of the State Council to the letter from the Archbishop, dated 14 March 1758 (A.H.U., box 108, published by us in *Epistolário* ..., p. 59).

reducing the expenses of the *comunidade*, without any concern for the danger that these youngsters would be exposed to.[115]

With regard to their moral conduct in Bardez, the regular parish priests lived freely out of the convent and, in the opinion of the Archbishop, this was what most discouraged the Franciscans from continuing in these churches. Sometimes they led a licentious life: 'they bring up lads in great luxury, build them houses, get them married and scandalously live in their houses'. In the opinion of the Archbishop, Neiva Brum, it was the regular parish priests who, were slack, for those who lived by the convent rule would not aspire to work in the parish. He further stated that during the pastoral visits to Bardez, the Franciscans were denounced much more than the secular clerics, hardly an edifying moral sight, contributing to aggravate the dissension between the regular and the secular clergy.[116]

Towards the end of the sixteenth century, there had been attempts on the part of the diocesan prelates to appropriate full jurisdiction over the parishes of Bardez.[117] In the first half of the eighteenth century, the question of replacing the Franciscans with secular clerics in Bardez was raised by the Chamber General of this province, who complained to the King about the abuses noticed. Hence, D. João V ordered the Franciscans to be removed from these lands and replaced by secular clerics; but this royal determination was thwarted by the said regulars.[118]

It must be said that the Chamber General of Bardez actively participated in this process. They often wrote directly to the

[115] See the Archbishop's letter of 1770 to the Secretary of State, referred to in fn. 113. Cf. A.H.U., *Índia,* maço 134 (134).

[116] Ibid.

[117] F. Félix Lopes, 'Os Franciscanos no Oriente Português de 1584 a 1590', in *Stvdia,* 9, Lisbon, 1962, pp. 46-8. The author stated that the argument of ignorance of the local language by the Franciscans was a pretext for the prelates to keep the entire jurisdiction of these lands. By the information that we have collected and described, the situation appears to have evolved in the second half of the eighteenth century, with a great emphasis on the language argument.

[118] Ibid. Back in the seventeenth century, several royal determinations ordered the Archbishops of Goa to appoint secular clerics in the parish churches by competition. See C.C. Nazareth, op. cit., p. 302.

King about the Franciscan irregularities. Indeed, before the final decision to expel the Franciscans from this province in 1766 there had been another 'representation' from this institution.[119]

This royal order was promptly executed by Archbishop Neiva Brum who since the beginning had conveyed this question with solid arguments, as evidenced by his *Dissertação jurídica sobre a jurisdição do diocesano de Goa, nas egrejas administradas pelos regulares.*[120] There was soon a competition for nineteen out of the twenty-four churches of Bardez and these were permanently entrusted to secular clerics. The remaining five remained under the Franciscan jurisdiction for, though all of them belonged to the Crown Patronage, their founders had gifted them to the Franciscan Order. It was only later that they joined the parishes.[121]

Several village *comunidades* as well as the General Procurator of the Province of S. Tomé that belonged to the Franciscan Order had appealed to the King in favour of these regulars, highlighting the work of evangelization that they had done, their knowledge of Portuguese, the injustice and violence that the act represented. But, in spite of having received royal attention, their voice fell on deaf ears.[122] The process was

[119] Ibid.

[120] C.C. Nazareth, op. cit., p. 275, published in the *Boletim Oficial do Estado da Índia,* 1879, nos. 43-57.

[121] Report on the missions sent by the Franciscan Provincial to the Province of S. Tomé, dated 29 January 1770, transcribed by Fr. Achilles Meersman OFM, *Annual Reports of the Portuguese Franciscans in India 1713-1833,* Lisbon, Centro de Estudos Históricos Ultramarinos, 1972, pp. 191-2. The five churches that remained in the possession of the Franciscans for the said reason were: Pomburpá, Penha de França, Reis Magos, Oxel and S. Lourenço de Linhares. Cf. the certificates of the curates of these churches accompanying the representation by the General Chamber of Bardez [January 1779] (H.A.G., *M. Reino,* Book 148-B, ff. 577-578v and 579-581v).

[122] Several villages protested in 1767 against the expulsion of the Franciscans from twenty-four churches of Bardez. The *ganvkars* of Sangolda (7 February) appealed 'in favour of the learned, exemplary and charitable friar, of smooth speaking Portuguese, with zeal and activity that is Franciscan, in contrast with the timid and slack local secular clerics, having no penchant for knowledge' (H.A.G., *M. Reino,* Book 143-B, ff. 841-2). The *ganvkars* of Mapusa (5 February) made a representation to the effect that the appeal by the General Chamber of Bardez was nothing short of 'insanity of some

irreversible indeed, given the new reality: the Franciscan Order had become very lax; numerous clerics who had passed out from the Goa seminaries were in need of a posting – they had a better formation, adaptation to the climate and knowledge of Konkaṇi as well as the locality, for they were locals. Besides this, the fact that these clergymen depended on the jurisdiction of the local Bishop counted a lot. As such, if they infringed on the law, the ecclesiastical authority could immediately intervene without bothering about the complicated privileges of the regulars.[123]

---

people', for it was known from the books of the Chamber and of this village that no powers had been given to make any such application. They alleged that the Franciscans had set up this church with unspeakable zeal and had put up with the poverty of that land (B.N., box 1, ff. 3-3v). Those of Nerul appeared to be worried that their daughters would remain unmarried, since in this way many lads wished to become priests. Cf. A.H.U., *Índia,* maço 26 (50). The General Procurator of the Province of S. Tomé stressed the violence that the royal order meant, as for many years [about two centuries and a half] the Franciscans had held the evangelization of Bardez. Cf. A.H.U., *Índia,* maço 85 (108). By virtue of these protests, the King asked the Governor and the Archbishop to give their opinion on the question. In their letters to the Secretary of State, dated 8 February 1770 and of the year 1770, respectively, these authorities countered the reasons advanced by the Provincial of the Observants. Both stated that their complaint would be worthy of note considering the valuable services rendered by the Franciscans in the 'India of old and in the subsequent years', but that it was unjustified in the epoch in question. Although they tackled the problem differently, generally speaking, they pointed the most serious anomalies of these regulars, contrasted them with the secular clerics and stood by the advantages that the latter offered over the former. Hence their opinion that the 19 parishes ought not to be restored to the Franciscans.

[123] In the beginning of the second half of the eighteenth century, there was a similar situation in the Philippines, inasmuch as the regular clergy enjoyed a supreme position vis-à-vis the ecclesiastical authority and in some fields even with relation to the civil authority. Whereas in Goa, the religious scene inflected in the sense of a progressively higher implantation of the local secular clergy to the detriment of the regular European clergy, in the Philippines the victory belonged to the religious Orders who maintained the curacy of the parishes and as such their importance in this insular society. On the subject, see Maria Fernanda Arcos, *Estado y Clero en las Filipinas del Siglo XVIII,* Mexico, 1988.

From the viewpoint of canon law too, the Franciscan position in Bardez had changed. The bull *Exponi nobis* of 1552 had entrusted the twenty-four parishes of Bardez to the Observant Franciscans, in the absence of secular clerics. It was thus a privilege 'precarious, interim and conditional'. During the time under consideration secular clerics abounded, and in the opinion of some contemporaries, they were better prepared and cultured. Consequently this privilege should have stopped, as in fact it had happened with the parishes of Salsete and the island of Goa. It may indeed be noted that the bull *Quamvis ad confirmandum* (1746) of Benedict XIV forbade the regulars from taking up services that involved the curing of souls.[124] Also, in relation to the five parishes still administered by the Franciscans, it was argued that the concession had been made to the Franciscans as parish priests.

Indeed the events evolved in the sense of having even those five parishes and their parish houses entrusted to seculars, notwithstanding the great resistance put up by the Franciscans. At the end of the eighteenth century, there was not a single church in Goa, or even in the province of Ilhas, under administration of these regulars.[125]

[124] The General Chamber of Bardez invoked some legal points, at the level of canon law, in their 'representation' of 30 January 1770 (H.A.G., *M. Reino,* Book 148-B, ff. 577-578v and 579-581v).

[125] Several royal provisions to the Archbishop determined that the regulars should be substituted by local parish-priests, through competition (charter of 7 April 1774; Instruction of 1774). Cf. A.H.U., *Índia,* maço 124 (109). But the Franciscans several times presented their desire to keep the said five churches of Bardez as they had been gifted to the Order. Their provincial too vouched for the good conduct of his ecclesiastics. Thus the question dragged on for many years. As D. Maria had ordered that the missions be restored to the religious Orders, there rose the doubt whether this determination should be extended to the parishes, with the regulars put back in them. See the letter from the Archbishop for [...], of 20 April 1778 [A.H.U., *Índia,* maço 125 (110)] and C.C. Nazareth, op. cit., p. 302. Finally the royal charter of 5 March 1779 decided on the removal of the regulars from the parishes. In the face of new resistance from the Franciscans, the Board of Conscience and Orders opined that the said charter be observed and if the parties felt oppressed they would used the caveat of 'obreption e subreption'. Cf. the letter from M.M. Castro to Frederico Guilherme de Sousa, dated 9 March 1781 (A.H.U., *Índia,* cod.

The Primatial See had been once a prestigious institution, with a large chapter. In the second half of the eighteenth century, though the chapter still remained so, there were some signs of decadence. This situation was possibly a reflection of the degeneration which the city of Goa found itself in and whose pristine splendour the central government sought to maintain at all cost.[126]

Portuguese-born secular clerics used to be traditionally appointed dignitaries of the Primatial See. At the time under consideration, this norm too was to be altered by the central government. Truly, to be fair to the 'representation' by the General Chamber of Bardez, there prevailed indeed a case of injustice and uncouth ambience in the See, for not a single local cleric was admitted and it was full of 'men provided they were whites, so ignorant that they do not even know the Latin language perfectly'.[127]

517, ff. 58-58v, 61-61v). He was also of the opinion that the residential houses of the churches, the gifts and testamentary provisions made to the church should continue to belong to the secular parish-priests (Opinion of 2 April 1783. A.C.P.G., *Cópia de cartas régias* [illegible], ff. 156-8 in F.U.P. 18-1-9, 51/1-4). On 13 March 1784, the Archbishop informed M.M. Castro about the expulsion of the Franciscans from the [church residential] houses of Reis Magos, Penha de França and Pomburpa. Cf. A.H.U., *Índia,* maço 115 (122).

[126] In the pastoral visit to the See in 1779, the witness of the denouncers pointed towards certain symptoms of decline (A.C.P.G., *Visitas Pastorais,* 1779, Primatial See, vols. 16-17, ff. 1-17v). In 1557 the chapter of the See comprised five dignitaries: dean, chantor, treasurer, archdeacon, and *mestre escola*; 10 canons, 4 semi-canons and 2 quartenarius; 1 *mestre de canto,* 12 singers, 6 choir boys and 1 grammar teacher (cf. our study, *Um Importante Documento* ..., p. 244). In 1779, even though still numerous, it had fewer members: 10 canons, 7 chaplains, 1 chantor, 1 subchantor, 1 quartenarius, 1 curate and 1 subtreasurer (*V. Pastorais,* 1779, Primatial See, vols. 16-17, ff. 2-17v).

[127] See the *Cópia da Representação que os Ecclesiásticos Seculares Naturais de Goa* ... (B.P.A.D.E., cód. CXVI/2-11, no. 32) and *Instrucções* ..., Third Instruction to the Archbishop, pp. 13-14. The former stated that in the absence of Portuguese ecclesiastics [read Reinóis], instead of admitting Goans the Chinese and illegitimate were appointed, 'both by defect of birth, as of the caste of the Portuguese, with whom there is only a small

These scandals resulting from exclusiveness of the clerics of Portuguese lineage in the See and from the presupposition that the locals were not fit to rise to these high posts, pretty much prompted the drafting of the charter of 2 April 1761. And there having been complaints that it was not being implemented in Goa, the charter of 7 April 1774 and the Instrucções to the Governor and the Archbishop were issued in the same year.

Thus, with regard to the appointment of dignitaries, canonships and other privileges of the Primatial See the alternate selection of a local secular cleric and clerics of Portuguese lineage in the appointment of the ecclesiastical dignitaries was implemented. The same criterion was to be adopted for the appointment of other members of the chapter, but with a two-third Indian component.[128]

All the same, this norm was probably not always respected, as testified by the representation of the General Chamber of Bardez (1781). The complaint, therefore, was that the canonships and dignitaries of the See were being occupied by Reinóis with little culture and qualities to the detriment of locals and it was requested that the royal charter of 7 April 1774 be observed.[129]

This testimony leads us to believe that something must have happened similar to what we have seen with regard to the entry of Indians into religious Orders. However, in spite of the local resistance to the royal determinations, Goan ecclesiastics did enter gradually into this institution. Though we do not have exhaustive data to quantify it, the few pieces of information on the capitularies of the See, in the period under study, are suggestive of such a situation.[130]

---

ratio of whites, being children of Ordinary Parents ...'. Hence in the See there was total idiocy. The Marquis of Pombal referred to the existence of 10,000 clerics, which is a highly exaggerated number.

[128] *Instrucções* ..., Third Instruction to the Archbishop, p. 18.

[129] Representation made by the General Chamber of Bardez, dated 27 January 1781. Cf. A.H.U., *Índia,* maço 82 (78).

[130] There is no list of capitulars in the See for the period before Archbishop Santa Catarina. Canon Francisco Xavier da Costa sought to fill in this lacuna by collecting matter on them from the chapel records, deeds, wills, etc., wherefore it results that the list is, evidently, very inadequate.

Besides entry in the Cathedral Chapter, the locals aspired to other ecclesiastical posts, such as advocates of the court-room and the ecclesiastical court, vicars, visitors, episcopal Governors.[131]

In the last quarter of the eighteenth century, the conflicts between the Patronage and the Propaganda became more intense: the vicars apostolic entered the lands of the Patronage clandestinely, exercised pastoral activity unmindful of the norms of the royal sanction and the Goa Metropolitan jurisdiction.[132] Thus the entry and exit of the missionaries in the East went out of hand. Several measures were taken to maintain the Portuguese Patronage of the Orient; the propagandists present in the East were even sent to Goa under arrest, and the Pope was urged to punish the criminals, but to no great avail.[133]

Hence, it is not possible to draw safe conclusions (*Série dos Capitulares da Sé Primacial de Goa com Apêndices e Notas,* Nova Goa, 1915).

[131] Cf. *Memória Histórico-Eclesiástica* ..., pp. 175-84, 210 and 215, and *A Voz de S. Francisco Xavier,* Year III, nos. 41 and 45, Goa, 1934. About the duties of the dignitaries, as also those of the other members comprising the chapter, see the regiment of the See, 1614, still in force in the year 1792, in *Studia,* 9 (1961), pp. 251 and ss.

[132] Though the present study is limited to Goa, we present here in broad outline the Patronage-Propaganda conflict at the end of the eighteenth century for it was a quite a serious problem of the archbishopric of Goa. Letters by the prelate make a reference to attempts of the Propagandists in the churches of their diocese, to money and power they wield. Cf. A.H.U., *Índia,* maço 110 (126). In his letter [to D. Frei Manuel de Santa Catarina], dated 10 March 1781, M.M. Castro referred to the 'erratic behaviour of Father Matias Therpensel and his ally Ricardo da Silva who did not wish to recognize subjection to the Metropolis nor to the ecclesiastical Governor sent by the Archbishop Primate' (A.C.P.G., *Cópia de Vários Documentos,* ff. 114, in F.U.P., 18-1-8, 40/5).

[133] *Instrucções* ..., Sixth Instruction, 'Attempts of the alleged Missionaries and Vicars Apostolic appointed by the Propaganda ..., inflexible resistance with which their violent encroachments should be repelled in a natural and necessary defence of the Royal Patronage ...', pp. 37-43. Several grounds of juridical and moral nature are invoked, such as the exclusion of foreigners from the services of any kingdom, the existence of 'more than ten thousand local clerics' [a false figure, though]. It also considered the possible action against them: that the Propagandists making a confession or absolution should be denounced, without licence and that the crown judge should proceed against them.

In some cases, the authorities temporized with the Congregation of the Propaganda Fide. It was so in 1780, when two priests whom the said Congregation had assigned to mission stations in China were authorized to reside in Macao.[134]

The problem turned particularly serious in Bombay, where the vicars apostolic, besides assailing the jurisdiction of the Archbishop of Goa, requested the British company to transfer the churches of this circumscription and of Mahim to the Propagandists so as to put an end to the disorders. It so happened that the Portuguese priests in these churches, being subjects of the Archbishop of Goa, would not swear allegiance to that government. The Company acceded and the Portuguese priests were consequently removed from ten to twelve parishes.[135] After the British conquest of Bassein in 1775, the Propagandists requested a similar action in the nineteen churches of that city, which were entrusted to a dean under the jurisdiction of the Archbishop of Goa. Even though the president of the Company did not grant the request, yet the risks facing the mission stations of Salsete and Thana were obvious.[136]

[134] By virtue of the pretensions of the Propagandists and the great inconvenience they had been causing and since it was the first time that ecclesiastics of the Propaganda were being allowed to reside in Macao, the Queen ordered that the missionaries sign a stipulation in the Secretariat of State. Cf. the letter from M.M. Castro to [the Bishop of Cochin] dated 15 March 1780 (A.C.P.G., *Cópia de Vários Documentos,* ff. 108v-109, in F.U.P., 18.1.8, 39, 1/3). Also in 1770, D. João José de Melo was of the opinion that the Propaganda Fide Bishop should be rewarded who had solicited permission to embark from the Goa port, in order to undertake a visit to the Christian population of Bombay and Surat. This Bishop with the title of *Assuritano* resided in Karwar, of the jurisdiction of Hyder Ali Khan. Cf. the letter to Francisco Xavier de Mendonça Furtado [A.H.U., *Índia,* maço 107 (84) and H.A.G., *M. Reino,* Book 145-A, f. 243].

[135] The vicar apostolic of Mogol, Frei Maurício de Santa Teresa left for Bombay along with his confreres. On this occasion, a proclamation was made without the intervention of London, but only by the Company. The Propagandists settled in Bombay requested that they be issued a provision in the name of the King of Great Britain and of the Company, to serve them as a title (A.C.P.G., *Cópia de Vários Documentos,* ff. 185-186v), in F.U.P., 18-1-8, 40/5.

[136] Ibid., ff. 187-8. After the conquest of Bassein, Frei Carlos de S.

The existence of two parallel powers – the Crown Patronage and the Propaganda – made the situation particularly difficult. Arguments invoking fidelity to the respective superiors were frequent. On their part, the Propagandists stated that the oath made in Lisbon to not act against the Patronage did not carry any water and that the Portuguese Crown Patronage did not extend beyond their dominions.[137]

After many years, in 1786, the Court of Rome offered to resolve the problem, by having the Propagandists removed from the mission areas of the Patronage; but perhaps because the Queen hesitated and the Archbishop of Goa adopted an intransigent attitude, the problem remain unresolved and worsened in the following century.[138]

Conrado, vicar apostolic of the Mughal Empire entered and other Propagandists as well, particularly Frei Clemente and Frei Angélico de S. José.

[137] Ibid., ff. 188-9.

[138] Cf. the letter from M.M. Castro to the Archbishop, dated 26 February 1786, in which he asks him to certify the number of clerics existing in Goa. He wished to know if they were sufficient for the pastoral ministry and if they Propagandists could be dispensed with [A.H.U., *Índia,* maço 150 (158) and cód. 519, ff. 38-40]. In his reply of 20 January 1787 the Archbishop opined that there was no need for the Propagandists since at the head of almost all the parishes there were clerics or friars from Goa. Cf. A.H.U., *Índia,* maço 1-A (728). In another letter from 11 February 1787, he stated that he was not insisting on the Propagandists leaving Bombay, for he thought it would lead to greater disorders, as they would approach the Anglican government; nevertheless, if M.M. Castro found the task easy, he would be doing a great service to God. Cf. A.H.U., *Índia,* maço 1-A (728). On 7 March 1789 the Archbishop communicated to M.M. Castro the decision of the Governor of Bombay to order the exit of the Propagandists but on condition of reserving for himself the possibility of expelling from the churches those ecclesiastics who did not have a good conduct or were offensive to the government. The Archbishop did not agree, 'for being heretics and most of them perverts, they will seize the opportunity to get rid of those they cannot stand'. Cf. A.H.U., *Índia,* maço 1-A (728).

THE NEW CONSTITUTIONS OF THE ARCHBISHOPRIC

Way back in 1606, at the time of celebrating the Fifth Provincial Council of Goa, the Constitutions of this archbishopric had become obsolete and needed reform. It was the Archbishop D. António T.N. Brum da Silveira who, rising to the occasion, drew from the Constitutions of Oporto and Bahia and at the same time sought to adapt the existing ecclesiastical laws to the customs and practices in India. The experience gathered on his pastoral visits to the provinces of Ilhas, Bardez and Salsete also played an important role in the composition of this eighteenth-century religious work.[139]

It may be noted that, in Brazil too, the Archbishop of Bahia, D. Sebastião Monteiro de Vide (1702-22), had adapted ecclesiastical laws to the local situation, despite attempts by the Inquisition to annul any innovation. Thus appeared the *Constituições Primeiras do Arcebispado da Bahia.*[140]

A man of his age who directed important tasks in the archbishopric he was heading (as referred to earlier), he could not afford to turn away from the change of mentality that was operating in Goa. The new Constitutions thus stood as a symbol of the changing times.

As compared to their sixteenth-century counterparts, there are perceptible differences both in the structure of the work and its contents. The author indeed divided these Constitutions

[139] See the prologue to these Constitutions. Cf. the letter from D. Frei Manuel de Santa Catarina to [...], dated 16 January 1781 (A.H.U., *Índia,* maço 134 (134). In fact, the Constitutions of Oporto and Bahia figure in the list of books belonging to the Archbishop Neiva Brum (cf. M.J.M. Lopes, *Epistolário* ..., p. 185). The first Constitutions had been approved in 1567 at the First Provincial Council of Goa (*Constituiçoens do Arcebispado de Goa Approvadas pello Primeiro Cõcilio Prouincial. Anno 1568,* Lisbon, 1592, or 'Constituições do Arcebispado de Goa 1568', published in *Documentação para a História do Padroado Português do Oriente. Índia,* coligida e anotada por António da Silva Rego, vol. 10 (*1566-1568*), Agência Geral do Ultramar, 1953, pp. 481-809).

[140] Cf. Caio C. Boschi, 'As Visitas Diocesanas e a Inquisição na Colónia', in *Inquisição. Actas do 1° Congresso Luso-Brasileiro sobre Inquisição,* coord. by Maria Helena Carvalho dos Santos, vol. II, Lisbon, 1989, pp. 965-6.

into five books on broad thematic areas, further subdivided into titles and these into constitutions, which resulted in a better arrangement of topics.[141]

But it is the theme that best sets it apart from the earlier Constitutions. However, it may be noted that the latter, being shorter, devote more attention to subjects of formal and extrinsic nature, which were considered less important in the Constitutions of the eighteenth century. On the other hand, the latter dwell in greater detail on other aspects that are not present in those of the sixteenth century. This is because the latter portray a rebellious society, little cultured and primitive, in which the lawmaker had to define the subjects with a lot of precision. Meanwhile, more than two centuries had gone by on Christianity and the consequent assimilation of cultures. Added to this there was the Hindu heritage and other Oriental philosophies, all of which had created a more developed society.

It can be said that the Constitutions of the eighteenth century were aimed at a basic objective, that of interiorising the acts and religious practice. Hence pecuniary penalties, so significant in the Constitutions of the sixteenth century, were now replaced by others in which the moral factor carried more weight, such as admonition, excommunication, etc.[142]

The entire work was imbued with great humanity and understanding which translated into an attitude of openness to bring the highest number of souls possible into the bosom of the Catholic Church. Hence various cases are considered in which children and adults can be baptized by persons other than priests; several options are presented allowing neo-converts to comply with baptism and Christian matrimony; attenuating factors and paths of Christian reconciliation are devised for

[141] The *Constituições* of the sixteenth century were not grouped into books but in titles and these into constitutions. Their titles are fewer in number and as such the work is smaller; the logical sequence between the subjects does not become as clear as in the Constitutions of the eighteenth century.

[142] Cf., for example, *Constituições* ..., Book III, Tit. I, Const. VII, pp. 182-3, in which games are forbidden to the clerics. No pecuniary penalties are specified. It only states that 'he shall be punished as deemed fit'.

excommunicated persons; the rights of the slaves are defended, etc.[143]

These Constitutions also endeavour to find a solution for the problems of the archbishopric. Thus, for example, as the want of clerics for the cure of souls, missionaries, and confessors was greater than that of minor Orders, it was determined that the tonsured should be ordained only if found to be fit in Latin and if capable of hearing confessions and tending to the souls.[144] These Constitutions also analysed the relations between Christianity and Hindu beliefs. In a multi-religious society like that of Goa, further enlarged by the incorporation of Hindu populations of the New Conquests, issues like the various forms of superstition and non-Christian religious practices, as also inter-religious marriages, were pressing issues, and were therefore given special attention in this religious work.[145]

It may be noted that the humanity and understanding present in dealing with the subjects did not in any way mean acquiescence on the fundamental points of Christian doctrine and living.[146] Quite the reverse. These aspects were dealt here with greater strictness and exigency than in the Constitutions of the sixteenth century and in the economy of the work they translated into a great number of titles and constitutions. It is the case of the qualifications demanded for the entry and the ordination of the clerics, in the selection of confessors and preachers, etc. Thus together with great humanity, the new Constitutions are very firm in the treatment of the subjects, above all the aspects considered being a priority. Hence, following the principles of the Tridentine reform, they do not temporize, among other things, with situations undefined between the sacred and the profane, neglect in the fulfilment of religious duties, the lack of respect towards the sacred.[147]

143 The midwife must be prepared to baptize babies in risk of life and even if there be a man it behoves her to do it, which is different in the constitutions of the sixteenth century (Tit. II). Cf. Book I, Tit. III, Const. VIII, p. 27.

144 Cf. Book I, Tit. VIII, Const. II, p. 87.

145 See Book I, Tit. IX, Const. XI, p. 125.

146 See Book I, Tit. I, Consts. V-VII, pp. 8-11.

147 Cf. Book II, Tit. I, Const. XI, pp. 152-3.

In order to better emphasize this attempt at characterising the Constitutions, let us review the five books they are made up of. Faith being 'the principle and basis of salvation', and the latter 'the final end of these Constitutions', it is treated in quite some detail.[148] Great stress is laid on the need for parents to teach their children the Christian doctrine, the lords, their slaves; the masters, their students; the parish priests, their parishioners.[149] Next comes a general inquiry into all the sacraments, the necessary requisites and their effects. In this respect, the interior dispositions to be adopted by the recipients and those administering the sacraments are highlighted.[150] In relation to baptism, what stands out is the concern for the salvation of all mankind, right from the handicapped child to the most humble slave so often forgotten.[151]

Hence, unlike the earlier Constitutions, the sacrament of Holy Eucharist, which in the structure of this work precedes that of Penance, is taken up with great seriousness. It highlights its vital importance as the spiritual sustenance for the soul. The practice of the Eucharist is sought to be extended to all those fit to receive it. Particular care is recommended with the infirm, not only in the administration of this sacrament but also that of confession and extreme unction.[152]

Regarding confession, it may be noted that these Constitutions do not deal with this duty as the final end. The penitent must have contrition of his sins committed and a firm resolution of correction. Perhaps herein lies the main difference between these Constitutions and those of the sixteenth century – the fundamental importance given to the interior conversion. A

[148] Cf. Book I, Tit. I, Const. I, p. 1.

[149] Cf. Book I, Tit. I, Consts. III-IV, pp. 6-7.

[150] Those who are going to receive Confirmation, Holy Eucharist, Extreme Unction, Holy Orders and Matrimony 'should go in a state of grace to God, repenting for all their faults with true contrition ...'.

[151] Cf. Book I, Tit. III, Consts. IV-VI, pp. 20-5.

[152] Parish priests ought to be not only diligent in taking the Eucharist to them, but also in finding out about the existing infirm and advising them to receive it. The same care must be taken in relation to confession and extreme unction of the sick (Book I, Tit. V, Const. VIII, pp. 47-51; Tit. VI, Const. VII, pp. 67-8; Tit. VII, Const. II, pp. 83-5).

certain benevolence in the penalties to be applied to the penitents is also noticed.[153]

As regards holy orders, these Constitutions are stricter than the earlier ones, distinguishing the aspects referring to each one of them. The degree of exigency attached to the qualifications for the priesthood increases progressively from the minor orders to the holy orders, culminating, thus, with that of the presbitery.[154]

When dealing with the sacrament of matrimony they propose a strict investigation of the impediments for its realization.[155] Clandestine marriages must not have been rare, and this led the Archbishop, a good judge of these problems, to legislate on them. And seeking to find other common problems in the archdiocese, relating to the marriage of the slaves and of the neo-converts, Neiva Brum considers them in two distinct constitutions. They made clear the slave's right to marriage and that no master could oppose it.[156]

In relation to the neo-convert, they also defend an attitude of understanding albeit blended with firmness. He need not cut off the already existing matrimonial ties but is invited to live according to God's law.[157]

[153] Penance should be proportional to the status, condition, sex, age, and faults. Public penances for hidden sins are forbidden however grave they may be. Cf. Book I, Tit. VI, Const. IV, p. 61.

[154] The presbyter could not say the new mass with special licence, without doing spiritual exercises for eight to ten days, without being examined by the *mestre-escola* (Chapter theologian) at the Primatial See on the ceremonies of the sung mass. Cf. Book I, Tit. VIII, Const. X, p. 103. The attribution of the first tonsure to an individual would be preceded by a confidential account of his life and habits and by a strict examination, made by authoritative persons. Cf. Book I, Tit. VIII, Const. II, pp. 86-7.

[155] Cf. Book I, Tit. IX, Consts. III-VIII, pp. 106-20.

[156] A careful religious preparation had to precede the reception of the sacrament of matrimony by the slave. Cf. Book I, Tit. IX, Const. X, pp. 122-3.

[157] If the neo-convert has a wife, he shall remain married to her, as long as the latter converts and he shall be given two months to do the same. If the wife does not wish to convert, the Christian shall consider having nothing to do with such a tie. If the convert had several wives during his

Let us proceed to Book II. Here the Mass is undoubtedly the fundamental theme treated at considerable length. Standing out among the important requisites for a priest celebrating Mass are interior purity, piety and the exterior devotion. An ambience of recollection and of respect for the sacred is also demanded, hence the ban on 'profane songs, feasts, dances…'.[158] Then a mention is made of some related anomalies, such as the faulty method of prayer, the 'business' of Masses, their celebration by ecclesiastics having some impediment. They contrive measures to curb these deviations.[159] And absence from Mass because of work on Sundays, servile jobs and mechanical work are all categorically prohibited, except in cases of extreme necessity.[160]

Whereas Book II is directed essentially to the faithful, the object of Book III is the Clergy. The several aspects taken up in this book include the moral and religious profile of the clergyman in general, who after the ordination becomes 'a new man, different in all things from what he was earlier'. Title I of this book covers, among other points, moderation, moral integrity and unity of life, keeping in mind the efficacy of the example and as such the responsibility of the clergyman in living a virtuous life.[161]

Among the priestly duties, processions and preaching are the focus of attention. Considering processions as cultic acts in which God is acknowledged as the Supreme Lord from Whom material and spiritual benefits are implored, certain norms are set on its organization. Other indications aim at steering clear of controversies on pagan precedence and practices, with an express ban on 'lascivious figures, dishonest representations or any other profane ones'. Also interdicted are live figures in the procession on Maundy Thursday and Passion scenes.[162]

Hindu days, he shall consider the first one as the legitimate wife who, to be so in reality shall have to convert. Cf. Book I, Tit. IX, Const. XI, pp. 123-5.

[158] Cf. Book II, Tit. I, Const. XI, pp. 152-3.

[159] While saying Mass the priests 'shall not be so hasty as to cause scandal, nor as slow as to trouble the faithful' (Book II, Tit. I, Const. II, p. 141). See Book II, Tit. I, Consts. VII, VIII and XII, pp. 147-51 and 153-4.

[160] Cf. Book II, Tit. II, Const. II, p. 161.

[161] Cf. Book III, Tit. I, Const. I, pp. 177-8.

[162] Cf. Book III, Tit. II, Const. II, p. 191.

Another duty of the priest that the Constitutions lay great stress upon is that of 'giving his sheep the Spiritual Pasture of the word of God, very necessary for the salvation of their souls'. For the souls not to be deprived of the spiritual fruit of preaching, it was within the Archbishop's power to grant licences only to those priests who had a good theological background and impeccable moral conduct.[163]

The Constitutions devote Book IV to the church in its diverse aspects and, finally, Book V to various deviations and the application of penalties. We shall refer to them when we discuss Pastoral Visits.

ASSISTANCE AND WELFARE

The Portuguese missionaries in the East made their presence felt not only in the conversion of Hindus to the Christian faith; another facet of their activity consisted of assistance provided to the converts, the poor and socially disfavoured. The merit of taking the initiative in this field went to the missionaries, and their unconformity vis-à-vis the indigence of the local inhabitants certainly helped the progress of Christianization. Conversions and social welfare were, thus, the two great pillars and instruments of civilising action.

This had become a greater challenge in India, where race and caste prejudices would not allow the neo-converted Hindu to stay with the family. Missionaries had to ensure the subsistence and the social adjustment of the neo-converts. Hence, every religious Order established in Goa had orphanages, catechumenates and hospitals too. As is known, the State used to give these new Christians certain public offices, which with the passage of time often became associated with this ethnic-religious group.

Goa's charitable institutions of the second half of the eighteenth century mostly dated back to soon after the conquest. Worthy of mention are some hospitals and hospices, meticulously organized and with an acceptable quality of service. Also their pharmaceutical establishments used to supply the people with

[163] Cf. Book III, Tit. IV, Const. I, pp. 199-201.

ready medicines, reportedly, hygienic and reasonably priced.[164]

Meanwhile, other hospital establishments were set up in Goa by royal initiative. These include the Royal Hospital, at the time of Afonso de Albuquerque, the Hospital of All Saints, of Our Lady of Piety, all maintained by the Senate of Goa, and that of the Lazarists (suppressed in 1740), entrusted to the Holy House of Mercy. In these institutions too the missionaries generally worked with zeal and dedication.[165] In fact, the administration of the Royal Hospital was in Jesuit hands almost uninterruptedly from 1579 to 1759 and after their expulsion, with the Hospitallers of St. John of God.[166] Towards the end of the sixteenth century and beginning of the seventeenth, a European traveller to India was all praise for this institution of assistance. Hence, Pyrard de Laval (*c.* 1607) considered it the best in the world, stating that the Jesuits administered it with great dignity.[167] However, in the

[164] The Franciscans had a hospice at Monte de Guirim. Between 1550 and 1568 the Jesuit Paulo Camerino had founded a hospital for the poor Indians in the city of Goa, which was later transferred to Margão and Rachol. In 1690 the Hospitaller Brothers of St. John of God built a hospital in front of the Augustinian convent. The creation of a little hospital in Rachol by the Franciscans dates back to the second half of the eighteenth century (*c.* 1760). About the hospitals founded by the religious Orders in the sixteenth century and still functional in the second half of the eighteenth century, see C.C. Nazareth, *Clero de Goa, Seus serviços à Religião e à Nação,* Nova Goa, 1927, pp. 139-41; *Memória Histórico-Eclesiástica,* pp. 56-7, 336-8, and E.R. Hambye, op. cit., pp. 325, 326, 328.

[165] See *Memória Histórico-Eclesiástica* ..., pp. 336-8; and A. Lopes Mendes, *A Índia Portuguesa,* vol. I, pp. 61-2.

[166] On the subject, consult Banha de Andrade, 'Hospitaleiros de S. João de Deus na Índia', in *Portugal em África,* XIV (1957), 80, pp. 110-15; and Fátima da Silva Gracias, *Health and Hygiene in Colonial Goa (1510-1961),* New Delhi, 1994.

[167] The Jesuit administrator was the head of all the officials; he was in charge of the temporal and spiritual direction of the institution; two Jesuit priests were in charge of consoling the infirm and administering the sacraments to them. Jesuit novices went round the city collecting old linen clothes to provide thread for the hospital. More information about the building, the diet, aspects of in-house life, can be collected from *Viagem de Francisco Pyrard de Laval* ..., vol. II, pp. 11-19.

second half of the seventeenth century this hospital became increasingly decadent.[168]

The Holy House of Mercy, founded in Goa between 1516 and 1517, on the lines of the one is Lisbon, was a purely Portuguese institution transported to numerous cities overseas. Managed by fifteen brothers, it was presided over by a *provedor*, or purveyor, who was to administer it well. Frequently this post fell on prominent political figures, like the Governor Filipe Valadares Sotto Mayor and Archbishop D. António T.N.B. da Silveira. Hence, he was often substituted with the secretary who assisted him.[169]

Initially composed of Portuguese men married in India, the brotherhood of the Holy House of Mercy got its first Goan brother only in 1720. It enjoyed the same rights as its Lisbon counterpart, in 1765 it requested certain privileges that had been granted to the latter in the earlier century, such as exemption from military service and the benefit of life or triennial posts 'in the vacancy of the appointments', for its old department officials.[170]

Besides the subsidy given by the Crown, the Holy House

[168] Sometimes, the Jesuits were blamed for the lack of neatness and assistance in the hospital, and it was even proposed to replace them by the Brothers of St. John of God, which indeed happened in 1759 (Banha de Andrade, op. cit., pp. 110-12 and Fátima Gracias, op. cit., pp. 231-4).

[169] See E.R. Hambye, op. cit., pp. 322-3 and José F. Ferreira Martins, *História da Misericórdia de Goa,* 3 vols., Nova Goa, 1910, 1912 and 1914.

[170] Cf. the favourable opinion by the Attorney of the Crown and Royal Revenue dated [8] January 1765, on the application of the Holy House. The privileges they invoked dated 1639 (H.A.G., *M. Reino,* Book 137-A, ff. 47-47v). Also cf. the application made by this institution on 14 April 1766 (A.H.U., *Índia,* cód. 214, ff. 254v-256). There is information of certain jurisdictional conflicts between the Misericórdia and the Archbishops of Goa, but in the documentation consulted we did not find any that may have taken place in the second half of the eighteenth century. In 1610, Archbishop D. Manuel de Souza de Menezes ordained the suspension of the confessor appointed by the purveyor to hear confession and exempt the recluse women and declared excommunication of the said women in the retreat houses. See the copies of the letters of the King to the Count Viceroy, dated 27 November 1683, and that of the King to the purveyor and Brothers of the Misericórdia, dated 26 February 1686 (A.C.P.G., *Cópias de Vários Documentos,* ff. 6, 12-13, in F.U.P., 18-1-8/9).

received several gifts and legacies, as also some trade profits. Nevertheless, with the fall of the Northern Province and the consequent ruin of the bankrupt debtors, the Holy House lost many benefits. It is amidst these financial difficulties that its purveyor, Filipe de Valadares Sotto Mayor, requested that the assets of those dying *ab intestatio* and without heirs up to the tenth degree, in the State of India and on voyage ships, should revert to the said institution.[171] In 1788, the Mozambican Holy House was ordered to send the proceeds of the inheritances of the dead and absent, as was their duty.[172]

The Holy House had multiple duties. Besides managing their hospital, they looked after the orphans, widows, those in risk, sought to salvage the captives and cure the indigent sick, etc. They were also entrusted the administration of two institutions, from 1610 to 1611 – the Recolhimento de Nossa Senhora da Serra and the Santa Maria Madalena, founded in 1605 by the Archbishop, D. Frei Aleixo de Menezes, who was the pioneer of women's education in Goa.

The former looked after the education and instruction of spinster daughters of the 'honest' families; the latter sheltered women guilty of certain faults and desirous of correction.

The State consigned some amounts to these institutions and granted some benefits such as marriage dowry for the former orphans of the Recolhimento de Nossa Senhora da Serra. This privilege of the past was still the accepted norm in the beginning of the second half of the eighteenth century. This is attested by the various dowry letters to orphans of the principal families of the kingdom granting two posts, letters transferring benefits to family members, or promotion to the next post granted to soldiers marrying these orphans.[173]

[171] Letter from F. V. Sotto Mayor dated 16 January 1750. Cf. A.H.U., *Índia,* maço 77 (62). On 8 August 1761 the summary of the revenue and expenditure was as follows: Revenue 21,082xs 2tgs 40rs, expenditure 17862xs 1tgs 10rs; there remained for dowries, alms and works 3,220xs 1tgs 30rs. Cf. A.H.U., *Índid,* maço 89 (100).

[172] Letter from 24 January 1782. Cf. A.H.U., *Índia,* maço 136 (129).

[173] Filipe de Valadares Sotto Mayor (1749-51) fixed the dowries for the sheltered women who married while in the Recolhimento da Serra. Among

It may be noted, however, that the political and economic decline of Portugal in the East and the ensuing financial difficulties caused a restriction in the number and amount of dowries, curtailed by the royal letter of 1773. The precarious situation of the orphan girls and widows of the nobility resulting from these measures prompted the Board of Mercy to intercede the Crown for restoration of the former dowries through revenue accruing from the *namoxins* (*namoxi*) that formerly belonged to the Jesuits.[174] The Governor responded with great humanity and understanding by considering their application for restoring those benefits, for this could 'succour those miserable sheltered women in their poverty, reward the services of their parents and husbands, facilitate their marriage, increase the population and thus help to cultivate in the vassals a greater love for service'.[175]

During the period under consideration, this Recolhimento

---

the various letters of concession of triennial benefits. Cf., for instance, the charters of 1 July 1755, 20 May 1756, 26 January 1764, 17 October 1764, 13 December 1764, 3 September 1765, 19 October 1765, 24 October 1765, 6 March 1766 (A.N./T.T. *Junta da Real Fazenda do Estado da Índia,* Book 46, ff. 167-8; Book 40, ff. 32v-33v; Book 51, ff. 8-8v; Book 54, ff. 29v-30v; Book 54, ff. 53-58v; Book 51, ff. 120v-121; Book 54, f. [in a deteriorated state]; Book 54, f. [in a deteriorated state]; Book 51, ff. 160-2, respectively]. The triennial benefits consisted mainly of 300 xerafins for the 'King's orphans', 200 for those of the *fabrica* (administrators of church property), 100 for the 'portionists' and 150 to those married the second time and living in the Recolhimento de Santa Maria Madalena (cf. José F. Ferreira Martins, *História da Misericórdia de Goa,* vol. II, Nova Goa, 1912, p. 112). The posts granted were, for example, that of the Customs judge in the city, factor of Mangalore, factor of the Diu fortress, minor broker and *drupo* of cotton at the Diu fortress, of the Rachol office of the crown judge, etc. Also see the publication of 11 April 1759 granting the promotion to the next post (A.H.U., *Índia,* cód. 447, ff. 68v-69).

[174] On the *namoxins,* consult the Glossary.

[175] Cf. the letter from the Governor to M.M. Castro, dated 14 April 1786 (H.A.G., *M. Reino,* Book 167-C, ff. 1176-7, 1179); cf. also the following documents: application of the Board of Mercy dated 3 March 1784 [A.H.U., *Índia,* maço 2 (246)]; A.H.U., *Índia,* maço 149 (155); letter from the High Court judge Sebastião José Francisco Barroco to Francisco da Cunha e Menezes [A.H.U., *Índia,* maço 36 (285)].

must have sheltered twenty orphan girls and some widows. They received the education customarily imparted to girls then and some elementary instruction. Apparently a moral objective rather than an educational one was behind its creation![176]

At the end of the century the possibility of establishing a gratuity fund for the widows and orphan girls of the military officials, through a plan meant for the overseas dominions was considered.[177]

As regards the Recolhimento de Santa Maria Madalena, in 1763, it was in a state of neglect. Archbishop Neiva Brum therefore prescribed certain reform measures in his capacity as purveyor of the Holy House of Mercy, preventing the entry of strangers into the Recolhimento without proper permission and the undue communication in the confessionals.[178]

The old practice of sending women of this Recolhimento and marrying them off to soldiers in Ceylon, was current at this time (1765), as it now was to Brazil or Angola too.[179]

As these two shelter homes were mainly for women coming from the Kingdom and for Luso-descendents, in 1763, there was a plan, albeit unsuccessful, to open one in Bardez for daughters of locals.[180] Several other aspects of assistance and welfare had

[176] Cf. letter of concession of benefits of 13 December 1764, op. cit. (A.N./T.T., *Junta da Real Fazenda do Estado da Índia,* Book 54, ff. 53-58v). For example, see *Memória Histórico-Eclesiástica ...,* op. cit., p. 333 and Father Caetano Francisco de Souza, *Instituições Portuguesas de Educação e Ensino no Oriente,* Bombay, 1890, p. 227.

[177] Cf. the letter from D. Rodrigo de Souza Coutinho to F.A.V. Cabral, dated 24 January 1798 (A.H.U., *Índia,* cód. 520, f. 114).

[178] Cf. the order of the purveyor of the Holy House of Mercy, Goa, D. António T.N.B. da Silveira, dated 1 September 1763 (H.A.G., *Misericórdia de Goa,* Book 10429 'Estatutos do Recolhimento de Santa Maria Madalena', ff. 42v-43).

[179] Cf. Chapter 19 of the statutes of the Recolhimento de Santa Maria Madalena (H.A.G., *Misericórdia de Goa,* Book 10424, f. 29). Details such as the ethnic origin of the sheltered women, the houses in which the institution functioned, etc., can be obtained from the works of L.A. Rodrigues, 'The Recluse Houses of Goa', in *Boletim do Instituto Menezes Bragança,* no. 106, Goa, 1974, pp. 29-42; Father Caetano Francisco de Souza, op. cit., pp. 225-8; A. Lopes Mendes, *A Índia Portuguesa,* vol. 1, Chap. I, pp. 61-74.

[180] Cf. C.C. Nazareth, *Mitras ...,* p. 279.

to be mentioned, but dearth of information makes it impossible to go deeper into the subject.

Many of these charitable institutions have survived up to our days. This is quite significant, for it proves that the Portuguese presence in the East was not only by way of its political sovereignty but also by its spiritual and social action.

MECHANISMS OF SOCIAL NORMALIZATION

The alliance between the *Throne* and the *Altar* in the Old Regime showed in the most diverse sectors of community life. Thus, in a conjunction of efforts, the secular and ecclesiastical institutions promoted a normalising action for social control, seeking behavioural uniformity among individuals, according to established archetypes.

In order to study how the lawful authorities used to collect information about the moral and religious situation of the Christian communities and intervene to curb misdemeanours; we need to reflect on the social vigilance processes in use at that time. These included the Rolls of Penitents and Communicants, Pastoral Visits and the Inquisition.

In Europe of the Old Regime, particularly in countries more intensely influenced by the Council of Trent, the impact of these mechanisms of social supervision was of great significance. In Portugal, the Tridentine norms of discipline and defence of quite a formal and traditional morality were mostly well accepted. The processes of social-religious vigilance that came to Goa remained in force for centuries. It may remembered that the spread of Western and Portuguese culture in Goa was intimately related with spreading of the Christian message. And since the cultural assimilation was a unique aspect of Goan colonization, it is no wonder that these mechanisms were also introduced in its religious structure and sometimes applied here more strictly than on the Continent.

The Church Rolls furnished concrete information on the number of souls, penitents, and communicants; on Christians who for some reason were obliged to postpone fulfilling these precepts; on defaulters and absentees. This helped the ecclesiastical authorities to inquire into the religious situation of the Christian community at different levels and to calculate the percentage of orthodox or heterodox people who did or did not submit themselves to the Church directives.

Evidently, there was an intimate connection between pastoral visits and the Church rolls. These would return to the parish, after being registered in the Ecclesiastical Chamber, in order to furnish data to the Bishop when he called on it.[181] His visit would concentrate on the state of preservation of the church building and the religious paraments, the religious principles and behavioural norms being complied with or not, and the functioning of the administrative and economic system of the church.

The Inquisition Tribunal had a different purpose. Falling under its jurisdiction were cases of dogmatic-religious nature, like heresy, blasphemy, whereas the diocesan jurisdiction in the pastoral visits was on moral faults (concubinage, intrigue, etc.). Pastoral visits permitted the diagnosing of cases that thereafter used to be sent to the Holy Office, if necessary. That is, the visit had a normative character, indicative, routine, with some coercive force. As the Inquisition dealt with rare cases considered very serious and perhaps with some political implications, it was more selective and enjoyed a larger judicial jurisdiction. Hence the action of these three mechanisms of social control – Church Rolls, Pastoral Visits and Inquisition – was complementary.[182]

CHURCH ROLLS

The preparation of the *Róis da Cristandade,* or Church Rolls, obeyed certain norms and determinate periods fixed by the Constitutions, bearing in mind their credibility and efficacy. We may consider several stages in its preparation. Thus the parish priest had to first go around the parish at fixed times, to collect precise information on its population. With this data, he would compose a roll giving the place, the year, the complete identi-

[181] Cf. *Constituições do Arcebispado de Goa,* Book I, Tit. VI, Const. V, Lisbon, 1810, pp. 64-5.

[182] See José Pedro de Matos Paiva, 'Inquisição e Visitas Pastorais. Dois Mecanismos Complementares de Controle Social?', in *Inquisição ...*, vol. II, Lisbon, 1989, pp. 865-79.

fication of the individual, including his family and social-professional position in the midst of each aggregate.[183]

Thereafter, on three Sundays before Lent, the parish priests would instruct the faithful on how to mention the members of the household and on how to confess properly: the importance of the interior disposition for reconciliation with God and neighbour.

The third stage corresponded to the careful filling in of the said form. He would also especially refer to the defaulters and their reasons, the absent, the impeded, those whom he had advised, for some reason, to postpone their confession. He would also refer to the manner in which the clergy of the parish had confessed and received communion. When there were the *declared* (defaulters by rebellion), he would attach to the list of the confessed another one with the name of the transgressors.

Finally, the parish priest would submit the roll to the diocese within the specified period; there it would be registered in the Book of the Ecclesiastical Chamber. As stated before, the roll would thereafter return to the parish priest, and an account of it given at the pastoral visit.[184]

In spite of the clear constitutional instructions reiterated by the pastoral letters of the Archbishops on how to prepare the roll, irregularities were quite rampant. Prelates would therefore remind the parish priests to duly perform this pastoral duty.[185] There are in fact reports of abuses like that of making the roll

[183] The parish priests had to trudge the whole parish between the third and the fifth Sunday before Lent. Since during Lent the navies would retreat bringing many to the confessional, the parish priest once had to rush through the parish. The information had to be as per a specific printed form (*Constituições* ..., Book I, Tit. VI, Const. V, pp. 62-3).

[184] Ibid., pp. 64-5. The roll had to be delivered to the purveyor within fifteen days from the Sunday of the Good Shepherd.

[185] See the pastoral letter from 14 October 1782 ordering the parish priests to begin a careful preparation of the roll in January. They were also reminded to find out if the servant slaves had been baptized and if they fulfilled the religious duties (cf. Father Manuel J.S. Albuquerque, *Decretos do Arcebispado de Goa. Summário Cronológico, 1775-1900*, Goa, Bastora, 1900, p. 21).

and 'unloading' it, or making use of the earlier roll and having the data systematically altered.[186]

Furthermore, the nomenclature used in the rolls was quite arbitrary; this vitiated the data collected on the Christian population of Goa.[187]

The Church Rolls of the eighteenth century cover only the years from 1773 to 1800.[188] And there is no information on all the years and parishes, either because some folios are in a damaged state or missing. Hence, the totals of certain parishes are quite low, possibly altering the final tally. To minimize these omissions, we have worked mostly with averages.

Supplying as they do information that is very rich and significant for our objectives, we made a systematic collection of the annual figures. As we propose to analyse the rolls as a mechanism of social control, we have not made use of all the data collected, but only attempted to interpret them precisely within the scope of our rationale.

One difficulty in handling the data came from the lack of uniform nomenclature. For example, if some parish priests used the term *rebel* to classify an individual who flagrantly disobeyed the annual Easter precept, others would classify him as *declared excommunicated.* There were repeated instructions from the Bishops on the use of a common typology; nonetheless a great variety of terms, sometimes difficult to tabulate, were in use by

[186] See the pastoral letter from 15 January 1795 and the circular of 25 July of the same year denouncing these irregularities. The parish priests were also asked to make sure to accept the confession bills only after they had fulfilled this duty. The last circular even stated the manner of classifying the presented, the granted and the defaulters and the manner of going about in relation to the expected, rude, granted and the absent (cf. *Mitras* ..., pp. 358-9 and Archive of the Pomburpa parish, Book of Decrees and Pastoral Letters (1796-1810), ff. 8v-13).

[187] Cf. A.C.P.G., *Ofícios e Portarias,* 2, ff. 1-6.

[188] All the data given hereafter was culled from the codices in the Archive of the Patriarchal Curia of Goa: Book I (*1773-5*), Book II (*1775-84*), Book III (*1784-97*), and Book IV (*1798-1810*). All the data has been computerized and shall be the object of a later study. Here we only present the data thought to be essential for the understanding of the subject under consideration.

parish priests.[189] Thus, for example, the terms *bestialised, rude,* are applied to persons who were not in a position to receive the sacraments because of their lack of breeding. To circumvent this difficulty, we have clubbed together terms with similar meanings upon a critical examination of the context in which they were used in each parish.[190]

On comparing the number of souls in the provinces of Ilhas, Bardez and Salsete, it was found that Salsete and Bardez had a higher average per parish, in the period in which there is data – 2,909.9 and 2,906.9, respectively. Ilhas was quite far from these averages – 1,088.6. This data matches with some of the observations made in Chapter II, regarding the higher number of Christians in Salsete.[191] However, we note that the nature of the data presented there is different from what we have commented upon just now, for it refers to averages of 8 to 24 years for each of the parishes. This aspect becomes clearer indeed when the percentages of those complying with the Easter precept are compared with the total number of souls. Thus, their number was higher in Ilhas (75.2) than in Salsete (66.5) and in Bardez (64.2), indicating a higher religious conformity in Ilhas than in the other provinces.

The observance of the religious principles by the faithful of these communities is curious indeed. Contrary to expectation in

[189] See the *Cópia da Carta Circular Suplemento da Pastoral de 15 de Janeiro de 1795 expedida a 25 de Julho do mesmo ano, em que determina o tempo em que deve principiar e findar a desobriga annual e mais providencias* (A.C.P.G., *Ofícios e Pastorais,* Book 2 (*1795-1827*), ff. 1-6 and Archive of the Pomburpa Parish, *Livro de Decretos e Pastorais,* ff. 1-6v). After referring to the *dolos* (frauds) employed by the bad Christians to elude the annual Easter precept and the excesses committed by some parish priests in the elaboration of the rolls, it indicates the correct meaning of the terms *presented, deferred, defaulting, expected, absent.*

[190] Included among the clergy were the priests, deacons, subdeacons and minor canons; in the group of *alienated* were the *fatuous, insensate, insensible, insane*; in that of *rebels* were included the *incurring, warned, obstinate, stuporous, declared, mundane, adversary, disobedient, excommunicated, negligent,* those who *had not fulfilled, the non-obliged, the non-satisfying, those yet to fulfil the Easter precept.*

[191] Cf. Chapter II – The population in ethnic-religious terms.

view of what we have just stated, Ilhas has a higher percentage of rebels (0.3) against 0.22 per cent in Bardez and 0.17 per cent in Salsete. However, the percentage differences challenge the hypothesis that there was a greater social control in the province of Ilhas than in the other two.

The number of Christians per cleric in the period under study and in the parishes generally is substantially different in the three provinces: Ilhas has the best inhabitants/clerics ratio, touching 175.9. Salsete is close on its heels, although with a proportion ten times lower than that of Ilhas (1,914.4) and Bardez has 27 times fewer clerics than Ilhas, that is, 4,765.4.

Ilhas

In this province the parishes with a higher average of souls were, in decreasing order, the following: Taleigão (2,885.6), Pangim (2,796.9), Ribandar (2,781.2), Agaçaim (2,718.5). There were many parishes with a very high religious practice. Between 90 and 97 per cent, were Santa Luzia (97.1) and Collegiate of Our Lady of Light (91.0).[192] A little lower were the Primatial See (89.8), Collegiate of Our Lady of the Rosary (86.2), Saint Alex (84.1), and some others around 81 per cent (S. Bartolomeu and Our Lady of the Grace, in Chorão; Daugim, Saint Ignez). An analysis of the table reveals, however, that the lowest percentage of penitents and communicants is two-thirds of the Christian population, which obviously refers to their almost total conformity with the Church commandments. It may be noted, in addition, that Pangim, which in 1760 became the seat of government, had quite a high religious practice (three-fourths of the Christians).[193]

A complementary aspect of the religious behaviour control is what we observe from the number of rebels. As it is natural in a population with a great religious compliance, as we have noticed,

[192] We have not taken into account in this critique the case of Mandur where the number of annual penitents and communicants recorded in the statistics is higher than that of the souls.

[193] Cf. *Tratado de Todos os Vice-Reis e Governadores da Índia,* Lisbon, 1962, p. 188.

their percentages are quite low, not reaching 1.5 per cent. Considering that the differences detected are not significant, it is noted, however, that the parishes with a greater relative number are the following, in decreasing order: Collegiate of Our Lady of the Rosary, Saint Alex, Corlim, Santa Luzia, Carambolim, and Pangim.

It may noted that many of these parishes we earlier registered as having a high percentage of annual penitents and communicants; this shows that the two phenomena are not complementary, and can coexist. It is quite possible that the excessive compliance may cause, by the need for differentiation, behaviour of non-compliance expressed in the numbers of rebels.

Bardez

Taking into account that the percentage of penitents and communicants is relatively low in this province (as compared to Ilhas); the percentages of the respective parishes are also quite low. Thus, the maximum level attained by them is 76.1 per cent (Reis Magos). Only two parishes have percentages in the 1770s: Penha de França (75.6 per cent) and Pomburpa (71.7 per cent). A great majority of them stand between 60 per cent and 67.8 per cent (fifteen parishes out of twenty-four).[194] In the rest of the parishes more than 50 per cent of the Christian population are penitents and communicants.

The highest percentage of 'rebels' (0.5 per cent) is attained by four parishes (Nagoa, Pilerne, Penha de França and Moira). Close on their heels (with 0.4 per cent) are the parishes of Candolim and Pomburpa. However, all the others have a percentage of less than 0.3 per cent.

Salsete

In this province too the highest percentages of penitents and communicants range between 70 per cent and 77.6 per cent. This includes six parishes, the ones with the strongest practice

[194] The Royal Legion has a higher percentage of religious practice (91.7 per cent). We have not considered it in the commentary on the parishes, it being a military unit.

being Mormugão (77.6 per cent) and Sancoale (74.8 per cent). Eighteen out of twenty-five parishes have percentages between 60 and 70 per cent and one only slightly below the lower limit of this category: Carmona, with 58.6 per cent.

The percentage of rebels of this province is generally on a par with the other provinces, as stated above. However, though with a relatively insignificant percentage, the parish of Cuncolim stands out: with 0.7 per cent it comes close to the percentage recorded in Corlim which occupies the third place in the rebel category of the parishes of Ilhas. This detail helps us to understand that in Bardez and Salsete there was no correlation between the greater percentages of penitents and communicants and of rebels, as we made out in the commentary on the province of Ilhas. Indeed, the rebel percentages in Bardez and Salsete are too low for the effect supposed in the earlier commentary to have taken place.

PASTORAL VISITS

Following Gabriel Le Bras, scholars have brought out the importance of the pastoral visits as a historical source and developed a more or less systematic research.[195] As far as we know, those available in the Archives of the Patriarchal Curia of Goa, in 29 volumes corresponding to the second half of the eighteenth century (1747 to 1803) have not yet been tapped for the purpose of a systematic study of the religious aspects of this people.[196] Indeed, the pastoral visits furnish another side of the

[195] See Gabriel Le Bras, *Études de Sociologie Religieuse,* 2 vols., Paris, P.U.F., 1955 and 1956, and Jean Delumeau, *Le Catholicisme entre Luther et Voltaire,* Paris, P.U.F., 1971.

[196] Teotónio R. de Souza, 'The Voiceless in Goan Historiography', in *Indo-Portuguese History: Sources and Problems,* ed. John Correia-Afonso, Bombay, 1981, pp. 114-31, called the attention to the importance of these sources. Also see our studies, 'A Sociedade Goesa da Segunda Metade do Século XVIII Analisada pela Hierarquia Católica: os Textos das *Visitas Pastorais*', in *Povos e Culturas,* no. 5: *Portugal e o Oriente: Passado e Presente,* Lisbon, Centro de Estudos dos Povos e Culturas de Expressão Portuguesa, Universidade Católica Portuguesa, 1996; and 'Mendicidade e maus costumes...', op. cit.

people's day-to-day living that wishes to throw light on the religious practice. Thus, historical analysis today prefers the actual behaviours to the principles, that is, the lived reality as against the prescribed: today we judge on the same strength that those principles had in the day-to-day life. And if the pastoral visits show some lacunae (every inquiry has an objective), they are a reflection of the daily life.[197]

Although the tradition of pastoral visitations did exist before the Council of Trent, after it they gained more dynamism and came to be an important means of vigilance and of religious edification. As in other parts of the Kingdom and overseas dominions, in the archdiocese of Goa too, in the second half of the eighteenth century, pastoral visits found a fertile field of work, 'because with it holy Doctrine is sown, Ecclesiastical discipline restored, true rites are exercised, heresies extirpated, superstitions banished, good customs preserved, the bad ones reproved, the sins corrected …'.[198]

The visitation in Goa in the second half of the eighteenth century was quite intense. As we shall see later, the Archbishops did carry the Tridentine determinations of going round the diocese annually or every two years, depending on the size of the diocese.[199]

Save the visits to Barcelore in 1764 and to Bardez and Ilhas in 1765/7, which Neiva Brum entrusted to competent priests for ponderous reasons, all others were held by the Archbishops themselves, which certainly made them very important.[200] It is

[197] Cf. Jean Delumeau, in *Histoire Vécu du Peuple Chrétien,* Toulouse, 1979.

[198] Cf. *Constituições* …, Book V, Tit. XXVI, Const. I, p. 370.

[199] See *Concílio de Trento,* Session 24, Chapter III, *De Reformatione,* and *Constituições* …, Book V, Tit. XXVI, Const. I, p. 370. See *Visitas Pastorais,* vols. 1-28 (A.C.P.G.) containing these records with respect to the second half of the eighteenth century. Hereinafter we shall refer to this corpus as *V.P.*

[200] Barcelore (13° 38' lat. N and 74° 45' long. E), in south Kanara, was a long distance from Goa and access to it was difficult, posing a danger to Neiva Brum's health, who was already weak. From 1765 to 1768, D. António belonged to the Twelfth Government Council. The visitor of Barcelor was Father Caetano Pires da Silva, dean of Mangalore (*V.P.,* vol. 8, f. 3v) and that of Bardez and Ilhas, Father Simão Perestrelo Dantas, chantor of the

important to bring out this aspect, since on the Continent the visit was normally held by a visitor other than the Bishop. Perhaps because it was a very heterogeneous milieu, as was that of Goa, the presence of the Bishop was perhaps important, with all the solemnity imposed by his vestments and his very person.

Besides this, the Bishop's visit permitted the immediate resolution of certain infractions that sometimes had dragged on for a long time. Archbishop D. António T.N.B. da Silveira refers to the itinerancy of the episcopal power in his *ad limina* visits from 1757 to 1769, when he states that he visits the parishes annually, 'leaving nothing to be corrected and resolving everything directly, whenever necessary'.[201]

It may be noted, in fact, that the same had happened in some parts of Brazil, as well portrayed, for example, by the pilgrimage of the Archbishop D. Frei Caetano Brandão through the lands of Para.[202]

At any rate, these higher ecclesiastical authorities showed great concern to know the parishioners' problems *in loco* and to find solutions for them. In fact, the prelates revealed that several pastoral letters had resulted precisely from the knowledge of problems they had got through the visits, as we shall shortly see.

According to canon law and, in a temporal perspective, we could consider three stages in pastoral visits: the first and preceding stage of preparation, when an edict announced the date of the Bishop's arrival in the parish and a questionnaire for the visit; second, the visit per se when accusers' opinions were

---

cathedral (*V.P.,* vol. 10, ff. 4-8 and vol. 11, ff. 4-16). Also cf. *Constituições ...,* Book V, Tit. XXVI, Const. I, p. 371 and *Regimento do Auditório Ecclesiastico,* Tit. XV, which determined that the priest should be 'virtues Priests, prudent and zealous ..., and being learned or, at least, persons with understanding, and experience'.

[201] See our study, 'Um importante documento para a história da Diocese de Goa no Ano de 1757: A Visita *ad limina* de D. António Taveira da Neiva Brum da Silveira', in *Arquipélago,* Série Ciências Humanas, no. V, 1983, pp. 247-8, and *Arquivo Secreto do Vaticano,* S. Congr. Concilii Relations: *ad limina* visit of 1769 of the Goa archbishopric.

[202] See Luis A. de Oliveira Ramos, *Diários das Visitas Pastorais no Pará de D. Fr. Caetano Brandão,* Porto, 1991.

collected, penalties announced and the accused were talked to;[203] and the third phase, after the visitor had considered the main abuses and deviations prevailing in the parish, he would leave behind his notes and decrees in the Church for the religious and moral perfection of his faithful.[204]

The success of the visit depended somewhat on the prior preparation for it. Hence it was important for the parish priests to make the faithful co-responsible in the correction of errors, by having them denounced, for 'failure in this obligation, [is] the cause for the visit not achieving its holy end, that is the correction of vices, extinction of bad customs, and introduction of good, and holy Doctrine'. Evidently, this denouncement had to stem from the zeal for the things of God and love of neighbour and not from hate and desire for vengeance.[205]

Added to the preparation of consciences for the visitations act was the preparation of the church building in general with its religious accoutrements, paraments, books, in short, everything that could make the occasion more solemn and circumspect. Thus, the ceremony surrounding the pastoral visit would engage the numerous clergy, confreres, the parish administrative board, and the people in general.[206]

[203] See the publication with the questionnaires of the visit in *Regimento* [...], Tit. XV, pp. 62-5.

[204] There existed norms for the visitor to follow, advising them on their manner in a pastoral visit. They ministered indications on, e.g. the arrival ceremony, the review of the liturgical things, the practice of the sacraments, the state of the church books, the judicial inquest, the verification of the faults, the judgement, etc. Cf. *Theatro Ecclesiastico de varias figuras, que expoem, e declarão as qualidades, que devem ter obrigaçoens e resoluçoens que devem seguir os R.R. Visitadores deste Arcebispado* (ms. belonging to the author). A. Franquelim S. Neiva Soares, in his study 'A Sociedade do Antigo Regime nas Visitações e Inquéritos Paroquiais do Distrito de Braga', in *Theologica: Revista de Ciências Sagradas,* 2nd series, vol. XIII, fascs. III-IV, Braga, 1978, pp. 438 and ss., describes quite in detail these moments of the visit.

[205] Cf. *Constituições ...*, Book V, Tit. XXVI, Const. I, p. 373.

[206] By way of example about the pastoral visits on the Continent and in Brazil, refer to the [studies] by Eugénio dos Santos, 'Os Açores na Época Moderna: Religião e Sociedade', in *Os Açores e o Atlântico* (séculos XIV-XVII), Angra do Heroísmo, 1984, pp. 729-92; Maria Fernanda Dinis Teixeira

From the historical-documentary point of view, the stages of the pastoral visit began with a registration, usually done by transcribing the provisions for appointing the coadjutor and the clerk for the visit. Then followed the record of the arrival and description of the visit to the church. A substantial part of this declaration is covered by the opinions expressed by witnesses on the questionnaire of the visit, opinions which undoubtedly constitute a very rich source of material on various aspects of the Goan society and their religious practice. Finally, there is a mention of the penalties that judicial inquest obliges the accused. Besides this, the final part in every volume of these Pastoral Visits generally contains records of correction by the accused in compliance with the sanction given.

It may be noted that in the parish were filed the visitors' considerations on the state of the church and the instruments of cult, on the pastoral activity by the parish priest and his reformatory orders. However, there is a record of only a few registers, commonly known as *Livros de Capítulos,* Books of Chapters.[207]

Before we present the data, it may be noted that for several reasons strict quantification has quite a relative value. Firstly, the study is qualitative rather than quantitative in nature. On

---

Enes, *As Visitas Pastorais da Matriz de São Sebastião de Ponta Delgada* (1674-1739), Secretaria Regional de Educação e Cultura/Universidade dos Açores, 1986; Francisco Barbosa da Costa e João de Sousa, *Visitas de Gulpilhares,* Vila Nova de Gaia, 1986; Joaquim Ramos de Carvalho e José Pedro de Matos Paiva, 'Reportório às Visitas Pastorais em Coimbra nos Séculos XVII, XVIII e XIX', in *Boletim do Arquivo da Universidade de Coimbra,* vol. VII, Coimbra, 1985, pp. 111-21; Caio C. Boschi, 'As Visitas Diocesanas e a Inquisição na Colónia', in *Inquisição,* op. cit., vol. II, pp. 963-96; António Franquelim Sampaio Neves Soares, *A Arquidiocese de Braga no Século XVII. Sociedade e Mentalidades pelas Visitações Pastorais (1550-1700)*, Braga, 1997.

[207] We have only managed to find chapters in a book of the church of Penha de França (A.C.P.G., *Livros de Conventos e Igrejas,* no. 13 – Penha de França). We admit that in other churches there may exist books with chapters. It may be noted that the documentation of the churches of Ilhas, Bardez and Salsete, of the Ecclesiastical Chamber and of the various religious congregations was sent to Lisbon. On the subject see 'Relação dos documentos ...', in A.H.U., *Índia,* maço 110 (126).

the other hand, quantification was not the dominant preoccupation for people in the eighteenth century. In fact, the accused being in the plural without indicating the number of defaulter is a proof of this. Besides, quantification was never a major concern in the sources we have dealt with.

What were the major deviations from the ideal model of religious patterns of the Counter-Reformation, according to the civil and ecclesiastical authorities?

Before we take up the subject proper, it may be worth mentioning the difficulties we have come across in the nomenclature and listing of certain delicts. Denouncements of concubinage and prostitution are a case in point. It is not rare for a woman leading a corrupt life with many men to have at the same time a more lasting bond with one person in particular. The dividing line between a 'brothel' and prostitution is sometimes very uncertain. We sought to overcome these difficulties by counting the accused in both delicts, whenever the situations were sufficiently clear.

From the methodological standpoint and in order to better systematize deviations imputed to the accused, yet without building water-tight compartments, we thought it fit to consider three large social areas: The first one comprising the clerics accused of having infringed on the ecclesiastical statutes. The second area covers all the faithful accused of non-compliance with the Church commandments. The third refers to the non-Christians who sometimes came under ecclesiastical jurisdiction. It is this third group that comes out as truly peculiar to Goan society, in contrast with the totally Christianized societies of Europe; it is the coexistence of the Christians and non-Christians that, in certain cases, makes the latter subject to the ecclesiastical regulations. Evidently, the non-Christians would be answerable to the episcopal authority only in quite a limited number of cases, since they were not obliged to comply with the moral norms or rituals set for the Christians.

Let us next consider the clerics. The faithful have to be a reflection of what the clerics are. Were the latter exemplary? What was their formation? Of what offences are they mainly accused? Are these infractions of a dogmatic-religious incidence or of a social nature?

Out of 3,677 individuals denounced in the pastoral visits that took place between 1750 and 1800, 452 were ecclesiastics (12.3 per cent).[208] Even though there were sporadic references to their social provenance and religious formation, the witnesses did not pronounce on that, sometimes only indicating their age and position in the ecclesiastical hierarchy. Quite often, they were accused of slackness in complying with their ecclesiastical duties: absence from meetings on moral theology and casuistics, processions; carelessness in the preparation of the Church roll, non-attendance at the confessional, even during Lent; very hasty and imperfect celebration of the mass; absence of sacramental assistance to the dying; negligence in the maintenance of the religious paraments and tidiness in the church; indifference to the dress-code, etc.[209]

Another aspect to emphasize is, no doubt, the secular spirit, ambition and materialistic spirit of some priests who would retaliate, if the parishioners did not fulfil their plans. To illustrate, we found priests who would detain the bridal couples in the doctrine tests if they did not promise them gifts; or order the confiscation of things from fishermen's houses if they did not

[208] The sum total of the denounced results only from the quantifiable data, wherefrom it can be concluded that the real number of accused must have been much higher. It is quite probable that it went beyond four thousand. The same is noticeable with respect to the global number of ecclesiastics that in reality must have also been quite high, for we find denouncements in the following terms: 'The Priests of this parish say mass very early...' (*V.P.,* Mercês, 1774, vols. 13-15, f. 60v); 'Quite a few clerics show themselves to be remiss in the renewal of the Blessed Sacrament ...' (*V.P.,* Neura, 1767, vols. 11-12, f. 168); 'Priests do not attend the processions of the souls ...' (*V.P.,* São Pedro de Panelim, 1794, vols. 24-6, f. 3), etc. Evidently, these cases cannot be quantified.

[209] By way of example we would cite the case of Father João Luís, a 'modern priest. He says Mass without the collar of the cassock' (*V.P.,* S. Tomé de Salsete, 1771, vols. 11-12, f. 30). Father Pascoal Lourenço de Sousa wears cabaan out in the streets (*V.P.,* Assolna, 1792, vols. 21-3, f. 67v). He is 'defective' in the ceremony of the Mass and says it in less than 15 minutes (*V.P.,* Margão, 1760, vols. 5-6, f. 100). See *V.P.,* S. Matias de Malar, 1753, vols. 3-4, ff. 51 and 99; Panelim, 1788, vols. 21-3, f. 4, and 1794, vols. 24-6, f. 3v; Parra, 1798, vols. 27-9, f. 48).

give them fish; or not grant confession to those who did not send them presents; or refuse to bury the dead until the family advanced the money for the funeral expenses. At other times, they used to undertake business, like buying rice and coconuts and reselling them or 'Balghat contracts by oxen caravans', etc.[210]

Although there may be parallel cases of simony in Europe, yet one can perceive here an influence of the traditional behaviour of the Brahmins and Hindu temple servers who largely live off alms and donations that they demand from members of various castes in exchange for the rites that they celebrate as priests.

Similarly, we witness the rural activity of certain priests who at times even stooped down to working in the fields, dressing quite freely, like typical farmers. Was it for a livelihood? An excessive attachment to material goods?[211]

The interference by ecclesiastics in parish affairs, especially the management of the village *comunidades* and in the *sacadoria* (treasury) of the same, attending meetings, collecting taxes, etc., is also mentioned. This active involvement of particular priests in worldly tasks and public life – in fact also confirmed by other sources of Goan history – can supply information on the

[210] The priest [the name is not mentioned] tore the clothes of the bridegroom and took an ornament from the bride for not having sent him piglings but only female piglings (*V.P.*, Colva, 1787, vols. 18-20, ff. 148-53). Father Pascoal Cardoso too on the occasion of the blessing of houses takes more than what he is given: chicken, onions, coconuts, eggs (*V.P.*, Nagoa, 1753, vols. 3-4, f. 57). Also see *V.P.*, Goa Velha, 1797, vols. 24-6, f. 55; Carmona, 1764, vols. 9-10, f. 90; Margão, 1787, vols. 18-20, ff. 160, 164v; S. Bartolomeu, 1753, vols. 3-4, f. 26; Anjuna, 1795, vols. 24-6, ff. 21-21v.

[211] Father António João Mascarenhas goes to work in the fields dressed in a *langotim* (*langoti*) (*V.P.*, Guirim, 1792, vols. 21-3, ff. 88-88v). *Langotim,* 'sheet worn between the buttocks, with one end tied to a cord behind the waist and the other hanging in front' (S.R. Dalgado, op. cit., vol. I, pp. 509-10). The curate of Nagoa was accused in 1798 of obliging the people to work in his field and only then, he would grant them confession. 'He does not have the spirit for the post he occupies' (*V.P.*, vols. 27-9, ff. 60-5). In addition, Father António do Rosário used to deal with the lands and the business of his nephew to the detriment of his priestly obligation (*V.P.*, Colva, 1764, vols. 9-10, ff. 53-53v).

social position of the clerics and on their sphere of influence seemingly considerable at the village level.[212] Here too the parallel with the rural Brahmin community in a Hindu ambience is notorious.

Though not specified, in practice, parishioners used to always oblige their priest with the best of food and *mimos* (gifts), on the occasion of the paschal blessing of houses, religious feasts, baptisms, marriages, etc. This practice in fact endured in the customs of the people, as seen even today in the Goan villages, as well as on continental Portugal and the Islands. By the Constituições, they had right also to the *primícias* (first fruits) of the production. They had the ecclesiastical jurisdiction over the parish; they could therefore admonish and reprehend the faithful, fine them, prohibit certain performances like the *brinco* and the *zagor.*[213]

However, when priests extorted money, punished the parishioners severely and unjustly when they infringed ecclesiastical norms, their power was far from being put at the service of their faithful; though rarely, it did turn rather discriminatory and exploitative.[214] And if his personal life favoured him, if he belonged to a powerful family and could

[212] *Sacador* was the tax collector of the *comunidade* and the one responsible for the revenue (S.R. Dalgado, op. cit., vol. II, p. 268). Father Custódio de Barros goes to the *ganvkari,* manages the village *sacadoria,* makes collections, charges interest at the rate of 9 per cent to 10 per cent (*V.P.,* Carambolim, 1782 and 1788, vols. 16-17, ff. 109-109v and vols. 21-3, f. 37v). The priests António do Rego, Vicente do Rego, Bernardo Tolentino Ribeiro, Francisco X. Miranda frequent the *ganvkari* and even go to Margão when the *comunidade* is meeting there (*V.P.,* Verna, 1787, vols. 18-20, f. 134).

[213] On the subject see the part referring to entertainment in Chapter VI.

[214] The parish priest of S. Tomé (Salsete) severely punished the laundry man who when questioned said it had been for personal reasons, with respect to his wife (*V.P.,* vols. 27-9, f. 24). Father Francisco Caetano Carvalho does not give the cloth or cloth for turban or *langoti* to the poor, but to his *mundkars* (*V.P.,* Chinchinim, 1764, vols. 9-10, f. 116v). Father Miguel Caetano Carvalho charges twenty vintém per person who goes to him to confess, to register his name in the Church roll, 'thus hindering his conduct the right of the *língua* (interpreter) who is responsible for the collections (*V.P.,* Navelim, 1800, vols. 27-9, f. 63v).

expect support from a family member, his high-handedness knew no bounds.[215]

A considerable number of defaulting ecclesiastics (33 per cent) were accused of the vice of drunkenness; their condition made it almost impossible for them to carry out their spiritual functions.[216]

Besides, priests found in such conditions would not be able to fulfil their pastoral duties, and this would have an adverse effect on parish assistance. Vices assuming proportions that are more serious would tarnish the priest's image and have quite a negative influence on the faithful. This aspect was indeed worse in villages whose inhabitants had little faith, as in the case of Ucassaim (Bardez).[217]

If the denouncers told the truth, what factors could have been responsible for this large number of alcoholics? Was the vice so widespread in society that the cleric too would suffer from it, in keeping with the 'fashion' of his parishioners? It may thus be noted that alcoholism attained a high percentage, though not the highest, in the general calculation of offences. In fact, we do not have enough data to answer satisfactorily all the complex issues that this raises. However, we believe that it was the isolation of Goan villages, and perhaps even a certain social tolerance of such behaviour, that were relevant factors accounting for the high incidence of alcoholism among ecclesiastics.

However, if drunkenness became quite widespread among clerics, cases of sexual misbehaviour too were not rare (21 per cent). From an analysis of the testimonies at the visits and in spite of the great diversity of cases having a varying degree of seriousness, many common situations have been collected that

[215] Father Francisco de Mendonça 'scolds the people who come to church and causes some troubles, under the wing of his brother-in-law, captain Miguel Anjo' (*V.P.,* Ucassaim, 1772, vols. 13-15, f. 22v).

[216] Out of the 452 ecclesiastical defaulters, 150 were denounced as drunkards. In Moira, 1795, the priest 'when he went to the pulpit he was drunk and made indecorous actions, gnashing his teeth' (*V.P.,* vols. 24-6, f. 40).

[217] Cf. *V.P.,* Ucassaim, 1772, vols. 13-15, ff. 25v-26; S. Matias de Malar, 1791, vols. 21-3, f. 89v; Pangim, 1794, vols. 24-6, ff. 25v, 26v; Chicalim, 1771, vols. 11-12, f. 6; Pilerne, 1783, vols. 13-15, f. 129v.

are worthy of mention. Thus it is not rare to find a priest that has sinned with his own servant or cook or that of some family member.[218] Illicit relations with widows and with his in-laws were not infrequent either, and quite a few times they resulted in births.[219] And it was certainly to avoid scandal for the faithful, that the Constitutions prescribed that 'if both a father and his son are Priests, one should not serve the Mass of the other, nor both be Beneficiaries, or serve in the same Parish'.[220]

Besides the above-mentioned accusations, other faults include particular forms of robbery, induction of false witnesses, lack of patrimony or titles of ordination and licences, fights. Indeed, some priests were accused of being quarrelsome and disturbing the people, when priests ought to have been a conciliatory force, by epithet. For example, recalling the Carmona (Salsete) incident, in 1764, involving brothers of the confraternity, two priests, 'instead of mediating, got involved in the fight, tearing *opas* (sleeveless garments of the confreres)'.[221]

Although it would be ideal to find in Goa clerics solely in the service of their communities, in Europe too ecclesiastics were not particular about sporting an impeccable conduct.[222]

[218] For example, see, *V.P.*, Benaulim, 1783, vols. 16-17, ff. 73-73v; Betalbatim, 1764, vols. 9-10, f. 45; R. Magos, 1783, vols. 13-15, ff. 80-80v; Ucassaim, 1792, vols. 21-3, f. 31v.

[219] Cf. *V.P.*, Nagoa, 1795, vols. 24-6, f. 66v; Calangute, 1795, vols. 24-6, f. 71v; Ucassaim, 1772, vols. 13-15, f. 64v; on illicit relations with female in-laws cf. *V.P.*, Sirula, 1772, vols. 13-15, f. 14v; Santa Inês, 1785, vols. 18-20, f. 41v; Taleigão, 1785, vols. 18-20, f. 50v. References to children of priests are found in *V.P.*, Piedade (Divar), 1750, vols. 3-4, f. 40v; Candolim, 1798, vols. 27-9, f. 80v; Moira, 1761, vols. 18-20, f. 50v.

[220] Cf. *Constituições ...*, Book III, Tit. I, Const. X, p. 187.

[221] Cf. *V.P.*, Carmona, 1764, vols. 9-10, f. 90v. The priests José de Jesus Maria and André de Monserrate have hatred and enmity against certain families (*V.P.*, Ribandar, 1774, vols. 13-15, ff. 6-6v). See *V.P.*, Agaçaim, 1797, vols. 24-6, f. 62v; Carambolim, 1767, vols. 11-12, f. 152; Nagoa, 1786, vols. 18-20, ff. 84-85; Pomburpa, 1798, vols. 27-8, f. 116v; Cortalim, 1771, vols. 11-12, f. 185; Sirula, 1799, vols. 27-9, ff. 40-40v.

[222] See Eugénio dos Santos, 'Os Livros das Visitas Pastorais da Região Portuense. Questões e Perspectivas de Abordagem', in *Revista de História*, vol. II, Porto, 1979, pp. 242-3; Luís A. de Oliveira Ramos, *Diários das Visitas Pastorais no Pará de D. Frei Caetano Brandão*, Porto, 1991, p. 22.

From this table of delicts attributed to clergymen, it is clear that their faults are mainly in violation of ecclesiastical statutes; these were moral aberrations with social incidence and not of a dogmatic-religious nature.

Most of those who denounced these ecclesiastics were also ecclesiastics. Bound by their conscience? Was it a regulatory point? Spite? Settling of scores? A very delicate question this, like all the affairs of the private conscience; nevertheless this appears to be quite normal, for who could be better informed about priests than their own colleagues in the apostolic work?

The incidence of ecclesiastical defaulters was bigger in the province of Bardez. Was it a mere coincidence or a situation inherited from earlier times? Recall that, in the past, there had been somewhat serious anomalies (already referred to in this chapter) in the administration of the parishes of Bardez. Seemingly, the substitution of secular local clerics for the Franciscans did not totally improve the morals of that region, for there continued to be some irregularities, especially in the private chapels.

Obviously, one cannot write the history of the Goan clergy solely from the behavioural deviations culled from the pastoral visits. In addition, whereas it is interesting to study the so-called anomalous conduct, in the final analysis, collective or psychosocial phenomena and individualistic aspects must be taken into account. On the other hand, the importance that the Catholic Church assumed in the Goan society and the role it played as an instrument of acculturation in the East must be noted. In spite of these sometimes hardly flattering observations, the clergy generally appear to have done justice to their duties.

At any rate, the documentation that we have utilized clearly shows that the higher echelons of the ecclesiastical hierarchy were always concerned about avoiding or suppressing deviations, if so required. These deviations were more common at the rural parish levels which, given their geographical isolation, were not as well controlled by their superiors.

It is evidently impossible to make out if behind the denunciations registered there is solely 'zeal for the house of God' or if simply human jealousies and misunderstandings as well.

However, this is not of interest to us, as we do not intend to pass judgements on them. It suffices to note that the system as a whole was functional: in Goa, in the second half of the eighteenth century, the ecclesiastical institution had a capacity for self-control and self-repression; its external image was thus acceptable to and compatible with the mission that the Christian community expected of it.

Let us next turn to the last two sociological areas that in fact represent 87.7 per cent of the accused. In an attempt to characterize them, we shall show the human groups that the Church aimed to control.

If women convicts are few in the lists of the Inquisition of Goa, in the pastoral visits, on the other hand, their numbers are quite striking. That is because many delicts are more easily detectable in women than in men, though in some other cases precisely the contrary happens. Or was it that being always considered some sort of temptation women presented themselves as the weaker element of established society and hence more vulnerable?[223]

There is no mention of the civil status of a large part of these accused. As regards the rest, we can say that singles slightly outnumber the married, followed by the widows, in a similar significant percentage.[224]

Social provenance is usually not mentioned. Thus, the denouncers do not pronounce on the social class of majority of the denounced, with the result that the little data we have at our disposal are not very significant. Yet, whenever social origin of the denounced is given, it generally happens to be the lower strata.[225]

How to explain this fact? Did the members of the higher

[223] The male percentage is 60.8 per cent and the female 39.2 per cent.

[224] Out of a total 3,677 accused, about 46.2 per cent are not identified as regards their civil status; 22.3 per cent are singles; 21.0 per cent are married; 10 per cent are widows and 0.5 per cent are widowers.

[225] With a very high percentage are the Shudras (0.78 per cent), followed by the Mahars (0.73 per cent); then the Kunbis (0.48 per cent), the Africans (0.43 per cent) and in a very low percentage the Brahmins (0.2 per cent) and the Kshatriyas (0.2 per cent).

social groups truly have an irreproachable conduct? Perhaps we may formulate the problem the other way round. It seems the lower caste individuals were more exposed to denouncements whereas the higher social strata were better placed to denounce. There was perhaps tacit solidarity among members of the higher classes that prompted them to spare each other, seeking scapegoats among people of a lower station.

Further, let us examine the professional activity of the accused. Here in addition, the percentage of non-identified persons is much higher; as such, any conclusion has only a relative value. The accused were from a variety of professions, mainly shopkeepers, tax collectors and soldiers. What stands out, however, is that the greater part of them could be clubbed together under the designation of occupations and trades.[226]

We can therefore conclude that people from various social strata and professions deserved corrections from the visitors, an aspect that speaks for the need and efficacy of similar intervention by the Church with the people.

Let us now analyse the delicts attributed to the accused of the Goan pastoral visits. Most of them refer to moral cases of concubinage and of prostitution by people of different lifestyles. Christians, Hindus and Muslims; white women, *mestizas,* natives, Chinese, African, mulattas; civil, military (from soldiers to higher officials) and prominent public figures, march past in these documents, leaving an impression of voluptuousness and lasciviousness.[227]

226 The professions of the accused cover, in a decreasing order, the soldiers, shopkeepers, the tax collectors. Various professions of arts and craft are indicated, such as, tailors, cobblers, bangle sellers, ironsmiths, toddy-tappers, fishermen, and goldsmiths. Also figuring are sacristans, bailiffs, confraternity callers, cooks, etc.

227 The woman 'relaxes her head on his lap, in the shade of the fig tree. When the lover does not go to her house, she goes to visit him in Mapusa'. The husband consents (*V.P.,* Moira, 1795, vols. 24-6, f. 38). Among the upper class figures of the political-military life of Goa and accused of deviations of sexual nature, are, for example: Manuel Godinho de Mira, Colonel of the legion, living in concubinage with a temple dancing girl (*V.P.,* Colvale, 1786, vols. 18-20, ff. 54v, 59); José Pasca Pessinga, Sergeant-Major and Engineer lives with a married woman (*V.P.,* Reis Magos, 1773,

Many individuals assumed more or less stable and lasting connections, sometimes building up large families, as if they were genuine marriages. Sometimes, the cook or the server with the pretext of cooking, or looking after the children, in case of widowers, would become companions in a conjugal life.[228]

We have identified situations of concubinage between individuals feigning intention of getting married or being engaged to be married that would thereafter cohabit without marriage. In the spirit of the Tridentine reform, these cases were regarded as deviations from Christian life and punished as such.[229]

There were many cases of concubinage and of prostitution registered against women whose husbands were absent, mainly in Balghat, or sometimes in Mozambique, Macao and Timor, on business or to fulfil deportation penalties.[230] Such sexual

---

vols. 11-15, ff. 123v-124); João Baptista Vieira Godinho, Lieutenant-Colonel, 'communicates' with worldly women (*V.P.*, Santa Inês, 1794, vols. 24-6, ff. 14-14v). From among the 3,677 denounced, about 2,071 were imputed of sexual deviations and among these 848 for living in concubinage (41 per cent), 653 of prostitution (32 per cent), 314 of practising sensual acts (15 per cent), 129 of living separately (6 per cent) and 127 of having a 'bawdy-house' (6 per cent).

[228] In Taleigão (1767), the wife of a *ganvkar* and sergeant of the village was living in concubinage with an artillery adjudant for more than 12 years; another, in identical circumstances, for more than three years (*V.P.*, vols. 11-12, f. 234). One Reinol, commander of the Cortalim post (1767) keeps a woman 'behind closed doors' with the pretext that she is his cook. He has two children. They had been denounced in earlier visits (*V.P.*, vols. 11-12, f. 188). A widower lives in concubinage with a widow, on 'pretext of being the nurse of his children. She was pregnant of him and has also aborted a few times' (*V.P.*, Rachol, 1764, vols. 9-10, f. 143). A Portuguese Sub-Lieutenant lives in concubinage as if she were his legitimate wife. He already has grown-up children (*V.P.*, Calangute, 1772, vols. 13-15, f. 96). The adjudant of the General of Bardez, José Silva Marques, lives with a widow and has children from her (*V.P.*, Guirim, 1761, vols. 7-8, f. 152).

[229] Cf. *V.P.*, Calangute, 1792, vols. 21-3, f. 74; Orlim, 1771, vols. 11-12, ff. 84-5.

[230] Cf. *V.P.*, Mormugão, 1771, vols. 11-12, ff. 15v-16; Chicalim, 1764, vols. 9-10, f. 10; Oxel, 1792, vols. 21-3, f. 60v; Cortalim, 1771, vols. 11-12, f. 188.

misdemeanours sometimes took place with the connivance of parents. Besides the cases in which the parents consented or even favoured such behaviour, there were others in which the father had turned his house into a brothel, offering his own wife and daughters to other men.[231]

Although sexual misconduct was rampant irrespective of the civil status, the number of widows is quite high. Was it for economic reasons? Quite possibly so, though reasons of religious and mental nature were not lacking. We may recall that in Hinduism there were certain taboos against widows, considered as an element of bad omen, hence socially undesirable. The higher castes did not allow widow remarriage. These beliefs remained in Goan Christianity and only gradually, with the passage of time, did the widow conquer her place in society. In the second half of the eighteenth century, widows finding remarriage difficult quite often resorted to concubinage or prostitution.

Against this background of the Goan pastoral visits, we must also refer to the presence of the *bailadeiras,* or dancing girls, the only Hindu caste whose social elements, dedicating their life to the temple, admitted carnal contacts with foreigners. They were sought after by civilians, militiamen and even ecclesiastics, either on 'the other bank' and 'mainland' or on Goan soil.[232] Often

[231] In Daugim (1785) 3 women were denounced as prostitutes (mother and 2 daughters) and 2 for debauching their daughters (*V.P.,* vols. 16-17, ff. 149v-150); in Chorão (1767) one woman was conniving in the prostitution of her daughter (*V.P.,* vols. 11-12, f. 35v). In Sancoale (1772) daughter-in-law and mother-in-law prostitute themselves; the husband gives 'bawdy-house' (*V.P.,* vols. 11-12, ff. 196, 197v); in Reis Magos (1783), mother and daughter prostitute themselves; the father consents and gives 'bawdy-house' (*V.P.,* vols. 13-15, ff. 80v-81). One parishioner in Candolim (1765) 'brings men to misuse his wife. They say his own brother-in-law sins with her' (*V.P.,* vols. 9-10, f. 21).

[232] A priest goes in cabaan to the other bank to meet the dancing girl (*V.P.,* Tivim, 1772, vols. 11-13, ff. 43v-44); a dancing girl has been living in the house of Captain Sebastião Lopes de Lavra, who justified himself with the argument that she had only come to visit a son of theirs whom he, the Captain, kept in his company, already baptized (*V.P.,* Daugim, 1788, vols. 21-3, f. 4); Captain António Pereira, Sub-Lieutenant Manuel da Silveira

other protagonists were the 'new Christians' communicating with the non-Christians out of matrimony. Was their conversion only a formality and superficiality? Maybe. Let us also bear in mind that Hindu society from where the converted Hindu comes is many a time polygamic.[233]

With regard to the cases of separation, the deponents refer to the reasons invoked by the accused in justification of their behaviour. These included drunkenness, theft, lack of sustenance by the husband, bad treatment by him, the mother-in-law or the sister-in-law.[234] It may be recalled that in Goa, the son often continued living at his parents' house after marriage, and understandably the mother-in-law/daughter-in-law relationship was not always easy. Its aggravation could sometimes compel the latter to leave the husband and return to her maiden house. Hence, in the wake of directives from the Tridentine reform, the Archbishop forbade parents from taking back their married daughters without their husbands' permission, as can be read from the 'books of records'.[235]

The witnesses also cite arguments forwarded by the husband to explain his wife's separation: her bad conduct or the fact that the father-in-law did not give the stipulated dowry or, more flagrantly, that he had 'taken back the chest-coffer of jewellery that was part of the marriage dowry'. These customs were quite

---

and some military men sent for dancing girls from the other side of the river; also the canons Rodrigo Lobo and S. Bernardo de Noronha often go to the other bank (*V.P.*, Santo Estêvão, 1753, vols. 3-4, f. 66).

[233] Cf. *V.P.*, Calangute, 1792, vols. 21-3, f. 74; Oxel, 1798, vols. 27-9, f. 34v; Tivim, 1772, vols. 13-15, f. 42.

[234] A woman separated from her husband for the bad life that he and the mother-in-law used to give her (*V.P.*, Colva, 1759, vols. 5-6, ff. 54-54v). The husband orders the wife to do the 'indecent work'; denies her maintenance (*V.P.*, Navelim, 1764, vols. 9-10, f. 120v). The wife separates from the husband as he provokes her to do dishonest acts, since he has the vice of theft; hence it repels her to live with him (*V.P.*, Navelim, 1764, vols. 9-10, f. 121).

[235] The wife made a stipulation promising never to return her parents' home without due permission (*V.P.*, Benaulim, 1799, vols. 27-9, f. 110). The mother promised not to receive her daughter without the husband's permission (*V.P.*, Aldona, 1798, vols. 27-8, f. 162).

deeply rooted in the minds of the people and hence greatly influenced the people's conduct.[236]

Although the lack of a solid moral formation was perhaps the main reason for the behavioural deviations we have just analysed, yet we cannot forget that other reasons – economic, social and of habit of mind – can help to explain them. For many, concubinage, prostitution, sensuality, were a form of social promotion. And to add to it, many a time the denouncers invoked economic reasons; the large number of widows running bawdy houses and parental acquiescence in certain cases explain it as being so.

Drunkenness with clergymen, also referred to earlier, is another vice that attained considerable proportions, judging from testimonies of the pastoral visits.[237]

Witness reports clearly expose the social-moral effects of alcoholism and above all the unwholesome consequences it had for the family: bad treatment meted out to wife and children; squandering of ancestral property; bad temper; absence from Mass and failing in the annual Easter precept; gambling; theft; separation; concubinage, etc. Informants state that the parish priests sought to combat such evils by denying the sacraments to the defaulters and sometimes even by excommunicating them, but such measures did not yield the desired results.[238]

Therefore, this vice sometimes brought about other behavioural problems. We do not know why it spread in Goa. Perhaps the hard life in the villages would cause some people to drink for amusement or momentary escape from reality. The easy

[236] In Benaulim (1759), the father-in-law withdrew the chest-coffer of jewellery given to his daughter in dowry, which caused the separation (*V.P.*, vols. 5-6, ff. 66v, 67 and 70v). The parish priest of Nagoa made efforts to reconcile the separated couple, but was unsuccessful as he was repelled by the husband and as she had trudged the lands of Balghat without wishing to be united with the husband (1772) (*V.P.*, vols. 13-15, f. 55v).

[237] Cf. the general table of delicts.

[238] Cf., for example, *V.P.*, Betalbatim, 1787, vols. 18-20, f. 144; Sancoale, 1772, vols. 11-12, f. 189v; Anjuna, 1772, vols. 13-15, f. 63v; Colvale, 1792, vols. 18-20, f. 8v; Moira, 1772, vols. 13-15, f. 36; Oxel, 1792, vols. 21-3, ff. 60-60v; Siolim, 1792, vols. 21-3, f. 53; Santa Cruz de Calapor, 1794, vols. 24-6, f. 23v; Taleigão, 1767, vols. 11-12, f. 233, and 1797, vols. 24-6, ff. 28v, 29v.

availability of *sur* must have helped too, never mind the grape wine from the Kingdom being scarce and dear.

In the overall picture of the faults imputed to the faithful in their complying with the Church precepts, most prominent are cases of individuals who neither attended Mass nor fulfilled their Paschal duty. Nevertheless they constitute a very small percentage (4.5 per cent or 2.0 per cent, respectively), which perhaps speaks volumes for Goan religiosity and spirit of discipline. Or else, did the Catholic religion carry social prestige? Was not the so-called *conformity* or *social mimetism* one of the values better appreciated by the hierarchy?

Many of these defaulters were also accused of alcoholism and of sexual misbehaviour, which were obviously interrelated. Naturally an individual drunk or debauched could not at the same confess and receive communion, without deciding privately to change his behaviour. Finally, is not the *oneness of life* a strong aspect of Christianity and so favoured by the Tridentine reform?[239]

By a careful reading of the denouncers' testimonies, we note that the most common arguments invoked by the accused to justify absence from Mass would be of the economic order, alleging that they had 'no clothes nor even a sheet to cover themselves with'.[240] It may be noted that this reason was always refuted by the informants who had a different explanation for this fault. They said, for example, 'the young lasses do not go for Mass, through the fault of their parents, either because they do not want their daughters to be seen or because they do not wish to give them dresses'. Curious ways of thinking that could have influenced the persons and which we must keep in mind in order to understand their behaviour.[241]

Based on testimonies like these, we wonder if the priests too were at times hand in glove with the situation, given that they

[239] Cf., e.g. *V.P.,* Sancoale, 1772, vols. 11-12, f. 197; Pangim, 1788, vols. 21-3, f. 25v; Moira, 1792, vols. 21-3, f. 35v.

[240] Cf. *V.P.,* Bambolim, 1797, vols. 24-6, f. 34; Candolim, 1772, vols. 13-15, f. 108.

[241] Cf. *V.P.,* Santo Estêvão (Jua), 1753, vols. 3-4, f. 65v.

did not exercise due control on the defaulters, neglecting as they did to draw up the Church rolls.[242]

It may be observed that some individuals drifted away from the parish at the time of the annual Easter precept. On the other hand, there were defaulters who never made an effort to ask for absolution or, upon being absolved of the excommunication, they would not bother about the Easter precept.[243]

Besides these two types of faults, the accusations further fell upon the non-fulfilment of religious pensions and the negligence of religious education of the servants, mainly the non-Christian female kaffirs. However, there are very few cases, not worth quantifying.

The informants also denounce 'backbiting', bad tempers and the quarrelsome attitude of some parishioners. Even though references and numbers are scarce (2.0 per cent) in this respect, it is quite interesting to note the presence of intra-caste webs of solidarity; inimical groups and little communities (members of confraternities, for example), that were responsible for greater social tensions in the microcosmic world of the village.[244] It may be noted that the above mentioned mission stations of the Vincentine fathers of Rachol sought to dismantle these webs of false solidarity and replace them with others of authentic Christian solidarity.

Bad treatment to daughters-in-law, fights between husband, wife and mother-in-law, quarrels between opposing groups,

[242] Cf. *V.P.*, Ribandar, 1774, vols. 13-15, f. 12; Ucassaim, 1760, vols. 7-8, f. 120.

[243] Cf. V.P. Betalbatim, 1799, vols. 27-9, f. 33; Carmoná, 1764, vols. 9-10, f. 92; Velsáo, 1799, vols. 18-20, ff. 19-19v; Penha de Frahça, 1798, vols. 27-8, ff. 101v, 103v; Pomburpá, 1772, vols. 13-15, ff. 3v, 5v, 1798, vols. 27-8, ff. 111v-112.

[244] The people of Assolna are divided, their main causes being, on the one hand, two Kshatriyas, Teotónio Vaz and Manuel Pais, and on the other, a Brahmin, José de Jesus Maria. In the elections of the confraternity of Our Lady of Martyrs the people divide among themselves, for each one wishes to elect the officials of their party, making unjust applications for the purpose. Father Álvaro Cardoso foments this disunity, taking the side of José de Jesus Maria (*V.P.*, Assolna, 1760, vols. 5-6, f. 132v). In Curca (1788), 'there are two factions that are mutually opposed and hinder the plans, with which they show their mutual hatred' (*V.P.*, vols. 21-3, f. 56).

hatred and enmity, are the main characteristics of the latent pugnacity that resound more in smaller milieus.[245]

There are quite a few cases of theft when compared with figures of other misdemeanours (1.0 per cent). The few references at our disposal show that many a time the targets of theft range from church property and liturgical paraments to coffers and pawns belonging to confraternities. There are also cases of minor stealing of wax, candles, oil.[246] The culprits were quite often (whenever the source specifies their profession) sacristans, church bailiffs, 'confraternity summoners', masons, kaffirs who frequently appear as material perpetrators of the crime, sometimes acting at the behest of their masters.[247]

Sale of underweight bread, acceptance of objects stolen by slaves, undue appropriation of fruits, poultry, rice, etc., were other theft objects revealing the rural character of this society.[248]

It may be noted that in other regions of the Kingdom and of Brazil these vices also scoured the country as earlier studies demonstrate. One case in point is Coimbra, where cases of concubinage were high on the list, followed by drunkenness, 'backbiting', etc.[249]

With reference to delicts imputed on the accused that we

[245] Cf. *V.P.*, Nagoa, 1772, vols. 13-15, f. 9; Moira, 1772, vols. 13-15, f. 27v, 1798, vols. 27-8, f. 15v; Chorão, 1766-7, vols. 11-12, f. 18v.

[246] There are references, for example, to the jewellery of the 'decoration' of St. Sebastian, images of the Infant Jesus, St. John and St. Sebastian (*V.P.*, Chinchinim, 1764, vols. 9-10, f. 116); silver candlestick of the church of St. Lawrence, Agaçaim (1788) that are found with the jeweller to be cleaned (*V.P.*, vols. 21-3, f. 68v); antependium of the side altar of Mandur (1794) (*V.P.*, vols. 24-6, f. 53v), etc. Further cf. *V.P.*, Nagoa, 1772, vols. 13-15, f. 86v; Carambolim, 1791, vols. 21-3, f. 74; Santa Luzia, 1767, vols. 11-12, f. 72v.

[247] Cf. *V.P.*, Piedade, 1797, vols. 24-6, f. 93; Oxel, 1792, vols. 21-3, ff. 60-60v; Chinchinim, 1764, vols. 9-10, f. 116.

[248] At Santa Inês (1767) one individual robbed a pan with pork meat (*V.P.*, vols. 11-12, f. 221v). Also cf. *V.P.*, Moira, 1772, vols. 13-15, f. 36; Pomburpa, 1761, vols. 7-8, f. 128v.

[249] Cf. Joaquim Carvalho and José Pedro Paiva, 'A Evolução das Visitas Pastorais da Diocese de Coimbra nos Séculos XVII e XVIII', in *Ler História*, no. 15, Lisbon, 1989, pp. 32-3.

have included in the third sociological area (non-Christians) too, there stand out some cases of sexual deviation. It is needless to repeat that in such a case, the partner is always a Christian or else the non-Christian would not fall under the ecclesiastical jurisdiction. It goes without saying that same is the case with delicts of sexual nature (concubinage, prostitution, etc.) in which only Christians are implicated. Suffice it to mention that the same delict was considered more serious if involving a non-Christian, for in addition to the delict per se there was some danger of apostasy or at least the risk of religious taint. However, it is important to dwell on practices attributed mainly to non-Christians: usury, irregularities in collecting tithes, keeping Christian servants in the household, the cohabitants of neo-converts with their non-Christian family members, and trading on Sundays.

The deponents at the visits mention several types of usurious agreements: of money, rice, tobacco. Moneylending at 10 per cent on mortgage of gold and silver; money lending at a profit of 20 per cent to 60 per cent (for example, when made to Balaghateers for the month-long voyage); sale of tobacco at one tanga to receive later two or three tangas; money taken in advance for *bat* to receive rice at harvest time cheaper than the seasonal price; lending of *bat* at higher price, etc. – these are only some ways in which money and food was extorted, which is quite illustrative of the unbridled exploitation often practised.[250]

This rather old and widespread problem in the diocese received special attention from Archbishop Neiva Brum who asked for support of the central government to control it. It may be recalled that usury was always considered a very serious crime given its moral and social consequences and hence of mixed

[250] In Nagoa an individual used to lend money on interest and later threaten to impose waiting charges, used to collect gifts of hens, cows, piglings, without deducting from the profits (*V.P.*, Nagoa, 1772, vols. 13-15, f. 88v). In Tivim, limited sums of money used to be lent out as also that of *bat* and legumes, at 'gains and regains' (*V.P.*, Tivim, 1795, vols. 24-6, f. 1v). In Anjuna (1792) an individual lent the Conchory *bat* at the harvest time of this *bat*, demanding the Sorty *bat* which is worth double at its harvest time (*V.P.*, vols. 21-3, ff. 62-62v).

jurisdiction. In accordance with the Constitutions, clergymen would be punished with incapacitation for benefits. Besides this, clerics and laymen would be denied ecclesiastical burial and the sacraments if, in spite of having the means, they failed to return what they had extorted.[251]

Despite their non-Christian faith, Hindus could not escape the clutches of the authorities, in this case ecclesiastical, considering the bearing their conduct had on the Christian society. However, although most individuals accused of usury were Hindus, we did come across Christians too, widows included.

The Church also forbade the Sunday sale of provisions by non-Christians, that is, it being a day consecrated to the Lord and believing that this distracted the faithful from their religious duties.

The presence of Christian servants in non-Christian households, 'behind closed doors', no doubt shows the peaceful co-existence of the different creeds, a characteristic feature of Goan society down the ages. Whereas on the one hand, this perfectly translated the policy of the New Conquests, on the other hand, it meant exposing Catholic orthodoxy to risk. It was precisely the fear of ideological and religious contamination that prompted ecclesiastical authorities to punish such happenings, thus precluding the fatality of religious syncretism and reversion into Hindu beliefs.

DELICT-PLACE

It is sometimes possible to establish a certain correlation between given delicts and geographical areas. Thus, many inhabitants of Ucassaim used to fail to attend Mass and the precept of Easter communion. Was that a region Christianized later? Was it a population whose conversion was somewhat extrinsic? This can be gathered from the opinion of an informant who denounced an alcoholic priest: He stated that 'such a priest should not live in that village, whose inhabitants are of a weak faith'. Evidently,

[251] Cf. Constitutions, Book V, Tit. VII, p. 312.

this ecclesiastic would have a deleterious effect on a village with characteristics like this one.[252]

In Margão, for unknown reasons, the index of alcoholism is quite high (including many alcoholic priests), the same being the case in two parishes of Bardez, Guirim and Nagoa. On the other hand, it is also explicable that the practice of usury was quite widespread in the parishes of Moira, where 'all those who have limited money invest it for excessive gains', and of Tivim, where they also 'make investments and reinvestments ...'. This can have a relation with the market necessities, motivated by the weekly Mapusa Fair, which by now had been drawing large crowds.[253]

In Mapusa too, where there were many Hindus connected with industry and trade, all the non-Christian tinkers in the year 1772 continued to work on Sundays and holy days and almost all of them had Christian servants in their houses notwithstanding the promises they had made at the previous visit.

There were many cases registered of prostitution in Pangim and Panelim, where 'many worldly women enter and leave'.[254] If we consider the large number of women corrupting themselves with soldiers (both whites and locals), we understand the natural *delict-place* correspondence: there were many military barracks in those parishes, and in Panelim the Royal Hospital too, where the Portuguese soldiers used to go for treatment. The Viceroy's court, another focal point of servants and employees, had its headquarters in Panelim until its transfer to Pangim in the administration of the Count of Ega (1760).

[252] Cf. *V.P.*, Ucassaim, 1772, vols. 13-15, ff. 25v-26. The people of the village of Bastora in Ucassaim used to normally not respect the duty of Mass. There being 900 Christians, only 50 used to hear Mass in the chapel (*V.P.*, Ucassaim, 1760, vols. 7-8, f. 120).

[253] Cf. *V.P.*, Tivim, 1795, vols. 24-6, f. 1v, op. cit.; Moira, 1772, vols. 13-15, f. 36v. With respect to the Mapusa fair, it is read in the Bardez town council proceedings, of 12 February 1785, which 'in their tents sell with the greatest abundance, liberty and safety all the commodities of victuals, clothes, copper, tin; there also come people from Ilhas and Salsete and from foreign lands' (Central Library, Pangim, manuscript 46B, f. 64).

[254] Cf. *V.P.*, Panelim, 1782, vols. 16-17, f. 186; Pangim, 1788, vols. 21-3, ff. 25v-30.

DELICT-PENALTIES

First, the episcopal visit aimed at correcting public sins. Let us see, therefore, if the Church had an appropriate judicial apparatus to allow its action in society.

In Portugal, the Council of Trent had rather reinforced the episcopal jurisdiction. As the 'spiritual censorship', applied by the Church during the past centuries, had fallen into discredit, it was sought to reformulate it; hence, its replacement by pecuniary penalties, imprisonment, change of residence, deportation, etc. In fact, it had been stipulated that the ecclesiastical authority should award 'real and personal' penalties only when they actually had measures to enforce their application.[255]

The Church had in fact established an administrative-judicial board comprising among others, one bailiff and one Church interpreter, allowing him to act immediately. The former was duty-bound to inform the parish priest about the worldly women; prevent servile tasks on Sundays and holy days; find out if people had heard Mass and fulfilled their Easter precept; if Christians were in the employ of non-Christians, and so on. The interpreter had specific functions too, such as to register the names of the faithful in the Church rolls. These parish employees thus made it possible for the Church to take legal action against the people. On the other hand, it was the bailiff's duty to fulfil the sanctions determined by the Archbishops, such as taking the transgressor to their presence or to the *aljube,* or prison of the ecclesiastical court.[256]

[255] See Joaquim Ramos de Carvalho, 'A Jurisdição Episcopal sobre Leigos em Matéria de Pecados Públicos: as Visitas Pastorais e o Comportamento Moral das Populações Portuguesas de Antigo Regime', in *Revista Portuguesa de História,* vol. XXIV, F.L.U.C., 1988, pp. 135-7.

[256] Cf. *V.P.,* Varca, 1760, vols. 9-10, f. 77, 1771, vols. 11-12, f. 78; Anjuna, 1772, vols. 13-15, f. 65v. It was also the bailiff's duty to warn the people, when they corrupted themselves (*V.P.,* S. Tomé de Salsete, 1799, vols. 27-9, f. 24; Pilerne, 1798, vols. 27-9, f. 93v; Benaulim, 1764, vols. 9-10, f. 70v; Candolim, 1798, vols. 27-9, f. 81). The parish administrative board further comprised the Church caller, the *boiás* (*boya,* men who carried the umbrella, when the parish priest took the viaticum to the sick) (*V.P.,* Panelim, 1797, vols. 24-6, f. 5; Salsete, 1764, vols. 9-10, f. 31v).

The correlation between the delict and the penalty stipulated is not always clear; it is not easy either to classify the different types of penalties imposed on the accused at the pastoral visits. In fact, there were different sentences prescribed for a given crime in apparently identical circumstances. Meanwhile, there seems to have been also certain general tendencies, which it is important to note.

Generally, the heavier penalties of imprisonment and deportation were only applied to serious cases, to notorious public sinners or in case of relapse (almost always for the third time). The amount of pecuniary penalty would depend on several factors, such as seriousness of the fault, the professional position of the delinquent and his social status. The cleric who, in the spirit of the Tridentine reform, was one of the main targets of pastoral visits, would be subject to a great number of penalties, such as his retirement into a seminary, spiritual exercises, confession, etc. He would also have to pay more than the layman in identical circumstances.

Let us now analyse the correlation between certain crimes and the respective penalties. Those accused of fomenting fights or discord would be reprehended or asked to sign an undertaking to live in peace and concord, to confess and, at times, to pay a fine. There was a higher penalty for priests; they could even face imprisonment.[257]

In theft cases, pecuniary fines were generally applied, restitution of assets when possible and, in certain cases, deprivation of the job as, for example, that of the Church bailiff or sacristan. In Velsão (Salsete), a public thief was put behind bars, obviously because of the seriousness of the case.[258]

In the event of civilians indulging in alcoholism, either admonition or undertaking, confession and pecuniary penalty would be employed; but for clerics, the penalty prescribed was retirement, spiritual exercises, high fine and, at times, imprisonment.

[257] Cf. *V.P.,* Orlim, 1764, vols. 9-10, f. 84v; Curca, 1788, vols. 21-3, f. 56; Sirula, 1772, vols. 13-15, ff. 14, 16v; Curtorim, 1783, vols. 27-9, ff. 40-40v.

[258] Cf. *V.P.,* Majorda, 1764, vols. 9-10, f. 37; Bambolim, 1791, vols. 21-3, f. 49v; Mandur, 1794, vols. 24-6, f. 53v; Velsão, 1799, vols. 18-20, f. 20v.

Coming next to penalties for sexual deviations: There was a great variety of penalties, apparently considering diverse aggravating and attenuating factors. Women who debased themselves were often shunted to another parish or, very rarely, kept in an honest household and commended to the vigilance of the párish priests. The use of certain corporal punishments like the ferule and head shaving to 'correct and deter others' is curious to note. It is like a reminiscence of the penalties quite widespread in the first days of the Christianization of Goa, consigned in the Constitutions of the sixteenth century.[259]

In some cases the soldiers too were removed or deported to other provinces.[260] The corruption of non-Christians (with Christians, evidently) was punished with admonition or undertaking, which could be repeated probably up to the third 'lapse'. Thus, the penalty for non-Christian culprits was lighter, given the lower degree of responsibility on his part as compared to Christians and clerics.[261]

Sexual demeanour was also punished with imprisonment and deportation, in more serious cases, or relapse, or in the case of married people.[262] Consent or connivance of family members in concubinage or prostitution also attracted imprisonment. This

[259] Cf. *V.P.*, Sancoale, 1772, vols. 11-12, f. 197. The denounced woman was taken to 'Cortarim' [Cortalim] and handed to the parish priest whence she would not leave for 3 years. Denounced in three earlier visits, she did not fulfil the deportation to Navelim; Nagoa, 1765, vols. 9-10, f. 32v; in Pilerne, 1779, vols. 13-15, ff. 19-22, one denounced woman was kept in an honest household; another, punished with a ferule and with her head shaven; yet another was deported to Calangute (*V.P.*, Penha de França, 1779, vols. 13-15, ff. 10v-11).

[260] The official José Pasca Pessinga was deported to Angediva (*V.P.*, R. Magos, 1773, vols. 13-15, ff. 123-123v).

[261] One non-Christian living in concubinage with a married Christian, after having been reprehended several times, was obliged to make a stipulation, confessing the fault and paying 4 xerafins (*V.P.*, Calangute, 1798, vols. 27-9, f. 75v). It may be observed, thus, that firstly he was warned and only later, by virtue of his persistence in this fault, he was punished. Also cf. *V.P.*, Candolim, 1765, vols. 9-10, f. 22v.

[262] An adjudant of the General of Bardez, José da Silva Marques, was living in concubinage for many years with a widow from whom he had children. He was punished with imprisonment (*V.P.*, Guirim, 1761, vols. 9-10, f. 43).

speaks of the importance attached to the morally responsible and to the deeper motives of human conduct. For the same reason perhaps, those accused of running brothels were also punished with imprisonment.[263]

At the first fault, the priest was either warned or asked to sign an undertaking of self-correction. If he persisted in the vice, punishments could range from spiritual exercises and withdrawal into a seminary up to deprivation of a post, imposition of high pecuniary penalties or imprisonment.

As noted earlier, the Tridentine council focussed on reformation of the clergy, seeking to improve and dignify their behaviour. The parish priest, thanks to the efficacy of his example, was the basic human factor of this spiritual renewal. Hence, at the pastoral visits the ecclesiastical jurisdiction was particularly strict with the clergy who would not 'satisfy, or fulfilled their ecclesiastical duties badly.' And when this lack of observance was linked to other deviations, penalties would evidently become heavier, going up to excommunication, temporary or permanent suspension of the Orders, and the entrusting of the process to the High Court.[264]

The typical coexistence of Christians and non-Christians that was once (and continues to be) very peaceful in Goa does raise, however, the problem of the influence of non-Christians on Christians. The Church therefore forbade Christians from living in non-Christian households. It was for this very reason that the visitors ordained the non-Christians to disengage their Christian servants or to send them back to their original parishes. Now, as regards the Christian *kaffirs*, the penalty was to have them sold immediately to any Christian.[265]

[263] Cf. *V.P.,* Benaulim, 1759, vols. 5-6, f. 71; Carmona, vols. 5-6, ff. 128v-129; Daugim, 1785, vols. 16-17, ff. 149v-150.

[264] On the behaviour of the clergymen, see D. António Xavier de Sousa Monteiro, *Manual de Direito Ecclesiástico Parochial para Uso dos Párocos,* 3rd edn., Coimbra, University Press, 1890, pp. 629-48 (The 1st edn. is dated 1867 and the work is based on various Constitutions of the Kingdom, Bahia, Goa and Angra).

[265] Cf. *V.P.,* S. Brás (Gondolim), 1767, vols. 11-12, f. 65; Santa Luzia, 1767, vols. 11-12, ff. 73-74v and 1791, vols. 21-3, f. 13; Pangim, 1797, vols. 24-6, f. 19v.

Against usury, the sanction most frequently applied was payment to the injured parties or returning of the surplus, though it could also attract a pecuniary penalty or appearance before the Archbishop and, in more serious cases, major excommunication.[266]

OUTLINE OF QUANTITATIVE ANALYSIS OF THE DATA COLLECTED FROM THE BOOKS OF JUDICIAL INQUESTS AND UNDERTAKINGS[267]

Visiting Activity of the Archbishops

In half a century (1750-1800) there were twenty-five years of pastoral visits; that means an average of one visit held to the diocese every two years. Archbishop D. Frei Lourenço de Santa Maria (1744-50) visited Ilhas in 1750 (see Table III.1).

Archbishop D. António held ten visits in his twenty-four year administration (1750-74) which means a visit every two years. He touched an average of 132 cases and heard 162 denouncers (see Table III.2).

The table shows 1767 and 1772/3 as being very active years for Ilhas and Bardez; they had a success rate of 1.0 and 0.8, respectively.[268] Despite the lack of figures for the visits of 1752 and 1754, we can say that the number of cases and denouncers increased considerably in the decade between 1764-74. Thus, whereas 243 cases were registered and 325 informants heard between 1752 and 1761, in the said decade the number of cases rose to 945 and denouncers to 1200, that is, the cases and the witnesses more than trebled.

[266] Cf. *V.P.*, Bambolim, 1753, vols. 3-4, f. 103; Carambolim, 1788, vols. 21-3, f. 86v; S. Matias de Malar, 1767, vols. 11-12, f. 48. Father João Jordão Pereira gives the *bat* seed to the needy for a higher price and accepts mortgages. He was punished with major excommunication and reclusion in Chimbel *(V.P.,* Benaulim, 1771, vols. 11-12, f. 65).

[267] For the treatment of the amounts of the visits, the methods presented by Joaquim Ramos de Carvalho and José Pedro Paiva in their study, op. cit., were very helpful.

[268] The success rate of the visit was obtained based on the relation between the number of cases and that of the denouncers.

TABLE III.1: VISITS REALISED BY FRIAR D. LOURENÇO DE SANTA MARIA

Year	Province	Churches visited	Total cases	Total denouncers	Ratio cases/church	Ratio cases/denouncer
1750	Ilhas	12	67	99	5.5	0.6

Note: Some figures are illegible and the table is therefore slightly incomplete.

TABLE III.2: VISITS REALISED BY D. ANTÓNIO T.N.B. DA SILVEIRA

Year	Province	Churches visited	Total cases	Total denouncers	Ratio cases/church	Ratio cases/denouncer
1752/3	Ilhas	10	77	87	7.7	0.8
1759/60	Salsete	23	90	148	3.9	0.6
1760/1	Bardez	24	76	90	3.1	0.8
1764	Salsete	21	134	232	6.3	0.5
1765/6	Bardez	17	113	146	6.6	0.7
1767	Ilhas	33	228	227	6.9	1.0
1771/2	Salsete	25	141	223	5.6	0.6
1772/3	Bardez	22	226	272	10.2	0.8
1774	Ilhas	10	103	100	10.3	1.0
–	–	185	1188	1525	6.7	0.7

Note: The records of the visits to Bardez in 1752 and 1754 are almost impossible to read and therefore their datat has not been included this table.

TABLE III.3: VISITS REALISED DURING THE TIME OF D. FRANCISCO DE ASSUNÇÃO E BRITO

Year	Province	Churches visited	Total cases	Total denouncers	Ratio cases/church	Ratio cases/denouncer
1779	Bardez	5	19	22	3.8	0.8

TABLE III.4: VISITS REALISED BY FRIAR D. MANUEL DE SANTA CATARINA

Year	Province	Churches visited	Total cases	Total denouncers	Ratio cases/church	Ratio cases/denouncer
1782	Ilhas	42	249	222	5.9	1.1
1782/3	Bardez	23	153	119	6.6	1.2
1783/4	Salsete	25	195	258	7.8	0.7
1785	Ilhas	30	123	144	4.1	0.8
1786	Bardez	22	117	167	5.3	0.7
1787	Salsete	24	50	58	2.0	0.8
1788	Ilhas	27	224	215	8.2	1.4
1791	Ilhas	35	105	87	3.0	1.2
1792	Bardez	24	167	238	6.9	0.7
1794/5	Ilhas	36	146	143	4.0	1.0
1795	Bardez	23	155	179	6.7	0.8
1797/8	Ilhas	29	211	131	7.2	1.6
1798/9	Bardez	24	218	253	9.0	0.8
1799/1800	Salsete	25	174	164	6.9	1.0
–	–	389	2287	2378	5.9	0.9

In the brief administration of D. Francisco de Assunção e Brito (1774-80) there was only one visit held in 1779 (see Table III.3).[269]

D. Fr. Manuel de Santa Catarina (1780-1812), in the twenty years of governance between 1780-1800, undertook fourteen visits to the diocese, with a rough average of one visit per year (see Table III.4).[270]

The year 1788 registered the highest number of cases. In the final years of this century, the number of denouncers and cases as well as the efficacy of the visits continued to be considerable. We can possibly conclude that the visits conducted by the diocesan prelates in the second half of the eighteenth century were relevant indeed.

Delicts

Bearing in mind that the figures can be precarious, as said above, we conclude that the Goan pastoral visits held between 1750 and 1800 present the following crime table: Concubinage topped the list (24 per cent); then followed prostitution (18.5 per cent), and finally, drunkenness, also with a high incidence (15.0 per cent).

Other deviations of sexual nature, like those marked 'sensuality', touched 10 per cent and at a certain distance from these, but quite seriously positioned, figure faults of non-compliance of duties by priests (8.0 per cent).

[269] D. Francisco de Assunção e Brito was called to the court in order to deal with affairs relating to the diocese. He left Goa in January 1780. Substituting him as Governor and Administrator of the archbishopric was D. Frei Manuel de Santa Catarina, Bishop of Cochin. The Archbishop of Goa, D. Francisco de Assunção e Brito renounced the mitre on 1 January 1783. Cf. the letters of Frederico Guilherme de Sousa, dated 1 January 1780, and of D. Frei Manuel de Santa Catarina to M.M. Castro, dated 2 January 1780, giving the news.

[270] It may be noted, in fact, that in the year 1795 the visits were most successful during the administration of D. Frei Manuel de Santa Catarina (1.6).

Cases of lesser incidence in the over-all picture of delicts were those of absence from Mass (4.5 per cent), those designated as 'bawdy house', separation and usury with 4.0 per cent. Finally, in decreasing order, came cases that we have termed as 'services by Christians to non-Christians' (3.0 per cent), quarrels and Easter precept default (2.0 per cent) and theft (1.0 per cent) (see Table III.5).

TABLE III.5: TABLE OF DELICTS IN THE TERRITORY OF GOA (1750-1800)

Deviations	% of occurencies	% of denouncers
Brothel	4.0	4.0
Quarrels	2.0	2.0
Alcoholism	15.0	18.5
Theft	1.0	2.0
Absence from communion	2.0	1.5
Absence from mass	4.5	3.5
Concubinage	24.0	17.0
Non-fulf. duties	8.0	13.0
Prostitution	18.5	17.0
Sensuality	10.0	10.0
Separation	4.0	4.5
Services to heathens	3.0	2.5
Usury	4.0	4.5

The said table also shows that the number of denouncers almost matches that of the respective deviations. Only in relation to drunkenness and defaulting in their priestly duties, the percentage of informants was higher than that of the cases invoked. Above all, in relation to the priests' deviations, the number of witnesses was quite higher than that of the cases (8.0 per cent against 13.0 per cent for denouncers). Further, it is clear that a smashing majority of the informants themselves were priests.

Let us now analyse the crime scene in each province (see Tables III.6, III.7 and III.8).

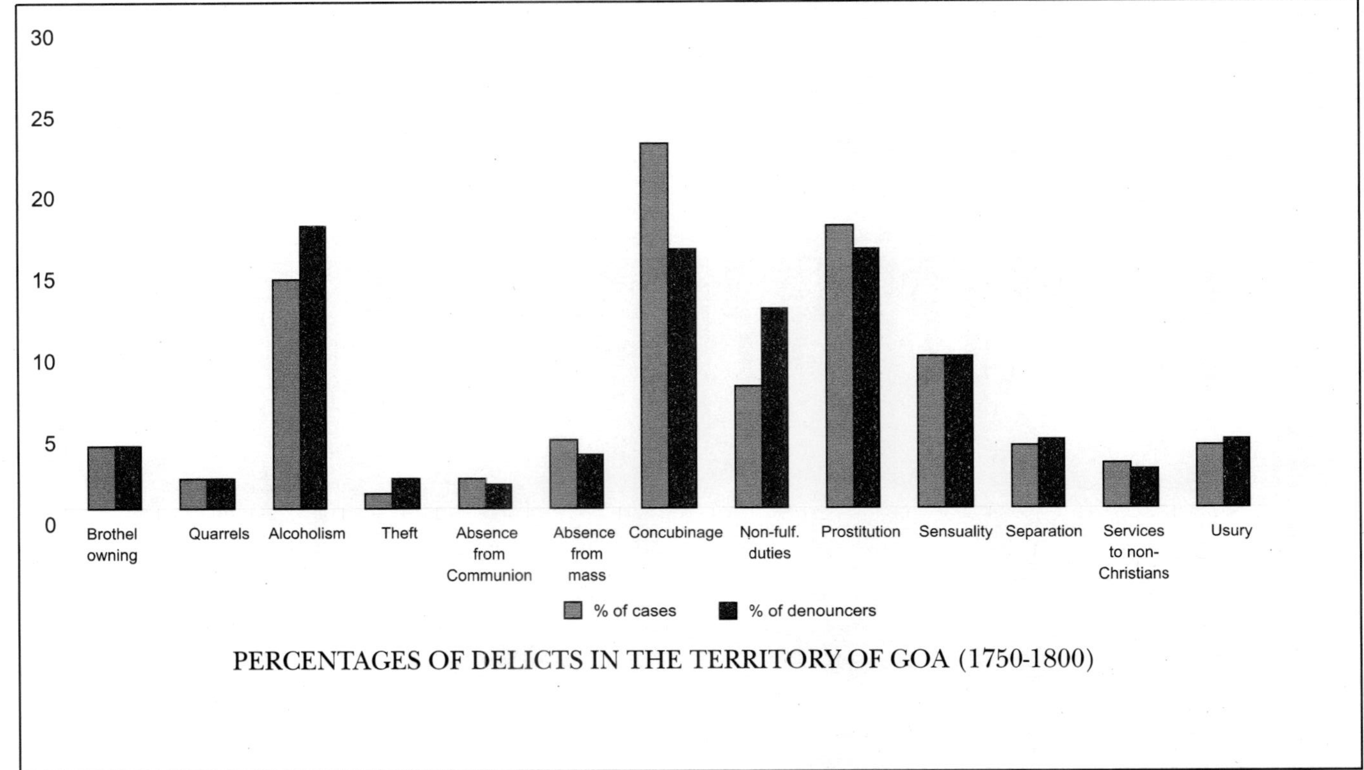

PERCENTAGES OF DELICTS IN THE TERRITORY OF GOA (1750-1800)

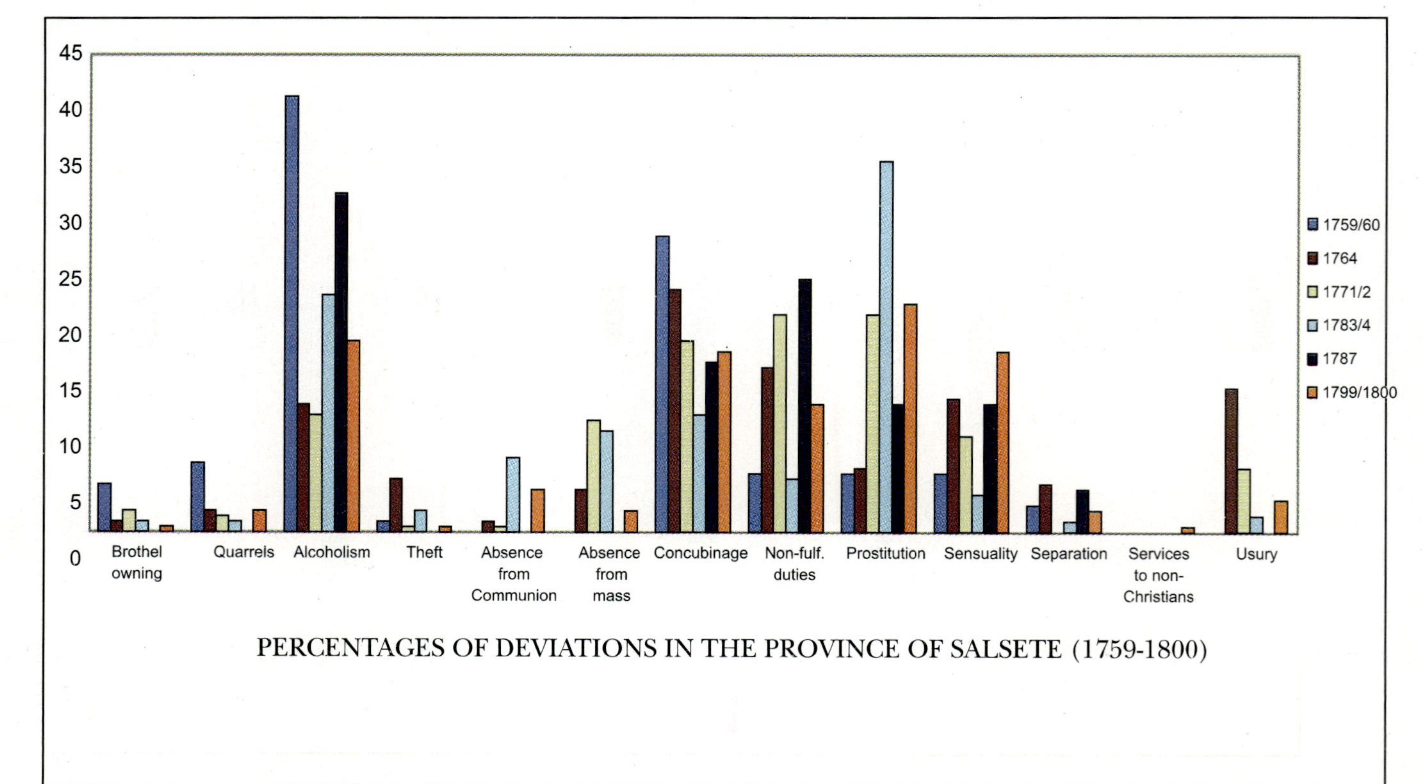

PERCENTAGES OF DEVIATIONS IN THE PROVINCE OF SALSETE (1759-1800)

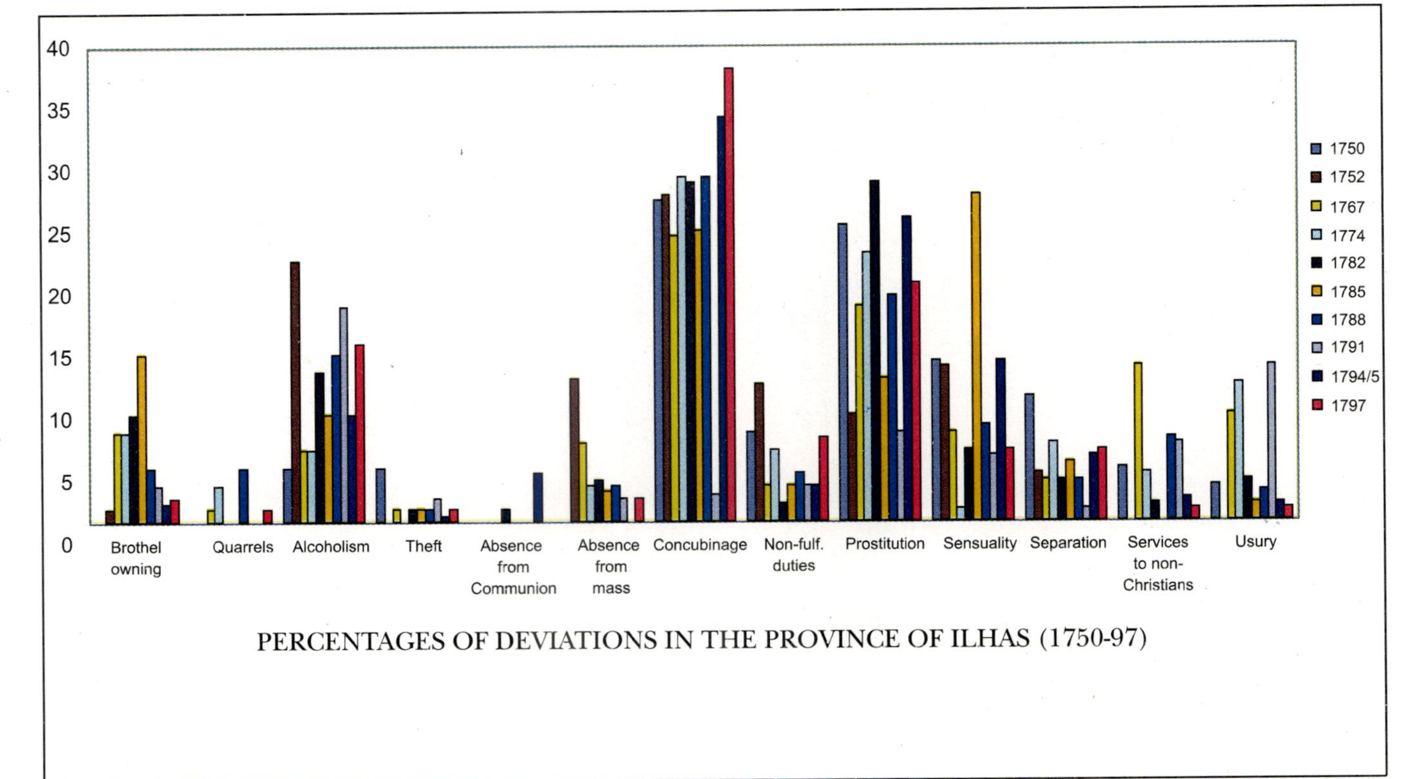

PERCENTAGES OF DEVIATIONS IN THE PROVINCE OF ILHAS (1750-97)

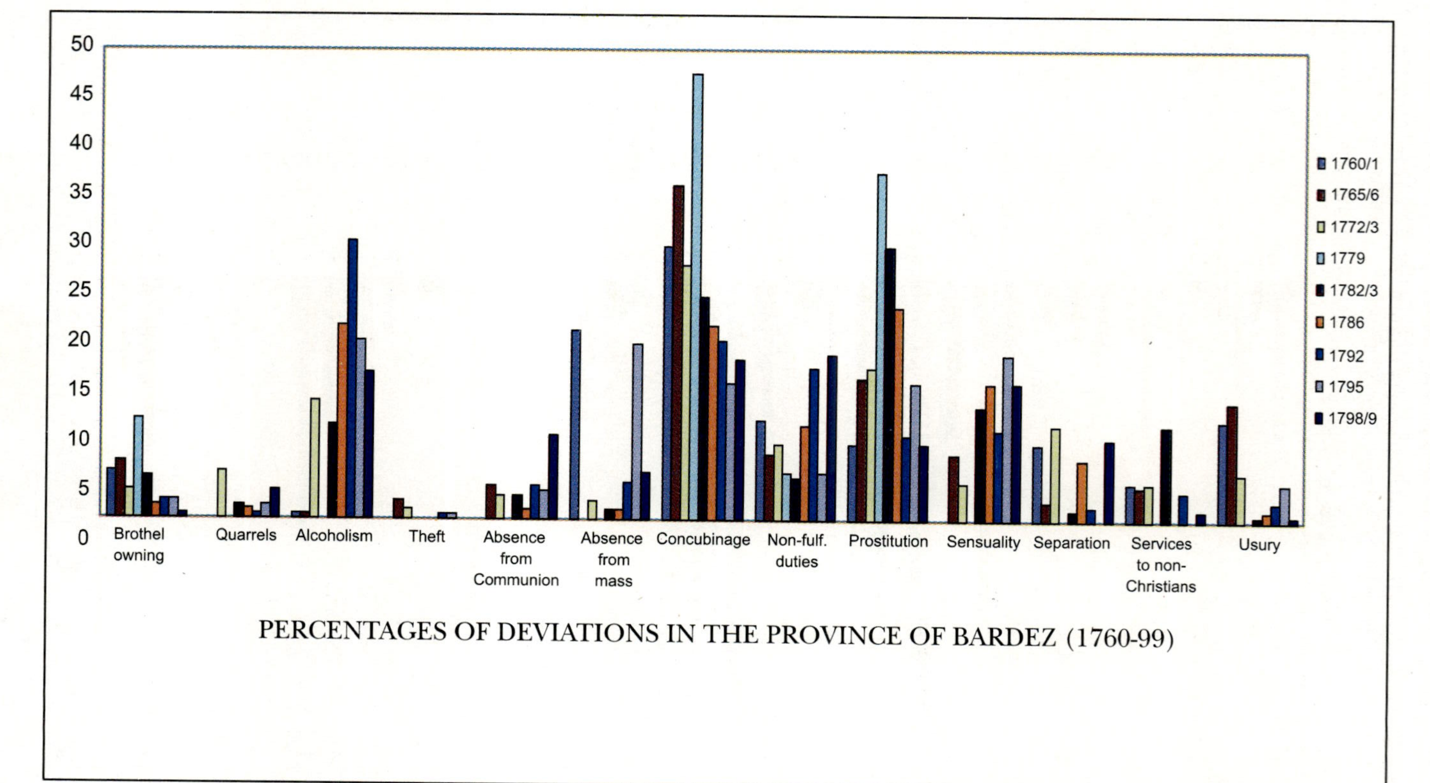

PERCENTAGES OF DEVIATIONS IN THE PROVINCE OF BARDEZ (1760-99)

TABLE III.6: PERCENTAGES OF DEVIATIONS IN THE PROVINCE OF ILHAS (1750-97)

Deviations	1750	1752	1767	1774	1782	1785	1788	1791	1794/5	1797	Total
Brothel owning	–	1	7.5	7.5	9	14	4.5	3	1.5	2	6
Quarrels	–	–	1	3	–	–	4.5	–	–	1	2
Alcoholism	4.5	22	6	6	12.5	9	14	18	9	15	11
Theft	4.5	–	1	–	1	1	1	2	0.5	1	1
Absence from Communion	–	–	–	–	1	–	–	–	4	–	0.5
Absence from Mass	–	12	6.5	3	3.5	2.5	3	2	–	2	3.5
Concubinage	27	27.5	24	29	28.5	24.5	29	2.2	34	38	28
Non-fulf. Duties	7.5	11.5	3	6	1.5	3	4	3	3	7	4
Prostitution	25	9	18	22.5	28.5	12	19	7.4	25.5	20	21
Sensuality	13.5	13	7.5	1	6	27.5	8	5.5	13.5	6	9.5
Separation	10.5	4	3.5	6.5	3.5	5	3.5	1	5.5	6	4.5
Services to non-Christians	4.5	–	13	4	1.5	–	7	6.5	2	1	4.5
Usury	3	–	9	11.5	3.5	1.5	2.5	13	1.5	1	4.5

TABLE III.7: PERCENTAGES OF DEVIATIONS IN THE PROVINCE OF BARDEZ (1760-99)

Deviations	1760/1	1765/6	1772/3	1778/9	1782/3	1876	1792	1795	1798/9	Total
Brothel owning	5.0	6.0	3.0	10.5	4.5	1.5	2.0	2.0	0.5	3.0
Quarrels	–	–	5.0	–	1.5	1.0	0.5	1.5	3.0	2.0
Alcoholism	0.5	0.6	12.5	–	10.0	20.5	29.5	19.0	15.5	15.5
Theft	–	2.0	1.0	–	–	–	0.5	0.5	–	1.0
Eas. precept def.	–	3.5	2.5	–	2.5	1.0	3.5	3.0	9.0	5.5
Absence from Mass	20.0	–	2.0	–	1.0	1.0	4.0	18.5	5.0	5.5
Concubinage	29.0	35.5	27.0	47.5	23.5	20.5	19.0	14.5	17.0	23.0
Non-fulf. duties	10.5	7.0	8.0	5.0	4.5	10.0	16.0	5.0	17.5	10.0
Prostitution	8.0	15.0	16.0	37.0	29.0	22.5	9.0	14.5	8.0	15.0
Sensuality	–	7.0	4.0	–	12.0	14.5	9.5	17.5	14.5	10.0
Separation	8.0	2.0	10.0	–	1.0	6.5	1.5	–	8.5	5.0
Services to non-Christians	4.0	3.5	4.0	–	10.0	–	3.0	–	1.0	3.0
Usury	10.5	12.5	5.0	–	0.5	1.0	2.0	4.0	0.5	3.5

Ilhas

Concubinage attained the highest numbers not only as a whole but also in individual years (405 cases out of total 1,443, which represented 28 per cent of the totality of deviations in this province, between 1750 and 1800). Quite close on its heels was the prostitution record (300 cases, meaning 21 per cent of the total). However, in the year 1752 prostitution was overtaken by alcoholism and in 1785 by brothels.

In the third place comes drunkenness (11 per cent), followed by sensuality (9.5 per cent) and brothels (6 per cent). In the sixth place stood the practices of separation, usury and what we have termed 'services by Christians to non-Christians' – all of them with the same percentage (4.5 per cent). In the seventh place figure cases referring to the non-fulfilment of duties by priests and at the foot of the scale, non-attendance at Mass (3.5 per cent), theft (1 per cent), and non-performance of the annual Easter precept (0.5 per cent).

The year 1782 had the highest incidence of cases (249 deviations), followed by 1767 (with 228 faults) and 1788 (with 224 illicit practices).

Bardez

Concubinage reaches the highest numbers (23 per cent), followed by cases of drunkenness (15.5 per cent) and of prostitution (15 per cent) with almost the same percentage. In the fourth place come cases of non-fulfilment of clerical duties and of sensuality; after them and in decreasing order figure the faults of non-fulfilment of the annual Easter precept and Mass, in equal percentage; cases of separation, usury, brothels and services of Christians to non-Christians, with identical percentages, and last of all, theft.

The year 1772-3 had the highest number of deviations (226 cases), followed by 1798/9 (with 218 faults) and 1795 (with 155 illicit practices).

Salsete

The highest percentage of deviations was related to drunkenness (20 per cent) (159 cases out of 784). Very close to those numbers

TABLE III.8: PERCENTAGES OF DEVIATIONS IN THE PROVINCE OF SALSETE (1759-1800)

Deviations	1759/60	1764	1771/2	1783/4	1787	1799/1800	Total
Brothel	4.5	1.0	2.0	1.0	–	0.5	1.5
Quarrels	6.5	2.0	1.5	1.0	–	2.0	2.0
Alcoholism	41.0	12.0	11.0	22.5	32.0	18.0	20.0
Theft	1.0	5.0	0.5	2.0	–	0.5	1.5
Eas. Precept def.	–	1.0	0.5	7.0	–	4.0	3.0
Absence from Mass	–	4.0	10.5	9.5	–	2.0	5.5
Concubinage	28.0	23.0	18.0	11.0	16.0	17.0	18.0
Non-fulf. Cler. duties	5.5	15.5	20.5	5.0	24.0	12.0	12.5
Prostitution	5.5	6.0	20.5	35.0	12.0	21.5	19.5
Sensuality	5.5	12.5	9.0	3.5	12.0	17.0	10.0
Separation	2.5	4.5	–	1.0	4.0	2.0	2.0
Services to non-Christians	–	–	–	–	–	0.5	0.1
Usury	–	13.5	6.0	1.5	–	3.0	4.4

are the cases of prostitution (19.5 per cent) and of concubinage (18 per cent).

This is followed by deviations in ecclesiastical duties by priests (12.5 per cent); sensuality (10 per cent) and, quite down the line, absence from Mass (5.5 per cent), usury (4.4 per cent) and non-fulfilment of the annual Easter precept (3 per cent). In the crime table, separation has a position close to cases with a smaller percentage, like fights (2 per cent) and theft (1.5 per cent). In the last place figures service to non-Christians by Christians (0.1 per cent).

The year 1783/4 had the biggest number of cases (195 deviations), followed by 1799/1800 (with 174 faults) and 1771/2 (with 141 illicit practices).

COMPARATIVE ANALYSIS OF DELICTS IN THE THREE PROVINCES

Sexual deviations like concubinage, prostitution, sensuality, and brothels, touched the highest numbers in the province of Ilhas (see Table III.9). This can probably be explained by its

TABLE III.9: COMPARISON OF PERCENTAGES OF DELICTS IN THE THREE PROVINCES IN DECREASING ORDER (1750-1800)

Province of Ilhas		Province of Bardez		Province of Salsete	
Delicts	%	Delicts	%	Delicts	%
Concubinage	28.0	Concubinage	23.0	Drunkenness	20.0
Prostitution	21.0	Drunkenness	15.5	Prostitution	19.5
Drunkenness	11.0	Prostitution	15.0	Concubinage	18.0
Sensuality	9.5	Sensuality	10.0	Non-ful. Cler. duty	12.5
Brothels	6.0	Non-ful. Cler. duty	10.0	Sensuality	10.0
Separation	4.5	Absence of Mass	5.5	Absence of Mass	5.5
Serv. to Hindus	4.5	Eas. Pr. Def.	5.5	Usury	4.4
Usury	4.5	Separation	5.0	Eas. Pr. Def.	3.0
Non-ful. Cler. duty	4.0	Usury	3.5	Quarrels	2.0
Absence of Mass	3.5	Serv. to Hindus	3.0	Separation	2.0
Quarrels	2.0	Brothels	3.0	Brothels	1.5
Theft	1.0	Quarrels	2.0	Theft	1.5
Eas. Pr. Def.	0.5	Theft	1.0	Serv. to Hindus	0.1

more urban and cosmopolitan setting; great affluence of soldiers, above all Reinóis; more contacts with the external world through the port and more promiscuity. It may be noted, for example, that the brothel or the 'lenocinium' figures in the fifth place in the over-all crime picture of Ilhas, whereas in Bardez it is in the eighth place and in Salsete in the tenth place.

In relation to the deviation that we have termed as services to non-Christians by Christians, there are inter-provincial differences. Thus, at the sixth place in Ilhas its percentage was higher than in the other two, whereas in Bardez it was in the eighth and in Salsete the eleventh place. In spite of the decadence of the city of Goa and of its trade too, many merchants, tithe collectors, Hindu shopkeepers to whom the Christians rendered services, continued to live in Ilhas. In Salsete, there were few Hindus and hence it is not surprising to find a low percentage of services to non-Christians by Christians.

Drunkenness, considerably widespread in Goa, reached considerable proportions in Salsete. Could it be because of a higher production of *sura*[271] due to a bigger number of coconut trees there? The fault in complying with religious duties by clergymen and faithful was more pronounced in Bardez and Salsete than in Ilhas. As is known, with regard to deviations by priests, this situation was since long true of the regulars administering parishes in Bardez. In Ilhas, they were more under the Archbishop's watchful eye. Could absenteeism of the faithful from Mass and their non-fulfilment of the annual Easter precept have a relation with non-fulfilment of duties by the priests? For instance, in Bastora (Ucassaim), the priests were accused of not drawing up the roll of the Christian population and of setting a bad example to the faithful.

Usury was quite widely practised in the three provinces and indeed its place is almost identical in the comparative table of the delicts.

Since the efficacy of the visit is a result of the ratio between the total number of cases and the total number of denouncers, this data has to be used with due care. Thus, the number of

[271] See the Glossary.

cases and denouncers is usually linked to the number of churches visited. When the churches are few, the percentage rises proportionally. This was noticed about the Bardez visit in the year 1779, where a high percentage of cases of concubinage (47.5 per cent) is accounted for by its reduced number of churches (only 5) and denouncers (31). Thus, it turns out to be quite an artificial percentage.

A year-wise comparative analysis is not possible, as the visitation years of Ilhas, Bardez and Salsete are not the same.

Higher global as well as year-specific figures relating to number of churches visited and delicts recorded came from the province of Ilhas, followed by Bardez and a little way down, Salsete, as shown by the following tables (see Tables III.10, III.11 and III.12).

It was in 1782 that the number of cases reached their highest point in comparison with all the visits held in Goa in the second half of the eighteenth century. That happened in Ilhas with 249 cases and a visit success rate of 1.1 per cent. Next came the year 1767, again in Ilhas, with 228 cases and a success rate of 1.0 per cent, followed by Bardez in 1772/3, with 226 cases and a success rate of 0.8 per cent.

TABLE III.10: NUMBER OF CASES, DENOUNCERS AND CHURCHES IN THE PROVINCE OF ILHAS (1750-97)

Years	Cases	Denouncers	Churches	Ratio cases/ denouncers	Ratio cases/ church
				effectiveness of visits	
1750	67	99	12	0.6	5.5
1752	77	87	10	0.9	7.7
1767	228	227	33	1.0	6.9
1774	103	100	10	1.0	10.3
1782	249	222	42	1.1	5.9
1785	123	144	30	0.8	4.1
1788	224	215	27	1.0	8.2
1791	105	87	35	1.3	3.0
1794/5	146	143	36	1.0	4.0
1797	111	131	29	0.8	3.8
Total	1,433	1,455	264	0.9	5.4

TABLE III.11: NUMBER OF CASES, DENOUNCERS AND CHURCHES IN THE PROVINCE OF BARDEZ (1760-99)

Years	Cases	Denouncers	Churches	Ratio cases/ denouncers	Ratio cases/ church
				effectiveness of visits	
1760/1	76	90	24	0.8	3.1
1765/6	113	146	17	0.8	6.6
1772/3	226	272	22	0.8	10.2
1779	19	22	5	0.9	3.8
1782/3	153	119	23	1.3	6.6
1786	117	167	22	0.7	5.3
1792	167	238	24	0.7	7.0
1795	155	179	23	0.9	6.7
1798/9	218	253	24	0.8	9.0
Total	1,244	1,486	184	0.8	6.8

TABLE III.12: NUMBER OF CASES, DENOUNCERS AND CHURCHES IN THE PROVINCE OF SALSETE (1759-1800)

Years	Cases	Denouncers	Churches	Ratio cases/ denouncers	Ratio cases/ church
				effectiveness of visits	
1759/60	90	148	23	0.6	4.0
1764	134	232	21	0.6	6.3
1771/2	141	223	25	0.6	5.6
1783/4	195	258	25	0.7	7.8
1787	50	58	24	0.9	2.0
1799/1800	174	164	25	1.0	7.0
Total	784	1,083	143	0.7	5.5

As regards the number of denouncers, global as well as year-specific figures were the highest in Bardez, followed by Ilhas and Salsete.

* * *

A reading of the denouncers' testimonies brings us to the conclusion that it was as though parish life was dissected at the time of episcopal visit. In a very special way, families portrayed here constituted the most conspicuous and evident aspect of the pastoral visits of Goa. All those deviations – anomalies in the husband/wife, parent/children, daughter-in-law/mother-in-law relationships, family consent or connivance in concubinage, prostitution, sensuality and separation, the behaviour of parents whore-mongering their daughters, the social-moral effects of alcoholism – show Christian life, the true Christian family, the importance and role attributed to it, in a negative light. This rich religious source-material also gives the reader a glimpse into the Christian family life and the life of other larger communities, like the confraternities. That is to say, they reconstruct the various forms of socialization present in the parish and gravitating around the Church. The faults denounced are quite varied and they broadly cover the questionnaire of the edicts.

At times, the denouncements include certain graphic details of great interest for the study of the customs, daily life and mentality, such as the exchange of *saguates* (gifts) between 'lovers', 'offering of fish', the habit of having *kanji*, the concession of dowry to the bride, etc. However, the pastoral visits of Goa have failed to answer certain questions that could provide aids to the study of the religion, such as attitudinal changes that took place in the Archbishops' pastoral policies, the specific deeds of each visitor, the Bishops' doctrinal preoccupations. We believe that these lacunae can be filled in by the *Livros dos Capítulos* (Books of Chapters) since in them the prelates used to register their directives and pastoral orientations.

INQUISITION

While analysing the behaviour of the faithful, the visitor used to work in close association and practically with the Inquisition. Indeed, making use of the denouncements of the clergymen and parishioners themselves he would diagnose the behavioural deviations and send certain types of cases to that tribunal for punishment. Thus, the visit afforded an understanding of the region and a much more systematic identification of faults than the inquiry made by family members and commissioners of the Holy Office.

The material furnished by the visitor used to be treated judicially by the Inquisition, which had a greater coercive force than the visitor did. In some cases, if the situation so demanded and as a precautionary measure, the visitor could even order the immediate imprisonment of the delinquent.

There was thus a conventional demarcation of the fields of action between the diocesan visit and the Inquisition. Moral cases we have mentioned came within the jurisdiction of the visitor. But according to the new regiment of the Inquisition of Goa (1778) crimes of heresy, blasphemy, idolatry, Hindu beliefs, bigamy, *sollicitatio ad turpia,* sodomy came under the tribunal of the Holy Office.[272]

Similarly, in the Kingdom and Brazil of the eighteenth century, the episcopal action through the visits and that of the Inquisition were complementary.[273]

Let us focus our attention on the lists of convicts of the Inquisition in the second half of the eighteenth century, given the fact that, through several vicissitudes, the rest of the documentary body on this institution is no more. Who was at the receiving end of the greatest convictions and punishments?[274]

Although there are a large number of women figuring in the pastoral visits; on the other hand, their number is quite low in the cases of the Inquisition. In the second half of the eighteenth century around 1997 persons were punished, out of which 1612 were men (82 per cent) and the remaining 376 were women (18 per cent). This low female percentage is no wonder, given the times in which it happened and, more importantly, the well

[272] See the *O Último Regimento e o Regimento da Economia da Inquisição de Goa,* leitura e prefácio de Raul Rêgo, Lisbon, 1983.

[273] See José Pedro de Matos Paiva, 'Inquisição e Visitas Pastorais. Dois Mecanismos Complementares de Controle Social?', in *Inquisição,* vol. II, Lisbon, 1989, pp. 865-79 and Caio C. Boschi, 'As Visitas Diocesanas e a Inquisição na Colónia', in ibid., pp. 963-96. On the inquisition in other countries of Europe refer to Francisco Bettencourt, *História das Inquisições. Portugal, Espanha e Italia.* Lisbon, Círculo de Leitores, 1994.

[274] On the sources existing for the study of the Holy Office of Goa, see our work, *A Inquisição de Goa na Segunda Metade do Século XVIII. Contributo para a sua História,* Lisbon, 1989, offprint of *Stvdia* (1989), 48, pp. 241-2.

known effacement suffered by Goan womenfolk – Muslim, Hindu or even Christian – in Indian society.

Age-wise, the group most punished by the Inquisition is the 26/30 year bracket (21.5 per cent) followed by 36/40 year bracket (14.7 per cent), and the 31/35 year bracket (12 per cent) and finally, the 21/25 year bracket (11.5 per cent). It thus refers to a period of the individual's statement of spiritual and religious convictions.

The age of marriage being relatively low in Goan society, it follows that the above mentioned age groups would mainly comprise married persons. Truly, their number reaches 59 per cent, whereas that of singles is 12 per cent and the widowed, 14 per cent.

The social provenance of 57 per cent of the convicts is known and professions of only 10 per cent cases are indicated. Hence some of the conclusions are merely indicative and not to be taken in absolute terms (see Table III.13). As in the pastoral visits, the inferior castes, namely, Sudras (18.5 per cent) and Kunbis (17.5 per cent) figure more prominently, whereas Chardós and Brahmins appear in a much smaller number, recording 7 per cent and 5 per cent, respectively.

Even other so-called inferior castes supply contingents for the Inquisition, though in a smaller percentage. It is the case of the Vannis (1 per cent), Mahars (0.8 per cent), Kolis (0.3 per cent), Gaudde (0.2 per cent). Although these numbers may appear insignificant, yet they do stress the humble origins of the defendants.

The cultural factor may also be noted. Indeed, the more educated members of society were less affected by the action of this tribunal. On the other hand, less cultured individuals, firmly rooted in the tradition of their religious convictions, were an easy catch for the Inquisition. We may say that the Tribunal of the Holy Office found abundant penitents in the lower strata of the different castes, particularly the lower ones, more illiterate and affected by Hindu customs, perhaps because their Christianization was rather superficial.

The higher population density of the inferior castes, weaker legal protection and even the fact that they had very little to lose could in some measure account for this situation.

TABLE III.13: SOCIAL GROUPS

Group	No.	Percentage
Brahmins (Bamonn)	97	4.80
Chardós (Chardde)	148	7.40
Sudras (Sudir)	369	18.50
Kunbi*	348	17.50
Vanni*	20	1.00
Farazes (Mahar)*	16	0.80
Koli*	6	0.30
Gaudde*	94	4.70
Bhandhari*	1	0.05
Ranne*	1	0.05
Forrros	3	0.10
Slaves	12	0.60
Adopted*	2	0.10
Marathas*	1	0.05
Europeans (Portuguese)	6	0.30
Total	1,124	56.00
Non identified	895	44.00
Total no. of sentenced	2,019	

Note: *See the Glossary.

In the pastoral visits, '*occupations and trades*' were among the most punished professional groups at the Holy Office of Goa, comprising 34 per cent out of a known total of 57 per cent. Also to note is the fact that the professional activity connected with the tertiary sector is at about 10 per cent only. Significantly, farmers (9.6 per cent), 'workers' (5 per cent), fishermen (5 per cent), *varzeiros* (3 per cent) and masons (3 per cent) also stand out among those accused by the Inquisition (see Table III.14).

Besides the more numerous groups, we find a long list of professions also related to the primary and secondary sectors (see Table III.15), such as day-labourers, grave-diggers, jewellers, potters and many others. And, whereas the tertiary sector has a much smaller percentage of representation (10 per cent), here too are detailed various professional activities like scribes, bailiffs, schoolmaster and soldier, presbyters, porters, priests, solicitors, etc.

TABLE III.14: TRADES

Designation	No.	Designation	No.
Tailor	7	Farmer and businessman	1
Oilman	8	Laundryman*	4
Barber	2	Bangle seller*	2
Boatman	2	Maid	2
*Begarins**	16	Potter	21
Embroiderer	1	Jeweller	12
Shopkeeper	1	Baker	1
Digger	16	Midwife	6
Carpenter	11	Shepherd	1
Coalman	1	Mason	46
Wax vendor	2	Mason and merchant	1
Seamster	1	Mason and farmer	2
Cook	3	Mason and soldier	1
Coin maker	1	Painter	1
Salt pan farmer	1	Fisherman and sailor	1
Toddy tapper*	4	Linen keeper	2
Wine distiller	5	Bleeder	1
Salt manufacturer	3	Wood cutter	2
Ironsmith	7	Bar tender	15
Iron founder	2	Barrelmaker	3
Day labourer	19	Worker	105
Farmer	161	Worker and *ganvkar*	1
Farmer and merchant	1	*Varzeiro**	64
Farmer and barman	5	*Varzeiro* and *ganvkar*	1
Farmer and wine distiller	2	Seller	18
	Total	694	

Note: * See the Glossary.

This so-called holy tribunal thus targeted a good number of persons from a large gallery of professionals.

As for the nature of crimes, heresy was considered the 'principal ground for the Holy Office to proceed against the accused'.[275] It is curious to note that way back in the Middle Ages the heretic was compared to a counterfeiter spreading ideas compromising the religious and political unity of the

[275] Cf. *O Último Regimento* ..., Tit. II, § 1, p. 54.

TABLE III.15: PROFESSIONS OF THE TERTIARY SECTOR

Designation	No.	Designation	No.
Laceseller	1	Military men	1
Second-Lieutenant	3	'Mocadão'	1
'Avançal do rendeiro do tabaco'	1	Wine Merchant	1
'Bandeira'	1	Naique (Naik)*	2
Corporal	7	Businessmen	2
Village corporal and seller of table wine	1	Patamar*	1
Captain	5	Patel*	4
Surgeon	2	Presbyter	4
Cleric	4	Porter	1
Fort Commandant	1	Tax collector	48
Merchant	3	Nuns	81
Merchant and farmer	1	Secular priest	14
Peon	1	Sacristan	2
Contractor of pork meat	1	Sergeant	3
Broker	1	Server in the hospital of the poor	2
Curate	1		
Scribe	2	Sepoy*	17
Herbalist, herbal medico and physician	6	Soldier	24
		Solicitor	1
Bailiff	2	Solicitor and naique (naik)	1
Trader	1	Subdeacon	1
Schoolmaster	3	Lieutenant	4
Music master and musician	3	Parish Priest	1
	Total	191	

Note: *See the Glossary.

community. Hence, the regiments of the Inquisition take up the issues of denouncements and confessions by heretics in detail.

Mutatis mutandis, blasphemy, idolatry, Hindu beliefs were considered heretic manifestations, constituting a deviation from the Christian orthodoxy that the Tridentine reform sought to preserve. That is because the main objective was to create a homogeneous social body in which religious and cultural unity would ensure political stability.

A large number of convicts (74 per cent) were imputed of

TABLE III.16: DELICTS

Delict		No.
Bigamy		7
Falsity		38
Fleeing, help to flee		24
Hindu practices		1,290
Islam		23
Joining the Society of Free Masons		3
Heretical propositions	Blasphemies	85
	Manifestations against dogma	50
	Judgements against the Church	3
Relapse		10
Against the Holy Office		27
Sodomy		2
Solicitatio ad turpia		16
Superstition		152
Participation in Hindu temple works		144
Miscellaneous		13
Not identified		54

Hindu beliefs or *Hindu practices*. Much lower down the scale are crimes of heresy and apostasy (1.5 per cent); and with identical percentages were abuses of authority and perturbation in the ministry of the Holy Office; fleeing, absence or help in escapes; conversion to Islam and the sale of people in order to prevent conversions or dissuading people from converting to the Christian faith, blasphemies, *sollitatio ad turpia*, etc. (see Table III.16).

Heresy was considered the most serious crime and hence it came under the jurisdiction of the Inquisition. By spreading their pernicious sects, heretics were apt to ruin the basis of the State; they were considered as harmful as those who made attempts on the life of the monarchs were.

Matrimony as the basis of the family attracted special attention from the Council of Trent. Hence, all deviations that might endanger it were severely punished. This also explains why bigamy came under the jurisdiction of the Inquisition.

The regiments of the Holy Office always recommended

avoiding public penalty for the crime of sodomy, thus preventing infamy.[276]

As regards Free Masons, it was determined that their cases be referred to the General Council, though there are no reports on their contents.[277]

There was also a watch on social behaviour through censorship of books; strict measures were taken on forbidden books. Hence, the customs offices of the city of Goa and other ports inspected books carefully. Thereafter book lists were made and registered (detailed as: books totally prohibited, 'without expurgation'; those banned 'with expurgation'; the doubtful books).[278]

The need or justification for the Holy Office was an issue debated at the very time of its creation but it lingered down the centuries. In fact, its extinction in 1774 and later revival in 1778 is good proof of this fact. Nevertheless the question remains. It is intrinsic to the very tribunal and the inquisitors' attitude of greater or lesser strictness in the face of the crime, may clarify this issue.

With the reestablishment of the Inquisition of Goa in 1778, there were voices vouching for or against this tribunal. The Inquisitor General pointed out serious troubles that would come from its extinction, such as the loss of schools of Catholic doctrine and Portuguese language, proliferation of bad Christians and non-Christians who would then freely spread their errors. But there were those who vehemently refuted these arguments and even stated that, when 'the Inquisition, with force, with terror, and with the sword, provoked the rancour of the Peoples; many of the converts returned to their errors; Christendom diminished considerably; the Businessmen fled our States, and the

[276] See the copy of the *assento que se tomou no Conselho Geral sobre o procedimento contra as mulheres sodomitas umas com outras* [1760] (B.N. Rio de Janeiro, Armário 25, 2, cód. 9, doc. 95, f. 158).

[277] Letter from Manuel Ferreira de Mesquita to Fr. António de Pádua, dated 28 February 1792, ordering to inform this order to all the Inquisitions (B.N. Rio de Janeiro, Armário 25, 2 cód. 9, doc. 78, ff. 136-136v).

[278] Letter from the Secretary [of the General Council of the Inquisition] to the inquisitors of Goa, dated 2 April 1760 (B.N. Rio de Janeiro, Armário 25, 2, cód. 9, doc. 36, ff. 68-70v and doc. 37 (second copy), ff. 71-73v).

Portuguese Language came to be generally hated, that the more civilized Indians consider it as a point of honour for their families not to speak it. ...' This same critic said that the establishment of the Inquisition was followed by the creation of many convents accommodating a large number of friars; and thus, in his opinion, the empire of the Portuguese sovereign in India changed to the Roman Curia and destroyed commerce.[279]

There is no doubt that the Holy Office had its days numbered. The progress of the Lights spread by science and philosophy created an ambience hostile to the functioning of the Inquisition, which finally became extinct in 1812.[280]

ASPECTS OF EVANGELIZATION

The training of clergy done in the diocesan seminaries in accordance with the principles of the Tridentine reform has to be analysed in strict relation with the needs of evangelization. The clergymen had to charm the faithful and attract them to the bosom of the Church by their example. In the recruitment of the clergy, the main idea was to fill in the posts of confessors and the curates of souls. Let us then see the human aims of Christianization, what directives they followed and the degree of popular support to the Catholic religion.

Whereas in the Old Conquests the Christian population was predominant, on the other hand, the territories annexed in the second half of the eighteenth century were mostly inhabited by Hindus. Obviously, the task of evangelization needed the teaching of Christian doctrine on a priority basis, which had, indeed, been stressed a lot in the Tridentine programme but which in

[279] Cf. B.N. cód. 235, f. 102v, 'Inquisição em Geral e Particularmente nos Estados da Índia'.

[280] We have dealt with the Goa Inquisition only as a mechanism of social control. Other aspects, mainly institutional, remained untackled. In A.N./T.T. there is documentation on the subject (Correspondência para a Inquisição de Goa, Livro 4, 1750-1804 e Conselho Geral do Santo Ofício, maços 31-9). On the Inquisition of Goa between 1700-50 see our study: 'A Inquisição de Goa na primeira metade de Setecentos. Uma visita pelo seu Interior', in *Mare Liberum*, no. 15, Lisbon, Comissão Nacional para as Comemorações dos Descobrimentos Portugueses, 1998.

India assumed a fundamental aspect for it was not totally Christianized society.

This teaching had to be above all attractive and effective. The *Instrucções* therefore recommended the imparting of a suitable catechesis, with simple and short terms, using catechism manuals in accordance with the age groups. The neophytes had to learn simple rules of natural ethics and revealed morality.[281]

Several pastoral letters reiterate the teaching of catechism on holy days before Mass, in churches and chapels alike, and sometimes a mention is made of the manual to be followed. It is a point to be analysed in the pastoral visits and the prelates refer to it in the *ad limina* visits, given its importance as the basis of Christianization. Thus, in 1802, Archbishop D. Frei Manuel de Santa Catarina informed the Pope that in the course of the pastoral visits he had noted a clear progress in the learning of catechism by the children.[282]

Although not theoretical, there was some interest evinced in the study of Oriental languages as a means of catechising the non-Christians. The substitution of the local clergymen for the Franciscans in the parishes of Bardez certainly contributed to the spread of Konkani and its use in the teaching of catechism.[283]

As is known, in modern times evangelization assumed new aspects with the mission fields held by certain religious Orders, including the Jesuits, Oratorians, Apostolic Missionaries, Lazarists. In order to plug loopholes of the secular clergy in pastoral action, these missionaries sought to free the local inhabitants

[281] See the *Instrucções* ..., Third Instruction for the Archbishop, p. 19.

[282] Cf. Secret Archives of the Vatican, *S. Congr. Concilii Relationes: ad limina* visit in 1802 of the archbishopric of Goa. He also refers to this fact in his letter of 17 March 1784 to M.M. Castro. Cf. A.H.U., *India,* maço 115 (122). The manual mentioned in 1781 and 1784 is the one entitled *Idea de hum parocho instruido nas suas obrigações, e instruindo as suas ovelhas na solida piedade* (cf. C.C. Nazareth, *Mitras* ..., p. 327).

[283] See the letter from the Count of Ega to Father Manuel da Conceição, of the Franciscan Order, Superior of the Malabar Mission, feting him for his success in learning the Malabar language and for being fit for confessions in this idiom. He asks for information on the remaining priests as regards their knowledge of this language and Tamil (A.H.U., *India,* cód. 430, ff. 98v-99).

from ignorance and social conformity. This was true mainly of far-flung and more obscure locations that were more in need of education and social assistance.

Using suitable strategies, such as spectacular ceremonies, suited to the Baroque taste, preaching was centred on fixed themes such as fear of the eternal punishment in order to prod people to the confessional, these missions did have very clear results. They often brought about reconciliation of persons at variance and, by and large, harmony among the faithful; produced many confessions, attracted vocations, and finally, aroused an authentic religious fervour in numerous Christian communities.[284]

This movement, which had a great push in the sixteenth century from the Ignatians, witnessed a new religious fervour in the second half of the eighteenth century. In Goa, several religious Orders had mission stations in some parts of the territory. Above all, the Theatines and the Oratorians were chosen, as they knew the local language. In the *ad limina* visit of 1802, Archbishop D. Frei Manuel de Santa Catarina refers to their efforts and apostolic zeal to convert to the Christian faith the people of Combarjua and the New Conquests, namely Ponda, albeit without encouraging results. [285]

However, with the arrival of the Lazarists in 1779 these evangelatory incursions into the hinterland witnessed a fresh religious upsurge. The mission stations in Rachol, Margão,

[284] On the 'missions', their evolution from the 16th to the nineteenth century, the methodologies used, the stages of a mission and the results achieved, see E. dos Santos, *Les Missions des Temps Modernes au Portugal,* offprint of *Histoire Vécue du Peuple Chrétien,* Toulouse, 1979.

[285] Secret Archive of the Vatican, *S. Congr. Concilii Relationes*: *ad limina* visit of 1802. Cf. the letter from Archbishop D. Frei Manuel de Santa Catarina to M.M. Castro, dated 17 March 1784, op. cit. On some missions held by the Oratorians of Goa, see our studies: 'Espiritualidade e Cultura nos Oratorianos de Goa, em Setecentos', paper presented at the colloquium *Portugal e a Índia. Referências e vivências culturais,* 7 to 10 November 1993, Lisbon, Casas de Fronteira e Alorna; and 'Pedagogic and Pastoral Innovation of the Oratory Congregation of Goa and its Repurcussions in Society (17th and 18th centuries)', in XIth International Seminar on Indo-Portuguese History, held in Goa, 21-25 September 2003.

Pangim and Ribandar were crowned with success, thanks to a great rush of people to sermons and confessions. Besides this, there were other lasting effects, such as the daily practice of mental prayer in common and the creation of a school for education and instruction of girls in Rachol and Margão.[286]

Given the multi-religious nature of Goan society, with a great predominance of non-Christians with whom the Christians inevitably communicated, the principles to be followed in relation to Hindu beliefs needed to be defined. Was it an attitude of rejection? Segregation of the non-Christians? Religious tolerance? Was it unconditional? Within certain limits? These issues in the second half of the eighteenth century cannot be studied as a monolith, since the matter is quite complex and had several nuances, in accordance with various factors. However, some guidelines adopted, largely, can be remembered which persisted in the course of this half century.

In the age of royal absolutism, when religious unity was the strength of political unity, the authorities could not afford to let rites and practices spread so easily. Besides, it would endanger Christian orthodoxy, with the diffusion of certain forms of religious syncretism.

It may be said that generally the authorities would not allow the public celebration of non-Christian ceremonies, in order to avoid scandal in Christian lands and religious contamination of the faithful. Hence, they allowed only Christians to render public cult to God, but Hindus and Muslims had to practise their religions privately. This aspect is very clear from the available documentation and apparently remained constant in this age.[287]

[286] Cf. Father Bráulio Guimarães, op. cit., pp. 157-8. On some aspects of the missions namely in the north of Portugal, see Eugénio dos Santos, *Missões e Missionários do Interior da Região de Guimarães,* offprint of the *Congresso Histórico de Guimarães e sua Colegiada. Actas,* vol. III, Guimarães, 1981 and 'Os Lazaristas e as Missões Populares em Portugal: 1734-1834. Um balanço', in *Congresso Internacional de História e Encontro de Culturas. Actas,* Braga, 1993.

[287] On 19 January 1768, the non-Christians asked for the transcript of the royal order in which reference was made to the 32,000 xerafins paid by them by way of donations, for being allowed to hold marriages. This order came up in the year 1726, cf. A.H.U., *India,* maço 16-A (291). See, for

The requests for permission to hold non-Christian marriages in Goan territory are so many and suggestive that reflecting on them is almost like capturing the evolution of the religious policy in that territory. Thus, although normally allowed within the house and behind closed doors, to avoid the inflow of Christians, there were certain variants in its observance. Thus in times of greater religious freedom, marriages used to be held in private houses, with the participation of dancing girls and musical instruments used in non-Christian ceremonies. Conversely, on other occasions, so many restrictions were imposed, like the presence of the inquisitorial authority at the ceremonies, that the non-Christians were obliged to go to the Bhonsale and Sunda lands to celebrate those acts.[288]

Nevertheless, there were moments when the policy changed towards a greater religious freedom for the non-Christians. It thus happened in the government of the Count of Alva (1754-6) that, in order to give an impetus to populating the lands conquered from the Bhonsales, he authorized the building of temples and the public celebration of their religion. This attitude, however, was totally displeasing to the Crown who ordered its immediate revocation.[289]

---

example, the petition of the Hindus, dated 6 April 1769 for their *bhatt* to be authorized to come to State territory to celebrate the rites and the marriages, in accordance with the established orders. Cf. A.H.U., *India,* maço 91 (102).

[288] See the representation of the Hindus asking for permission to celebrate their marriages in the manner they employed before 1774. They used to cite examples of tolerance by the Kings of Spain. They alleged that during the administration of the Governor D. João de Saldanha da Gama marriages were made simply with permission from the Governor and without the presence of a *naik* of the Holy Office, and were allowed the use of pipes and dancing girls. Reference was made to Hindu marriages celebrated in private homes at the time of the Marquis of Louriçal, D. Luís Caetano de Almeida, the Count of Alva and in the first year of administration of the Count of Ega. They also argued that in the Kanara and Mughal lands, Mysore and many missions there was great freedom for Hindu practices and nonetheless the Christian population was increasing (H.A.G., *M. Reino,* Book 159-D, ff. 1068-1072v).

[289] See the royal letter of 27 March 1756 to the Count of Alva, ordering

The prosecution of the conquest of lands populated mainly by non-Christians required an alteration in the religious policy. In Europe, the prevailing cultural ambience of the Lights put a question mark on the Counter-Reformation spirit of intolerance. Hence, the Inquisition lost its power and ended in 1774; the religious bases of political power were also shaken up. It may also be recalled that the Society of Jesus was suppressed in 1759. It was in this climate that the Count of Ega acted upon a royal order and aimed at having the new territories populated. For this end, he published notices and proclamations promising to preserve the usage and customs of the Hindu inhabitants in the annexed territories. Public ceremonies of non-Christian marriages were permitted. The earlier mentioned royal charter of 15 January 1774 noted the excessive application of ex-communication by the Church and ordained its regulation.[290]

From the religious point of view, Pombaline Goa was thus similar to Albuquerque's Goa, given that the non-Christians used to hold public celebrations of their festivities and marriages, with a lot of singing, many instruments and dances. In addition, according to a contemporaneous source, Christians did not pervert themselves with these public non-Christian festivities as they used to attend them either to mock them or for pastime only.[291]

This religious freedom granted to the non-Christians seems to have caused an eruption of Hindu beliefs with the construction

---

the demolition of the temples constructed and banning public acts of Hindu worship. It further stated that in similar cases the Viceroy should not have decided without taking into confidence the Board of the Holy Office. Cf. A.H.U., *India,* maço 86 (107). According to Mira Mascarenhas, the attitude of the Count of Alva might have been the first serious step in favour of a liberalization of the official religion. Cf. 'The Church in Eighteenth Century Goa', in *Essays in Goan History,* ed. Teotónio R. de Souza, New Delhi, 1989.

[290] Cf. *Instrucções ...*, Third Instruction, p. 16.

[291] See the letter from the Attorney of the Crown and Revenue, João Diogo Guerreiro Camacho de Aboim, dated 13 December 1779. Cf. A.H.U., *India,* maço 131 (137).

of several temples and an ablution tank as well as public celebrations of their festivals.[292]

The historical moment known in political circles as *'viradeira'* (turnabout), which covered the first times of the reign of D. Maria I, corresponded to a temporary return to the old religious intolerance in Goa. This had determined the destruction of the said tank, prohibition of public rites, re-establishment of the Inquisition in 1778, and extinction of temples in Daman. In short, it was a return to the *status quo ante* 1774, the year of the great religious liberalization. Now many restrictions were imposed on the holding of Hindu marriages and the 'thread' ceremony,[293] and this compelled the Hindus to celebrate these events in the lands of the Bhonsles and Sunda.[294]

In the 1790s, however, the religious policy mellowed down in favour of the non-Christians and the power of the Inquisition was restrained. The cultural winds blowing in Europe created a

[292] The royal *Instrucções* to Governor Frederico Guilherme de Sousa refer to the opening of a tank in which the Hindus used to do their superstitious washing and purification. They were permitted to publicly hold the marriage ceremonies or the *entrudos,* that is, the Ganesh or *Shigmo* festivals (A.H.U., *India,* cód. 516, ff. 131-145v). Ganesh, god of wisdom, is one of the gods most adored by the Hindus. *Shigmo,* 'licentious Hindu festival in the Konkan, similar to our carnival' (cf. S.R. Dalgado, *Glossário Luso-Asiático,* vol. I, pp. 420-1 and vol. II, p. 305).

[293] It is an initiation ceremony that confers on the Hindu child the religious status of a Brahmin. Certain mystical powers are attributed to the holy thread, hence it is given great importance in ceremonial life. The description of the ceremony and more information can be collected from Mariano Feio, *As Castas Hindus de Goa,* Lisbon, 1979, pp. 28-9.

[294] Ibid., See the letters from the Governor F.G. de Sousa [to the King], dated 27 December 1779. Cf. A.H.U., *India,* maço 129 (143); the letters from the said Governor to M.M. Castro, dated 1 January 1780, stating that everything had been reduced to the way it was done before 1774 (H.A.G., *M. Reino,* Book 159-A, f. 110) and which had ordained, in compliance with the royal determinations that the use of temples should be abstained from in Daman and that those that had already been built be extinct (H.A.G., *M. Reino,* Book 159-A, ff. 111-12). He further informs on the same date that the tank had been destroyed and that the *bhat* had to leave Goa but without violence [A.H.U., *India,* maço 132 (140)]. On this subject there is a lot of documentation referring to the years between 1780 and 1782.

climate conducive to the toleration of the usage, the religious customs of the people, and hence, they did not favour the Inquisition, which became definitively extinct in 1812.[295]

Besides the non-Christians who converted to Christianity of their own accord, catechumens were also recruited from among non-Christian orphans and illegitimate children of non-Christian mothers, minors of 12 years, if boys; and minors of 16, in case of girls. They were handed over to the Father of the Christians for instruction and baptism.

Nevertheless, the fact that children were converted to Christianity, contrary to the wishes of their collateral relatives, if any, and of non-Christian mothers, in case of illegitimate children, became controversial and sometimes gave rise to 'great disorder ... in the matter of propagation of the faith'.[296] Numerous laws sought to clarify ambiguous situations and justify the religious, moral and social principles underlying this provision. One of the arguments invoked was that this practice was 'rational and very fair also because of the lapse of so much time without the least objection from the government'. It was thought, therefore, that the State would not have tolerated it for so long if it were not correct.

Besides this, the fact that these illegitimate children were born in Christian lands would *ipso facto* mean that they were born of Christian parents, since their mothers were generally

[295] See the letter from D. Rodrigo de Sousa Coutinho to Francisco António da Veiga Cabral, dated 30 March 1797, communicating the order of the Queen favouring and protecting the non-Christians assistants in Goa by virtue of the advantages that come from their staying in this territory (A.H.U., *India,* cod. 520, f. 107); letter from Frederico Guilherme de Sousa to the King, dated 11 May 1797 (A.H.U., *India,* cód. 215, ff. 84-84v); letter from D. Maria, dated 12 July 1797, permitting the non-Christian marriages in their houses behind closed doors with the presence of a person appointed by the Governor (H.A.G., *M. Reino,* Book 178-B, f. 676). On 8 March 1799 the Regent Prince writing to F.A.V. Cabral states that he wishes to reanimate trade and attract businessmen in Daman and Diu, and therefore sets up some freedom of worship (H.A.G., *M. Reino,* Book 179-A, ff. 9-12).

[296] Cf. the royal charter of 11 July 1718 incorporated in that of 8 December 1744 (A.C.P.G., *Cópia de Vários Documentos,* f. 42v, in F.U.P., 18-1-8/9).

public women. Finally, another argument, a strong one indeed, was the 'sure and common' opinion of the doctors in favour of baptism for such children.[297]

Nevertheless, it was ordained that these children be treated with understanding and respect towards their different creeds. Their ages, and with the more grown up, their wish and free will too, had to be taken into consideration.[298]

Save some exceptions, these were the directives followed for recruiting catechumens since the beginning of Christianity.[299] The charters indeed always go back to earlier times, incorporating

[297] See the letter from D. José to the Count of Alva [*sic*], dated 30 March 1757 (A.C.P.G., ibid., ff. 44-44v), published by José Wicki, S.J., *O Livro do Pai dos Cristãos,* Lisbon, 1969, pp. 349-51.

[298] The orphans without ancestors had to be handed to the Father of the Christians who would carry on with the immediate baptism in case of minors of less than 7 years old. The older ones would be instructed with the purpose and before they decided they were not forbidden from communicating with their relatives and other non-Christians. Those of doubtful ages, close to puberty, had to be kept in the custody of competent people and examined by doctors and proper authorities to state their age; out of them, those considered minors or probably had not reached puberty, would be handed to the Father of the Christians to be catechized if they wished to 'already, being in the age of will and free choice' and hence they were also allowed the said communication. If they were thought to be in puberty already, they would be admonished 'gently, manner and good counsel to follow Christ's law'. If they did not spontaneously adhere to the Christian faith they would be handed to their relatives. See the royal charter of 5 April 1754 (published by J. Wicki, ibid., pp. 352-7) and taken up again on 18 January 1782 (A.C.P.G., *Cópia de Vários Documentos,* ff. 41-3, F.U.P., 18-1-8/9). The said charter confirms and incorporates the charters of 11 July 1718 and 8 December 1744. It mentions the heavy sanctions infringed on those trangressing these orders.

[299] Ibid. In this last charter is referred an occasion in which the normally set style is altered. The Father of the Christians had collected two illegitimate children and baptized them as they were in risk of life. One non-Christian asked for these children, but his request was not granted as they had already been baptized. However, the Father of the Christians was asked not to collect such illegitimate children in such circumstances, by virtue of a letter from D. Pedro II of 24 March 1702. But by royal resolution of 19 April 1756 it is ordained that he continue to practise the usual style. See the royal letter to the Count of Alva, dated 20 April 1756 (A.H.U., *India,* cód. 214, ff. 119-119v and H.A.G., *M. Reino,* Book 129-A, ff. 204-6).

earlier diplomas in their texts and reiterating the need to preserve them intact. However, it is true that many times orphans were not made known and handed over to the Father of the Christians.[300]

Let us see the aspects of evangelization in Goa and the impact that it had on this society. In Goa, as in other Portuguese Overseas territories, there was the institution of Father of the Christians. According to *O Livro do Pai dos Cristãos,* he acted on three fronts, viz., services towards the conversion of infidels, teaching of Christian doctrine and assistance to new Christians. As regards the first aspect, it may be noted that, since in India conversions did not occur through preaching and doctrine, other means had to be employed, such as preventing idolatry, punishing those who practised it, denying favours to the non-Christians and granting them to the Christians instead so as to attract others to convert. Hence, the Father of the Christians had to be well versed in all the provisions in favour of Christianity.[301]

From the lists of catechumens and neo-converts that have come down to us it is seen that non-Christians of the most diverse castes and professions and sometimes some or all the members of a particular family embraced the Catholic faith. There figure also many kaffirs and some foreigners, mainly English.[302]

It was sought to find godfathers who would be in a position to protect the neo-converts and to have these neo-converts adopt

[300] Cf. the order of the inquisitors to the Father of the Christians to intimate the *mukaddams* to denounce the same, within six days, publ. by J. Wicki, S. J., op. cit., pp. 283-4. Reference is made to the 'many omissions in denouncing the Father of the Christians the orphans, children of the non-Christians vassals of His Highness, to be baptized ...'.

[301] See *O Livro do Pai dos Cristãos,* op. cit., pp. 16 ff.

[302] On 26 July 1759, the director of the catechumens, Belchior José Vaz de Carvalho, informed [the Count of Ega] about the baptism of a non-Christian lady from Kanara, belonging to a very distinguished caste, to be held that day, which would be followed by the handover of the treaty [with the Kanara King] (A.N./T.T., *Reino,* maço 603). On 1 December 1759 the Count of Ega communicated this news to the said King (A.H.U., *India,* cód. 430, f. 183). See, for example, the letter from the Count of Ega to Francisco Xavier de Mendonça Furtado, dated 10 January 1762, accompanied by the list of the new Christians who got baptized between 1 October 1759 and 31 December 1761. Cf. A.H.U., *India,* maço 100 (85)

surnames of families from the Kingdom. This was perhaps to bring about a clean break with the non-Christian past and to achieve an easier acculturation and social integration. According to the Marquis of Pombal, this was also meant to create an attitude different from the 'Jesuit policy that put those miserables into that confusion'.[303]

As is known, the task of evangelization was filled out by the social assistance rendered to the neo-convert, which often translated as monetary concessions, exemption from the harvest tithe, dress subsidy, dwelling place, legal protection and appointment to offices 'that are generally given to the people of the land'.[304] As a result, in the field of justice, there was since the sixteenth century a competent authority – the registrar and judge of the Christians of the land – to resolve their legal problems and avoid dilatory court cases. Imprisonment in civil cases was also abolished.[305]

The old practice of granting certain posts to new Christians now occasioned abuses and expenses for the Royal Treasury, which the authorities sought to put an end to.[306]

[303] See the letters of the Secretary of State Francisco Xavier Mendonça Furtado to the Count of Lousã, dated 13 April 1766, and the reply [from the Governors] to the Secretary of State, dated 26 January 1767 (H.A.G., *M. Reino,* Book 139, f. 351 and A.H.U., *India,* cód. 514, f. 8v and cód. 515, ff. 139-139v).

[304] Cf. *O Livro do Pai dos Cristãos,* pp. 59-61, 75-6, 106-8, 188-9. Cf. the letter to Teodoro de Barros e Azevedo, a neo-convert, appointing him to the post of 'interpreter' of the court of the court of the senior civil crown judge, dated 9 June 1764. In his petition, the applicant stated that the King had recommended to the Viceroys by letter of 1714 'increase of the neo-converts' (A.N./T.T., *Junta da Real Fazenda do Estado da Índia,* Book 50, ff. 129-129v). Among the posts given to the new Christians are included that of the clerk of the (Indian) governorship and agreements for three years in the vacancy of the appointments (ibid., Book 46, ff. 164v-165), that of 'interpreter' of the court of the senior civil crown judge, already cited, that of *naik* of the court of the crown judge, that of *mukdam,* village clerk, doctor, etc. Cf. *O Livro do Pai dos Cristãos,* pp. 109-10, 208-9, 255-6, 319-20.

[305] Cf. *O Livro do Pai dos Cristãos,* pp. 71-4, 286-95. The people of the land could not be imprisoned for a debt lower than 20 pardaus.

[306] By letter of 10 February 1767 it was noted that certain persons, in their capacity as new Christians, had the rank of sepoys; they were ordered

From the numerous provisions favouring the neo-converts it is indeed clear that they enjoyed great privileges, whereas the non-Christians were subjected to restrictions in the forms of treatment and access to certain posts, and in the sixteenth century had to carry a self-identification badge.[307] The orientation followed was that of 'denying the favours that they can be legitimately denied and to give them to the neo-converts ... so that others may thus be converted'.[308] Non-Christians who voluntarily agreed to embrace Christianity were also rewarded.[309]

The support given by the Count of Ega to the prosecution of the evangelatory and civilizational action must be emphasized. He thus transferred the catechumenate from the insalubrious location at S. Paulo-o-Velho to Betim, which, besides having healthier air, afforded a panoramic view of the inlet of the river Mandovi and the entry of the bar. He endowed this institution with independent resources for its financial stability. Designated as *Nova Colónia da Fé* (New Colony of the Faith), this young institution had a very meritorious social and educational work to its credit, sheltering the converts in its houses built for the purpose and teaching them some trades.[310] Here many non-Christians were baptized and married, like Sudras, Vannis, fishermen, dancing girls, Africans and some foreigners too.[311]

---

to be relieved because of the expenses and because the new Christians had to be admitted only in the posts that were habitually given to the locals. Cf. A.H.U., *India,* maço 63 (321).

[307] Cf. *O Livro do Pai dos Cristãos,* pp. 77-8.

[308] Cf. ibid., pp. 16-17.

[309] If they became Christians within six months, the women and daughters of the dead non-Christians would inherit their properties. Ibid., pp. 110-12, 290-1.

[310] See the letter from Belchior J.V. de Carvalho to the Count of Ega, dated 15 January 1763 (H.A.G., *M. Reino,* Book 135-B, ff. 567-572v).

[311] From 1750 to 1782, 996 catechumens were baptized; there are no indications for the years 1783 and 1784. From 1785 to 1800, 557 were baptized, which means that in the second half of the eighteenth century, an average of 31 baptisms per year (32.3) were held in the House of the Catechumens. Every year Africans were baptized, 23 English, 2 Irish, one German and one Danish. For a more detailed study on this institution and the work carried out by it, consult our works: 'Conversion as a Means to

Taking up earlier provisions, Archbishop Neiva Brum permitted the Father of the Christians to celebrate marriages in the chapel of the said house. Moreover, to avoid 'the inconvenience and grave detriment' involved in transporting the dead to the parish church (Reis Magos), he granted the catechumens the privilege of burial in the said chapel.[312]

It was also during the administration of the Count of Ega and that of D. António T.N.B. da Silveira that the Christianization of new territories, namely Ponda and Zambaulim, received a boost with the construction of some churches, which were well received by the non-Christians.[313]

The adherence by Hindus to Christianity was not always immediate and unconditional, since there were several barriers to their conversion. Above all, there were great difficulties arising from the fact that the religious and moral principles of Christianity were very different from those of the non-Christian religions. Besides, at the time of conversion, the family of the neophyte would try to cheat him by feigning poverty and withholding his share in the estate. Or else, they would approach

---

Cultural Adaptation. The Catechumens of Betim in the eighteenth century', in *Goa and Portugal. Their Cultural Links,* New Delhi, Concept Publishing Company, 1997; 'Converts, Protegés and Assimilated Natives: The Advantages of Christianisation and the Beliefs of Goan Christians (Eighteenth Century)', in *Vasco da Gama and the Linking of Europe and Asia,* ed. Anthony Disney and Emily Booth, New Delhi, Oxford University Press, 2000; 'A Problemática da Conversão ao Cristianismo em Goa; os catecúmenos de Betim (séculos XVIII-XIX)', in *Anais de História de Além-Mar,* vol. III: *Homenagem a Luis Filipe Thomaz,* Lisbon, Centro de História de Além-Mar, da Faculdade de Ciências Sociaise Humanas da Universidade Nova de Lisboa, 2002. See the *Relação dos Baptismos de Catecúmenos da Casa de Betim de 1750 a 1800* (H.A.G., *Assentos de Baptismos dos Catecúmenos,* Book 1554 (*1733-82*), ff. 77-239v and Book 1555 (*1785-1843*), ff. 2-116v).

[312] See the provisions of the Archbishop D. António, of 30 July 1766 and of 6 May 1772, in *O Livro do Pai dos Cristãos,* op. cit., pp. 358-60; 364-5.

[313] Cf. the letter from the Count of Ega to Francisco Xavier de Mendonça Furtado, dated 28 February 1764 (A.H.U., *India,* maço 100 (85) and cód. 428, ff. 34-5). He stated that the celebration of the first Mass in the church of Saint Anne in Ponda had an abundance of non-Christians that was comparable to the great Portuguese pilgrimages to Rome (A.H.U., *India,* cód. 438, ff. 34-35).

the court with the sole objective of delaying the cases and burdening the neo-converts who, once reduced to extreme poverty, would shy away from their shares in the inheritance.

In order to curb dodges like these employed by the Hindus, the Father of the Christians, in accordance with a fifteenth-century provision, asked for the creation of the post of registrar-judge to resolve matters arising between the Hindus and the neo-converts. In spite of this, the former would circumvent the law alleging that 'they could dispute in another court not only as defendants but also as plaintiffs, or further if the opposing parties were not privileged or did not have their private counsel'.[314] The task of evangelization was also conditioned quite a lot by scarcity of resources, aggravated at times by critical situations in the Kingdom.[315]

Some lists of neo-converts provide an estimate of the number of conversions, at times also indicating their social provenance and professions. However, this information is quite fragmentary and does not allow any numerical formulations.[316]

[314] See the representation by the Father of the Christians Frei Manuel de S. Tomás to the King, dated 20 January 1781, accompanied by the transcript of the charter of 21 February 1581, exposing the subterfuge resorted to the non-Christians to invalidate the law that provides for a judge registrar for the causes of the new Christians. He requested the resumption of the said charter which had instituted that post. Cf. A.H.U., *India,* maço 134 (134).

[315] The Count of Ega appeared wary that his evangelatory fervour would not have a follow-up because of the lack of revenue. King D. José praised the zeal, stating that the purposes of a war (Seven Years' War) and the peace negotiations had not permitted the establishment of sufficient resources for the task but he averred that he would do so thereafter (A.H.U., *India,* cód. 515, ff. 50-50v and 4v). Also see the letter from the Count of Ega to the Secretary of State, dated 19 January 1762, referring to the smallness of the revenue and the expenses and proposing measures to solve that problem such as to revert some of the mission money for this end (A.H.U., *India,* cód. 441, ff. 351v-352v).

[316] The list that accompanies the letter from the Count of Ega, dated 10 January 1762, comprises 33 newly baptized persons, mentioning the name, caste, address or origin. Cf. A.H.U., *India,* maço 100 (85). Another list of 278 converts comes appended to the letter from the director of the catechumens Belchior J.V. de Carvalho, to the Count of Ega, dated 15 Janu-

Furthermore, we think it a secondary issue, for it would be more interesting to establish what was behind these numbers, that is, to what extent the Christian message had penetrated into the consciences of those Hindu converts, transforming their behaviour and lifestyle. These points call for a reflection on aspects of their religious sensibility, that is, the cultic forms, religious habits, etc.

Of the feasts in the liturgical calendar, the one held in honour of St. Francis Xavier drew such a large number of people that this saint became the spiritual patron of India by epithet. In fact, this devotion was always very strong in Goa and for which reason it was encouraged in many ways. Archbishop D. António allowed the faithful to venerate a few relics of the saint and beginning from the eighteenth century some solemn expositions of his body were held, two of which took place in the second half of this century (1761 and 1782).[317]

Touching is the popular piety that comes into sight during the novena, whereby they seek to remain away from the crowds swarming the Convent of the Good Jesus, to advance in their intimacy with God. And diverse are their manifestations of religiosity: rosaries, litanies, ejaculations, hymns that never fail

---

ary 1763, op. cit. (H.A.G., *M. Reino,* Book 135-B, ff. 567.572v). There exists a list of 85 persons baptized from 1 February 1763 to the end of January 1764 (A.H.U., *India,* cód. 428, ff. 36-36v). The Letter from the Provincial Fr. António de Pádua to the Count of Oeiras, dated 17 December 1765, states that on 4 December of this very year 69 non-Christians were baptized (A.N./T.T., *Reino,* maço 603). A list of converts of the year 1783 mentions 25 baptized persons (H.A.G., *M. Reino,* Book 164-C, ff. 1153-1154v).

[317] Archbishop D. António cut some hair and some of the skin of the body of St. Francis Xavier to expose them to the faithful. Cf. Maria de Jesus Mártires Lopes, *O Epistolário ...*, p. 35. In his circular of 15 January 1782, Archbishop D. Frei Manuel de Santa Catarina announces the exposition of the body of the Saint, with royal authorization, on 10, 11 and 12 February of that year. He prescribes lights in the parishes and the pealing of bells, as also the conditions to gain indulgence. Cf. C.C. Nazareth, *Mitras ...*, p. 330. On 3 December 1991 we attended the feast of the Saint held in the old city and witnessed a great multitude of people of diverse ethnic groups and creeds, who had turned up from several parts of India and abroad to attend the ceremony.

to include the Saint's anthem, which goes beyond its religious form to assume a wider character. It becomes an appeal to Goan unity and an invitation to a return to the homeland.[318]

The bulk of people also include Hindus, Muslims, and Parsis who implore or acknowledge with thanks the favours received. That is because the devotion to St. Francis Xavier has penetrated not only the life of Christians but also, more than expected, into the lives of the non-Christians as well, who in their daily routine turn to him and implore his intercession.[319]

The religious customs of the Christians of Goa were at times arrayed in unique forms and betrayed a strong local influence. Thus, the Holy Week services used to adopt various figures and devices as also musical instruments used in the pagan festivals. The picturesque depiction of the Lord's Supper, the descent from the Cross on triumphal Palm Sunday, the tableau in the procession of the *Senhor dos Passos* (Our Lord in the Steps of the Passion), the meeting of the Virgin and Our Lord, accompanied by the artificial motion of the images, and the blood simulated by *brindão* in the *Ecce Homo*; the arrangement of live figures in Moorish caps and heathen costumes, the real presentation of the Supper with local fruits and foodstuffs – these were some aspects of the way of life during the Holy Week in Goa. They illustrate a fondness for baroque theatricality and the inter-penetrating of rituals culled from diverse religions.[320] Some of these performances were forbidden and set down to rules by Archbishops D. Francisco da Assunção e Brito and D. Frei Manuel

[318] We have not come across any eighteenth century description of the feast of the Patron of the Indies. However there exists an article by Professor Orlando Ribeiro which is very current and, *mutatis mutandis,* can be used for the past, since this feast has gone beyond the temporal frontiers and as a manifestation of religiosity had and shall have aspects that shall remain eternal.

[319] It is frequent to find images of the Saint in public places with garlands hanging down the neck, as if with non-Christian gods. Cf. L.F.F.R. Thomaz, *O Cristianismo e as Tradições Pagãs* ..., p. 9.

[320] *Brindão* is a fruit which 'has a very fine red colour inside resembling blood' – Garcia de Orta, coll. X, quoted by S.R. Dalgado, op. cit., vol. I, p. 151.

de Santa Catarina in order to safeguard Christian orthodoxy and prevent it from sliding into heathenism.[321]

The ceremonies of the *Santos Passos* (a representation of the holy steps of Christ's Passion) dating back to the early days of Christianity in Goa, make up intense moments of Christian life. The rite comprises the 'singing of *motets*, followed by sermon by a preacher who at a certain point calls attention to the tableau in the chancel; there follows the procession with the *andor* (a kind of sedan chair) carried by the confreres'. Also incorporated in the Lenten rites are the processions of the flagellants, proscribed by Archbishop D. Francisco da Assunção e Brito in 1775.[322] So great is the importance given to these and other religious acts during the Holy Week that attending them figures as an essential duty in the statutes of all the brotherhoods of Goa.[323]

Another characteristic of the religious sensibility of the Christian community of Goa is the tenor of the solemn public processions, in keeping with the ancient traditions of the land. In fact, already in the sixteenth century they lent an extraordinary liveliness and colour to the city of Goa, the centre of Christian expansion in the East.[324] There are reports that some grand processions, like those of *Corpus Christi*, *Senhor dos Passos*,

[321] Cf. the edict of Archbishop D. Francisco da Assunção e Brito of 6 April 1775 (B.P.A.D.E., cód. CXVI/2.11, no. 32), published by C.C. Nazareth, *Mitras* ..., pp. 307-10. It refers *inter alia* to the playing of the drum accompanied by the pipe and to the fact that two men had shed their blood in exchange for one or two pardaus. Also see circular of 4 March 1780 containing directives on the manner of conducting the holy ceremonies (concerning the image of Veronica, the face of Our Lord is not to be wiped) (C.C. Nazareth, *Mitras* ..., pp. 325-6); the edict of 6 March 1781, which refers to and forbids the use of live figures and *brindão* juice to simulate blood (ibid., pp. 328-9); the edict of 6 March 1781, stating the norms to be followed in these ceremonies and warning that, in case there be abuses, Lenten functions would be prohibited in India (ibid., p. 328).

[322] See Leopoldo da Rocha, op. cit., p. 169.

[323] Ibid., pp. 157-61, which traces the origin and evolution of the ceremonies of the *Santos Passos* and describes some typical features.

[324] Ibid., pp. 156-7. Refer to the mystery plays by people disguised as fictitious animals, dances of great folk interest; they were healthy forms of entertainment and aimed at mystifying the non-Christians.

Our Lady of Immaculate Conception, and St. Francis Xavier, used to be conducted in the second half of the eighteenth century, with great pomp and large attendance.[325]

The Constitutions and episcopal decrees laid down strict norms concerning their organization, which did not lack in directive on the rank and seniority of some authorities in relation to others, as protocol was of great consequence to the mentality of the times and often caused controversies.[326]

Other processions used to take place in the city and villages, less solemn but nonetheless significant for the people from a religious point of view. Owing to the large participation of the local inhabitants they were truly the religious manifestation of the parish. It must be noted that the authorities sought to nurture the tradition of processions, quite rooted in the religious customs of this population, by preserving the existing ones and reviving those that had withered.[327]

Donning flaming capes and vestments and carrying impressive

[325] See letter of 31 December 1756 from the Senate of Goa to D. José I, and the exchange of letters that followed on the incident at the feast of Our Lady of Conception whence some Franciscans wrested violently from the hands of the citizens the staff of the canopy they were carrying in that procession. Joaquim Heliodoro da Cunha Rivara published these documents, *Ensaio Histórico da Língua Concani,* Nova Goa, 1858, pp. 402-5. For Pietro della Valle there is no country in the world where there are more processions than in Goa and he ascribes this to the numerous religious Orders existing here. Quoted by Menezes Bragança, 'A Educação e o Ensino na Índia Portuguesa', in *A Índia Portuguesa,* vol. II, Nova Goa, 1923, p. 63.

[326] According to the *Constituições,* the brotherhoods and confraternities had to go first, followed by the Religious Orders, the clerics and parish priests and finally the Cathedral Chapter (cf. *Constituições,* Book III, Tit. II, Const. I, p. 189).

[327] The chapter considered discontinuing the procession of St. Martin held in memory of the glorious victory of Diu, since the Revenue Office had not paid the 40 xerafins that it used to contribute every year for the act. The proposal of the Senate President to have this amount paid for holding the procession was approved. Cf. the proceedings of the Senate of Goa, 20 December 1777 (H.A.G., *Assentos e Juramentos da Câmara de Goa,* 7762, ff. 161-161v). On 11 May 1797 the Senate officials informed the Crown that the chapter had again stopped holding the said feast and the procession that the Prince Regent had ordered to be maintained with the said deposit paid [A.H.U., *India,* maço 118 (118) and cód. 215, ff. 79v-80v].

and nearly life-size statues of saints, the confraternities made the processions resplendent indeed.[328] If in fact these cultic acts have much in common with the pilgrimages held in the Kingdom, with a ceremonial in the Portuguese style, they do not lack a certain local and original touch. There appear distinctive costumes, live representations of Biblical figures, Hindu musical instruments, in an interpenetrating of Christian and Hindu elements. It may be noted that the ecclesiastical authority in fact sought to prevent, albeit unsuccessfully, the spread of somewhat pagan practices.[329]

But if the external splendour of the processions was grand, so was the interior recollection and spirit of penance, for the faithful used to partake of them by praying and singing religious hymns, thus contributing to turn the procession into an act of authentic Christian dignity.

Introduced by the Dominicans through the confraternities of the Rosary that they had set up, Marian devotion and the praying of the Rosary became an essential part of the religious habits of Goan Christians who still, at the fall of day, pray the same as a family, at the oratory in their homes.[330] And quite numerous are the feasts in honour of Our Lady, as noted from the fact that many churches, chapels and confraternities have the Virgin Mary for their patroness, under diverse invocations.[331] There was also the custom of intoning the doctrine and the rosary at once.[332]

The Goan religious tradition is indeed rich. Different feasts

[328] See Leopoldo da Rocha, op. cit., p. 157.

[329] The *Constituições* go to the point of punishing with excommunication the ostentation of 'lascivious figures, dishonest or any other profane representations, nor go men and women representing men Saints, or women saints, dances, *folies*, dances, nor masks, and that they should not do in them morality plays of profane things, nor some colloquys of figures, even if to the Divine' (*Constituições* [...], Book III, Tit. II, Const. II, pp. 191-2). The same spirit is obvious in some episcopal decrees of D. Francisco de Assunção e Brito and D. Frei Manuel de Santa Catarina.

[330] L. Rocha, op. cit., pp. 35-6.

[331] In the province of Ilhas, nine out of the thirty-nine churches have the Virgin as their patroness with diverse names, seven out of twenty-four in Bardez, and in Salsete fourteen out of twenty-five.

[332] Cf. *Livro dos Capítulos* of the Church of Penha da França (A.C.P.G., *Livro de Conventos e Igrejas,* no. 13).

filled with symbolism, in which the interpenetrating of cultures is truly deep, producing combinations of a moving but lasting piety. The confraternities played their part in the perpetuation of those traditions. Here and there, parishes are agog with the celebration of religious feasts with the spontaneous participation of Hindus and Muslims alike, lending the village a semblance of ethnic bustle. This is what happens (to cite just one case) at the feast of Saint Anne in Talaulim. As the wife of St. Joachim and the mother of Mary, she is considered spiritually very powerful, miraculous, and adored almost as a goddess (*devi*). At this feast, the offerings in her honour comprise cucumbers, bangles, spoons, *udid*, etc. Childless couples thus present a cucumber and mouth the following rhyme: '*Toma pepino, dá cá menino*' (Take a cucumber, give us a babe). In addition, parents desiring a girl-child, offer a bangle, imploring the '*devi*' Saint Anne: '*Toma manilha, dá cá filha*' (Take this bangle, give us a daughter).

Researchers who have explored the meaning of these offerings assert that, by their forms, the cucumber is suggestive of the *linga* or phallic element; the bangle or spoon, the ionic element of Hindu mythology, that is, the symbols of male and female energy. This religious tradition documents the symbiosis of elements from Christianity and Hinduism.[333]

At other times, there are principles from different religions standing side by side in a totally harmonious ambience. A clear illustration is the presence of a cross in the place of the *tuloss*, the sacred plant for the Hindus, 'as if Hinduism and Christianity had been born in the shade of the same palm groves'.[334]

Some Hindu practices remained but were adapted to the Christian cult, an example of which is the *oratório* (oratory),

[333] See J. A. Ismael Gracias, *A Índia em 1623 e 1624. Excertos das Memórias do viajante italiano Pietro Della Valle Compilados e Anotados por ...*, Nova Goa, Imprensa Nacional, 1915, pp. 41-2, and Joseph de Barros, 'A Religious Tradition at St. Anne's Church', paper read at the History Seminar, Goa University, 19-20 February 1991, organized by the University of Goa and the Historical Archives of Goa.

[334] See Orlando Ribeiro, 'A Cruz e o Tulôsse (Imagens de Goa)', in *Aspectos e Problemas da Expansão Portuguesa,* p. 188 and L.F.F.R. Thomaz, op. cit., p. 10.

piece of furniture in Christian homes substituting for the Hindu household deity. The votive flame of the Hindu houses now burned before the crucifix or images of saints. The agricultural festival called *addav* was Christianized too with the blessing of the first sheaves of paddy.[335]

The propagation of the Christian cult in the parishes, especially in the first times of Christian Goa, was a lot due to the confraternities that had indeed found a fertile ground in these eastern stations.[336] Several factors contributed to their amazing multiplication, one of them being the restricted spirit of their statutes blending with the impervious caste system. In every church there was at least one, and at times up to four, confraternities.[337]

Being essentially associations of piety and cult for the parishioners, the confraternities instituted and ensured the celebration of Christian feasts, contributing towards the continuance of religious traditions that otherwise would have been lost in the mists of time. Thus, thanks to chapels and the pensions bequeathed by their donors, they had financial resources that gave stability to the church cult.[338]

The principal objective of the confraternities was spiritual and religious formation, which, in fact, is obvious from the

[335] Cf. Mira Mascarenhas, op. cit., p. 85. *Addav* is 'a religious and civil festival celebrated on the Islands of Goa with sham fencing, on the occasion of the rice harvest'. Also cf. L.F.R.R. Thomaz, op. cit., p. 9. Also see Chapter V.

[336] On the confraternities of Goa the indispensable work is Leopoldo da Rocha's *As Confrarias de Goa,* Lisbon, 1973, which deals with the various aspects that accompany the evolution of these institutions.

[337] Ibid., p. 2. See E.R. Hambye, op. cit., p. 330. Even the Santa Mónica Convent had a confraternity in 1717, with 191 confrères in 1774, and 231 in 1783. Cf. R.T., in *A Voz de S. Francisco Xavier,* year XI, no. 3, 1941, p. 23. The episcopal decree of 24 February 1780 recommends the institution of the confraternity of the Most Blessed Sacrament in the churches which had a tabernacle. Cf. Father Manuel J.S. d'Albuquerque, *Decretos do Arcebispado de Goa,* Bastorá, 1900, p. 10.

[338] See the list of pensions and chapels that each confraternity administers, dated 26 January 1766 (H.A.G., *M. Reino,* Book 138-A, ff. 230-252v, publ. by J.A. Ismael Gracias, 'Legados e Pensões a cargo das fábricas e confrarias de Goa', in *O Oriente Português,* vol. X, Nova Goa, 1913, pp. 62-86, quoted by L. Rocha, op. cit., p. xx).

Constitutions that define them as a 'voluntary personal college, convened for the purpose of the religion, glory and honour of God, and veneration of the Saints'.[339] This and the fact that confraternities were widespread in Goa, shows how effective its action must have been in the Christianization of the neo-converts.[340]

Besides this, these typical institutions of the Portuguese Crown Patronage were certainly important models for the social-religious adjustment of the Christian population. This was true especially of the new converts who were finding themselves rejected by their families and socially uprooted. Now, they began to have a new place in the society, by introducing themselves into that structure. In fact, this was the case a little all over the Kingdom, Islands and Overseas. In the Oporto region, for example, 'with chapels, their own vestments, solemn public processions, masses for the dead, organising funerals or banquets, they [the confraternities] constitute a means of affirmation and public recognition, of sociability, essentially male'.[341] It may be noted that they bore the expenses of education in parishes and also had an economic function, granting loans on mortgages.[342]

[339] *Constituições* ..., Book IV, Tit. IX, Const. única, p. 300.

[340] This religious scope is quite clear from the statutes of the confraternities. Thus, by their statutes of 1747, the brothers of the confraternity of Our Lady of Deliverance, in the church of St. Philip and St. James, Cortalim, undertook to pray the daily rosary, one Our Father and Hail Mary for the souls in Purgatory, one Our Father and Hail Mary for the conversion of the non-Christians, three Hail Marys in honour of the purity of the Virgin, examination of conscience at night, one quarter of an hour of mental prayer and many other religious duties (A.C.P.G., *Ofícios e Portarias,* Book 1, pp. 77 ss). See L. Rocha, op. cit., pp. 382-5, which transcribes a part of the statutes of the confraternity of the Mother of God, Daugim, and refers to other statutes of the second half of the eighteenth century.

[341] See Eugénio dos Santos, 'Os Livros das Visitas Pastorais da Região Portuense. Questões e Perspectivas de Abordagem', in *Revista de História,* vol. II, Porto, 1979, p. 244; and Maria Manuela Martins Rodrigues, 'Confrarias da Cidade do Porto: Espaços de enquadramento espiritual e polos difusores da mensagem da Igreja', in *Congresso Internacional de História. Missionação Portuguesa e Encontro de Culturas. Actas,* vol. I, Braga, 1993, pp. 381-410.

[342] A.C.P.G., *Livros dos Conventos e Igrejas,* no. 6 (Nossa Senhora de

In the second half of the eighteenth century, the juridical and economic situation of the confraternities was quite precarious. The jurisdictional conflicts between the Bishop of the diocese and the secular authority as a representative of the Grand Master of the Order of Christ aggravated the situation even further. The prelate sought to impose his tutelage and accordingly Archbishop Neiva Brum's action was quite incisive, decreeing as he did certain norms to bring order into the confraternities. D. Francisco de Assunção e Brito too ordered the formulation of new statutes[343] and D. Frei Manuel de Santa Catarina asked the parish priests of Bardez to send the list of the existing confraternities, mentioning their designation, origins, immovable properties, *fábricas* (administrators of the church properties), titles and income.[344] But the provision of 1801 finally clinched the matter by placing the confraternities under royal jurisdiction, with the purveyor ministers being entrusted with its accounts. Gradually, these institutions begin to lose the nature of religious associations as originally defined.[345]

As is known, some customs and superstitions rampant with the Hindus, relating to birth, marriage and death had pervaded the life of Christians. The Inquisition and the prelates always

Daugim). See Artur Teodoro de Matos, 'Um Quotidiano Diferente: Empréstimos e Penhores de uma Confraria de Goa no Século XVIII', paper presented at the international meeting *O Quotidiano na História Portuguesa,* Faculdade de Ciências Sociais e Humanas da Universidade Nova de Lisboa, 22–24 April 1993; Maria de Jesus dos Mártires Lopes and Artur Teodoro de Matos, 'Religiosidade e Aculturação do Povo Goês', in *Histórias de Goa,* Lisbon [1997].

343 Copy of the letter dated 3 July 1977 (A.C.P.G., *Livros de Conventos e Igrejas,* no. 13, Penha de França).

344 Archive of the Pomburpa Parish, *Livro de Decretos e Pastorais* (1796-1810), f. 20.

345 Provision of the Board of Conscience and Orders of 13 February 1801. Cf. Leopoldo da Rocha, op. cit., p. 213. On the interventions of the secular authority in the jurisdiction of the Archbishop of Goa, the legal nature of the confraternities and the analysis of the controversy, see ibid., pp. 210-13 *passim* and 275-6; at pp. 225-31 it deals with the reform measures of the administration of the confraternities and at pp. 240-2, the diocesan laws of the second half of the eighteenth century, relating to the statutes.

sought somewhat systematically to ban this religious hybridism, however, without great results. It may be noted, in fact, that some practices, earlier banned by this tribunal do figure even today in the life of Christians, under different aspects that nevertheless betray their origin. Thus, with a ban on betel offerings, areca and ritual ablutions, something remained in the guise of an elaborate exchanges of gifts and feasts lasting days together. There was a ban on funeral banquets, but the pomp of the funerals did not disappear. As seen, the interpenetrating of Christian and Hindu elements is deep-seated and has produced a very typical religiosity.[346]

But, even though the religious manifestations of the Goan Christians present deep imprints of the interpenetrating of Christianity and Hinduism and there is a marked Hindu influence amidst the lower social strata, yet the acts of Christian cult do have characteristics that set them apart from the Hindu religious festivals. As observed by Professor Orlando Ribeiro, there is no stridency and frenzy in the Christian ceremonies as there is in the Hindu celebrations. Some of its ostentation translates only in the church interior decoration sometimes similar to that of the Hindu temple: wreaths of flowers decorating the roofs; incense at the throne of the Blessed Sacrament; flower garlands decorating frames and images. However, the acts of the Christian cult speak of a personal faith, of true Christian unction.[347]

[346] Many Hindu customs entered the day-to-day life of the Christians. Nevertheless we are not listing them as there is a lot of material on the same. See the edict of the Inquisition of Goa, dated 14 April 1736, publ. by A. Lopes Mendes, op. cit., vol. I, pp. 250-60. L.F.F.R. Thomaz, op. cit., pp. 6-7; Mira Mascarenhas, op. cit., p. 85; Maria de Jesus Mártires Lopes, *A Inquisição de Goa,* op. cit., pp. 253-5 and 'A Inquisição de Goa na primeira metade de Setecentos. Uma visita pelo seu interior', in *Mare Liberum,* no. 15, Lisbon, Comissão Nacional para as Comemorações dos Descobrimentos Portugueses, 1998, pp. 128-9. The following episcopal decrees prohibit the Christians from holding certain non-Christian practices: that of 30 May 1783, paragraph 11; 1 January 1793, paragraphs 18 and 30; 22 April 1780 and 27 April, paragraph 3, pub. by C.C. Nazareth, *Mitras* ..., pp. 326-7, 330, 335, 354-5, 356-7.

[347] Cf. O. Ribeiro, op. cit., p. 192. The pastoral letter of 18 July 1784 prohibited the use of aromatic substances at the throne of the Blessed Sacrament. Cf. C.C. Nazareth, *Mitras* ..., pp. 337-8.

As stated by Archbishop D. Frei Manuel de Santa Catarina in his report on the *ad limina* visit of 1802, the Goan people were mostly pious and zealous in promoting the divine cult. This was especially true of the women, who are better inclined to devotion and hold fast to the sacraments of penance and holy Eucharist for the profit of their souls and their salvation.[348]

Let us try to sketch the religious and moral framework of the diocese in the final years of the eighteenth century. The cultic acts were held in parish churches, chapel and private oratories which by their large number and artistic beauty left an indelible mark on the landscape.[349] In 1798, these churches gathered in prayer about 1,81,579 souls in the Old Conquests and 9,052 in the New Conquests, spread over parishes which in Salsete and Bardez became quite populous.[350]

A similarly reduced clergy shepherded this flock. In 1798, there were no longer regulars exercising the healing of souls in the parishes, work which was performed by secular clerics.[351] About 792 priests worked in the parishes of Ilhas, Bardez and Salsete and 7 missionary parish priests in the new territories. Out of these, 281 priests were not confessors and attended to the cult in chapels and private oratories, besides helping out in the parishes, where they said Mass. In spite of the creation

[348] Secret Archives of the Vatican, *S. Congr. Concilii Relationes, ad limina* visit in 1802.

[349] 39 parish churches, 2 collegiate churches and 60 chapels in Ilhas, 24 churches and 68 chapels in Bardez and 25 churches and 51 chapels in Salsete, totalling up to 88 churches and 173 chapels. Cf. the Archbishop D. Frei Manuel de Santa Catarina's letter of 20 March 1798 to D. Rodrigo de Sousa Coutinho [A.H.U., *India,* maço 172 (186)].

[350] In 1798, the province of Ilhas had 36,539 souls, that of Bardez had 67,306 and Salsete 77,734 members of the faithful. The most populous parishes were those of Assolna, with 7,166 souls, and Anjuna with 7,000. They were followed by Chinchinim with 6,828, Margão with 6,333 and Curtorim with 6,111 faithful; Calangute had 4,728 and Mapusa 4,087 souls (ibid., f. 5).

[351] The only exception was a Dominican in the church of Santa Bárbara (Ilhas) which was under the jurisdiction of the Archbishop and who worked faithfully (Secret Vatican Archives), *S. Congr. Concilii Relationes, ad limina* visit of 1802).

of diocesan seminaries, there were still priests with a deficient formation.[352] Nevertheless, already in the final years of the eighteenth century, they produced fruits, with pupils trained to occupy the vacant parishes and teachers for the seminaries.[353]

The chapter of the See had more or less the same composition as in the earlier years and the Cathedral choir strictly fulfilled its duty.[354]

The regular clergy was fading out, 'both because there were no persons to administer them, and because they were done with'. The surviving regulars lived in monasteries, according to the convent rule. The Monica sisters, who were the only nuns in the territory, guarded their cloister inviolably and their revenue was administered faithfully.[355]

From the moral viewpoint and going by the Archbishop's testimony, the situation relating to the clergy seems to have improved, thanks to the efforts put in training them, by promoting meetings on moral theology and casuistics, sacred rites,

[352] 82 confessors and 60 non-confessors in Ilhas; 120 confessors and 87 non-confessors in Bardez; 222 confessors and 134 non-confessors in Salsete, totalling 705 priests. The Archbishop refers to 792, which includes the parish priests.

[353] Two seminaries were functioning, one in Chorão and the other in Rachol, and in each of them 15 pupils received formation. The Archbishop prohibited the going of these pupils to feasts in the parishes since he thought that nothing of profit could come therefrom for them, as they were initiated in the ecclesiastical discipline, modesty and strictness of customs (Secret Vatican Archives, *S. Congr. Concilii Relationes, ad limina* visit in 1802). Cf. the letter from the Archbishop, dated 20 March 1798, op. cit., A.H.U., *India,* maço 172 (186). It may be noted that besides these 15 pupils boarding at State expense, the seminaries gave formation to a considerable number of boys frequenting the public classes of these institutions. See the part referring to the seminaries in Chapter IV.

[354] Secret Vatican Archives, *S. Congr. Concilii Relationes, ad limina* visit of 1757, 1769 and 1802. Besides the dignitaries, the canons, semicanons, quartenarii, chaplains, etc., who are identical in number, the report of 1801 specifies other personnel connected to minor services. The number of singers too is higher here (15 instead of 12).

[355] Cf. the letter from the Archbishop, dated 20 March 1798 and the *ad limina* visit of 1802, op. cit.

spiritual exercises. The parish priests used to reside in their own parishes and observe a certain discipline.[356]

With regard to the faithful, the prelate drew the following picture: the people, particularly women, were diligent in going to church and exercising works of sanctification. Nevertheless, there was only a thin line between the sacred and the profane, which translated as games, dances, comedies on vespers and feasts, late into the night. There also continued some traditional Hindu religious practices particularly suppers on the sixth day of childbirth.

It becomes quite difficult to take stock of the religious situation and practice in this territory, given the nature of the issue and the lack of systematic studies. The essential problems, such as deviations in the moral conduct of the clergy and the people, non-Christian infiltration in the religious life of Christians, as well evidenced by the results of the pastoral visits, seem to continue. Meanwhile, the efforts made towards reforming customs and controlling human conduct must have contributed to a certain moralization of society or, at least, to avoiding its collapse. Thus, with regard to imparting doctrine – one of the prize targets of the Tridentine Council – there are testimonies attesting to progress made by catechesis mainly at the children's level.[357]

There is a new interest in the religious renewal of Goa in the second half of the eighteenth century as shown especially by the setting up of diocesan seminaries that trained local staff to be better attuned to the needs of Christianization.

Though there had been some moments of religious intolerance, it can be said that the balance sheet was in the black and that was when the foundations of religious freedom were laid. Henceforth, this has been a characteristic of Goa.

The interpenetrating of religious elements of Christianity and Hinduism is very deep in Goa, creating harmonious syntheses. Hence, even repeated efforts by the Inquisition and the ecclesiastical authority did not manage to dismantle the system.

[356] Ibid. The parish priests kept in order the books of marriages and of baptism.

[357] Cf. the *ad limina* visit of 1802, op. cit.

The rising access of local clergymen to diocesan posts may also have helped that interpenetrating, contributing towards a certain 'Indianization' of religious customs.

APPENDIX III.1

Mortgage of the Islands of Corjuem and Ponolem to the Jesuits by the Crown: Measures for its Redemption

The Mombassa expedition in 1727, during the viceroyship of D. João de Saldanha da Gama, compelled the mortgaging of the islands of Corjuem and Ponolem to the Jesuits for 1,39,000 xerafins, at the interest rate of 8 per cent and they were handed over to them with full administrative powers [cf. letters of King D. João V to the Viceroy, dated 25 and 27 March 1750. A.H.U., *Índia,* maço 77 (62) and cód. 205, f. 180]. It may be noted that in a letter to the Provincial of the Society of Jesus, dated 3 October 1750, the Viceroy, the Marquis of Távora, had stated that this rate of interest was exorbitant, 'when the villages take loans at the rate of 5 to 5.5 per cent' (H.A.G., *Cartas e Ordens,* Book 880, ff. 49-49v). By 1746 the Jesuits had already charged 1,76,173 xerafins and a half and the remainder was 1,59,000 and odd xerafins. Considering that at this rate these islands would never be redeemed or would be so in the very distant future, 3,497 xerafins were despatched (cf. letter of D. João V to the Viceroy, dated 27 March 1750. A.H.U., *Índia,* maço 17 (14) or H.A.G., *M. Reino,* Book 123-A, f. 120, or also B.N., *Pomb.* 742, ff. 32-32v). However, silver, converted into money in Goa, was spent on the payment of the troops and other expenditure. By deed of 13 January 1751 the interest rate was reduced to 5 per cent, with effect from 1 November 1750. Meanwhile, on 27 June 1753, with the threat of the King of Sunda to the Estado da Índia, the Jesuits lent another 80,000 xerafins on the same islands, also at the rate of 5 per cent, thus raising the debt considerably. See the letter of Francisco de Oliveira to the King, dated 22 September 1755, in which he details the payments effected from 1726 up to this date. Cf. A.H.U., *Índia,* maço 84 (105). Since the expenditure was higher than the revenue, it was decided at the Overseas Council that interest tables be drawn, at the rate of 5 per cent, on the State revenue (cf. letter of D. José to the Count of Alva, dated 3 March 1757, A.H.U., *Índia,* cód. 205, ff. 222-222v). At the Revenue Council on 12 January 1758 the endorsement to the deeds whereby the islands had been mortgaged to the Jesuits was decided. Cf. A.H.U., *Índia,* maço 23 (294). They were incorporated in the Royal Revenue and leased for the same (cf. letters of interim Governors to the King, dated 24 January 1758 and 30 March 1759, H.A.G., *M. Reino,* Book 130-A, ff. 12-14 and A.H.U., *Índia,* maço 26 (196), respectively). In 1755 the Jesuits of the Malabar Province lent the Royal Treasury 1,000 xerafins, at the rate of 5 per cent interest, for the revenues of the villages of Sirigão and Mulgão, in Bicholim (New Conquests). See the deed regiment of 26 March 1755 (A.N./T.T., *J.R.F.E.I.,* Book 37, ff. 24v-26v). On 26 March 1759, Tomé Joaquim da Costa Corte Real wrote to the Count of Ega that the malfunctioning of the Jesuits were on the rise, as seen from the papal briefs. Thus by brief no. 1, Pope Benedict XIV constituted a reformer for the said missionaries; brief no. 2 curbed the *'scandalous trade they were engaged in'*; brief no. 3 banned them from hearing confessions and preaching ..., cf. A.H.U., *Índia,* cód. 439, ff. 73-7, or maço 23 (294).

APPENDIX III.2

Daily Schedule at the Chorão Seminary

The daily schedules at the Seminaries of Rachol and Chorão were quite similar. The same amount of time was allotted to classes, meals, religious duties, and almost always, the same timings.

By way of example, let us see how time was used at the Chorão Seminary.

5:00 a.m. – Rising;
5:00-6:00 a.m. – Mental prayer (vocal prayers, followed by silent meditation);
6:00-7:00 a.m. – Studies in the cells;

7:00 a.m. – Mass, by the grammar master;
7:30 a.m. – Breakfast (canji, bread and figs);
8:00-10:00 a.m. – Classes;
10:30-10:45 a.m. – Spiritual lesson in the chapel and private examination of conscience;
11:00-11:30 a.m. – *Jantar* (Lunch) (Bread, rice, figs and seasonal fruit; fish, seasoned, baked or fried;
11:30-12:45 a.m. – Study (in the respective classes, for exchange of views);
12:45-14:00 p.m. – Silence for rest;
15:00-17:00 p.m. – Class;
18:00 p.m. – Rosary in the chapel;
After Rosary up to 19:15 p.m. – Silent study, by candlelight;
19:15-20:00 p.m. – Mental prayer and litany to Our Lady, accompanied by the professors;
20:00 p.m. – Supper (Bread, figs, rice, curry, fish; on solemnities, there were extra courses). Both at lunch and supper, there was the reading of the life of saints or church history, after the Bible lesson;
20:30-21:15 p.m. – Meetings for academic discussions;
21:15 p.m. – General examination of conscience in the chapel.

After this, each one would retreat silently to his cell. Any extra time after these exercises was properly spent, for there was silence and study; some of that time was used for their priestly duties, like Holy Scriptures, ceremonies of the sung mass, plainchant, catechism. The youth were not treated with strictness, for on holidays they had one hour for 'recreative conversation' in the morning and similarly in the evening. They were also allowed a stroll outside the seminary building and on other holidays when they would not go out, they would entertain themselves with the ball. Cf. the letters of the rectors of the Seminary of Chorão, Sebastião Mascarenhas, dated 12 April 1801 and of Rachol, Father Joaquim Cabral to [the Archbishop], dated 27 April of the same year, which they wrote in fulfilment of the orders received, the study syllabus and the internal regulation observed in these houses (H.A.G., *M. Reino,* Book 180-A, ff. 170-173v and 174-7, respectively).

CHAPTER IV

Education and Culture

In the cultural field, the eighteenth century saw the dawn of a new era in Europe. Enlightenment or the 'Lights', a cultural movement that characterized this century, made its presence felt in diverse fields of social life. Gradually a new mentality was forming in which the taste for scientific innovations gave birth to a richer cultural life. This atmosphere was conducive for reflecting upon the problems of education and occasioned studies on science and pedagogy, since its mentors were conscious of the important role played by education in mental transformation. Several reforms sought to adapt teaching to the scientific discoveries; while at the same time new progresses in science and culture were springing out from the 'modern' schools.[1]

Portugal kept up with this movement endeavouring to be on par with the ideas that were gaining currency outside its borders. It distanced itself in some ways from Spain and gravitated more towards the cultural orbit of France, England, Italy and Germany. The frenchified and the rather foreign agents played an important role in the profound cultural mutation that was underway in the country and Luís António Verney 'symbolizes the social transformation that was under way'.[2]

As in Europe, so it was in Portugal that pedagogical literature arose which had a definite influence on the change of mentality.[3] Educational reforms did not come up at one stroke. There was

[1] See Rómulo de Carvalho, *História do Ensino em Portugal,* Lisbon, Fundação Calouste Gulbenkian, 1986, pp. 393-9.

[2] Ibid., p. 406. See A.H. de Oliveira Marques, *História de Portugal,* vol. II, Lisbon, Palas Editora, 1983, pp. 322 and ss.

[3] For Verney a general reform in teaching was indispensable for the transformation of the mental life. Cf. Rómulo de Carvalho, op. cit., p. 408.

a long gestation period at the ideological level and another of practical application. Earlier, under the patronage of D. João V, the Oratorians had tried new teaching methods and introduced some alterations in the syllabi, but it was indeed with the Marquis of Pombal that educational reform assumed a deeper and more objective countenance.

TEACHING INSTITUTIONS

It was sought to extend the educational reform to Goa and in fact to other overseas dominions as well. Let us find out, then, what measures were adopted and the possible effects they had. However, it may perhaps be important to have a look at the formal teaching structure in force in this territory, in the beginning of the second half of the eighteenth century. The institutional scene, the type of teaching administered and the public for whom it was meant, would elucidate on the general state of teaching and the impact that the Pombaline reforms could possibly have on Goa.

Since very long, still in the first half of the sixteenth century, there used to be parish-run schools in Goa. According to some researchers, it is possible to trace back its remotest origin to the meetings that St. Francis Xavier used to organize for studying the Christian doctrine.[4] Meanwhile, a royal order in 1545 determined the opening of schools for the education of lads in Christian-populated villages, teaching them catechism and liturgical singing. These parish schools always had a religious scope, for which reason the schools created by D. João III can be considered their embryo.[5]

[4] According to Father Caetano Francisco de Souza, the Apostle of the Indies used to improvise catechism schools at places in the city of Goa where the sound of the bell could be heard inviting the faithful to come to learn the Christian doctrine. D. João de Albuquerque, the first Bishop of Goa, impressed by the good results achieved by Xavier, ordered the extension of this study to all the parishes of the diocese. Cf. *Instituições Portuguezas de Educação e Instrucção no Oriente. Estudos Histórico-Archeológicos,* Bombay, 1890, p. 202. It may be noted, in fact, that the schools in the Christian countries depended on the advances of Christianity.

[5] Filipe Nery Xavier considers that the origin of the parish schools stems

They were institutions of very humble origin, functioning here and there, in verandas of old temples or corridors of the parish schools, and employing rudimentary pedagogical methods. However, they had an introductory and fundamental role in the education and instruction of the Goan people. The passage through the 'schools for reading, writing, counting, song, violin and organ' was indispensable for entry into colleges of the religious Orders. Besides catechism, they used to administer the basics of reading and writing in Portuguese, arithmetic, arts and craft. They further made a remarkable contribution to music teaching, which was simultaneously a vehicle for the teaching of language and doctrine taught in song or story form. Meant to ensure the liturgical singing at religious ceremonies, the parish schools were responsible for the great development of the polyphonic song and music in general, soon opening the regular course of emigration and of the musical profession.[6]

The *mestres-escola*, paid by the village communities and the confraternities, were at the same time *mestres-capela*, in charge of

---

from the schools ordered to be created in 1545. Cf. Father Caetano Francisco de Souza, op. cit., p. 202.

[6] Susana Sardo and Rui Simões, 'A música e o seu papel no processo da cristianização em Goa', in *Goa* (revista da Casa de Goa), no. 1, Lisbon, 1989, p. 15. The *mestres-capela* have the duty to 'singing at the organ the weekly Masses of the Confraternities, Rosaries, and Litanies, accompany the dead when called, and to do all the other acts, both ordinary and solemn of their respective Churches, for this end making use of the Lads, who learn the Art of Singing, and Musical Instruments'. As *mestres-escola*, 'they have the duty of teaching the Lads to read, write, count, Catechism', see the *Rellação dos Mestres de Capella das Igrejas, e Escollas das Freguezias das Ilhas de Goa, e Provincias de Salcete, e Bardes, e das suas obrigaçoens em 1801* (H.A.G., *M. Reino*, Book 180-A, ff. 168-169v). According to Luís F. Thomaz, polyphony entered Goan folklore through its teaching in the parish schools (cf. L.F. Thomaz, *O Cristianismo e as Tradições Pagãs na Índia Portuguesa*, in *Actas do Congresso International de Etnografia*, Lisbon, 1965, p. 9). Goan musicians became well known in their land, in neighbouring India and abroad. Almost all the bands of the local regiments of British India consisted of musicians from Goa. Cf. Father Caetano Francisco de Souza, op. cit., pp. 203-5 and Father Amaro Pinto Lobo (ed.), *Memória Histórico-Eclesiástica da Arquidiocese de Goa 1533-1933*, Nova Goa, 1933, pp. 334-5.

teaching catechism and liturgical singing. Hence, the criterion for selecting these teachers was, above all, their musical qualities and knowledge of doctrine rather than their literary and scientific training. Hence this teaching naturally had several limitations. The study of Portuguese language was of secondary importance, taught only inasmuch as it was necessary to understand catechism and some liturgical hymns. In fact, the catechism manual was used as the language primer, a practice that was followed up to the nineteenth century.[7]

It must be pointed that these public teaching institutions in Goa are quite old, in fact, older than some of their counterparts in Europe; and they continued till 1831 when State primary schools were opened by determination of the Viceroy D. Manuel de Portugal e Castro.[8] These aspects, added to the age-old school tradition in India, must have contributed to creating certain habits of mind and helped to understand the importance that education had on the fate of these peoples.[9]

Although the founding of the retreats called Recolhimento de Nossa Senhora da Serra and Santa Maria Madalena had well defined religious and moral objectives, yet the nuns and the lay

[7] Cf. Menezes Bragança, 'A Educação e o Ensino', in *A Índia Portuguesa,* vol. II, Nova Goa, 1923, p. 18.

[8] Father Caetano Francisco de Souza cites the example of France where Christian schools were opened at the end of the seventeenth century, by St. John Baptist de la Salle, thus, one century after those in Goa. Cf. de Souza, op. cit., p. 201.

[9] Menezes Bragança refers to the teaching that probably existed in Goa before Afonso de Albuquerque and draws attention to the 'difference between a society that, for some reason, stopped short of its progressive evolution and a human grouping which did not succeed to come out of the almost gregarious state of primitive life'. Cf. 'A Educação e o Ensino', op. cit., pp. 15-16. It is possible to have an idea of how this teaching took place through the Hindu schools existing in the New Conquests, under the porch of the *guru*'s house, the boys seated on the ground learnt to read, write and do arithmetic, 'on a board covered with fine sand, or with a piece of bamboo on banana leaves, the letters, while at the same time they go on pronouncing or singing aloud'. Cf. A. Lopes Mendes, op. cit., vol. I, p. 106.

servants working there were also taught basics of reading, writing, arithmetic and stitching.[10]

In this retrospective view of teaching in Goa from the time of its conquest up to the Pombaline reforms, we must highlight the educational action by the colleges of the religious Orders. It may be noted, however, that the uncertainty of their names sometimes makes it difficult to judge the extension of the syllabi and the degrees conferred by them. Colleges, seminaries, orphanages taught the first letters as well as medium- and higher-level courses.[11]

The first college or seminary in Goa – the Seminary of the Holy Faith – was founded very early, in 1541, and 'marks our first literary and academic age'. This institution, meant to train Asian missionaries for the Oriental missions, was entrusted soon thereafter to the Jesuits settled in Goa. Their work was noteworthy and soon they began to direct two teaching establishments, the Seminary of the Holy Faith and the College of Saint Paul. In the former, the pupils who showed an inclination toward religious life and intellectual capacity learned music, grammar, rhetoric, philosophy and theology, besides the liturgical offices. The college, with three Latin classes, one course in philosophy and the subject of morals, became well known in the East and the starting point of other Jesuit colleges in Asia, all with the same name. Hence, these priests are also known as St. Paul fathers or Paulist priests.[12] Later, this college came to be known as 'University of Goa', but the unhealthy nature of the place obliged its transfer to the Monte do Rosário or Holy Mount, and it was

[10] Cf. *Memória Histórico-Eclesiástica* ..., p. 333. On the teaching of girls in this house, refer to Propércia Correia-Afonso, 'A mulher indo-portuguesa', in *Boletim do Instituto Vasco da Gama,* no. 8, Nova Goa, 1930, pp. 43-4.

[11] Ibid., p. 329.

[12] The Seminary of the Holy Faith with all its revenue was handed to St. Francis Xavier who took charge of everything, in the name of the Society of Jesus. On this seminary and on this College of St. Paul, see Father Francisco de Sousa, S.J., *Oriente Conquistado* ..., vol. I, 1.D.1. §47 and 1.D.2ª §14, publ. by Felipe Nery Thomé Caetano de Souza, *Noticia Historica e Legislação da Instrucção Publica Primaria, Secundaria e Superior na India Portugueza,* Nova Goa, 1879, p. 9 and F.X. Gomes Catão, *O Primeiro Seminário de Goa,* Bastora, 1955, p. 18.

called S. Paulo-o-Novo, or S. Roque (1614). Here, according to Pyrard de Laval, they 'taught two thousand students or more both Portuguese and Indians'.[13]

In the second half of the sixteenth century the Jesuits began to evangelize the lands of Salsete where they set up a college with that name (1574), definitively established in Rachol in 1610. Besides the hospital, there functioned one seminary for poor lads, house of catechumens, school for reading, writing, counting and catechism. They even had a Kanari language school for the missionaries.[14]

We have not come across any documentation specifically treating the methodology followed in the Ignatian colleges of Goa. Meanwhile, it is common knowledge that, by the opening of various colleges in Europe and Overseas, the Jesuits felt compelled to follow some general directives for teaching, which were summed up in the *Ratio Studiorum* (1599), 'the didactic magna carta of the Order'. Nonetheless, this was the result of a long training, which was preceded by various plans and projects, subjected to successive corrections and adaptations.[15]

Given the uniformity of rules for the Jesuit teaching establishments (which, however, used to permit sporadic alterations), their colleges in Goa obviously followed the directives of the *Ratio*. For the higher and secondary courses, it had three curricula: theological, philosophical and humanistic. In the first course, which was of four years' duration, there was Scholastic Theology, Moral Theology and Holy Scriptures. In the second, they taught Logic and introduction to the Sciences (1st year); Cosmology, Psychology, Physics and Mathematics (2nd year), Psychology, Metaphysics and Moral Philosophy (3rd year).

[13] *Viagem de Francisco Pyrard de Laval Contendo a Noticia de sua Navegação* . . . etc. Portuguese version of Joaquim Heliodoro da Cunha Rivara, vol. II, pp. 45-6.

[14] F.N.T.C. Rosario e Souza, op. cit., pp. 12-15.

[15] William V. Bangert, S.J., *História da Companhia de Jesus,* Porto, Livraria Apostolado da Imprensa, 1985, pp. 41-2; Leonel Franca, S.J., *O Método Pedagógico dos Jesuítas, O 'Ratio Studiorum',* introdução e tradução de ..., Rio de Janeiro, Agir Editora, 1952, pp. 41-2, and P. Charmot, *La Pédagogie des Jésuites, ses principes, son actualité,* Paris, Spés, 1943.

Finally, the humanistic syllabus, by and large corresponding to the modern secondary school, covered three classes: Rhetoric, Humanities and Grammar with three levels (higher, medium, lower).[16]

The doctrine of St. Thomas was followed in Scholastic Theology and Aristotle in philosophy (in fact, common to the other schools), except when in contradiction with the faith.[17] The students of Physics and Mathematics had to learn the Euclidian elements, some concepts of Geography, sphere, etc.[18] Introduced in the humanistic curriculum, Rhetoric broadly comprised rules of oratory, style and erudition, based on Ciceronian and Aristotelian books of rhetoric. In grammar, the compendium of Father Manuel Álvares was followed. Jesuit teaching laid great stress on the study of Latin, which had to be spoken by all pupils, especially the students of the Humanities.[19]

In pedagogy, as recommended by the *Ratio*, lectures were considered the fundamental process of teaching, being 'an anticipated lesson, an explanation of what the pupil had to learn', more formative than informative, its objective was not theoretical, but artistic, having in mind the vivid analysis of a model. It employed an active method wherein the teacher was helped by the pupils and resorted much to emulation, with a great variety of exercises and prizes; physical punishment was only used in extreme cases.[20]

But, although the Jesuits were in the forefront of teaching, other religious Orders also did set up colleges, like the Dominicans who, having competent teachers, trained Thomist theologians and local clerics in the College of St. Thomas Aquinas (1623). The Franciscans founded the Reis Magos College (1555), with the St. Jerome Seminary for the education of orphan lads (1595) as also the college of St. Bonaventure (1602) in the city of Goa. Here the ecclesiastics were taught philosophy and theology. In the Augustinian Populo College, there were public

[16] Leonel Franca, S.J., op. cit., pp. 47-8.

[17] Ibid., pp. 152, 155, 159.

[18] Ibid., pp. 164, 192.

[19] Ibid., pp. 215-16.

[20] Ibid., pp. 57-60, 64, 84.

classes for Latin, Philosophy and Theology and the diocesan clergy were trained at the St. William College.[21] Possibly, they did not use the right methods in these colleges, where teaching was somewhat dogmatic and rigid. That is because, by and large, new currents of humanism and experimentalism, widespread in sixteenth century Europe and Portugal, had not been adopted by the colleges belonging to the regulars in Goa. Here, pedagogy and thinking remained quite imbued with the medieval spirit.[22]

Essentially regulars, who gave prime importance to training future ecclesiastics, directed the studies in these colleges. But also many external students, even from outside Goa, received formation here, which later allowed them to become bureaucrats, private teachers, advocates and physicians.

These teaching institutions managed by regulars were still functioning around 1758 and most probably throughout the second half of the eighteenth century, despite the vicissitudes they went through. Standing out among them were the colleges of St. Paul the New and Rachol, belonging to the Jesuits. It may be recalled that the Society of Jesus was, since its founding, an

[21] F.N.T.C. Rosário e Sousa, op. cit., pp. 15-18 and Benedito Gomes, 'Instituto Vasco da Gama', in *Boletim do Instituto Vasco da Gama,* no. 16, Bastora, 1932, p. 44. When they arrived the Viceroys used to be accommodated in the Franciscan College at Reis Magos, founded in 1555. On 7 August 1761, the Count of Ega exhorted the Franciscan Provincial to have the college cleaned and the Viceroys' room whitewashed, for with the impending arrival of the ships from the Kingdom, his substitute could be coming (cf. A.H.U., *Índia,* cód. 442, ff. 212v-213). On the foundation of the Franciscan colleges, see the *Copia dos sinco Capitulos do mapa junta a informação que o Exmº Governador e Capitão General da India deo no anno de 1770 sobre as Igrejas da Provincia de Bardez* (H.A.G., *M. Reino,* Book 148-B, ff. 537-538v).

[22] Menezes Bragança deals quite in detail with the type of teaching imparted in the colleges of the Jesuits and other regulars, adopting a very critical attitude. He states the 'when the Jesuits and other Orders that were exclusive holders of public education for a span of almost three centuries exited from Goa, they left it in a mental state that, for three hundred years, had ceased to be in Europe', 'A Educação e o Ensino na Índia Portuguesa', in *A Índia Portuguesa,* vol. II, Nova Goa, 1923, pp. 37-44. This judgement appears unduly severe; in fact, we have no knowledge about what he has based his statements on.

Order with a vocation for teaching. In Goa too, these missionaries were the main agents of the teaching magisterium until the date of their expulsion in 1759. At this time, teaching at the college of St. Paul the New tended towards the Humanities, Law, Philosophy and Theology, meant for both the local clergy as also the Jesuit students. At the Rachol Seminary there functioned a seminary-college for the children of Salsete.

At the college of Reis Magos the Franciscans ministered courses of clerical formation for the seminarians and for the youth of Bardez. At the college of the Mother of God, Pomburpa (Bardez), the lads were taught the 3 R's, i.e. Reading (W)Riting, Rithmatic though in a much reduced number than earlier.

The Dominicans trained the diocesan clergy in their St. Thomas Aquinas College. The Populo College of the Augustinians was mainly devoted to educating the novices of the Order, but also opened their classes to other students, even though not future ecclesiastics.[23]

The religious Orders founded by the local Goans like the Oratorians (1682) and the Discalced Carmelites (1750), more recent in origin than the European congregations, had an impact on teaching a little later, above all, during the second half of the eighteenth century. Hence we shall not dwell on them.

The historical vicissitudes facing the European religious Orders headquartered in Goa and the slackness that characterized some of their members certainly jeopardized teaching which for more than two centuries they gave the youth.[24] Subjects like Theology, Metaphysics, Morals, Canon law carried a lot of weight in the curriculum as the college curriculum was meant for the formation of regulars. This was, for example, to the detriment of science that had begun to create an interest in some continental colleges. This was, broadly speaking, the academic scene in Goa, in the

[23] Some data on the colleges of the missionaries can be found in *Memória Histórico-Eclesiástica ...*, pp. 331-2 and in Benedito Gomes, 'O Instituto Vasco da Gama', in *Boletim do Instituto Vasco da Gama,* no. 16, Bastora, 1932, p. 44.

[24] Of all the religious Orders of European origin the Society of Jesus was the one with the least number of signs of lack of discipline and insubordination. They were mainly accused of a materialist spirit and holding large businesses.

first years of the second half of the eighteenth century, that is, in the beginning of the Josephine epoch.

As is commonly known, two moments marked the Pombaline reform for minor studies: the Directoria Geral de Estudos, or Directorate-General of Studies (1759-71) and the period in which the Real Mesa Censória, or Royal Censor Board (1771-7) superintended the studies.

In this context, the charter of 28 June 1759 marked the beginning of the Pombaline reform and was an important milestone in the history of teaching in Portugal. With it came to a close a long period of pedagogic activity of the Jesuits who, in reality, presided over the greater part of teaching.[25]

Reference may also be made to the ban on the use of methods and compendiums. Thus the Instrucções which accompanied the charter ordained the use of the Sellecta Latini Sermoni by Chompré, the grammars of the Oratorian António Pereira de Figueiredo and António Félix Mendes, instead of the much-criticized *Arte* by Manuel Álvares. Bento Pereira's *Prosódia* was prohibited and replaced by Pedro José da Fonseca's *Diccionario.*[26]

There was a deeper ideological bias underlying this list of compendiums. That is because following the new books meant assuming a political orientation that would guide the spirit culturally, to serve unconditionally the enlightened despot. But it is also certain that in Portugal the pedagogical works produced in Europe were spread.[27]

In the opinion of Rómulo de Carvalho, though the term *reform* appears in the text of the diploma, it does not formulate any reform of the minor studies; it only devises an alternative to the Jesuit pedagogy. Thus, the disciplines and the teaching objectives remain unaltered, that is, the study of Latin, Greek and Rhetoric with a view to perfecting the monarchy.[28]

[25] On the said charter and its importance, see Rómulo de Carvalho, op. cit., p. 429.

[26] Other books proposed for the new pedagogy have been mentioned by A.A.B. Andrade, *A Reforma Pombalina* ..., vol. I, pp. 70-2, 83.

[27] Ibid., p. 72.

[28] In order to substitute the method of the Jesuits it was proposed to adopt a method that was in use prior to the entry of the Jesuits, albeit duly updated. Cf. R. Carvalho, op. cit., pp. 429-30.

This charter brought about a single authority, subordinated to the royal power, to preside over teaching in Portugal. In practice, however, it meant imposing the will of the Marquis of Pombal.

Free classes were set up for Latin, Greek, Rhetoric and Hebrew in the Kingdom, but they never became functional. Latin continued to be the basic language for school training, but inasmuch as it would help to learn Portuguese correctly. Hence, Latin grammar was taught in Portuguese, and even the study of Portuguese grammar would progress whenever there was an analogy between their language rules.[29]

The Pombaline reform of the minor studies was quickly carried to Goa where the charter of 28 June 1759 came into force in 1760, through the Chancellor Commissioner of the Director-General of Education.[30] Accordingly, they sought to know the number of teaching staff and students, later compiled as *Lista do numero dos Mestres e discipulos que havia na cidade de Goa e suas Ilhas e Provincias de Salsete e Bardês*. However, no such documentation is available giving the post-examination list of candidates to allow a comparison of the pre- and post-Charter situation. Nonetheless, this statistical data provides information on the amplitude of the school network and its possible evolution.[31]

There was an exchange of correspondence between the Commissioners of Goa and the Director-General in Lisbon to the effect of keeping themselves informed of the progress of the reform. It covers issues related to the prices of books that were locally considered exorbitant, teachers' salaries, the ban on certain books, the greater or lesser openness to higher orders, etc. Thus on 24 April 1762, Tomás de Almeida agreed with the Commissioner's decision to scrap a teaching post in the city of Goa because of its unhealthy location; however, disagreeing with

[29] Ibid., p. 433 and A.H. de Oliveira Marques, op. cit., p. 337.

[30] Quite detailed information on the manner in which this first moment of the Pombaline reform (1759-71) went on in Goa is given by A.A.B. de Andrade, op. cit., vol. II, pp. 768-87. A total of 49 teachers used to lecture to 612 students.

[31] Ibid., pp. 769-70.

the Commissioner's position, he consented to a Latin language class in the former Jesuit building in Rachol. The General Council of Salsete had not only made a request for the said subject, but had created and taken responsibility for it.[32]

Like in the Kingdom, violent means were ordained to exterminate the reminiscences of Jesuit presence, such as sudden inspections to the classes, the booksellers, and imprisonment of obstinate teachers. ... Nonetheless, the Commissioner gave an account of the local resistance to the introduction of the new method, the holding of exams, concession of licences, with even mutinies having taken place in Salsete. That was to say that repression was not to succeed as it had in the Kingdom.

It would have been of interest to study the topics prized in these classes, the textbooks adopted, the pedagogic systems used, but we have not come across any syllabus for such an analysis. Moreover, since the Pombaline reform adopted common criteria to Ilhas and Overseas they must have surely evolved in a similar manner.[33]

This first phase in the reform of minor studies in the Kingdom and Ilhas as well as Overseas must have redounded in the inefficacy of the structural measures. There are several reasons to explain these poor results, more importantly the lack of competent teachers and of funds to ensure that the classes would be held free of cost.[34]

As stated by Banha de Andrade, it must be remembered that Latin grammar schools in Goa functioned with a higher or lower degree of success, directed by approved teachers or by teachers who had never answered exams. That is because the authority

[32] Ibid., pp. 774-6.

[33] Studies on the reform of the minor studies in Ilhas and Brazil include A.A.B. de Andrade, op. cit., pp. 205-35; idem, *A Reforma Pombalina dos Estudos Secundários no Brasil,* S. Paulo, 1978; Maria Beatriz Nizza da Silva, 'Instituições culturais', in *Nova História da Expansão Portuguesa,* direcção de Joel Serrão e A.H. de Oliveira Marques, vol. VIII, *O Império Luso-Brasileiro 1750-1822,* coordenação de Maria Beatriz Nizza da Silva, Lisbon, Estampa, 1986, pp. 445-51.

[34] See A.A.B. de Andrade, 'A Reforma Pombalina dos Estudos Secundários no Arquipélago dos Açores (1ª Fase 1759-71)', in *Arquipélago. Revista da Universidade dos Açores,* Special edition, 1983, pp. 219-20.

realized that no strict or violent measures would of use in this territory as they were in the Kingdom, moreover because the government in India was too unstable to allow it.[35]

Furthermore, another option for the reformation of teaching was gaining ground in Goa. That was because the Oratorian regulars – a young congregation comprising Goan Brahmins were animated by a great religious fervour and had obtained encouraging results in their pastoral work – though devoid of the many pedagogical and scientific abilities of their brothers in Lisbon (perhaps because of lack of opportunities).[36] The great interest evinced by the Marquis of Pombal to have his educational projects enforced without much ado prompted him to entrust teaching in Goa to the said ecclesiastics, who used to accept only Indians and exercise the letters and virtues by 'giving religious examples'.[37] These ecclesiastics were untouched by the softening that was then assuming serious proportions among members of some religious Orders. For these reasons, they were delegated to teach in the diocesan seminaries. The clear need for a larger number of Oratorians in the tasks of evangelization and teaching made the Crown authorize the opening of another house. This was at a time when the religious policy tended to favour the spread of the diocesan secular clergy to the detriment of the regular.[38]

[35] Ibid., pp. 781-2.

[36] See in Chapter III, what we have said about the regular clergy; and A.A.B. de Andrade, op. cit., vol. II, p. 782.

[37] Cf. the King's letter to the Prepositus of the Congregation of St. Philip Nery, Goa, dated 4 April 1761 (A.H.U., *Índia,* cód. 513, ff. 146-146v). He also ordained that whenever the Archbishop or the Count of Ega asked for the ecclesiastics of this congregation to be teachers of the new studies, he should grant them. Also see the letter from Francisco Xavier de Mendonça Furtado to the Count of Ega, dated 2 April 1761, publ. by Filipe Nery Thomé Caetano do Rosário e Souza, op. cit., pp. 19-24.

[38] The letter from D. José to the Archbishop, dated 4 April 1761, authorized the founding of a third house of the Oratorian Congregation to function in the Rachol college which belonged to the Jesuits (cf. A.H.U., *Índia,* cód. 513, ff. 141-142v and A.C.P.G., *Cópia de Vários Documentos,* ff. 54-5 in F.U.P., 18-1-8/9). It may be noted, however, that priority was given to the '2nd founding of local clergymen of the Orient and ... only finding for

It is noteworthy that, on the one side, the educational projects in Goa were strictly in keeping with the general teaching reform undertaken in the Kingdom; on the other, it was sought to adapt them to the local circumstances. Hence, there can be a correlation made of the happenings here and in the Kingdom. As is known, the education of the nobles was another issue that engaged the pedagogues and the politicians in Europe, in the eighteenth century. A new nobility was sought to be formed, versed in the scientific and cultural innovations of the age and 'domesticated' according to the principles of enlightened despotism.[39] It is in this context that, in the first phase of the Pombaline reform of the minor studies, the Collegio Real dos Nobres, or Royal College for the Nobles (1761) was created, with quite an ambitious syllabus; equipped with the most modern material and staffed with foreign teachers.[40]

The establishment of the Collegio de Meninos e Clerigos Naturaes do Oriente, or College for Local Lads and Clerics of the East, in Goa was, so to say, an answer to that institution. This one sought above all to train local ecclesiastics and prepare them for evangelising their country-cousins, by resuming the objectives that had presided over the foundation of the Seminary of the Holy Faith.[41] The students of this institution had 'to be

---

this invincible difficulties recourse would be had to the remedy of establishing a third house of congregates' (A.H.U., *Índia,* cód. 513, ff. 145v-146). 'The said two new Colleges are the two Poles, in which most safely and opportunely can be sustained the conservation and propagation of our Holy Law ...'. Cf. F.N.T.C. Rosário e Souza, op. cit., p. 23.

[39] It is the case of the work of Martinho de Mendonça de Pina e Proença, *Apontamentos para a Educação de um Menino Nobre* which gave rise to the critical edition by Joaquim Ferreira Gomes, Coimbra, 1964. Also L.A. Verney, *Verdadeiro Método de Estudar* and Ribeiro Sanches, *Cartas,* refer to the education of the nobles. See R. Carvalho, op. cit., pp. 443 and ss.

[40] On some aspects related to the creation of and the studies in the College of the Nobles, see Rómulo de Carvalho, *História da Fundação do Colégio Real dos Nobres de Lisboa (1761-1772),* Coimbra, 1959.

[41] See the King's letter to the Prepositus of the Congregation of St. Philip Nery, dated 4 April 1761, op. cit., in which he refers to the restoration of the establishment made in 1541 by Miguel Vaz and Diogo de Borba for the education of the boys born in the East, 'who returning to their

noble in their local communities and of legitimate matrimony' and, what is more, they would all be treated equally. The statutes of this teaching establishment were to draw inspiration from those of the College of the Nobles, for which reason they were despatched to Goa.[42]

With regard to the curriculum, this college sought to give an all-round education: The two sides – that of Christian practice and civil obligations, on the one hand, and scientific training, on the other – were to go hand in hand.

The college students had to know reading, writing and arithmetic; they would be taught Philosophy, Theology and Morals, besides the Latin language, Rhetoric, Poetry, Logic, History and Oriental languages. The teaching of philosophy came before that of Physics, considered 'a very useful part of philosophy'. Students were given a summary information of the history of old and modern physics and instruments of recent innovation had to be used.

Theology included two papers on speculative theology of the doctrines of St. Thomas Aquinas and St. Augustine, while completely excluding casuistics as developed by the Jesuits. It also included the study of the more necessary subject of positive scholastic theology, Holy Scriptures, and Christian morals, for two or three years.

The Latin language was a strong component of the curriculum; it was taught to all students and only those who successfully answered the exams would be promoted to the class of Rhetoric and Poetry, which was followed by Logic by the new method. Also included in their syllabus was the history of Portugal and its dominions, with particular attention to the Oriental conquests and the progress made by religion before the arrival of the Jesuits. Finally, all students would be initiated in the Marathi and

---

countries ... would therein fruitfully preach the Gospel. ...' Therefore, it meant a second founding of the local clerics in the East, of the habit of St. Peter. See the same document in A.C.P.G., *Cópia de Vários Documentos,* ff. 54-5 and H.A.G., *M. Reino,* Book 118-A, ff. 118-118v in F.U.P., 18-1-8/9.

[42] See the draft of the *Estatutos do collegio de meninos e clerigos naturaes do Oriente* (A.H.U., *Índia,* cód. 441, ff. 364-367v), publ. by F.N.T.C. Rosario e Souza, op. cit., p. 25.

Tamil languages besides which they would be taught rudiments of 'languages of the lands where there are churches and mission stations'.[43]

Because of the unhealthy location of the college of St. Paul, they had it shifted to the island of Chorão, contiguous to that of Goa. The educational objectives that had determined the creation of this college were not totally fulfilled. This was in fact the case in the Kingdom too, where the College of Nobles had not been very successful, perhaps because of its great scientific and disciplinary requirements. However, in Chorão, the college was transformed into a diocesan seminary, where, apparently, it fulfilled its mission.[44]

Let us, however, return to the Pombaline reform of the minor studies. As seen above, a second stage began in 1771 when the management of the studies was entrusted to the Royal Censor Board. They were governed by the regiment of the charter of 28 June 1759 which had created the Directorate-General of Studies and all other statutes issued till then.[45] This determination was followed by the organization of a plan presented by the Censor Board for minor schools in the Continent, Islands, Africa, Asia and Brazil. It indicated the places where they would function and the number of teachers to be appointed for reading and professors of Latin, Greek, Rhetoric and Philosophy. According to this plan Goa would have two readers, two professors of Latin, and one each for Greek, Rhetoric and Philosophy.[46]

[43] Ibid., the teaching of the Latin language occupied two and half-hours of the morning session and two of the evening.

[44] Cf. the letter from the [Count of Ega] to Francisco Xavier de Mendonça Furtado, dated 15 January 1762, publ. by F.N.T.C. Rosario e Souza, op. cit., pp. 32-3. The daily schedule was also strict with rising at 5.30 a.m., with 5 class hours, one study hour, besides time for religious practice, study of Christian doctrine, conferences or debates on speculative theology. Cf. the draft of the statutes of the said college, referred to above (A.H.U., *Índia,* cód. 441, ff. 364-367v and 513, ff. 130-133v; H.A.G., *M. Reino,* Book 118-A, f. 178, in F.U.P., 7-1-1, 38/5, 39/1-5 and 40/1).

[45] Cf. the royal charter of 4 June 1771, publ. by F.N.T.C. Rosario e Souza, op. cit., p. 78 and the fn. of p. 77.

[46] It was the school staff organized by the Censor Board and which was published in annexe to the law of 6 November 1772. See R. Carvalho, op. cit., pp. 453-5.

Customarily, the teachers of reading, writing and counting had to teach calligraphy, general rules of Portuguese orthography and syntax, arithmetic, catechism and good manners. In the spirit of the reform, which began in 1759, the study of the mother tongue was further stressed. There was no ban on private teaching but it needed to have due approval. Then the teachers had to answer an examination and to be approved by the Board. For the financial viability of the reform, the literary subsidy tax was imposed.[47]

As a whole (and keeping in mind the two stages referred to above), it was the Pombaline reform of the curricula that introduced the idea, and later the practice, of free public State-sponsored education in Portugal, Islands and Overseas. It allowed duly authorized private schools to function; made the competitive system the regular procedure of recruiting teachers, and one entity responsible for educational affairs.

This second stage of Pombaline reform (1771-7) in Goa took place as follows: A Literary Board, comprising the Archbishop, Governor, theologians and jurists, was made responsible for enforcement of royal laws, edicts, orders of the Board and censorship on books.[48] Competition for the appointment of royal teachers and professors was announced, in accordance with instructions from the higher authorities. It must be noted that preference was given to locals in the selection of the candidates.[49] In Goa too the literary subsidy was imposed on meats and liquors.[50]

[47] See the royal letters of 6 and 10 November 1772, publ. by F.N.T.C. Rosario e Souza, op. cit., pp. 79-83.

[48] See the deliberation of the Board, submitted to the royal sanction and confirmed on 22 March 1773, publ. by F.N.T.C. Rosario e Souza, op. cit., pp. 84-5. 'That all the major prelates be called to the state who have convents in Asia, and that they be intimated to restore the banned books, and be imposed the responsibility for the choice of individuals to whom the teaching was entrusted'.

[49] Cf. the letter from D. José I to the crown judge of the Estado da Índia, dated 7 April 1774 (ibid., p. 85).

[50] In Goa, the tax collection consisted of one real per pound of meat cut in the slaughterhouse and 10 réis per *canada* (measure equivalent to 2 litres) of brandy. Cf. the letter from D. José I to the Governor D. José Pedro da Câmara, dated 17 October 1773 (ibid., pp. 83-4).

Let us now turn to the candidates' qualifications, the examiners, the profile of teachers and professors selected, and finally, some practical aspects of the Pombaline reform in Goa. The examinees had 'to be competent and very knowledgeable about life and habits. All education agents, and especially royal professors of Latin Grammar and Rhetoric, needed to have a Latin background. Evidently the professors of philosophy had to have training in Philosophy.[51] Finally, the situation did not change much as compared to 1759. A jury comprising the high court chancellor and *padres mestres* (priest-teachers), who included Dominicans and Franciscans, tested the candidates.[52]

In the list of royal professors selected in the first competition, and in the ensuing ones, there were regulars, secular priests and laymen. Perhaps there were more laymen and individuals with minor orders, as masters of reading than as royal professors.[53] This was perhaps because the academic qualifications required

[51] See the Instructions on the exams accompanying the letter from D. José to the crown judge, dated 7 April 1774, op. cit. (ibid., p. 85). The candidates for the subject of philosophy were expected to have knowledge of logic, ontology, those of rhetoric, 'two orations of Cicero, beauties of a Portuguese author of good note, defects of another of bad repute'.

[52] See the charters of licence issued to the teachers of reading or the royal professors, authorising the teacher of the syllabi. One of 1774 refers to the examiners, priest teachers Fr. Manuel de S. Joaquim Cabral and Fr. Narciso e Sª Machado, of the Dominican order. Those of 1776 refer to the high court judge Dr. Feliciano Ramos V. Mourão, as a member of the jury. These documents obey quite a similar format. Almost always they refer to the place of birth, to the place of teaching for which they were appointed, to the syllabi to be taught, their examination results, the jury, the capacity and information about the life and habits, etc. Cf. among others, the statute of 13 September 1774 (A.N./T.T., *Junta da Real Fazenda do Estado da Índia,* Book 61, ff. 101v-102); the charter of 22 March 1776 (Book 63, ff. 148v-149); the temporary licence of 6 July 1776 (Book 63, ff. 174v-175).

[53] The persons selected in the first competition were: one Augustinian for the chair of philosophy, an advocate for rhetoric, a cleric and a layman each for each of the two classes of Latin grammar. A cleric and a layman for the two reading, writing, counting and catechism classes. For the year 1776 we counted among the masters of reading 5 laymen, 1 priest and 1 tonsured and among the royal professors 2 ecclesiastics and 2 laymen. These persons are, however, very few and there might have been others.

of the former were not so demanding. Though the religious Orders had thrown open their doors to external students, there probably was more learning among ecclesiastics, because they had already been the principal educational agents as well as because teaching was, above all, oriented towards the priestly formation.

Pombaline reform so thoroughly changed the educational structure in Portugal that efforts made to backtrack, in the period of the *viradeira* (turnabout), could not go beyond the secondary aspects. However, the reforms planned by the Marquis would not be feasible without a spontaneous participation from the right people with their own initiative, which did not happen. The iron will of the minister of D. José I stifled everything and everybody!

By D. Maria's reform of minor studies, dated 16 August 1779, primary education once again came under the ecclesiastics. As regards the curricular subjects of middle-level education – Rational Philosophy, Rhetoric, Greek language, Latin grammar and drawing – 'did not make up a course but were taught perhaps in accordance with the possibilities of the teaching places'. In contrast with the Pombaline reform, it is noted that there was an increase in the number of primary schools, but a reduction in the number of classes of the subjects at the medium-level education. The management of studies in the primary schools, and the administration of the literary subsidy, in 1787, requisitioned the Tribunal of the Royal Board of the General Commission on the Exam and Censorship of Books, which was in charge of examining and reforming the earlier provisions.[54]

Let us see the repercussion that these educational measures had in Goa. As in the Pombaline government, the system of masters and royal professors seems to have become popular also during the reign of D. Maria I, an age in which public education was extended to Salsete and Bardez, with a master of reading

---

Hence, they are only indicators. Cf. A.N./T.T., *J.R.F.E.I.*, Books 61 and 63, deteriorated ff.

[54] See Rómulo de Carvalho, op. cit., pp. 488-90.

and a professor of Latin appointed in each province.[55] At the close of the century there functioned in Goa ten royal subjects (four in the city of Goa, two in Pangim, two in Salsete and two in Bardez).[56]

Nonetheless, from a reading of the charters of professorial appointments, one realizes that, down the years, public classes were created in several villages of Goa, in response to people's requests for schools at more accessible localities. It so happened that earlier, to attend the royal classes, they had to bear the inconvenience and expense of travelling long distances.[57]

How to explain this apparent contradiction? Those were perhaps classes conducted by private teachers and parish schoolmasters, duly authorized upon the holding of the exams. It may be recalled that in the Pombaline reform itself, freedom of private education was safeguarded as long as it had the required authorization. In such cases, the expenses were borne not by the literary subsidy but by the village communities and the confraternities. It was thus quite a malleable system: Royal schools, private classes and parish schools were functional, besides education in the convents, in colleges founded by secular clerics and in the seminaries.[58] Interestingly, there are no traces of

[55] See D. Maria I's letter of 9 April 1778, publ. by F.N.T.C. Rosario e Souza, op. cit., p. 87 and Menezes Bragança, op. cit., p. 74.

[56] See the *Demonstração do Rendimento do Subsidio Literario ... Do Numero das Cadeiras e dos Logares em que Foram Estabelecidas ...*, publ. by F.N.T.C. Rosario e Souza, op. cit., p. 90.

[57] For the year 1776, for instance, there exist charters of interim appointment of masters of reading for the city of Goa (Ilhas), for the villages of Betalbatim, Majorda, Verna, Navelim (Salsete), Guirim, Moira, Pomburpa (Bardez) (A.N./T.T., *Junta da Real Fazenda do Estado da Índia,* Book 63, ff. 146-146v, 151v, 152v-153v, 158, 165-165v); for the royal professors of philosophy, rhetoric in the city of Goa; for philosophy in Margão. All of them obeyed the customary format with references to the constitutive members of the examination jury, to the information about their life, their qualifications, etc. (Book 63, ff. 145v-146, 148v-149, 174v-175). The charter of licence passed on 7 October 1786 to Father Mateus Fernandes to teach Latin grammar to the young lads of Navelim, because their parents could not send their wards to Rachol, being far, nor to Margão, being epidemic and there being need of hostels (Book 73, ff. 79-79v).

[58] Reference may be made to the private college of St. Francis Xavier,

teaching institutions in the New Conquests; perhaps because no efforts had been made to Christianize them, also none were made to develop education similar to that in the Kingdom, leaving the same to them and their Hindu tradition.

The royal classes were discontinued in 1798 by the Governor Francisco António da Veiga Cabral: On the one hand, State expenses were alleged, and on the other, the existence of public schools for minor studies in the seminaries of Chorão and Rachol, with proper and competent professors.[59] Later on, following the reaction of the professors who had appealed to the central government, he maintained that the teachers had been negligent and the pupil attendance poor.[60] Could they have been the real reasons?

Meanwhile, it may be noted that by the balance sheet of the literary subsidy of 1800 it was found that the Governor had paid the royal professors' salaries only up to 1797, and a certain amount had been withdrawn from the coffer by way of loan. Although the literary subsidy had been created especially to

---

founded by Father Rafael Pereira, on the Benaulim mount, where in 1760 they taught Latin, Philosophy and Theology. Cf. Benedito Gomes, 'Instituto Vasco da Gama', in *Boletim do Instituto Vasco da Gama,* no. 16. A provision of temporary licence, of 17 June 1789, after appointing the master of reading, makes reference to the schools that functioned in the churches (A.N./T.T., *J.R.F.E.I.,* Book 74, f. 155v). The same seems to be said in the charter of temporary licence of 3 October 1791 issued to Vitorino Luís Gonçalves to be a master of reading, 'by the *nemos* (decisions) given by the *comunidades* ..., as also local originals benefactors of the same parish to teach escola to the youngsters ...' (Book 78, deteriorated f.).

[59] Cf. the administrative rule from the Governor dated 4 January 1798, publ. by F.N.T.C. Rosario e Souza, op. cit., p. 88 and the letter from the same to D. Rodrigo de Souza Coutinho, dated 24 March 1798 (H.A.G., *M. Reino,* Book 177-B, ff. 547-8).

[60] See the letter from the Governor to D. Rodrigo de Souza Coutinho, dated 16 April 1800. He states that after some years the classes became useless and that the rhetoric classes were attended only by 2 students 'to whom the master used to pay to keep him company and to serve as a title to unduly receive his salary'. It further states that the same happened with the Latin grammar classes and in those of reading, writing ... (H.A.G., *M. Reino,* Book 179-A, ff. 96-96v), publ. by F.N.T.C. Rosario e Souza, op. cit., p. 88.

help defray the expenses on teaching,[61] the abolition of the public schools had compelled their students to enrol in the royal classes held at the State-financed seminaries. Former royal professors now unemployed were to be paid one-fourth of their old salary.[62] Years later, in 1808, the Viceroy Count of Sarzedas instituted five chairs of Latin, acknowledging its usefulness in Goa.[63]

The diocesan seminaries of Chorão, founded in 1761, and of Rachol a year later, and Bom Jesus in 1781, constituted another facet of the State-sponsored education. It is the crisis that the regular clergy was undergoing and similarly the teaching entrusted to them, that prompted the government to set up the royal classes, on the one hand, and on the other, to conceive of a new type of seminary directed by the episcopal authority and destined to train ecclesiastics for the modern times. Besides this, the diocesan seminaries were most evidently turned outwards by institutionalising the public classes for the population.

Earlier we referred to the aspects related to the creation, financing, installation and direction of the seminaries. Let us now turn our attention to the teaching imparted therein.[64]

In the seminary of Chorão there functioned the courses of Theology, Philosophy, Rhetoric and Latin grammar. The first consisted of theology per se and morals; in the philosophy course, Logic was taught in the first year, Physics in the second and Metaphysics in the third. These subjects were taught by masters of the Oratorian congregation and by secular priests.

The texts and authors adopted illustrate the pedagogy that pontificated in this seminary. Thus, in Physics they followed

[61] See the letter from José Joaquim Pereira Marinho to D. Rodrigo de Sousa Coutinho, dated 29 March 1802, publ. by F.N.T.C. Rosário e Souza, op. cit., p. 91 and Menezes Bragança, op. cit., pp. 76-7.

[62] Cf. the letter from D. Rodrigo de Sousa Coutinho to the Governor, dated 17 April 1801, publ. by F.N.T.C. Rosario e Souza, op. cit., pp. 90-1.

[63] The chairs of Latin were spread over the following places: one in Ilhas (in the old city of Goa, commonly known as the old city); two in the Salsete province (in Majorda and Chinchinim) and two in the Bardez province (in Mapusa and Candolim). Cf. António de Salvador Fernandes, *O Liceu Nacional Afonso de Albuquerque em Nova Goa,* Lisbon, 1946, p. 6.

[64] See in Chapter III, the part relating to the seminaries.

Gassendo, Descartes, Leibnitz, which meant the elimination of the traditional peripathetism; in the Latin grammar class it was the new method by Father António Pereira instead of the *Arte* by Father Álvares, which showed that here, as in the other diocesan seminaries of Goa, teaching had moved away from the Jesuit methods and taken new paths of openness and innovation. It was the triumph of the Oratorian methodology characterized *inter alia* by the 'importance assigned to the mother tongue, simplification of the study of Latin grammar, the stress laid on historical and geographical knowledge, acceptance of a certain experimentalism and rationalism in the philosophical studies'.[65] That was the educational contribution made by the Oratorians to the transmission of new ideas of the age of enlightenment in Goa.

Every subject had four class hours daily (two in the morning and two in the evening) that the professor divided in a most fitting manner, making time to dictate and comment, explain, judge, discuss and solve doubts. The students had roughly three hours of study every day.[66]

The student population of this seminary generally consisted of fifteen seminarians sponsored by the State; the 'portionists' who contributed a certain amount and external students who studied free of cost. In his *Glozas,* Father Caetano Vitorino de Faria stated that in 1781 the seminary had five hundred students.[67]

[65] Cf. Eugénio dos Santos, *O Oratório no Norte de Portugal. Contribuição para o Estudo da História Religiosa e Social,* Porto, 1982, p. 309. In theology, they followed: Thourneli, Lhermeniel, João Lourenço, Baptista, Habert, St. Augustine, St. Thomas, Ricardo, Vitorino ... and the more modern ones; logic by Baptista, Almeida, Tosca, Malebranchio and 'the others of the modern System'. The rhetoric compendium was by Francisco Pomei and others. See the 'plan of everything is done in this royal Seminary ...', divided into 11 chapters (H.A.G., *M. Reino,* Book 180-A, ff. 170-173v). On the Oratorians of Goa, see Manuel Costa Nunes, *Documentação para a História da Congregação do Oratório de Santa Cruz dos Milagres do Clero Natural de Goa,* Lisbon, 1966.

[66] 1h:45m of individual study and 1h:45m of studying with companions. See the internal schedule of the seminary, in Appendix III.2.

[67] Cf. 'Glosas do padre Caetano Vitorino de Faria à informação de D. Fr. Manuel de Santa Catharina ...', in J.H.C. Rivara, *A Conjuração de*

In the year 1801 there were sixteen seminarians, five 'portionists' and external students whose number was appreciable but difficult to determine because at the beginning of the course there would be many but by and by would reduce. Indeed, in the year of Logic, more than 150 students joined the philosophy class alone; 80 for the Theology class and an equal number for Rhetoric and Latin grammar. Nonetheless, this number went on shrinking to forty or fifty in each class.[68]

The staff of the Rachol Seminary was quite similar to that of Chorão; the same courses, the same triennial schemes, the same methodology, which is not surprising, since the management too was committed to the missionaries of St. Philip Nery. It is a well known fact that the same texts and authors used to be followed in all the houses connected with the congregation, which proves the solidarity existing among these ecclesiastics.[69]

In Chorão and Salsete, the number of students who flocked to the respective seminaries was so large in the beginning of the academic year that 'the Readers find it difficult to pave their way to go up to their chairs'. However, at the end of the year there were about fifty students in each discipline, which is still a good number.[70]

We do not know what was the syllabus in the seminary of the Good Jesus. Nonetheless, being also entrusted to the Oratorians and for the reasons stated above, naturally it would not differ very much from the rest. Besides this, given its short existence, its action was more restricted.

1787 ..., Nova Goa, 1785, reed. by Asian Educational Services, New Delhi, Madras, 1990, p. 54 (documented part).

[68] The 'portionists' paid Rs. 7 monthly. They and the seminarians lived in the same manner, in what concerns food, studies and spiritual exercises. In 1801 the 5 portionists were from Macao. Cf. F.N.T.C. Rosario e Souza, op. cit., pp. 40-1.

[69] Also as regards the daily schedule and the timetable, there were great similarities in what happened in the Chorão and Rachol seminaries. See Appendix III.2 and Eugénio dos Santos, *O Oratório no Norte de Portugal* ..., pp. 309, 310, 318.

[70] See the letter from the rector of the Rachol Seminary to the Archbishop, dated 27 April 1801 (H.A.G., *M. Reino,* Book 180-A, ff. 174-7).

With the extinction of the royal classes in 1798, the so-called secondary education was practically limited to studies in the diocesan seminaries. It does not seem out of purpose to highlight the important role played by these institutions in Goan culture and formation of the cultural elite. Thus, the public classes put education within the reach of many Goans, allowing them new cultural flights. We suspect that the diocesan seminaries functioned virtually as a fountain from which Indians drank to keep abreast of the cultural currents that were blowing in the West. How much this mental ambience influenced Goan culture at the end of the eighteenth century is what we propose to examine ahead.

In some documents of the time some colleges and seminaries were called universities.[71] Thus, for example, Theology, Philosophy and Holy Scriptures taught in the Jesuit college of St. Paul (founded in 1544-8), the Dominican College of St. Thomas Aquinas (1623), in the diocesan seminaries of Chorão (1761) and Rachol (1762) came to be regarded as higher studies. There are also reports that in the administration of D. Constantino de Bragança (1558-61) the first medical classes took place in the college of St. Paul. Some matters, then, were taught at the higher level though they did not covering the totality of learning; and this is why the title of University seems a trifle exaggerated. However, it was modelled on the European Universities of the day, where only certain areas were studied in depth.[72]

It must be observed that in the Philippines too there was a growth in education with the setting up of public schools, colleges and seminaries. In 1645, the Dominican college of St. Thomas was promoted to a University for perpetuity.[73] On the other

[71] The Chamber General of Bardez asked the central government, by a 'representation' of 30 January 1770, that it be authorized to set up a University in this province, as there were the other two, in Salsete (Rachol) and in Ilhas (Chorão). Cf. H.A.G., *M. Reino,* Book 148-B, ff. 577-578v, 579-581v.

[72] Refer to *Memória Histórico-Eclesiástica ...*, pp. 324-8 and Américo Cortez Pinto, *'Talant de Bien Faire': A Divisa do Infante e a Criação do Estado da Índia,* Lisbon, 1955, pp. 38-9.

[73] António M. Molina, *História das Filipinas,* pt. I, Madrid, 1984, p. 123.

hand, in the Dutch Indies, the influence of Calvinist doctrine of predestination ('he is ignorant whom God predestined for ignorance') produced a much greater stagnation in education for its local inhabitants than in the Catholic countries where the religious Orders were in charge of education as well as to train the clergy. In Indonesia, it was only in the present century that the secondary education was thrown open to locals the first establishment dating back to 1920; and it was only in 1942 that the first University was set up.

* * *

It is common knowledge that the idea of checking the decadence and re-establishing the Estado da Índia in a new garb was really a plan of action always brewing in the second half of the eighteenth century. Education became a fundamental means of social transformation. Besides the minor studies in traditional moulds, other forms of practical teaching were promoted in Goa. The Count of Ega, seeking to control the decadent state of the navy and to reorganize it, created a class on the subject. Thus, thanks to the zeal of its masters and the co-operation of some officials of the navy corps of Lisbon, both theoretical and practical knowledge of great utility was imparted.[74]

The Governor Frederico Guilherme de Sousa gave the naval classes a further push: He sought to create an autonomous body of pilots in Goa who would not be dependent on a despatch from Lisbon, as was customary in other parts of Asia. For this

[74] See the letter from Tomé Joaquim da Costa Corte Real to the Count of Ega, dated 29 March 1760, whereby the King takes cognizance of the creation of the naval school (A.H.U., *Índia,* cód. 425, ff. 170-170v). António Rodrigues dos Santos who served many years in the State as pilot was given the charge of *lente* of the navigation class and provided good collaboration [A.H.U., *Índia,* maço 126 (142) and cód. 441, ff. 360-360v]. To the request of the Count of Ega asking for pilots of the Kingdom, 'those practising at the naval school that there is in Goa being incapable of any navigation other than that of the Malabar Coast', M.M. Castro replies, on 3 February 1784, that this is impracticable, because in the Kingdom too there is a lack of capable pilots [A.H.U., *Índia,* maço 55 (300) and cód. 517, f. 101].

purpose, he appointed a competent *lente* (professor) who later agreed to publish his lectures, and many practitioners were admitted to learn piloting.[75] In 1786, he reformed the naval class, gave it new statutes and stimulated the better students with prizes and post promotions. Experience as a methodological attitude received prime importance.[76]

The artillery class set up also showed positive results. Its *lente*, João Baptista Vieira Godinho (1777), dynamized the studies and won followers, thanks to his training and talent.[77] Like in the naval class, here too a practical orientation was planned, taking the officials of the artillery corps to work on board the war frigates so that they might be of help in navigation. It is from this class perhaps that the Military Academy was born in 1817.[78]

In keeping with the same spirit of creating local staff in Goa who would make the territory self-sufficient without having to be strictly dependent on the Kingdom, the central government

[75] Cf. the Governor's letter to M.M. Castro, dated 3 February 1784 (H.A.G., *M. Reino,* Book 164-A, f. 166). José Joaquim de Vasconcelos, *lente* of the naval class had answered his exams in the Kingdom with approval, prize and the voyages determined in the statutes. Cf. the letter from Frederico Guilherme de Sousa to M.M. Castro, informing him of this appointment [A.H.U., *Índia,* maço 143 (128)].

[76] Cf. letter [of the Governor] to M.M. Castro, dated 26 March 1786 (H.A.G., *M. Reino,* Book 167-A, ff. 101-101v). 'The *lente* or master of piloting must possess this art, not only theoretical but practical and in the same way he should teach his disciples it making them first masters of the theory and after this he shall apply the manner of putting it into practice'. See the *Ordens que se hão-de observar na aula da marinha de Goa e metodo que se deve seguir no ensino da pilotagem,* Chapter 1 (B.P.A.D.E., cód. CXVI/1-39, no. 16).

[77] See *o Plano que S. Magestade manda seguir no estabelecimento, estudos e exercícios das aulas do Regimento de Artilheria da Cidade de Goa,* of 15 July 1763. Cf. A.H.U., *Índia,* maço 40 (315).

[78] Cf. the letter from D. José Pedro da Câmara to D. João [general of the Royal Navy], dated 3 January 1779 (H.A.G., *M. Reino,* Book 160, f. 168). Also see the *Relação dos oficiais inferiores ... que dão lição na aula do Regimento de Artilharia de Goa e dos progressos que cada um tem feito* (H.A.G., *M. Reino,* Book 170-A, ff. 164-165v). On the creation of the Military Academy, see António de Salvador Fernandes, op. cit., p. 7.

urged the locals to take up medical education. It was also very difficult to have doctors sent down from the Continent. Hence, in the period under study, a class functioned in the Royal Hospital of Goa, under a qualified doctor usually from the University of Coimbra and attended by locals. Besides acquiring theoretical knowledge in the said class, the Goan students used to do their apprenticeship in the hospital practice.[79]

After graduation, which according to the opinion of the traveller Richard Burton, used to take four years, the students had to answer an examination. If successful, the Viceroy or Governor would award them a diploma of medicine or physician and surgeon, in the name of the King. Hence, these diploma holders were called *médicos* or *cirurgiões por Sua Magestade* (surgeons by His Majesty).[80]

With the return to the Kingdom, in 1782, of the physician-major Dr. Luís da Costa Portugal, who had apparently not given a good account of himself in the mission to Goa, the series of physician-majors of the eighteenth century came to a close and medical education was in serious jeopardy. Thus, 'the medically

[79] The medical students used to visit infirmaries, work in the company of approved physicians and sometimes continued in the Hospital after having ended their studies, in order that they may acquire more practice. Those who dedicated themselves to what today we call pharmacy, would attend the manufacturing of medicines in the *botica* (pharmacy) of the hospital and work therein for years. Cf. by way of example, some letters authorising certain locals to exercise the functions as physicians, pharmacist, surgeon or bleeder (A.N./T.T., *J.R.F.E.I.,* Book 73, ff. 131-131v, 73-73v; Book 74, ff. 79v-80, 81v-82, 115-116v, 178v-179; Book 77, ff. 146-147; Book 78, ff. 72-72v; 86-86v; Book 79, ff. 19-19v, 39-39v, 40v-41, 47-47v, 177-177v, 189v-190).

[80] The traveller Richard Burton who visited Goa in the middle of the nineteenth century refers to several halls in the Hospital and to the recourse to French and English books in the medical course, though the essential apprenticeship was done in Portuguese. See Richard Burton, *Goa and the Blue Mountains or six months of sick leave,* London, 1951, pp. 150-1. Also see the list of books on medical subjects requested by the Goa Hospital (H.A.G., *M. Reino,* Book 180-A, f. 49). There are references to doctors graduating in Goa, in 1797 to 1800, in the study by J.A. Ismael Gracias, 'Alguns médicos antigos de Goa, 1797-1839', in *O Oriente Portuguez,* vol. XI, nos. 9 and 10, September and October 1914, Nova Goa, 1914, pp. 214-24.

curious passed off as professional doctors'.[81] The situation appears to have been particularly precarious at this time: There was an absence of well qualified doctors and competent professionals; the activity was exercised by persons without scientific training; infrastructure conditions were unfavourable and inadequate for the purpose, and there was a scarcity of medicines.[82]

For all these reasons, the mortality index in the Goa Hospital was high during the second half of the eighteenth century, in spite of continuous appeals by the central government and efforts made by the Governors, who never failed to pay daily visits to the building.[83] To a certain extent, the problem was perhaps due to the acute unavailability in Goa of good doctors who could teach. This would not be difficult at all given the Goan aptitude for medicine.[84] This lack of doctors was seriously deplored by the Governors who in their correspondence with the central government repeatedly sought a solution to the problem.[85]

It may be noted, in fact, that the locals showed a particular aptitude for this activity and that its practice was deep rooted in Goa, at the family level and a more extended level as

[81] See the Governor's letter of 14 March 1798. Cf. A.H.U., *Índia,* maço 170 (163). M.M. Castro, in his letter of 8 February 1779, refers to the 'bad behaviour of the physician-major, for the irregularity of his bad genius, presumptions about his knowledge and excessive ambition' (A.H.U., *Índia,* cód. 516, f. 207). On 2 April 1782, the government notes the same to the Secretary of State: as lente da aula, the physician-major was obliged to instruct the locals in medicine, which he does not alleging that they do not have the necessary qualifications of rhetoric and philosophy (H.A.G., *M. Reino,* Book 161-D, ff. 2149-2149v).

[82] See, for example, F.A. Veiga Cabral's letter to Luís Pinto de S. Coutinho, dated 21 February 1797. Cf. A.H.U., *Índia,* maço 167 (165).

[83] See in Chapter VI, the part relating to health and hygiene.

[84] L.F.F.R. Thomaz writes that 'the predilection of the Goans from good families for the liberal professions (medicine and law) must be interpreted as a survival from the horror of caste to manual or technical work' (*O Cristianismo e as tradições pagãs* ..., p. 5).

[85] See, e.g. the Governor Frederico Guilherme de Sousa's letters to M.M. Castro of 2 April 1782 and 15 March 1784 (H.A.G., *M. Reino,* Book 161-D, ff. 2149-2149v and Book 164-C, f. 1057, respectively) and that of the Governor F.A. Veiga Cabral's to the Marquis Major-domo, of 29 April 1799 (H.A.G., *M. Reino,* Book 178-B, f. 644).

well.[86] Some researchers aver that the medical-surgical apprenticeship in Goa dated back to the first half of the sixteenth century, when in 1534 the physician-major Garcia de Orta arrived in India. More than a century later, in 1691, two doctors had been appointed to assist the sick and to train the locals in medicine and make them the subject teachers in future. However, this attempt came to nothing, as the professor-designates had desisted from changing to Goa.[87] In the Jesuit College of St. Paul there used to be a medicine class which, coupled with that of surgery in 1716, was the germ of the Escola Médico-Cirúrgica (School of Medicine and Surgery), officially established in 1842.[88]

There were apparently better staff for surgery, thanks to pains taken by the surgeon-major Francisco Manuel and his assistant Carlos Eloy Bossé.[89] However, this is not to deny that at the end of the century (1799) the Governor Veiga Cabral informed the central government that 'in this State there is not a single Portuguese Doctor with University training, that from those of

[86] M.M. Castro states in his letter of 8 February 1779 that there is great difficulty in sending a doctor from the Kingdom and that the lack of a professor in Goa 'should be compensated with medical and surgical schools and with the hospital practice, for which the local Indians are capable' (A.H.U., *Índia,* cód. 516, f. 207). There is reference to a very capable Brahmin, Inácio Afonso, gifted in medicine, but who used to get drunk. He became the physician-major. Cf. A.H.U., *Índia,* maço 170 (163) and maço 2 (713).

[87] Cf. Alberto C. Germano da Silva Corrêa, *História do Ensino Médico na Índia Portuguesa,* Nova Goa, 1917, pp. 3-4 and ibid., *A Escola Médico-Cirúrgica de Goa. Monografia,* Goa, 1959, pp. 6-7.

[88] Cf. L.F.F.R. Thomaz, *Goa: Une Société Luso-Indienne,* op. cit., p. 21.

[89] The Governor Francisco da Cunha e Menezes takes note of the appointment of Francisco Manuel Barroso da Silva as surgeon-major of the Estado da Índia. He was a student of Constância who gave a lot of good information about him. Cf. his letter to M.M. Castro, of 29 January 1787 [A.H.U., *Índia,* maço 151 (157)]. On 22 December 1794 we find him exercising his activity in Goa, but the idea that there is of him at this date changes a little: he is 'able' in his art and must have exercised it with utility if he did not rush into an illicit friendship'. This connection, as per the document, 'discredits one of Goa's main families' (H.A.G., *M. Reino,* Book 176-B, ff. 430-430v). The post of surgeon coexisted with that of physician-major, having the private practice of his profession.

the Hospital as well as others, none of them studied the faculty with Method, and that all of them should be considered as mere Practitioners'.[90]

By way of a balance sheet of the evolution of education and the academic staff in the final years of the eighteenth century, we can draw some conclusions. That primary education was quite widespread in this age, with schools in all parishes, is a well-known fact. Thus, in each of the ninety-one churches of Goa, a *mestre de capela e de escola* was appointed to teach the 3 R's and catechism and make provision for singing in the liturgical acts.[91]

The education that we call 'secondary' covered the courses in the diocesan seminaries and the convents, the classes in the said seminaries where students of the royal classes had been transferred to, upon their extinction in 1798; the artillery and naval classes.

As stated earlier, some diocesan seminary courses (especially Theology) were perhaps considered higher studies. Education imparted in the Royal Hospital was regarded so, for the final examination that followed, conferred the diploma of physician, pharmacist or surgeon.

PLANTS AND ANIMALS: LOCAL HISTORY

The transfer of Asian plants to other overseas territories and the Kingdom, for economic reasons, aroused some interest in their

[90] Cf. letter from F.A. Veiga Cabral to the Marquis Major-domo, dated 29 April 1799, op. cit. (H.A.G., *M. Reino,* Book 178-B, f. 644). On the books followed in the different branches of medicine, see the *Rellação dos Livros Precizos,* of 2 March 1801 (H.A.G., *M. Reino,* Book 180-A, f. 49).

[91] Each of the 34 churches of the Ilhas province had a *mestre de capela e de escola,* appointed by the parish priests, examined and approved by the *mestres de capela* and subchanter of the Primatial See; in the Salsete province there were 25 masters in the respective churches and another 8 in the affiliated chapels; in Bardez, there were 24 masters corresponding to a similar number of parish churches of this region. In 1801, therefore, there were 91 *mestres de capela e de escola* in the territory of Goa. In the Salsete province, some mestres had coadjutors by the 'multiplicity of the duties, and of boys'. Cf. the Archbishop's letter to D. Rodrigo de Souza Coutinho, dated 20 March 1798 [A.H.U., *Índia,* maço 172 (186)].

description, stages of cultivation, medicinal qualities and properties. 'Drugs', medicinal plants from the Kingdom used to be sent to Goa, mainly for the pharmacy of the Royal Hospital.

There seems to have been a considerable exchange, particularly between Goa and Brazil, in the second half of the eighteenth century.[92] There were also plans to introduce the cultivation of cinnamon, cloves, nutmeg, pepper, tea, ginger and indigo in Maranhão. The plan had the support of the director of the Company of Grão-Pará and Maranhão, influenced by the mercantilist ideas of Duarte Ribeiro de Macedo. They sought to produce more spices, by cultivating them in Brazil in order to develop its trade. They even anticipated that the Company would appropriate the trade of this commodity 'which the foreigners wrested from us'.[93]

[92] For the earlier times (sixteenth-seventeenth centuries and first half of the eighteenth century) there is a study by Luís Ferrand de Almeida, *Aclimatação de plantas do Oriente no Brasil durante os séculos XVII e XVIII,* Coimbra, 1976, offprint of the *Revista Portuguesa de História,* XV (1976). It supplies even some data for the second half of the eighteenth century (cf. pp. 399-405). Abundant information on the names of the plants, their origin, their adaptation to other regions, can be collected in José E. Mendes Ferrão, *A Aventura das Plantas e os Descobrimentos Portugueses,* Lisbon, Instituto de Investigação Científica Tropical, 1992. Some correspondence between the transplantation of Asian plants to Brazil is found at A.H.U. and at H.A.G. It being impossible to mention all of them, we selected those in which there really was the said transplantation. Cf. letter from the Count of Oeiras to the Count of Ega, dated 5 April 1760. In it he states that he is convinced that pepper never developed in Brazil in such proportions that the Indian will be left unused (A.H.U., *Índia,* cód. 425, f. 202); the Governor Francisco da Cunha Menezes' letter to M.M. Castro, of 30 January 1794, referring to the annual remittances made [A.H.U., *Índia,* maço 167 (165)]; letter from the said Governor to Luís de Vasconcelos e Sousa, Governor of Brazil, dated 29 February 1788 (H.A.G., *M. Reino,* Book 169-B, ff. 720-721v); F.C. Menezes' letter to M.M. Castro, dated 30 January 1794 on the remittance of sandalwood seeds to Bahia and pepper and sandalwood seeds to Pará [A.H.U., *Índia,* maço 165 (168)].

[93] See the letters from [Domingos de Basto Viana, director of the Companhia Geral do Grão-Pará e Maranhão] to [Sebastião José de Carvalho e Melo], dated 31 March 1758, and from the Count of Ega to Sebastião J. de C. Melo, dated 9 December 1758 (H.A.G., *M. Reino,* Book 131-B, f. 519). Duarte Ribeiro de Macedo's plan (of which there are many copies, v.g.,

We have no information about the evolution of this project but there are reports of frequent requests for plants, which the local authorities in Goa tried to fulfil promptly. Plant nurseries of cloves, nutmeg, cinnamon, pepper, ginger, 'breadfruit', teak, sandalwood from different parts of India and South-East Asia went to Brazil.[94] The Governor of India, Francisco da Cunha e Menezes refers to the annual dispatch of parcels to Rio de Janeiro, Bahia and Pará.[95]

The interest of the central government in this project of naturalising Asian plants in America is quite clear from the request for information on the cultivation and even technical methods.[96]

We do not know if the economic objective was achieved. There are reports that, in 1800, pepper and cinnamon cultivation did

---

B.N.R.J., 10, 1, 29, no. 2, 'Discurso sobre se poderem transplantar todas as plantas, que na Azia, na nossa America, e conveniencias, que disso podem rezultar ao Reino', Paris, 15 March 1675) was resumed a century later with the aim of developing it in Brazil and preventing that, imitating North America, this colony should rebel against the metropolis (B.N.R.J., 9, 2, 24, no. 2, 'Discurso sobre a transplantação de plantas indiáticas para a América'). On the subject, also see João Paulo Costa, 'O Império e os Diplomatas da Restauração', in *Stvdia* , 48, Lisbon, 1989, pp. 307 and ss.

[94] Clove plants used to come from Moluccas; nutmeg from the island of Banda; cinnamon from Ceylon, pepper and ginger were found in Goa itself, 'breadfruit' tree, from the islands of the South Sea, particularly Otaite; teak, from Daman; sandalwood, from Timor, Solor and Goa. Cf. the letters of D. Rodrigo de S. Coutinho to F.A.V. Cabral, dated 18 March 1797 and of 14 November 1798 (A.H.U., *Índia,* cód. 520, ff. 99 and 129, respectively). In 1798, S. Coutinho referred to the introduction in Brazil of the cultivation of breadfruit, Indian cloves, pepper, cinnamon and other precious plants. Cf. Luís Ferrand de Almeida, op. cit., p. 404. 'Breadfruit' (*Artocarpus communis* Forst.) is originally from Malaysia and according to De Candolle it used to be cultivated in the islands of the Asian archipelago of the Indian Ocean, between Sumatra and the Marquesas, when the Europeans arrived there. Cf. José E. Mendes, op. cit., pp. 180-1.

[95] Cf. Governor F. C. Menezes' letter to M.M. Castro, dated 30 January 1794 [A.H.U., *Índia,* maço 167 (165)].

[96] Cf. the letter, op. cit., from D. Rodrigo de S. Coutinho to F.A.V. Cabral, dated 2 April 1800, in order to send from India a cultivator of pepper and another for cinnamon to Bahia.

exist in Bahia and was to be expanded.[97] However, it is a fact that the people gradually became familiar with the cultivation of exotic items and the botanical interest was always on the rise. Private parties used to bring different seeds on the Indian ships. It is perhaps symptomatic that the Governor of India, Francisco da Cunha Menezes, should have sent a parcel of cinnamon seeds to his cousin, the Governor of the State of Brazil, and to the Baron of Messamenes.[98]

Given the good quality of sugar on the Malabar Coast there was a request for despatch of sugar cane plants, which did materialize, and of teak as well.[99]

Over and above the mere despatch of seeds and plants with a commercial purpose, there was an attitude of openness and curiosity for new knowledge. This was a result of the meeting of different cultural ideas in which physiocracy certainly played a vital role. It is in this mental climate – quite evident in the activity developed by the Academy of Sciences – that the Botanical Garden is opened in Goa, in the last years of the eighteenth century, in order 'to take care of the cultivation of more interesting plants from India, China and their Adjacent Islands ...' as done on the Continent and Overseas.[100]

[97] Cf. the letter from D. Rodrigo de S. Coutinho to F. A.V. Cabral, dated 2 April 1800 (A.H.U., *Índia,* cód. 520, f. 185).

[98] See this Governor's letter to Luís de Vasconcelos e Sousa, Governor of Brazil, op. cit., dated 29 February 1788; it was communicated that he had earlier sent 1 box of Indian pepper and 2 containing its seeds, as also an instruction on the manner of cultivating it; he further informed that on this date he had sent 3 boxes of cinnamon seeds to the Baron of Messamenes who had to give him half of it. The pepper and cinnamon seeds should be sent to Bahia and to Rio (H.A.G., *M. Reino,* Book 169-B, ff. 720-721v).

[99] Cf. letter from D. Rodrigo de S. Coutinho to F.A.V. Cabral, dated 15 December 1797 (A.H.U., *Índia,* cód. 520, ff. 112-112v and H.A.G., *M. Reino,* Book 178-A, f. 125).

[100] See D. Rodrigo de S. Coutinho's letter to F.A.V. Cabral, dated 5 December 1800, informing him that the Regent Prince was again recommending the Botanical Garden, whose establishment had earlier been ordered (however, he does not mention the date) (H.A.G., *M. Reino,* Book 181-A, f. 119). On 18 April 1802, the Viceroy informed the Secretary of State that the Botanical Garden was ruined much before its take-over but

Finally, this transmutation of Asian plants to Brazil confirms 'the expansion of certain plants encountered by the Portuguese in the course of the Discoveries and were finally extended to every place on the Earth where its cultivation was possible'. This is how, in the words of Orlando Ribeiro, a 'tropical agrarian heritage' was formed, common to all the Overseas territory.[101]

Natural History was another branch of learning that developed with the sending of Asian products to the Kingdom. In 1783, a team went to Goa to explore the territory.[102] Materials of this nature were collected and rich collections formed in the Ajuda Office, the Queen's private museum and the museum of the Academy of Sciences, Lisbon. It may be noted that copies of the *Instrucções* of the Academy of Sciences reached Goa regarding the despatch of products and containing information on natural history; and the Governor was directed to impart the information to people likely to put it to good use. In fact, the same instructions were sent to the Viceroy and Captain General of the State of Brazil and the Governor of Bahia.[103]

---

that he was requesting the physician-major of the State to select another site, as he did not find it possible to reform it at the old site (H.A.G., *M. Reino,* Book 181-A, f. 119).

[101] See Orlando Ribeiro, *Aspectos e Problemas da Expansão Portuguesa,* Lisbon, 1962, pp. 29-31.

[102] The team consisted of the naturalist Manuel Galvão da Silva who was to be the Governor of Mozambique, scriber António Gomes and José da Costa, botanical gardener. Cf. the letters of M.M. Castro to Frederico Guilherme de Sousa, dated 1 April 1783 and 20 March 1784 [A.H.U., *Índia,* cód. 517, ff. 185-186v and maço 144 (169)]. In the report presented later Manuel Galvão da Silva stated 'not having found gold in Goa; and that, with respect to pearls, only some shells were found that produced small seed-pearls of low value. See Joaquim Heliodoro da Cunha Rivara, *Observações sobre a História Natural de Goa feitas no anno de 1784 por Manuel Galvão da Silva e agora Publicadas por …,* Nova Goa, Imprensa Nacional, 1862 and Vicente Philippe de Sá, 'Um Naturalista Portuguez em Goa no Século 18°', in *O Oriente Portuguez,* Year 7, 1910, nos. 9 and 10, September and October, pp. 276-94 and nos. 11 and 12, November and December, p. 329.

[103] 20 copies of the *Instrucções* of the Academy of Sciences were sent. Cf. M.M. Castro's letter to Frederico Guilherme de Sousa, dated 8 March 1782 (A.H.U., *Índia,* cód. 517, f. 104v).

Furthermore, in the field of scientific development, the contribution of the central government towards promoting Goan history needs to be stressed. They ordered the Municipal Councils to register in annual *memórias* (papers) all events of historical interest in the respective provinces. Little is known on the execution of this norm, which, if properly undertaken, would have provided important historical aids on Goa. To be appreciated, nonetheless, is the historical sensibility of the people.[104]

In 1778, the Queen ordered the despatch of books of the Secretariat of the Estado da Índia to the Kingdom to be stopped and determined that all those that had been sent earlier should be returned to Goa, for 'they contain memorials required on many occasions, and it is only fair that the State should not forget them'. That was the same idea of promoting the study of the history of Goa, by keeping the materials in the land itself![105]

ORIENTAL LANGUAGES

Save certain moments in which the use of Konkani was opposed, the general orientation followed in this matter was to favour the learning of this local language and that of other Oriental idioms as well.[106] The importance of Konkani for preaching and

[104] On 12 February 1787, the Council of Goa communicated that they had nothing historically worthy to record, since 1 January 1785 up to the end of the year; that of Salsete, ditto; that of Bardez informed that it had only registered 'an underground thundering noise that was later understood to have been a type of earthquake in the Britona ward up to the Church of Salvador do Mundo of the village Sirula' (H.A.G., *M. Reino,* Book 168-A, ff. 23-7). From the beginning of 1789, there exist two reports of the Senate of the Councils of Goa and Bardez regarding the Pinto conspiracy, as a noteworthy case and sent to the central government. Cf. the Memoria do Senado da Câmara de Goa de 28 de Fevereiro de 1789 (H.A.G., *Anais Históricos da Câmara de Goa,* ff. 3-6) and the copy of the proceedings and the paper of the Council of [Bardez], dated 4 March 1789 (H.A.G., *M. Reino,* Book 170-A, ff. 23-24v).

[105] Cf. M.M. Castro's order to the Governor, dated 2 April 1778 [A.H.U., *Índia,* maço 23 (294)] and the Governor's letter to M.M. Castro, dated 2 January 1781 [A.H.U., *Índia,* maço 140 (132) and H.A.G., *M. Reino,* Book 161-A, ff. 96-7].

[106] The exceptional moments in which the use of Konkani was banned

catechising the locals as well as objectives of trade, diplomatic and political nature so required it.

Not much is known about how it was taught in Goa in the second half of the eighteenth century. Until their expulsion in 1759, the Jesuits were the great mentors of Konkani, Tamil, and Marathi and published several books. With regard to the Franciscans, despite their eradication from the parishes of Bardez in 1766, they did stay in certain places in Goa; and some of them contributed their mite for the spread of Konkani. In the mission stations, where mastery of the Oriental languages was even more pressing, it was more widely taught than in Goa. Thus, in 1759, there functioned a school of languages teaching Tamil and Malayalam in Travancore.[107] Konkani was possibly better diffused in Goa as a result of the access that Goans had to the religious Orders and the implementation by the local secular clergy.

SURVEILLANCE AND CENSORSHIP OF BOOKS

Adhering to the ideas of the Enlightenment did not mean in any way that in Portugal there was freedom of the press. Book censorship continued, though the system had been reformed with the Royal Censor Board created in 1768. In fact, this legal

---

were: the years that followed the conquest of Goa with the razing of the temples and destruction of the books in this language; the viceroyalty of the Count of Alvor, after the charter of 27 June 1684 according to which the locals had to learn Portuguese within 3 months; and during the government of Archbishop D. Frei Lourenço de Santa Maria with the pastoral letter of 21 November 1745 that disallowed the marriage of any individual not knowing Portuguese. Cf. A.B. de Bragança Pereira, *Etnografia da Índia Portuguesa,* vol. II, Bastora, 1940, p. 199; A. Lopes Mendes, op. cit., vol. II, pp. 110-11.

[107] In the first part of the eighteenth century, the Franciscan friar Domingos de S. Bernardino wrote an explanation of the credo in Konkani. He was a rector in Revora; in 1713 he was the commissioner of the Holy Office in Bardez; in 1726 he became vicar of the province of St. Thomas. It must be presumed that, during his career, he did promote the study and use of Konkani. For the second half of this century, the residence of Olicare in Travancore was transformed into a language school where, in 1769, the Franciscan Friar Joaquim de S. Diogo used to teach Tamil and Malayalam.

authority hitherto belonged jointly to the Holy Office, the Bishop and the Palace Replevin Court. Everything was to be centralized into one institution in the interest of greater unity and speed and, perhaps, for easier political control. Later, in the government of D. Maria I, this tribunal was called Real Mesa da Comissão Geral sobre o Exame e Censura dos Livros (Royal Board for the General Commission on Examination and Censorship of Books).[108]

It must be stressed that in Goa not only was the vigilance on books, reviews and papers in circulation quite strict but sometimes there were even discrepancies between the list of books banned by the Board and by the pastoral letters of the Archbishop. In fact, the said royal letter of 1787 setting up the Royal Board gave ample powers to the Bishops. Hence, perhaps, in practice there was some inter-lapping of jurisdictions.[109] Thus, this higher

---

See Fr. Achilles Meersman, O.F.M., 'Notes on the study of Indian languages by the Franciscans', in *Newe Zeitschrift fur Missionswissenschaft Nouvelle Revue de science missionaire,* sixteenth year, Switzerland, 1960, pp. 53-4.

[108] By the law of 5 April 1768 the Royal Censor Board was created which by the charter of law published on 23 June 1787 began to be called Real Meza da Comissão Geral sobre o Exame, e Censura dos Livros. It was composed of eight deputies, cultured and well bred. Their activity consisted of examining and censoring 'Books, Pictures, and all the papers in which to be printed, drawn and get published, of those that have already been introduced in the Kingdoms, and their Dominions, as well as entering therein afresh, and forbidding the bad one, or those suspect, both by the Holy Office and the State ...'. With the institution of this tribunal the jurisdiction of the ministers of the Holy Office came to an end. See the royal letter of 23 June 1787 (A.C.P.G., *Cópia de Vários Documentos,* ff. 188-195v, in F.U.P., 18-1-8/9). Also cf. Rómulo de Carvalho, op. cit., p. 452. It may be noted that the royal charter of 22 August 1791 grants powers to the Bishop Inquisitor General of the Kingdom and its dominions to proceed against those who buy, sell, read or possess pernicious books (A.C.P.G., *Cópia de Vários Documentos,* ff. 225-226v).

[109] 'I declare that it is not My Real Intention ... that to the Bishops in this part is diminished something of the jurisdiction that Christ Our Lord, and by the Church was given them ... '. And ahead, after referring to the action of the tribunal, the document reads: 'However when you feel that in your bishoprics there circulate some bad Books, and dangerous, you

ecclesiastical authority ordered the removal of Voltaire's *Théâtre,* which, 'its Author being what he was, should have been burned'. In vain did the bookseller take refuge in the permission given by the said Board, whereas the Bishop retorted that 'if they governed there, he governed here'.[110] The Archbishop D. Frei Manuel de Santa Catarina was referring to the dangers of the doctrines in vogue in his times, such as materialism, licentiousness, etc.[111]

---

may, and should by reason of your High, and Holy Ministry, censure: and if being necessary to write their letter to the said Tribunal, in order to disallow their circulation, and to make the necessary measures, which I much recommend you; or have recourse to Me immediately' (ibid., ff. 191-191v).

[110] See the letter from the [factor of Surat] to Francisco Rolland, dated 14 November 1790, which referred to the sale of books in Goa, which had reached in the previous monsoon. He stated that he was selling them very slowly, as they were considered expensive (recall the expensiveness of life and the poor purchasing power, mainly, of the locals) and by the fact that some were in Italian and in Latin. He considered that the Goa-bound books should be in Portuguese, some in French and none in Italian and Latin. He was reporting the 'some ignorant Priests of whom there are many in Goa ..., on the occasion of the arrival of the said box of Books, will come ... Voltaire's *Théâtre,* and this name sufficed, to fill them with horror, they went to denounce him to the Archbishop, who without any further information or perhaps going by the same principles, ordered that the said work be taken ...' (H.A.G., *Feitoria de Surrate,* 2604, pp. 17-18). We wish to thank Professor Doctor Ernestina Carreira for making this document available to us.

[111] Cf. the letter of 2 July 1789 [A.H.U., *Índia,* maço 158 (150)]. Archbishop Santa Catarina's pastoral letter of 12 July 1789 referred to the creation of the tribunal of the Royal Board, earlier referred to and the prohibition; under penalty of excommunication, of the following banned books: the works of Voltaire and Rousseau, *Diccionario philosophico,* Spinozza, *Exame critico dos apologistas da religião christã, Historia philosophica e politica, Espirito de Helvecio, Espião Chinez, Espião turco, Comedia de Mahomet,* works by Pope Bayle, João Guilherme Velisario, João Lourenço, Moshein and others which had not been approved by the said tribunal (C.C. Nazareth, *Mitras* ..., p. 346). Also see the pastoral letter from D. Frei Manuel de Santa Catarina, of 2 July 1789 (A.C.P.G.), *Livros de conventos e igrejas,* no. 13 (Igreja de Nossa Senhora de Penha de França).

It appears that Goa received books that constituted in fact the fulcrum of contemporaneous thought; their diffusion in the territory made it possible for the local élite to be in contact with the cultural ideas in vogue in Portugal and Europe. Unfortunately, the documentation sometimes only mentions that lists were sent to Goa, without specifying any of them, which obviously makes it impossible to know them fully. Nonetheless, it is absolutely certain that Goa received anti-Jesuit literature, like the *Dedução Chronologica*; similarly the *Instrucções* of the Academy of Sciences, Lisbon, the collection of laws against Sigilism, edicts of the Royal Censor Board, gazettes with news from the Kingdom and Europe, manuals most widely used on the Continent, such as the *Pároco Instruído,* Montpellier's *Catecismo,* etc.[112]

The booksellers had to obey the rules such as not to sell more than one copy to a buyer, and to sell them only to those 'determined by chits from the Governor and the Archbishop Primate'. Upon selling, they would still have to produce the list of buyers' names. This measure was meant to prevent the purchase of books 'sound and advantageous to people of the reproved doctrines of the Jesuits and Casuists', therefore, the books did not reach the people who needed them.[113]

Besides book censorship, there was a ban on establishment of printing presses in the Estado da Índia in 1774, whether privately-owned or belonging to the convents and other communities.[114]

[112] See the 'list of books and papers ready to be encased for Goa', on 24 March 1774. Cf. A.H.U., *Índia,* maço 120 (112). A short letter from the Count of Ega, dated 2 December 1774, acknowledged the receipt of gazettes and an epistle from D. João José de Melo to Francisco Xavier de Mendonça Furtado, dated 4 February 1770, stated having received copies of the *Dedução Chronologica* [A.H.U., *Índia,* maços 90 (99) and 107 (84), respectively].

[113] Cf. the letter from the Marquis of Pombal to D. José Pedro da Câmara, dated 2 April 1774 (H.A.G., *M. Reino,* Book 152-C, ff. 710-710v).

[114] See the letter to the Viceroy, the Count of Alva, dated 20 March 1754. Cf. A.H.U., *Índia,* maço 86 (107) and António dos Mártires Lopes, *Imprensa de Goa* ..., Lisbon, 1971, p. 12. The private press resumed in the liberal age.

It may be noted that the press had first started functioning in 1556, in the Jesuit College of St. Paul (in Greece it did only in 1850). However, in spite of the strictness of censorship, books were spreading among the people.[115]

[115] In 1557 the catechism compiled by St. Francis Xavier was printed in the printing press of the Society. It was one of the first books, if not the first book, to be published from Goa (according to Leão Fernandes, in the previous year there had been printed the *Conclusiones Philosophicas*). Then followed the printing of many other works. On the subject, refer to Tomás Estêvão [Thomas Stephens], S.J., *Doutrina Cristã em Língua Concani* ..., introduction, notes and glossary by Mariano Saldanha, Lisbon, 1945, pp. 3 and ss; Bragança Pereira, *S. Francisco Xavier, Esboço Histórico,* Goa, 1952, p. 21; Benedito Gomes, op. cit., pp. 75-6 and [João Baptista] Amâncio Gracias, 'Os Portugueses e os Estabelecimentos da Imprensa na Índia', in *Boletim do Instituto Vasco da Gama,* no. 37, Nova Goa, 1938.

CHAPTER V

The Pinto Conspiracy: A Consequence of the Growth of Education?

That in Goa there circulated 'banned' books and the non-banned ones as well, spreading the ideas of liberalism, was a reality and as a second proof of this fact could perhaps be found in the much spoken of Pinto Conspiracy.[1] To scrutinize what it consisted of, who were responsible for it and, above all, the true leitmotifs of the revolt – this is a problem that creates a lot of interest, but raises a lot of controversy. It has indeed caused some reflection among Goan researchers, enriching the historiography of this territory with new explanatory theses.

On 5 August, the clerk of the *comunidade* of Aldona, António Eugénio Toscano, denounced to the Governor the plan of a conspiracy plotted by clergymen in order to expel the Portuguese and to form an independent government. The news, which at first did not worry the Governor, was confirmed on the same day

[1] There are studies on the subject, some of which are: J.H. da Cunha Rivara, *A Conjuração de 1787 em Goa e varias cousas desse Tempo. Memoria Historica,* Nova Goa, 1875, reed. of Asian Educational Services, New Delhi, Madras, 1990; João Manuel Pacheco de Figueiredo, 'O Marquês de Pombal visto por Escritores Goeses', in *Memórias da Academia das Ciências de Lisboa, Classe de Ciências,* pt. XXIII, Lisbon, 1980, pp. 480-7; Mariano Dias, 'Fr. Caetano Vitorino de Faria', in *Essays in Goan History,* ed. Teotónio R. de Souza, New Delhi, 1989; Carmo Azevedo, 'Pinto's Revolt of 1787', in *Armed Coups Against Portuguese Regime,* Goa, 1986; Ernestina Carreira, 'Goa in the Reign of Tipoo Sultan: International Politics and the Pinto's Conspiracy', paper presented at the 5th International Seminar on Indo-Portuguese History, Cochin, January 1989. A new modified version of the said paper was published by the author under the title 'Portuguese India in the Reign of Tipoo Sultan', in *Moyen Orient et Océan Indien,* vol. 6, 1989.

by the commander of the Bardez legion and by the Archbishop of Goa, leading to a strict judicial action to capture the conspirators.[2]

How does one account for an eruption of this nature in Goa? The answer to this question calls for an exploration into the socio-cultural profiles of its mentors, the remote and proximate antecedents of the event. The Pinto Conspiracy was a movement delineated by the members of the secular, local clergy, mainly of the Brahmin caste. Thus the heads of the conspiracy were Fathers Caetano Francisco Couto and José António Gonçalves and, besides them, one more dozen clergymen supported and gave consistency to this plan. However, the support of this conspiracy was more diversified: local military men, assistant surgeons, *varzeiros* (farmers), porters and students. Though the documentation is silent on their station in society, everything suggests that largely these people were not from the higher social strata.

With regard to the geographical origin of the accomplices, it is noted that, whereas the main ringleaders were locals from the provinces of Bardez or Salsete, the other supporters of the revolt, on the other hand, were from the New Conquests, namely Ponda. This geographical incidence appears symptomatic, once the lands of Bardez and Salsete, being a part of the State of India for more than three centuries, were the cradle of people with quite a settled culture and open to the ideas of the age. On the contrary, it is perfectly understandable that Ponda, a land that had been then recently annexed to the Portuguese dominions, without the Portuguese historical and cultural traditions, should supply men to make possible a separatist movement.

As regards the intellectual profile of its principal mentor, Father José António Gonçalves (1748-1818), he exercised the royal professorship of Rhetoric and Philosophy and later in the seminary of Chorão. In the public examination that preceded his educational activity, he revealed, using the form of appointment letters, 'capacity to teach' and about him, there were 'good

[2] See J.H. da Cunha Rivara, *A Conjuração de 1787 em Goa ...*, pp. 6 and ss. and doc. no. 1, p. 3. Also cf. M.J. Gabriel de Saldanha, *História de Goa (Política e Arqueológica)*, vol. I, Nova Goa, 1925, pp. 225-6.

reports of life and habits'. We find him as the parish priest of S. Bartolomeu (Chorão) between 1778 and 1780, when he resigned the post to teach at the Chorão Seminary. In 1781, he sailed for Lisbon.[3]

His travel companion was Father Caetano Francisco Couto who did the minor and major studies up to theology, in the seminary of Chorão. In this institution and through the Oratorian pedagogy, he as well as Fr Gonçalves acquired their formation, adapting it in to the contemporaneous Western thought. A brilliant student, he was invited by Archbishop D. António T.N.B. da Silveira to be his 'chamberlain' and visit secretary, then becoming the dean of Honavar, Kanara. By virtue of the good services rendered, he was promoted by the Bishop D. Francisco de Assunção e Brito to Governor of the bishopric of Cochin.

However, the ambitions harboured by both did not end with these posts. They desired the mitre. With this in mind, they journey to Lisbon in order to secure some vacant suffragan bishopric.[4]

From another perspective, a Goan community settled in Lisbon and having as their 'patriarch' Father Caetano Vitorino de Faria could not remain alien to the ideas of the times. This

[3] Son of Domingos Gonçalves and of Maria de Sousa, from of Piedade, on the island of Divar, he graduated in the seminary of Chorão with distinction and was ordained in the year 1772, at the age of 25 years. In 1777, he applied for the royal chairs of rhetoric and philosophy created in the city of Goa. The priest teachers were publicly examined, in the presence of Dr. Feleciano Ramos Nobre Mourão, and he answered satisfactorily. In the year 1780, he held these chairs in the seminary of Chorão. In 1781, he left for Portugal and in the following year, he secured a doctorate in Rome. Cf. 'Licença para o Padre José António Gonçalves poder ensinar retórica e filosofia em qualquer das provincias e Ilhas', dated 21 October 1777 (A.N./T.T., *J.R.F.E.I.,* Book 66, f. 84v); Mariano Dias, 'Fr. Caetano Vitorino de Faria', in *Essays in Goan History,* p. 150; and J.H.C. Rivara, op. cit., pp. 13, 54-5. The author wishes to acknowledge with thanks the information furnished here by Mariano Dias.

[4] Father C.F. Couto was from Pangim, son of Pascoal do Couto and of Pascoela Pereira. Father Caetano Vitorino de Faria greatly praised him in his *Glosas* which he, in fact, wrote with his collaboration. See J.H.C. Rivara, op. cit., pp. 42 ff.

priest probably had good relations with Verney, whom he knew when in Rome.[5] Some students who were a part of this group would later play an active role in the ideological groundwork of the revolt. The younger people who had graduated from the Portuguese and foreign universities, at a certain moment began to aspire to have their own government, a model for which, though not very well defined, was of Western inspiration.[6]

Once a married man, Caetano Vitorino de Faria, received holy orders and went to Rome with his son, José Custódio de Faria. His wife joined the Santa Monica monastery. In the pontifical city he admitted his son in a college of the Propaganda Fide, got to know the authorities of the Roman Curia and Portuguese nationals residing there.[7] Then he settled in Lisbon, where his accomplishments have been interpreted in a number of ways. In the words of the Secretary of State, Martinho de Melo e Castro, Father Faria 'clamours against the ministers, military men and finally against everything Portuguese in India, on account of the vexation and humiliation to which they subject the locals'.[8] Nonetheless, this leader of the Goan community seems to have used some influence to secure a few privileges for his countrymen. He is supposed to have thus advanced some reforms in Lisbon that were then undertaken for Goa by the

[5] Cf. Mariano Dias, op. cit., p. 143.

[6] Included among the Goans residents of Lisbon who interacted with Father Faria, and sharing, therefore, the same aspirations, were the student José António Pinto, scion of the Pinto family of Candolim; Joaquim António Vicente, naval student and Narciso Vicente, probably his brother; Father José Custódio de Faria, son of Father Caetano Vitorino de Faria, known as *Abade Faria* and who in France became known for his research on hypnotism; Fr. Custódio de Santa Maria, an Augustinian friar. Cf. J.H.C. Rivara, op. cit., pp. 13, 19, 21. Also, see our study, *A Colónia Goesa em Lisboa e o Ideário da Conspiração dos Pintos (1787),* offprint of *Arquipélago ...,* in Memoriam Maria Olímpia Rocha Gil, vol. I, Ponta Delgada, 1995, pp. 247-8.

[7] Cf. M.M. Castro's letter to Frederico G. de Sousa, dated 22 March 1779 (A.H.U., *Índia,* cód. 516, ff. 186-7 or H.A.G., *M. Reino,* Book 159-B, ff. 499-500) and the order sent to the Estado da Índia in the year 1779. Cf. A.H.U., *Índia,* maço 26 (296).

[8] A.H.U., *Índia,* cód. 516, ff. 186-7.

Secretary of State, Martinho de Melo e Castro, such as the reaffirmation of the access of locals to civil and military posts and the religious Orders; the abolition of the differences in the nuns' veil, whether they were of Portuguese lineage or Indians; the reiteration of the canonical powers to the Archbishop of Goa to reform the Franciscan Order in India.[9] Controversial, however, is the support given by Father Faria to the stay of the Lazarists in Goa, the religious Order that by virtue of the work they did, mainly in the diocesan seminaries, won a pride of place in the history of these institutions. If the Vicentians are said to have gone to Goa thanks to his influence, the adverse criticism made by this priest against the said ecclesiastics must also to be noted.[10]

In Rome, this ecclesiastic managed to see the resumption of the statutory law of the College of Propaganda Fide, according to which six seats had been reserved for Brahmin students, a right which in fact had been theirs for over a century. He also proposed that the Archbishop of Goa be granted the privilege of delegating onto the vicar-generals or foranes of the diocese and on various missionaries, the faculty of conferring the sacrament of confirmation and minor orders as well. Further, he successfully spoke on the Malabar rites to some cardinals.[11] Called to opine on the state of the diocese of Goa, he wrote the

[9] See Mariano Dias, op. cit., pp. 143-4.

[10] According to Mariano Dias, Father Faria was responsible for the decision to have Lazarist priests sent to Goa (op. cit., p. 150). In reply to D. Frei Manuel de Santa Catarina, M.M. Castro wrote as follows: 'Similarly you point the sinister voices that have been spread in this kingdom against the two Portuguese priests [António Luís dos Santos and Manuel Correia Valente], making Father Caetano Vitorino their author. . . . The same Lady [Queen] is quite persuaded about the merit, zeal and virtue of the said priests, nor will the vague declarations which Father Caetano and other persons may have risked ever be able to put the slightest note against the said Priests, mainly after Y. Excellency went from here knowing the image that there was of the said Father Caetano. . . .' Letter of 17 April [1786], transcribed by Father Braulio Guimarães, *Memorias da Congregação da Missão em Portugal,* op. cit., pp. 196-7.

[11] Father Caetano V. Faria must have reached Rome in 1772. 'Brahmin by Nation ... knowing that this College of Propaganda Fide used to receive

Glosas (Comments) on the reports by the Archbishop of Goa.[12]

Another project that became important in Faria's spirit was the securing of some mitres for Goans. However, his plan failed in relation to the bishoprics of the Propaganda. Hence, he returned to the Crown Patronage, which presently had some mitres vacant. This explains why he wanted the priests José António Gonçalves and Francisco Caetano Couto to get their training in Rome to become future Bishops. In addition, he certainly viewed the appointment of Joseph Cariatil as Archbishop of Cranganore, in 1782, yet another hope for the success of his plan.

These were the broad guidelines for his operations in Rome and Lisbon. He maintained contacts with some prominent public figures and thus some of his countrymen looked upon him as a patriot enjoying great prestige and power in the Court and thanks to whom those benefits that came their way.[13] In fact, he himself used to insinuate that he had great authority and influence with the King. But, perhaps from the 1780s, he began to fall into disrepute with the governmental authorities and his plan was thwarted.[14] The archbishopric of Goa was finally entrusted to a

---

six students of his Nation, he wanted his son to enjoy this right; however, as the funds constituted for the sustenance of the Brahmin Alumni for some years had been used elsewhere ..., he would surely not have been successful if not for the fortune he had of being sponsored by the Viscount of Vila Nova'. Later, as the cardinals and those in charge of directing the said college were 'so happy with the rare talent of the new Alumnus, and of the progress in his studies, which they never failed to mention, that they would happily prefer the Brahmins to other Asians', he asked that this old provision be resumed. He also requested for the Archbishop of Goa the right to confer the sacrament of confirmation and minor orders. Cf. the letter from Manuel Marques Brandão to José Gomes da Costa, official of the Secretary of State, department of Overseas Affairs, written in Rome on 2 July 1775, accompanied by a transcript on Caetano Vitorino Faria (B.P.A.D.E., cód. CXVI/2-11, no. 27).

[12] See J.H.C. Rivara, op. cit., doc. 45, pp. 53-64, of the documentary part.

[13] He used to frequent the house of the apostolic nuncio in Lisbon, the cardinal of Cunha, etc. Cf. J.H.C. Rivara, op. cit., p. 16.

[14] In Lisbon it was thought that this cleric was 'well behaved, disinter-

Portuguese from the Kingdom, D. Frei Manuel de Santa Catarina (1784) who had already been exercising the function of a governor and administrator of this archbishopric since 1780.[15]

Some researchers have forwarded the hypothesis of probable external support to the conspirators, extended by European and Asian powers that, on the other hand, coveted Goa. The issue has to be analysed with due care. First of all, it must be remembered that the political and military situation of Goa was precarious: war with the Bhonsales, though stopped by a ceasefire; threat of invasion by Nawab Tipu Sultan who, having occupied the lands of Kanara and Sunda, had emerged as the most dangerous neighbour. Added to it, the dislodged King of Sunda, having sought Portuguese asylum, was planning to recover his kingdom, at the cost of territories that he had lost to the Marathas and which the Portuguese had later conquered. Now these territories had to function as 'buffers' against incursions by Tipu Sultan and hence the re-conquest by Sunda could mean a grave threat to the Portuguese.[16] To add to these difficulties, the state of the Portuguese army was deplorable indeed: Field-

---

ested as regards his people, but at the same time a little crazy and lacking sincerity, tending to be very wily to achieve his ends'. Cf. M.M. Castro's letter dated 22 March 1779, op. cit. (H.A.G., *M. Reino,* Book 159-B, ff. 499-500). In his letter of 13 February 1788 the Archbishop General Inquisitor stated to D. Frei Manuel de Santa Catarinas that his idea about his priest was confirmed. Indeed, knowing him from Lisbon, he considered him an *anti-Christ.* Later events showed that he and his companions were in fact animated by a 'bad spirit' which took them to conspire against the State (B.A. 54-XI-39, no. 77). Also, see the Governor Frederico Guilherme de Sousa's letter of 4 February 1780, in which he mentions the great influence of Father Faria [A.H.U., *Índia,* maço, 133 (139)]. Cf. the excerpt of the letter of 17 April [1786].

[15] Discalced Carmelite, D. Frei Manuel de Santa Catarina was appointed Governor and Administrator of the archbishopric of Goa, when Archbishop D. Francisco de Assunção e Brito was asked to return to the Kingdom. He arrived in Goa on 3 October 1779 and took charge on 5 February 1780. On 19 July 1783, he was confirmed as Archbishop of Goa; he took charge in the Primatial See on 21 November 1784. Cf. C.C. Nazareth, *Mitras ...*, pp. 319-25 and F.N.T.C. Rozario e Souza, op. cit., p. 34.

[16] Cf. J.H.C. Rivara, op. cit., pp. 5-6.

Marshal Francisco António da Veiga Cabral was serving a term of imprisonment for the conflict with the Governor and the military cadres were in the red.[17]

This situation helps to understand the policy of neutrality followed by Portugal in India, vis-à-vis the two power blocs – the British, allied to the Marathas, against the kingdom of Mysore supported by the French. Goa emerges as a 'neutral centre for disputes' playing the role of an 'international mediator'. This is noticed above all in relation to the French, who needed Portuguese India as a base for commercial and diplomatic contacts between their factories and Europe. The Governor Frederico Guilherme de Sousa therefore followed a policy of rapprochement with France and reconciliation with Tipu.[18]

In this context it is not likely that the Maratha chief, Nana, or the Nawab Tipu Sultan or the French should have wished to expel the Portuguese or been implicated in the Pinto uprising. There is no doubt that the Marathas were the traditional enemies of Goa but given Tipu's successes they tried to seek Portuguese support. Besides, an attack on Goa could have triggered a fresh war against Tipu who also might have coveted the same territory. Added to this was the fact that Nana had expanded his army at the expense of the Portuguese deserters. The political asylum given to Father Gonçalves by the Pune court is understandable by the fact that he belonged to the Brahmin caste, which was extremely influential at this court. It may be noted in fact that the Maratha intervention is not mentioned in the Lisbon process.[19]

Among the probable causes of the revolt, much has been made of the alliance between Tipu and the French against Goa. As seen above, a neutral port was much more suited to the latter's needs. After the correspondence with the court of Lisbon,

[17] 'The French Brigadier Jacques Milles de Noyers, made to retire due to senility, two infantry colonels dead the last one surviving, the French Hércules de Chermont, colonel of the only artillery regiment, had just then been appointed Governor of Diu.' Cf. Ernestina Carreira, 'Goa in the Reign of Tipoo Sultan ...', op. cit., p. 3.

[18] Ibid., pp. 11-12.

[19] Ibid., pp. 20-1.

Governor Francisco da Cunha e Menezes never again believed in the French involvement in this revolt.

As regards Tipu, it is important to remember his policy of religious intolerance since 1784, ordaining the destruction of the Christian missions of Kanara and Mysore. The point can be put differently: it was not the said alliance but the fear of an invasion by Tipu that led the Goan priests to make the wild scheme since, in their view, the Portuguese, being in a weak position, would have left and they would be the sacrificed.[20]

The conspirators feigned foreign help to win adherents to their party, but in reality, there was no external intervention in the scheme of the Pinto Conspiracy; and the latter must be understood in the context of the internal dynamics of the local society. There might have been many motives, some of them implicit, in spite of the rights and privileges conferred to the Goans by Pombal. In a reflection on the possible causes of the conspiracy, it must be understood that some situations that may have in some measure created a climate conducive for the explosion. Thus and in spite of the rights given to the locals by the Pombaline reforms there was still resistance to their entry into the religious Orders. In 1779, the Franciscan Provincial refused to admit Indians, calling them 'niggers', and in 1786, the same happened again. In the Monica nunnery too, there still prevailed the distinction of the black veil for the European nuns and the white one for the Indians.

These discriminations were still more flagrant in the Primatial See, where despite the availability of local clergymen trained in the diocesan seminaries and approved in the competitions, they were left out in favour of the Portuguese born. In 1781, if the Chamber General of Bardez can be believed, Goans were still not allowed to become canons, and this preference for the Reinóis was not based on competence or moral fitness. It was rather a case of racial segregation.[21] D. Frei Manuel de Santa

[20] Ibid., p. 25.

[21] The Câmara Geral of Bardez in its 'representation' of 27 January 1781, after quoting the royal charter of 7 April 1774, which provided for the canonship and dignities to be filled in by locals and Reinóis, preferring locals at the first vacancy, stated that this was observed by D. Francisco de

Catarina (1784-1812) was governing the archbishopric of Goa, whose action was by and large characterized by preference for the European clergy, who were considered more cultured and virtuous. Hence, the discontent of the local clergy was further increased, also because they were already accustomed to some promotion during the Pombaline administration.

Inequalities in the military are referred to in a letter from a Goan student in Lisbon to a family member in India, stating that 'Goans could not hope for high posts from the Portuguese because both in Portugal as in Goa the ruling authorities had the same mentality'.[22] It is not known whether these statements were true to fact. And in case they are genuine, it would be important to know the reasons why higher posts were not granted to the Goans, the orientation followed by the central government was that of recruiting local military cadres.

Nevertheless, it must be pointed out that this complaint was sometimes formulated in the documentation of the epoch and that, curiously, the persons implicated in the conspiracy were, above all, clerics and military personnel.[23]

Off and on, here and there, it is possible to detect some signs of discontent and lack of social stability. Within the Goan territory, there were some that were enemies of Portugal, among them individuals of Portuguese lineage, like Colonel Henrique Carlos Henriques. Having occupied posts of great responsibility, he took the side of the Nawab Hyder Ali Khan who in the end of

---

Assunção e Brito with regard to one canonship only and by his successor, Archbishop Frei Manuel de Santa Catarina, in none. Cf. A.H.U., *Índia*, maço 8 (278).

[22] See the letter from the student José António in Lisbon to his brother, Father João Baptista Pinto, residing in Goa, dated 15 March 1787. He mentions about his refusing the Cross of Christ, 'for why to tire us, putting ourselves under the feet of four deportees in order to obtain their vile protection'. Cf. A.H.U., *Índia*, maço 155 (153).

[23] Ernestina Carreira states that the Pinto conspiracy was 'essentially a revolt by the clergy and the military men, the main classes hurt by the discriminatory policies. The tradesmen and the people had a restricted participation'. 'Goa in the Reign of Tipoo Sultan', op. cit., p. 26.

the eighteenth century was an imminent danger for Goa.[24] The number of Portuguese deserters who used to move to Bombay and neighbouring kingdoms of India was, in fact, considerable.[25] Certainly from 1750 to 1800, this number went on diminishing, but it must also be remembered that the aids sent to Goa were also reduced.[26]

On the occasion of the recruitment of the troops and by the 'natural antipathy' of the Indians to the military service, there

[24] See the letter from Father Benedito Caetano Gracias to the Governor D. José Pedro da Câmara (1770). Cf. A.H.U., *Índia,* maço 125 (110).

[25] There are reports that in 1757 there were more than 500 Portuguese deserters in Bombay whom the British had provided asylum, mainly in their factory at Vengurla, situated in the Bhosale lands (cf. the letter from the Governors to the King, dated 23 January 1757, H.A.G., *M. Reino,* Book 129-B, ff. 424-424v and 433, and letter from M.M. Castro to the Governor Frederico Guilherme de Sousa, dated 5 March 1781. A.H.U., *Índia,* cód. 517, f. 37). At other times, they used to desert for the dominions of Hyder Ali Khan. This was the case of the Lieutenant-Colonel Alexandre António de Sousa Pereira, apparently for not having been promoted to the post of Colonel [see the judgement delivered on 18 March 1769. A.H.U., *Índia,* maço 55, (300)]. In the opinion of the Count of Ega, the high number of runaways was because the aids for India were made up of *fascínoras.* (Letter from the Count of Ega to the Secretary of State, dated 8 January 1762. A.H.U., *Índia,* cód. 441, f. 345v.) It was sought to check this evil, offering pardon to the deserters who returned (cf. the pardon granted by the Governors on 25 August 1756. H.A.G., *Serviços,* 1374, f. 107v and the proclamation by the Governor Francisco da Cunha e Menezes, dated 7 November 1786. H.A.G., *Serviços,* 1375, ff. 86-7). At times, more drastic measures were taken such as to ordain their imprisonment and remittance to the Kingdom or that of offering prizes for those who captured them, and even being allowed to freely kill them. (See the order of the Count of Ega dated 12 December 1758. A.H.U., *Índia,* cód. 447, ff. 33-33v and the letter from Francisco Xavier de Mendonça Furtado to the Governors of the State of Brazil, *Arquivo Público do Estado da Baía,* vol. 64 de *Cartas Régias,* f. 252.)

[26] In the year 1753, 143 soldiers absent themselves from Goa (*Matrícula Geral,* 5 January 1754. H.A.G., *M. Reino,* Book 126-C, ff. 964-968); in the year 1769, 67 soldiers [A.H.U., *Índia,* maço 109 (123)]; in 1771, 41 soldiers (Matrícula Geral, 4 February 1771. H.A.G., *M. Reino,* Book 147-B, ff. 568-575v); in 1780, 34 soldiers (H.A.G., *M. Reino,* Book 161-C, f. 648v); in 1792, the number of deserters and incapacitated is 96 (H.A.G., *M. Reino,* Book 175, f. 192).

emerged some hurdles spurred by certain people.[27] In 1760, the Count of Ega complained to the Archbishop, about the behaviour of a priest for 'tumultuously fomenting the spirits of the said locals adding to this act scandalous and petulant words'. It may be noted, then, that a priest had manifested himself on the acts of public life, infringing on the norms of the Constitutions.[28]

That the Goan clergy, mainly the secular, had a great power of intervention in this society at the end of the eighteenth century is truly a fact. We found priests opposing the military recruiting, attending meetings and dictate orders in the *comunidades*, hold businesses, teach at the royal schools and diocesan seminaries, etc.[29]

These considerations call for a reflection on the place of the local clergy in Goan society. As against the decline of the European clergy was contrasted the progressive relevance of the secular clergy, recruited from among the locals. Goan clerics, trained in episcopal seminaries, also from Goa, began to exercise activities at the level of assistance and education formerly performed by regulars, mainly European. However, the policy of the local recruitment of the secular clergy, would have other results. Besides the large – even excessive – number of clerics, such an action, in the measure that brought about a greater school education of a good lot of locals, would simultaneously bring them a greater awareness of their importance not only in religious terms but also civic and even political.

This explains the pretension of the Goan priests in ascending to the highest posts in the ecclesiastical hierarchy, for which

[27] See the letter from Father Benedito Caetano Gracias, cited earlier. He stated that various Christians had arrived from Salsete to Madras, who expressed unhappiness about their children being conscripted; this animosity was fomented by a local from that province called Pedrinha, 'who is the head of all the locals of that province and that is a minion of Brigadier Henrique Carlos Henriques'.

[28] Cf. the letter of 17 November 1760. The priest should be punished 'so that the example may serve as a deterrent for others, to which I am told that not so decent references are being made' (A.H.U., *Índia,* cód. 432, f. 195).

[29] Opinions of this nature at the pastoral visits held during the second half of the eighteenth century may be recalled.

they sought support from the Congregation of the Propaganda Fide. It may in fact be noted that the first Goan Bishops were ordained by this institution, like the case of Mateus de Castro in 1637.[30]

The priests who planned the scheme belonged to the Brahmin caste. Now, the Pombaline reforms proclaiming the equality of the baptized Indians with the Reinóis, created propitious conditions for the rise of the members of this caste, more than those of other castes did. In the evening of this century, many Brahmins were occupying posts, and some very prominent ones, in the public administration. Others occupied leadership positions in the neighbouring kingdoms of India. They wish to intervene now in the civil and ecclesiastical government of their land.

Conscious of their value – and of their superiority – they entered in latent conflict with another social layer who enjoyed a privileged social position – the Luso-descendants, whom not even the Pombaline reforms, could bring down. Much to the contrary, one gets the impression that it was the social class that best benefited from the above-mentioned charters.[31]

The attempt to analyse the motivations for this revolt and of their characterization raises very complex problems. Since the movement was aborted and as its main mentor, Father José António Gonçalves was never captured, many aspects remained – perhaps forever – silenced. Let us, however, investigate some issues. Since the conspiracy was formulated by a group of priests of the Brahmin caste, could it be said that it was a revolt by the entier Goan population? Is it correct to identify the Brahmin caste with the people of Goa, if individuals of social echelons regarded as lower, especially the Sudra caste constitute the bulk of the population? In the same way, it would be necessary to investigate whether the discontent was general or if on the

[30] Matheus de Castro was the first vicar apostolic in India. Cf. Mariano Dias, op. cit., p. 146.

[31] See Appendix II.2, which gives the list of Luso-descendants ennobled in the second half of the eighteenth century. L.F.F.R. Thomaz refers to their prominent position in Goan society, which could have been the cause of the Pinto Conspiracy. Cf. *Goa: une société luso-indienne*, op. cit., p. 27.

contrary it was restricted to the higher class. It does not seem likely that there was a generalized discontent, for we did not detect any rising of the population for the second half of the eighteenth century.

The phases of this conspiracy can be situated as follows: first, the priests, conscious of their abilities, and enjoying a certain ascendancy in the society, aspired to occupy the mitres vacant in their diocese, and this made them travel to Lisbon and study in Rome (1781-2). Second, the idea of their possible appointment as Bishops did not materialize and much to the contrary, one *catanar* of the Oriental church was paradoxically promoted to the post of Bishop (1782-5). Third, the spite and consciousness of an injustice – the Goan priests did not have great regard for Cariattil whom they considered inferior – made them conceive the conspiracy (1785-7). Today it is a settled point that it was the appointment of the said *catanar* as Bishop that prompted the conspirators.[32]

In view of this picture, supported by chronology, it can perhaps be legitimately asked if this plot did in fact begin as a dispute restricted to a group of priests, then ending up as a wider movement. Let us have in mind that today, as if yesterday, the human species is self-seeking. Moreover, in many cases ideological reasoning only hides a more personalized motivation. It is undeniable that some Goan priests desired mitres and that their ambitions would not stop at the posts that they had occupied earlier. The arousal of a nationalist sentiment in Goa, certain inequalities that prevailed, the social-cultural status of the

[32] Cf. E.R. Hambye, op. cit., p. 298. *Catanar, caçanar* or *cassanar* was the 'priest of the Christians of St. Thomas in India, who follow this Syrian rite'. Cf. S.R. Dalgado, *Glossário Luso-Asiático,* vol. I, p. 161. Joseph Cariattil and Thomaz Periamakel must have come from Lisbon in 1779. The former was appointed by the Queen and confirmed by the Pope as Archbishop of Cranganore. According to Rivara, 'the principal ground for this appointment that was unprecedented, was undoubtedly that His Majesty and the Pope hoped that by putting in that diocese a local prelate and belonging the same Syro-Chaldean rite that prevails there, they would be reduced to the bosom and subjection of the Roman church in a real and effective manner, which despite so much diligence, had still not been achieved since the days of D. Fr. Aleixo de Menezes'. Cf. J.H.C. Rivara, op. cit., pp. 57-8.

clergyman, the cultural level of certain sectors of the population, especially that of the higher strata of society, comfortable with the liberal ideas – all these factors determined the adherence of a large number of people, lending the conspiracy the aspects and proportions with which it had.

It seems to us also important to relate the Pinto Conspiracy to the development of learning and culture in Goa, which helps to understand the presence of a whole class of learned and pretty Westernized people in this territory. Two cases in point for these times are Sebastião do Rego (1699-1765) who, by his fluent discourse and impeccable language won the epithet of 'António Vieira of India', and Paulo António Dias da Conceição (1769-1853).[33] Truly, the Pinto Conspiracy cannot be understood without this human and ideological support.

[33] Sebastião do Rego was a missionary and parish priest of the church of Bedour (Kanara) and later dean of the missions of this region. Returning to Goa, he entered the Oratorian Congregation and thence to the convent of St. Cajetan where he was the prefect. He wrote *Chronologia Da Congregação Do Oratorio De Goa,* whose manuscript we are in the process of editing; *Vida do Veneravel Padre José Vas,* 1745, 2nd edn., Margão, 1867, the first historical biography of this Blessed, still indispensable for the study of his life and work; *Sermão da Santa Cruz dos Milagres,* preached in 1745 and printed in Lisbon in 1759. Here, the author 'does not seek a theological justification for the caste system, but makes use of the most extraordinary means to prove that the Portuguese were sent by God to India' to be 'the new Pauls and Peters, chosen to exalt the holy name of Christ'. See Vimala Devi and Manuel de Seabra, *A Literatura Indo-Portuguesa,* Lisbon, 1971, pp. 118-20 and Casimiro Cristóvão de Nazareth, *Clero de Goa ...*, op. cit., pp. 120-1. *Father José Custódio de Faria* (1756-1819) got his doctorate in theology in the city of Rome (1780). He joined the revolutionary party in France (1793) taking part in the march against the Convention and the extinction of the Gironde. He gave up the political life when Napoleon took over the reins of power, and devoted himself to teaching philosophy. In 1813, disillusioned with the official education system, he began the series of talks on Hypnotism, which made him famous (*Memória Histórico-Eclesiástica ...*, p. 220). However, this Goan spent the greater part of his life out of his birth place. Paulo António Dias da Conceição studied theology in the Seminary of Rachol, where he was made to substitute the masters of Latin and Philosophy. Later he worked as a professor and director of the seminary of Chorão. He was an advocate of the ecclesiastical court, by archiepiscopal

The relevant role of the Oratorians of Goa as disseminators of the liberal ideology may also be noted. They had an important influence on the gestation of the Goan intelligentsia. In fact, in the propaganda made in Ceylon in favour of the revolt, Father Gonçalves had depended on the priests of St. Philip Nery and that the religious justification of the same was defended, among others, by Oratorian theologians. It is a known fact that Father Caetano Vitorino de Faria, the 'patriarch' of the Goans in Lisbon, had very close links with the Oratorians in the capital, through whom he attained the good graces of the Court. Besides this, as observed by Martinho de Melo e Castro, this priest 'was suggesting in the Secretariats of State different plans of reform, all directed mainly in favour of the Congregation of St. Philip Nery', established in Goa in 1682.[34] It cannot be inferred therefrom that the Oratorians had been the cause of the conspiracy. They did represent the human instrument for spreading new ideas. It may be noted that two Oratorians considered accomplices in the plot were pardoned soon thereafter.

Let us dwell on the correspondence exchanged between the Goan community residing in Lisbon and their country cousins at home. An analysis of it shows to what extent the Indians in 1787 were in possession of the ideology of the Enlightenment and of the very proximate French Revolution. Nationalism is a sentiment quite evidenced by the promoters of the conspiracy. It is like a background that involves these missives and that is externalized in the love for the land, the identity of a people or, more precisely, of a group, anxious to return to India immediately, wishing to ponder on the 'ways for the future happiness of Goa'. 'Nobody can think better than ourselves, for we know

---

provision. He wrote for the *Pregoeiro da Liberdade,* 1839, nos. 88, 92, 93, 94 and wrote *Resposta dum amigo a outro, refutando a escandalosa pastoral do Cabido da Sé Primacial de Goa,* Nova Goa, 1839. Cf. C.C. Nazareth, op. cit., pp. 108-9. More information on his *curriculum vitae* can be found in *Illustração Goana,* year 1, Margão, 1864-5, pp. 1-4, and in A.N./T.T., *Conselho Geral do Santo Ofício,* maço 32, doc. 16, where around 1779, he had applied for the post of promoter of the Goa Inquisition.

[34] Cf. M.M. Castro's letter to Frederico Guilherme de Sousa, dated 22 March 1779 (A.H.U., *Índia,* cód. 516, ff. 186-7).

what Goa is, and what is Europe', wrote the Goan student José António from Lisbon to his priest-brother in Goa.[35]

The development of agriculture constitutes another side of political action of these revolters, which establishes the link between their idiosyncrasy and the physiocratic ideas. In the above mentioned letter, its author urges his compatriots to cultivate the fields, mainly in Ponda (New Conquests), where there was still a large area to cultivate and consider that 'these are the best posts that we can have'. This Goan also makes an appeal to personal work and 'serious' education as 'sources' for an honourable life. Referring to the career of a family member, he advises him to learn French and join the seminary of Rachol, for 'the beautiful time of the children should not be wasted'.[36]

He further propounded the formation of a Goan association that would ensure quick contacts with Italy, 'for it is supremely advantageous for us to have direct correspondence with Italy'.[37] It would be interesting to check the political and ideological connections of these rebels. Their links, though not very direct, do let us understand something of what was happening in Europe and America. As stated earlier, some of the conspirators like Caetano Vitorino de Faria, his son José Custódio de Faria, José António Gonçalves, Caetano Francisco do Couto, stayed in Italy, which was a great centre for the diffusion of ideas, and here they established contacts with civil and ecclesiastical entities, and held important inquiries, assimilating, evidently, the liberal ideology. Furthermore, since Portugal had severed relations with the Holy See during the Pombaline period, it interested the rebels to explore this channel. It may be noted, in fact, that the support sought from the Congregation of Propaganda Fide and the somewhat hostile attitude adopted by the principal mentor of the conspiracy, Father José António Gonçalves, corroborates this

[35] See this student's letter of 15 March 1787 to his brother, Father João Baptista Pinto, very rich in ideological content. It can be said that it confirms the fundamental points endorsed by these conspirators. Cf. A.H.U., *Índia,* maço 155 (153), published by us in *A Colónia Goesa em Lisboa …*, in the cited place, pp. 253-4.

[36] Ibid.

[37] Ibid.

position in relation to the Portuguese Patronage in the East.[38]

One of those implicated in the conspiracy, the Italian Luis Ginete, confesses that the Goan rebels 'manifested the displeasure in which they lived in subjection and obedience in this State, recalling the rebellion of the American English and envying their luck'.[39] Father Couto confessed that he had surreptitiously brought a book on the 'New British America', from Europe.[40]

In 1786, that is, approximately one year before the discovery of the conspiracy, the English inhabitants of Calcutta had vigorously opposed a parliamentary determination establishing strict control on the properties held by the functionaries of the Company of India at their return to Europe. They were determined not to subject themselves to these provisions, 'thinking of becoming independent from Great Britain as the Americans had done'. Naturally the rebels, namely, Caetano Vitorino de Faria, who used to be on close terms with members of the Court, must have known of this fact that created the due caution of the central government.[41]

On the other hand, the relations of India with Europe and Brazil through the *Carreira da Índia* brought about a mutation of ideas that the more literate absorbed better.

The Pinto Conspiracy has had a wide range of interpretations and its existence as a planned revolt even denied at times. According to Carmo Azevedo, it was the 'second anti-colonial revolt in modern times' (the first one evidently being the independence of the United States of America). It was Goa's first organized effort to get rid of the colonial overlords. This

[38] The letter of 18 February 1789 refers to a pastoral letter by Father José António Gonçalves aspiring to encroach upon the rights of the Patronage (H.A.G., *M. Reino,* Book 170-A, ff. 77-8).

[39] Cf. Ernestina Carreira, op. cit., p. 27.

[40] Ibid.

[41] This Act of the English Parliament established a new tribunal to judge the causes of the said functionaries. The English inhabitants of Calcutta formed a junta to solicit its revocation, which they were successful in doing. On 18 January 1787, the Governor gives this news to the Secretary of State who urged much vigilance in Goa (A.H.U., *Índia,* cód. 159, ff. 28v-29v or H.A.G., *M. Reino,* Book 168-B, ff. 595, 597).

researcher looked at it as 'a progressive movement aimed at establishing a republican form of government, with a new social order, based on Liberty, Equality and Fraternity, from which it drew inspiration'.[42]

Ernestina Carreira disagrees with Carmo Azevedo's description of the Pinto Conspiracy as the second anti-colonial revolt. That is, whereas in the United States a group of individuals of 'European origin' reacted against the metropolis, in Goa it was the 'indigenous people from the colonies who feel hurt in relation to the Europeans'; it is thus 'the first political organization of a colonized people to expel a colonial power and secure its independence'.[43]

Besides this, in her opinion, the principles of the sovereign people, of liberty, equality and fraternity cannot be applied to Goa. Almost all the conspirators were of the Brahmin caste that was traditionally in power, which seeks to take over Goa. The people had to be used solely as a means of pressurising. 'Wanted is the freedom of the Goan people against the colonizers, but in the Indian context of the times it is unthinkable to speak of the same rights and of fraternity for all the castes.' Ernestina Carreira further minimizes the external influences as, for example, possible foreign help to the plotters, and considers that this 'conspiracy is rather an internal phenomenon and the revolt of 1789 in Brazil shows that it was the general malaise of the Portuguese colonial world'.[44]

For Frederico Diniz d'Ayalla, a Luso-descendant, the Pinto Conspiracy was no more than an attempt to restore the old Brahmin hegemony. A.A. Bruto da Costa and the men of the *Partido Ultramarino* around the periodical *O Ultramar* took the extreme position of denying the existence of the revolt considering it impossible to have it with such a reduced force, commanded by priests. They consider it only a movement to secure equal political and civil rights for Goans and metropolitans alike. Taking the same line, another researcher, Claude F. Saldanha opines that the revolt was only a public manifestation

[42] Cf. Carmo Azevedo, 'Pinto's Revolt of 1787', op. cit., pp. 14-15.

[43] Ernestina Carreira, op. cit., pp. 27-8.

[44] Ibid., pp. 28-9.

to draw attention to the reasons that the Goans had to complain and to their citizenship rights guaranteed by Afonso de Albuquerque and restored by the Marquis of Pombal, there being no intentions to expel the Portuguese. Vimala Devi states that the conspiracy of 1787 was nothing more than a pretext to crush the 'Brahmin intelligentsia' which, after Pombal's Instructions, had begun to conquer positions and become predominant.[45]

Without passing value-judgements on the Pinto Conspiracy, it seems that it emanated from a whole lot of circumstances that characterized Goan society at the end of the eighteenth century, as also the level of education of some individuals, mainly the ecclesiastics. Men of all times, nobles or plebeians, clergymen or politicians cannot escape from determinate influences that act with greater or lesser force. Thus, it happened in 1787, with a group of Goan clergymen. The ideas of the conspirators were precociously liberal. The movement that they developed was close in time to the independence of the United States of America and the Minas Gerais Conspiracy, in Brazil. It is, however, early by more than a century to the Asian nationalist movements.[46] It may also appear that this conspiracy could safely indicate the way in which the Goans partook of European ideas and concerns, that is, how they were getting Westernized.

[45] Cf. Carmo Azevedo, op. cit., p. 21. *O Ultramar* was the first privately owned newspaper founded in Margão, on 6 April 1859, by Bernardo Francisco da Costa. Cf. António dos Mártires Lopes, *Imprensa de Goa (Monografia)*, Lisbon, Comissariado do Governo para os Assuntos do Estado da Índia, 1971, p. 45.

[46] Cf. L.F.F.R. Thomaz, *Goa: Une Société Luso-Indienne ...*, p. 28.

CHAPTER VI

Aspects of Daily Living

Modern historiography has rightly been stressing the study of everyday life as being an integral part of the reconstruction of the past. Indeed, a judicious analysis of the traditions and customs can help to understand some aspects of the historical life that elude the written document. The manner in which individuals and social groups fill up their day acts as a sort of spine for their conduct; the habits and customs influence the life of the people and speak about their mentality. In addition, if one keeps in mind that it largely determines historical facts, we can appreciate the significance of this study for a broader understanding of the human past.

If, on the one hand, its historical source value is clear, there remains, nonetheless, the great difficulty of collecting and interpreting the usable sources. Besides the more or less sparse data culled from manuscripts we turned, in the present case, to ethnographic collection, namely by Bragança Pereira, who left behind a vast compilation on the subject. From among the sources, note the contribution made by the travellers who visited Goa and who in their reports put in concrete form their impressions about this land and its people. These are different writings, and with a very variable degree of trustworthiness, but they are nonetheless important sources for the study of the title subject.[1]

[1] Richard Burton, *Goa and the Blue Mountains or, six months of sick leave,* London, 1951. Maria dos Remédios Castelo Branco and Fernando Castelo Branco, after making a critical balance on the value of the opinions of travellers, called the attention of the researchers of Indo-Portuguese history to these reports. See 'Goa vista por alguns viajantes estrangeiros (de seiscentos até oitocentos)', by the authors, in *Stvdia,* no. 49, Lisbon, 1989, pp. 139-41.

The characteristics observed both before and after the eighteenth century (referred to by subject experts) are constant. This does allow us to acknowledge the use of a wider kaleidoscope of sources beyond those of the eighteenth century. Thus, Richard Burton supports some habits that the traveller Biervillas had referred to, when in Goa probably around 1736, a century later. This proves that these habits had stayed on during the second half of the eighteenth century.

BIRTHS

Some Hindu customs related to the birth of children persisted in Christian society.[2] The cultural influences of Hinduism were marked, mainly in the lower Christian classes. It is the case of the festivities on the sixth day of the birth of a child, to ward off the devil trying to stay in the new-born. Hence, after singing pious prayers, the invitees used to spend the night keeping a watch on the house, making bonfires near the door and singing noisily in order to prevent the entry of the demon. The newborn (swaddled in black cloths) and his mother would be constantly kept watch over during the night. This practice was quite widespread even among the families of European Reinóis. It has still lived on, in spite of being forbidden by the charter of 28 December 1681, by the edict of the Inquisition of 14 April 1736 and episcopal decree of 27 July 1784.[3]

[2] Even today it is a habit to put vegetable black *(kajal)* on the children's eyelashes, in order to keep away the 'evil eye'. It is current among Hindus and among some Christians. The same must be mentioned about rubbing the body of new-borns with coconut oil in order to strengthen them. Cf. A.B. Bragança Pereira, op. cit., vol. II, pp. 272, 275 and L.F.F.R. Thomaz, *O Cristianismo e as influências pagãs ...*, p. 7.

[3] Edict of the Inquisition of Goa, 1736, in A.C.P.G., *Livros dos Conventos e Igreja,* no. 6 (Igreja de S. José de Daugim). Also see Manoel Felicíssimo Louzada d'Araujo d'Azevedo, 'Segunda Memória ...', in *Annaes Marítimos Coloniaes,* 2nd series, no. 6, Lisbon, 1842, p. 431; See our article 'Hinduism in the Quotidian of the Christians of Goa in the 18th Century' in *The Portuguese Indian Ocean and European Bridgeheads: Festschrift in Honour of Prof. K.S. Mathew,* ed. Pius Malekandathil and T. Jamal Mohammed, Lisbon, Fundação Oriente, 2001, pp. 354-63.

Another frequent custom was that of women not going for Mass during the forty postpartum days. The episcopal decree of 1784 banned this practice on penalty of mortal sin to those missing Mass without a proper impediment and considered it to be like an influence of the Jewish rite. Perhaps vestiges of Hindu beliefs could be seen also, since the Hindu parturient used to be advised rest, secluded at home, during forty days.[4]

Among the Hindus, a series of prescriptions filled the period of pregnancy and the postpartum period. Curiously, although without a code on the matter, many traditions circulated among the Christians; they were observed strictly, such as not to touch the expectant women in order not to harm the child and to preventing 'evil eye'. Anyway, aspects of an age-old tradition and of superstition could probably explain such a situation.

The new-born used to be christened on the eighth day, in principle, with Christian names; that is why the first Provincial Council (1567) had use of Hindu names and the episcopal decree of 9 October 1782 recommended that the parents should refrain from giving them names other than those of the saints.[5]

MARRIAGES

The parents, sometimes with the help of intermediaries who found out information about the spouses' families, their assets, the conditions of engagement, etc., arranged marriages. A Konkani proverb *Eka cheddvak kazar korunk bara zotim zhorounk zay* (To marry off a girl, you must wear off twelve slippers) referred to the trouble involved in finding a son-in-law.[6] By the dowry

[4] A.B. de Bragança, op. cit., vol. II, pp. 271-2.

[5] Padre Manuel J.S. Albuquerque, op. cit., pp. 19-20. The same decree prohibited baptism at home, except in cases of risk of life, with a fine of 2 xerafins.

[6] Cf. S.R. Dalgado, *Florilégio de Provérbios Concanis* ..., Coimbra, 1922, p. 34. The intermediary who used to deal with marriages was called Raibari. There were, and still are, cases in which the old servants used to undertake to find marriage proposals for the children of the greater families. Many a time their services used to bear fruit and they would be rewarded with a cloth-piece, some money, and even some gold beads. See Joseph Barros,

system, the groom used to receive from the future in-laws an amount of money obliging the bride to give up the legal paternal share of inheritance.[7] The non-fulfilment of the conditions stipulated could create difficulties that, in extreme cases, could lead to the couple's separation.[8]

It must be noted that dowries sometimes meant great sums of money. Thus it so happened in Bardez where in a few years they moved from two to eight to ten thousand xerafins.[9] Excessive spending on dowry and marriage celebrations would sometimes bring the family to ruin. The prelates intervened by soliciting help from the civil authority, by way of suitable laws. Thus, Archbishop D. Lourenço de Santa Maria published a pastoral letter in 1745 regulating the number of persons who could attend a wedding, in accordance with the amount of dowry.[10]

Sometimes the marriage dowry was provided in the form of government or military posts: This is what happened with orphan girls educated in the Recolhimento de Nossa Senhora da Serra. Others received remuneration for part or all of the

---

Goan Society: Luso-Tropical Experiment in India. At other times, the Malo (barber) was the Raibairi, who going as he did from house to house, knew the families inside out. Cf. Teotónio R. de Souza, *Goa Medieval: A Cidade e o Interior no Século XVII,* Lisbon, Editorial Estampa, 1994 (Portuguese version of *Medieval Goa: A Socio-Economic History,* New Delhi, 1979, p. 80). The following saying is frequently used, which proves that match-makers were in great vogue: *Barem zalyar haklê-navryachem, vaitt zalyar malyachem* (If successful, it is due to the groom or bride; if unsuccessful, it is the match-maker's fault). Cf. S.R. Dalgado, op. cit., Coimbra, 1922, p. 35.

[7] See the letter of 12 December 1796 on the betrothals. Cf. A.H.U., *Índia,* maço 170 (163).

[8] The *Visitas Pastorais* refer to some cases of separation. It was the case, for example, in Siolim, in 1786 (A.C.P.G., *V.P.,* vol. 18-20, ff. 62-5).

[9] Ofícios da Câmara de Bardez de [1777]. Cf. A.H.U., *Índia,* maço 102 (87).

[10] The pastoral letter of 21 November 1745 'banned the attendance of more than 8 to 10 persons at local weddings, the dowry being 100 xerafins, more than ten if the dowry was up to 500 xerafins and 20 if higher than 500, failing which the bridal couple would be fined 20 xerafins and 2 to the accompanying party' (A.B. de Bragança Pereira, op. cit., vol. II, p. 294).

services rendered by the father or any other family member in India.[11]

By the Charter of 6 October 1784, nuptials not celebrated by a deed became invalid. Nonetheless, in the last years of the following decade (1798), that provision was revoked, considering those engagements and agreements to be true nuptials which had been ratified in the presence of the parish priests and three witnesses. They alleged lack of resources of the Goan population and the manner of preventing the parents from cheating, for they used to make new engagements without their children's consent.[12] It must be borne in mind that marriage was contracted at a tender age (before puberty) and as such without the voluntary and mature assent of the spouses.

An ambience of manifest joy and great ostentation marked the marriage celebrations. Two aspects seem to be of consequence in these functions. One is the multiplicity of function that used to be held ever since the groom's family accepted the marriage proposal up to several days after the religious ceremony. Thus, in the act of handing the dowry and the exchange of presents (when these two functions used to be held in a single ceremony), the bride's father or eldest brother and in their absence the bride's 'commissioner', would place a chain or a ring on the ring-finger and hand over the stipulated dowry, thus making the discharge.

Another important moment in these celebrations was the ceremony called *pitam,* which consisted of grinding rice all night, to the sound of verses in praise of the bridal couple, in the company of some women and neighbours. The liturgical

[11] The orphan girls sheltered in this institution were white and usually married Reinóis. On the remuneration of the services of others, see the case, e.g. of Sebastiana, daughter of António de Albuquerque, who was given possession of the letter of *contador* of the Bardez Court in her lifetime, for her marriage dowry, in remuneration of part of her father's services (A.N./T.T., *J.R.F.E.I.,* Book 27, deteriorated f.)

[12] The royal charter of 27 January 1798 (H.A.G., *M. Reino,* Book 178, ff. 4-4v). Also, see the diploma of 1 May 1799 on the charter of law of 6 October 1784 and the Archbishop's letter to D. Rodrigo de Sousa Coutinho of even date. Cf. A.H.U., *Índia,* maço 170 (163).

marriage, wedding reception, *mesada*, were some other marriage celebrations. This last one (also called *torna-boda*) consisted of a reception at the house of the parents of the bride, with the same pomp and style as the marriage feast thrown by the bride's parents. Interestingly, in the course of the first year of marriage gifts and invitations for meals were continually made to the newly-married.[13]

Besides these celebrations, the families exchanged gifts such as flowers, areca and betel, *foguéus*, *merendas*, *ojem*. There would also be animals, foodstuffs or fruits. In order to escape the jurisdiction of the Inquisition, the Christians replaced some items with others, but the tradition of exchange of gifts was kept up.[14]

Another aspect to be remembered about these festivities was the magnificent show of the musical cortège, the orchestra, the large number of invitees, the sumptuous dress code, the heavy concourse of palanquins, the rich banquets and the great balls. All these aspects, carefully planned, made the weddings exceptionally colourful. This penchant for ostentation is connected no doubt with the desire of a social statement by the families and with the caste-stratified Goan society.

Marriage functions were as a rule accompanied by a lot of music. It was customary to sing, both in public and in private, certain songs in the local language, called *vovio,* which in fact had been banned by the Inquisition. At the ball, after the wedding feast, there was the *mando* dance to the tune of songs which has marriage-related themes. It was a habit (now outmoded) of singing highly sentimental verses bidding adieu to the bride, when she left her parents' house. At the reception at the house of the groom's parents, soon after the religious ceremony, they used recite verses in honour of the bridal couple, especially for

[13] After the *mesada,* the bridal couple used to prolong their stay at the bride's parents' house for some days, during which time the groom used to be the victim of some tricks, with which he used to entertain those present (A.B. de Bragança Pereira, op. cit., vol. II, pp. 299-300).

[14] Cf. the edict of the Goa Inquisition of 1736 published by A. Lopes Mendes, op. cit., vol. I, pp. 250-1; and A.B. de Bragança Pereira, op. cit., vol. II, pp. 290, 296 (the latter published only the part referring to the marriage).

the bride who would be living at the in-laws' place. In some cases, the *Laudate* or *Te Deum* was recited at the family oratory.[15]

A comparison of Hindu and Christian marriage celebrations allows shows some parallels in the habits and at other times an adaptation of the earlier practices. Such is the case of the bridal songs, common at these functions, but among the Christians followed by the singing of the *Te Deum*. In this perspective, particularly important is the edict from the Inquisition in 1736 which, banning certain Hindu practices among Christians, thus allows to judge the manner in which the marriage ceremonies of the eighteenth century Goan Christians were held. From its analysis and comparison with other studies, it can be deduced that some habits, not exactly religious, were common to these two ethnic-religious groups.

ATTITUDE TOWARDS DEATH

Christian funerals, quite different from those of the Hindus, who generally opt for cremation, used to be held with much ceremony: long cortèges, luxurious dress, display of jewellery, imposing mausoleums, many lights, walls and benches in black, etc. In 1789, the Archbishop solicited from the central government the publication of etiquette on the matter, in order to avoid the total destruction of the people. His pastoral letter of 1 January 1793 regulated some aspects relating to funerals, with a view to avoiding certain excesses.[16]

At the time of the burials, sometimes there were excesses, which the authorities sought to curb, but were not always successful. Thus, there used to be a row, while the body was at

[15] A. Lopes Mendes, op. cit., vol. I, pp. 42, 251, and A.B. de Bragança Pereira, op. cit., vol. II, pp. 298-9.

[16] See the Archbishop's letter to M.M. Castro, dated 19 February 1789, and his long pastoral letter mentioned in the text (A.H.U., *Índia,* maço 1 (731) and C.C. Nazareth, *Mitras* ..., pp. 354-6, respectively). In the said pastoral letter, *inter alia* it prohibited the practice of covering the church walls or benches with black, restricted the number of candles and the signs by the clerics in the offices, stipulated the persons responsible for praying and singing the office of the dead.

home, or at its exit and, closer to our days that moment which remained in our customs can sometimes surprise us in the villages. The departure of the dear ones for the eternal resting place no doubt causes feelings of profound sadness; but then there used to be also some artificiality, a 'studied crying, at certain hours of the day and for a certain number of months, accompanied by words vouching for the deceased person, and in such a loud voice as to be heard by neighbours and passers-by'.[17]

There was also the custom of narrating the deeds of the deceased and of preventing the exit of the coffin. These and other habits have been explained as reminiscences of paganism and Hindu beliefs. This aspect is clear from the attitude of refusing extreme unction, upon the belief that was a signal for the devil to enter in the house. There was also the custom of the mourning people not moving out of the house for some time.[18]

Some habits surround the death of people and seem to translate the sentiments of solidarity among the family members, face-to-face with this event. Indeed, the relatives used to get together in the house of the mourning family for some days: it was the custom called *novendio.* In addition, on the day of the death, the mourning family, as well as the relatives who gathered at the house of the deceased person, would not do the cooking. Hence, the neighbours and friends would send them cooked food, as was the practice in Portugal too. This custom was called *dukatto.*[19]

[17] The decrees of 30 May 1783, # 11 and of 27 July 1784, by the Archbishop D. Frei Manuel de Santa Catarina, forbid the 'abuse of loud cries at the time of removing the body and of crying poetically narrating the deeds of the deceased, failing which they would have to pay a fine of 1 rupee to the *fabrica* and of preventing the exit of the coffin by throwing themselves on it, failing the parish priest would go away along with the confreres without taking the body'. Published by Father Manuel J.S. Albuquerque, *Decretos do Arcebispado de Goa, Summario Chronologico 1775 a 1900,* Bastora, 1900, p. 25 and C.C. Nazareth, *Mitras* ..., p. 335.

[18] Ibid., p. 25.

[19] From an unknown author, 'Documentos da Comissão Archeologica da India Portuguesa. Ethnografia goesa' do 'Anglo-Lusitano' de Bombaim, in *O Oriente Portuguez,* vol. IV, Jan., Feb. and Mar. 1907, Nova Goa, [1907], pp. 86-8.

In the second half of the eighteenth century, gradually the practice of building cemeteries begins to spread. However, the people, being long accustomed to burying their dead inside the churches, begin to resist the determinations, as is evident from the successive renewal of the Archbishop's orders. There was opposition from the priests too. Centuries-old customs which would indeed take their own time to disappear![20]

Well known is the fact that Hinduism had prescribed *sati* (immolation in the husband's funerary pyre) for the Hindu widow. Although Albuquerque had kept up the Hindu usages and customs, he positively did away with *sati*, for its flagrant inhumanity. The traveller Biervillas (*c.* 1736) referred to the custom of the women burning themselves with their husbands' bodies. Those who feared it would poison themselves as soon as their husbands died, and then both the bodies would be cremated together. If they refused cremation, they would face the worst of infamies from their own family members and friends.[21]

The Hindus used to perform this rite outside the Goan territory and in 1759, the widow of Satrogi Rane sought permission for *sati*, a request that was contrary to royal orders and hence refused. Furthermore, it was said that there had never been a similar case, which means that it was the only case.[22]

In Christian society, the widow had quite a subaltern position. She lived like a recluse at her in-laws, who looked down upon a second marriage. Even a fortuitous meeting with a widow was considered a bad omen. The Church and the civil authorities protected the widows, asserting their right to remarriage, without jeopardizing their economic interests. Already in 1575, the second Provincial Council of Goa had solicited legal support from the Government against the compulsory practice of the

[20] See what is said thereafter on the subject, in the part referring to health and hygiene.

[21] See *Voyage de D'Innigo de Biervillas ...*, pp. 193-5. He also refers to the origin of *sati*.

[22] The Hindus used to go to the other side of the river with one or more *bhats* (Hindu priests) and in the presence of the family members.

widow having to shave her head after the death of the husband, as a sign that they could not get married again.[23]

HABITATION

Excepting the mansions of the rich, the houses were generally humble and with simple furnishings: walls of clay or laterite, palm-thatched roofs, girders made from coconut tree trunks, cow dung floor, narrow windows sometimes covered with *karepo,* in the case of some Hindu houses.[24] The houses were built adjacent to each other, as a form of protection against assaults, common during the Maratha wars.

By their vastness and architectural beauty, the residences of the affluent stood out in the scenery. An external staircase led to the portico or *balcão* and the verandas where the family enjoyed the rural quietude and refreshed themselves on warm nights. One or two halls, dining room, oratory (in the older constructions), bedrooms, kitchen, and toilet made up the main living quarters. Every house had a larder and a well to provide for the domestic needs and for baths. Often there were outbuildings for servants' toilets and for stocking firewood. It can possibly be said that in the eighteenth century the Indo-Portuguese style of architecture was formed, with cornices on the façades for protection against sun and rain; the multiple roofs, wide windows, the street-fronts sporting broad verandas, etc.[25] Variegated furniture with Eastern and Western motifs, on strong Oriental woods, as also China porcelain, from the Macao trade, made up the effects of these country-houses.[26]

[23] Cf. *Memória Histórico-Eclesiástica* ..., p. 155.

[24] A coating of cowdung was used for sanitary reasons and for the purpose of purification. *Karepo,* 'translucent oyster shell *Placuna placenta* that filters soft and discreet light' (A.B. de Bragança Pereira, *Etnografia da Índia Portuguesa,* vol. II, p. 82).

[25] See Mário Cabral e Sá, 'Thresholds of Leisure: Manors, Mansions, Villas', in *Goa: Cultural Patterns,* Marg Publications, Bombay, 1983, p. 108.

[26] The Archbishop of Goa, D. António Taveira da Neiva Brum da Silveira, sent home to his family in Azores pieces and sets of chinaware bought in Goa. Cf. Maria de Jesus Mártires Lopes, *Epistolário,* op. cit., pp. 66, 72, 73, 106, 107, 124, 125.

The Hindu houses generally followed a well-delineated plan. The bedrooms surrounded an inner or central patio (*razangonn*), comprising the core of the living quarters. The sacred *tullôs* plant was venerated here; and it was here that they chatted, far from the indiscreet public gaze, put their clothes up for drying and the children entertained themselves. In the front gallery was the drawing room (*vosro*), in the back one, the dining room and in the side galleries were the rooms. Like in the Christian houses, there was a porch or *balcão*, with seats all round.[27] Their furniture was particularly simple, although from the eighteenth century onwards some Hindu families with business connections began furnishing their homes with European style items.[28]

FOOD

The importance of alimentary habits on the life of the people is well known. One suggestive example was the introduction of fat corn in the diet of north Portugal; its effects were so salutary that Orlando Ribeiro called it the *revolução do milho* (corn revolution).[29] Since times immemorial, Indians believed that the food that was consumed influenced the intellectual and moral faculties; thus they justified the fact that food habits differed from caste to caste, in accordance with the professions entrusted to each one of them, as found codified in the Puranas. The staple diet was rice, consumed by everyone. However, since their priestly function demanded a greater intellectual activity, the Brahmins fed themselves on milk products, vegetables, and never meat. The Khetri, who mainly had military duties, and so required physical strength, ate vegetables as well as meat, though not beef.[30] The Vaishyas, who were devoted to trade, fed them-

[27] A.B. de Bragança Pereira, op. cit., pp. 81-2 and Caroline Ifeka, 'The Image of Goa', in *Indo-Portuguese History: Old Issues, New Questions*, ed. Teotónio R. de Souza, New Delhi, 1985, pp. 188-90.

[28] Mário Cabral e Sá, op. cit., p. 104.

[29] Orlando Ribeiro, 'Milho', in *Dicionário de História de Portugal,* dirigido por Joel Serrão, vol. II, Lisbon, 1968, p. 63.

[30] See the Glossary.

selves on fruits, milk products and fish; and the Sudras, besides these foodstuffs, also ate birds.[31]

Goan Christian cuisine was essentially traced out from the Hindu cuisine, for 'the Christian influence was passive, consisting of the elimination of the vegetarian items'.[32] It is for this reason that the food habits of the lower Christian castes, who show a stronger Hindu influence, as we have seen, are practically the same as theirs too.

The most popular course in the Goan menu was rice-curry (*xit-coddi*), accompanied by several others or *toca-boca,* such as fried fish, spicy vegetable dishes, several pickles generally called *achar, papads,* etc. In the Christian household, besides these delicacies, there used to be also the *balchanv,* of Malayan origin, *pará, mol* and other conserves of salted fish and fruit, a daily feature in the rainy season, when fresh fish was scarce.[33] On

[31] The Puranas, legendary books of Hindu mythology, established norms on food to be consumed at meals, the religious duties to fulfil before meals, the care to be taken by the Hindus not to be touched by impure objects. See A. Lopes Mendes, *A Índia Portuguesa* ..., vol. I, pp. 122-3.

[32] L.F.F.R. Thomaz, *O Cristianismo e as Tradições Pagãs,* op. cit., p. 8.

[33] Curry is prepared by grinding together coconut, red chillies and a few spices. In its making are also used onions, garlic, ginger and fish, prawns or meat. *Papads,* 'a fine and dry, circular shaped dough, made from some vegetable flour, kneaded with some hot spices' (S.R. Dalgado, op. cit., vol. II, pp. 166-7). Just before eating, it is deep fried in hot oil. *Balchão* (*balchanv*), made of chopped and fermented prawns, *bilimbins, ambadde* and hot spices. *Bilimbins* and *ambadde* are fruits used not only in this delicacy but also in several preserves (S.R. Dalgado, op. cit., vol. I, pp. 30, 86, 127). *Pará,* a kind of sauce used to preserve cooked fish or meat, made from vinegar, tamarind or a little brandy, malaguetta powder, turmeric and other condiments, where salted fish or dry fish are preserved for one or more years. When fried just at the time of eating, it goes well with rice-curry (S.R. Dalgado, op. cit., vol. II, p. 169 and A.B. de Bragança Pereira, *Etnografia da Índia Portuguesa,* vol. II, Bastora, 1940, p. 74). *Miscutt,* a preserve of green (or raw) mangoes, previously seasoned in vinegar, water and salt. These are then boiled and prepared with a filling of red chillies, salt, asafoetida, mustard and oil (A.B. de Bragança Pereira, op. cit., vol. II, p. 139). See our study, *As Especiarias e a Culinária Goesa,* in A. Epopeia das Especiarias, ed. Inácio Guerreiro, Lisbon, I.I.C.T. - Inapa, 1999, pp. 134-45.

Archivum Romanorum, S.I. *Goana*, 34-1, f. 158v (mid 17th century)

festive occasions, people from the lower social groups used to have beef, pork and chicken. The higher castes ate in the European style.

Like the locals who could not do without rice-curry, the Reinóis too, with the passage of time in India, and especially their children, could not dispense with this dish. Ferreira Barroco, who was the Secretary of State in India in the last years of the eighteenth century, recounts the commotion at the arrival of the said dish during a meal, for the educated lot used to take to it in such a manner that it 'seemed as if they had eaten the rest as a favour and this for its taste'.[34]

Another dish, quite popular and commonly served to the sick, was *pez,* also accompanied by a few courses; in the villages, it used to be the night meal, perhaps being a light dish. There is also the habit, though less frequent, of having *pez* in the morning itself.[35]

Hindu confectionery is quite diverse with their *laddu, bessan-laddu, neureo, jilebi, dudh-pendde,* etc., by and large without eggs or sugar; the latter is substituted by a treacle called jaggery.[36]

[34] Sebastião José Ferreira Barroco, *Reflexões sobre a cauza da decadencia do Estado da India, oferecidas ao Illustrissimo e Excellentissimo Senhor Vicente da Anadia, por* ..., (1802) Biblioteca da Academia das Ciências de Lisboa, *Ms vermelho,* no. 634, ff. 61v-62.

[35] Dellon mentions that the prisoners of the Goa Inquisition had a different food regimen, depending on whether they were Negroes or whites; thus, the former used to have *pez,* a sort of thick rice, at breakfast. Cf. Maria dos Remédios Castelo Branco and Fernando Castelo Branco, op. cit., p. 145. In Parra (Bardez), a priest was accused in 1798 of not having attended the administration of *pez* and the later burial of a parishioner. This happened at the time of the smallpox epidemic, which proves the food habit of *pez* in sickness (A.C.P.G., *V.P.,* vol. 27-9, f. 48). The decree of Archbishop D. Francisco de Assunção e Brito of 25 September 1778 condemns the use of *pez* with *'toca boca'* on days of fasting (C.C. Nazareth, *Mitras* ..., p. 315). On the habit of having *pez* at breakfast, see Dinis L. Cottineau de Kloguen, *Bosquejo Histórico de Goa* ..., Nova Goa, 1858, p. 162.

[36] Jaggery, 'sweetener produced from toddy, which hardens on evaporation'. *Sur,* white, sweet liquid, extracted from a bunch of tender coconuts. For this, the Chaudhuris, people engaged in this work, climb the coconut trees and with a curved knife, open the peduncle of the bunch,

Since the Christians rarely make these cakes at home, they normally consume those made by Hindus. The typical *bolos* (cakes) of the Christians include *doce de grão, dodol,* also of Malayan origin, and *bebinca.*[37]

Hindu cuisine is rich in dishes made from different types of flour, legumes and vegetables, fruit, milk products, in such a way that 'with these ingredients a good cook could prepare a dinner with four hundred dishes or more'.[38] This variety is visible in the many types of salted *bolos* that go with and complete the meals, such as *chapatis, sandnam, bhakri, vodde,* etc. They largely correspond to bread in the West.[39]

The lower castes, mainly the Kunnbi, live especially on gruel or broth made of cereals, quite nutritive and very eco-

---

before the calyx overflows and attach it to a rush, hanging a vessel into which the liquid trickles' (*Instrucções ...*, fn. 45 by the editor, p. 80). *Laddu,* little balls prepared with sugar and different types of flour and cashew nuts. *Bessan-laddu,* prepared from previously roasted gram flour, butter, sugar and sesame. *Neureo,* puff pastry tarts with a sweet filling. *Jilebi,* prepared from gram flour, cardamom powder and syrupy sugar. *Dudh-pendde,* made by condensing milk with sugar. A little butter is added to the mass, which is then shaped into small balls or squares.

[37] The pudding-like cake, *bebinca,* is made of a batter of coconut milk, egg yolk, sugar, which is flavoured with nutmeg and cardamom. This pap is oven-baked in successive layers, in such a way that when it is ready and cut into slices, the layers are easily seen. Depending on the number of layers, the *bebinca* is designated as being five-, seven-, or nine-layered. It is decorated with peeled almond cut into fine strips. *Doce de grão* is prepared from fresh coconut, ground gram cereal, sugar and cardamom powder.

[38] Cf. A. Lopes Mendes, op. cit., vol. I, p. 124.

[39] *Sandnam,* 'a very spongy cake made of ground rice with water to which toddy is added for its fermentation and cooked in a steam bath' (Father Filinto Cristo Dias, 'Vocábulos Portugueses de Origem Concani', in *Boletim do Instituto Menezes Bragança,* no. 112, Pangim, 1976, p. 76: *Bhakri,* a type of Indian bread made of rice flour. *Foguéus,* a type of cake made of rice flour and fried in coconut oil (S.R. Dalgado, op. cit., vol. I, p. 400). *Vodde,* small cakes prepared from concentrated rice water fermented in advance, in which *nachinim* [*sic*] flour is kneaded to form a mass as thick as baker's flour, which is spread on a board by means of sieve, cut in the form of hosts, and then fried in coconut oil' (A.B. de Bragança Pereira, op. cit., vol. II, p. 68).

nomical.[40] The favourite dish of the Muslims is *pulau* or *bringe*, and their food never contains pork meat.[41]

In Goan cuisine as a whole a characteristic feature is the widespread use of coconut and other ingredients got from the coconut tree, such as *sur* and jaggery made from it, in the preparation of food items. This palm tree is indeed a basic in the life of the Indians. It has a great number of uses, not only in cuisine, but also in habitation, furniture, dress, etc. Hence, the coconut is the symbol of felicity and normally figures in Hindu religious ceremonies.[42] It may be noted that white sugar entered Goan daily life only in the last years of the nineteenth century, when the Anglo-Portuguese Treaty of 1880 sanctioned the entry of British merchandise, to the detriment of the sale of the local products, such as coconut jaggery (*maddachem-chakam*) and sugar cane jaggery (*depichem godd*). The locals earlier consumed the latter as a sweetener.[43]

Drinks commonly accompanying the meals is water cooled in clay pots known as *gorgoleta*, and in the higher social classes, table wines, mainly the Portuguese.[44] As a drink, there is the

---

[40] The poor eat pap of *kullit*, an Indian legume, or *nachnim* flour (*ragi* or *eleusine coracona*), slightly fermented, known as *ambil*, being cheap (S.R. Dalgado, op. cit., vol. I, pp. 31, 332, 333 cited by Father F. Cristo Dias, op. cit., pp. 65-8). The higher classes too have *tisanas*, especially to recuperate strength.

[41] Stewed meat with rice, butter, spices, almonds, raisins, etc. (A.B. de Bragança Pereira, op. cit., vol. II, p. 74).

[42] The Hindu name for the coconut tree is *kalpa-vrucxa*, which means a tree that gives everything that is wanted of it. The groom carries a coconut in his hand when he goes to the bride's house for the nuptial ceremony (ibid., vol. II, p. 123. Also see *Voyage d'Innigo de Biervillas*, op. cit., p. 187).

[43] See F. X. Fernandes, *Índia Portuguesa. Estudos económico-sociais*, Bastora, 1905, and Ernestina Carreira, 'Índia', in *Nova História da Expansão Portuguesa*, direcção de Joel Serrão e A. H. de Oliveira Marques, vol. X, *O Império Africano 1825-1890*, coordinated by de Valentim Alexandre and Jill Dias, Lisbon, Estampa, 1998, pp. 703-7.

[44] The *gorgoleta* caught Dellon's eye; he referred to it in his narration on the Inquisition of Goa. Among other utensils given to the prisoners there was this one, with fresh drinking water. Maria dos Remédios Castelo Branco and Fernando Castelo Branco refer to this aspect in their op. cit., p. 146. Pyrard de Laval, who visited Goa in the first years of the seventeenth cen-

juice of the pseudo-fruit (developed peduncle) of the cashew – *niró*, *brindão* juice, tender coconut water, etc. Among the alcoholic drinks, there are *urrak*, *fenni*, cashew liquor, more widespread among the lower castes.[45]

In Goa, as in India and South Asia, it is customary to chew *areca* rolled up in betel leaves, a habit often mentioned by Indian and European writers.[46] In the current opinion of the locals, this masticator is palatable and produces an aesthetic effect by the redness in the mouth. Medicinal properties are attributed to it like that of a digestive and circulatory aid, for the areca 'strengthens the teeth and gums, controls the blood flow, vomiting and intestinal indispositions'.[47] Hence, Indians serve their visitors and friends rolls of areca with betel, as a sign of courtesy and hospitality.[48]

Cuisine is a marked element of culture and, together with

---

tury, refers to another type of *gorgoleta*, made of very fine clay, with a few symmetrical holes and little stones inside which would not come out, serving to clean the vase; water would be let out slowly, not pouring out even with its mouth downwards. Later this type of vase, originally from the lands of the south, fell into disuse (*Viagem de Francisco Pyrard de Laval*, op. cit., vol. II, pp. 57-8).

[45] Of the *brindão* fruit (*Garcinia purpurea*, from the Konkani *bhirând*) a light red-coloured syrup is obtained (see Chapter III, fn. 320). The tender coconut liquid is a pleasant and healthy drink, hence widely used by the Indian armies in the past. *Niró* is distilled *sura*. 'Of distilled *sura* comes *urrak*, a type of brandy, which in a stronger degree is called *fenni*; and it is the common spirit among the ordinary people' (S.R. Dalgado, op. cit., vol. I, p. 394).

[46] Cf., e.g. *Voyage d'Innigo de Biervillas* ..., pp. 98-9.

[47] In the opinion that the local medicos gave on Count of Ega's illness in 1762, they advised as 'stomach corroborants' the betel leaves with areca (A.H.U., *Índia*, maço 89 (100). Also see S.R. Dalgado, op. cit., vol. I, pp. 53-4).

[48] The Goan writer, Francisco Luís Gomes, has a description of the areca grove (plantation or areca tree forest) in his novel *Os Brahamanes*, Lisbon, 1866, pp. 83-4. 'Like the oasis in the desert so God created the areca garden for shelter against the ardour and activity of the Indian sun. The areca garden has the majesty of a temple and the freshness of the garden ...'.

music, it constitutes a point of convergence for the Goans, outside their land.

DRESS

The dress code in India – mainly that of women – has always been diverse and colourful, lending the human landscape a startling note of joy and vivacity. It is not only the woman, but also the Hindu male who sports variegated pieces of clothing, depending on his caste. Thus, they cover the head with a *topi* or with a piece of cloth rolled up in various forms and different effects, which have their own names.[49] They wear the vest, shirt and a type of overcoat; they roll up a piece of cloth round the waist, covering the thighs and partly the legs (*puddvem* or *dhontor*). In addition, only the Dessais wear narrow trousers.[50] They wear sandals, slippers or shoes curved at the end and clogs. Some adornments are also a part of the male dress code, such as rings in the earlobes, gold chains on the neck, bracelet or band on the right arm, rings.[51]

The Hindu women garments are generally attractive and elegant. Particularly the *saris* make the woman quite slim. There is a great variety of them, according to their quality and design. A short blouse goes with the *sari*. The Kunnbi women drape the cloth in a peculiar fashion, covering the forearm with copper bangles. The widows, besides shaving their head, wear red *saris*, perhaps in imitation of the Buddhist monks.[52]

[49] See the drawing in *Etnografia da Índia Portuguesa*, op. cit., between pp. 72-3, of the forms of head gear with the *pâgddi, topi, pagottem, mandir, mundaxem, rumal* and *fentó*. The dessais and Ranne wear the *mandir, fento* or *pâgddi*; the other rich classes, the *pâgddi,* and the Hindu of the Old Conquests, *topi,* which according to tradition is the distinctive sign of the Jews. ibid., p. 75.

[50] The *puddvem* is made of white cotton cloth, sometimes with colour-striped or gold-lined.

[51] Cf. A.B. Bragança Pereira, op. cit., vol. II, p. 76. Only the princes and the Ranne wear pearl necklaces.

[52] When it is cotton cloth, the dress is called *kapodd,* instead of *saddi*. There are two ways of wearing it, whether or not 'one of the extremities goes under the thighs at the lumbar region' (A.B. de Bragança Pereira,

Some accessories that are almost indispensable, so to say, in the physical make-up of the Hindu woman give her the feminine touch of graciousness. These include the very fragrant, natural flower necklaces, which they arrange round their hair combed into a *xenddo* or in plaits.[53] Very early in the morning the hawkers sing and display them in their great diversity. This aspect is very characteristic and has even become part of Goan folklore.[54] It must be noted that Christian women do not put flowers in their hair when they go out though they love to do so when indoors. Perhaps this habit dates back to the Provincial Council ban on *fulan* (flower) arrangement on the head. The reason for the ban was that petals were in use in temples for guessing the divine will.

Other adornments for Hindu woman comprise gold jewellery and precious stones which they flaunt on the hair knot, in the earlobes, the nose, on the chest, the arms, and silver ones on the fingers and toes. Some traditional jeweller designs, in fact quite rich, remained and certain motifs were assimilated by Indo-Portuguese art.[55] Besides their decorative value, jewellery has other functions in India in general and in Goa as well. They indicate the social-economic status of the woman and her family. Besides this, they are a form of saving for a rainy day or even some important undertaking in their lifetime.[56]

---

op. cit., vol. II, pp. 76-7). This last manner is called *kas* (from the cloth *caixa*), worn by women when they worked in the fields or when they go selling their produce in the market. *Saddi* is a finer cloth and is not used by the lower classes. Thus, the woman's social status could be known from whether she dressed the *kapodd*, *saddi*, or the dress.

[53] See the Glossary.

[54] In one of the most typical and popular dances of *deknni*, the woman asks the sailor to transport her to the other river bank, and offers him gratefully the flowers she has on her head: 'xinvtim, mogrim haddtolim; matear mavunk haddtolim ...' ('I'll give you the chrysanthemums and mogarins I have on my head ...').

[55] See the beautiful and varied designs of Hindu jewellery presented by A.B. de Bragança Pereira, op. cit., vol. II, between pp. 76-9.

[56] Ibid., pp. 78-9 and Mira Mascarenhas, *The Pombaline Era in Goa (1750-1777)*, Bombay, 1977, photostat. The author states that 'the use of jewellery was a social duty and each adornment had its own meaning, whether in relation to the caste or the woman's family status ...'.

The Muslim and Hindu dress codes have very much in common. Over the knee-long shirt, they usually wear an embroidered waistcoat; they wear trousers or *puddvem* (*dhontor*) and coat. The main difference between the dresses of the Hindu and Muslim women is that the latter wear some narrow trousers underneath the cloth and a vaporous mantle.

Christian men dressed in the Western style. Middle-class individuals would be seen in cloth coats, shorts and shoes without socks; the poorer lot, excluding the slaves, used to wear a shirt, jacket and *calção,* without hat or shoes.[57] However, many from the lower strata in the villages wore Hindu costumes like the *langotti,* the cloth to cover the thighs, the cabaan. As regards the womenfolk, the more affluent used to follow the European style and some others wore the old Portuguese dress comprising 'a cape made of fine linen, long kimono',[58] striped silk skirt and a big black veil over the head when out of the house'. Others stuck to the *saddi.* To church, many used to wear a long white sheet covering from head to toe. Still others wore typical dresses like the *pan-bajú* and the *pan-paló.* The Brahmin and Chardó ladies did so if they did not dress in the European style; the former wore the *pan-bajú* and the latter a white cloth with red or black border.[59] Married ladies, spinsters and widows dressed differently, though we do not have any description of the respective costumes.[60]

For protection from the bright sun in summer and rain in the monsoons, the people used sombreiros.[61] Pyrard de Laval

[57] Cf. Diniz L. Cottineau de Kloguen, op. cit., pp. 161-2.

[58] Quimão, long dressing gown, with sleeves, a la Japanese dress.

[59] *Pan-bajú* 'comprising a cloth (*saras* or *todôp)* which only covers the waist downwards (and is called *fota,* being made of a rich cloth, silk with gold embroidery, *tisso*) and *quimão*', ibid., p. 80 and the drawing at pp. 80-1. *Pan-paló* is the cloth without the *kas,* that is, one of the extremities passing through the thighs is not safe in the higher portion of the waist'. Ibid., p. 89 and the drawing between pp. 76-7.

[60] A married lady living as a concubine adopted the dress of a widow and said that she wished to continue the concubinage (*V.P.,* Tivim, 1772, vols. 13-15, ff. 43v-44). A married lady used to dressed differently from the spinster (*V.P.,* R. Magos, 1786, vol. 18-20, f. 4).

[61] This is a type of umbrella.

observed, curiously, that 'all these open sombreiros touch each other, appearing like a single roof'.[62]

HEALTH AND HYGIENE

Indigenous medicine was quite widespread above all in the villages, given the unavailability of modern medicos, the high cost of Western medicine, the difficulty in transportation and access to the hinterland and the mentality of the people accustomed as they were to traditional healing methods.[63]

The indigenous medical practice had its own remedies (based on local herbs), forms of treatment, diets and resorted to certain magic rites and superstition. This knowledge, not imparted in medical schools but handed down from generation to generation, was collected along the generations. The Vaidyas, Hindu professionals of Ayurvedic medicine, transmitted their knowledge in a secret book to their children who used to preserve it religiously.[64]

Not only the locals but the Reinóis too, including Viceroys, Archbishops and other authorities, sometimes approached the local doctors, as did the Count of Ega when ill in 1762.[65] The restrictions on this medical practice as imposed by the civil and ecclesiastical authorities, invoking reasons of faith and morality, dated back to the sixteenth century.[66]

Regarding health and hygiene, mention may be made of the Hindu practice of rubbing the body, head and even the ears with coconut oil, considered to be a coolant and useful for health as it blocked excessive transpiration. The Christians inherited the custom of using coconut oil on the head in order to strengthen the hair. Hindus, local Christians and Portuguese

[62] *Viagem de Francisco Pyrard de Laval ...*, vol. II, p. 50.

[63] Fátima Gracias, *Health & Hygiene in Colonial Goa, 1510-1961*, New Delhi, Concept Publishing Company, 1994.

[64] Ibid., pp. 280 and ss. and A.L. Mendes, vol. I, pp. 107-14.

[65] See fn. 47 of this chapter.

[66] On these restrictions, see Fátima Gracias, op. cit., pp. 285-8. Besides the Vaidyas and the Hakims (Muslim professionals) who constituted the local medical elite, there were the herbalists, charlatans, witch doctors, bleeders, snakebite healers, etc.

born in India used to rub the body dry in order to activate blood circulation in the body.[67]

In the period under study, medical assistance at the Royal Hospital was quite precarious, and this reflected on the mortality index.[68] The imperfection of the building, inadequate for the purpose, the insufficient ventilation and circulation of air, in addition to the lack of competent doctors, scarcity of medicines, were factors that certainly determined such a situation.[69] Many patients, admitted to the hospital with scurvy contracted during the voyage, ended up dying here.[70] The central government was interested in checking these evils. The Governor even visited the buildings personally and ordered improvements. What is certain is that the number of dead diminished in 1794 (198 dead) when compared to the immediately earlier years (259 and 246). Yet, the situation did not improve substantially.[71]

As said earlier, it was during the second half of the eighteenth century that cemeteries were ordered to be built for reasons of health and hygiene.[72] Considering that one of the causes of

[67] Cf. A. Lopes Mendes, *A Índia Portuguesa,* vol. I, Chap. II, p. 114.

[68] The original hospital was in the city of Goa, next to St. Catherine's Chapel. Transferred to Mormugão because of the Maratha invasion in 1739, it was shifted back, this time to the Panelim Palace in 1760, during the government of the Count of Ega (Manoel Felicissimo Louzada d'Araujo d'Azevedo, 'Segunda Memória ...', in *Annaes Maritimos e Coloniaes,* 2nd series, no. 4, Lisbon, Imprensa Nacional, 1842, p. 210).

[69] The Governor's letters to M.M. Castro, dated 1 February 1787 and 11 February 1788. Cf. H.A.G., *M. Reino,* Book 166, ff. 160-160v and A.H.U., *Índia,* maço 156 (148).

[70] The Governor's letter to M.M. Castro, dated 12 February 1788 (A.H.U., *Índia,* maço 154 (154) and H.A.G., *M. Reino,* Book 169-A, ff. 308-9).

[71] The average number of dead in the Hospital between 1775-94 was 173.7, with a minimum of 79 dead in 1779 and a maximum of 259 in 1792. In 1793, 246 troops died and in 1794, 198 (A.H.U., *Índia,* maços 156 (148), 158 (150), 159 (149), 162 (171), 35 (282), 164 (169), 167 (165) and cód. 520, ff. 41-41v; H.A.G., *M. Reino,* Book 172-A, f. 123 and Book 176-B, ff. 436, 438-56).

[72] The Governor's letters to M.M. Castro, dated 1 February 1787, op. cit., and from the latter to the Governor, dated 3 April 1788 (A.H.U., *Índia,* cód. 519, f. 109v).

serious illnesses in the city of Goa was the burials inside the church buildings, not very deep into the ground, exhaling 'corrupt vapours' and infecting the air, Governor Frederico Guilherme de Sousa ordered the construction of cemeteries enclosed by high fences. The same was true about Pangim, where the local cemetery was situated in a lowland, liable to cause serious illnesses in the population.[73] Archbishops D. Francisco de Assunção e Brito and D. Frei Manuel de Santa Catarina also issued statutes on this subject, with directives on the construction, as the epidemics in Ilhas, Bardez and Salsete had been caused presumably by the burials inside the church buildings. It may be noted that, nevertheless, even at the beginning of the nineteenth century not all parishes had cemeteries.[74]

AMUSEMENTS

Friends visiting filled the moments of leisure; there were also card games, sometimes *gamão* and ball, chess, draughts. ... References to cock fights, as in fact registered in the place-names of Goa, makes us believe that this was possibly yet another popular entertainment, somewhat introduced in the rural life and festivities, as in the other parts of India and South-East Asia where the cock fights were a great attraction.[75]

[73] Cf. the letter from Frederico Guilherme de Sousa to the Archbishop Primate, dated 19 September 1779. He stated that digger-rats would overturn the mud of the graves up to the surface; hence, there were corrupt airs in the temples especially in the morning. He further referred to the fevers that attacked the ecclesiastics from the College of St. Thomas until they ordered the plastering of the church (H.A.G., *Cartas e Ordens,* Book 901, ff. 142v-143v).

[74] Edict of 26 September and decrees of 13 December 1779 and 15 April 1783. Among other things, the cemetery had to be situated in highlands and their dimensions proportional to the population of the parish (H.A.G., *M. Reino,* Book 159-C, ff. 739-740v, 741-3; Father Manuel J.S. d'Albuquerque, *Decretos do Arcebispado de Goa ...*, pp. 7-9 and A.C.P.G., *Copia de Varios Documentos,* f. 113, in F.U.P., 18-1-8/9).

[75] In the city of Goa, in the middle of a square called *Bazar Pequeno* [Little Bazaar], there exists a fenced elevation – the *Terreiro dos Galos* – so called, in the opinion of Pyrard de Laval, being the place of sale of birds

The Reinóis used to probably spend their Sundays and feast days in horse races 'throwing oranges and playing canes with each other' or in pleasant river cruises in their *manchuas*. They also had the habit of seating themselves on armchairs, at the door of their houses, in a friendly chat. They wished that the passers-by should stop to talk to them. Apparently, these customs remained in Goa, through the Luso-descendants, until their return to Portugal in 1961.[76]

On festive occasions there were *brincos* (clown processions) which attracted many people and there used to be some very busy fairs that gathered hawkers and articles coming from different parts of Goa and India in general.[77] There used to be objects ranging from trinkets, sweets and ceramics, to clothes and a rich variety of cloth.[78] Besides the fairs on the occasion of religious festivals, there were others on specific days of the year and on certain days of the week, like the Mapusa fair which was a place for business and work for some people, and for others a form of entertainment and a pastime.[79]

---

and eatables. But it seems reasonable that it was rather the site where 'cock fights were held', an entertainment that although banned by the charter of Viceroy Matias de Albuquerque, dated 18 May 1594, it continued in vogue (*Viagem de Francisco Pyrard de Laval ...*, vol. II, p. 44). Animal combats, especially sheep, peacocks and cocks took place in various regions in India, with high bets. Cf. Jeannine Duboyer, *A Vida Quotidiana na Índia desde o século II a.C. até ao século VII d.C.*, Lisbon, Livros do Brasil, undated pp. 199-200.

76 *Viagem de Francisco Pyrard de Laval ...*, vol. II, pp. 84-5, 89. Even in 1961, we witnessed this pleasant scene in the old Ourém Road.

77 *Brinco* (masquerades or group of clowns, who sing, play, dance and fence on the occasion of Carnival or in the civic cortège of great revelry (S.R. Dalgado, op. cit., vol. I, p. 150).

78 This is what happens on the occasion of the feasts of St. Francis Xavier, in Old Goa, and Immaculate Conception, Pangim, where the people stock certain articles and entertain themselves.

79 In 1842, the grand annual fairs in Goa were held at Goa Velha, Siridão, Reis Magos Fort, Mapusa, Navelim and S. Tomé of Salsete, and the weekly fairs at Mapusa, Marcela, S. Lourenço, S. Tiago, Bicholim, Sanquelim, Sanguem and Quepem (Manoel Felicissimo Louzada d'Araujo d'Azevedo), 'Segunda Memoria Descriptiva e Estatistica das Possessões Portuguezas na

GRAND FEASTS

Especially on certain religious festivals, there was the custom of holding a coarse and biting drama known as *zagor,* in the course of which they sang songs in Konkani. These comic representations were held in the open air, normally at some coconut grove, engaging a large part of the night and attracting many spectators.[80] For these reasons the ecclesiastical authorities banned the *zagor,* with its concomitant superstitious practices, as seen from the pastoral letters and the opinions at the pastoral visits. However, they were not any more immoral than many of the European dramas. At the time of the Christian act of *fama* which consisted of the solemn blessing of a picture of the saint whose feast was going to be celebrated, some *folies* used to be held which were prohibited by the Archbishop D. Frei Manuel de Santa Catarina.[81] According to Dalgado, probably this custom has come from Hinduism in which there is a similar ceremony (Holi), but, on the other hand, the same was apparently seen in some regions in Portugal, possibly imported from India.[82] In short, whether in relation to the *zagor* or in relation to the *fama,* it meant the mixing up of the profane and the sacred, as referred to in Chapter III, and this is what the post-Tridentine Church sought vigorously to combat.

The Hindu festival of Holi, festival of the areca tree or *shigmo* was the *entrudo* (carnival) of the Hindus, as the *al'labo* was the carnival of the Muslims. Being a lewd festival, with the part-

Asia e seu estado actual', in *Annaes Maritimos e Coloniaes,* 2nd series, no. 8, Lisbon, 1842, p. 378.

[80] The word *zagor* derives from the Konkani *zagar* (vigil) and *zag* (to rise); hence it is understandable that it was held in the night.

[81] After stressing the true finality of the cult which was to create interior dispositions in the believer, he lamented that this happened only outwardly and being an occasion for sin and scandal. He condemned the way of celebrating with folies the Christian act of *fama* and the entertainment called *zagor.* He used to threaten the transgressors with excommunication and if the parish priest came to know in advance that these spectacles were going to be held, he would warn the laity that he would not hold the religious feast (C.C. Nazareth, *Mitras* ..., p. 336, condensed by Father Manuel J.S. d'Albuquerque, op. cit., p. 23).

[82] S.R. Dalgado, op. cit., vol. I, p. 386.

icipation of dancing girls and Hindu musical instruments, the authorities often forbade its celebration in public, which does not mean that it was not held in Goa.[83] Celebrated by Christians, Hindus and Muslims, carnival had, as we shall see later, a long tradition in this land, where till today *brincos* and civic processions of colourful dresses are held, with dances and wriggling of bodies, in an ambience of great hilarity.[84]

Besides *shigmo* and the carnavalesque merry-making, another very typical Goan festival, continuing the Hindu tradition, is the *addav*, which takes place on 24 August, on the rice harvest. Grateful for the help rendered by the residents of Taleigão in the fight against the Moors, Albuquerque granted them the privilege of being the first to cut the paddy sheaves, the staple food of the people. Hence, on this day, the *ganvkars* of the said village, after reaping, solemnly, the first sheaves, go to the Primatial See and the Governor's Palace, accompanied by armed men and strident drums. They place at the altar of the See the firstlings of their rice and offer them to the Governor and the authorities too. The somewhat martial spectacle is surprising indeed held annually in front of the Governor's Palace (in Pangim, and formerly in Old Goa) with agricultural workers, Kunnbi, with armed men fencing with two long and broad swords, *potkar*, and with the *ganvkars* wearing coats and top hat carrying the Portuguese flag and a tray with sheaves of paddy.[85]

It may be noted that the *addav,* celebrated in all the villages of Goa, although not as solemnly as in Taleigão, is one of the few Hindu festivals to be Christianized.

In the Christmas season, the roads and windows of the houses

[83] Cf., e.g. the Governors' proclamation prohibiting the holding of *shigmo,* dated 10 January 1757, and the letter from Governor Frederico Guilherme de Sousa to M.M. Castro, dated 1 January 1780, interdicting the public festivities and reducing the status quo ante 1774 (H.A.G., *M. Reino,* Book 159-A, f. 110).

[84] Some indications on the *brincos* of the nineteenth century are found in S.R. Dalgado, op. cit., vol. I, pp. 150-1.

[85] The *poto* or long double-edged sword is quite heavy and only manageable by people used to it since their childhood, who are hence called *potkar.* On this subject and the *addav,* see A. Lopes Mendes, op. cit., vol. I, pp. 45-6 and S.R. Dalgado, op. cit., vol. I, p. 10 and vol. II, p. 223.

are decorated with coloured balloons and paper stars which are lit up at night, imparting a festive air to the hamlets.[86] The midnight Mass attracts many faithful, some from the parish and others from the neighbouring villages. People wear their best clothes. The crib, mainly large-sized ones, scattered with human and animal figures, rocks, lakes and artificial waterfalls, dominates the interior of the church. After the Mass, the family gathers together at home to enjoy the *consoada* (Christmas supper) in which the seasonal sweets are never overlooked (*dodol, vodde, manddare, cake, bebinca,* etc.).

Pyrard de Laval notes that on Christmas day the mysteries of the Nativity were represented, with live figures, at churches, homes and cross roads; here they used to put up for sale, on large tables laid with rich napery, sugar-plums and dry comfits for the feast of Christmas. This traveller further noted that people went around by night placing large bills inscribed with an *Ano Bom* (Happy New Year), to the accompaniment of music.[87] Such customs outlived the centuries and today they are a part of the Christmas tradition in Goa.

For Lent and the Holy Week, there used to be great processions and religious ceremonies with live representations. It may be recalled that several pastoral letters and episcopal decrees prohibited some of the more extravagant manifestations such as the use of *brindão* syrup evoking the blood of Christ or the scene of the meeting with Veronica.[88] Church interiors used to be richly put up and decorated, normally with palms and the floor strewn with flowers and palm leaves. The area around the church was also taken care of, where they used to plant grass, flowers and bushes, as also make palm avenues.[89]

We have not come across eighteenth century reports on Carnival; meanwhile, a curious report in the *Illustração Goana* describes the seasonal festivities at the beginning of this century, with variegated Western human types and figurines in vogue.

[86] *Viagem de Francisco Pyrard de Laval,* op. cit., vol. II, p. 77.

[87] Ibid., p. 78.

[88] See Chap. III, fns. 320, 321 and the respective text.

[89] *Viagem de Francisco Pyrard de Laval,* op. cit., p. 78.

The imagination, humour and social criticism that it comprises make it a very interesting cultural phenomenon. The Goan carnival still has this characteristic. Could these spectacles have dated back to the second half of the eighteenth century?[90]

DANCES AND SONGS

Notwithstanding its Indian cultural heritage and Western influences, Goan music is an original creation of this people. It stands out from the Hindustani and Western musical traditions. Indeed it presents some similarities with the Indian choreographic tradition, vocal interpretation, use of *gumott* and with the Western tradition in its musical structure and thematic.[91] The music of the Hindu community is different from that of the Christian community, following as it does Indian classical models developed since the Vedic beginnings. We shall now deal with it.

With the conversion to Christianity, the Goan Christian captured without difficulty the tempered scale and sacred music, essentially characterized by the single melody and the Gregorian chant. For this, it contributed its dominion of the art of melody, developed in the Indian compositions and the fact that it was intrinsic to its musical conscience. In this way, polyphony was also introduced, with good results. Sacred music was learnt in the teaching institutions of the religious Orders in the city of Goa and in the parish schools.

Masses, *motets*, litanies in Latin, hymns in this language and in Portuguese and Konkani, constituted a rich musical repository

[90] The author of the report states that everything came out on display – 'the jackets, the morning coats, the silk dominos, coats of yellow cotton prints, large-brimmed hats, white tunics, red tapis – many funny masks – many balloon skirts, many dancers, Hindus, Parsis, Muslims, sailors, lords, coquettes, princes, senators, magistrates, – the *fadistas*, how many musical instruments were seen. ...' Referring to social criticism, he says that there was a march past of 'hen-pecked husbands, wives ill-treated by their husbands, – style figurines for 1868 ...' (*Illustração Goana*, ano segundo, Nova Goa, 1868).

[91] See Mira Mascarenhas, 'Impact of the West on Goan Music', in *Goa: Cultural Trends,* Goa, 1988, p. 190. She refers *inter alia* to the Indian heritage in Goan music, in the predominant forms of the Hindustani music.

of past times. *Motets* became particularly famous, as they were sung at the *Santos Passos* scenes (Via Crucis) at Lent; they were quite distinct from the European, corresponding to a type of representation that found meaning in everyday religious life, lived with great intensity. All these religious hymns had 'a distinctive Goan stamp ...'.[92]

Soon the influence of sacred music became clear in secular music, because the former was taught in schools and the ecclesiastical authorities and the Inquisition had banned the Hindu cultural forms for the local Christians, to prevent religious contamination.[93] There developed in the territory various types of dances and songs, all in Konkani, although influenced by Marathi in the north and Portuguese in the Old Conquests.[94] Among them are the *palnnam* (lullabies), *zoti* and *pittam* (nuptial chants of the Bardez Christians), *zagor* (drama songs of the Kunnbi and also used on festive religious occasions), *dhalo* (wedding songs), *fugddi* (harvest songs), story songs, work songs, dirges, etc. All these songs correspond to a monophonic tradition and perform the social function of music in Goa.[95]

Nonetheless, the dances and songs known as *mandde, dulpodam* and *deknni* occupy pride of place in Goan folklore, their oldest models dating back to the middle of the eighteenth century. Mainly the cultured aristocracy influenced by the Portuguese way of life and the moral patterns of the Church promoted the *mando*, a song generally accompanied by the violin and gumott. Personal and possessive loves, political problems, the apology of everyday situations like the monsoons, the sea, the sun were often their themes.

The *mando*, as a dance form, is always followed by the *dulpod*

[92] Mira Mascarenhas, op. cit., p. 193.

[93] Maria de Jesus Mártires Lopes, 'A Persistência Hindu no Quotidiano dos Goeses Cristãos em Setecentos', paper presented at the international meet on *O Quotidiano na História Portuguesa,* Lisbon, 22 to 24 April 1993.

[94] Portuguese words like *'adeus', 'casamento', 'feliz',* appeared in the *mandde* and *dulpodam*.

[95] Teotónio R. de Souza, 'A Presença Portuguesa nas Expressões Folclóricas do Quotidiano da Goa Portuguesa', paper presented at the international meet on *O Quotidiano na História Portuguesa,* 22 to 24 April 1993.

in which the melancholy gives way to the rhythmic vivaciousness and the *gumott* stands out. The *mando* begins slow, soft and solemn and then picks up tone and rhythm in the *dulpod* sequence, till the end is unrecognizably different from the beginning.[96] The *dulpod* sequence presents a great thematic richness, providing information on the seasons of the year, the fauna, flora and historical facts. It is also clothed in sarcasm chastising dishonest and immoral actions.

Whereas in the *mando* the Portuguese and Christian influence is obvious and the local cultural resistance in the *dulpod*, in the *deknni* there prevails the Indian matrix, symbolized by the dancing girl as a protagonist of impersonal love.[97]

Western influence made itself felt in the Goan melody by the adoption of the tonal system, based on the seven natural sounds of the Western scale, the treatment of the voices and by the organization of the sounds through shorter melodic curves and supported by a Western harmony.[98] The tradition of the litany is quite widespread in Goa; it was always and continues to be, albeit less frequently, a very popular social-religious act in the daily life of the Goan Christian. Any occasion is good enough to hold a litany at the oratory in a home or a large cross, or even at wayside crosses. The hymns are in Latin, Portuguese and Konkani, to the accompaniment of the violin.[99]

Familiar with Indian musical instruments, Goans received others from the West, like the violin, viola, organ, flute, trumpet, horn, drum, etc. The *gumott* is a membranophone used on all traditional occasions. By its richness and originality, the dances and songs of Goa undoubtedly become an important source for the study of the daily life.

* * *

[96] Ibid., and Mira Mascarenhas, op. cit., p. 194.

[97] Teotónio R. de Souza, op. cit.

[98] On these influences see Mira Mascarenhas, op. cit., p. 195 in which she mentions, for example, the Neapolitan and Basque songs.

[99] The religious part is followed by some social exchanges with a generous flow of *fenni* and boiled gram with coconut pieces. It would end with the greets of *'dev borem korum'* (may God bless you) and '*bonoite*' (Teotónio R. de Souza, 'A Presença Portuguesa ...').

It becomes difficult to study the day-to-day living of the Hindus, given the reserved nature of their habits. It may be recalled that Hindus were not allowed public celebration of Ganesh, *shigmo,* for example, two of their most important festivals, as also the marriage and 'thread' ceremonies.[100] Hence we have not dwelt on these aspects. It may be noted, in fact, that until date certain Hindu families, like the Mhamais, celebrate the Ganesh festival with paper image, since the times when its celebration had been prohibited. A proverb refers to *shigmo* as being an indispensable entertainment: *Haka nagoi, taka nagoi, shigmeachi porob zagoi* (He robs this one, and he robs that one, but *shigmo* with pomp he does celebrate).

If the culture of a people is what persists after centuries of existence and in spite of historical vicissitudes, Goa is a case in which the meeting of multiple influences did produce a peculiar idiosyncrasy.

* * *

Although it was not included in the daily life of the larger part of the population, given its sporadic aspect, royal births used to be celebrated in Goa, with the pealing of bells, lighting and *Te Deum.* So it happened in 1761 with the birth of D. José, Prince of Beira; in 1770, with Princess D. Mariana; in 1776, when Infanta D. Maria Clementina was born, and in 1801, with Princess D. Maria Francisca.[101] These festivities were seen as a means of helping the Goans to strengthen their ties of fidelity with the Mother Country.

[100] Ganesh, god of wisdom, with body of a man and head of an elephant, it is one of the most popular festivals of the Hindu pantheon.

[101] On 21 August 1761, a royal letter informed the Count of Ega of the birth of the Prince of Beira, D. José, in order to celebrate as was customary on such occasions (H.A.G., *M. Reino,* Book 135-B, f. 380) and on 26 January 1763, the Viceroy replied that he and the Senate had commemorated the event with jubilation (A.N./T.T., *Reino,* maço 602). Cf. the *Treslado do assento de parabens ...,* of 24 January 1770, of the Chamber General of Bardez, on the birth of Princess D. Mariana (H.A.G., *M. Reino,* Book 148-B, ff. 579-81). Also see C.C. Nazareth, *Mitras ...,* pp. 311, 358, 364, and the royal letter of April 1800 (A.H.U., *Índia,* cód. 520, f. 187).

Marriages of Portuguese princes and other members of the royal family were also celebrated in Goa with *luminárias* (festive lighting) and *Te Deum,* as in 1778, on the marriage of the Prince of Beira. In addition, in the year 1787 a solemn act of thanks took place in the Primatial See for the marriages of the Infants D. João and D. Mariana Vitória, children of D. Maria I.[102]

In Goa, as in other parts of the Overseas territories, solemn ceremonies marked the exequies of the monarchs, according to the custom of the Kingdom. Thus, the tolling of bells in all the churches and convents in the territory was followed by the ceremony of the breaking of the coat-of-arms at certain places; then followed at the Primatial See the vespers and exequies, officiated by the Archbishop who would recite the funeral oration.[103] Other forms of mourning were established, such as closing of the Senate as a sign of mourning and the ecclesiastic mourning for a stipulated period.[104] Seemingly, the General Chambers used to hold funeral ceremonies on the death of the

[102] The purveyor's notice dated 15 March 1778 (C.C. Nazareth, *Mitras* ..., p. 314). On 13 and 15 February 1787, thanksgiving was held in the See (ibid., p. 323). See the Queen's letter to [...], dated 12 April 1785 (A.C.P.G., *Copia de Varios Documentos,* f. 175). M.M. Castro's letter to the Archbishop, dated 19 April 1785, informed of the conclusion of the betrothals of the Infantes D. João and D. Mariana Vitória, even before the customary royal letter and informed that on the 22 April the royal family would be going to Alentejo where they would be doing the mutual exchanges of D. Mariana to Spain and D. Carlos to Portugal (ibid., f. 181).

[103] See the Appendix to this chapter: *Ceremonial das exequias de D. José I.* Also cf. C.C. Nazareth, *Mitras* ..., p. 274, which refers to the exequies of D. João V and the funeral oration pronounced by the Archbishop D. António T.N.B. da Silveira.

[104] The Senate used to remain closed for eight days (H.A.G., *Vice-Reis,* 650, f. 46) and by the notice of the purveyor of the Archbishop of 30 January 1778 the ecclesiastics had to put on deep mourning of 6 months and light for the remaining six. The circular of 9 December 1781 ordained mourning for the death of Queen D. Maria I (C.C. Nazareth, *Mitras* ..., p. 330). The letter [from the Archbishop] to the parish priests of Bardez, dated 30 January 1778 determined the same, with one year of strict mourning and six months of light mourning. Cf. A.C.P.G., *Livros de conventos e igrejas,* no. 13 (Penha de França).

sovereigns.[105] Exequies were also held on the death of members or relations of the royal family, as also on the death of a Pope.[106]

[105] A representation by the Chamber General of Bardez on 2 March 1779, among other accusations made against the Governor, complained that he had not permitted spending 800 xerafins of their *corpo commú* (common body) for the exequies of D. José I, depriving it of this honour. It stated that other 'common figures in similar demonstrations spend in common and not on their own as the governor had ordered' [A.H.U., *Índia,* maço 2 (246), f. 5].

[106] In March 1755 there were exequies for the Queen Mother D. Mariana of Austria (C.C. Nazareth, *Mitras* ..., p. 276) at the See of Goa, and on 18 February 1783 for the Queen D. Mariana Vitória, the mother of D. Maria I (A.C.P.G., *Copia de Varios Documentos,* f. 148, in F.U.P., 18-1-8/9); on 26 September 1799, on the death of the Pope (ibid., f. 260).

APPENDIX VI.I

Ceremonies of the Exequies of D. José I

The public ceremonies began on 25 February 1778, at 3 o'clock in the afternoon, with the exit from the Senate buildings of a cortège formed as follows: the Chamber scribe, 48 citizens in two files flanking three ministers in the middle row; finally, the tribunal of the Senate with its president, *fidalgo* councillors and noblemen, the attorney, the masters, etc. The Council scribe on horseback and in black attire carried a large black flag; each of the three ministers carried a black coat-of-arms up to the black-coloured dais erected in advance at the steps of the Old See; close to the Church of Mercy and before the yard of the Bom Jesus he uttered the following words: 'Cry, oh noblemen, cry, oh people, for Your Most Faithful King Dom Joze the First of Portugal has died'. And, soon thereafter, he broke the coat-of-arms and let it fall to the ground. In this ceremony the Artillery Regiment rendered military honours.

Then there were the vespers and the funeral in the Cathedral, with the tolling of bells in all the churches and respecting the manner of address typical of the age. After the vespers, the Archbishop left, but the chapter continued praying the matins, after which, the troops fired three rounds and the pieces of the new invention the funeral salvo; besides, during the day, all the ships and fortresses fired.

A majestic mausoleum had been erected in the See, with grand columns, a canopy and a tomb decorated with gold and many candles; at the four corners of the said mausoleum hung rich crystal candelabra with silver candlesticks. The music was divided into two choirs. See H.A.G., *Vice-Reis,* 650, ff. 44-8.

Conclusion

The acquisition of the New Conquests, broadening the frontiers up to the natural limits, conferred geo-political amplitude to the Goan territory. This simultaneously brought prestige to the State helping it to recover from the damage caused by the loss of the Northern Province in 1739.

With a marked ethnic and religious population structure, albeit suffering a demographic recession; with a government centred on the person of the Governor or the Viceroy, notwithstanding the attempts made to simplify the administrative and bureaucratic machinery, Goa, as well as other parcels of the Portuguese Empire, attended to important social reforms absorbed in the larger context of the Lights and the humanitarian measures in vogue in Europe.

The intervention of the central government in the destinies of India translated into a copious legislation aimed at reformulating the economy, finances, administration, religious practice, education and teaching. Pombaline reforms then gave way to some important happenings, such as the suppression of the Jesuits; the extinction of the Inquisition tribunals and the High Court of Goa; a policy of tolerance toward non-Christians; the filling up of local cadres with Indians; new educational models and objectives, etc.

This period thus witnessed the promotion of the local Goans who gradually rose to the ranks of the army and the various posts of public administration, which aspect is still more evident in relation to the local, and mainly secular, clergy. Directing the parishes, the clergy then began to have an active role and considerable influence with the populations. The Goan priest was certainly an important agent in the gestation of a culture marked by the interpenetrating of Eastern and Western elements and by a certain 'Indianization' of the local habits. He decidedly contributed toward the formation of an autonomic conscience, soon resisted by the local and central government. It is in this context that the Pinto Conspiracy took place, which was delineated by ecclesiastics.

The social repercussions of these measures were felt before long. They may have not been spectacular (consider the slow evolution of the social events), but they did represent an irreversible impetus in the progressive conquering of civil rights by the Christian Goan, with a great impact on his future.

It was in this age and social-cultural ambience that the Goan exercised his adaptability, in a quest for his own identity in habitation, furniture, music, cuisine, as witnessed by his rich day-to-day living. In the field of architecture, the Indo-Portuguese style, contrived in the eighteenth century, according to some researchers, could be interpreted as a form of affirmation by this people who not only assimilated the artistic tendencies of the West but also filtered them though their Oriental sensibility. We believe, therefore, that the Goan – perhaps better than any one else – combines the inter-culturality that has always characterized him and is now well defined in the Indo-Portuguese culture of our time.

[illegible]

[illegible] the Pinto Conspiracy took place, which [illegible]

[illegible]

[illegible] the Goan [illegible]

[illegible] of the Indo-Portuguese [illegible] of that time.

*Glossary**

Addav	The cutting of paddy sheaves, which used to take place on 24 November, first in Taleigão, and continued at the Cathedral and in front of the Government Secretariat, in the capital city. Here it had a martial nature.
Ayurvedic Medicine	Largely employs plants to cure illnesses. The medicines are prepared from leaves, roots and barks, collected on particular days and following certain criteria. This knowledge is kept secret and handed on from father to son, and is never give away.
Bhandari	People of the Sudra caste, whose work is to extract *sur* and distil *urrak*.
Begarim	Worker, day labourer, who carries loads on the head.
Bosta	Cowdung used for flooring. Among the Hindus the act of coating the floor with dung has a liturgical meaning, for the cow and its excrement are considered holy.
Cartaz	Safe-conduct or passport issued by the Portuguese authorities, indispensable for navigation by non-Christians. This practice

* In the preparation of this Glossary we mainly made use of the following works: Sebastião Rodolfo Dalgado, *Glossário Luso-Asiático,* vols. I & II, Coimbra, Imprensa da Universidade, 1919, 1921; *Hobson-Jobson: A Glossary of Colloquial Anglo-Indian Words and Phrases ...,* by Col. Henry Yule and A.C. Burnell, new edition, New Delhi, Munshiram Manoharlal, n.d. Since in footnotes along the text we did explain the meanings of many other terms, we do not think it necessary to have them included here.

	was in vogue in the eastern seas, before the arrival of the Portuguese.
Crioulo	Indo-Portuguese term used with two meanings: adopted son and famulus brought up at home from infancy.
Dessaiado, or *deshmukhi*	A type of feud granted to a local chief of the highest castes (Desai) on the condition that he will serve the overlord in peace and war.
Dharmashastra	One of the codes of Hindu law, organized by authoritative jurists, with guidelines on political, civil, social, domestic and religious life.
Dukatto	Custom of not cooking on the day of death of any family member and consuming food offered by neighbours.
Fama	A solemn blessing of the picture of the main saint of the parish, whose feast is to be celebrated. It takes place on the eve of the novena. The picture is hoisted in the churchyard for the information of the public.
Faraz	Person belonging to one of the two of meanest castes in Goa, doing menial jobs, as grave-diggers, palanquin or *machila* carriers, village criers, etc.
Feni	Coconut or cashew liquor.
Gumott	Drum used for accompanying songs and folk dances.
Jains	Followers of Jainism, one of the three great Indian religions that, like Buddhism, believes in the transmigration of souls. They live mainly in Gujarat and as businessmen they are also spread throughout South Asia and East Africa. The Europeans usually know them as Banias.
Karepo	Translucent conch shell used in windowpanes instead of glass.
Khetri	Konkani for the Sanskrit word Kshatriya (warrior caste).

Koli	Sudra caste which in Gujarat and Konkan is engaged in fishery and horticulture.
Kulkarni	Scribe of the village *comunidade.*
Kumb	Measure of dry capacity. It has 20 *khandi* = 20 *kuddav.* One *kuddav* = 2 *paili*; 1 *paili* = 4 *poddi*; 1 *podd,* or measure = 2 *naktti*; 1 *naktti* = 2 *ardnaktti*; 1 *ardnaktti* = 2 *girnatti*; 1 *girnatti* = 2 *solavem*; 1 *solavem* = 2 *bot-solavem.* The litre is to a podda 1:099825. As the khandi has 160 poddi, it is equal to 159.62 litres and a kuddav, 7.986 litres.
Kunnbi	Person of the Sudra caste and farmer on the western coast of India.
Tangoli	Sheet worn between the buttocks, with one end tied to a cord behind the waist and the other hanging in front.
Mainato	Laundry man.
Manilheiro	Bangle and bracelet vendor.
Mantra	Formula used during sacrifices in Vedic times.
Maratha	Name of a warrior caste or a people of meridional India, whose language is Marathi, from the Indo-Aryan group of languages.
Mesada or *torna-boda*	Reception at the house of the bride's parents, a few days after the wedding.
Mit-Gauddo (saleiro)	Member of one of the Goan castes, commonly known as *saleiro,* as his main occupation is to salt-making.
Mocadão (Mukddam)	Skipper or owner, chief of crew, overseer, major-domo, farm manager, coconut garden administrator. In the eighteenth century he often appears as a chief of crew or coconut garden administrator.
Naique (Naik)	Generic term for 'captain or chief of native infantry men' and sometimes 'corporal or captain' in general.
Namoxi	Cultivable land belonging to an agricultural community whose produce is devoted to the cult or sustenance of the village servers.

Novendio	A practice whereby the relatives keep company to the mourning family, staying in their house for nine days.
Patamar	Messenger, wayfarer, 'land courier'.
Patel	Village chief managing its affairs and acting as the instrument of communication with the governmental authorities.
Purana	Legendary book of Hindu mythology, with norms on different aspects of life.
Ranne	Noble caste in the New Conquests, with belligerent tendencies.
Razangonn	Central or inner patio around which rooms are arranged in a Hindu household.
Sardessaiado, or *Sardeshmukhi*	An area larger than a *dessaiado (deshmukhi)*, owned by a *sar-dessai* or principal Dessai (Sardeshmukh).
Sati	Ceremony of voluntary immolation in the husband's pyre by a Hindu widow.
Sepoy	Local soldier, disciplined and uniformed almost in the European style, in India and Portuguese Africa.
Sura, Sur	Juice extracted from the spathe of several Indian palm trees, especially the coconut tree.
Tullos	Sacred plant adored by the Hindus. Normally found in the inner patio of the house or at the main door.
Urrak	A kind of liquor obtained in the first distillation of *sur.* A stronger variety is called *feni.*
Vaidya	Hindu professional ayurvedic doctor (see Ayurvedic medicine).
Vanni	Caste related to the Chardós. Its members are brokers or merchants.
Varzeiro	Very frequently used to refer to the owner or cultivator of a rice field in India.
Xenddo	Hair bun at the back of the neck, around which it is customary to fit a flower wreath.

Xerafins, tangas and réis	Monetary unit of the age. One xerafim had 5 tangas and one tanga, 60 reis.
Zagor	Comic, rough and sarcastic drama in Konkani.

Bibliography

1. PRIMARY SOURCES

BRAZIL

ARQUIVO PÚBLICO DO ESTADO DA BAÍA (S. Salvador)
Ordens Régias: cód. 63-5 (1744-61; 1761; 1762).

BIBLIOTECA NACIONAL DO RIO DE JANEIRO
Armário 25, 2;
Cód. 1-32, 28, 29 no. 1;
Cód. 1-25, 28, 6;
Cód. 1-32, 34, 25;
Cód. 1-32, 34, 20;
Cód. 1-32, 34, 21.

INSTITUTO HISTÓRICO E GEOGRÁFICO BRASILEIRO (Rio de Janeiro)
Lata 52, doc. 2;
Lata 81, doc. 3;
Lata 88, doc. 2;
Lata 125, doc. 8;
Lata 205, doc. 1.

INDIA

ARCHIVES OF THE PATRIARCHAL CURIA OF GOA (Panjim)
Livros de Conventos e Igrejas (Books of Convents and Churches):
No. 6 (Church of S. José de Daugim);
No. 13 (Church of Nossa Senhora da Penha de França).
Oficios e Portarias, Books 1, 2.
Róis da Cristandade (Church Rolls):
Book I (*1773-1775*);
Book II (*1775-1784*);
Book III (*1784-1797*);
Book IV (*1798-1810*).
Visitas Pastorais (Pastoral Visits):
Book I. Salsete. 1 May 1747 - 26 October 1784;
Book II. Ilhas. 23 July 1747 - 17 April 1750;

Book III. Salsete. 1 March 1752 - 27 May 1752;
Book IV. Ilhas. 21 February 1752 - 30 March 1753;
Book V. Salsete. 24 October 1754 - 8 February 1755;
Book VI. Salsete. 20 November 1759 - 16 March 1760;
Book VII. Bardez. 12 October 1760 - 13 January 1761;
Book IX. Salsete. 5 November 1764 - 19 December 1764;
Book X. Bardez. 10 December 1765 - 1 February 1766;
Book XI. Ilhas. 1 December 1766 - 23 September 1767;
Book XII. Salsete. 21 November 1771 - 12 January 1772;
Book XIII. Bardez. 17 October 1772 - 21 September 1773;
Book XIV. Ilhas. 17 February 1774 - 5 March 1774;
Book XV. Bardez. 4 September 1779 - 14 June 1783;
Book XVI. Ilhas. 22 April 1779 - 31 May 1782;
Book XVII. Salsete. 10 October 1783 - 12 January 1785;
Book XVIII. Ilhas. 6 November 1785 - 30 December 1786;
Book XIX. Bardez. 22 October 1786 - 23 December 1786;
Book XX. Salsete. 17 October 1787 - 16 December 1787;
Book XXI. Ilhas. 19 October 1788 - 17 December 1788;
Book XXII. Ilhas. 25 September 1791 - 22 November 1791;
Book XXIII. Bardez. 18 October 1792 - 17 December 1792;
Book XXIV. Ilhas. 19 October 1794 - 30 November 1794;
Book XXV. Bardez. 19 October 1795 - 17 December 1795;
Book XXVI. Ilhas. 5 November 1797 - 14 December 1797;
Book XXVII. Bardez. 21 October 1798 - 11 January 1799;
Book XXVIII. Salsete. 21 October 1799 - 21 February 1800;

Note: Book VIII refers to visits to the Canara region, outside the territory of Goa and has therefore not been included.

HISTORICAL ARCHIVES OF GOA (PANJIM)

Acordãos e Assentos da Câmara de Goa: cód 7742 (1793-1823);
Almotaçaria: cód. 7767, 7768 (1791-7);
Alvaras e Provisões de Sua Magestade: cód 2614 (1764-6);
Anais Históricos: cód. 7868 (1787-1849);
Anais da Câmara de Goa;
Assentos e Juramentos da Câmara de Goa: cód 7762 (1765-1793).
Cartas e Ordens:
Cód. 879 (1748-59);
Cód. 880 (1750-1);
Cód. 892 (1768-81);
Cód. 912 (1787-8).
Catecúmenos de Betim: cód. 1554-5 (1733-1843). Registration of Baptism.
Cristandade: cód. 7693 (1562-1843). Laws in favour of Christendom.

Feitoria de Surrate: cód. 2604 (1790-1792).
Santa Casa da Misericórdia de Goa: cód. 10424, 10429.
Monções do Reino: Books 118-A, 118-B, 122-A, 122B, 123-A, 123-B, 124-A, 124-B, 125-A, 125-B, 126-A, 126-B, 126-C, 127-A, 127-B, 128-A, 128-B, 129-A, 129-B, 130-A, 130-B, 131-A, 131-B, 132-A, 132-B, 133-A, 133-B, 134-A, 134-B, 135-A, 135-B, 136, 137-A, 137-B, 138-A, 138-B, 138-C, 138-D, 139, 140-A, 140-B, 141-A, 141-B, 142-A, 142-B, 142-C, 143-A, 143-B, 144-A, 144-B, 144-C, 145-A, 145-B, 146, 147-A, 147-B, 148-A, 148-B, 149-A, 149-B, 150-A, 150-B, 151, 152-A, 152-B, 152-C, 154, 156, 157-A, 157-B, 158-A, 158-B, 158-C, 159-A, 159-B, 159-C, 159-D, 160, 161-A, 161-B, 161-C, 161-D, 161-E, 161-F, 162-A, 162-B, 162-C, 163-A, 163-B, 164-A, 164-B, 164-C, 164-D, 164-E, 164-F, 164-G, 165-A, 165-B, 165-C, 166, 167-A, 167-B, 167-C, 167-D, 168-A, 168-B, 168-C, 168-D, 169-A, 169-B, 169-C, 170-A, 170-B, 170-C, 171-A, 171-B, 172-A, 172-B, 173, 174-A, 174-B, 175, 176-A, 176-B, 177-A, 177-B, 178-A, 178-B, 179-A, 179-B, 180-A, 180-B, 181-A, 181-B, 182.
Pensões de sendi: cód. 1921, 1925.
Senado de Goa:
General Registration No. 7710 (1777-8);
General Registration No. 7711 (1777-1800).
Serviços:
No. 1374 (1751-75);
No. 1375 (1775-1829).

ARCHIVE OF THE CHURCH OF POMBURPÁ (Bardez)
Livro de Decretos e Pastorais (1795-1810).

CENTRAL LIBRARY (Panjim)
Manuscript 46-B.

Italy

ARQUIVUM SECRETUM APOSTOL. VATICANUM (Rome)
S. Congr. Concili Relationes: Ad limina visits of the Archbishopric of Goa: 1757, 1769, 1802.

Portugal

ARQUIVO HISTÓRICO ULTRAMARINO (Lisbon)
Caixas 46, 46-A (372) (1706-50).
Caixas sem número de ordem:
1750-4;
1755-6;
1757-8;
1760-4.

Caixas sem número de ordem e sem data (3).
Cód. 205, 206, 214, 215, 425, 428, 430, 438, 439, 441, 442, 444, 447, 494, 496, 512-520.
Cód. 1308, nos. 119, 121, 125, 186.
Maços 2 (25), 2 (246), 3 (244), 4 (245), 7 (26), 7 (279), 11 (21), 11 (275), 14 (11), 14 (274), 15 (13), 15 (271), 16-A (291), 17 (14), 17 (265), 18 (264), 26 (59), 26 (296), 33 (53), 33 (288) 35 (300), 44 (42), 53 (303), 58 (81) 59 (298), 63 (321), 64 (75), 64 (322), 65 (295), 76 (63), 77 (62), 78-A (55), 79 (56), 80 (57), 81 (104), 82 (103), 83 (106), 84 (105), 85 (108), 86 (107), 87 (98), 88 (97), 89 (100), 90 (99), 91 (102), 91 (101), 93 (91), 94 (92), 95 (94), 96 (93), 97 (96), 98 (95), 99 (86), 100 (85), 101 (88), 102 (87), 103 (90), 104 (89), 105 (82), 106 (83), 107 (84), 108 (124), 109 (123), 110 (126), 111 (125), 112 (120), 113 (119), 115 (122), 116 (116), 117 (115), 118 (118), 119 (117), 120 (112), 121 (111), 122 (114), 123 (113), 124 (109), 125 (110), 126 (142), 127 (141), 128 (144), 129 (143), 130 (138), 131 (137), 132 (140), 133 (139), 134 (134), 135 (133), 136 (129), 137 (136), 138 (130), 139 (135), 140 (132), 141 (131), 142 (127), 143 (128), 144 (160), 145 (159), 146 (162), 147 (161), 148 (156).

ARQUIVOS NACIONAIS / TORRE DO TOMBO (Lisbon)
Conselho Geral do Santo Oficio, Papéis avulsos: maço 6-2434
Ministério do Reino, maços 313, 317, 603.
Junta da Real Fazenda do Estado da India. Books 27, 32, 37, 38, 40, 41, 46, 50, 51, 54, 60, 61, 63, 66-9, 73, 74, 77, 78.

BIBLIOTECA DA ACADEMIA DAS CIÊNCIAS DE LISBOA
Série Vermelha, cód. 284, 286, 287, 634.

BIBLIOTECA DA AJUDA (Lisbon)
51-VII-27, nos. 1, 33;
51-VII-33
54-XI-39, no. 77;
54-V-12, no. 6.

BIBLIOTECA NACIONAL (Lisbon)
Cód. 166, 175-7, 203, 233, 235, 308, 607, 853, 866.
Manuscripts:
1, no. 4;
28, no. 24;
75, no. 18;
79, no. 10;
174, no. 176;
201, no. 176;

211, no. 13;
245, nos. 129, 146, 154;
247, no. 23.
Pombalina 610, 614, 618, 641, 643, 684, 742, 743.

FILMOTECA ULTRAMARINA PORTUGUESA (Lisbon)
Cópias de Vários Documentos (1603-1793).
Provisões e alvaras a favor da Cristandade (1533-1831).

BIBLIOTECA GERAL DA UNIVERSIDADE DE COIMBRA
Reservados: cód. 634.

BIBLIOTECA PÚBLICA E ARQUIVO DISTRITAL DE ÉVORA
Cód.:
CXVI/2-11, nos. 27, 32;
CXVI/1-39, no. 16;
CXVI/2-21, 1788;
CXVI/1-19.

AUTHOR'S COLLECTION
Cód containing instruction for the Visitors (eighteenth century).

2. PUBLISHED SOURCES

ABREU, Miguel Vicente de, *Noção de Alguns Filhos Distinctos da India Portugueza Que se Illustraram Fora da Patria,* ordenada por ..., Nova Goa, Imprensa Nacional, 1874.

———, *Real Mosteiro da Santa Monica de Goa. Memoria Histórica,* Nova Goa, Imprensa Nacional, 1882.

AFONSO, Pedro Correia, 'A contribuição portuguesa para o desenvolvimento dos recursos naturais da Índia e do Oriente', in *Boletim do Instituto Vasco da Gama,* no. 47, Bastorá, Tip. Rangel, 1940.

AFONSO, R. Correia, 'A Evolução do Municipalismo na India Portuguesa', in *A Índia Portuguesa,* vol. II, Nova Goa, Imprensa Nacional, 1923.

ALBUQUERQUE, Diogo Vieira de Tovar e, *Index Alfabetico, Chronologico e Remissivo das Reaes Ordens expedidas para o Governo do Estado da India, desde o anno de 1568, até o de 1811, e de muitas partes dadas pelo mesmo Governo á Corte, comprehendidas em 192 Livros, que existem na Secretaria de Estado da India,* Nova Goa, Imprensa Nacional, 1918.

ALBUQUERQUE, Justiniano, 'Famílias portuguesas estabelecidas no Chorão', in *O Oriente Português,* vol. XVI, nos. 5-6, 9-10; vol. XVII, nos. 3-4, Nova Goa, Imprensa Nacional, 1920.

d'ALBUQUERQUE, Padre Manuel João Socrates, *Summario Chronologico dos Decretos Diocesanos do Arcebispado de Goa desde 1775 até 1900,* Goa, Bastorá, 1900.

Albuquerque, Viriato A. Caetano Brás de, 'Baptismos solemnes em Goa', in *O Oriente Português,* vol. II, no. 9, Nova Goa, Imprensa Nacional, 1905.

——, 'Casa de Catechumenos em Goa', in *O Oriente Portuguez,* vol. I, no. 7, Nova Goa, Imprensa Nacional, 1904.

——, 'Congregação do Oratório de S. Filipe Nery em Goa', in *O Oriente Português,* vol. II, no. 7, Nova Goa, Imprensa Nacional, 1905.

——, 'Ilha dos Fidalgos', in *O Oriente Portuguêz,* vol. I, nos. 10-11, Nova Goa, Imprensa Nacional, 1904.

——, 'O Seminario de Chorão', in *O Oriente Portuguez,* vol. I, no. 4, Nova Goa, Imprensa Nacional, 1904.

Almeida, Fortunato, *História da Igreja em Portugal,* new edition prepared and organized by Damião Peres, vols. III-IV, Porto, Livraria Civilização, 1970-1.

Almeida, Luis Fernand de, *Aclimatação de plantas do Oriente no Brazil durante os séculos XVII e XVIII,* offprint of *Revista Portuguesa de História,* XV, Coimbra, 1976.

——, *Alexandre de Gusmão, o Brazil e o Tratado de Madrid,* Coimbra, Instituto Nacional de Investigação Científica - Centro de História da Sociedade e da Cultura - Universidade de Coimbra, 1990.

Alorna, Marques de, *Instrucção do Exm° ..., ao seu Successor o Exm° Vice-Rei Marques de Tavora,* 2nd edn., rectificada ... por Felippe Nery Xavier, Nova Goa, Imprensa Nacional, 1856.

Andrade, António Alberto Banha de, *Contribuição para a História da Mentalidade Pedagógica em Portugal,* Lisbon, Imprensa Nacional, 1982.

——, 'Os Hospitaleiros de S. João de Deus na Índia', in *Portugal em Africa,* vol. XIV, no. 80, Lisbon, March-April 1957.

——, '*Luís António Vernei, soldado na India*', offprint of *Boletim do Instituto Vasco da Gama,* no. 75, Bastorá, Tip. Rangel, 1958.

——, 'Pombal e os Oratorianos', in *Brotéria,* vol. LXXVII, Lisbon, 1963.

——, *A Reforma Pombalina dos Estudos Secundários no Brazil,* S. Paulo, Saraiva-Edusp, 1978.

——, *A Reforma Pombalina dos Estudos Secundários (1759-1771) (Contribuição para a História da Pedagogia em Portugal),* vol. I (2 pts.), Coimbra, Acta Universitatis Conimbrigensis, 1981-4.

——, 'A reforma pombalina dos estudos secundários no arquipélago dos Açores (1st phase, 1759-71)', in *Arquipélago. Revista da Universidade dos Açores,* Série Ciências Humanas, special edition, 1983.

——, *Vernei e a Cultura do seu Tempo,* Coimbra, Acta Universitatis Conimbrigensis, 1966.

Anthony, Philomena, 'Colonial Brazil and Goa—Visible and Invisible links', in *Purabhilekh-Puratatva,* vol. VII, no. 1, Goa, January-June 1990.

ARAUJO, D. Manoel do Monte Rodrigues de, *Compendio de Theologia Moral,* 2 pts., Porto, 1853.

ARCOS, Maria Fernanda, *Estado y Clero en las Filipinas del Siglo XVIII,* Mexico, Universidad Autonoma Metropolitana - Unidad Iztapalapa División de Ciencias Sociales y Humanidades, 1988.

Arquivo das Colónias, vol. I, no. 15, Lisbon, Ministério das Colónias, 1917.

ARRUDA, José Jobson de Andrade, 'A produção económica', in *Nova História da Espansão Portuguesa,* dir. de Joel Serrão, A.H. de Oliveira Marques, vol. VIII: *O Império Luso-Brazileiro. 1750-1822,* coordinated by Maria Beatriz Nizza da Silva, Lisbon, Estampa, 1986.

d'AYALLA, Frederico Diniz, *Goa Antiga e Moderna,* Lisbon, 1888.

AZEVEDO, A.E. de Almeida, *As Comunidades de Goa. História das Instituições Antigas,* Lisbon, 1890.

AZEVEDO, António do Carmo, 'Pintos' Revolt of 1787', in *Armed Coups Against Portuguese Regime,* ed. Vikas V. Desai, Canacona, Centro Promotor de Instrução, 1986.

AZEVEDO, Carlos de, 'A Cidade do Porto nos Relatórios das Visitas 'Ad Limina' do Arquivo do Vaticano', in *Revista de História,* vol. II: *Actas do Colóquio "O Porto na Época Moderna",* Porto, Instituto Nacional de Investigação Científica, 1979.

d'AZEVEDO, Manuel Felicíssimo Louzada d'Araújo, 'Asia Portugueza. Primeira memoria sobre as principaes causas remotas da decadencia dos Portuguezes na Asia, pelo Socio e Secretario da Associação, ...', in *Annaes Maritimos e Coloniaes,* 2nd series, no. 2, Lisbon, Imprensa Nacional, 1842.

———, 'Memoria acerca da educação Publica nos Estados da India', in *Annaes Maritimos e Coloniaes,* 2nd series, no. 1, Lisbon, Imprensa Nacional, 1841.

———, 'Segunda Memoria descriptiva e estatistica das Possessões Portuguezas na Asia, e seu estado actual', in *Annaes Maritimos e Coloniaes,* 2nd series, nos. 4-11, 1842; 3rd series, nos. 1-2, and 4-11, 1843; 4th series, nos. 1-2, 7, 9, 1844, Lisbon, Imprensa Nacional (parte não oficial).

BAIÃO, António, *A Inquisição de Goa,* vol. I, Lisbon, Academia das Ciências, 1949.

———, 'Origem e Estabelecimento da Inquisição de Goa', in *I Congresso da História da Expansão Portuguesa no Mundo. Publicações. 2nd section.* O Oriente, Lisbon, 1938.

BARRETO, Antoni[No] José Nicolau, *Resumo das Ceremonias Eclesiasticas, que se devem observar nas Funções Publicas e Solemnes, Festivas e Funebres, Frequentes nas Igrejas Parochiaes,* Nova Goa, Imprensa Nacional, 1846.

BARRETO, Padre [Francisco Xavier da] Expectação, *Quadros Biográphicos dos Padres Illustres de Goa,* Bastorá, 1899.

Barreto, Justiniano Augusto da Piedade, *Summario chronologico da legislação portugueza desde as ordenações do reino de 1603 até 1860,* Margão, Imprensa, Nacional, 1864.

Barros, Caetano Manuel de, *Novas Aplaudidas em Obséquio da Notícia que veio de chegar com vida à cidade de Goa a ... Senhora Marquesa de Távora e o ... Senhor Marquês do Mesmo Título, seu Esposo, Vice-Rei e Capitão-general de Aqueles estados,* Lisbon, 1752.

Barros, Joseph, 'Língua e Cultura Portuguesa em Goa. (Sua génese histórica)', offprint of *Boletim do Instituto Menezes Bragança,* no. 147, Bastorá, 1985.

——, 'A Religious Tradition at St. Anne's Church', paper presented at the University of Goa, seminar held between 19 and 20 February 1991.

Bayly, Chris A., *Indian Society the Making of the British Empire,* Cambridge, Cambridge University Press, 1988.

Beaumont, Souvenir de [pseudonym], *Voyage d'Innigo de Biervillas, Portugais, a la côte de Malabar, Goa, Batavia & autres lieux des Indes Orientales,* Paris, Chez Gregorie-Antoine-Dupuis, Grand' Salle du Palais, au Saint Esprit, 1736.

Biker, Júlio Firmino Judice, *Collecção de tratados e concertos de pazes que o Estado da India Portugueza fez com os reis e senhores com quem teve relações nas partes da Asia e Africa Oriental desde o principio da conquista até ao fim do século XVIII,* pts. VII, VIII, Lisbon, 1885; rpt. Asian Educational Services, New Delhi-Madras, 1995.

Blanco, Maria Manuela Sobral, 'O Estado Português da Índia da Rendição de Ormuz à Perda de Cochim (1622-1663)', vol. I: Estudo Histórico, Lisbon, 1992 (doctoral thesis, photostat).

Boléo, Oliveira, *Apontamentos para uma Geografia Física de Goa,* Lisbon, Agência Geral do Ultramar, 1955.

Boletim do Conselho Ultramarino. Legislação Antiga, vol. II, Lisbon, 1867.

Boletim Oficial do Estado da Índia, nos. 43-57, Nova Goa, 1879.

Borges, Charles J., *The Economics of Goa Jesuits. An Explanation of their Rise and Fall, 1542-1759,* New Delhi, Concept Publishing Company, 1994.

Boschi, Caio César, *O assistencialismo na Capitania do Ouro,* offprint of *Revista de História,* no. 116, S. Paulo, 1984.

——, *As directrizes metropolitanas, a realidade colonial e as irmandades mineiras,* Brazil, Belo Horizonte, 1987.

——, *Os leigos e o poder. Irmandades laicas e política colonizadora em Minas Gerais,* S. Paulo, Editora Ática, 1986.

——, 'As Visitas Diocesanas e a Inquisição na Colónia', in *Inquisição* (comunicações apresentadas ao 1º Congresso Luso-Brazileiro sobre Inquisição, realizado em Lisboa de 17 a 20 de Fevereiro de 1987), vol. II, Lisbon, Univ. Editora, 1989.

Boxer, Charles R., 'Casados and Cabotagem in the Estado da Índia, 16th/17th Centuries', in *II Seminário Internacional de História Indo-Portuguesa. Actas,* Lisbon, Instituto de Investigação Científica Tropical - Centro de Estudos de História e Cartografia Antiga, 1985.

——, *A Idade de Ouro do Brazil,* S. Paulo, Editora Nacional, 1969.

——, *O Império Colonial Português (1415-1825)*, Lisbon, Edições 70, 1981.

——, *A Índia Portuguesa em meados do século XVII,* Lisbon, Edições 70, 1982.

——, *Portuguese Society in the tropics. The Municipal Councils of Goa, Macao, Bahia and Luanda (1510-1800),* Madison and Milwaukee, Univ. of Wisconsin Press, 1965.

——, 'Some Possible Fields of Research in the History of Portuguese India (16th-18th Centuries)', in *Indo-Portuguese History. Sources & Problems,* ed. John Correia-Afonso, S.J., Bombay, Oxford University Press, 1981.

Bragança, Menezes, 'A Educação e o Ensino na Índia Portuguesa', in *Índia Portuguesa,* vol. II, Nova Goa, Imprensa Nacional, 1923.

Bras, Gabriel Le, *Études de Sociologie Religieuse,* 2 vols, Paris, P.U.F., 1955-6.

Brito, Raquel Soeiro de, *Goa e as Praças do Norte Revisitadas,* 2nd edn., Lisbon, Comissão Nacional para as Comemorações dos Descobrimentos Portugueses, 1998.

——, 'Notas para o estudo dos modos de vida em Goa', in *Garcia de Orta,* special edition, Lisbon, 1956.

——, 'Notícia do inquérito das aldeias de Goa', in *Garcia de Orta,* vol. 5, no. 4, Lisbon, 1957.

——, 'A terra e a gente na Índia Portuguesa', in *Ultramar,* nos. 7-8, Lisbon, 1962.

Burton, Richard Francis, *Goa and the Blue Mountains or, six months of sick leave,* London, 1851; rpt. California, University of California Press, 1992.

Caetano, Marcello, *O Conselho Ultramarino,* Lisbon, Agência Geral do Ultramar, 1967.

——, 'As reformas pombalinas e post-pombalinas respeitantes ao Ultramar. O novo espírito em que são concebidas', in *História da Expansão Portuguesa no Mundo,* vol. III, Lisbon, Editorial Ática, 1940.

The Cambridge History of India, vol. V, ed. H.H. Dodwell, Cambridge, Cambridge University Press, 1963.

Camilleri, Jean-Luc, 'L'Aculturation des catholiques dans les Vieilles Conquetes de Goa', Aix-en Provence, 1980 (graduate thesis, photostat).

Campos, Plácido da Costa and Francisco Xavier Vas, *Monumenta Goana Eclesiastica,* Nova Goa, 1918.

CARRREIRA, Ernestina, 'Portuguese India in the reign of Tipoo Sultan', in *Moyen Orient at Océan Indien,* vol. 6, 1986.

——, 'Les Kamat et le commerce français en Inde, 1778-1819', in *Moyen Orient & Océan Indien, Middle East & India Ocean XVIe-XIXe s,* no. 7, Paris, Sociéte d' Histoire de l'Orient, 1990.

——, 'Moçambique, Goa e Macau durante as Guerras Napoleónicas. 1801-1810', in *As Relações entre a Índia Portuguesa, a Ásia do Sueste e o Extremo Oriente. Actas do VI Seminário Internacional de História Indo-Portuguesa,* Macao, Lisbon, 1993.

——, 'Os últimos anos da Carreira da Índia', in *A Carreira da Índia e as Rotas dos Estreitos. Actas do VIII Seminário Internacional de História Indo-Portuguesa,* Angra do Heroísmo, 1998.

——, "Índia", in *Nova História da Expansão Portuguesa,* direcção de Joel Serrão e A.H. de Oliveira Marques, vol. X, *O Império Africano 1825-1890,* coordinated by Valentim Alexandre and Jill Dias, Lisbon, Estampa, 1998.

CARVALHO, Joaquim Ramos de, 'A Jurisdição Episcopal Sobre Leigos em Matéria de Pecados Públicos: as Visitas Pastorais e o Comportamento Moral das Populações Portuguesas do Antigo Regime', in *Revista Portuguesa de História,* pt. XXIV, F.L.U.C. - Instituto de História, 15, Lisbon, Teorema, 1989.

—— and José Pedro de Matos Paiva, 'A evolução das visitas pastorais da diocese de Coimbra', in *Ler História,* 15, Lisbon, Teorema, 1989.

—— and José Pedro de Matos Paiva, 'Reportório das Visitas Pastorais da Diocese de Coimbra Séculos XVII, XVIII e XIX', in *Boletim do Arquivo da Universidade de Coimbra,* vol. VII, Coimbra, 1985.

CARVALHO, Rómulo de, *História do Ensino em Portugal,* Lisbon, Fundação Calouste Gulbenkian, 1986.

CASTELO-BRANCO, Maria dos Remédios and Fernando Castelo-Branco, 'Goa vista por alguns viajantes estrangeiros (de seiscentos a oitocentos)', in *Stvdia,* no. 49, Lisbon, 1989.

CATAO, Padre Francisco Xavier Gomes, *O Primeiro Seminário de Goa,* Bastorá, Tip. Rangel, 1955.

——, *Regimento de 1614 e os Actuais Estatutos do Cabido da Sé Metropolitana de Goa e Damão Primacial do Oriente e Patriarcal das Índias Orientais,* com prefácio e notas de ..., offprint of *Stvdia,* no. 9, Lisbon, 1961.

——, 'Vigários colados na Arquidiocese de Goa', in *Boletim Eslesiástico da Arquidiocese de Goa,* year XIII, Bastorá, 1954.

CHARMOT, P., *La Pédagogie des Jésuites, ses principes, son actualité,* Paris, Spés, 1943.

CHAVES, Baltasar Manuel de, *Anal Indico Historico do Governo do Ilustrissimo e Excelentissimo Senhor Marques de Tavora, Vice-Rei, Capitão-General da India,* Lisbon, Imprensa Nacional, 1754.

CIDADE, Hernani, *A literatura portuguesa e a expansão ultramarina,* 2 vols., Coimbra, Arménio Amado Ed., 1963-4.

COLAÇO, Agostinho da Piedade, 'A abolição da escravatura', in *Boletim do Instituto Vasco da Gama,* no. 38, Bastorá, Tip. Rangel, 1938.

Constituiçoens do Arcebispado de Goa Approvadas pello Primeiro Cõcilio Prouincial, Anno 1568, Lisbon, 1592.

Constituições do Arcebispado de Goa, Compostas, e Addicionadas pello Excelentissimo e Reverendissimo Senhor Dom Antonio Taveira de Neiva Brum ..., corregidas, e Accrescentadas pelo Ecellentissimo e Reverendissimo Senhor Dom Frei Manoel de Santa Catharina ..., Lisbon, Impressão Regia, 1810.

CORREIA, Alberto Carlos Germano da Silva, *Les bayadères et les autres courtisantes de L'Inde Portugaise,* Bastorá, Imprensa Nacional, 1940.

——, 'Cruzamentos indo-europeus', in *O Oriente Português,* no. 34, Lisbon, 1916.

——, 'O Culto de Agni em Goa — Uma Visão dos Tempos Védicos', in *O Mundo Português,* vol. 1 (9-10), Lisbon, 1934.

——, *O ensino de Medicina e Cirurgia em Goa nos séculos XVII, XVIII e XIX. História do ensino médico-cirurgico no Hospital Real de Goa, antes da fundação da Escola Médico-Cirúrgica de Nova Goa,* Bastorá, Tip. Rangel, 1941.

——, *Les Eurasiens de l'Inde Portugaise,* Bastorá, Tip. Rangel, 1940.

——, *História da Colonização Portuguesa na Índia Portuguesa,* Nova Goa, Imp. Nacional, 1917.

——, 'Os Luso-Descendentes da Índia', in *Boletim Eclesiástico da Arquidiocese de Goa,* 2nd series, year IV, nos. 1-2, 4, 6-7, Bastorá, Tip. Rangel, 1945, 1946.

——, *Les Musulmans de l'Inde Portuguaise, Histoire, Demographie, Anthropometrie, Morphologie médicale, Anthropo-sérologie, Ethnographie,* Bastorá, Tip. Tangel, 1937.

——, *La Vieille Goa,* Bastorá, Imprensa Nacional, 1931.

CORTESÃO, Jaime, *Alexandre de Gusmão e o Tratado de Madrid,* vol. 1, Lisbon, Livros Horizonte, 1984.

——, 'Domínio Ultramarino', in *História de Portugal,* directed by Damião Peres, vol. VI, Barcelos, Portucalense Editora, 1934.

CORTE-REAL, António de Mendonça, 'Familias portuguesas estabelecidas na India, cuja varonia se extinguiu', in *O Oriente Português,* vol. XVI, nos. 3-4, Nova Goa, Imprensa Nacional, 1919-20.

COSTA, A.D., *The Christianisation of the Goa Islands,* Bombay, St. Xavier's College, 1965.

COSTA, Adolfo, 'Orfãs d'El-Rei e as Mulheres Portuguesas vindas à Índia durante o século XVI', *Boletim do Instituto Vasco da Gama,* no. 47, Bastorá, Tipografia Rangel, 1940.

Costa, Aleixo Manuel da, 'Perfis dalguns goeses de antanho vistos pelos seus contemporâneos', in *Boletim do Instituto Menezes de Bragança,* nos. 111, 114, 117, Bastorá, Tip. Rangel, 1976-7.

———, *Dicionário de Literatura Goesa,* 3 vols., Macao, Instituto Cultural de Macau e Fundação Oriente, undated.

Costa, Bernardino C. da, 'Geografia Física e Política', in *A Índia Portuguesa,* vol. I, Nova Goa, Imprensa Nacional, 1923.

Costa, C.F. Alvares de, 'Um Boticário e dois médicos antigos de Goa (1700-1800)', in *O Oriente Portuguez,* vol. XIV, nos. 9-10, Nova Goa, Imprensa Nacional, 1917.

Costa, Constâncio Roque de, *Les Communautés des Villages à Goa,* Lisbon, Imprensa Nacional, 1892.

Costa, Francisco Barbosa da and João de Sousa, *Visitas de Gulpilhares,* Vila Nova de Gaia, 1986.

Costa, Francisco Xavier, *Série dos capitulares da Sé Primacial e Patriarcal de Goa com Apêndices e Notas,* Nova Goa, Tip. Bragança & Co., 1915.

Costa, João Paulo, 'O Império e os Diplomatas da Restauração', in *Stvdia,* 48, Lisbon, Instituto de Investigação Científica Tropical, 1989.

Costa, Maria Helena de Teves, 'Livros Escolares de Latim e Grego adoptados pela Reforma Pombalina dos Estudos Menores', in *Arquivos do Centro Cultural Português,* XIV, Paris, Fundação Calouste Gulbenkian, 1979.

Coutinho, Sales da Veiga, 'Medicina Portuguesa na India', in *Boletim do Instituto Vasco da Gama,* no. 47, Bastorá, Tip. Rangel, 1940.

Couto, José Jorge da Costa, 'O Colégio dos Jesuitas do Recife e o destino do seu património', Lisbon, Fac. de Letras, 1990 (Masters thesis, photostated) Lisbon.

Cruz, António, *A reforma pombalina do ensino das Humanidades (Novos subsídios para o seu estudo),* Porto, Faculty of Letters, University of Oporto, 1956.

Cruz, Soror Isabel da (Prioress), 'Relação completa das religiosas do Mosteiro de Santa Monica de Goa', in *O Oriente Português,* no. 203, Nova Goa, Imprensa Gonçalves, 1932.

Dalgado, Sebastião Rodolfo, *Glossário Luso-Asiático,* 2 vols., Coimbra, Imprensa da Universidade, 1919, 1921.

———, *Florilégio de Provérbios Concanis, Traduzidos, Explicados, Comentados e Comparados com os de Línguas Asiáticas e Europeias,* Coimbra, Imprensa da Universidade, 1922.

Deleury, Gui, *Les Indes Florissantes. Anthologie des Voyageurs Français (1750-1820),* Paris, Ed. Robert Laffont, 1991.

Dellon, *Narração da Inquisição de Goa, escripta em francez por Mr. ... vertida em portuguez e accrescentada com varias memorias, notas, documentos, e um appendice, contendo a noticia que da mesma inquisição deu o inglez*

Claudio Buchanan, por Miguel Vicente de Abreu, Nova Goa, Imprensa Nacional, 1866.

DELUMEAU, Jean M., *Le Catholicisme entre Luther et Voltaire,* Paris, P.U.F., 1971.

———, *Histoire Vécu du Peuple Chrétien,* Toulouse, 1979.

DESSAI, Naraina B. Sar, 'Fundamentos para uma Universidade em Goa', in *Boletim do Instituto Menezes Bragança,* no. 84, Bastorá, Tip. Rangel, 1963.

DEVI, Vimala, and Manuel de Seabra, *A Literatura Indo-Portuguesa,* Lisboa, Junta de Investigações do Ultramar, 1971.

DIAS, Filinto Cristo, 'Vocábulos portugueses de origem concani', in *Boletim do Instituto Menezes Bragança,* no. 112, Bastorá, Tip. Rangel, 1976.

DIAS, João José Alves, 'Para uma Abordagem do Sexo Proibido em Portugal no século XVI', in *Inquisição* (comunicações apresentadas ao 1st congresso Luso-Brazileiro sobre Inquisição realizado em Lisbon, 17-20 February 1987), vol. 1, Lisbon, Sociedade Portuguesa de Estudos do Século XVIII - Universitária Editora, 1989.

DUBOYER, Jeannine, *A Vida Quotidiana na Índia desde o século II a.C. até ao século VII d.C.,* Livros do Brasil, Lisbon, undated.

DIAS, Mariano, 'Fr. Caetano Vitorino de Faria', in *Essays in Goan History,* ed. Teotónio R. de Souza, New Delhi, Concept Publishing Company, 1989.

ENES, Maria Fernandes Dinis Teixeira, *As Visitas Pastorais da Matriz de São Sebastião de Ponta Delgada (1764-1739),* Introduction, transcription and notes by notas de ..., Ponta Delgada, Universidade dos Açores, 1986.

ENTHOVEN, R.E., *The Tribes and Castes of Bombay,* vol. III, Delhi, 1975; 1st edn. 1922, reed. by Asian Educational Services, New Delhi and Madras, 1990.

A Escola Medico-Cirurgica de Goa. Monografia, Col. de Divulgação e Cultura, no. 31, Goa, Imprensa Nacional, 1959.

FARINHA, Padre António Lourenço, *A Expansão de Fé no Oriente. (Subsídios para a História Colonial),* vol. II, [Lisbon], Agência Geral das Colónias, 1943.

FEIO, Mariano, *As castas hindus de Goa,* Lisbon, Junta de Investigações Científicas do Ultramar - Centro de Estudos de Antropologia Cultural, 1979.

———, 'Problemas da geomorfologia de Goa', in *Garcia de Orta. Revista da Junta das Missões Geográficas e de Investigações do Ultramar,* special edition, Lisbon, 1956.

FERNANDES, António de Salvador, *O Liceu Nacional Afonso de Albuquerque em Nova Goa,* Lisbon, Agência Geral das Colónias, 1946.

FERREIRA, Octaviano Guilherme, *Catálogo dos Livros, Opúsculos e Manuscritos pertencentes à Biblioteca Nacional de Nova Goa,* 2 vols., Nova Goa, 1907, 1909.

Figueiredo, Caetano de, 'As Comunidades de Goa', in *A Índia Portuguesa,* vol. II, Nova Goa, Imprensa Nacional, 1923.

Figueiredo, João Manuel Pacheco de, *O Marquês de Pombal visto por Escritores Goeses,* offprint of *Memórias da Academia das Ciências de Lisboa,* Classe de Ciências, pt. XXIII, Lisbon, 1980.

Figueiredo, Propércia Correia Afonso, 'A mulher indo-portuguesa', in *Boletim do Instituto Vasco da Gama,* nos. 2-9, Nova Goa, 1928-31.

Fonseca, Félix Feliciano da, *Relação dos Felicissimos Sucessos Observados na Índia Oriental, em o Vice-Reinado do ... Snr. Marquês de Távora, etc., Extraída de Algumas Cartas Remetidas a esta Corte,* Lisbon, 1753.

França, Padre Leonor, S.J., *O Método Pedagógico dos Jesuitas: O 'Ratio Studiorum',* introduction and translation, Rio de Janeiro, Agir Editora, 1952.

Freire, Romualdo Glohysio, *Descrição Funebre das Exequias que a Inquisição de Goa Dedicou à Memoria do ... Sr. Nuno da Cunha Ataide,* Lisbon, 1753.

Furber, Holden, *Rival Empires of Trade in the Orient, 1600-1800,* New Delhi, Oxford University Press, 1990.

Furtado, Álvaro de Loyola, 'Os primórdios da imprensa e do jornalismo em Goa e no resto da Índia', in *Boletim do Instituto Menezes Bragança,* nos. 100-4, 116, Bastorá, 1973-4, 1977.

Garden, Maurice, 'A Índia: o começo de um declínio', in *História Económica e Social do Mundo,* directed by Pierre Léon, Portuguese translation., vol. III, pt. 1, Lisbon, Sá da Costa, 1983.

Gomes, Francisco Luís, *Os Brahamanes,* Lisbon, Typ. da Gazeta de Portugal, 1866.

———, *Os brigadeiros Henrique Carlos Henriques e Joaquim José Xavier Henriques,* Nova Goa, Tip. Universal, 1929.

Gomes, J. Benedito, 'O Instituto Vasco da Gama ...', in *Boletim do Instituto Vasco da Gama,* nos. 16, 18, 25, 27-9, Bastorá, 1932-6.

Gomes, Padre João Pereira, "Jesuítas", in *Dicionário de História de Portugal,* directed by Joel Serrão, vol. II, Lisbon, Iniciativas Editoriais, 1965.

Gonsalves, Sebastião, *História dos Religiosos da Companhia de Jesus,* vol. III, Coimbra, Atlântida, 1962.

Gracias, António, 'Algumas notas sobre a Imprensa Periódica de Goa', in *O Mundo Português,* vol. X, no. 110, Lisbon, 1943.

Gracias, Caetano Francisco Xavier, *Velha Goa e seus monumentos e reliquias da antiga-glória dos Portugueses e da civilização cristã.* Memória histórico-arqueológica, 2nd edn., Nova Goa, Tip. Central, 1931.

———, *Velha Goa e seus monumentos. Breve memoria historica dos seus actuais edificios religiosos e civis para os visitantes da Velha Cidade,* Lisbon, Tip. Literaria, 1922.

Gracias, [José António de] Ismael, 'Alguns Advogados Antigos de Goa', in *O Oriente Portuguez,* vol. XI, Nova Goa, Imprensa Nacional, 1914.

——, 'Alguns médicos antigos de Goa 1797-1839', in *O Oriente Portuguez,* vol. XI, nos. 9-10, Nova Goa, Imprensa Nacional, 1914.

——, 'Aula de Artilharia em Goa, no século XVIII', in *O Oriente Portuguez,* vol. XIV, nos. 5-6, Nova Goa, Imprensa Nacional, 1917.

——, *O Bispo de Halicarnasso D. António José de Noronha. Memória Histórica,* Nova Goa, Imprensa Nacional, 1903.

——, *Catálogo dos livros do assentamento da gente de guerra que vem do Reino para a India desde 1731 até 1811,* Nova Goa, Imprensa Nacional, 1893.

——, 'Clero em Goa. Providencias para a sua redução em 1750', in *O Oriente Portuguez,* vol. XI, Nova Goa, Imprensa Nacional, 1914.

——, 'Os 2 Padres Coutos Implicados na conjuração de 1787', in *O Oriente Portuguez,* vol. V, nos. 11-12, Nova Goa, Imprensa Nacional, 1908.

——, 'Feriados Concelhios na Índia Portugueza', in *O Oriente Portuguez,* vol. XII, nos. 1-2, Nova Goa, 1915.

——, 'O Governador Filippe de Valladares Soutomaior', in *O Oriente Portuguez,* vol. XI, nos. 1-2, Nova Goa, 1914.

——, *A Imprensa em Goa nos séculos XVI, XVII e XVIII. Apontamentos Histórico-Bibliográficos,* Nova Goa, Imprensa Nacional, 1880.

——, 'Legados e pensões a cargo das fábricas e confrarias de Goa em 1766', in *O Oriente Portuguez,* vol. X, nos. 3-6, Nova Goa, Imprensa Nacional, 1913.

——, *Legislação para a Administração das confrarias (Coligida e Anotada),* Nova Goa, 1886.

——, 'Novos Documentos sobre o Bispo de Halicarnasso', in *O Oriente Portuguez,* vol. III, nos. 5-6, Nova Goa, Imprensa Nacional, 1906.

——, 'Uma pagina da historia dos Theatinos de Goa', in *O Oriente Português,* vol. II, Nova Goa, 1905.

——, 'Reforma da Religião Franciscana em Goa no século XVIII', in *O Oriente Portuguez,* vol. VII, nos. 1-2, 11-12, Nova Goa, Imprensa Nacional, 1910-11.

——, *A India em 1623 e 1624. Excertos das Memorias do viajante italiano Pietro Della Valle Compilados e Anotados por ...,* Nova Goa, Imprensa Nacional, 1915.

Gracias, João Baptista Amâncio, 'Regimen alimentar no Convento de S. Domingos', in *A Voz de S. Francisco Xavier,* year IV, no. 47, 1935.

——, 'Bens pensionados em Goa da Congregação de S. Filipe Nery', in *O Oriente Portuguez,* no. 14, Bastorá, Tip. Rangel, 1937.

——, 'Bens pensionados em Goa das Capelas do Convento de N.ª S.ª da Graça', in *O Oriente Portuguez,* vol. XVI, nos. 3-4, Nova Goa, Imprensa Nacional, 1919.

——, 'Bens pensionados em Goa das Capelas do Convento de S. Francisco', in *O Oriente Portuguez,* vol. XVI, nos. 11-12, Nova Goa, Imprensa Nacional, 1920.

——, 'Bens pensionados em Goa das Capelas e Pensões do Convento de S. Caetano', in *O Oriente Portuguez,* vol. XVI, nos. 7-8, Nova Goa, Imprensa Nacional, 1920.

——, 'Bens pensionados em Goa do Convento de N. Sra da Graça', in *O Oriente Portuguez,* no. 14, Bastorá, Tip. Rangel, 1936.

——, 'Uma embaixada científica portuguesa à corte dum rei indiano no séc. XVIII', in *O Oriente Português,* nos. 19-21, Bastorá, Tip. Rangel, 1938.

——, 'Ingleses em Goa', in *Boletim do Instituto Vasco da Gama,* nos. 4, 22-4, Nova Goa, 1928, 1934.

——, 'Médicos europeus em Goa e nas cortes indianas nos séculos XVI a XVIII', in *O Oriente Português,* nos. 24-5, Bastorá, Tip. Rangel, 1939.

——, 'Notulas para a historia das ordens religiosas na India. Os dominicanos', in *O Oriente Portuguez,* vol. IV, no. 4, Nova Goa, Imprensa Nacional, 1907.

——, 'Os portugueses e o estabelecimento da imprensa na Índia', in *Boletim do Instituto Vasco da Gama,* no. 37, Bastorá, Tip. Rangel, 1938.

——, 'Portugueses na Índia', in *O Oriente Português,* no. 10, Bastorá, Tip. Rangel, 1934-5.

——, *Portugueses na Índia – Catálogo dos que Vieram à Índia nas Monções de 1690, 1774, 1776 e 1780, com Notas Biográficas acerca de alguns Deles,* Nova Goa, Imprensa Nacional, 1934.

Gracias, Fátima da Silva, *Health & Hygiene in Colonial Goa 1510-1961,* New Delhi, Concept Publishing Company, 1994.

Guillermou, Alain, *Les Jésuites,* Col. Que sais-je?, no. 936, Paris, P.U.F., 1961.

Guimarães, Padre Bráulio, *Memórias da Congregação da Missão em Portugal* (unpublished), A.P.C.M.

Habib, Irfan, "Population", in *The Cambridge Economic History of India,* vol. I, ed. T. Raychaudhuri and I. Habib, Cambridge, Cambridge University Press, 1982.

Hambye, E. R., "Goa", in *Dictionnaire D'Histoire et de Géographie Ecclésiastiques,* sous la direction de R. Aubert, fasc. 121, Paris, Letouzey and Ané, n.d.

Higgs, David, 'A Inquisição de Goa no fim do século XVIII', in *Ler História,* 24, Lisbon, ISCTE, 1994.

Hoppe, Fritz, *A Africa Oriental Portuguesa no tempo do Marquês de Pombal 1750-1777,* Lisbon, Agência Geral do Ultramar, 1970.

Illustração Goana. Publicação mensal, Margão, Tip. do Ultramar, 1864-6.

Instrucção do Exmº Vice-Rei Marques de Alorna ao seu Sucessor o Exmº Vice-Rei Marquez de Tavora ..., 2nd edn., rectificada, e enriquecida com novas peças do mesmo autor e 380 notas históricas por Filippe Nery Xavier, Nova Goa, Imprensa Nacional, 1856.

Instrucções com que El-Rei D. José I mandou passar ao Estado da India o Governador, e Capitão General e o Arcebispo Primaz do Oriente, no Anno de 1774 Publicadas e Annotadas por Claudio Lagrange Monteiro de Barbuda, ..., Pangim, 1841.

KAMAT, Pratima, 'Some Protesting Priests of Goa', in *Essays in Goan History*, ed. Teotónio R. de Souza, New Delhi, Concept Publishing Company, 1989.

KLOGUEN, Dinis L. Cottineau de, *Bosquejo Historico de Goa,* vertido em portuguez e accrescentado com algumas notas e rectificações por Miguel Vicente d'Abreu, Nova Goa, Imprensa Nacional, 1858.

LAPA, José Roberto do Amaral, 'O Brazil e a navegação portuguesa para a Ásia (séculos XVI, XVII e XVIII)', in *Estudos Históricos,* no. 7, Marília, 1968.

LARDINOIS, Roland, 'Deserted Villages and Depopulation in Rural Tamil Nadu, c. 1780-c.1830', in *India's Historical Demography: Studies in Famine, Disease and Society,* ed. Tin Dyson, London, Cruzon Press, 1989.

LIMA, José Joaquim Lopes de and continued by por Francisco Maria Bordalo, *Ensaios sobre a Estatistica das Possessões Portuguezas na Africa Occidental e Oriental na Asia Occidental na China e na Oceania Começados a Escrever de Ordem do Governo de Sua Magestade,* Lisbon, Imprensa Nacional, 1862.

LOBATO, Alexandre, 'A Política Ultramarina Portuguesa no século XVIII', in *O Ultramar,* no. 30, year VIII, vol. VIII, no. 2, Lisbon, 1967.

LOPES, António dos Mártires, "Goa, criação de Portugal", in *Boletim Geral do Ultramar,* year XXXII, no. 373, Lisbon, 1956.

———, *Imprensa de Goa.* Monografia coordenada por ..., Lisbon, Comissariado do Governo para os Assuntos do Estado da Índia, 1971.

LOPES, David, *A Expansão da Língua Portuguesa no Oriente, nos séculos XVI, XVII e XVIII,* Barcelos, Portucalense Editora, 1936.

Lopes, Francisco Félix, O.F.M., 'Os Franciscanos, no Oriente Português de 1584 a 1590', in *Stvdia,* no. 9, Lisbon, Centro de Estudos Históricos Ultramarinos, 1962.

Lopes, Maria de Jesus dos Mártires, *O Arcebispado de Goa no Tempo de D. António Taveira da Neiva Brum da Silveira (1750-1755). Alguns elementos para o seu estudo,* offprint of *Arquipélago.* Revista da Universidade dos Açores, série Ciências Humanas, no. VI, Ponta Delgada, 1984.

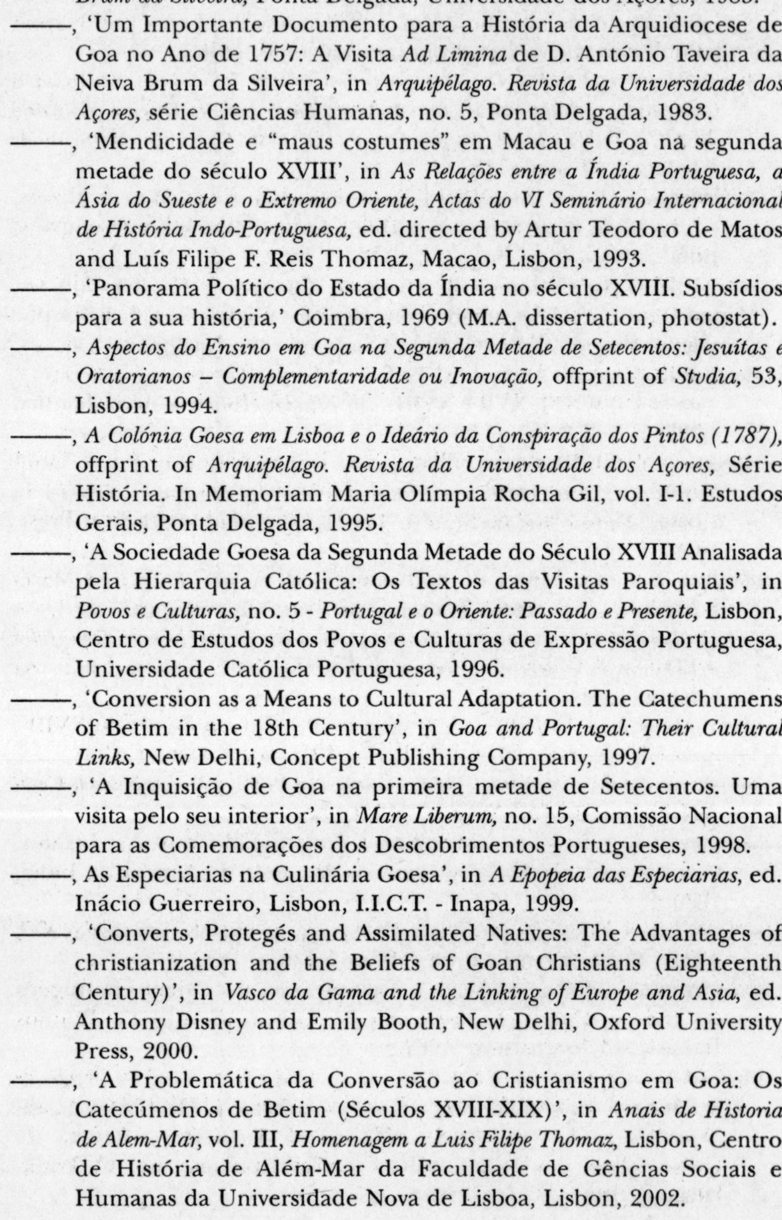

——, *Epistolário de um Açoriano na Índia: D. António Taveira da Neiva Brum da Silveira,* Ponta Delgada, Universidade dos Açores, 1983.

——, 'Um Importante Documento para a História da Arquidiocese de Goa no Ano de 1757: A Visita *Ad Limina* de D. António Taveira da Neiva Brum da Silveira', in *Arquipélago. Revista da Universidade dos Açores,* série Ciências Humanas, no. 5, Ponta Delgada, 1983.

——, 'Mendicidade e "maus costumes" em Macau e Goa na segunda metade do século XVIII', in *As Relações entre a Índia Portuguesa, a Ásia do Sueste e o Extremo Oriente, Actas do VI Seminário Internacional de História Indo-Portuguesa,* ed. directed by Artur Teodoro de Matos and Luís Filipe F. Reis Thomaz, Macao, Lisbon, 1993.

——, 'Panorama Político do Estado da Índia no século XVIII. Subsídios para a sua história,' Coimbra, 1969 (M.A. dissertation, photostat).

——, *Aspectos do Ensino em Goa na Segunda Metade de Setecentos: Jesuítas e Oratorianos – Complementaridade ou Inovação,* offprint of *Stvdia,* 53, Lisbon, 1994.

——, *A Colónia Goesa em Lisboa e o Ideário da Conspiração dos Pintos (1787),* offprint of *Arquipélago. Revista da Universidade dos Açores,* Série História. In Memoriam Maria Olímpia Rocha Gil, vol. I-1. Estudos Gerais, Ponta Delgada, 1995.

——, 'A Sociedade Goesa da Segunda Metade do Século XVIII Analisada pela Hierarquia Católica: Os Textos das Visitas Paroquiais', in *Povos e Culturas,* no. 5 - *Portugal e o Oriente: Passado e Presente,* Lisbon, Centro de Estudos dos Povos e Culturas de Expressão Portuguesa, Universidade Católica Portuguesa, 1996.

——, 'Conversion as a Means to Cultural Adaptation. The Catechumens of Betim in the 18th Century', in *Goa and Portugal: Their Cultural Links,* New Delhi, Concept Publishing Company, 1997.

——, 'A Inquisição de Goa na primeira metade de Setecentos. Uma visita pelo seu interior', in *Mare Liberum,* no. 15, Comissão Nacional para as Comemorações dos Descobrimentos Portugueses, 1998.

——, As Especiarias na Culinária Goesa', in *A Epopeia das Especiarias,* ed. Inácio Guerreiro, Lisbon, I.I.C.T. - Inapa, 1999.

——, 'Converts, Protegés and Assimilated Natives: The Advantages of christianization and the Beliefs of Goan Christians (Eighteenth Century)', in *Vasco da Gama and the Linking of Europe and Asia,* ed. Anthony Disney and Emily Booth, New Delhi, Oxford University Press, 2000.

——, 'A Problemática da Conversão ao Cristianismo em Goa: Os Catecúmenos de Betim (Séculos XVIII-XIX)', in *Anais de Historia de Alem-Mar,* vol. III, *Homenagem a Luis Filipe Thomaz,* Lisbon, Centro de História de Além-Mar da Faculdade de Gências Sociais e Humanas da Universidade Nova de Lisboa, Lisbon, 2002.

——, 'The Sisters of Santa Monica in the 18th Century. Details of Their Daily Life', in *Goa and Portugal. History and Development,* ed. Charles J. Borges, Óscar G. Pereira, Hannes Stubbe, New Delhi, Concept Publishing Company, 2000.

——, 'Hinduism in the Quotidian of the Christians of Goa in the 18th Century', in *The Portuguese Indian Ocean and European Bridgeheads: Festschrift in Honour of Prof. K.S. Mathew,* ed. Pius Malekandathil & T. Jamal Mohammed, Lisbon, Fundação Oriente, 2001.

Lourenço, Agapito, 'O Clero de Goa Através dos Tempos', in *Boletim do Instituto Menezes Bragança,* no. 96, Número Especial Comemorativo do Centenário da Fundação do Instituto (1871-1971), Bastorá, 1971.

'Mappa Geral, Estatístico e Histórico da Índia Portuguesa ...' de 1848, in *Boletim Oficial,* no. 45, Goa, Imprensa Nacional, n.d.

Marques, A.H. de Oliveira, *História de Portugal Desde os Tempos Mais Antigos até à Presidência do Sr. General Eanes,* vol. II, Lisbon, Palas Editores, 1983.

Marques, Maria Adelaide Salvador, *A Real Mesa Censória e a Cultura Nacional: Aspectos de Geografia Cultural Portuguesa no século XVIII,* offprint of the *Boletim da Universidade de Coimbra,* vol. XXVI, Coimbra, 1963.

Martins, José Frederico Ferreira, *Crónica dos Vice-Reis e Governadores da Índia,* vol. I, Nova Goa, Imprensa Nacional, 1919.

——, *História da Misericórdia de Goa,* 3 vols., Nova Goa, Imprensa Nacional, 1910, 1912, 1914.

——, *Os Vice-Reis da Índia (1505-1917),* Lisbon, Imprensa Nacional, 1935.

Mascarenhas, Constâncio, 'Bocage e suas impressões da India', in *Boletim do Instituto Menezes Bragança,* no. 102, Bastorá, Tip. Rangel, 1973.

——, *As Castas da Índia. Esboço de estudo antropo-social,* Porto, Imprensa Nacional, 1924.

Mascarenhas, Mira, 'The Church in Eighteenth Century Goa', in *Essays in Goan History,* ed. Teotónio R. de Souza, New Delhi, Concept Publishing Company, 1989.

——, 'Impact of the West on Goan Music', in *Goa: Cultural Trends,* ed. P.P. Shirodkar, Goa, Directorate of Archives, Archaeology and Museum, 1988.

——,'The Pombaline Era in Goa (1750-1777)', Bombay, 1977 (M.A. thesis, photostat, guided by B.S. Shastry).

Matos, Artur Teodoro de, 'Um Quotidiano Diferente: Empréstimos e Penhores de uma Confraria de Goa no Século XVIII', paper presented at the international meet on *O Quotidiano na História Portuguesa,* Faculdade de Ciências Sociais e Humanas da Universidade Nova de Lisbon, 22-4 April 1993.

———, 'Teres e haveres das Ordens Religiosas de Goa em finais do século XVI', in *Stvdia,* Lisboa, 53 (1994).

———, 'Sistema tributário e rendimento fundiario de Goa no século XVI', in *Las Relationes entre Portugal y Castilla en la Época de los Descubrimientos y la Expansión Colonial,* ed. Ana Maria Carabias Torres, Salamanca, Ediciones Universidad de Salamanca, 1994.

MAX, Frédéric, 'Le Procès Inquisitorial et la Captivité du Médicin François Charles Dellon à Goa et à Lisbonne (1673-1677). Essai d'Étude Critique', in *Inquisição,* Lisbon, Universitária Editora, 1989.

MEERSMAN, Fr. Achilles, O.F.M., *Annual Reports of the Portuguese Franciscans in India 1713-1833,* coligidas e anotadas por ..., Lisbon, Centro de Estudos Históricos Ultramarinos, 1972.

———, 'Notes on the study of Indian languages by the Franciscans', in *Neue Zeitschrift für Missionswissenschaft Nouvelle Revue de Science Missionnaire, XIII,* Switzerland, 1957.

———, 'The Question of Admitting Indians to the Franciscan Order', in *Neue Zeitschrift für Missionswissenschaft Nouvelle Revue de Science Missionnaire,* XIII, Switzerland, 1957.

MELO, Afonso José de, 'O Deão da Sé de Goa José Paulo de Almeida Fundador da povoação de Quepém', in *Boletim do Instituto Vasco da Gama,* no. 66, Bastorá, Tip. Rangel, 1950.

Memória Histórico-Eclesiástica da Arquidiocese de Goa, 1533-1933, ed. Padre Amaro Pinto Lobo, Nova Goa, Tip. A Voz de S. Francisco Xavier, 1933.

MENDES, A. Lopes, *A India Portugueza. Breve Descripção das Possessões Portuguezas na Asia,* 2 vols., Lisbon, Imprensa Nacional, 1886; reed. by Asian Educational Services, New Delhi and Madras, 1989.

MENEZES, José António, *Almanach Recreativo para 1883 ... Segundo Anno,* Nova Goa, Imprensa Nacional, 1882,

MIRANDA, Jacinto Caetano Barreto de, *Quadros Históricos de Goa. Tentativa Histórica,* 3 cadernetas, Margão, Tip. do Ultramar, 1863, 1864, 1865.

———, 'O Sermão de Santa Cruz dos Milagres de Sebastião do Rego', in *O Ultramar,* Margão, 1867.

MOLINA, António M., *Historia de Filipinas,* pt. I, Madrid, ed. Cultura Hispanica Del Instituto de Cooperacion Iberoamerica, 1984.

MONCADA, Luís Cabral de, *Estudos de História do Direito,* vol. III, Coimbra, Acts Universitatis Conimbrigenses, 1950.

MONIZ, Egas, 'Vida e obra do Abade de Faria', in *Boletim Geral das Colónias,* year XXI, nos. 242-3, Lisbon, 1945.

MONIZ (Júnior), António Francisco, 'Um curioso documento para a História da Conversão', in *O Oriente Portuguez,* vol. I, nos. 10-11, Nova Goa, 1904.

———, 'Relação completa das religiosas do Mosteiro de Santa Monica de

Goa', in *O Oriente Portuguez,* vol. XVII, nos. 5-6, Nova Goa, Imprensa Nacional, 1920.

MONTEIRO, D. António Xavier de Souza, *Código das Confrarias,* Coimbra, Imprensa Nacional, 1870.

——, *Manual de Direito Ecclesiastico Parochial para Uso dos Parocos,* 3rd edn., Coimbra, Imprensa da Universidade, 1890.

MORAES, G.M., "Padre Cetano Victorino de Faria – a would-be Archbishop of Goa", in *Boletim do Instituto Menezes Bragança,* no. 96, Special Commemorative Issue on the Centenary of the Establishment of the Institute, Bastorá, Tip. Rangel, 1971.

MORAIS, A. Faria de, *A Índia e as Castas,* Lisbon, Agência Geral das Colónias, 1944.

MOTA, Avelino Teixeira da, *Cartas antigas da Índia existentes em Portugal (séculos XVIII, XIX e XX),* offprint CXVI of the Centro de Estudos de Cartografia Antiga, Lisbon, Junta de Investigações Científicas do Ultramar, 1979.

——, 'Cartas antigas do Estado da India Existentes em Paris e Londres', in *II Seminário Internacional de História Indo-Portuguesa. Actas,* Lisbon, Instituto de Investigação Científica Tropical - Centro de Estudos de História e Cartografia Antiga, 1985.

MOURA, Jacinto José do Nascimento, 'Uma aula de artelharia em Goa no século XVIII', in *Boletim Geral das Colónias,* year VIII, no. 82, Lisbon, 1932.

MOUSNIER, Roland, and Ernest Labrousse, 'O século XVIII', in *História Geral das Civilizações,* directed by Maurice Crouzet, pt. V, 2 vols., S. Paulo, Difusão Europeia do Livro, 1961.

NAZARETH, Padre Casimiro Cristóvão de, *Clero de Goa, Seus serviços à Religião e à Nação* (collection of studies published in journals in Lisbon and Goa) with a biographical profile of the author by J. B. Amâncio Gracias, Nova Goa, Casa Luso-Francesa, 1927.

——, *Mitras Lusitanas no Oriente. Catalogo dos Prelados da Egreja Metropolitana e Primacial de Goa e das Dioceses Suffraganeas com a recopilação das Ordenanças por ellas emitidas dos factos notaveis da História eclesiastica de Goa,* 2nd edn. corrigida e aumentada, Nova Goa, Imprensa Nacional, 1897.

NAZARETH, J.M. do Carmo, 'Beneficencia publica na India', in *O Oriente Portuguez,* vol. I, nos. 10-11, Nova Goa, Imprensa Nacional, 1904.

——, 'Início de Estudos Militares na India', in *O Oriente Portuguez,* vol. VI, Nova Goa, Imprensa Nacional, 1908.

——, 'Occidentais e orientais nos conventos religiosos de Goa', in *O Oriente Portuguez,* vol. IV, Nova Goa, Imprensa Nacional, 1907.

NIGHTINGALE, Pamela, *Trade and empire in Western India 1784-1806,* Cambridge, Cambridge University Press, 1970.

NORONHA, Percival, 'Levantamento arqueológico de Velha Goa e tentativas para a sua preservação', in *Leba–Estudos do Quaternário, Pré-História e Arqueologia,* no. 7, Lisbon, Centro de Pré-História e Arqueologia, IICT, 1993.

NUNES, Manuel da Costa, *Documentação para a história da Congregação do Oratório de Santa Cruz dos Milagres do clero natural de Goa,* vol. I: *1681-1721,* Lisbon, Centro de Estudos Históricos Ultramarinos, 1966.

OLIVEIRA, J. P. Bacelar e, 'Arrest, Spoliation and Exile of the Goa Jesuits according to Father Caeiro's *De Exilio*', in *Indo-Portuguese History. Old Issues, New Questions,* ed. Teotónio R. de Souza, New Delhi, 1985.

PACHECO, António Caetano, *Plano geral da Instrucção Publica nos Estados Portuguezes da India,* Lisbon, 1948.

PAIVA, José Pedro de Matos, 'Inquisição e Visitas Pastorais. Dois mecanismos complementares de Controle Social?', in *Inquisição,* vol. II, Lisbon, Universitária Editora, 1989.

PALHA, Francisco Mourão Garcês, 'Familias portuguesas estabelecidas na India, cuja varonia se extinguiu', in *O Oriente Portuguez,* vol. XVI, nos. 5-8, Nova Goa, Imprensa Nacional, 1920.

PEARSON, M.N., 'Goa-based Seaborn Trade (17th-18th Centuries)', in *Goa Through the Ages: An Economic History,* vol. II, ed. Teotónio R. de Souza, Goa, Goa University, 1990.

———,'Indigenous Dominance in a Colonial Economy: The Goa Rendas, 1600-70', in *Mare Luso-Indicum,* pt. II, Geneva, Centre de Recherches d'Histoire et de Philologie de la IVe Section de l'École Pratique des Hautes Études, 1973.

PEREIRA, A.B. de Bragança, *Etnografia da India Portuguesa,* vol. II, Bastorá, Tip Rangel, 1940.

———, *História Religiosa de Goa,* offprint of *O Oriente Português,* vol. I, Bastorá, Tip. Rangel, 1932-4.

———, 'Os ranes, os quetris, os oixos, os chardós e os bramanes de Goa', in *O Oriente Portuguez,* vol. XVI, nos. 7-8, Nova Goa, Imprensa Nacional, 1920.

———, *S. Francisco Xavier, Esboço Histórico. Publicação comemorativa da Exposição do Corpo do Apóstolo das Indias pelo 4° Centenário da sua Morte,* Goa, Imprensa Nacional, 1952.

———, *O sistema das castas. Ensaio Histórico-Sociológico,* offprint of *O Oriente Portuguez,* vol. XVII, nos. 1-4, Nova Goa, 1920.

PEREIRA, [Armando] Gonçalves, *Índia Portuguesa,* Lisbon, Agência Geral do Ultramar, 1953.

PEREIRA, Francisco Raimundo de Morais, *Anal Índico Lusitano dos Sucessos mais Memoráveis e das Acções Particulares do Primeiro Ano do Fedelíssimo Governo do ... Senhor Francisco de Assis de Távora, Marquês de Távora,*

Conde de S. João ... Vice-Rei e Capitão-General da Índia, Lisbon, 1758.

———, *Relação da viagem que do porto de Lisboa, fizerão à India os Illmos e Excmos Senhores Marquezes de Tavora ...,* Lisbon, Oficina de Miguel Manescal da Costa, 1752.

PEREIRA, José da Silva, *A assistência pública no Estado da Índia,* Goa, Agência Geral das Colónias, 1952.

PERY, Gerardo A., *Geographia e Estatistica Geral de Portugal e Colonias com um Atlas,* Lisbon, Imprensa Nacional, 1875.

PESSOA, D. João Chrisostomo d'Amorim, *Memoria sobre o Real Padroado Portuguez,* Tome III, pt. I, Lisbon, Tip. Universal (Imprensa da Casa Real), 1887.

PINTO, Américo Cortez, '*Talant de Bien Faire*', *A Divisa do Infante e a Criação do Estado da Índia,* Lisbon, Agência Geral do Ultramar, 1955.

PINTO, Celsa, 'At the dusk of the second empire Goa-Brazil commercial links 1770-1820', in *Purabhilekh Puratatva,* vol. VII, no. 1, Jan.-June, 1990.

———, 'Goa-based Overseas and Coastal Trade (18th-19th Centuries)', in *Goa Through the Ages,* vol. II: *An Economic History,* ed. Teotónio R. de Souza, Goa University, 1990.

———, *Trade and Finance in Portuguese India: A Study of the Portuguese Country Trade (1770-1840),* New Delhi, Concept Publishing Company, 1994.

PINTO, Virgílio Noya, *O Ouro Brazileiro e o Comércio Anglo-Português (Uma Contribuição aos Estudos da Economia Atlântica no Século XVIII),* Braziliana, vol. CCCLXXI, 2nd edn., S. Paulo, Companhia Editora Nacional, 1979.

PISSURLENCAR, Panduronga, *Agentes da Diplomacia Portuguesa na Índia. Hindús, Muçulmanos, Judeus e Parses,* Bastorá, Tip. Rangel, 1952.

———, *Contribuição ao estudo etnológico da casta indo-portuguesa denominada "chardó", à luz de documentos inéditos encontrados no Arquivo Histórico da Índia,* offprint of *Actas do I Congresso Nacional de Antropologia Cultural,* Porto, 1934.

———, 'O Elemento Hindu da Casta Chardó', in *O Oriente Português,* nos. 12-13, Bastorá, Tip. Rangel, 1936.

———, 'O Enigma da morte do Vice-Rei Conde de Alva, esclarecido á luz de documentos maratas', in *Memórias,* pt. VI, Lisbon, Academia das Ciências de Lisboa, 1957.

———, 'Um Frade Capucho na Côrte de Puném', in *Boletim do Instituto Vasco da Gama,* no. 24, Bastorá, Tip. Rangel, 1934.

———, *Perfil Biográfico de Abade Faria,* Nova Goa, Imprensa Nacional, 1918.

———, *Portugueses e Maratas,* Nova Goa, Imprensa Nacional, 1937.

———, *Os Portugueses nas literaturas indianas dos séculos XVI, XVII e*

XVIII, offprint of *Boletim da Sociedade de Geografia*, nos. 7-9, Lisbon, 1955.

——, *Roteiro dos Arquivos da Índia Portuguesa*, Bastorá, Tip. Rangel, 1955.

——, 'Servidores Hindus do Estado Portugues da India: Seculos XVI-XVIII', in *Defesa Nacional*, year XVI, no. 187, Lisbon, 1949.

Prakash, Om, *The New Cambridge History of India*, vol. 5: *European Commercial Enterprise in Pre-Colonial India*, Cambridge, Cambridge University Press, 1998.

Priolkar, Anant Kakba, *The Terrible Tribunal for the East: The Goa Inquisition*, Bombay, Bombay University Press, 1961.

Províncias Ultramarinas Portuguesas. Dados Informativos, Lisbon, Agência Geral do Ultramar, 1961.

Ramos, Luís A. de Oliveira, *Da Ilustração ao Liberalismo. Temas Históricos*, Porto, Lello & Irmão, 1979.

——, *Diários das Visitas Pastorais no Pará de D. Fr. Caetano Brandão*, Porto, Instituto Nacional de Investigação Científica - Centro de História da Universidade do Porto, 1991.

——, 'Novo Estilo Pastoral na Arquidiocese de Braga pelos Fins do século XVIII', in *Congresso Internacional de História. Missionação Portuguesa e Encontro de Culturas, Actas*, Braga, 1993.

——, *Portugal e a Revolução Francesa (1777-1834)*, Porto, Trabalhos e Documentos do CEMPA-8, 1991.

——, *Projecções do Reformismo Pombalino*, offprint of *Boletim do Arquivo da Universidade de Coimbra*, VI, Coimbra, 1984.

——, *Situações e propostas de mundança em* Portugal no final do antigo regime, offprint of Revista *Bracara Augusta*, vol. XXXIV, fasc. 78 (91), Braga, 1980.

Rangel, Jaime, 'José Custódio de Faria', in *Boletim do Instituto Vasco da Gama*, no. 72, Bastorá, Tip. Rangel, 1956.

Regimento do Auditorio Ecclesiastico do Arcebispado Primacial de Goa e da sua Relação .., Lisbon, Impressão Regia, 1810.

Rego, António da Silva, 'Adaptação missionária e assimilação colonizadora no ultramar português', in *Boletim Geral do Ultramar*, year XXXIV, no. 402, Lisbon, 1958.

——, 'Em louvor da Arquidiocese de Goa: quatro séculos de história', in *Boletim do Instituto Menezes de Bragança*, no. 120, Bastorá, 1978.

——, *Fontes para a História do Antigo Ultramar Português*, vol. I: *Estado da Índia*, pt. I, Lisbon, Academia Portuguesa da História, 1978.

——, 'Goa - a realenga', in *Ultramar*, nos. 7-8, Lisbon, 1962.

——, *História das Missões do Padroado Português do Oriente*, vol. I: *1500-1542*, Lisbon, Agência Geral das Colónias, 1949.

——, *O Padroado Português do Oriente, Esboço Histórico*, Lisbon, Agência Geral das Colónias, 1940.

——, *O Padroado Português no Oriente e a sua Historiografia (1838-1950)*, Lisbon, Academia Portuguesa de História, 1978.

——, *O Ultramar Português no século XVIII (1700-1833)*, Lisbon, Agência Geral do Ultramar, 1970.

RÊGO, Raul, *O Último Regimento e o Regimento da Economia da Inquisição de Goa*, Leitura e prefácio de ..., Lisbon, Biblioteca Nacional, Série Documental da Biblioteca Nacional, 1983.

REGO, Sebastião do, *Sermão da Santa Cruz dos Milagres*, Lisbon, Miguel Manescal da Costa, 1759.

——, *Vida do Veneravel Padre Joseph Vas*, with notes by J.C. Barreto Miranda, 2nd edn., Margão, Tip. do Ultramar, 1867.

RIBEIRO, Orlando, 'Aspectos e problemas da Expansão Portuguesa', in *Aspectos e problemas da Expansão Portuguesa*, Lisbon, Junta de Investigações do Ultramar, 1962.

——, 'A festa de São Francisco Xavier em Velha Goa', in *Aspectos e Problemas da Expansão Portuguesa*, Lisbon, Junta de Investigações do Ultramar, 1962.

——, 'Originalidade de Goa', in *Aspectos e Problemas da Expansão Portuguesa*, Lisbon, Junta de Investigações do Ultramar, 1962.

RICHARDS, John F., *The New Cambridge History of India*, vol. 1, 5: *The Mughal Empire*, 2nd edn., Cambridge, Cambridge University Press, 1995 (1st edn., 1993).

RIVARA, Joaquim Heliodoro da Cunha, *Archivo Portuguez Oriental*, fasc. 4º, Nova Goa, Imprensa Nacional, 1862.

——, *Cartas de Luis Antonio Verney, e Antonio Pereira de Figueiredo aos Padres da Congregação do Oratorio de Goa*, publicadas por ..., Nova Goa, Imprensa Nacional, 1838.

——, *A Conjuração de 1787 em Goa, e varias cousas desse Tempo. Memoria Historica*, Nova Goa, Imp. Nacional, 1875; reed. by Asian Educational Services, New Delhi and Madras, 1990.

——, *Demonstrativo Juris Patronatus Portugaliae Regum, a Clarissimo Viro D. Ludovico de Sousa Archiepiscopo Bracharense, Apud Romanum Curiam Legato, jussu Serenissimi principis Portugaliae Regnorum Regentis Summo Pontifici Innocencio XI Anno MIMDCLXXVII oblata*, Nova Goa, Imprensa Nacional, 1880.

——, *Ensaio Histórico da Lingua Concani*, Nova Goa, Imprensa Nacional, 1858.

——, *Grammatica da lingua concany escripta em portuguez por um missionario italiano e publicada por ...*, Nova Goa, Imprensa Nacional, 1859.

——, *Observações sobre a Historia Natural de Goa, feitas no anno de 1784 por Manoel Galvão da Silva e agora publicadas por ...*, Nova Goa, Imprensa Nacional, 1862.

——, *Reflexões sobre o Padroado Português do Oriente*, Nova Goa, Imprensa Nacional, 1858.

Rocha, Leopoldo da, *As Confrarias de Goa (séculos XVI-XX). Conspecto Histórico-Jurídico,* Lisbon, Centro de Estudos Históricos Ultramarinos, 1973.

Rodrigues, L.A., 'Noteworthy "luso-descendentes" of Portuguese India', in *Boletim do Instituto Menezes Bragança,* no. 111, Bastorá, Tip. Rangel, 1976.

——, 'Portuguese-blood communities in India', in *Boletim do Instituto Menezes Bragança,* no. 109, Bastorá, Tip. Rangel, 1975.

——, 'The Recluse Houses of Goa', in *Boletim do Instituto Menezes Bragança,* no. 106, Goa, Tip. Rangel, 1974.

Rodrigues, Maria Manuela Martins, 'Confrarias da cidade do Porto. Espaços de enquadramento espiritual e pólos difusores da mensagem da Igreja', in *Congresso Internacional de História. Missionação Portuguesa e Encontro de Culturas, Actas,* vol. I, Braga, 1993.

Sá, Renato, 'A língua portuguesa antes e depois das reformas pombalinas em Goa', paper presented at the Iberian and Ibero-American Seminar, Naples, in *Boletim Geral do Ultramar,* year XLI, no. 478, Lisbon, 1965.

Sá, Vicente Philippe de, 'Um naturalista portuguez em Goa no século 18º', in *O Oriente Portuguez,* vol. VII, nos. 9-12, Nova Goa, Imprensa Nacional, 1910.

Sáinz Ramírez, José, *Imperios Coloniales,* Madrid, Editora Nacional, 1942.

Saldanha, António de Souza e Vasconcelos Simão de, *As Cartas de Manuel de Saldanha 1º Conde da Ega e 47º Vice-Rei da Índia a Sebastião José de Carvalho e Melo e seus Irmãos (1758-1765). Subsídios para a História Política, Económica e Social da Índia Portuguesa de Setecentos,* Lisbon, Gabinete Português de Estudos Humanísticos, 1984.

——, *A Índia Portuguesa e a Política do Oriente de Setecentos. Manuel de Saldanha, 1º Conde da Ega e 47º vice-rei da Índia,* Biblioteca da Expansão Portuguesa, Lisbon, Publicações Alfa, 1989.

Saldanha, Padre M.J. Gabriel de, *História de Goa (Política e Arqueológica),* vol. 1: *História Política,* Nova Goa, Livraria Coelho, 1925.

Sampayo, João de Mello, 'Breve noticia da origem e divulgação dos estudos superiores em Goa, por methodos europeus e em lingua portugueza', in *O Oriente Portuguez,* vol. II, no. 3, Nova Goa, Imprensa Nacional, 1905.

Santa Maria, Fr. Agostinho de, *História da Fundação do Real Convento de Santa Mónica da Cidade de Goa,* Lisbon, A. Pedroso Galram, 1699.

Santos, Alfredo Rodrigues dos, 'Abade Faria', in *Boletim do Instituto Vasco da Gama,* no. 26, Bastorá, Tip. Rangel, 1935.

Santos, Domingos Maurício Gomes dos, 'Para a história do cartesianismo entre os jesuítas portugueses no século XVIII', in *Revista Portuguesa de Filosofia,* no. 1, Lisbon, 1945.

SANTOS, Eugénio dos, 'Os Açores na Época Moderna: Religião e Sociedade', in *Os Açores e o Atlântico (Século XIV-XVII),* Actas do Colóquio Internacional realizado em Angra do Heroísmo, 8 to 13 August 1983, Angra do Heroísmo, 1984.

——, 'Os Lazaristas e as Missões Populares em Portugal, 1734-1834: Um balanço', in *Congresso Internacional de História Missionação Portuguesa e Encontro de Culturas, Actas,* vol. I, Braga, 1993.

——, 'Os Livros das Visitas Pastorais da Região Portuense. Questões e perspectivas de abordagem', in *Revista de História,* vol. II: *Actas do Colóquio 'O Porto na Época Moderna',* Porto, Instituto Nacional de Investigação Científica, 1979.

——, *Les Missions des Temps Modernes au Portugal,* offprint of *Histoire Vécue du Peuple Chrétien,* Toulouse, Editions Privat, 1979.

——, 'Missões e Missionários do Interior da Região de Guimarães', in *Congresso Histórico de Guimarães e sua Colegiada. Actas,* vol. III, Guimarães, 1981.

——, *Os Oratorianos e o Iluminismo: Algumas Reflexões,* offprint of vol. II, seminar proceedings, *A Recepção da Revolução Francesa em Portugal e no Brazil,* no date, no place.

——, *O Oratório no Norte de Portugal. Contribuição para o Estudo da História Religiosa e Social,* Porto, Instituto Nacional de Investigação Científica, Centro de História da Universidade do Porto, 1982.

——, *Para a História da Cultura em Portugal no século XVIII,* offprint of *Arquipélago. Revista da Universidade dos Açores,* Série Ciências Humanas, no. 11, January, 1980.

SCHOLBERG, Henry with the collab. of Archana Ashok Kakodker and Carmo Azevedo, *Bibliography of Goa and the Portuguese in India,* New Delhi, Promilla & Co. Publishers, 1982.

SEN, S.P., *The French in India 1763-1816,* 2nd edn., New Delhi, Munshiram Manoharlal, 1971.

SERRÃO, Joaquim Veríssimo, *História de Portugal,* vol. VI: *1750-1807,* Lisbon, Editorial Verbo, 1982.

SHASTRY, B.S., 'Commercial Relations Between the portuguese and the Sunda Chiefs: 1693-1764', paper presented at the 5th International Seminar on Indo-Portuguese History, Cochim, 1989.

—— and V.R. Navelkar, *Bibliography of Dr. Pissurlencar Collection,* pts. I, II, III, Bambolim, Goa University, 1989.

SILVA, A.D. da, *Collecção de Legislação Portuguesa,* (Legislação de 1750 a 1762), Lisbon, Imprensa Nacional, 1830.

SILVA, João José da, *Repertório Alphabetico e Chronologico ou Indice Remissivo da Legislação Ultramarina,* desde a época das descobertas até 1882 inclusive, Lisbon, 1886.

SMITH, Vincent A., C.I.E., ..., *The Oxford History of India from the Earliest*

Times to the End of 1911, 2nd edn., Oxford, Oxford University Press, 1923.

Soares, A. Franquelim S. Neiva, 'A Sociedade do Antigo Regime nas Visitações e Inquéritos Paroquiais do Distrito de Braga', in *Theologica. Revista de Ciências Sagradas,* 2nd series, vol. XIII, fascs. 3-4, Braga, 1978.

———, *A Arquidiocese de Braga no Século XVII. Sociedade e Mentalidades pelas Visitações Pastorais (1500-1700),* Braga, Universidade do Minho, 1997.

Soriano, Simão José da Luz, *História do Reinado de El-Rei D. José e da Administração do Marquez de Pombal,* 2 vols., Lisbon, 1867.

Souza, Bento Graciano d', *Goan Society in Transition: A Study in Social Change,* Bombay, Popular Prakashan, 1975.

Souza, Felipe Nery Thomé Caetano do Rosario e, *Noticia Historica e Legislação da Instrucção Publica Primaria, Secundaria e Superior na India Portuguesa,* Nova Goa, Imprensa Nacional, 1879.

Souza, Padre Francisco Cetano de, S.J., *Instituições Portuguezas de Educação e Instrução no Oriente. Estudos Históricos Archeologicos,* Bambolim, Job Printing Press, 1890.

Souza, Teotónio R. de, 'Capital Input in Goa's Freedom Struggle: the Bombay connection', in *Indo-Portuguese History: Old Issues, New Questions,* New Delhi, Concept Publishing Company, 1985.

———, 'French slave-trading in Portuguese Goa (1773-1791)', in *Essays in Goan History,* New Delhi, Concept Publishing Company, 1989.

———, 'Glimpses of Hindu Dominance of Goan Economy in the Early Seventeenth Century', in *Indica,* XII, Bombay, 1975.

———, 'Goa-based Portuguese Seaborne Trade in the Early Seventeenth Century', in *The Indian Economic and Social History Review,* XII, New Delhi, 1976.

———, *Mar no Quotidiano Popular Goês,* Lisbon, Academia da Marinha, 1993.

———, 'Mhamai House Records: Indigenous Sources for Indo-Portuguese Historiography', in *II Seminário Internacional de História Indo-Portuguesa. Actas,* Lisbon, Instituto de Investigação Científica Tropical - Centro de Estudos de História e Cartografia Antiga, 1985.

———, 'Oratorians of Goa (1682-1835)', in *Goa: Cultural Trends,* ed. de Shirodkar, Goa, Directorate of Archives, Archaeology and Museum, 1988.

———, 'A Presença Portuguesa nas Expressões Folclóricas do Quotidiano da Goa Portuguesa', paper presented at the international meet on *O Quotidiano na História Portuguesa,* Lisbon, 22 to 24 April 1993.

———, 'Rural Economy and Life', in *Goa Through the Ages,* vol. II: *An Economic History,* New Delhi, Concept Publishing Company, 1990.

———, 'The Voiceless in Goan Historiography: A Case for the Source-

Value of Church Records in Goa', in *Indo-Portuguese History: Sources and Problems,* ed. John Correia-Afonso, Bombay, Oxford University Press, 1981.

——, *Goa Medieval: A Cidade e o Interior no Século XVII,* Lisbon, Editorial Estampa, 1994 (Portuguese version of *Medieval Goa: A Socio-Economic History,* New Delhi, Concept Publishing Co., 1979).

——, *Goa to Me,* New Delhi, Concept Publishing Company, 1994.

——, *Uns Confessionários Inéditos: Instrumentos de Missionação e Fontes para a História de Goa,* offprint of *Amar, Sentir e Viver a História.* Estudos de Homenagem a Joaquim Veríssimo Serrão, Lisbon, ed. Colibri, 1995.

SPEAR, Percival, *India: A Modern History,* new edn., University of Michigan Press, Chicago, 1961, 1972.

THOMAZ, Luís Filipe Ferreira Reis, *O Cristianismo e as Tradições Pagãs na Índia Portuguesa,* offprint of *Actas do Congresso Internacional de Etnografia,* sponsored by the Câmara Municipal de Santo Tirso, 10 to 18 July 1963, vol. IV, Lisbon, Junta de Investigações do Ultramar, 1965.

——, 'Estrutura Política e Administrativa do Estado da Índia no século XVI', in *II Seminário Internacional de História Indo-Portuguesa. Actas,* Lisbon, Instituto de Investigação Científica Tropical - Centro de Estudos de História e Cartografia Antiga, 1985.

——, *Goa: Une Société Luso-Indienne,* offprint of *Bulletin des Études Portugaises et Brésiliennes,* pts. 42-3, Paris, 1983. This study was recently translated into Portuguese and included in *De Ceuta a Timor,* Lisbon, Difel, 1994.

Tratado de todos os vice-reis e governadores da Índia, Lisbon, ed. Enciclopédia, 1962.

TUNON de Lara, Manuel, Metodología de la Historia Social de España, 4th edn., Madrid, Siglo Veintiuno de España Editores, 1979; 1st edn., 1973.

VAZ, Francisco Xavier, 'Agostinianos no Oriente', in *O Oriente Português,* vol. XVI, nos. 11-12, Nova Goa, Imprensa Nacional, 1920.

——, 'Vigarios Provinciaes dos Religiosos da Ordem de Santo Agostinho na India', in *O Oriente Portuguez,* vol. V, nos. 1-2, Nova Goa, Imprensa Nacional, 1908.

VIGIÉ, Marc, *Dupleix,* Paris, Fayard, 1993.

A Voz de S. Francisco Xavier, year III, nos. 41, 45, Goa, 1934; year XI, no. 3, Goa, 1941.

WACHSMANN, Fred, 'Os Padres Faria', in *Boletim do Instituto Vasco da Gama,* no. 65, Bastorá, Tip. Rangel, 1949.

WICKI, Josef, S.J., *O Livro do 'Pai dos Cristãos',* edição crítica anotada por ... Lisbon, Centro de Estudos Históricos Ultramarinos, 1969.

Witte, Charles Marital de O.S.B., *Les Lettres Papales Concernat L'expansion Portugaise au XVI siècle,* [Switzerland], Nouvelle Revue de Science Missionnaire, 1986.

Xavier, Carlos, 'Catalogo dos Religiosos que professaram no Convento de S. Domingos de Goa nos anos de 1744 a 1796 e 1814 a 1834', in *Boletim do Instituto Vasco da Gama,* no. 65, Bastorá, Tip. Rangel, 1949.

——, 'A Inquisição e a Sociedade Indo-Portuguesa', in *Inquisição,* vol. I, Lisbon, Universitária Editora, 1989.

Xavier, Filippe Nery, *Bosquejo Histórico das Communidades das Aldeias dos Concelhos das Ilhas, Salsete e Bardez,* ed. revista e acrescentada por José Maria de Sá, com um esboço biographico do autor por J.B. Amâncio Gracias, 3 vols., Bastorá, Tip. Rangel, 1903-7.

——, *Descripção do Coqueiro, Arequeira, Arroz e Moedas da Goa,* Nova Goa, Imprensa Nacional, 1866.

——, *Gabinete Litterario das Fontainhas,* 4 vols., Nova Goa, Imprensa Nacional, 1846-9.

——, e Diogo Luís da Fonseca, *Nobiliarchia goana ou catálogo das pessoas que desde 1640 a 1893 foram agraciadas pelos soberanos com títulos de nobreza e fidalguia, cartas de conselhos, condecorações ...,* Nova Goa, Imprensa Nacional, 1862-3.

Xavier, P.D., *Goa: A Social History (1510-1640),* Goa, Rajhauns Vitran, 1993.

List of Viceroys and Governors of India (1750-1807)

1750-4	Francisco de Assis de Távora, 3rd Marquis of Távora, 72nd Governor and 45th Viceroy.
1754-6	Luís de Mascarenhas, 2nd Count of Alva, 73rd Governor and 46th Viceroy.
1756	12th Government Council: Dom António Taveira da Neiva Brum da Silveira, João de Mesquita Matos Teixeira and Filipe de Valadares Sottomayor.
1756-65	Manuel de Saldanha e Albuquerque, 1st Count of Ega, 74th Governor and 47th Viceroy.
1765	13th Government Council: Dom António Taveira da Neiva Brum da Silveira, João Baptista Vaz Pereira and João José de Melo.
1768-74	João José de Melo, 75th Governor.
1774	Filipe de Valadares Sottomayor, 76th Governor.
1774-9	José Pedro da Câmara, 77th Governor.
1779-86	Frederico Guilherme de Sousa Holstein, 78th Governor.
1786-94	Francisco da Cunha e Meneses, 79th Governor.
1794-1807	Francisco António de Veiga Cabral da Câmara Pimentel, 1st Viscount of Mirandela, 80th Governor.

List of Archbishops of Goa (1750-1812)

1750-75	Dom António Taveira da Neiva Brum da Silveira.
1775-83	Dom Francisco de Assunção e Brito.
1783-1812	Dom Frei Manuel de Santa Catarina.

Index